Exploring Critical Approaches of Evolutionary Computation

Muhammad Sarfraz
Kuwait University, Kuwait

A volume in the Advances in Computer and
Electrical Engineering (ACEE) Book Series

Published in the United States of America by
    IGI Global
    Engineering Science Reference (an imprint of IGI Global)
    701 E. Chocolate Avenue
    Hershey PA, USA 17033
    Tel: 717-533-8845
    Fax: 717-533-8661
    E-mail: cust@igi-global.com
    Web site: http://www.igi-global.com

Library of Congress Cataloging-in-Publication Data

Names: Sarfraz, Muhammad, editor.
Title: Exploring critical approaches of evolutionary computation / Muhammad
  Sarfraz, editor.
Description: Hershey, PA : Engineering Science Reference, [2019] | Includes
  bibliographical references.
Identifiers: LCCN 2017059208| ISBN 9781522558323 (hardcover) | ISBN
  9781522558330 (ebook)
Subjects: LCSH: Evolutionary computation.
Classification: LCC TA347.E96 E98 2019 | DDC 006.3/823--dc23 LC record available at https://lccn.loc.gov/2017059208

This book is published in the IGI Global book series Advances in Computer and Electrical Engineering (ACEE) (ISSN: 2327-039X; eISSN: 2327-0403)

British Cataloguing in Publication Data
A Cataloguing in Publication record for this book is available from the British Library.

For electronic access to this publication, please contact: eresources@igi-global.com.

Advances in Computer and Electrical Engineering (ACEE) Book Series

Srikanta Patnaik
SOA University, India

ISSN:2327-039X
EISSN:2327-0403

MISSION

The fields of computer engineering and electrical engineering encompass a broad range of interdisciplinary topics allowing for expansive research developments across multiple fields. Research in these areas continues to develop and become increasingly important as computer and electrical systems have become an integral part of everyday life.

The **Advances in Computer and Electrical Engineering (ACEE) Book Series** aims to publish research on diverse topics pertaining to computer engineering and electrical engineering. **ACEE** encourages scholarly discourse on the latest applications, tools, and methodologies being implemented in the field for the design and development of computer and electrical systems.

COVERAGE

- VLSI Design
- Programming
- Chip Design
- Analog Electronics
- Electrical Power Conversion
- Qualitative Methods
- Optical Electronics
- Digital Electronics
- Circuit Analysis
- Applied Electromagnetics

IGI Global is currently accepting manuscripts for publication within this series. To submit a proposal for a volume in this series, please contact our Acquisition Editors at Acquisitions@igi-global.com or visit: http://www.igi-global.com/publish/.

Titles in this Series

For a list of additional titles in this series, please visit: www.igi-global.com/book-series

Electronic Nose Technologies and Advances in Machine Olfaction
Yousif Albastaki (University of Bahrain, Bahrain) and Fatema Albalooshi (University of Bahrain, Bahrain)
Engineering Science Reference • copyright 2018 • 318pp • H/C (ISBN: 9781522538622) • US $205.00 (our price)

Quantum-Inspired Intelligent Systems for Multimedia Data Analysis
Siddhartha Bhattacharyya (RCC Institute of Information Technology, India)
Engineering Science Reference • copyright 2018 • 329pp • H/C (ISBN: 9781522552192) • US $185.00 (our price)

Advancements in Computer Vision and Image Processing
Jose Garcia-Rodriguez (University of Alicante, Spain)
Engineering Science Reference • copyright 2018 • 322pp • H/C (ISBN: 9781522556282) • US $185.00 (our price)

Handbook of Research on Power and Energy System Optimization
Pawan Kumar (Thapar University, India) Surjit Singh (National Institute of Technology Kurukshetra, India) Ikbal Ali (Jamia Millia Islamia, India) and Taha Selim Ustun (Carnegie Mellon University, USA)
Engineering Science Reference • copyright 2018 • 500pp • H/C (ISBN: 9781522539353) • US $325.00 (our price)

Big Data Analytics for Satellite Image Processing and Remote Sensing
P. Swarnalatha (VIT University, India) and Prabu Sevugan (VIT University, India)
Engineering Science Reference • copyright 2018 • 253pp • H/C (ISBN: 9781522536437) • US $215.00 (our price)

Modeling and Simulations for Metamaterials Emerging Research and Opportunities
Ammar Armghan (Aljouf University, Saudi Arabia) Xinguang Hu (HuangShan University, China) and Muhammad Younus Javed (HITEC University, Pakistan)
Engineering Science Reference • copyright 2018 • 171pp • H/C (ISBN: 9781522541806) • US $155.00 (our price)

Electromagnetic Compatibility for Space Systems Design
Christos D. Nikolopoulos (National Technical University of Athens, Greece)
Engineering Science Reference • copyright 2018 • 346pp • H/C (ISBN: 9781522554158) • US $225.00 (our price)

Soft-Computing-Based Nonlinear Control Systems Design
Uday Pratap Singh (Madhav Institute of Technology and Science, India) Akhilesh Tiwari (Madhav Institute of Technology and Science, India) and Rajeev Kumar Singh (Madhav Institute of Technology and Science, India)
Engineering Science Reference • copyright 2018 • 388pp • H/C (ISBN: 9781522535317) • US $245.00 (our price)

701 East Chocolate Avenue, Hershey, PA 17033, USA
Tel: 717-533-8845 x100 • Fax: 717-533-8661
E-Mail: cust@igi-global.com • www.igi-global.com

Table of Contents

Detailed Table of Contents

Chapter 1

Heisnam Rohen Singh, NIT Silchar, India
Saroj Kr Biswas, NIT Silchar, India
Monali Bordoloi, NIT Silchar, India

Classification is the task of assigning objects to one of several predefined categories. However, developing a classification system is mostly hampered by the size of data. With the increase in the dimension of data, the chance of irrelevant, redundant, and noisy features or attributes also increases. Feature selection acts as a catalyst in reducing computation time and dimensionality, enhancing prediction performance or accuracy, and curtailing irrelevant or redundant data. The neuro-fuzzy approach is used for feature selection and classification with better insight by representing knowledge in symbolic forms. The neuro-fuzzy approach combines the merits of neural network and fuzzy logic to solve many complex machine learning problems. The objective of this article is to provide a generic introduction and a recent survey to neuro-fuzzy approaches for feature selection and classification in a wide area of machine learning problems. Some of the existing neuro-fuzzy models are also applied to standard datasets to demonstrate their applicability and performance.

Chapter 2

Muhammad Sarfraz, Kuwait University, Kuwait
Mohammed Jameel Ahmed, King Fahd University of Petroleum and Minerals, Saudi Arabia

This chapter presents an approach for automatic recognition of license plates. The system basically consists of four modules: image acquisition, license plate extraction, segmentation, and recognition. It starts by capturing images of the vehicle using a digital camera. An algorithm for the extraction of license plate has been designed and an algorithm for segmentation of characters is proposed. Recognition is done using neural approach. The performance of the system has been investigated on real images of about 610 Saudi Arabian vehicles captured under various conditions. Recognition of about 90% shows that the system is efficient.

Chapter 3

Sanjay Kumar, G. B. Pant University of Agriculture and Technology, India
Kamlesh Bisht, G. B. Pant University of Agriculture and Technology, India
Krishna Kumar Gupta, G. B. Pant University of Agriculture and Technology, India

In this chapter, an application of dual hesitant fuzzy set (DHFS) in intuitionistic fuzzy time series forecasting is proposed to handle fuzziness and non-determinism that occurs due to multiple valid fuzzification method for time series data. Advantages of the proposed DHFS-based time series forecasting method are that it includes characteristics of both intuitionistic and hesitant fuzzy sets to handle the non-determinism and hesitancy corresponding to single membership grade multiple membership grades of an element. In the present study, universe of discourse is partitioned and fuzzified the time series data by two different fuzzification methods (triangular and Gaussian) to construct DHFS. Further, elements of DHFS are aggregated to construct the intuitionistic fuzzy sets. Proposed method is implemented over the share market prizes of SBI at BSE, India and SENSEX of BSE to confirm its out performance over existing time series forecasting methods using RMSE and AFER.

Chapter 4

Shamim Akhter, East West University (EWU), Bangladesh
Sakhawat Hosain Sumit, Socian Ltd., Bangladesh
Md. Rahatur Rahman, Simplexhub Ltd., Bangladesh

Intelligence traffic management system (ITMS) provides effective and efficient solutions toward the road traffic management and decision-making problems, and thus helps to reduce fuel consumption and emission of greenhouse gases. Software-based real-time bi-directional TMS with a neural network was proposed and implemented. The proposed TMS solves a decision problem, dynamic road weights calculation, using different environmental, road and vehicle related decision attributes. In addition, the development of the real-time operational models as well as their solving challenges has increased in a rapid manner. Therefore, the authors integrate the design and development of a neural-based complete real-time operational ITMS, with the combination of software modules including traffic monitoring, road weight updating, forecasting, and optimum route planning decision. Collecting, extracting the insights and inherit meaning, and modeling the tremendous amount of continuous data is a challenging task. A discussion is also included with the future improvements on ITMS.

Chapter 5

Manisha Rathee, Jawaharlal Nehru University, India
Kumar Dilip, Jawaharlal Nehru University, India
Ritu Rathee, Indira Gandhi Delhi Technical University for Women, India

DNA fragment assembly (DFA) is one of the most important and challenging problems in computational biology. DFA problem involves reconstruction of target DNA from several hundred (or thousands) of sequenced fragments by identifying the proper orientation and order of fragments. DFA problem is proved to be a NP-Hard combinatorial optimization problem. Metaheuristic techniques have the capability to handle large search spaces and therefore are well suited to deal with such problems. In this chapter, quantum-inspired genetic algorithm-based DNA fragment assembly (QGFA) approach has been proposed to perform the de novo assembly of DNA fragments using overlap-layout-consensus approach. To assess the efficacy of QGFA, it has been compared genetic algorithm, particle swarm optimization, and ant colony optimization-based metaheuristic approaches for solving DFA problem. Experimental results show that QGFA performs comparatively better (in terms of overlap score obtained and number of contigs produced) than other approaches considered herein.

Hundreds of lives in India are lost each day due to the delayed medical response. In the present scenario, the victims completely rely on the passersby for almost every kind of medical help such as informing the hospital or ambulance. This project aims to automate the process of detecting and reporting accidents using accident detection kits in vehicles. The kit has a system on chip and various sensors which sense various parameters that change drastically during the occurrence of accidents such as the vibration levels, orientation of vehicles with respect to the ground. The accident is said to occur when these values cross the permissible threshold limit. As soon as this happens, the latitude and longitude of the accident spot is tracked using the GPS module present in the kit. The nearest hospital and police station is computed by the GPS module, which uses the latitude and longitude values as the input. The accident notifications are sent to the concerned hospital and police station over the web interface accordingly. The assignment of particular ambulance and the required traffic policemen to the accident cases is done using the web interface. The android application guides the ambulance driver as well as the policemen to the accident spot and also helps in the detailed registration of the accidents. The closest doctor facility and police headquarters is processed by the GPS module, which utilizes the scope and longitude esteems as the information. The accident warnings are sent to the concerned healing facility and police headquarters over the web interface as needs be. The task of specific rescue vehicle and policemen to the accident cases is finished utilizing the web interface. An intelligent analysis of the last five years' rich dataset uncovers the patterns followed by the accidents and gives valuable insights on how to deploy the existing resources such as ambulances and traffic-police efficiently. Various types of analysis are done to identify the cause-effect relationships and deal with this in a better way. Such technical solutions to the frequently occurring problems would result in saving many lives as well as making the cities safer and smarter.

Chapter 7

Nature has always been a source of inspiration for human beings. Nature-inspired search-based algorithms have an enormous computational intelligence and capabilities and are observing diverse applications in engineering and manufacturing problems. In this chapter, six nature-inspired algorithms, namely artificial bee colony, bat, black hole, cuckoo search, flower pollination, and grey wolf optimizer algorithms, have been investigated for scheduling of multiple jobs on multiple potential parallel machines. Weighted flow time and tardiness have been used as optimization criteria. These algorithms are very efficient in identifying optimal solutions, but as the size of the problem increases, these algorithms tend to get stuck at local optima. In order to extract these algorithms from local optima, genetic algorithm has been used. Flower pollination algorithm, when appended with GA, is observed to perform better than other counterpart nature-inspired algorithms as well as existing heuristics and meta-heuristics based on MOGA and NSGA-II algorithms.

Chapter 8

Habib Shah, King Khalid University, Saudi Arabia
Nasser Tairan, King Khalid University, Saudi Arabia
Rozaida Ghazali, Universiti Tun Hussein Onn Malaysia, Malaysia
Ozgur Yeniay, Hacettepe University, Turkey
Wali Khan Mashwani, Kohat University of Science and Technology, Pakistan

Some bio-inspired methods are cuckoo search, fish schooling, artificial bee colony (ABC) algorithms. Sometimes, these algorithms cannot reach to global optima due to randomization and poor exploration and exploitation process. Here, the global artificial bee colony and Levenberq-Marquardt hybrid called GABC-LM algorithm is proposed. The proposed GABC-LM will use neural network for obtaining the accurate parameters, weights, and bias values for benchmark dataset classification. The performance of GABC-LM is benchmarked against NNs training with the typical LM, PSO, ABC, and GABC methods. The experimental result shows that the proposed GABC-LM performs better than that standard BP, ABC, PSO, and GABC for the classification task.

Chapter 9

Ritu Garg, National Institute of Technology Kurukshetra, India

The computational grid provides the global computing infrastructure for users to access the services over a network. However, grid service providers charge users for the services based on their usage and QoS level specified. Therefore, in order to optimize the grid workflow execution, a robust multi-objective scheduling algorithm is needed considering economic cost along with execution performance. Generally, in multi-objective problems, simulations rely on running large number of evaluations to obtain the accurate results. However, algorithms that consider the preferences of decision maker, convergence to optimal tradeoff solutions is faster. Thus, in this chapter, the author proposed the preference-based guided search mechanism into MOEAs. To obtain solutions near the pre-specified regions of interest, the author has considered two MOEAs, namely R-NSGA-II and R-ε-MOEA. Further, to improve the diversity of solutions, a modified form called M-R-NSGA-II is used. Finally, the experimental settings and performance metrics are presented for the evaluation of the algorithms.

Chapter 10

Reda Mohamed Hamou, Dr. Moulay Tahar University of Saida, Algeria
Abdelmalek Amine, Dr. Tahar Moulay University of Saida, Algeria
Mohamed Amine Boudia, Dr. Tahar Moulay University of Saida, Algeria
Ahmed Chaouki Lokbani, Dr. Tahar Moulay University of Saida, Algeria

The clustering aims to minimize intra-class distance in the cluster and maximize extra-classes distances between clusters. The text clustering is a very hard task; it is solved generally by metaheuristic. The current literature offers two major metaheuristic approaches: neighborhood metaheuristics and population metaheuristics. In this chapter, the authors seek to find the optimal configuration of sensitive parameters of the PSO algorithm applied to textual clustering. The study will go through in dissociable steps, namely the representation and indexing textual documents, clustering by biomimetic approach, optimized by PSO, the study of parameter sensitivity of the optimization technique, and improvement of clustering. The authors will test several parameters and keep the best configurations that return the best results of clustering. They will use the most widely used evaluation measures like index of Davies and Bouldin (internal) and two external: the F-measure and entropy, which are based on recall and precision.

Chapter 11

Jayapriya J., National Institute of Technology, India
Michael Arock, National Institute of Technology, India

In bioinformatics, sequence alignment is the heart of the sequence analysis. Sequence can be aligned locally or globally depending upon the biologist's need for the analysis. As local sequence alignment is considered important, there is demand for an efficient algorithm. Due to the enormous sequences in the biological database, there is a trade-off between computational time and accuracy. In general, all biological problems are considered as computational intensive problems. To solve these kinds of problems, evolutionary-based algorithms are proficiently used. This chapter focuses local alignment in molecular sequences and proposes an improvised hybrid evolutionary algorithm using particle swarm optimization and cellular automata (IPSOCA). The efficiency of the proposed algorithm is proved using the experimental analysis for benchmark dataset BaliBase and compared with other state-of-the-art techniques. Using the Wilcoxon matched pair signed rank test, the significance of the proposed algorithm is explicated.

Chapter 12

Kanika Gandhi, University of Skövde, Sweden
P. C. Jha, University of Delhi, India

Supplier selection is one of the most important decisions within SCM since suppliers have emerged as value adding partners in industrial relationship. In the current study, supplier selection on the basis of information pertaining to quality and delivery time is explained. The cost aspects are taken care while coordinating procurement and distribution in the echelons. The deteriorating nature of the product creates imprecision in demand and fuzziness in different stages of the coordination. A fuzzy bi-objective mixed integer non-linear model is developed, where the first objective minimizes the combined cost of holding, processing, and transportation in all the echelons and the second objective maximizes combination of lot acceptance percentage and on-time delivery percentage. The solution process converts the model into crisp form and solves using a fuzzy goal programming technique.

Chapter 13

Marwa Elhajj, University of Versailles, France
Rafic Younes, Lebanese University, Lebanon
Sebastien Charles, Universite de Versailles Saint Quentin en Yvelines, France

Due to their large application quantities with extremely low efficiency, pollutant emissions, high fuel consumption, and oil price, researches on the environment protection and the energy saving of construction machinery, especially hydraulic excavators, become very necessary and urgent. In this chapter, the authors proposed a complete study for the excavators' hydraulic energy recovery systems. This study is divided into two parts. In the first one, an overview for the energy saving principles is discussed and classed based on the type of the energy recovered. In the second part and once the energy recovery system is selected, the authors proposed a new approach to design the energy recovery system under a typical working cycle. This approach, the global optimization method for parameter identification (GOMPI), uses an optimization technique coupled with the simulated model on simulation software. Finally, results concluded that applying GOMPI model was an efficient solution as it proves its accuracy and efficiency to design any energy recovery patent applied to hydraulic systems.

Chapter 14

Alok Ranjan, National Institute of Technology Rourkela, India
H. B. Sahu, National Institute of Technology Rourkela, India
Prasant Misra, TCS Research & Innovation, India

To ensure the safety of miners, reliable and continuous monitoring of underground mine environment plays a significant role. Moreover, such a reliable communication network is essential to provide speedy rescue and recovery operations in case of an emergency situation in a mine. However, due to the hostile nature and unique characteristics of underground mine workings, emergency response communication and disaster management are very challenging tasks. This chapter presents an overview of evolving technology wireless robotics networks (WRN) which may be a promising alternative to support search and rescue (SAR) operation in underground mine emergencies. The chapter first outlines the introduction followed by a detailed discussion on the current state of the art on WRNs and their development in the context of underground mines. Finally, this chapter provides some insights on open research areas targeting the current wireless research design community and those interested in pursuing such challenging problems in this field.

Chapter 15

Tarun Kumar Ghosh, Haldia Institute of Technology, India
Sanjoy Das, Kalyani University, India

Grid computing is a high performance distributed computing system that consists of different types of resources such as computing, storage, and communication. The main function of the job scheduling problem is to schedule the resource-intensive user jobs to available grid resources efficiently to achieve high system throughput and to satisfy user requirements. The job scheduling problem has become more challenging with the ever-increasing size of grid systems. The optimal job scheduling is an NP-complete problem which can easily be solved by using meta-heuristic techniques. This chapter presents a hybrid algorithm for job scheduling using genetic algorithm (GA) and cuckoo search algorithm (CSA) for efficiently allocating jobs to resources in a grid system so that makespan, flowtime, and job failure rate are minimized. This proposed algorithm combines the advantages of both GA and CSA. The results have been compared with standard GA, CSA, and ant colony optimization (ACO) to show the importance of the proposed algorithm.

Chapter 16

The findings of image segmentation reflect its expansive applications and existence in the field of digital image processing, so it has been addressed by many researchers in numerous disciplines. It has a crucial impact on the overall performance of the intended scheme. The goal of image segmentation is to assign every image pixels into their respective sections that share a common visual characteristic. In this chapter, the authors have evaluated the performances of three different clustering algorithms used in image segmentation: the classical k-means, its modified k-means++, and proposed enhanced clustering method. Brief explanations of the fundamental working principles implicated in these methods are presented. Thereafter, the performance which affects the outcome of segmentation are evaluated considering two vital quality measures, namely structural content (SC) and root mean square error (RMSE). Experimental result shows that the proposed method gives impressive result for the computed values of SC and RMSE as compared to k-means and k-means++. In addition to this, the output of segmentation using the enhanced technique reduces the overall execution time as compared to the other two approaches irrespective of any image size.

Preface

Evolutionary Computation is an active and important area of study and research today. It is a source revolutionizing for facilitating and enhancing the exchange of information among researchers involved in both the theoretical and practical aspects of computational systems drawing their inspiration from nature, with particular emphasis on evolutionary models of computation such as genetic algorithms, evolutionary strategies, classifier systems, evolutionary programming, genetic programming, and related fields such as swarm intelligence, and other evolutionary computation techniques.

The chapters in this comprehensive reference explore the latest developments, methods, approaches and applications of Evolutionary Computation in a wide variety of fields and endeavors. This book is compiled with a view to provide researchers, academicians, and readers of backgrounds and methods with an in-depth discussion of the latest advances. It consists of sixteen chapters from academicians, practitioners, and researchers in different disciplines of life.

Heisnam Rohen Singh et al. begin the book with a discussion on Feature Selection and Classification. Feature Selection and Classification are the extremely important phases in recognition process. Classification is the task of assigning objects to one of the several predefined categories. However, developing a classification system is mostly hampered by the size of data. With the increase in the dimension of data, the chance of irrelevant, redundant and noisy features or attribute also increases. Feature selection acts as a catalyst in reducing computation time and dimensionality, enhancing prediction performance or accuracy, and curtailing irrelevant or redundant data. This chapter, "Recent Neuro-Fuzzy Approaches for Feature Selection and Classification" by Heisnam Rohen Singh et al., introduces a Neuro-fuzzy Approach to detect and classify with better insight by representing knowledge in symbolic forms. The neuro-fuzzy approach combines the merits of neural network and fuzzy logic to solve many complex machine learning problems. The objective of this chapter is to provide a generic introduction and a recent survey to neuro-fuzzy approaches for feature selection and classification in a wide area of machine learning problems. Some of the existing neuro-fuzzy models are also applied on standard datasets to demonstrate their applicability and performance.

Sarfraz and Ahmed, in Chapter 2 of the book, follow with a discussion of "An Approach to License Plate Recognition System Using Neural Network." Their work aims at presenting an approach for automatic recognition of license plates. They have developed an automated and working intelligent system which consists of four phases. Image acquisition, license plate extraction, segmentation and recognition. The system starts by capturing images of the vehicle using a digital camera. They have designed algorithms for the extraction of license plates as well as segmentation of characters. They have adopted neural network approach for the Recognition phase in the propose system. The performance of the system has been investigated on real images of about 610 Saudi Arabian vehicles captured under various conditions. Recognition of about 90% shows that the system is efficient.

Application of Dual hesitant fuzzy set (DHFS), in intuitionistic fuzzy time series forecasting, is important to handle fuzziness and non-determinism that occurs due to multiple valid fuzzification method for time series data. Chapter 3, "Intuitionistic Fuzzy Time Series Forecasting Based on Dual Hesitant Fuzzy Set for Stock Market: DHFS-Based IFTS Model for Stock Market," by Sanjay Kumar et al. presents a typical study. Advantages of the proposed DHFS based time series forecasting method are that it includes characteristics of both intuitionistic and hesitant fuzzy sets to handle the non-determinism and hesitancy corresponding to single membership grade multiple membership grades of an element. In this chapter, the authors have partitioned the universe of discourse and fuzzified the time series data by two different fuzzification methods (triangular and Gaussian) to construct DHFS. Further, elements of DHFS are aggregated to construct the intuitionistic fuzzy sets. Proposed method is implemented over the share market prizes of SBI at BSE, India and SENSEX of BSE to confirm its out performance over few existing time series forecasting methods using RMSE and AFER.

In the modern age today, an Intelligence Traffic Management System (ITMS) provides effective and efficient solutions toward the road traffic management and decision-making problems. It helps to reduce fuel consumption and emission of greenhouse gases. Software based real time bi-directional TMS with a neural network has been proposed and implemented in the next chapter, "Design and Implementation of an Intelligent Traffic Management System: A Neural Approach," by Shamim Akhter et al. It proposes a TMS which solves a decision problem, dynamic road weights calculation, using different environmental, road and vehicle related decision attributes. It integrates the design and development of a neural based complete real time operational ITMS, with the combination of software modules including traffic monitoring, road weight updating, forecasting, and optimum route planning decision. This integration is done because of the development of the real time operational models as well as their solving challenges has increased in a rapid manner. Collecting, extracting the insights and inherit meaning, and modeling the tremendous amount of continuous data is a challenging task. This chapter, finally, includes the discussion with the future improvements on ITMS.

This is followed by "DNA Fragment Assembly Using Quantum-Inspired Genetic Algorithm" by Manisha Rathee et al. DNA fragment assembly (DFA) is one of the most important and challenging problem in computational biology. DFA problem involves reconstruction of target DNA from several hundred (or thousands) of sequenced fragments by identifying the proper orientation and order of fragments. DFA problem is proved to be a NP-Hard combinatorial optimization problem. Metaheuristic techniques have the capability to handle large search spaces and therefore well suited to deal with such problems. In this chapter, Quantum inspired Genetic algorithm-based DNA Fragment Assembly (QGFA) approach has been proposed to perform the de novo assembly of DNA fragments using overlap-layout-consensus approach. To assess the efficacy of QGFA, the authors have compared genetic algorithm, particle swarm optimization and ant colony optimization-based metaheuristic approaches for solving DFA problem. Experimental results show that QGFA performs comparatively better than other considered approaches here. This improvement is in terms of overlap score obtained and number of contigs produced.

Motivated by recent results in prevention and reduction in the rate of accidents, Chapter 6, "Effective Prevention and Reduction in the Rate of Accidents Using Internet of Things and Data Analytics" by Sowmya BJ et al., addresses the issue of automating the process of detecting and reporting accidents using accident detection kit in vehicles. The kit has a System on Chip and various sensors which sense various parameters that change drastically during the occurrence of accidents such as the vibration levels, orientation of vehicles with respect to the ground. The accident is said to occur when these values cross the permissible threshold limit. As soon as this happens, the authors demonstrate, the latitude and longitude of the accident spot is tracked using the GPS module present in the kit. The nearest hospital and police station is computed by the GPS Module, which uses the latitude and longitude values as the input. The accident notifications are sent to the concerned hospital and police station over the web interface accordingly. The assignment of particular ambulance and the required traffic policemen, to the accident cases, is done using the web interface.

Nature has always been a source of inspiration for human beings. Nature-inspired search-based algorithms have an enormous computational intelligence and capabilities and are observing diverse applications in engineering and manufacturing problems. In the following chapter, Kawal Jeet has described "Nature-Inspired Algorithms for Bi-Criteria Parallel Machine Scheduling." This chapter presents six nature-inspired algorithms, namely, Artificial Bee Colony, Bat, Black Hole, Cuckoo Search, Flower Pollination, and Grey Wolf Optimizer algorithms have been investigated for scheduling of multiple jobs on multiple potential parallel machines. Weighted flow time and tardiness have been used as optimization criteria. These algorithms are very efficient in identifying optimal solutions but as the size of the problem increases, these algorithms tend to get stuck at local optima. In order to extract these algorithms from local optima, Genetic Algorithm has been used. Flower Pollination algorithm, when appended with GA, is observed to perform better than other counterpart nature-inspired algorithms as well as existing heuristics and meta-heuristics based on MOGA and NSGA-II algorithms.

The nature activities and prettiness of social insects such as birds, bees, fish etc., have motivated scientific researchers to develop new bio-inspired methods for solving complex optimization problems. Some of the bio-inspired algorithms include Cuckoo Search, Fish Schooling, Artificial Bee Colony (ABC). ABC uses the inspiring behaviors of the real honey bees. Sometimes, these algorithms cannot reach to global optima due to randomization and poor exploration and exploitation process. Habib Shah et al., in Chapter 8, "Hybrid Honey Bees Meta-Heuristic for Benchmark Data Classification," proposed GABC-LM algorithm which will use and train Neural Network (NN) for obtaining the accurate parameters, weights and bias values for benchmark dataset classification. The performance of GABC-LM is benchmarked against NN training with the typical LM, PSO, ABC and GABC methods. The experimental results show that the proposed GABC-LM performs better than the standard BP, ABC, PSO and GABC for the classification task.

The computational grid provides the global computing infrastructure for users to access the services over a network. However, grid service providers charge users for the services based on their usage and QoS level specified. Therefore, in order to optimize the grid workflow execution, a robust multi-objective scheduling algorithm is needed considering economic cost along with execution performance. Generally, in multi-objective problems, simulations rely on running large number of evaluations to obtain the accurate results. However, algorithms that consider the preferences of decision maker, convergence to optimal tradeoff solutions is faster. Chapter 9, "Guided Search-Based Multi-Objective Evolutionary Algorithm for Grid Workflow Scheduling: Multi-Objective Evolutionary Algorithm for Grid Workflow Scheduling," by Ritu Garg, proposes a preference based guided search mechanism into MOEAs. To obtain solutions near the pre-specified regions of interest, the author has considered two MOEAs namely R-NSGA-II and R-ε-MOEA. Further, to improve the diversity of solutions, a modified form called M-R-NSGA-II is used. Finally, at the end of the chapter, the experimental settings and performance metrics are presented for the evaluation of the algorithms.

The combinatorial problems of clustering, specially of textual data, are solved generally by meta-heuristics. In Chapter 10, "An Optimal Configuration of Sensitive Parameters of PSO Applied on Textual Clustering," Reda Mohamed Hamou et al. have optimized operational research problem. That is, they are minimizing intra-class distance and maximizing extra-classes distances in a pattern of clustering data. This chapter has proposed an algorithm where a swarm of agents have been utilized to solve a problem of clustering. It aims to conclude optimal configuration of sensitive parameters of the technique of Particle Swarm Optimization (PSO) applied on the textual clustering. Several PSO parameters have been tested to keep the best configurations that return the best results of clustering using the conventional evaluation measures like index of Davies and Bouldin (internal), F-measure and entropy (external). Each of the parameters is fixed after experimentation on its optimal value. The study goes through in dissociable steps, namely, representing and indexing textual documents, clustering by biomimetic approach, optimizing by PSO, the study of parameter sensitivity of the optimization technique and the improvement of clustering.

In Bioinformatics, sequence alignment is the heart of the sequence analysis. Sequence can be aligned locally or globally depending upon the biologist need for the analysis. As local sequence alignment is considered as an important one like global, there is demand for an efficient algorithm. Due to the enormous sequences in the biological database, there is a trade-off between computational time and accuracy. In general, all biological problems are considered as computational intensive problems. To solve these kinds of problems, evolutionary based algorithms are proficiently used. Jayapriya J and Michael Arock, in Chapter 11, propose an improved Hybridized Evolutionary Algorithm based on rules for local sequence alignment. They focus on local alignment in molecular sequences using Particle Swarm Optimization and Cellular Automata (IPSOCA). The efficiency of the proposed algorithm is proved using the experimental analysis for benchmark dataset BaliBase and compared with other state-of-the-art techniques. Using the Wilcoxon matched pair signed rank test, the significance of the proposed algorithm is explicated.

Globally changed requirements extend wing of interdependent organizations, outsourcing of products, parts and services. This has led more importance to supply chain management (SCM). Supplier selection is one of the most important decisions within SCM as recently, suppliers have emerged as value adding partners in industrial relationship. In Chapter 12, Kanika Gandhi and P. C. Jha have proposed bi-objective Supply Chain Optimization with supplier selection. In this study, supplier selection on the bases of information pertaining to quality and delivery time is explained. The cost aspects are taken care while coordinating procurement and distribution in the echelons. The deteriorating nature of the product creates imprecision in demand and fuzziness in different stages of the coordination. A fuzzy bi-objective mixed integer non-linear model is developed, where the first objective minimizes the combined cost of holding, processing and transportation in all the echelons. The second objective maximizes combination of acceptance percentage & on-time delivery percentage. The solution process converts model into crisp form and solves using fuzzy goal programming technique.

Due to their large application quantities with extremely low efficiency, pollutant emissions, high fuel consumption and oil price, researches on the environment protection and the energy saving of construction machinery, especially hydraulic excavators, become very necessary and urgent. Marwa Elhajj et al., in the next chapter, present an Overview and optimized design for energy recovery patents applied on hydraulic systems. In this chapter, they have proposed a complete study for the excavators' hydraulic energy recovery systems which is divided into two parts. In the first part, an overview for the energy saving principles are discussed. These principles are classed based on the type of the energy recovered. In the second part, once the energy recovery system is selected, the authors have proposed a new approach to design the energy recovery system under a typical working cycle. This approach, the Global

Optimization Method for Parameter Identification (GOMPI), uses an optimization technique coupled with the simulated model on simulation software. Finally, results have concluded that applying GOMPI model is an efficient solution as it proves its accuracy and efficiency to design any energy recovery patent applied on hydraulic systems.

Next, Alok Ranjan et al. explore "Wireless Robotics Networks for Search and Rescue in Underground Mines: Taxonomy and Open Issues." To ensure the safety of miners; reliable and continuous monitoring of underground mine environment plays a significant role. A reliable communication network is essential to provide speedy rescue and recovery operations in case of an emergency situation in a mine. However, due to the hostile nature and unique characteristics of underground mine workings, emergency response communication and disaster management are very challenging tasks. This chapter presents an overview of evolving technology for Wireless Robotics Networks (WRN) which may be a promising alternative to support search and rescue (SAR) operations in underground mine emergencies. The chapter, first of all, outlines the introduction followed by detailed discussion on the current state-of-the-art on WRNs and their development in the context of underground mines. Later, this chapter provides some insights on open research areas targeting the current wireless research design community and those interested in pursuing such challenging problems in this field.

Tarun Kumar Ghosh and Sanjoy Das, then, present "Solving Job Scheduling Problem in Computational Grid Systems Using a Hybrid Algorithm" in Chapter 15. The main function of the job scheduling problem is to schedule the resource-intensive user jobs to available Grid resources efficiently to achieve high system throughput and to satisfy user requirements. The job scheduling problem has become more challenging with the ever-increasing size of Grid systems. The optimal job scheduling is an NP-complete problem which can easily be solved by using meta-heuristic techniques. In this chapter, the authors present a hybrid algorithm for job scheduling using Genetic Algorithm (GA) and Cuckoo Search Algorithm (CSA) for efficiently allocating jobs to resources in a Grid system so that makespan, flowtime, and job failure rate are minimized. This proposed algorithm combines the advantages of both GA and CSA. The achieved results have been compared with standard GA, CSA and Ant Colony Optimization (ACO) to show the importance of the proposed algorithm.

The goal of image segmentation is to assign every image pixels into their respective sections that share a common visual characteristic. In Chapter 16, Bikram Keshari Mishra and Amiya Kumar Rath present an enhanced clustering method for image segmentation. In this chapter, the authors have evaluated the performances of three different clustering algorithms used in image segmentation viz, the classical K-Means, its modified K-Means++ and proposed Enhanced Clustering methods. Brief explanations of the fundamental working principles implicated in these methods are also presented in this chapter Thereafter, the performance which affects the outcome of segmentation are evaluated considering two vital quality measures namely: Structural Content (SC) and Root Mean Square Error (RMSE). Experimental results show that the proposed method gives impressive results for the computed values of SC and RMSE as compared to K-Means and K-Means++. In addition, the output of segmentation using the enhanced technique reduces the overall execution time as compared to the other two approaches irrespective of any image size.

Muhammad Sarfraz
Kuwait University, Kuwait

Chapter 1
Recent Neuro–Fuzzy Approaches for Feature Selection and Classification

Heisnam Rohen Singh
NIT Silchar, India

Saroj Kr Biswas
NIT Silchar, India

Monali Bordoloi
NIT Silchar, India

ABSTRACT

Classification is the task of assigning objects to one of several predefined categories. However, developing a classification system is mostly hampered by the size of data. With the increase in the dimension of data, the chance of irrelevant, redundant, and noisy features or attributes also increases. Feature selection acts as a catalyst in reducing computation time and dimensionality, enhancing prediction performance or accuracy, and curtailing irrelevant or redundant data. The neuro-fuzzy approach is used for feature selection and classification with better insight by representing knowledge in symbolic forms. The neuro-fuzzy approach combines the merits of neural network and fuzzy logic to solve many complex machine learning problems. The objective of this article is to provide a generic introduction and a recent survey to neuro-fuzzy approaches for feature selection and classification in a wide area of machine learning problems. Some of the existing neuro-fuzzy models are also applied to standard datasets to demonstrate their applicability and performance.

DOI: 10.4018/978-1-5225-5832-3.ch001

1. INTRODUCTION

The focus of this era is not simply serving the purpose of a work but to optimize the process involved, in order to minimize time and space complexity. Machine learning algorithms in pattern recognition, image processing and data mining mainly ensure classification. These algorithms operate on a huge amount of data with multiple dimensions, from which knowledge is extracted. However, the entire dataset in hand does not always prove to be significant to each and every domain. An important concept that contributes extensively in classification and better understanding of the domain is feature selection (Kohavi and John, 1997). Feature selection is a process of selecting a subset of features from a set of features in a balanced manner, without losing most of the characteristics and identity of the original object. There are two factors that affect feature selection – irrelevant features and redundant features (Dash and Liu, 1997). Irrelevant features are those which provide no useful information in that context and redundant features are those which provide the same information as the currently selected features.

Selection of an optimal number of distinct features contributes substantially to the improvement of the performance of a classification system with lower computational effort, data visualization and improved understanding of computational models. Feature selection also reduces the running time of learning algorithm, the risk of data overfitting, dimensions of the problem and cost of future data acquisition (Guyon and Elisseeff, 2003). Thus, in order to cope up with the rapidly evolving data, many researchers have been proposing different feature selection techniques for classification tasks.

The main goals of feature selection are to select the smallest feature subset that yields the minimum generalization error, to reduce time complexity and to reduce memory and money for handling large datasets (Vergara and Este´vez, 2014). In most common scenarios, feature selection methods are used for solving classification problems or are a part of a classification problem. Many classical techniques exist for the purpose of feature selection such as Mutual Information (MI), decision tree, Bayesian network, genetic algorithm, Support Vector Machine (SVM), K-nearest neighbor (K-nn), Pearson correlation criteria, Linear Discriminant analysis (LDA), Artificial Neural Network (ANN), Fuzzy sets. The choice of using a specific algorithm is a critical step as no such best algorithm exists that fits for considering every scope and solving every problem of feature selection and classification.

The use of Mutual Information (MI) for feature selection can be found in many contributions by different researchers (Vergara and Estevez, 2014; Peng et al.2005; Grande et al., 2007; Chandrashekar and Sahin, 2014; Battiti, 1994). Mutual information provides the dependencies between variables in terms of their probabilistic density functions. However, if one among the two variables is continuous, a limited number of samples obtained after feature selection makes the computation of the integral in the continuous space a bit challenging (Peng et al. 2005). It has also been found that MI does not work efficiently in high-dimensional spaces and there exists no standard theory for MI normalization (Vergara and Estevez, 2014).

Decision tree is a tree-based knowledge representation methodology used to represent classification rule; where at each node one can select the most useful feature for classification using some appropriate estimation criteria. Decision tree methods like ID3 and CART, in general, split a node using only a single attribute. However, use of combinations of attributes makes more sense in some cases (Setiono and Liu, 1997) Also, their performance degrades if they face many features which are unnecessary for the desired output prediction (Kohavi and John, 1997). In decision tree interpretation, the constructed tree may contain sub-tree(s) containing irrelevant attributes even when the data is not noisy and which misleads the user's interpretation and thus lead to over-fitting and even data fragmentation.

Bayesian networks are directed acyclic graphs representing the joint probability distribution over a set of random variables (features). However, it suffers from the limitation that the number of structure super-exponentially increases as a number of features increase and focuses more on the dependency of the features rather than the important features. In Naïve Bayes classifier, classification is done using posterior probability distribution by applying Bayes rule, but all attributes are assumed to be conditionally independent. Even if the relevant features are considered, the performance may degrade quickly if correlated features are added (Kohavi and John, 1997).

In genetic algorithm (GA), the chromosome bits represents if the feature is included or not, however, some kind of randomness is involved and it is very hard to select significant features. In GA, classifier accuracies for a feature that are already evaluated are not stored for future retrieval and thus lead to multiple evaluations of the same set of features.

K-nearest neighbor (K-nn) is based on the principle that instances within a dataset that have similar properties exist in close proximity to each other. However, the lack of a principled way of choosing K, except through cross-validation or similar computationally expensive procedure; larger storage requirement; larger computational time for classification and sensitivity to the choice of similarity function used to compare instances come under the limitations of K-nn.

Support vector machine (SVM) is one of the emerging supervised machine learning techniques based on statistical learning. But, SVM methods are binary, thus, in multi-class problems, one must reduce the problem to a set of multiple binary classification problems. Also, SVM suffers from poor interpretability.

Different limitations of different techniques as discussed above led to head away from them and think of a stronger technique to serve the purpose. Artificial neural network has emerged as a powerful tool to solve the problem of optimal feature selection for classification problems. Some of its merits, which aid to this purpose are: i) self-adaptive in data, ii) universal functional approximators, iii) flexibility in modeling real-world complex relationships, iv) robustness due to feedback based features weighting, v) generalization capability, vi) knowledge base learning (De et al. 1999). However, due to the presence of imprecise information, ambiguity or vagueness in input data, overlapping boundaries among classes of the different patterns of the dataset i.e. patterns belonging to more than one class and indefiniteness in defining features some uncertainties can arise at any stage of a data classification system. Moreover, ANN is regarded as black box in nature as it doesn't reveal its internal processing about how a decision is made. This black box nature hinders the application of ANN in some data mining and machine learning algorithms, where explanation and understanding to the internal problem-solving process while handling uncertainties are required. One explanation of the decision making is extracted, the decision can be taken only by the explanation without running the ANN repeatedly. The fuzzy logic (Dubois and Prade, 1980; Liu, 2004; Zadeh, 1965) is very flexible in handling different aspects of uncertainties or incompleteness about real-life situations. The use of If-Then rules by fuzzy logic, help to depict the internal working scenario of the classification process involved in order to reach a decision, with proper explanation and understanding. Both ANN and fuzzy systems are very adaptable in estimating the input-output relationships, in which ANN deal with numeric and quantitative data while fuzzy systems can handle symbolic and qualitative data.

Neuro-fuzzy hybridization leads to a crossbreed intelligent system widely known as NeuroFuzzy System (NFS) (Ghosh et al., 2014; Azar and Hassanien, 2015; Chakraborty and Pal, 2001; Vranesic, 1977) that exploits the best qualities of ANN and fuzzy logic efficiently. NFS combines the advantages of both ANN and fuzzy logic which covers up each other's disadvantages (De et al., 1999; Kar et al., 2014; Jang et al., 1993; Kasabov, 1996; Chakraborty and Pal, 2004; Castellano etal., 2003; Sen and Pal,

2007; Chen et al., 2012; Azar and Hassanien, 2014; Hayashi et al., 1992; Ishibuchi et al., 1993; Kasabov, 1996; Nauck and Kruse, 1997; Ghosh et al., 2009; Eiamkanitchat et al., 2010; Silva et al., 2012; Shosh et al., 2014; Khayat et al., 2009; De et al., 1997; Benitez et al.,2001; Li et al., 2002; Kulkarni and Shinde, 2013; Wongchomphu and Eiamkanitchat, 2014; Napook and Eiamkanitchat, 2015). The neuro-fuzzy approach enables us to handle any kind of information (numeric, linguistic, logical, etc.); manage imprecise, partial, vague or imperfect information and incorporates self-learning, self-organizing and self-tuning capabilities. The neuro-fuzzy approach does not need to have prior knowledge of relationships in data. It mimics human decision-making process and performs fast computation using fuzzy number operations. In the neuro-fuzzy system, the knowledge gained by the network in the form of linguistic interpretations can be used to generate rules for feature selection and classification. Rule extraction from NN for feature selection and classification enhances human understanding in problem-solving tasks. The current article presents different neuro-fuzzy approaches used for optimal feature selection and classification

The neuro-fuzzy system is a more helpful method for understanding and analysis of features. To generate neuro-fuzzy rules, the input features need to be labeled with some symbolic representation called linguistic variables. The knowledge extracted from the data is combined with the linguistic variables for rule-based classification. In order to determine proper linguistic feature, preprocessing of data is required before feeding to the neuro-fuzzy system. Therefore, the endeavor of this article is to present state-of-art of the neuro-fuzzy models for feature selection and classification tasks.

The rest of the paper is organized as follows. Section 2 provides a brief overview of feature selection techniques. Section 4 presents a brief discussion of the core concepts of neuro-fuzzy approach i.e. ANN and Fuzzy Logic. Section 4 includes an in-depth survey and classification of different neuro-fuzzy methods in the context of feature selection and classification problem. In Section 5 we present some of the experimental results in order to establish the effectiveness of neuro-fuzzy methods in classification and feature selection. In Section 6 we present the conclusion.

2. FEATURE SELECTION TECHNIQUE

Feature selection is a process of selecting an appropriate reduced set of attributes from the original set of attributes, which enables us to serve our purpose without degrading the desired performance while reducing the time and space complexity. The features may be continuous, categorical, or binary. A Higher number of features may sometimes produce almost the same accuracy for a particular algorithm as that with a fewer number of features but this may slow down the process involved to obtain the final output. Pruning the irrelevant and/or redundant variables and selecting fewer discriminative variables not only elevate the prediction accuracy but also abates the computational complexity to alleviate 'the curse of dimensionality' problem (Leng et al. 2010).

Feature selection methods can be broadly categorized into three types namely Filter (Vergara and Estévez, 2014; Chandrasekhar and Sahin, 2014; Mladenic, 2006; Peng et al., 2010) Wrapper (Vergara and Estévez, 2014; Chandrasekhar and Sahin, 2014; Mladenic, 2006; Peng et al., 2010) and Embedded methods (Vergara and Estévez, 2014; Chandrasekhar and Sahin, 2014; Mladenic, 2006; Peng et al., 2010). Filter method finds the optimized set of features using a measure which is independent of the learning algorithm. Here, feature subset selection can be considered as a preprocessing step which is applied prior to applying the learning algorithm. A random subset of features can be selected first and then tested using the independent evaluation measure. Another random subset is again selected, tested and then compared with the previous subset. Until the predefined stopping criterion is met, different random feature subsets are compared, and finally, the best subset is obtained (Peng et al., 2010).

Wrapper method makes use of learning algorithms to find the optimized feature subset Until the stopping criteria is met, here, each time a feature subset is evaluated using the learning algorithm and the accuracy obtained is used as a comparing parameter to select the best subset (Peng et al., 2010).

Embedded method or hybridized method is the combination of both filter and wrapper methods. A typical embedded method performs both an independent test and evaluation of the performance of the feature subset (Peng et al., 2010) as illustrated in the steps below:

1. The filter method is applied to a given set of features. Random subsets are chosen from the initial feature set and the best, say p_i, among them, is found out using some independent criteria;
2. Wrapper method is then applied to the best subset obtained in the previous step i.e. random subset of features, q_i is chosen from the features of p_i and then evaluated using the learning algorithm, to find the accuracy. The classification accuracy of the different random subsets (obtained by adding features to q_j from p_i or removing features from q_j) is compared with current best subset's accuracy and the one that yields the highest accuracy is considered the best subset, say r_i;
3. Go to step 'a' to consider a new random subset from the initial set of features to yield another best subset p_{i+1} and then r_{i+1}. Using another comparing strategy, the current best subset r_i is compared with r_{i+1}, where r_i is the best subset of step 'b' in the ith iteration;
4. Steps 'a' to 'c' are repeated until a predefined stopping criterion is met to finally yield the best subset, r, among all.

Filter method finds a good subset of features while computing feature evaluation weight, without performing any classification and wrapper method evaluates the goodness of subset of features by employing some inductive classification algorithms (Leng et al., 2010). In most of the filter methods, feature relevance score is calculated and the features with low scores are removed. The three feature selection techniques with different pros and cons are shown in Table 1.

Relief, Correlation-based feature selection, Fast correlated based filter, INTERACT, FOCUS, Sequential forward search, Sequential floating forward search, stepwise clustering, feature selection through clustering are some of the algorithms that come under filter methods. Most of the feature selection methods using neuro-fuzzy come under either wrapper or embedded methods. Traditional learning schemes like decision tree and artificial neural network come under the embedded methods.

3. ANN AND FUZZY LOGIC

The neuro-fuzzy approach requires two core concepts that are hybridized to formulate it. Therefore, before discussing the neuro-fuzzy method brief overviews on artificial neural network and fuzzy logic are presented in the following sections.

Table 1. Merits and demerits of filter, wrapper and embedded feature selection methods

Feature Selection Method	Merits	Demerits
Filter	Computationally cheaper as compared to wrapper and embedded. Fastest running time. Lower risk of overfitting. Ability of good generalization. Easily scale to high-dimensional datasets.	No interaction with classification model for feature selection. Mostly ignores feature dependencies and considers each feature separately in case of univariate techniques, which may lead to low computational performance as compared to other techniques of feature selection.
Wrapper	Interacts with the classifier for feature selection. More comprehensive search of feature-set space. Considers feature dependencies. Better generalization than filter approach.	High computational cost. Longer running time. Higher risk of overfitting as compared to filter and embedded. More computationally unfeasible with increased number of features. No guarantee of optimality of the solution if predicted with another classifier.
Embedded	Less computationally intensive as compared to the wrapper. Faster running time as compared to the wrapper. Interacts with the classification model for feature selection. Lower risk of over fitting compared to the wrapper. Outperforms filter in generalization error with the increased number of data points.	Identification of a small set of features may be problematic.

3.1 Artificial Neural Network (ANN)

ANN is a powerful data mining tool that is able to capture and represent complex input/output relationships. ANNs are computational models inspired by animals' central nervous system that can perform intelligent tasks similar to those performed by the human brain. Figure 1 shows the fundamental building block for neural networks i.e. the single input neuron along in association with the biological neuron.

Thousands of researchers adopted ANN as their tool to perform feature selection and classification by considering factors like ranking criteria, weights between layers, error function. Setiono et al. (1997) have performed backward feature selection using a 3 layered feed-forward ANN, Kabir et al. (2010) have presented a wrapper approach of feature selection using ANN starting with a random set of features and adopting forward selection process in a way which they termed as constructive approach for FS (CAFS). A backward feature selection based on the reaction of the cross-validation data set classification error using ANN was proposed by Verikas et al. (2002).

3.2 Fuzzy Logic

The judgment for classification always needs to be certain. However, problems which include reasoning with some approximation rather than precise cannot provide crisp judgment and are dealt with fuzzy set theory. Fuzzy set theory enables one to incorporate more flexibility in classification and thus to build more intelligent and adaptive systems that represent vague data and concepts on an intuitive basis, such as human linguistic description, e.g. the expressions approximately, large, young.

Figure 1. Neuron architecture

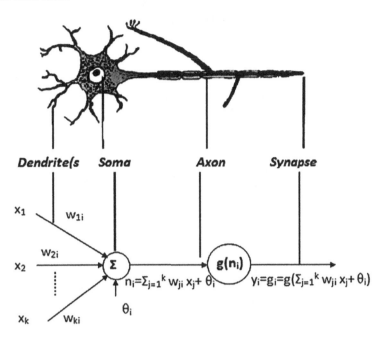

A fuzzy set A in X, is determined by a function called the "membership function", denoted by $\mu_A(x)$, defined for all $x \in X$. X is called the "support set", too. The membership function $\mu_A(x)$ states to what grade, x is a member of A. It is common to associate a number in the interval [0, 1] to $\mu_A(x)$. Mathematically, a fuzzy set A in X is defined by

$$A = \left\{ x, \mu A\left(x\right) | x \in X \right\} \tag{1}$$

where $\mu_A(x) \in [0, 1]$ is the MF of x in A.

According to Du et al. (2014), the fuzzy inference result is a combination of the fuzzy values of the conditions and the corresponding actions, given a set of fuzzy rules in the form "IF *condition* THEN *action*". Feature selection and classification using fuzzy concepts are performed using different methods like fuzzy entropy (Lee et al., 2001), fuzzy c-means (Marcelloni, 2003), fuzzy rules, fuzzy ISODATA (Bezdek and Castelaz, 1977).

4. NEURO-FUZZY SYSTEMS

Fuzzy logic provides an inference morphology that enables approximate human reasoning capabilities to be applied to knowledge-based systems. Fuzzy logic carries with it the advantage of uncertain or approximate reasoning and decision-making with incomplete or uncertain information. To make fuzzy reasoning work, numeric data must be mapped into linguistic variable terms (e. g. very high, young, small etc.) and so most of the fuzzy controllers and fuzzy expert systems must predefine membership functions and fuzzy inference rules to perform the mapping. The linguistic variables are usually defined as fuzzy sets with appropriate membership functions. A fuzzy system is intrinsically a rule-based system which is composed of a set of linguistic rules in the form of "IF–THEN". ANNs are good at recognizing patterns; however, they fail to explain how they reach their decision. Thus to compensate each other's deficiencies, fuzzy logic and neural network are hybridized to yield a system with the capability of learning, adapting, fault tolerance, knowledge representation, explanation of decision making, massive parallelism, robustness, handling any kind of information along with the ability to explore interpretable "IF-THEN" rules (De et al., 1999; Kar et al., 2014). This approach is termed as neuro-fuzzy system which was first proposed by Jang (Jang, 1993). Chakraborty et al. (2001) have classified neuro-fuzzy approaches into three main types: i) neural fuzzy systems, ii) fuzzy neural systems and iii) cooperative systems. All, these three paradigms are together known as neuro-fuzzy computing. Most of these systems perform feature selection and classification either in a combined or in an individual scenario or in association with some other phenomenon.

4.1 Neural Fuzzy Systems

When NNs implement fuzzy systems they are termed as neural fuzzy systems. The hybridization is done in order to enhance the adaptability, speed and flexibility of the fuzzy systems (Kasabov, 1996). Neural fuzzy systems have been successfully applied to various classification tasks while performing feature selection, however, systems with only classification or feature selection intentions also do exist.

Chakraborty et al. (2001) have proposed a neural fuzzy system for system identification along with feature selection. The basic structure of their model (Chakraborty et al., 2001) is illustrated in Figure 2.

Figure 2. The network structure for neuro-fuzzy model (Chakraborty & Pal, 2001)

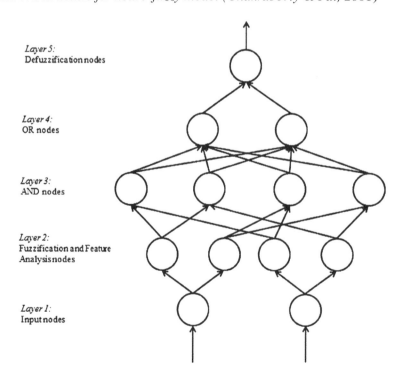

The nodes of the 1ˢᵗ layer, 2ⁿᵈ layer, 3ʳᵈ layer, 4ᵗʰ layer and 5ᵗʰ layer represent the features of the data, fuzzifiers and a feature analyzer, antecedents of the rules, consequents of the rules and defuzzifiers respectively. Each attribute is attached to a feature modulator β_p and the important features are selected based on the value of the modulator function:

$$\gamma_p = 1 - e^{-\beta_p^2} \tag{2}$$

To get optimal network architecture and to eliminate the conflicting rules, they pruned the nodes and the links.

Chakraborty et al. (2004) have proposed another neuro-fuzzy model for performing classification along with feature selection, which is almost similar to Chakraborty et al. (2001) except removing of defuzzification layer i.e. a 4 layered model is proposed which is shown in Figure 3.

This model considers the redundancy of the features depending on the value of and prunes the incompatible rules, redundant nodes, and links. However, unlike in Chakraborty et al. (2001), the tuning of membership function parameters and removal of less used or zero rules i.e. removal of antecedent nodes are performed in this model, which improves the performance of the system.

Castellano et al. (2003) have proposed a predictive neuro-fuzzy wrapper model shown in Figure 4, which uses a simple clustering procedure to initialize the structure of the model.

The feature selection based on a ranking criterion of features is done on the basis of relevancy index which also discards the highly correlated features and the ones with the smallest ranking. To adjust the network weights and consequently to tune the fuzzy rule parameters, a supervised learning process, based on a gradient descent technique, is performed which improves the final prediction results. The limitation of this model lies in the number of models that are generated for each property that needs to be predicted.

Sen et al. (2007) have proposed a neuro-fuzzy scheme for classification which greatly resembles the schemes (Battiti, 1994; Chakraborty et al., 2004), however, they design their scheme to select fuzzy sets

Figure 3. The network structure for neo-fuzzy model (Chakraborty & Pal, 2004)

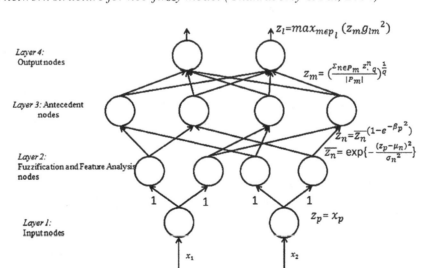

Figure 4. The neuro-fuzzy network (Castellano et al., 2003)

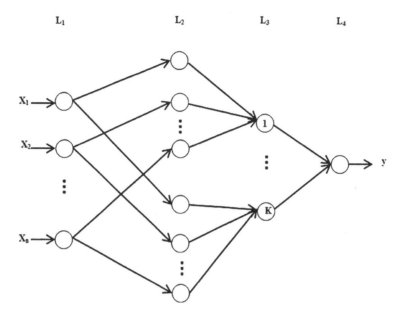

of the features instead of features and also to generate an optimal set of fuzzy rules to perform the classification and system identification. Here they assign a modulator function to each fuzzy set instead of a single modulator function for each feature as in (Chakraborty et al., 2001; 2004). However, the model fails to learn the modulator function which can aid in the feature selection.

Chen et al. (2012) have proposed an integrated mechanism for simultaneous fuzzy rule extraction and useful feature selection to solve classification problems which resemble mostly to that of (Castellano et al., 2003) to a great extent. The model uses k-means algorithm to find clusters for generating the fuzzy rules. The feature selection is done on the basis of modulator values described for each feature. These modulator values, denoted by λ are learned during the training. A feature is considered to be a good feature, only if for that particular feature, λ is less than 1.3. This model, however, may fail to curb the redundancy totally and thus has a scope of being extended to produce a controlled redundancy.

Cetisli (2010) have proposed an adaptive neuro-fuzzy classifier in which linguistic hedges is used. The linguistic hedges determine the importance of the fuzzy sets for fuzzy rules. This system improved the distinguishability of fuzzy sets by tuning the linguistic hedges.

Azar et al. (2015) have proposed a linguistic hedge neuro-fuzzy classifier with selected features (LHNFCSF) for dimensionality reduction, feature selection and classification to medical big data. This model proposes two criteria for feature selection: [i] features are selected that have biggest hedge value for any class and [ii] features are selected that have a bigger hedge value for every class. A selection function based on the linguistic hedge values for each feature is used in the feature selection process.

4.2 Fuzzy Neural Systems

NNs capable of handling fuzzy information are called fuzzy neural systems. The inputs, outputs, and weights of fuzzy neural networks could be fuzzy sets, often fuzzy numbers or membership values. Dated back to 1990's, Hayashi et al. (1992) have provided the basic model for the fuzzy neural systems along with three application areas while Ishibuchi et al. (1993) have proposed a model with fuzzy inputs and outputs along with a learning algorithm, which utilizes fuzzy if-then rules and the numerical data that were used for learning of neural network for classification and fuzzy control problems.

Kasabov et al. (1996) have proposed an algorithm which extracts weighted or simple fuzzy rules from adaptive fuzzy neural networks while addressing the issues of knowledge acquisition and approximate reasoning in hybrid neuro-fuzzy systems and is termed as REFuNN (Rule extraction from a fuzzy neural network). The FuNN architecture used for rule extraction is shown in Figure 5.

This model even introduces a knowledge engineering environment named as FuzzyCOPE (Fuzzy COnnectionist Production System Environment) which is shown in Figure 6 for facilitating different rule extraction methods.

Nauck et al. (1997) have proposed NEFCLASS (NEuro Fuzzy CLASSification) model to learn the fuzzy classification rules and to adopt membership functions for pattern classification in the neuro-fuzzy model. The model shown in Figure 7 determines the rule base by using three learning procedures namely Simple, Best and Best per class rule learning.

Ghosh et al. (2009) have proposed a fuzzy neural approach for classification that firstly performs fuzzification of the input patterns to yield a fuzzy membership matrix. The matrix is then converted into a vector and fed as input to the NN classifier. Defuzzification of the NN output is done using the MAX operation in order to assign the final classes to the patterns. The model shows that its scheme performs well for even a small training set and to deal with small training sets it uses β-index of homogeneity and Davies–Bouldin (DB) index of compactness and separability as a performance index. However, proposed work provides an inspiration to work on lowering the computational complexity of the scheme, which is found slightly high for data with a large number of classes and features.

Figure 5. An exemplar FuNN architecture for a simple set of two fuzzy rules (Kasabov, 1996)

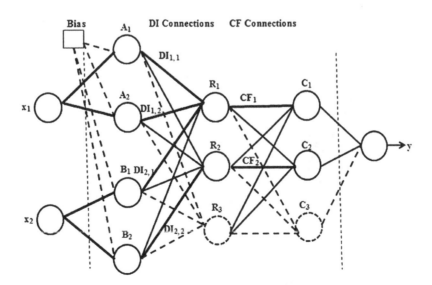

Figure 6. A block architecture of FuzzyCOPE (Kasabov, 1996)

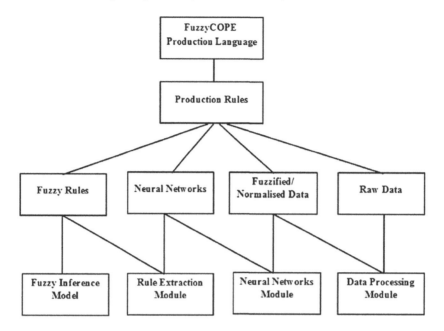

Figure 7. A NEFCLASS system with two inputs, five rules, and two output classes (Nauck & Kruse, 1997)

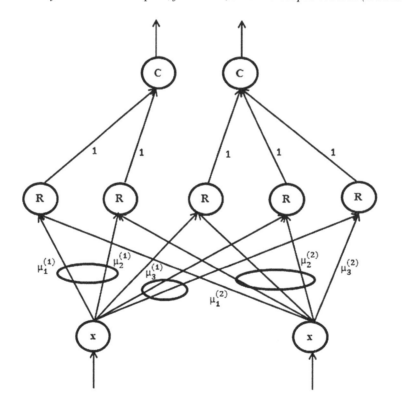

Eiamkanitchat et al. (2010) have proposed a fuzzy neural network which points out some of the drawbacks of (Chakraborty et al., 2004). Instead of using a random number of fuzzy sets for the features as in (Chakraborty et al., 2004), this model uses fixed three membership functions, i.e., {SMALL, MEDIUM, LARGE} for each feature. The model also presents a simpler network structure as compared to (Chakraborty & Pal, 2004) and selects top N linguistic features to generate classification rules. This model, however, does not provide any information on how and on what basis, the number of membership functions and the value 'N' while considering the top 'N' linguistic features, are fixed.

Silva et al. (2012) have proposed an adaptive feature selection (wrapper) method using an evolving fuzzy neural network which uses seven fixed membership function, though it is pointed that the decision upon the number of membership functions fairly depends on users. This model selects and uses two membership functions among all the membership functions for learning. In each candidate model, feature selection is done based on a statistical test that considers the accuracy and the number of free parameters of the model. The best candidate is finally selected. This model is, however, likely to suffer from stability, sensitivity and higher complexity issues because of the variable nature of the number of membership functions and the candidate models.

Ghosh et al. (2014) have proposed a neuro-fuzzy classification scheme that utilizes fuzzification matrix for the purpose of classification. Fuzzification of the input patterns to obtain the fuzzification matrix acts as a pre-processing step. The fuzzification matrix is then applied to the MLPBPN (Multi-Layer Perceptron Back-Propagation Network), RBFN and ANFIS classifiers.

Biswas et al. (2016) have proposed an interpretable neuro-fuzzy classifier without losing knowledge. In this model, classification rules are generated using the important feature which is determined by the frequencies of the linguistic variables.

4.3 Cooperative Systems

The cooperative systems are those which use different paradigms (neuro or fuzzy) to solve various facets of the same problem. Khayat et al. (2009) have proposed a cooperative system which is termed as self-organizing fuzzy neural network based on GA and PSO, though, this model is not meant for feature selection or classification. The model shows the use of Xie–Beni (XB) index to find the optimal number of fuzzy rules and the use of fuzzy C-means to initialize the firing strengths of the rules.

De et al. (1997) have proposed two schemes, one of which is employed to select a subset of features based on the feature ranking. The importance of a feature is calculated with respect to discriminating all the classes by using overall feature evaluation index ($OFEI_q$) in the first scheme. The model uses fuzzy entropy for calculating OFEI. In the second scheme, a multi-layer perceptron is trained for a dataset where the weights are so adjusted that the less important features (as detected by OFEI) do not affect the output vector much. Each feature is provided a rank based on the value of feature quality index (FQI) or feature devaluation index (FDIs) and few of the features are selected based on ranking to form a good subset of the feature. Among all the possible subsets, the subset with the lowest FQI or FDI is considered optimal.

Benitez et al. (2001) have proposed a feature selection method which is applied to different classification problems. Here, feature selection is done by ranking of a particular feature set and performing a backward selection of features one by one until unacceptable generalization accuracy is reached using ANN. The ranking is determined using relevance measure of inputs, which is derived by bounding the sensitivity of the network with respect to its inputs. When the problem to model is hard, different networks are employed to obtain their respective rankings of feature sets, and these rankings are aggregated using i-or operator (fuzzy aggregation operator) to obtain a final improved ranking which helps in obtaining the optimal feature set

Li et al. (2002) have proposed a feature-weighted detector (FWD) that can perform both classification and feature selection. The model uses two types of learning: i) unsupervised for memory learning and ii) supervised for weight learning. The feature selection is done based on the contribution of features of a particular pattern to the clusters representing the outputs according to the weight vectors associated with those clusters. The model employs Fuzzy Learning Law (FLL), in order to generate the outputs. The model also uses the interpretable If-Then rules to assist the classification.

Kulkarni and Shinde (2013) have proposed a hybrid fuzzy classifier which uses ANN to find the membership value of each feature value to each class. Feature selection is done based on information gain of an attribute. Starting with a single attribute with the highest information gain, all attributes are added one by one and the classification accuracy is measured. The feature subset with the highest accuracy is selected. SARR (sum aggregation reasoning rule) aggregation method is applied to the fuzzy membership matrix of the selected features, followed by a defuzzification process using MAX operator.

Wongchomphu et al. (2014) have proposed a neuro-fuzzy approach for classification using dynamic clustering to extend the work of Eiamkanitchat et al. (2010). The neuro-fuzzy model of (Eiamkanitchat et al., 2010) uses a fixed number of linguistic variables for each feature. However, fixing the equal number of linguistic variables for each feature is not a correct way of interpreting features. Therefore, the neuro-fuzzy model (Wongchomphu et al., 2014) determines proper linguistic variables for each feature by using dynamic clustering as a preprocessing step instead of fixing the number of linguistic variables. After, obtaining the proper number of clusters representing the appropriate number of membership functions (linguistic variables) for each feature, the fuzzification and classification using the neural network is performed using 10-fold cross-validation. However, this model produces unnecessarily large number of linguistic variables that degrade the accuracy of the model along with the increase in computational complexity.

Napook et al. (2015) have proposed a neuro-fuzzy approach for classification tasks to further extend Wongchomphu et al. (2014) using adaptive dynamic clustering algorithm. This model solves the problem of huge linguistic variables by the fuzzy union and Golden Section Search (GSS).

Singh et al. (2017) have proposed a neuro-fuzzy system for classification in which the problem of interpretability of the input features is tackle with a different approach. In this system the adaptive dynamic clustering algorithm is modified such that the more number of elements are appeared in each cluster, resulting in less and significant linguistic variables for each feature.

5. EXPERIMENTS AND RESULTS

In this section the following neuro-fuzzy approaches as discussed in the previous section have been applied to seven datasets to demonstrate the performance of neuro-fuzzy approaches in classification problems:

1. Eiamkanitchat et al. (2010)
2. Wongchomphu et al. (2014)
3. Napook et al. (2015)
4. Singh et al. (2017)

Eiamkanitchat et al. (2010) is a fuzzy neural network that solves the problem of Chakraborty et al. (2004). Wongchomphu et al. (2014), Napook et al. (2015) and Singh et al. (2017) belong to the cooperative neuro-fuzzy systems where Napook and Singh solve the problem of Wongchomphu with different approaches. The experimental results of above mentioned neuro-fuzzy approaches on seven datasets are shown in Table 2. The results show the effectiveness of the neuro-fuzzy system in feature selection and classification. It also shows how much accurate results can be produced using the neuro-fuzzy system in classification problems with great human interpretability and understandability. 10-fold cross-validation is used to measure the performance of the models. The datasets are divided into 90% training and 10% testing sets and the performance measure is the prediction accuracy of the test set.

It is observed from Table 2 that the fuzzy-neural systems have produced different accuracy for different datasets. The cooperative neuro-fuzzy model of (Wongchomphu et al. 2014) solves the limitation of blindly fixing the number of membership functions by (Eiamkanitchat et al., 2010) using dynamic clustering as a preprocessing phase, however, it suffers from yielding unnecessarily huge number of linguistic variables, thereby lowering the performance accuracy and increasing the computational complexity. The cooperative models of (Napook et al., 2015) and (Singh et al. 2017) lower the number of linguistic variables produced by the model of (Wongchomphu et al., 2014) using fuzzy union and modifying the cluster mechanism respectively; still, the accuracy produced is slightly low. As a whole, almost in all the datasets, accuracies are good using different neuro-fuzzy methods. It shows that neuro-fuzzy methods provide a fruitful contribution in feature selection and classification problems.

6. CONCLUSION

This paper provides an introduction and a recent survey of neuro-fuzzy approaches for feature selection and classification. The neuro-fuzzy approach combines the merits of the neural network and fuzzy logic

Table 2. Accuracy by different neuro-fuzzy approaches on different datasets

Datasets	Accuracy				
	Novel Neuro-Fuzzy Method (Eiamkanitchat et al.,2010)	Neuro-fuzzy system using dynamic clustering (Wongchomphu et al., 2014)	Neuro-fuzzy system using adaptive dynamic clustering by fuzzy union (Napook et al., 2015)	Neuro-fuzzy system using adaptive dynamic clustering by GSS (Napook et al., 2015)	Neuro-fuzzy (Singh et al. 2017)
Diabetes	72.97	69	71	71	74
Liver Disorder	72.44	59	58	56	54
Blood Transfusion	62.93	60.3	63	70	56.51
Breast cancer	94.72	91	90	85.6	90.2
Ionosphere	58.76	48	53	53	48.47
Iris	71.33	91	92	90	87.33
Sonar	57.86	62.1	62.8	63.3	67
Heart	68.89	68.1	68.5	56.3	67

to solve many complex machine learning problems. A neural network is widely regarded as a black box because it does not reveal its internal processing about how a decision is made. However, extraction of rules from neural networks provides humans understanding in decision making. Rules in natural form require less time to make a decision as it avoids repeated execution of ANN. Rules in natural form also help in enhancing their comprehensibility for humans, which is suitably handled using fuzzy set Feature selection and classification by rule extraction from data using neuro-fuzzy approach provide insight into the data, better classifier model, enhanced generalization and identification of irrelevant variables.

Comparison among some of the neuro-fuzzy approaches is shown on seven datasets to demonstrate the performance of the neuro-fuzzy approaches and it is observed that neuro-fuzzy approaches can produce good accuracy. As a future direction, readers can work more upon transparency of the neuro-fuzzy system which provides better visualization and understanding of the underlying domain. Wongchomphu et al. (2014), Napook et al. (2015) and Singh et al. (2017) all work in interpretability of the input features using linguistic variables. But further improvement can be done in the rule generation by augmenting effective classification rule and finding a new approach to select the important features, which ultimately improved the transparency with great accuracy.

Over the past decade, the neuro-fuzzy application has established its superiority over other existing methods and has grown vigorously to a greater extent finding its applicability in education, medical, economy, forecasting, industry, traffic control, social science, forecasting and prediction; and electronics and electrical system.

REFERENCES

Azar, A. T., & Hassanien, A. E. (2015). Dimensionality reduction of medical big data using neural-fuzzy classifier. *Soft Computing*, *19*(4), 1115–1127. doi:10.100700500-014-1327-4

Battiti, R. (1994). Using mutual information for selecting features in supervised neural net learning. *IEEE Transactions on Neural Networks*, *5*(4), 537–550. doi:10.1109/72.298224 PMID:18267827

Benitez, J. M., Castro, J. L., Mantas, C. J., & Rojas, E. (2001). A Neuro-Fuzzy Approach for Feature Selection. *IFSA World Congress and 20th NAFIPS International Conference, Joint 9th*. DOI: 10.1109/NAFIPS.2001.944742

Bezdek, J. C., & Castelaz, P. F. (1977). Prototype Classification and Feature Selection with Fuzzy Sets. *IEEE Transactions on Systems, Man, and Cybernetics*, *7*(2), 87–92. doi:10.1109/TSMC.1977.4309659

Biswas, S. K., Bordoloi, M., Singh, H. R., & Purkayasthaya, B. (2016). A NeuroFuzzy RuleBased Classifier Using Important Features and Top Linguistic Features. *International Journal of Intelligent Information Technologies*, *12*(3), 38–50. doi:10.4018/IJIIT.2016070103

Castellano, G., Castiello, C., Fanelli, A. M., & Mencar, C. (2003). Discovering Prediction Rules by a NeuroFuzzy Modeling Framework. Knowledge-Based Intelligent Information and Engineering Systems, 2773, 1242–1248.

Cetisli, B. (2010). Development of an adaptive neuro-fuzzy classifier using linguistic hedges: Part 1. *Expert Systems with Applications*, *37*(8), 6093–6101. doi:10.1016/j.eswa.2010.02.108

Chakraborty, D., & Pal, N. R. (2001). Integrated feature analysis and fuzzy rule-based System identification in a neuro-fuzzy paradigm. Systems, Man, and Cybernetics, Part B. *Cybernetics*, *31*(3), 391–400. PMID:18244802

Chakraborty, D., & Pal, N. R. (2004). A neuro-fuzzy scheme for simultaneous feature selection and fuzzy rule-based classification. *Neural Networks*, *15*(1), 110–123. doi:10.1109/TNN.2003.820557 PMID:15387252

Chandrashekar, G., & Sahin, F. (2014). A survey on feature selection methods. *Computers & Electrical Engineering*, *40*(1), 16–28. doi:10.1016/j.compeleceng.2013.11.024

Chen, Y. C., Pal, N. R., & Chung, I. F. (2012). An Integrated Mechanism for Feature Selection and Fuzzy Rule Extraction for Classification. *IEEE Transactions on Fuzzy Systems*, *20*(4), 683–698. doi:10.1109/TFUZZ.2011.2181852

Dash, M., & Liu, H. (1997). Feature Selection for Classification. *Intelligent Data Analysis*, *1*(1-4), 131–156. doi:10.1016/S1088-467X(97)00008-5

De, R. K., Basak, J., & Pal, S. K. (1999). Neuro-fuzzy feature evaluation with theoretical analysis. *Neural Networks*, *12*(10), 1429–1455. doi:10.1016/S0893-6080(99)00079-9 PMID:12662626

De, R. K., Pal, N. R., & Pal, S. K. (1997). Feature analysis: Neural network and fuzzy set theoretic approaches. *Pattern Recognition*, *30*(10), 1579–1590. doi:10.1016/S0031-3203(96)00190-2

Du, K. L., & Swamy, M. N. S. (2014). Introduction to Fuzzy Sets and Fuzzy Logic. Springer.

Dubois, D., & Prade, H. (1980). Fuzzy sets and systems: theory and applications. New York: Academic Press.

Eiamkanitchat, N., Theera-Umpon, N., & Auephanwiriyakul, S. (2010). A Novel Neuro-fuzzy Method for Linguistic Feature Selection and Rule-Based Classification. In *Computer and Automation Engineering (ICCAE)* (pp. 247-252). IEEE.

Ghosh, A., Shankar, B. U., & Meher, S. K. (2009). A novel approach to neuro-fuzzy classification. *Neural Networks*, *22*(1), 100–109. doi:10.1016/j.neunet.2008.09.011 PMID:19004614

Ghosh, S., Biswas, S., Sarkar, D., & Sarkar, P. P. (2014). A Novel Neuro-Fuzzy Classification Technique for data mining. *Egyptian Informatics Journal*, *15*(3), 129–147. doi:10.1016/j.eij.2014.08.001

Grande, J., Suárez, M. R., & Villar, J. R. (2007). A Feature Selection Method Using a Fuzzy Mutual Information Measure. *Innovations in Hybrid Intelligent Systems*, *44*, 56–63. doi:10.1007/978-3-540-74972-1_9

Guyon, I., & Elisseeff, A. (2003). An Introduction to Variable and Feature Selection. *Journal of Machine Learning Research*, *3*, 1157–1182.

Hayashi, Y., Buckley, J. J., & Czogala, E. (1992). Fuzzy Neural Network with Fuzzy Signals and Weights. *International Joint Conference on Neural Networks, IJCNN*, *2*, 696 - 701. 10.1109/IJCNN.1992.226906

Ishibuchi, H., Fujioka, R., & Tanaka, H. (1993, May). Neural Networks That Learn from Fuzzy If-Then Rules. *IEEE Transactions on Fuzzy Systems*, *1*(2), 85–97. doi:10.1109/91.227388

Jang, J. S. R. (1993). Adaptive network based fuzzy inference systems. *IEEE Transactions on Systems, Man, and Cybernetics*, *23*(3), 665–685. doi:10.1109/21.256541

Kabir, M. (2010). A new wrapper feature selection approach using neural network. *Neurocomputing*, *73*(16-18), 3273–3283. doi:10.1016/j.neucom.2010.04.003

Kar, S., Das, S., & Ghosh, P. K. (2014). Applications of neuro fuzzy systems: A brief review and future outline. *Applied Soft Computing*, *15*, 243–259. doi:10.1016/j.asoc.2013.10.014

Kasabov, N. K. (1996). Learning fuzzy rules and approximate reasoning in fuzzy neural networks and hybrid systems. *Fuzzy Sets and Systems*, *82*(2), 135–149. doi:10.1016/0165-0114(95)00300-2

Khayat, O., Ebadzadeh, M. M., Shahdoosti, H. R., Rajaei, R., & Khajehnasiri, I. (2009). A novel hybrid algorithm for creating self-organizing fuzzy neural networks. *Neurocomputing*, *73*(1-3), 517–524. doi:10.1016/j.neucom.2009.06.013

Kohavi, R., & John, G. H. (1997, December). Wrappers for feature subset selection. *Artificial Intelligence*, *97*(1-2), 273–324. doi:10.1016/S0004-3702(97)00043-X

Kulkarni, U. V., & Shinde, S. V. (2013). Hybrid fuzzy classifier based on feature-wise membership given by artificial neural network. *Fourth International Conference on Computing, Communications and Networking Technologies (ICCCNT)*. 10.1109/ICCCNT.2013.6726549

Lee, H. M., Chen, C. M., Chen, J. M., & Jou, Y. L. (2001). An Efficient Fuzzy Classifier with Feature Selection Based on Fuzzy Entropy. *IEEE Transactions on Systems, Man, and Cybernetics. Part B, Cybernetics*, *31*(3), 426–432. doi:10.1109/3477.931536 PMID:18244807

Leng, J., Valli, C., & Armstrong, L. (2010). A Wrapper-based Feature Selection for Analysis of Large Data Sets. *3rd International Conference on Computer and Electrical Engineering (ICCEE)*, V1-166-V1-170.

Li, R. P., Mukaidono, M., & Turkse, I. B. (2002). A fuzzy neural network for pattern classification and feature selection. *Fuzzy Sets and Systems*, *130*(1), 101–108. doi:10.1016/S0165-0114(02)00050-7

Liu, B. (2004). *Uncertainty theory: an introduction to its axiomatic foundations*. Berlin: Springer Verlag. doi:10.1007/978-3-540-39987-2_5

Marcelloni, F. (2003). Feature selection based on a modified fuzzy C-means algorithm with supervision. *Information Sciences*, *151*, 201–226. doi:10.1016/S0020-0255(02)00402-4

Mladenić, D. (2006). Feature Selection for Dimensionality Reduction. *SLSFS 2005. LNCS*, *3940*, 84–102.

Napook, P., & Eiamkanitchat, N. (2015). The adaptive dynamic clustering neuro-fuzzy system for classification. *Information Science and Applications*, *339*, 721–728. doi:10.1007/978-3-662-46578-3_85

Nauck, D., & Kruse, R. (1997). A neuro-fuzzy method to learn classification rules from data. *Fuzzy Sets and Systems*, *89*(3), 277–288. doi:10.1016/S0165-0114(97)00009-2

Peng, H., Long, F., & Ding, C. (2005). Feature Selection Based on Mutual Information: Criteria of Max-Dependency, Max-Relevance, and Min-Redundancy. *IEEE Transactions on Pattern Analysis and Machine Intelligence*, *27*(8). PMID:16119262

Peng, Y., Wu, Z., & Jiang, J. (2010). A novel feature selection approach for biomedical data classification. *Journal of Biomedical Informatics*, *43*(1), 15–23. doi:10.1016/j.jbi.2009.07.008 PMID:19647098

Sen, S., & Pal, T. (2007). A Neuro-Fuzzy Scheme for Integrated Input Fuzzy Set Selection and Optimal Fuzzy Rule Generation for Classification. *PReMI. LNCS*, *4815*, 287–294.

Setiono, R., & Liu, H. (1997, May). Neural-Network Feature Selector. *IEEE Transactions on Neural Networks*, *8*(3), 654–662. doi:10.1109/72.572104 PMID:18255668

Silva, A., Caminhas, W., Lemos, A., & Gomide, F. (2012). Evolving Neural Fuzzy Network with Adaptive Feature Selection. *11th International Conference on Machine Learning and Applications*. 10.1109/ICMLA.2012.184

Singh, H. R., Biswas, S. K., & Purkayastha, B. (2017, January). A neuro-fuzzy classification technique using dynamic clustering and GSS rule generation. *Journal of Computational and Applied Mathematics*, *309*, 683–694. doi:10.1016/j.cam.2016.04.023

Vergara, J. R., & Este'vez, P. A. (2014). A review of feature selection methods based on mutual information. *Neural Computing & Applications*, *24*(1), 175–186. doi:10.100700521-013-1368-0

Verikas, A., & Bacauskiene, M. (2002). Feature selection with neural networks. *Pattern Recognition Letters*, *23*(11), 1323–1335. doi:10.1016/S0167-8655(02)00081-8

Vranesic, Z. G. (1977). Multiple-Valued Logic: An Introduction and Overview. *IEEE Transactions on Computers*, *26*(12), 1181–1182. doi:10.1109/TC.1977.1674778

Wongchomphu, P., & Eiamkanitchat, N. (2014). Enhance Neuro-Fuzzy System for Classification Using Dynamic Clustering. *4th Joint International Conference on Information and Communication Technology, Electronic and Electrical Engineering (JICTEE)*, 1-6. 10.1109/JICTEE.2014.6804071

Zadeh, L. A. (1965). Fuzzy sets. *Information and Control*, *8*(3), 338–353. doi:10.1016/S0019-9958(65)90241-X

Chapter 2
An Approach to License Plate Recognition System Using Neural Network

Muhammad Sarfraz
Kuwait University, Kuwait

Mohammed Jameel Ahmed
King Fahd University of Petroleum and Minerals, Saudi Arabia

ABSTRACT

This chapter presents an approach for automatic recognition of license plates. The system basically consists of four modules: image acquisition, license plate extraction, segmentation, and recognition. It starts by capturing images of the vehicle using a digital camera. An algorithm for the extraction of license plate has been designed and an algorithm for segmentation of characters is proposed. Recognition is done using neural approach. The performance of the system has been investigated on real images of about 610 Saudi Arabian vehicles captured under various conditions. Recognition of about 90% shows that the system is efficient.

1. INTRODUCTION

Automatic vehicle identification system is of considerable interest because of a number of applications. It is used in many applications such as the payment of parking fee, highway toll fee collection, traffic data collection, crime prevention and so on. A number of techniques to recognize license plates have been developed during the past two decades (Sarfraz & Ahmed, 2005; Sarfraz, Ahmed, & Ghazi, 2003; Ahmed et al., 2003; Yusuf & Sarfraz, 2005; Yusuf & Sarfraz, 2006; Bakhtan, Abdullah, Rahman, 2016; CCTV Information, n.d.; Comelli et al., 1995; Hansen et al., 2002; Kim, et al., 2000; Lee et al., 1994; Naito et al., 1999; Neito et al., 2000; Nieuwoudt & van Heerden, 1996; Schalkoff, 1992; Yan et al., 2001; Wikipedia, n.d.). Several systems have been applied practically, especially into large-scale facilities. However, currently demands to apply license plate recognition into small-scale facilities are increasing. It includes, for example, managing a private parking lot and monitoring vehicle entry and exit (Naito et al., 1999).

DOI: 10.4018/978-1-5225-5832-3.ch002

License plate recognition (LPR) is realized by acquiring image of either front or rear of a vehicle by using a digital camera and then by further processing to detect the license plate. So the acquisition, extraction and recognition methods play an important role in the whole process.

The steps involved in recognition of a license plate are Image acquisition, License plate extraction, Segmentation, and Recognition. Image acquisition is the first step in an LPR system. There are a number of methods discussed in the literature for the image acquisition stage. Yan et. al. [23] used an image acquisition card that converts video signals to digital images based on some hardware-based image preprocessing. Comelli et. al. (1995) used a TV camera and a frame grabber card to acquire the image for the developed vehicle LPR system. The proposed system uses a high resolution digital camera for image acquisition.

License plate extraction is the key step in a LPR system, which influences the accuracy of the system significantly. Different approaches for the extraction of the license plate depending upon the back ground color of the image are presented in (Lee, Kim, & Kim, 1994). Hontani et. al. (2001) proposed a method for extracting characters without prior knowledge of their position and size in the image. Kim et. al. (2000) used two neural network-based filters and a post processor to combine two filtered images in order to locate the license plates. Kim G. M (Kim, 1997) used Hough transform for the extraction of the license plate. The proposed approach uses matching of vertical edges and then finding Black-to-White (B/W) ratio to extract the plate. This method is computationally better than using Hough Transform (Kim, 1997). This approach involves four steps, vertical edge detection, filtering, vertical edge matching and finding Black-to-White ratio.

In the Segmentation phase, individual characters are isolated from the license plate. Various approaches have been proposed in the literature. Nieuwoudt et. al. (1996) used region growing for segmentation of characters. Hansen et. al (2002) uses the connected component method to segment the characters. The proposed approach for segmentation is based on horizontal-and-vertical projection profiles on the extracted license plate.

Recognition of characters is the last phase in the LPR system. A wide variety of approaches have been considered for individual character recognition. Cowell and Hussain (2002) discussed the recognition of individual Arabic and latin characters. Their approach identifies the characters based on the number of black pixel rows and columns of the character and comparison of those values to a set of templates or signatures in the database. Hamami and Berkani (2002) adopted a structural or syntactic approach to recognize characters in a text document, this can be applied on individual characters to get good recognition. Naito et. al. (2000) used template matching. In the proposed system, recognition is done using neural approach.

This research work proposes an approach for automatic recognition of license plates which consists of four phases in the whole process of the LPR system. These phases are Image acquisition, license plate extraction, segmentation and recognition. A digital camera starts the first phase by capturing images of the vehicle. Phase two, for the extraction of license plate, is achieved by developing an algorithm. An algorithm. for segmentation of characters, is proposed for phase three. Finally, recognition phase is achieved using neural approach. The performance of the system has been investigated on a database (Sarfraz & Ahmed, 2005) of real images of 610 Saudi Arabian vehicles captured under various conditions. Recognition of about 90% shows that the system is efficient.

The chapter is organized as follows, Section 2 provides the description of the whole system. The image acquisition phase is explained in Section 3. Section 4 discusses the proposed method for license plate extraction. Section 5 gives a brief description of the segmentation of license plate into individual characters. Section 6 deals with recognition of characters using neural approach. Section 7 discusses analysis and demonstrates the achieved results. Finally, the chapter is concluded in Section 8.

2. SYSTEM DESCRIPTION

The proposed system presented is designed to recognize license plates from the front and rear of the vehicle. The system consists of four modules: Image acquisition, License plate extraction, Segmentation and Recognition of individual characters. The structure of the system is shown in Figure 1.

Image acquisition phase is used to acquire the image of a vehicle containing the license plate using a digital camera. In the extraction phase, the region containing the license plate is extracted. The segmentation phase isolates the extracted plate into six images, each containing individual character and finally neural network is used for the recognition of individual characters.

3. IMAGE ACQUISITION

This is the first phase in the LPR system. There are basically following three ways of acquiring an image (Cowell & Hussain, 2002). They are:

- Using a conventional analog camera and a scanner.
- Using a digital camera.
- Using a video camera and a frame grabber (capture card) to select a frame.

Figure 1. Typical structure of a license plate recognition system

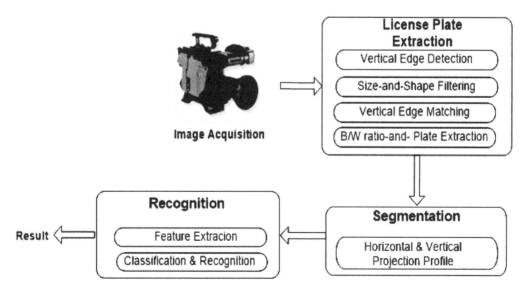

In the proposed system a high resolution digital camera is used to acquire the image, as shown in Figure 2(a). This is, first of all, converted to gray scaled image, as shown in Figure 2(b), which facilitates in further processing.

4. LICENSE PLATE EXTRACTION

License plate extraction is the key step in an LPR system, which influences the accuracy of the system significantly. The goal is to extract the region, with high probability of containing a license plate. In the adopted approach, extraction of the license plate is divided into four steps which are explained in the following subsections.

Figure 2. Results showing different stages in a license plate recognition system: (a) Original Image, (b) gray scaled image

(a)   (b)

Figure 3. Results showing different stages in a License Plate Recognition System: (a) Vertical Edges, (b) Vertical Edge Regions

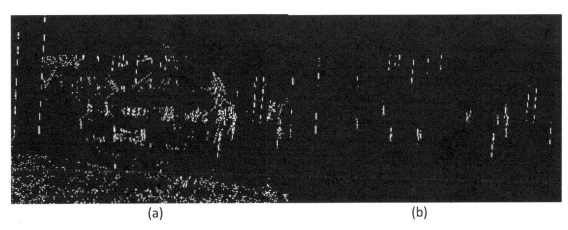

(a)   (b)

4.1 Vertical Edge Detection

For the transformed gray-scaled image, its corresponding vertical edges are detected using an edge detector. The proposed system uses Sobel edge detector because it gives better results. The Sobel edge detector uses a 3x3 mask, which is applied on the input image to give the resultant edged image. Figure 3(a) shows an image with vertical edges. It is observed that most of the vehicles usually have more horizontal lines than vertical lines. To reduce the complexity of algorithm, only the vertical edges are detected. If two of the vertical edges are detected correctly, four corners of the license plate can then be located. This helps in extracting the license plate exactly from the input image even if it is out of shape.

4.2 Size-and-Shape Filtering

Filtering is basically used to remove objects that do not satisfy some specific features. In the proposed approach, seed-filling algorithm by smith (Yan et al., 2001) is used to filter the unwanted objects. After filtering, the result is shown in Figure 3(b). The process of filtering starts by first detecting all the regions. Any group of white pixels is called a region if they are eight-connected pixels.

In Figure 4, the eight pixels around the shaded pixel are called eight-connected components of the shaded pixel (marked in gray). For the proposed system, all the eight components are not considered. Only the components to the South-West, South, South-East, East (marked in blue) of the shaded pixel, as shown in Figure 4, is considered. If any of the four pixels are marked as a white pixel, it is considered as the next pixel to be processed, and the pixel under consideration is marked as the processed pixel.

Once all the pixels of a region are marked, the region is checked for its size and shape. Through filtering our target is to select the regions that can serve as possible license plate boundaries and discard the others by filling it with black pixel. To achieve this target any region of interest must be a straight path of specific length. So for each region the size and shape filter is applied. As shown in Figure 5, the first pixel of the region is marked as P_o and the last is marked as P_{end}. If there are multiple paths from P_o to P_{end}, then the path with maximum distance is taken as a probable vertical region. In Figure 5, the region on the right hand side is chosen as the probable vertical region. Then this is checked for its size and shape. Shape of the region is detected through the slope of the line joining P_o and P_{end}. The size of the region is the distance between P_o and P_{end}. If the distance falls within the thresholded value, it is taken as the region of interest. A threshold of 30 to 100 pixels is taken as the distance between P_o and P_{end} with an angle of deviation of around $\pm 15°$. This threshold is taken since the image can be taken from a closer or farther view with some angle of deviation. The region in Figure 5 is discarded on the basis of slope of the line P_o, P_{end}.

4.3 Vertical Edge Matching

In this phase the width to height ratio of license plate is used to match the vertical edges for finding the region, where there is a high probability of license plate. The ratio of width-to-height of Saudi Arabian license plate is about 2:1. After the size-and-shape filtering, the image in Figure 3(b) is extracted with a number of vertical regions. Only two of the regions could be the possible boundary of the license plate. The task of vertical edge matching is to find out the correct pair of regions that include the license plate. To achieve this task, the width-to-height ratio of the rectangular area between two vertical regions is compared with the actual standard ratio of a license plate. The standard ratio is taken with certain

Figure 4. Eight connected components

*For a more accurate representation see the electronic version.

threshold to lie between 1.75: 1 to 2.25: 1 and the angle of deviation is ±15 with respect to the straight line perpendicular to x-axis. Figure 6 shows the extracted license plate for the matched vertical edges.

An algorithm for vertical edge matching is as follows:

```
for i=1 to no. of extracted regions
        for j=i+1 to no. of extracted regions
if width-to-height ratio of region(i) and region(j) falls in the range 1.75:1
to 2.25:1
select the two region in the list of possible license plate regions
            end if
      end for
end for
```

In some cases, there is a possibility of more than one pair of region that satisfying the above threshold. This case is shown in Figure 7, where there are two regions satisfying the constraint of width-to-height ratio. To overcome this problem, Black-to-White ratio of these pair of regions are taken to get the probable license plate.

Figure 5. The resultant vertical regions

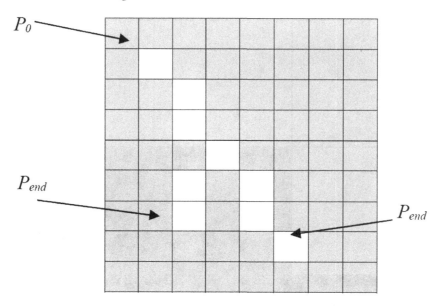

Figure 6. Extracted license plate for the matched vertical edges

4.4 B/W Ratio and License Plate Extraction

This phase is considered when more than one pair of probable license plate regions are obtained after the matching of vertical regions for their width-to-height ratio, as shown in Figure 7. All the coordinate points for every pair of matched regions are stored and the black to white ratio of the stored regions are calculated with respect to the Figure 4(a). Since the characters on the license plate in the Figure 4(a) contain white pixels, so the B/W ratio for the probable plate region is very less than the ratio of any of the extracted regions which does not contain a license plate. Therefore, if the pair is a possible license plate, then the ratio is within a specified threshold. The threshold is selected based on tests performed on a number of plates.

Figure 7. Extracted license plate regions of a vehicle satisfying the width-to-height ratio

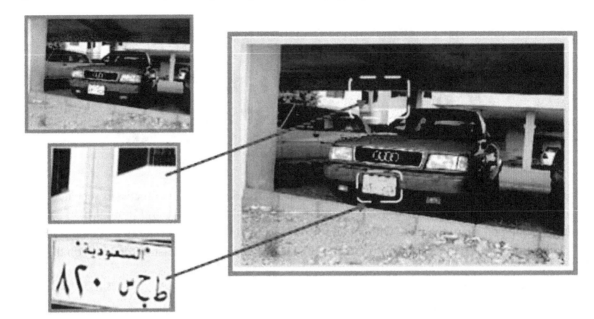

5. LICENSE PLATE SEGMENTATION

After the extraction phase, the License Plate is segmented into individual characters. To ease the process of identifying the characters, it is preferable to divide the extracted plate into six images. This is done because the Saudi Arabian license plates consist of 6 characters, with 3 letters and 3 numerals. Before the license plate is given as an input to the segmentation stage, the upper part of the plate is cropped to remove a part, as shown in Figure 8. This eases the process of segmentation based on the proposed techniques. Presence of bolts and logos in the license plates may prove to be cumbersome during the segmentation process, but the Saudi Arabian license plate template doesn't contain any logos. The bolts are usually on the upper part of the plate, and are removed in the process of cropping. For the segmentation phase the proposed strategy is based on horizontal and vertical projections.

5.1 Horizontal and Vertical Projection Profile

The Segmentation of extracted plate into individual characters is done using the horizontal and vertical projections on the license plate. This method first finds the horizontal profile of the binarized license plate and the resultant plate is extracted with any unwanted pixels removed from the top and bottom of the plate. vertical projections are performed on the resultant image of the plate to segment it into six individual characters.

Horizontal Projection Profile

The horizontal projection profile of the cropped binary plate shown in Figure 9(a) is found by counting the number of black pixels for all the columns corresponding to a particular row. The obtained count

Figure 8. Result of cropped license plate

is then plotted to obtain the resultant projection for that particular row. This process is repeated for all the rows and the resultant plot gives the overall projection profile as shown in Figure 9(b). The above result gives the portion of the plate without any white spaces at the top and bottom as shown in Figure 9(c). This information removes any unwanted black pixels obtained due to dust or scratches on the plate.

Vertical Projection Profile

The result obtained after horizontal projection, is given as an input to find the vertical projection profile. To obtain the vertical projection profile, the number of black pixels for all the rows corresponding to each column is found. The obtained count is plotted to get the vertical projection profile for particular column. This process is repeated for all the columns and the resultant plot gives the over all projection profile as given in Figure 9(d). There will be six projections for each of the six characters. The characters are now segmented depending on the transition from a group of black pixels to a white pixel. Figure 10 shows the resultant six characters. Some threshold is also taken to avoid unnecessary black pixels.

Figure 9. Results showing different stages in a license plate recognition system: (a) cropped binary license plate, (b) horizontal projection profile, (c) resultant cropped binary license plate after horizontal projection, (d) vertical projection profile on (c)

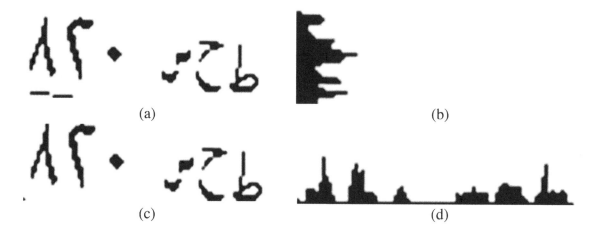

(a)

(b)

(c)

(d)

Figure 10. Segmented characters

6. CHARACTER RECOGNITION

The process of recognizing a pattern or character is basically dealt with three approaches: Statistical, Syntactic and Neural approaches (Schalkoff, 1992). Character recognition is one of the applications in the field of pattern recognition and it generally uses syntactic and neural approaches. This chapter discusses the recognition using neural approach.

In this approach stable state information is used to recognize the character under investigation. This chapter uses a multi-layer perceptron (MLP), which is a feed forward neural network. It consists of a number of layers, an input layer, several hidden layers, and an output layer. Before using MLP network, features of all the characters are extracted. These features are fed to the neural network as input. The following subsections discusses the feature extraction method and the process of classification.

6.1 Feature Extraction

The main advantage of feature extraction is that it removes redundancy from the data and represent the character image by a set of numerical features. These features are used by the classifier to classify the data. In the proposed strategy, horizontal projection profile, height-to-width ratio and black-to-white ratio of a character is taken as the input features. The horizontal projection profile gives the number of black pixels in each row of the character image. The height of a character is fixed as the maximum number of rows of a character in the group of 38 Arabic characters. If the height of a character is less than the maximum height, the remaining rows of that character is filled with zeros. So in our case the maximum height of a character is 28 along with the values of height-to-width ratio and black-to-white ratio. Therefore for each of the input character there will be 30 input neurons.

6.2 Classification & Recognition

Characters are classified according to their computed horizontal projection profile, height-to-width ratio and black-to-white ratio by means of artificial neural networks. Many neural network architectures have been used in OCR implementation. MLP is usually a common choice. MLP have been applied successfully to solve some difficult problems by training them in a supervised manner with error back propagation algorithm (Haykin, 1999).

In the proposed system, the MLP Network is implemented with three layers, as shown in Figure 11. First, is an input layer, a hidden layer and an output layer of linear neurons. The input layer is composed of thirty neurons. The thirty input neurons are the features extracted from the feature extraction phase. The hidden layer used consists of ten neurons. Based on the input features that are passed to the neural network the output layer gives the resultant character. The number of the output neurons depends on the number of the characters in the character set. Since the system consist of 27 characters (17 letters and 10 numerals), with some of the excluded characters as shown in Figure 12, the output for each character can be represented using 5 bits. Therefore, the output layer consists of five neurons, each representing a bit as an output. For example, one character is represented by 0 0 0 1 0. This approach gives a recognition rate of 90%. The reason for its low recognition rate is due to the closeness in is features.

7. ANALYSIS AND RESULTS

Experiments have been performed to test the proposed system using MATLAB (The MathWorks Inc, n.d.). The system is designed for recognition of Saudi Arabian license plates. The image to the system is a gray scale of size 640x480. The test images were taken under various conditions. For example, here are some experiments which were carried out for the following cases:

- License plates in normal shapes (Shown in Figure 13.)
- License plates that are leaned with some angle of view (Shown in Figure 14.)
- License plates that where the image taken under sunlight (Shown in Figure 15.)

Figure 11. Three-layer MLP network

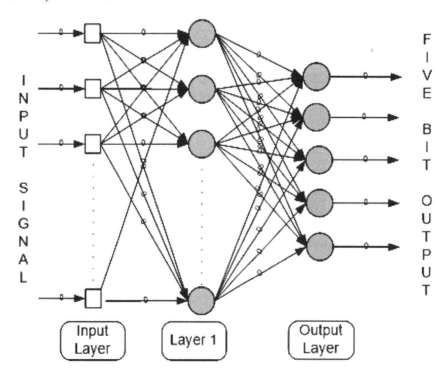

Figure 12. Excluded characters

ف غ ظ ض ش ز ذ خ ج ث ت

Table 1.

	License Plate Extraction	License Plate Segmentation	Recognition
Correct Recognition	587/610	574/610	550/610
Percentage Recognition	96.22%	94.04%	90.16%

Figure 13. The overall process of an LPR system with license plate in normal showing the rear end

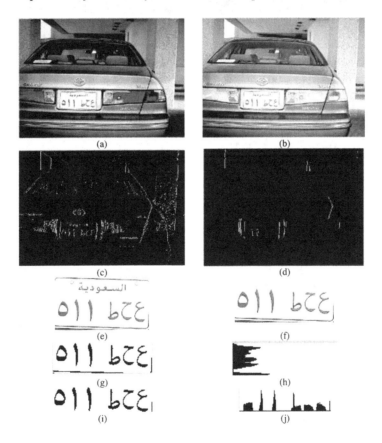

Figure 14. The overall process of an LPR system with the rear part of the car slanted towards left

- License plates with rear part of the car slanted towards right (Shown in Figure 16.)

The experiments for the above system were performed under different situations. The whole system is working fine achieving high recognition rate. Table 1 gives results for the percentage recognition of license plate extraction, segmentation, and character recognition. A failure results if a character of the license plate is incorrectly interpreted. This normally happens due to bad quality of extracted plate. It is shown that the system has correctly recognized 581 license plates out of 610 test images.

Figure 15. The overall process of an LPR system with the image taken under sunlight

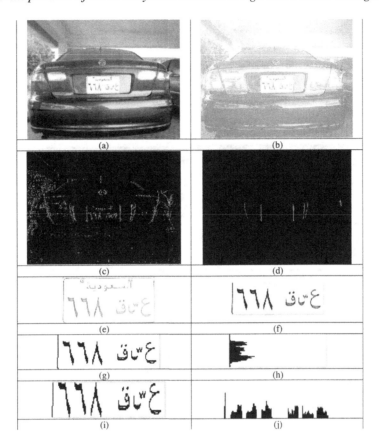

The experimental results show that the shortcoming of the proposed system is mainly due to bad quality of input image during the acquisition stage (i.e., the bad quality is due to the presence of dirty or unclear license plates), or unclear detection or extraction of the edges. The segmentation phase gives good results, because the image is converted into binary form. In character recognition there is some form of mis-recognition. This is due to the nuts and bolts within the character. Otherwise, there is a standard font for all the Arabic characters used in the license plates, which do not cause any problem during recognition phase.

8 CONCLUSION

Although there are many running systems for recognition of various plates such as Singaporean, Korean and some European license plates, the proposed effort is a one of its kind for Saudi Arabian license plates. The license plate recognition involves image acquisition, license plate extraction, segmentation, and recognition phases. Beside the use of Arabic language, Saudi Arabian license plates have several unique features that are taken care in the segmentation and recognition phases. The recognition is carried out using the neural approach. The system is tested over a large number of car images and is proved to be 90% accurate.

Figure 16. The overall process of an LPR system with rear part of the car slanted towards right

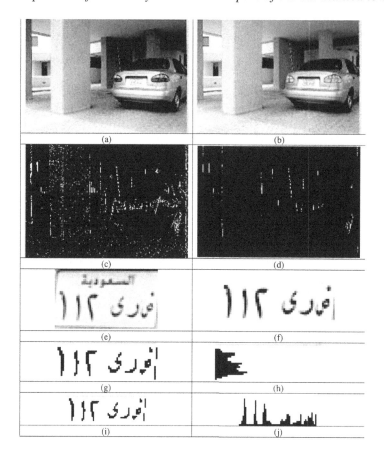

Although the data used here was compiled in year 2003, but the approach is manageable to adjust any data compiled after minor changes in the algorithm. Similarly, the scheme developed can also be oriented to a license plate for not just Saudi Arabian case, but it can be applied to some other countries license plates too with minor changes.

REFERENCES

Ahmed, M. J., Sarfraz, M., Zidouri, A., & Alkhatib, W. G. (2003). License Plate Recognition System. *Proceedings of The 10th IEEE International Conference On Electronics, Circuits And Systems (ICECS2003)*.

Bakhtan, M. A. H., Abdullah, M., & Rahman, A. A. (2016). A review on License Plate Recognition system algorithms. In *International Conference on Information and Communication Technology (ICICTM)* (pp. 84 – 89). IEEE Xplore.

CCTV Information. (n.d.). *An introduction to ANPR*. Retrieved 2018-02-03 from https://www.cctv-information.co.uk/i/An_Introduction_to_ANPR

Comelli, P., Ferragina, P., Granieri, M. N., & Stabile, F. (1995). Optical recognition of motor vehicle license plates. *IEEE Transactions on Vehicular Technology*, *44*(4), 790–799. doi:10.1109/25.467963

Cowell, J., & Hussain, F. (2002). A Fast Recognition System for Isolated Arabic Characters. In *Proceedings Sixth International Conference on Information and Visualisation*. IEEE Computer Society. 10.1109/IV.2002.1028844

Hamami, L., & Berkani, D. (2002). Recognition System for Printed Multi-Font and Multi-Size Arabic Characters. *Arabian Journal for Science and Engineering*, *27*(No. 1B), 57–72.

Hansen, H., Kristensen, A. W., Kohler, M. P., Mikkelsen, A. W., Pedersen, J. M., & Trangeled, M. (2002). *Automatic Recognition of License Plates*. Institute for Electronic System, Aalborg University.

Haykin, S. (1999). *Neural Networks: A Comprehensive Foundation*. Prentice Hall Inc.

Hontani, H., & Koga, T. (2001). Character Extraction Method Without Prior Knowledge on Size and Information. *Proceedings of the IEEE International Vehicle Electronics Conference (IVEC'01)*, 67-72. 10.1109/IVEC.2001.961728

Kim, G. M. (1997). The Automatic Recognition of the Plate of Vehicle Using the Correlation Coefficient and Hough Transform. *Journal of Control Automation and System Engineering*, *3*(5), 511–519.

Kim, K. K., Kim, K. I., Kim, J. B., & Kim, H. J. (2000). Learning Based Approach for License Plate Recognition. *Proceedings of IEEE Processing Society Workshop on Neural Networks for Signal Processing*, 2, 614-623. 10.1109/NNSP.2000.890140

Lee, E. R., Kim, P. K., & Kim, H. J. (1994). Automatic Recognition of a Car License Plate using Color Image Processing. *IEEE International Conference on Image Processing*, 2, 301-305. 10.1109/ICIP.1994.413580

Naito, T., Tsukada, T., Yamada, K., Kozuka, K., & Yamamoto, S. (2000). Robust License-Plate Recognition Method for Passing Vehicles under Outside Environment. *IEEE Transactions on Vehicular Technology*, *49*(6), 2309–2319. doi:10.1109/25.901900

Naito, T., Tsukada, T., Yamada, K., Kozuka, K., & Yamamoto, S. (n.d.). *Robust recognition methods for inclined license plates under various illumination conditions outdoors*. IEEE/IEEJ/JSAI

Nieuwoudt, C., & van Heerden, R. (1996). Automatic Number Plate Segmentation and Recognition. *Seventh Annual South African Workshop on Pattern Recognition IAPR*, 88-93.

Sarfraz, M., Ahmed, M., & Ghazi, S. A. (2003). Saudi Arabian License Plate Recognition System. In *Proceedings of IEEE International Conference on Geoemetric Modeling and Graphics-GMAG'2003-UK*. IEEE Computer Society Press.

Sarfraz, M., & Ahmed, M. J. (2005). *License Plate Recognition System: Saudi Arabian Case*. In M. Sarfraz (Ed.), *Computer-Aided Intelligent Recognition Techniques and Applications* (pp. 19–32). John Wiley and Sons. doi:10.1002/0470094168.ch2

Schalkoff, R. (1992). *J.: Pattern Recognition: Statistical*. Structural and Neural Approaches, John Willey & Sons Inc.

The MathWorks, Inc. (n.d.). *Matlab*. Retrieved 2018-02-03 from http://www.mathworks.com

Wikipedia. (n.d.). *Automatic number-plate recognition*. Retrieved 2018-02-03 from https://en.wikipedia.org/wiki/Automatic_number-plate_recognition#cite_note-29

Yan, D. (2001). A High Performance License Plate Recognition System Based on the Web Technique. *Proceedings IEEE Intelligent Transport Systems*, 325-329.

Yousuf, S. A., & Sarfraz, M. (2006). Identification of Number Plates under Extreme Outdoor Factors, International Journal of Pattern Reconition and Machine Intelligence. *International Scientific*, *01*(3), 69–78.

Yusuf, A. S., & Sarfraz, M. (2005). Color Edge Enhancement based Fuzzy Segmentation of License Plates. In *Proceedings of IEEE International Conference on Information Visualisation (IV'2005)-UK*. IEEE Computer Society Press.

Chapter 3
Intuitionistic Fuzzy Time Series Forecasting Based on Dual Hesitant Fuzzy Set for Stock Market:
DHFS–Based IFTS Model for Stock Market

Sanjay Kumar
G. B. Pant University of Agriculture and Technology, India

Kamlesh Bisht
G. B. Pant University of Agriculture and Technology, India

Krishna Kumar Gupta
G. B. Pant University of Agriculture and Technology, India

ABSTRACT

In this chapter, an application of dual hesitant fuzzy set (DHFS) in intuitionistic fuzzy time series forecasting is proposed to handle fuzziness and non-determinism that occurs due to multiple valid fuzzification method for time series data. Advantages of the proposed DHFS-based time series forecasting method are that it includes characteristics of both intuitionistic and hesitant fuzzy sets to handle the non-determinism and hesitancy corresponding to single membership grade multiple membership grades of an element. In the present study, universe of discourse is partitioned and fuzzified the time series data by two different fuzzification methods (triangular and Gaussian) to construct DHFS. Further, elements of DHFS are aggregated to construct the intuitionistic fuzzy sets. Proposed method is implemented over the share market prizes of SBI at BSE, India and SENSEX of BSE to confirm its out performance over existing time series forecasting methods using RMSE and AFER.

DOI: 10.4018/978-1-5225-5832-3.ch003

1. INTRODUCTION

Financial time series forecasting has been an important, challenging and intensive working area for researchers and practitioners. Prediction of stock price volatility which translates to high risk is important for investors to take investment decision for better return. Statistical techniques-based methods such as ARMA, ARIMA, ARCH and generalized ARCH were deployed for financial forecasting, but these methods fail to handle the uncertainty caused by the non-probabilistic and linguistic representation of financial time series data. Fuzzy set (Zadeh, 1965) based time series forecasting model proposed by Song & Chissom (1993, 1994) and Chen (1996) stand out as a key solution for financial instrument forecasting. Researchers and practitioners are more fascinated by fuzzy time series forecasting than traditional time series forecasting method because of their competent ness of handling uncertainty caused by aforesaid reasons. Various researchers (Chen et al., 2012; Hung & Lin, 2013; Wang et al., 2014; Diaz et al., 2016; Rubio et al., 2017) proposed numerous methods based on fuzzy approach for financial time series forecasting. Support vector machine (SVM), neural network, granular computing, genetic algorithm (GA), particle swarm optimization (PSO) and other nature based optimization techniques (Merh, 2012; Huang & Tsai, 2009; Roy, 2015; Lee et al., 2007; Chen & Chen, 2015; Efendi et al., 2015;Askari et al., 2015; Deng et al., 2016; Chen & Phuong, 2017) were integrated with fuzzy approach to propose intelligent fuzzy time series methods for enhancing accuracy in financial time series forecast.

Although fuzzy time series methods achieved great success in financial time series forecasting in environment of non-probabilistic uncertainty, but failed to handle non-determinism. Non-determinism in fuzzy time series forecasting occurs due to hesitation caused by use of single function in fuzzy set for both membership and non-membership and cannot be handled by random probability distribution. Atanassov (1986) generalized fuzzy set and defined Intuitionistic fuzzy set (IFS) to address issue of non- determinism caused by non- stochastic factors. IFS includes two distinct functions to determine membership and non- member ship grade of an element.

Application of IFS in time series forecasting was initiated by Joshi & Kumar (2011, 2012) to include hesitation in financial time series forecasting. Fuzzified IFS (Ansari, 2010) based financial time series forecasting method was proposed by Kumar & Gangwar (2015) to forecast SBI share price. Kumar & Gangwar (2016) defined intuitionistic fuzzy time series and used Cartesian product of IFSs to propose a methodology for intuitionistic fuzzy time series forecasting model. Recently, Wang, et al. (2016) established multidimensional intuitionistic fuzzy modus ponens inference and forecast rules based intuitionistic fuzzy approximate reasoning for time series forecasting. Fan et.al (2016) applied vector quantization and curve similarity measure to define long term intuitionistic fuzzy time series forecasting model to forecast TAIEX.

In real-world problems, it is arduous to define the membership grade of an element due to collection of possible membership values. In decision making problems, it is very general situation when decision maker disagree on the identical membership grade for an element. If fuzzify the time series data using the different fuzzification methods then this situation may also be occur in FTS forecasting. In this situation difficulty of constructing a common membership grade is not because of margin of error or possible distribution values (occurs in IFS or type-2 fuzzy sets, however, due to various possible membership values. To handle these situations, Torra and Narukawa (2009) and Torra (2010) introduced the hesitant fuzzy set (HFS) as a new generalization of fuzzy sets. Qian et al. (2013) introduced the generalized hesitant fuzzy sets and their application in decision support system. Fuzzification of time series data is a crucial step of any fuzzy time series forecasting method and is accomplish by opting the most appropriate fuzzification method. Motivated by the applications of HFSs in decision making problems (Xia & Xu, 2011). Bisht & Kumar (2016) proposed fuzzy time series forecasting model based on HFSs and claimed the out performance of proposed model in financial time series forecastingin hesitant environment.

Zhu et al. (2012) introduced dual hesitant fuzzy set (DHFS) as a new extension of fuzzy set. IFS consists two parts, membership and the non-membership hesitancy function; therefore, DHFS focused the many decision makers' approaches for providing more information about the ambiguity in the system. This is very flexible concept to assign values for every element in the domain and to handle non-determinacy and uncertainty as discussed in IFS and HFS. Zhu & Xu (2014) and Farhadinia (2014) used the concept of DHFSs.

In this paper, authors have presented novel approach of using DHFS in time series forecasting to remove the hesitancy in membership and non-membership grades of time series data. Jurio et al. (2010) method is applied over fuzzified data to construct dual hesitant fuzzy elements (DHFEs) and suitable aggregation operator is applied to aggregate DHFEs to have a single intuitionistic fuzzy element (IFE). After aggregation of DHFE, authors obtain IFEs, therefore authors apply the methodology of intuitionistic fuzzy time series to forecast time series data. Proposed method is implemented over the enrollment data and compared with other existing methods in terms of RMSE and AFER value.

2. PRELIMINARIES

Some basic definitions related to FS, IFS, DHFS and intuitionistic FTS are given below.

Definition 1: Let U be the discrete reference set. A fuzzy set A on U is defined as $A = \{< u_i, \mu_A(u_i) > \big| \forall u_i \in U\}$, where, $\mu_A(u_i)$ is the membership grade of u_i in fuzzy set A having any value between [0,1] depend upon the nature of membership function.

Definition 2: An intuitionistic fuzzy set I on U is defined as $I = \{< u_i, \mu_I(u_i), \nu_I(u_i) > \big| \forall u_i \in U\}$, where, $\mu_I(u_i)$ and $\nu_I(u_i)$ are the membership grade and non-membership grade of u_i in intuitionistic fuzzy set I having any value between [0,1] s.t. $0 < 1 - \mu_I(u_i) - \nu_I(u_i) < 1$, is known as degree of hesitancy.

Definition 3: A DHFS D over U is defined by following mathematical object:

$$D = \{< u, h(u), g(u) > \big| u \in U\}$$

$h(u)$ and $g(u)$ are possible membership degrees and non membership degrees of the element $u \in U$ to the set D respectively having values in the interval [0, 1] with the following conditions:

$$0 \leq \phi, \varphi \leq 1, 0 \leq \phi^+ + \varphi^+ \leq 1,$$

where $\phi \in h(u), \varphi \in g(u), \phi^+ = \max_{\phi \in h(u)} \{\phi\}, \varphi^+ = \max_{\varphi \in g(u)} \{\varphi\} \forall u \in U.$

Definition 4: Kumar and Gangwar (2015) defined the intuitionistic fuzzy time series as follows:

Assume, $Y(t)$, $(t = ...,0,1,2,...)$ is the sequential collection of data over a time interval or Universe of discourse and subset of real no. R. If $I_i(t), (i = 1,2,...)$ are the intuitionistic fuzzy sets defined in $Y(t)$ then the collection $\xi(t)$ of $I_i(t)$ is known as intuitionistic fuzzy time series.

If $I_i(t)$ is caused by $I_i(t-1) \in \xi(t-1)$ then the relationship can be expressed as $I_i(t-1) \rightarrow I_j(t)$.

3. PROPOSED METHOD AND ALGORITHM

In this section, the authors present the stepwise procedure of construction of DHFS, aggregation of DHFEs, construction of intuitionistic FLRs and intuitionistic defuzzification method for financial time series data as follows:

Step 1: Define the Universe of discourse (U) by observing maximum value of time series data (D_{max}), minimum value of time series data (D_{min}) and following given mathematical expression: $U = [E_{max}, E_{min}]$, where $E_{max} = D_{min} - D_1$, $E_{min} = D_{max} + D_2$ and D_1, D_2 are any proper positive integers.

Step 2: Partition U into equal length of intervals ($u_i, i \in N$) and construct triangular fuzzy set (A_i) and Gaussian fuzzy sets (G_i) according to the following rule:

$$A_k = [E_{min} + (k-1)h, E_{min} + kh, E_{min} + (k+1)h] \text{ for } k = 1,2,...,i-1, h = \frac{E_{max} - E_{min}}{no. \, of \, int \, ervals}$$

$$A_k = [E_{min} + (k-1)h, E_{min} + kh, E_{min} + kh] \text{ for } k = i$$

$$G_k = [\sigma, E_{min} + kh] \text{ for } k = 1,2,...,i, \sigma = \frac{h}{2}$$

Step 3: Fuzzify the time series data by using triangular and Gaussian membership functions. On each membership grades either occur by triangular membership functions or occur by Gaussian membership function authors apply the Jurio et al. (2010) method for finding the membership and non-membership grade for construction of DHFS. Procedure to finding the membership and non-membership grade by Jurio et al. (2010) method are given as follows:

Let $A_F \in FS_s(X)$, where $FS_s(X)$ represents collection of all fuzzy sets in X. Let $\pi : X \rightarrow [0,1]$ and $\delta : X \rightarrow [0,1]$ be two mappings.

$f : [0,1]^2 \times [0,1] \rightarrow L^*$ where $f(x,y,\delta) = (f_\mu(x,y,\delta), f_\nu(x,y,\delta))$, and f_μ, f_ν are given by following expression:

$$f_\mu(x,y,\delta) = x(1-\delta y)$$
$$f_\nu(x,y,\delta) = 1 - x(1-\delta y) - \delta y$$

Let $A_F \in FS_S(X)$, where $FS_s(X)$ represents collection of all fuzzy sets in X. Let $\pi : X \to [0,1]$ and $\delta : X \to [0,1]$ be two mappings.

Mapping $f : [0,1]^2 \times [0,1] \to L^*$ satisfies following properties:

1) If $y_1 \leq y_2$ then $\pi(f(x,y_1,\delta)) \leq \pi(f(x,y_2,\delta))$ for all $x,\delta \in [0,1]$.

2) $f_\mu(x,y,\delta) \leq x \leq 1 - f_\nu(x,y,\delta)$ for all $x \in [0,1]$.

3) $f(x,0,\delta) = (x, 1-x)$.

4) $f(0,y,\delta) = (0, 1-\delta y)$.

5) $f(x,y,0) = (x, 1-x)$.

6) $\pi(f(x,y,\delta)) = \delta y$.

Step 4: Each collection of membership grades and non-membership grades are aggregated to construct the IFSs. Following is the mathematical expression of aggregation operator:

$$O(\{x_1, x_2, ..., x_n\}) = 1 - \prod_{i=1}^{n} (1 - x_i)^{w_i}$$

here n is number of elements in the subset of [0, 1] and w_i is the weight of x_i where $i=1, 2, ...,n$. s.t. $\sum_{i=1}^{n} w_i = 1$.

Triangular and Gaussian membership functions are commonly used for fuzzification of time series data. To treat both fuzzification methods equally good and to remove any biasness during fuzzification of time series data, equal weight of 0.5 is assigned to both triangular and Gaussian membership grades in aggregation process.

Step 5: Use following algorithm for intuitionistic fuzzification of financial time series data.

for i= 1 to m (end of time series data)

for j= 1 to n (end of intervals)

choose

$$\mu_{ki} = max\left(\mu(x_1), \mu(x_2), ..., \mu(x_k), ..., \mu(x_n)\right), 1 \leq k \leq n$$

If I_K is intuitionistic fuzzy set corresponds to μ_{ki} then assign I_K to x_i.

end if

end for

end for

Intuitionistic fuzzy logical relations (IFLRs) are established using following rule:
If I_K is the intuitionistic fuzzy production of month n and I_j is the intuitionistic fuzzy production of month $n+1$, then the intuitionistic FLR is denoted as $I_K \rightarrow I_j$. Here, I_K and I_j are current and next intuitionistic fuzzy state respectively.

Step 6: Compute the first order intuitionistic fuzzy time invariant relation R_i, $i=$ number of intervals:

$$R_i = (I_i \times I_1) \cup (I_i \times I_2) \cup ... \cup (I_i \times I_k), k = \text{fuzzified time series data related with } i$$

$$R_i = R_{i1} \cup R_{i2} \cup ... \cup R_{ik}$$

$$R_i = \bigcup_l R_{il}$$

The intuitionistic fuzzy output is carried out as follows:

$$I_i = I_{i-1} \circ R_i$$

where, I_{i-1} and I_i the intuitionistic fuzzified production of previous state, current state respectively '$\circ$' is the max-min composition operator. If μ_i and ν_i are the row vector corresponding to the membership and non-membership respectively then the numerical forecast done by the given formula.

$$\text{Numerical forecast} = \frac{\sum_{i=1}^{n} \left|\mu_i - \nu_i\right| l_i}{\sum_{i=1}^{n} \left|\mu_i - \nu_i\right|}$$

Here, l_i is the mid-point of triangular or Gaussian fuzzy set and i vary from 1 to end of interval.

4. PERFORMANCE ANALYSIS

Performance of proposed forecasting method is analyzed using different error measures of root mean square error (RMSE) and average forecasting error (AFER). Following are expressions for RMSE and AFER.

$$\text{RMSE} = \sqrt{\frac{\sum_{i=1}^{n} \left(forecasted_i - actual_i\right)^2}{n}}$$

$$\text{AFER} = \frac{\sum_{i=1}^{n} \left|forecated_i - actual_i\right| / actual_i}{n} \times 100$$

5. IMPLEMENTATION OF PROPOSED METHOD

This section is divided into two subsections for implementation of proposed method over the financial database of share market prices of SBI at BSE, India and SENSEX of BSE.

5.1 SBI Share Price Forecasting

SBI is the largest Indian multinational government-owned public bank sector and finance service company. SBI is one of the top 50 global banks with balance sheet size of \$33 trillion. SBI share price is highly nonlinear database and is very much suitable to test the performance of proposed DHFS based intuitionistic fuzzy time series forecasting method. SBI share price dataset taken in this study includes observations from April 2009 to March 2010 (Table 1).

Following are some steps in forecasting SBI share prices as authors discussed in previous section:

Step 1: Observing the minimum and maximum value from Table 1 the Universe of discourse is defined as U= [1350, 2550]. Further, partition U into 6 equal intervals as follows:

Table 1. Actual SBI share price of year 2009-10

Month	Actual Share Price
April-09	1355.00
May-09	1891.00
Jun-09	1935.00
July-09	1840.00
August-09	1886.90
Sepember-09	2235.00
October-09	2500.00
November-09	2394.00
December-09	2374.75
January-10	2315.25
February-10	2059.95
March-10	2120.05

$$u_1 = [1350, 1550], u_2 = [1550, 1750], u_3 = [1750, 1950]$$
$$u_4 = [1950, 2150], u_5 = [2150, 2350], u_6 = [2350, 2550]$$

Step 2: Following six triangular and Gaussian fuzzy sets defined on U:

$$A_1 = [1350, 1550, 1750], A_2 = [1550, 1750, 1950], A_3 = [1750, 1950, 2150]$$
$$A_4 = [1950, 2150, 2350], A_5 = [2150, 2350, 2550], A_6 = [2350, 2550, 2550]$$

$$G_1 = [100, 1550], G_2 = [100, 1750], G_3 = [100, 1950]$$
$$G_4 = [100, 2150], G_5 = [100, 2350], G_6 = [100, 2550]$$

Step 3: Fuzzify the time series data by using triangular and Gaussian membership grades then apply the Jurio et. al (2010) method to construct the DHFS. Table 2 shows the DHFS for SBI share price data.
Step 4: Aggregate the DHFEs by given aggregation operator to construct the intuitionistic fuzzy set and shown in Table 3. Table 3 also shows the intuitionistic fuzzified SBI share price data.
Step 5: The intuitionistic fuzzy logical relations for SBI share price data are shown in Table 4.
Step 6: Apply the max-min composition operation over IFLR and also use the given numerical forecast to defuzzify the time series data. Table 5 shows the forecasted SBI share price by proposed method and also shows the forecasted outputs by Song and Chissom (1993), Chen (1996), Joshi and Kumar (2012). The reduced amount of RMSE and AFER value by proposed method over other compared model shows that proposed method has better accuracy and also least error.

Table 2. Dual hesitant fuzzy sets for SBI share price

Actual Share Price	D_1	D_2	D_3	D_4	D_5	D_6
1355.00	{0.024,0.149} {0.974,0.850}	{0,0.0004} {0,0.999}	{0,0} {0,0}	{0,0} {0,0}	{0,0} {0,0}	{0,0} {0,0}
1891.00	{0,0.002} {0,0.996}	{0.282,0.369} {0.675,0.629}	{0.411,0.840} {0.172,0.159}	{0,0.034} {0,0.963}	{0,0} {0,0}	{0,0} {0,0}
1935.00	{0,0.0006} {0,0.999}	{0.079,0.180} {0.886,0.819}	{0.539,0.988} {0.043,0.011}	{0,0.098} {0,0.898}	{0,0.00018} {0,0.999}	{0,0} {0,0}
1840.00	{0,0.0149} {0,0.984}	{0.527,0.6667} {0.431,0.332}	{0.262,0.546} {0.321,0.453}	{0,0.008} {0,0.989}	{0,0} {0,0}	{0,0} {0,0}
1886.90	{0,0.0034} {0,.996}	{0.302,0.391} {0.656,0.6080}	{0.399,0.819} {0.184,0.180}	{0,0.031} {0,0.966}	{0,0} {0,0}	{0,0} {0,0}
2235.00	{0,0} {0,0}	{0,0} {0,0}	{0,0.017} {0,0.982}	{0.384,0.695} {0.284,0.302}	{0,0.516} {0.449,0.48}	{0,0.0069} {0,0.986}
2500.00	{0,0} {0,0}	{0,0} {0,0}	{0,0} {0,0}	{0,0.0021} {0,0.995}	{0,0.324} {0.585,0.67}	{0,0.877} {0.22,0.11}
2394.00	{0,0} {0,0}	{0,0} {0,0}	{0,0} {0,0}	{0,0.0508} {0,0.947}	{0,0.907} {0.171,0.09}	{0,0.294} {0.707,0.69}
2374.75	{0,0} {0,0}	{0,0} {0,0}	{0,0.00012} {0,0.999}	{0,0.079} {0,0.918}	{0,0.969} {0.096,0.03}	{0,0.213} {0.794,0.77}
2315.25	{0,0} {0,0}	{0,0} {0,0}	{0,0.001268} {0,0.998}	{0,0.254} {0,0.743}	{0,0.941} {0.135,0.05}	{0,0.0631} {0.749,0.93}
2059.95	{0,0} {0,0}	{0,0.0081} {0,0.991}	{0,0.546} {0,0.453}	{0,0.665} {0,0.332}	{0,0.0148} {0.351,0.98}	{0,0} {0.498,0}
2120.05	{0,0} {0,0}	{0,0.0010} {0,0.998}	{0,0.235} {0,0.764}	{0,0.954} {0,0.043}	{0,0.071} {0.116,0.92}	{0,0} {0.771,0}

5.2. Forecasting SENSEX of BSE

In this section authors forecast the SENSEX of BSE by proposed DHFS based intuitionistic time series forecasting method. SENSEX is an abbreviation of the Bombay Exchange Sensitive Index, which is the benchmark index of the BSE. SENSEX is the oldest stock index in India composed of 30 of the largest and most actively-traded stocks on the BSE. The SENSEX is basically an indicator and gives us a general idea about whether most of the stocks have gone up or most of the stocks have gone down. Following are some steps in forecasting SENSEX of BSE:

Step 1: BSE SENSEX is taken from daily wise observation from month January 2012. Observing the minimum and maximum value from Table 6 the Universe of discourse is defined as $U = [15300, 17400]$. Further, partition U into 7 equal intervals as follows:

Table 3. Intuitionistic fuzzy set for market share price

Actual share price	I_1	I_2	I_3	I_4	I_5	I_6	Intuitionistic fuzzified data
1355.00	<0.089,0.938>	<0.0002,0.973>	<0,0>	<0,0>	<0,0>	<0,0>	I_1
1891.00	<0.001,0.944>	<0.327,0.653>	<0.693,0.165>	<0.0175,0.807>	<0,0>	<0,0>	I_3
1935.00	<0.0003,0.973>	<0.127,0.856>	<0.927,0.027>	<0.050,0.682>	<0,0.981>	<0,0>	I_3
1840.00	<0.0074,0.877>	<0.603,0.384>	<0.421,0.391>	<0.004,0.898>	<0,0>	<0,0>	I_2
1886.90	<0.0017,0.940>	<0.348,0.632>	<0.670,0.182>	<0.015,0.817>	<0,0>	<0,0>	I_3
2235.00	<0,0>	<0,0>	<0.008,0.868>	<0.567,0.293>	<0.431,0.466>	<0.003,0.88>	I_4
2500.00	<0,0>	<0,0>	<0,0>	<0.001,0.934>	<0.262,0.633>	<0.801,0.17>	I_6
2394.00	<0,0>	<0,0>	<0,0>	<0.025,0.769>	<0.809,0.132>	<0.248,0.70>	I_5
2374.75	<0,0>	<0,0>	<0,0.984>	<0.040,0.713>	<0.902,0.064>	<0.164,0.78>	I_5
2315.25	<0,0>	<0,0>	<0.0006,0.962>	<0.136,0.493>	<0.855,0.097>	<0.111,0.86>	I_5
2059.95	<0,0>	<0.0041,0.907>	<0.3264,0.260>	<0.421,0.183>	<0.250,0.901>	<0.230,0.29>	I_4
2120.05	<0,0>	<0.0005,0.963>	<0.1256,0.514>	<0.785,0.022>	<0.441,0.749>	<0.070,0.52>	I_4

Table 4. IFLR of SBI share price data

Intuitionistic Fuzzy Logical Relations		
$I_1 \rightarrow I_3$	$I_3 \rightarrow I_3$	$I_3 \rightarrow I_2$
$I_2 \rightarrow I_3$	$I_3 \rightarrow I_4$	$I_4 \rightarrow I_6$
$I_6 \rightarrow I_5$	$I_5 \rightarrow I_5$	$I_5 \rightarrow I_5$
$I_5 \rightarrow I_4$	$I_4 \rightarrow I_4$	

Table 5. Forecasted SBI share price data

Months	Actual and Forecasted SBI Share Price				
	Actual Share Price	Song and Chissom (1993)	Chen's Method (1996)	Joshi and Kumar (2012)	Proposed Method
April 2009	1355.00	-	-	-	-
May 2009	1891.00	2000.00	1600.00	1750.00	1785.464
June 2009	1935.00	2000.00	2000.00	1850.00	2101.426
July 2009	1840.00	2000.00	2000.00	1850.00	2101.426
August 2009	1886.90	2000.00	2000.00	1850.00	1824.036
September 2009	2235.00	2000.00	2000.00	1850.00	2101.426
October 2009	2500.00	2400.00	2400.00	2250.00	2114.719
November 009	2394.00	2000.00	2200.00	2350.00	2345.48
December 2009	2374.75	2000.00	2200.00	2350.00	2283.615
January 2010	2315.25	2000.00	2200.00	2350.00	2283.615
February 2010	2059.95	2000.00	2200.00	2250.00	2283.615
March 2010	2120.05	2000.00	2000.00	2050.00	2114.719
RMSE		25824.98	28000.43	25824.98	7434.62
AFER		5.31	7.351	5.316	3.15

$$u_1 = [15300, 15600], u_2 = [15600, 15900], u_3 = [15900, 16200]$$
$$u_4 = [16200, 16500], u_5 = [16500, 16800], u_6 = [16800, 17100], u_7 = [17100, 17400]$$

Step 2: Following seven triangular and Gaussian fuzzy sets defined on U:

$$A_1 = [15300, 15600, 15900], A_2 = [15600, 15900, 16200], A_3 = [15900, 16200, 16500]$$
$$A_4 = [16200, 16500, 16800], A_5 = [16500, 16800, 17100], A_6 = [16800, 17100, 17400]$$
$$A_7 = [17100, 17400, 17400]$$

$$G_1 = [150, 15600], G_2 = [150, `15900], G_3 = [150, 16200]$$
$$G_4 = [150, 16500], G_5 = [150, 16800], G_6 = [150, 17100], G_7 = [150, 17400]$$

Table 6. Dual hesitant fuzzy set for SENSEX data 1/1/2012 to 31/1/2012

Date	Index	D_1	D_2	D_3	D_4	D_5	D_6	D_7
1/1/2012	15454.92	{0.626,0.513} {0.373,0.481}	{0.012,0} {0.987,0}	{0,0} {0,0}	{0,0} {0,0}	{0,0} {0,0}	{0,0} {0,0}	{0,0} {0,0}
2/1/2012	15534.67	{0.909,0.778} {0.090,0.216}	{0.051,0} {0.948,0}	{0,0} {0,0}	{0,0} {0,0}	{0,0} {0,0}	{0,0} {0,0}	{0,0} {0,0}
3/1/2012	15640.56	{0.963,0.860} {0.035,0.134}	{0.224,0.117} {0.775,0.748}	{0.0009,0} {0.998,0}	{0,0} {0,0}	{0,0} {0,0}	{0,0} {0,0}	{0,0} {0,0}
4/1/2012	15967.49	{0.049,0} {0.950,0}	{0.903,0.670} {0.096,0.194}	{0.300,0.178} {0.699,0.613}	{0.001,0} {0.998,0}	{0,0} {0,0}	{0,0} {0,0}	{0,0} {0,0}
5/1/2012	15893.07	{0.148,0.022} {0.851,0.972}	{0.998,0.845} {0.001,0.019}	{0.123,0} {0.876,0}	{0.0002,0} {0.999,0}	{0,0} {0,0}	{0,0} {0,0}	{0,0} {0,0}
6/1/2012	15789.08	{0.451,0.367} {0.548,0.627}	{0.760,0.545} {0.239,0.320}	{0.023,0} {0.935,0}	{0,0} {0,0}	{0,0} {0,0}	{0,0} {0,0}	{0,0} {0,0}
7/1/2012	15893.03	{0.148,0.023} {0.851,0.972}	{0.998,0.845} {0.001,0.020}	{0.123,0} {0,0}	{0.0002,0} {0.999,0}	{0,0} {0,0}	{0,0} {0,0}	{0,0} {0,0}
8/1/2012	15848.80	{0.252,0.169} {0.747,0.825}	{0.943,0.717} {0.056,0.147}	{0.064,0} {0.867,0}	{0,0} {0,0}	{0,0} {0,0}	{0,0} {0,0}	{0,0} {0,0}
9/1/2012	15480.22	{0.726,0.597} {0.272,0.397}	{0.019,0} {0.979,0}	{0,0} {0.935,0}	{0,0} {0,0}	{0,0} {0,0}	{0,0} {0,0}	{0,0} {0,0}
10/1/2012	15898.32	{0.138,0.005} {0.861,0.989}	{0.999,0.860} {0,0.004}	{0.132,0} {0,0}	{0.0003,0} {0.999,0}	{0,0} {0,0}	{0,0} {0,0}	{0,0} {0,0}
11/1/2012	16222.37	{0.0001,0} {0.999,0}	{0.099,0} {0.900,0}	{0.988,0.732} {0.867,0.05}	{0.180,0.069} {0.819,0}	{0.0006,0} {0.998,0}	{0,0} {0,0}	{0,0} {0,0}
12/1/2012	16117.19	{0.002,0} {0.997,0}	{0.350,0.238} {0.649,0.626}	{0.858,0.573} {0.011,0.218}	{0.038,0} {0.961,0}	{0,0} {0,0}	{0,0} {0,0}	{0,0} {0,0}
13/1/2012	16144.57	{0.001,0} {0.998,0}	{0.264,0.159} {0.735,0.705}	{0.933,0.645} {0.141,0.146}	{0.060,0} {0.939,0}	{0,0} {0,0}	{0,0} {0,0}	{0,0} {0,0}
14/1/2012	16154.62	{0.001,0} {0.998,0}	{0.236,0.130} {0.762,0.734}	{0.955,0.672} {0.065,0.119}	{0.070,0} {0.929,0}	{0,0} {0,0}	{0,0} {0,0}	{0,0} {0,0}
15/1/2012	16121.46	{0.002,0} {0.997,0}	{0.336,0.226} {0.663,0.638}	{0.871,0.584} {0.044,0.207}	{0.041,0} {0.958,0}	{0,0} {0,0}	{0,0} {0,0}	{0,0} {0,0}

continued on following page

Table 6. Continued

Date	Index	D_1	D_2	D_3	D_4	D_5	D_6	D_7
16/1/2012	16086.74	{0.005,0} {0.994,0}	{0.46,0.326} {0.539,0.538}	{0.751,0.492} {0.128,0.298}	{0.022,0} {0.977,0}	{0,0} {0,0}	{0,0} {0,0}	{0,0} {0,0}
17/1/2012	16270.87	{0,0} {0,0}	{0.047,0} {0.952,0}	{0.894,0.604} {0.247,0.187}	{0.311,0.218} {0.688,0.707}	{0.001,0} {0.997,0}	{0,0} {0,0}	{0,0} {0,0}
18/1/2012	16502.42	{0,0} {0,0}	{0.0003,0} {0.999,0}	{0.130,0} {0.105,0.187}	{0.999,0.918} {0.0001,0.007}	{0.139,0.008} {0.859,0.984}	{0.0003,0} {0.999,0}	{0,0} {0,0}
19/1/2012	16573.87	{0,0} {0,0}		{0.044,0} {0.868,0}	{0.885,0.698} {0.114,0.228}	{0.320,0.244} {0.678,0.747}	{0.002,0} {0.997,0}	{0,0} {0,0}
20/1/2012	16745.01	{0,0} {0,0}		{0.001,0} {0.954,0}	{0.263,0.169} {0.736,0.756}	{0.934,0.810} {0.064,0.181}	{0.060,0} {0.938,0}	{0,0} {0,0}
21/1/2012	16739.01	{0,0} {0,0}		{0.001,0} {0.998,0}	{0.28,0.188} {0.718,0.737}	{0.920,0.790} {0.079,0.201}	{0.055,0} {0.944,0}	{0,0} {0,0}
22/1/2012	16621.32	{0,0} {0,0}		{0.019,0} {0.998,0}	{0.720,0.551} {0.278,0.374}	{0.491,0.401} {0.507,0.590}	{0.006,0} {0.993,0}	{0,0} {0,0}
23/1/2012	16667.02	{0,0} {0,0}		{0.007,0} {0.980,0}	{0.537,0.410} {0.461,0.515}	{0.674,0.552} {0.324,0.439}	{0.015,0} {0.984,0}	{0,0} {0,0}
24/1/2012	16806.72	{0,0} {0,0}		{0.0002,0} {0.991,0}	{0.123,0} {0.876,0}	{0.998,0.969} {0.001,0.022}	{0.147,0.021} {0.851,0.957}	{0.0004,0} {0.999,0}
25/1/2012	17068.85	{0,0} {0,0}		{0,0} {0.999,0}	{0.0007,0} {0.999,0}	{0.200,0.103} {0.798,0.889}	{0.978,0.877} {0.021,0.101}	{0.0874,0} {0.912,0}
26/1/2012	17077.18	{0,0} {0,0}		{0,0} {0,0}	{0.0006,0} {0.999,0}	{0.181,0.075} {0.818,0.916}	{0.988,0.904} {0.011,0.074}	{0.098,0} {0.901,0}
27/1/2012	17201.33	{0,0} {0,0}		{0,0} {0,0}	{0,0} {0,0}	{0.027,0} {0.971,0}	{0.795,0.648} {0.203,0.330}	{0.415,0.318} {0.583,0.624}
28/1/2012	17233.98	{0,0} {0,0}		{0,0} {0,0}	{0,0} {0,0}	{0.015,0} {0.984,0}	{0.670,0.541} {0.328,0.437}	{0.541,0.421} {0.457,0.522}
29/1/2012	17189.13	{0,0} {0,0}		{0,0} {0,0}	{0,0} {0,0}	{0.034,0} {0.964,0}	{0.837,0.688} {0.161,0.290}	{0.372,0.280} {0.627,0.663}
30/1/2012	17138.04	{0,0} {0,0}		{0,0} {0,0}	{0.0001,0} {0.999,0}	{0.078,0} {0.920,0}	{0.968,0.855} {0.031,0.124}	{0.217,0.119} {0.782,0.823}
31/1/2012	16965.58	{0,0} {0,0}		{0,0} {0,0}	{0.008,0} {0.991,0}	{0.5430.444} {0.455,0.547}	{0.669,0.540} {0.330,0.438}	{0.015,0} {0.984,0}

Table 7. Intuitionistic fuzzy set for SENSEX data 1/1/2012 to 31/1/2012

Index	I_1	I_2	I_3	I_4	I_5	I_6	I_7	Intuitionistic Fuzzified Data
15454.92	<0.573,0.429>	<0.006,0.887>	<0,0>	<0,0>	<0,0>	<0,0>	<0,0>	I_1
15534.67	<0.858,0.155>	<0.026,0.772>	<0,0>	<0,0>	<0,0>	<0,0>	<0,0>	I_1
15640.56	<0.929,0.086>	<0.172,0.762>	<0.0004,0.964>	<0,0>	<0,0>	<0,0>	<0,0>	I_1
15967.49	<0.025,0.776>	<0.821,0.146>	<0.241,0.659>	<0.0009,0.955>	<0,0>	<0,0>	<0,0>	I_2
15893.07	<0.087,0.935>	<0.985,0.010>	<0.063,0.648>	<0.0001,0.980>	<0,0>	<0,0>	<0,0>	I_2
15789.08	<0.411,0.589>	<0.670,0.280>	<0.011,0.845>	<0,0>	<0,0>	<0,0>	<0,0>	I_2
15893.03	<0.087,0.935>	<0.985,0.010>	<0.063,0.648>	<0.0001,0.980>	<0,0>	<0,0>	<0,0>	I_2
15848.80	<0.212,0.789>	<0.873,0.103>	<0.032,0.745>	<0,0>	<0,0>	<0,0>	<0,0>	I_2
15480.22	<0.668,0.338>	<0.010,0.857>	<0,0>	<0,0>	<0,0>	<0,0>	<0,0>	I_1
15898.32	<0.074,0.962>	<0.992,0.002>	<0.068,0.635>	<0.0001,0.979>	<0,0>	<0,0>	<0,0>	I_2
16222.37	<0,0.981>	<0.050,0.684>	<0.944,0.035>	<0.126,0.575>	<0.0003,0.965>	<0,0>	<0,0>	I_3
16117.19	<0.001,0.947>	<0.296,0.638>	<0.754,0.180>	<0.0194,0.803>	<0,0>	<0,0>	<0,0>	I_3

continued on following page

Table 7. Continued

Index	I_1	I_2	I_3	I_4	I_5	I_6	I_7	Intuitionistic Fuzzified Data
16144.57	<0.0006,0.960>	<0.214,0.720>	<0.846,0.107>	<0.030,0.754>	<0,0>	<0,0>	<0,0>	I_3
16154.62	<0.0005,0.964>	<0.185,0.749>	<0.878,0.083>	<0.0359,0.734>	<0,0>	<0,0>	<0,0>	I_3
16121.46	<0.001,0.949>	<0.283,0.651>	<0.769,0.168>	<0.020,0.796>	<0,0>	<0,0>	<0,0>	I_3
16086.74	<0.002,0.926>	<0.397,0.538>	<0.645,0.273>	<0.011,0.849>	<0,0>	<0,0>	<0,0>	I_3
16270.87	<0,0>	<0.023,0.782>	<0.795,0.147>	<0.266,0.698>	<0.0009,0.949>	<0,0>	<0,0>	I_3
16502.42	<0,0>	<0.0001,0.974>	<0.067,0.637>	<0.995,0.003>	<0.076,0.952>	<0.0001,0.973>	<0,0>	I_4
16573.87	<0,0>	<0,0>	<0.022,0.787>	<0.814,0.173>	<0.283,0.715>	<0.001,0.950>	<0,0>	I_4
16745.01	<0,0>	<0,0>	<0.0006,0.959>	<0.217,0.746>	<0.888,0.125>	<0.030,0.752>	<0,0>	I_5
16739.01	<0,0>	<0,0>	<0.0007,0.957>	<0.236,0.728>	<0.870,0.142>	<0.028,0.764>	<0,0>	I_5
16621.32	<0,0>	<0,0>	<0.009,0.859>	<0.646,0.328>	<0.448,0.551>	<0.003,0.919>	<0,0>	I_4
16667.02	<0,0>	<0,0>	<0.003,0.909>	<0.478,0.489>	<0.618,0.384>	<0.007,0.874>	<0,0>	I_5
16806.72	<0,0>	<0,0>	<0.0001,0.976>	<0.063,0.648>	<0.993,0.011>	<0.087,0.920>	<0.0002,0.975>	I_5
17068.85	<0,0>	<0,0>	<0,0>	<0.0003,0.970>	<0.153,0.850>	<0.948,0.062>	<0.044,0.703>	I_6

continued on following page

51

Table 7. Continued

Index	I_1	I_2	I_3	I_4	I_5	I_6	I_7	Intuitionistic Fuzzified Data
17077.18	<0,0>	<0,0>	<0,0>	<0.0003,0.973>	<0.129,0.876>	<0.966,0.043>	<0.050,0.685>	I_6
17201.33	<0,0>	<0,0>	<0,0>	<0,0>	<0.014,0.831>	<0.732,0.270>	<0.369,0.604>	I_6
17233.98	<0,0>	<0,0>	<0,0>	<0,0>	<0.007,0.874>	<0.611,0.385>	<0.485,0.490>	I_6
17189.13	<0,0>	<0,0>	<0,0>	<0,0>	<0.017,0.812>	<0.775,0.229>	<0.327,0.645>	I_6
17138.04	<0,0>	<0,0>	<0,0>	<0,0.984>	<0.040,0.718>	<0.931,0.079>	<0.170,0.804>	I_6
16965.58	<0,0>	<0,0>	<0,0>	<0.004,0.909>	<0.496,0.503>	<0.610,0.387>	<0.007,0.876>	I_6

Table 8. Intuitionistic fuzzy logical relations for SENSEX data

Intuitionistic Fuzzy Logical Relations for SENSEX Data					
$I_1 \rightarrow I_1$	$I_1 \rightarrow I_1$	$I_1 \rightarrow I_2$	$I_2 \rightarrow I_2$	$I_2 \rightarrow I_2$	$I_2 \rightarrow I_2$
$I_2 \rightarrow I_2$	$I_2 \rightarrow I_2$	$I_2 \rightarrow I_1$	$I_1 \rightarrow I_2$	$I_2 \rightarrow I_3$	$I_3 \rightarrow I_3$
$I_3 \rightarrow I_3$	$I_3 \rightarrow I_3$	$I_3 \rightarrow I_3$	$I_3 \rightarrow I_3$	$I_3 \rightarrow I_3$	$I_3 \rightarrow I_4$
$I_4 \rightarrow I_4$	$I_4 \rightarrow I_5$	$I_5 \rightarrow I_5$	$I_5 \rightarrow I_6$	$I_6 \rightarrow I_6$	$I_6 \rightarrow I_6$
$I_6 \rightarrow I_6$	$I_6 \rightarrow I_6$	$I_6 \rightarrow I_6$	$I_6 \rightarrow I_6$		

Step 3: Fuzzify the time series data by using triangular and Gaussian membership grades then apply the Jurio et. al (2010) method to construct the DHFS. Table 6 shows the DHFS for BSE SENSEX.

Step 4: Table 7 and 8 are shows the intuitionistic fuzzy set and IFLR for SENSEX data.

Step 5: The forecasted SENSEX data by proposed method is shown in Table 9. Table 9 also shows the forecasted SENSEX data by Song and Chissom (1993), Chen (1996), Joshi and Kumar (2012). Again, reduced amount of RMSE and AFER value by proposed method over other compared model shows that proposed method has better accuracy and also least error.

6. CONCLUSION

In this research paper, authors have proposed use of DHFS in time series forecasting and presented a DHFS based intuitionistic fuzzy time series forecasting model. The proposed model include characteristics of both intuitionistic and hesitant fuzzy sets, hence it is capable enough to handle both type of non-probabilistic nondeterminism that occurs due to hesitation and availability of multiple fuzzification methods for time series data. Out performance of proposed method is measured in terms of RMSE and AFER and it outperforms other existing fuzzy and intuitionistic fuzzy set based time series forecasting methods. On the basis of above discussion, it is concluded that proposed model is competent enough to handle the hesitation in financial time series forecasting.

Table 9. Forecasted SENSEX data

Date	Actual SENSEX Price	Song and Chissom (1993)	Chen's Method (1996)	Joshi and Kumar (2012)	Proposed Mathod
1/1/ 2012	15454.92	-	-	-	-
2/1/ 2012	15534.67	15600	15600.00	15750.00	15723.75
3/1/ 2012	15640.56	15600	15600.00	15750.00	15723.75
4/1/ 2012	15967.49	15900	15900.00	15750.00	15943.53
5/1/ 2012	15893.07	16050	16050.00	16200.00	15941.76
6/1/ 2012	15789.08	15900	15900.00	15750.00	15941.76
7/1/ 2012	15893.03	15900	15900.00	15750.00	15941.76
8/1/ 2012	15848.80	15900	15900.00	15750.00	15941.76
9/1/ 2012	15480.22	15900	15900.00	15750.00	15723.75
10/1/ 2012	15898.32	15600	15600.00	15750.00	15943.53
11/1/ 2012	16222.37	15900	15900.00	15750.00	16236.07
12/1/ 2012	16117.19	15350	15350.00	16450.00	16466.78
13/1/ 2012	16144.57	16050	16050.00	16200.00	16466.78
14/1/ 2012	16154.62	16050	16050.00	16200.00	16466.78
15/1/ 2012	16121.46	16050	16050.00	16200.00	16466.78
16/1/ 2012	16086.74	16050	16050.00	16200.00	16466.78
17/1/ 2012	16270.87	16500	16050.00	16200.00	16466.78
18/1/ 2012	16502.42	16500	15350.00	16450.00	16661.87
19/1/ 2012	16573.87	16800	16800.00	16650.00	16658.70
20/1/ 2012	16745.01	16500	16800.00	16650.00	16664.65
21/1/ 2012	16739.01	16500	16800.00	16650.00	16664.65
22/1/ 2012	16621.32	16500	16800.00	16650.00	16658.85
23/1/ 2012	16667.02	16800	16800.00	16650.00	16664.65
24/1/ 2012	16806.72	16800	16800.00	16650.00	16664.65
25/1/ 2012	17068.85	17400	17100.00	16650.00	17096.90
26/1/ 2012	17077.18	17400	17100.00	16650.00	17096.90
27/1/ 2012	17201.33	17100	17100.00	17100.00	17096.90
28/1/ 2012	17233.98	17100	17100.00	17100.00	17096.90
29/1/ 2012	17189.13	17100	17100.00	17100.00	17096.90
30/1/ 2012	17138.04	17100	17100.00	17100.00	17096.90
31/1/ 2012	16965.58	17100	17100.00	17100.00	17096.90
RMSE		51897.41	85856.17	38472.94	29717.54
AFER		1.0125	1.064	0.933	0.8177

REFERENCES

Ansari, A. Q., Philip, J., Siddiqui, S. A., & Alvi, J. A. (2010). Fuzzification of intuitionistic fuzzy sets. *International Journal of Computational Cognition, 8*(3).

Askari, S., Montazerin, N., & Zarandi, M. F. (2015). A clustering based forecasting algorithm for multi-variable fuzzy time series using linear combinations of independent variables. *Applied Soft Computing, 35,* 151–160. doi:10.1016/j.asoc.2015.06.028

Atanassov, K. T. (1986). Intuitionistic fuzzy sets. *Fuzzy Sets and Systems, 20*(1), 87–96. doi:10.1016/S0165-0114(86)80034-3

Bisht, K., & Kumar, S. (2016). Fuzzy time series forecasting method based on hesitant fuzzy sets. *Expert Systems with Applications, 64,* 557–568. doi:10.1016/j.eswa.2016.07.044

Chen, M. Y., & Chen, B. T. (2015). A hybrid fuzzy time series model based on granular computing for stock price forecasting. *Information Sciences, 294,* 227–241. doi:10.1016/j.ins.2014.09.038

Chen, S. M. (1996). Forecasting enrollments based on fuzzy time series. *Fuzzy Sets and Systems, 81*(3), 311–319. doi:10.1016/0165-0114(95)00220-0

Chen, S. M., Chu, H. P., & Sheu, T. W. (2012). TAIEX forecasting using fuzzy time series and automatically generated weights of multiple factors. *IEEE Transactions on Systems, Man, and Cybernetics. Part A, Systems and Humans, 42*(6), 1485–1495. doi:10.1109/TSMCA.2012.2190399

Chen, S. M., & Phuong, B. D. H. (2017). Fuzzy time series forecasting based on optimal partitions of intervals and optimal weighting vectors. *Knowledge-Based Systems, 118,* 204–216. doi:10.1016/j.knosys.2016.11.019

Deng, W., Wang, G., Zhang, X., Xu, J., & Li, G. (2016). A multi-granularity combined prediction model based on fuzzy trend forecasting and particle swarm techniques. *Neurocomputing, 173,* 1671–1682. doi:10.1016/j.neucom.2015.09.040

Diaz, D., Theodoulidis, B., & Dupouy, C. (2016). Modelling and forecasting interest rates during stages of the economic cycle: A knowledge-discovery approach. *Expert Systems with Applications, 44,* 245–264. doi:10.1016/j.eswa.2015.09.010

Efendi, R., Ismail, Z., & Deris, M. M. (2015). A new linguistic out-sample approach of fuzzy time series for daily forecasting of Malaysian electricity load demand. *Applied Soft Computing, 28,* 422–430. doi:10.1016/j.asoc.2014.11.043

Fan, X., Lei, Y., Wang, Y., & Lu, Y. (2016). Long-term intuitionistic fuzzy time series forecasting model based on vector quantisation and curve similarity measure. *IET Signal Processing, 10*(7), 805–814. doi:10.1049/iet-spr.2015.0496

Farhadinia, B. (2014). Correlation for dual hesitant fuzzy sets and dual interval-valued hesitant fuzzy sets. *International Journal of Intelligent Systems, 29*(2), 184–205. doi:10.1002/int.21633

Huang, C. L., & Tsai, C. Y. (2009). A hybrid SOFM-SVR with a filter-based feature selection for stock market forecasting. *Expert Systems with Applications, 36*(2), 1529–1539. doi:10.1016/j.eswa.2007.11.062

Hung, K. C., & Lin, K. P. (2013). Long-term business cycle forecasting through a potential intuitionistic fuzzy least-squares support vector regression approach. *Information Sciences, 224,* 37–48. doi:10.1016/j. ins.2012.10.033

Joshi, B., & Kumar, S. (2012). A computational method of forecasting based on intuitionistic fuzzy sets and fuzzy time series. In *Proceedings of the International Conference on Soft Computing for Problem Solving (SocProS 2011) December 20-22, 2011* (pp. 993-1000). Springer Berlin/Heidelberg. 10.1007/978-81-322-0491-6_91

Joshi, B. P., & Kumar, S. (2012). Fuzzy time series model based on intuitionistic fuzzy sets for empirical research in stock market. *International Journal of Applied Evolutionary Computation, 3*(4), 71–84. doi:10.4018/jaec.2012100105

Kumar, S., & Gangwar, S. S. (2016). Intuitionistic Fuzzy Time Series: An Approach for Handling Nondeterminism in Time Series Forecasting. *IEEE Transactions on Fuzzy Systems, 24*(6), 1270–1281. doi:10.1109/TFUZZ.2015.2507582

Lee, L. W., Wang, L. H., & Chen, S. M. (2007). Temperature prediction and TAIFEX forecasting based on fuzzy logical relationships and genetic algorithms. *Expert Systems with Applications, 33*(3), 539–550. doi:10.1016/j.eswa.2006.05.015

Merh, N. (2012). Stock Market Forecasting: Comparison between Artificial Neural Networks and Arch Models. *Journal of Information Technology Applications & Management, 19*(1), 1–12.

Qian, G., Wang, H., & Feng, X. (2013). Generalized hesitant fuzzy sets and their application in decision support system. *Knowledge-Based Systems, 37,* 357–365. doi:10.1016/j.knosys.2012.08.019

Roy, S. S., Mittal, D., Basu, A., & Abraham, A. (2015). Stock market forecasting using lasso linear regression model. In *Afro-European Conference for Industrial Advancement* (pp. 371–381). Cham: Springer. doi:10.1007/978-3-319-13572-4_31

Rubio, A., Bermúdez, J. D., & Vercher, E. (2017). Improving stock index forecasts by using a new weighted fuzzy-trend time series method. *Expert Systems with Applications, 76,* 12–20. doi:10.1016/j. eswa.2017.01.049

Song, Q., & Chissom, B. S. (1993). Fuzzy time series and its models. *Fuzzy Sets and Systems, 54*(3), 269–277. doi:10.1016/0165-0114(93)90372-O

Song, Q., & Chissom, B. S. (1993). Forecasting enrollments with fuzzy time series—part I. *Fuzzy Sets and Systems, 54*(1), 1–9. doi:10.1016/0165-0114(93)90355-L

Song, Q., & Chissom, B. S. (1994). Forecasting enrollments with fuzzy time series—part II. *Fuzzy Sets and Systems, 62*(1), 1–8. doi:10.1016/0165-0114(94)90067-1

Torra, V. (2010). Hesitant fuzzy sets. *International Journal of Intelligent Systems, 25*(6), 529–539.

Torra, V., & Narukawa, Y. (2009, August). On hesitant fuzzy sets and decision. In *Fuzzy Systems, 2009. FUZZ-IEEE 2009. IEEE International Conference on* (pp. 1378-1382). IEEE. 10.1109/FUZZY.2009.5276884

Wang, L., Liu, X., Pedrycz, W., & Shao, Y. (2014). Determination of temporal information granules to improve forecasting in fuzzy time series. *Expert Systems with Applications, 41*(6), 3134–3142. doi:10.1016/j.eswa.2013.10.046

Wang, Y. N., Lei, Y., Fan, X., & Wang, Y. (2016). Intuitionistic fuzzy time series forecasting model based on intuitionistic fuzzy reasoning. *Mathematical Problems in Engineering.*

Wang, Y. N., Lei, Y., Lei, Y., & Fan, X. (2016). Multi-factor high-order intuitionistic fuzzy time series forecasting model. *Journal of Systems Engineering and Electronics, 27*(5), 1054–1062. doi:10.21629/ JSEE.2016.05.13

Xia, M., & Xu, Z. (2011). Hesitant fuzzy information aggregation in decision making. *International Journal of Approximate Reasoning, 52*(3), 395–407. doi:10.1016/j.ijar.2010.09.002

Zadeh, L. A. (1965). Information and control. *Fuzzy Sets, 8*(3), 338-353.

Zhu, B., & Xu, Z. (2014). Some results for dual hesitant fuzzy sets. *Journal of Intelligent & Fuzzy Systems, 26*(4), 1657–1668.

Zhu, B., Xu, Z., & Xia, M. (2012). Dual hesitant fuzzy sets. *Journal of Applied Mathematics.*

Chapter 4
Design and Implementation of an Intelligent Traffic Management System:
A Neural Approach

Shamim Akhter
East West University (EWU), Bangladesh

Sakhawat Hosain Sumit
Socian Ltd., Bangladesh

Md. Rahatur Rahman
Simplexhub Ltd., Bangladesh

ABSTRACT

Intelligence traffic management system (ITMS) provides effective and efficient solutions toward the road traffic management and decision-making problems, and thus helps to reduce fuel consumption and emission of greenhouse gases. Software-based real-time bi-directional TMS with a neural network was proposed and implemented. The proposed TMS solves a decision problem, dynamic road weights calculation, using different environmental, road and vehicle related decision attributes. In addition, the development of the real-time operational models as well as their solving challenges has increased in a rapid manner. Therefore, the authors integrate the design and development of a neural-based complete real-time operational ITMS, with the combination of software modules including traffic monitoring, road weight updating, forecasting, and optimum route planning decision. Collecting, extracting the insights and inherit meaning, and modeling the tremendous amount of continuous data is a challenging task. A discussion is also included with the future improvements on ITMS.

DOI: 10.4018/978-1-5225-5832-3.ch004

INTRODUCTION

Intelligence Traffic Management System (ITMS) incorporates modern emerging technologies including information processing, intelligent embedded systems, internet and wireless communication, electronics, and etc., to provide continuous or pre-selected travel information, congestion alleviation, incident detection and/or guide optimal route (re-route) to travelers, vehicles and infrastructure. Four (4) major stages including data collection, data processing, decision making stages, and information delivery, are involved within an ITMS. Software based real time bi-directional traffic management system (TMS) with Artificial Neural Network (ANN) was proposed and implemented in (Rahman & Akhter, 2015a; 2015b; 2015c). The proposed TMS solved a decision problem, dynamic road weights calculation, using different environmental, road and vehicle related decision attributes. Back Propagation Neural Network (BPNN) with Levenberg-Marquardt (LM) optimization was adopted in (Akhter et al., 2016) to replace DT. NN classifies four (4) different decision classes, and they correspond to four (4) different weight increment/ decrement values. Cluster based classifications are able to find the optimum number of classifications in each attribute and can improve the classification performance of the ITMS. With this hypothesis, Hierarchical and K-means clustering were applied on environmental data in (Nawrin et al., 2017), and Dunn-Index cluster validation technique was performed better.

Current ITMS has two (2) different decision making frameworks- road weight updating and future road weight forecasting. Forecasting is helpful due to the estimation of optimum routes and reduces the effects of traffic jam in advance. Exponential Weighted Moving Average (EWMA) algorithm (Reporter, 2016) on time series data was used in (Rahman & Akhter, 2015c) to calculate the predicted factor values on time series rainfall data. However, the performance is not so adequate. Therefore, we incorporate an experimental measurement of accuracy level for other road weight factors separately. The evaluation results for weight influencing factors using EWMA achieves accuracy level 72.93% for rainfall, 85.81% for temperature, 45.15% for humidity, 18.52% for wind, and 16.45% for road status.

In addition, building the interoperability between classifications and clustering algorithms is necessary. BPNN was performing well by providing classification result only but the decision for the actual weight calculation or weight mapping was missing. Therefore, in this chapter, we integrate the design and development of a neural based complete real time operational ITMS, with the combination of software and hardware based modules including traffic monitoring, road weight updating, forecasting, congestion management, and optimum route planning decision. Figure 1 presents the integrated design framework.

Data collection is another dimension; for this kind of research. Intelligent data crawling feature is enhanced to collect required data automatically from assigned web domain. However, their coverage is limited to city level congregate information and location/area/road segment based high resolution information is necessary for real time TMS decision. Thus, in this chapter, a prospect of Internet of Things (IoT) based online integrated sensors are also included in future research directions section.

RELATED WORK

Radio and television are common service providers to broadcast traffic related estimated information. Several web sites contribute on-line based real time traffic condition services. Over the time, different solutions (Verma, 2012; Aloul et al., 2012; Dhar, 2008; Romão, 2006; Angel et al., 2003) have been proposed, to solve the traffic management related decision problems. The solutions vary in their core technologies, as some of them used infrared sensors, CCTV cameras, machine vision (image processing), GSM and/or cellular towers, RFID gateways, sound sensors, aerial surveillance, remote sensing, and etc. In (Romão, 2006), high quality CCTV cameras were used to capture vehicle images and machine vision technique was applied to process them, and to retrieve essential information. The procedure was very expensive, due to high cost of CCTVs, and also required heavy installations and regular maintenances. In addition, machine vision was not effective during heavy snowfall, sand storm, rainfall, and foggy weather circumstances. In (Aloul et al., 2012; Dhar, 2008), RFID Sensor was used, and this technology required installed RFID gates and vehicles were needed to pass through those gates. It was inefficient and ineffective procedure. Surveillance Drone and aerial imagery techniques were used in (Verma, 2012; Angel et al., 2003). They were only effective during the normal weather condition and could not be an option during bad weather condition. Furthermore, the deployment and the maintenance of such technologies carried high cost.

Bluetooth and Wi-Fi signals were used for measuring travel times (Reporter, 2013). Wireless connections, particularly in urban areas, get worse gradually. In addition, Bluetooth based solutions are suitable for unidirectional monitoring traffic flows only. Automatic number plate recognition (ANPR) systems were used in (ANPR, 2014); and they maintained more sophisticated control systems and more sensitive image processing technologies. However, ANPR systems required high quality cameras with fast frame rates to capture an image of the number plate, with enough definition for the system, to define the vehicle's registration number. Installation and maintenance of such cameras are relatively costly. Thus, many of those solutions are either very expensive or difficult to install and maintain over the periods of time. Moreover, their coverage zones are limited and most of the existing technologies use unicast communication. Bi-directional communication is already in use for different purposes like Named Data Networking (Almishari et al., 2014), video conferencing (Panagiotakis et al., 2013), chatting, telecommunication etc. However the benefits and the results of real time bi-directional communication are yet to be discovered especially for moving agents (i.e. the road traffic system). Questions were raised - whether any approach or technique would bring low operational-cost but flexible internet-based solution for road traffic system.

Therefore, a new internet-based (WebSocket (HTML5 Web Sockets, 2015) over HTTP) traffic management support system (ITMS) with real time bi-directional communication was implemented (in Rahman & Akhter, 2015a; 2015b; 2015c) to assist the traffic system. It supports low cost implementation, flexibility, maintainability and infrastructure security. Initially, decision tree (DT) (Rahman, 2012) was used to classify road weights (Rahman & Akhter, 2015a; 2015b; 2015c) and weighted moving average analytic was implemented to estimate or predict feature values and achieved 16.45% accuracy. However, DT did not work well with continuous data and reconstruction may require for exceptional situation (e.g. missing values). Later, Back Propagation Neural Network (BPNN) with Levenberg-Marquardt (LM) optimization was adopted in (Akhter et al., 2016) to replace DT and achieved 96.67% accuracy. The NN classification provided four (4) different decision classes and directly corresponded to four (4) different weight increments. In addition, the NN model attribute data sets were classified by instinct method and thus the ITMS suffers for optimal data classification strategies.

Figure 1. Proposed internet-based traffic management system

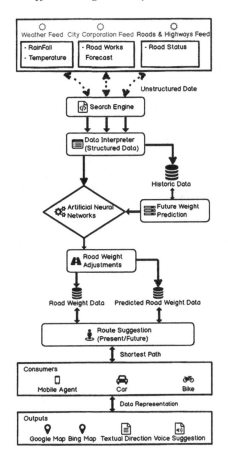

Cluster based classifications are able to find the optimum number of clusters in each attribute and can improve the performance. With this hypothesis, Hierarchical and K-means clustering were applied on environmental data for ITMS system in (Nawrin et al., 2017), and resulted Dunn-Index cluster validation technique was performed better. In addition, current ITMS has two (2) different decision making frameworks- road weight updating and future road weight forecasting. Forecasting is helpful due to the estimation of optimum routes and reduces the effects of traffic jam in advance. Exponentially Weighted Moving Average (EWMA) algorithm on time series data was used to calculate the estimated or predicted factor values. However, the performance is not so adequate.

Therefore, still the system insists potential improvements in several sectors including intelligent data crawling, building the interoperability between classifications and clustering algorithms, and future road weight forecasting models. This chapter contributes an experimental measurement of accuracy level for each road weight attributes, and combined them together with neural system, to improve the performance of the road weight forecasting model. In addition, the chapter highlights a proposed technique, to improve the interoperability between clustering algorithms into the neural system, and broadly discusses- IoT based feasible solutions for data collection problems.

Figure 2. Gulshan Thana and Ward 19 map

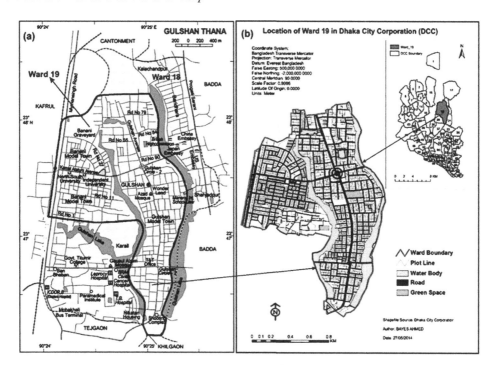

INTELLIGENCE TRAFFIC MANAGEMENT SYSTEM (ITMS)

Test Zones/Study Area

Demand for a feasible solution to the traffic problems is very high for a metro city- like Dhaka, Bangladesh. Losing valuable time (approximately 200%) being stuck in traffic jams and increases CO_2 emissions (approximately 300%) due to the present traffic situation.

Banani (Figure 2) area (Banani Intersection) is the heart of Dhaka road network system and thus has been selected as the test area for vehicle routings. Like other intersections at Dhaka city, it follows all way stop control intersections, resulting in a huge congestion of vehicles at peak hours which makes it almost impossible for the traffic police to control the vehicle flow in a nimble way. In addition, the road networks inside the Banani area shape as quadrangle and suitable for our test simulation.

All the roads will be divided into segments (Figure 3) and each segment will be marked as a rectangle and will have five points – the four corners and the midpoint. The four corners will identify the proper road segment and the midpoint of a road will be used as road marker. Client can easily decide the nearest road segment by using the difference between its location and segment's road marker. Thus, road segment location will be stored (in database) in terms of latitude and longitude of the five points and placed on the Google Map (Google Map, 2015).

Figure 3. Road segments at Banani

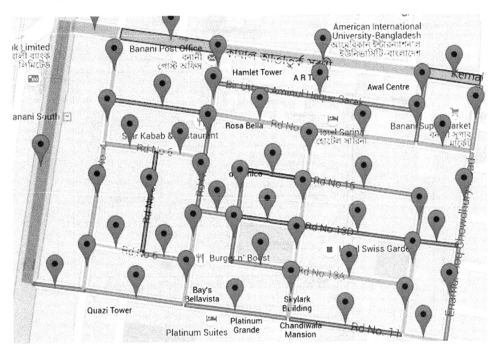

Search Engine

The search engine (referred as a web crawler) intelligently crawls three (3) predefined feed sites including weather, city corporation and government roads and highways authority. It searches the web sites directly for an HTML element with metadata indexing (title, predefined IDs, class names, description, keyword and etc). The crawler does not have any dependency on the position or the hierarchy of the HTML elements. A scheduler runs in the background and scraps data for each of the web site in a regular interval (e.g. every six (6) hrs). Once an HTML tag is detected, the crawler scraps the adjacent data rows using XPath (XPath, 2016), interprets unstructured data, converts them to simplified structured format, and then stores in the database table. Figure 4 represents the total search engine crawling sequence diagram.

UML Model Description

A .NET API "System.Web" namespace supplies classes and interfaces to enable communication between the browser and the server. It includes the HttpRequest class, the HttpResponse class, and the HttpServerUtility class. It also includes classes for cookie manipulation, file transfer, exception information, and output cache control. An application of type "HttpApplication" is selected and it calls a private method named "AddScheduledTask" with local parameters including method name and Seconds, and registers a cache object dependency callback for the web framework.

After a specified duration (in seconds), the web application framework calls "CacheItemRemoved" method to remove the web cache and the method whose name was passed during the cache registration, and starts crawling the feed sites using "ParseWeatherData" method of the "FeedParser" object. "Parse-

Figure 4. Search engine sequence diagram

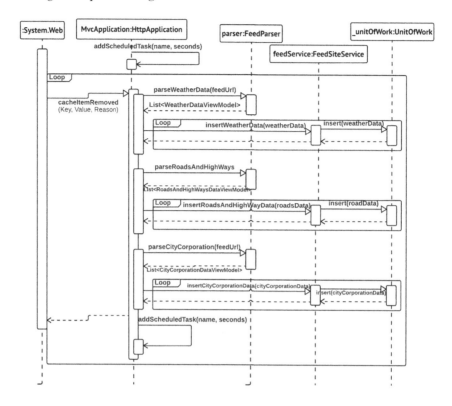

WeatherData" method successfully crawls the given URL site and returns a list of formatted weather data. Later, all crawled weather data are inserted into the database one by one in a loop. Figure 5 presents a snapshot of the weather database entries. Inside the loop the "HttpApplication" invokes "FeedSiteService" method and inserts the "weatherData" object into the database and returns to the "HttpApplication". "HttpApplication" does similar tasks for Roads and Highways, and City Corporation web feeds and stores formatted data into the database. At the end of all data collection, "HttpApplication" invokes the "AddScheduledTask" method and does all the above tasks repeatedly.

Road Weight Calculations

Decision Tree (DT) Based Road Weight Calculations

Decision tree based logic was implemented over the simplified data to adjust the route weights in database. For the test purpose four (4) different weather attributes were considered– rain fall, temperature, humidity and wind to determine the environmental status. The interpreted data (presented in Table 1) were evaluated against the generated decision tree (Figure 6) and based on the result; the application either increased or reset the weight of a road segment and replicated in the road weight matrix.

Figure 5. Snapshot of the weather database

	Id	RoadID	DateTime	Atmospheric Pressure	RainFall	WindSpeed	Surface Temperature	Relative Humidity	SolarFlux	BatteryV
1	1	2	2015-10-12 09:38:41.737	1010	0.000000	4.313000	27.000000	84.000000	0.131702	13.950000
2	2	3	2015-10-12 09:38:41.737	1010	0.000000	3.688000	27.000000	88.500000	0.121344	13.970000
3	3	4	2015-10-12 09:38:41.737	1010	0.000000	5.146000	28.000000	80.000000	0.179056	13.970000
4	4	5	2015-10-12 09:38:41.737	1009	1.500000	4.313000	28.000000	84.000000	0.124303	13.990000
5	5	19	2015-10-12 09:38:41.737	1010	1.500000	5.146000	25.000000	75.000000	0.124303	13.950000
6	6	20	2015-10-12 09:38:41.737	1012	1.000000	3.688000	24.000000	80.000000	0.121344	13.950000
7	7	21	2015-10-12 09:38:41.737	1012	1.500000	3.688000	25.000000	84.000000	0.131702	13.990000
8	8	22	2015-10-12 09:38:41.737	1010	2.000000	4.313000	24.000000	84.000000	0.183495	13.950000
9	9	2	2016-02-09 07:19.40.847	1013	2.000000	3.688000	23.000000	84.000000	0.183495	13.960000
10	10	3	2016-02-09 07:19.40.847	1009	2.000000	6.167000	23.000000	80.000000	0.183495	13.960000
11	11	4	2016-02-09 07:19.40.847	1012	0.500000	4.313000	24.000000	88.500000	0.131702	13.950000
12	12	5	2016-02-09 07:19.40.847	1009	1.500000	3.688000	24.000000	84.000000	0.124303	13.960000
13	13	19	2016-02-09 07:19.40.847	1010	0.000000	4.875000	26.000000	75.000000	0.121344	13.990000
14	14	20	2016-02-09 07:19.40.847	1009	1.000000	3.688000	24.000000	91.000000	0.131702	13.960000
15	15	21	2016-02-09 07:19.40.847	1012	2.000000	4.875000	25.000000	91.000000	0.179056	13.990000

Figure 6. Decision tree formulation from the data set in Table 1

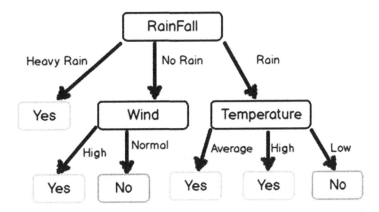

Figure 7. BP_NN with LM

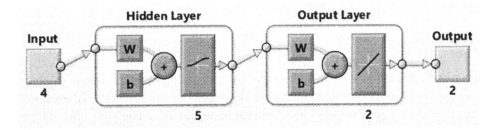

NN Based Dynamic Road Weight Calculations

DT was generated by ID3 (Rahman, 2012) algorithm and did not have any pruning procedures nor have the capability to handle numeric attributes or missing values. Thus, another alternative decision making system was required. (Akhter et. al., 2016) considered BP NN and established the capability of the neural system as a weight updating decision process. Thus, DT was replaced by the NN. Table II data

Table 1. Data set for decision tree formulation

Rain Fall	Temperature	Humidity	Wind	Increase Weight
No Rain	High	High	Normal	No
No Rain	High	High	High	Yes
Rain	High	High	Normal	Yes
Heavy Rain	High	High	Normal	Yes
Heavy Rain	Low	Normal	Normal	Yes
Heavy Rain	Low	Normal	High	Yes
Rain	Low	Normal	High	No
No Rain	Average	High	Normal	No
No Rain	Low	Normal	Normal	No
Heavy Rain	Average	Normal	Normal	Yes
No Rain	Average	Normal	Normal	No
Rain	Average	High	High	Yes
Rain	High	Normal	Normal	Yes
Heavy Rain	Average	High	High	Yes

were interpreted to numeric (0, 1, and 2) from corresponding linguistic (low, mid, high) formulations. DT implementation had two decision classes (Yes/No weight updates); however NN considered four decision classes (3-0) to increment the weight values. The weight matrix value was updated/adjusted by using a multi-layer fully connected BP NN and later the NN was upgraded with LM optimization (Hagan et al., 1995). The BP NN was optimized by using LM optimization (in Figure 7) with one hidden layer (with 5 neurons), and one output layer (with 2 neurons). The LM based BP NN was trained with 30 samples (12 from class 3, 9 from class 2, 5 from class 1, 4 from class 0) and tested with 15 samples (5 from class 3, 3 from class 2, 3 from class 1, 4 from class 0) and achieved 96.67% accuracy. In addition a k-fold cross-validation (Wiki-1, 2016) was applied to estimate the LM based BP model's true errors. Overall LM based BP achieved 94%- 96.67% accuracy.

Road Weight Forecast Model

Current future weight prediction module utilizes the structured data from the historic database to predict the future road weights. Weighted Moving Average algorithm (Moving Average Algorithm, 2016) was used to predict the factor values (rainfall, temperature, humidity and wind) and this algorithm prioritized the most recent data to have higher impact on the prediction. Different factors influence the road weights in different ways and thus, factor values were predicted independently and later decision tree was formulated together to calculate the estimated road weights. The estimated road weights were stored in "Predicted road weight" matrix. Thereafter, the application simulated and advised future routes based on the road weight values from the "Predicted road weight" matrix. The model achieved 72.93% accuracy for rainfall, 85.81% accuracy for temperature, 45.15% accuracy for humidity, 18.52% accuracy for wind and 16.45% accuracy for road status factors.

Figure 8. Client dashboard

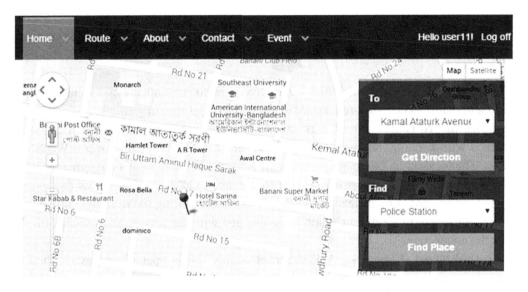

Figure 9. Server dashboard

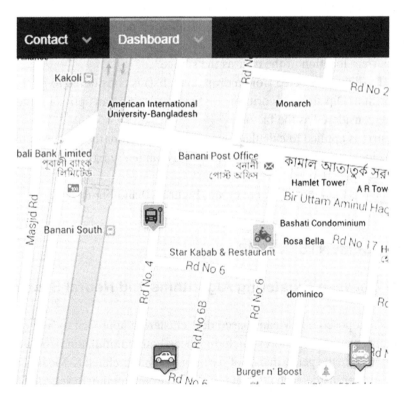

Route Formulation

A software application with ASP.NET platform was developed to monitor, operate and control the full Intelligence Traffic Management System (ITMS). The software covers the following activities:

- **Authentication:** Clients use predefined set of credential to authenticate as a valid user. Upon successful authentication clients are forwarded to the client dashboard.
- **Client Dashboard (Figure 8):** Clients can monitor his current location on a map. The location is marked with a marker and transmitted to the server at the same time over a WebSocket connection. The location on the map updates itself according to the client's movement. The test data for each of the clients comes from the Test Route table. On the real field this data would come directly from the GPS unit instead of the Test Route table. During the running phase of a client in the dashboard a Websocket connection is established with the server, and remains till the client closes the connection.
- **Server Dashboard (Figure 9):** A WebSocket connection is opened and established with the server application. The server transmits the location of each client (as the data is available) to the dashboard. Then the dashboard plots the locations of all the clients on a map. Both the clients and the dashboard are utilizing WebSocket based connections. Thus, the data transmission procedure consumes much lower bandwidth.
- **Route Suggestion:** Client dashboard does the following activities when a client requests for a route to a destination:
- Consider the current location of the user as the source.
- The selected "To Place" (selected from a drop down list) is considered to be the destination.
- Dijkstra's algorithm (Dijkstra's Algorithm, 2015) is used to find an optimal route. Only the weights of the roads are considered as the factors.
- The weight matrix is applied to calculate an optimal route from the source to the destination.
- The weights inside the weight matrix are changed dynamically based on the external factors with the help of the decision tree.
- A calculated route is then displayed on a map (Figure. 10 and Figure. 11).

RECENT ENHANCEMENTS IN ITMS

Interoperability Between Clustering Algorithms and Neural System

(Nawrin et. al., 2017) proposed a K-Means based data clustering approach to find optimal road weight values from the weight calculation features- including peek hour, rainfall, temperature, wind and humidity. The authors demonstrate the performance of partition and hierarchical K-Means clustering to outline the optimal number cluster inside each attribute of the environmental data sets of TMS. Subsequently, the optimal classes are cross-validated by using statistical analytics. Table II shows a sample set of road weight clusters using K-Means algorithm.

We are proposing a new neural model which forecasts road weight using K-Means clustering result. Two (2) different road forecast models are proposed. The first model includes, forecasting each feature values separately using Long Short Term Memory networks (LSTM) (Hochreiter and Schmidhuber, 1997), univariate time series model, and then put them in the K-Means model to estimate the future road weight value. The second model uses LSTM multivariate time series model to forecast the road weights directly from the current values of all features. In this model K-Means outcomes are used for training the NN.

Implementation of Road Weight Forecast Models

LSTM Univariate Time Series Model to Forecast Each Feature Value

LSTM is designed with two (2) layers and 15 units in each of them. Dropout regularization (Srivastava et al., 2014) 0.3 is used for avoiding overfitting. Activation layer- tanh is used to avoid vanishing and exploding gradient decent problems. LSTM needs a predefined window size to recognize the pattern of the time series data set. However, LSTM performance varies according to the values of the window size and choosing the suitable value for window size is also a crucial task. We experiment the grid search separately for each features with different window size, and evaluate their optimum window size. The grid search finds optimum window size 20 with minimum Mean Square Error (MSE) is 44.8 for rainfall, optimum window size 30 with minimum Mean Square Error (MSE) is 5.8 for temperature, optimum window size 5 with minimum Mean Square Error (MSE) is 15.7 for wind, optimum window size 40 with minimum Mean Square Error (MSE) is 106.67 for humidity, and optimum window size 5 with minimum Mean Square Error (MSE) is 0.02 for peek hour. The grid search results are presented

Table 2. Road weight clusters using K-Means algorithm

Peek Hour	Rainfall	Temperature	Wind	Humidity	Road Weight
1	0	20	1	55	2
1	0	18	3	62	2
2	0	20	3	62	2
4	0	20	0	64	2
2	0	21	1	69	4
3	0	22	1	61	2
0	0	21	0	68	4
1	0	22	0	69	4
1	0	22	1	68	4
2	0	22	0	69	4
4	0	23	1	69	4
2	0	19	5	66	4
3	0	18	1	50	6
0	0	20	3	60	2
1	0	20	1	67	4
1	0	22	3	61	2
2	0	20	0	70	4

in Figure 10 to Figure 14. Afterward, the optimum window sizes from each feature are used to generate their corresponding forecast results and present in Figure 15 to Figure 19.

LSTM Multivariate Time Series Model to Forecast Road Weight

This model uses two (2) layers LSTM with 25 units for each layer. Dropout regularization 0.3 is used for avoiding overfitting. tanh activation layer is used to avoid vanishing and exploding gradient decent problems. Grid search, based on number of input features and number of output features, is used to forecast the road weights. It results (Table 3), three (3) times input features and four (4) times output feature is the optimum model with minimum MSE 0.016 for multivariate time series road weight forecast. Afterwards, the optimum model is used for road weight forecasting. LSTM is trained with 600 data points (each has five (5) features) and tested with 150 data points.

CONCLUSION

In this chapter, we are sharing our experience on the design and implementation of an Intelligent Traffic Management System (ITMS) and discuss the recent advancements on this model. A neural base decision support system is developed with two (2) different modules including road weight calculation and road weight forecasting. Backpropagation Neural Network (BP-NN) and K-Means clustering were formulated for road weight calculation. BP-NN provides 94% classification accuracy and K-Means provides seven (7) optimal road weight clusters. Exponentially Weighted Moving Average (EWMA) algorithm was used as road weight forecasting model. However, the accuracy is not acceptable. Thus, we develop two

Figure 10. Grid search for rainfall

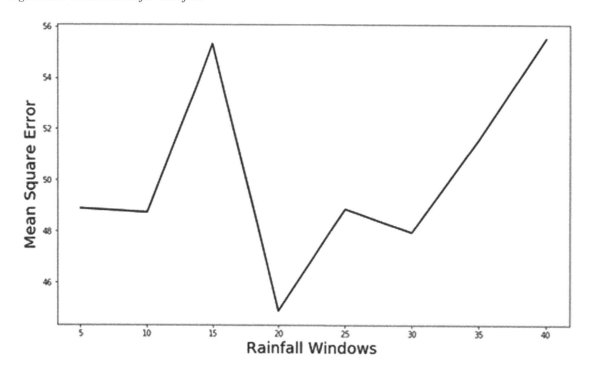

Figure 11. Grid search for temperature

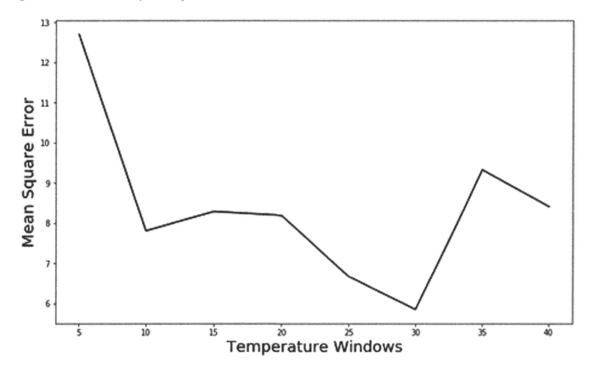

Figure 12. Grid search for wind

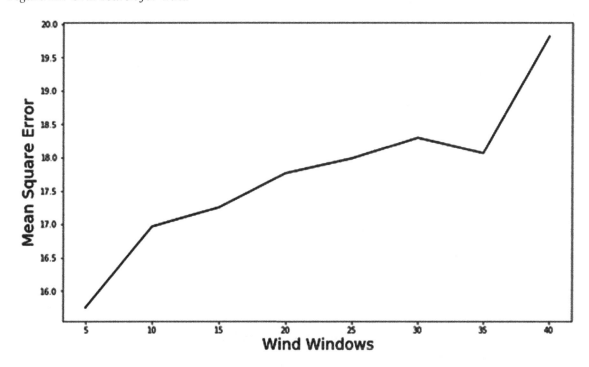

Figure 13. Grid search for humidity

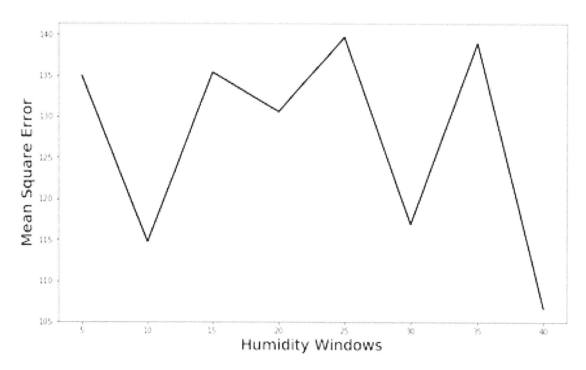

Figure 14. Grid search for peek hour

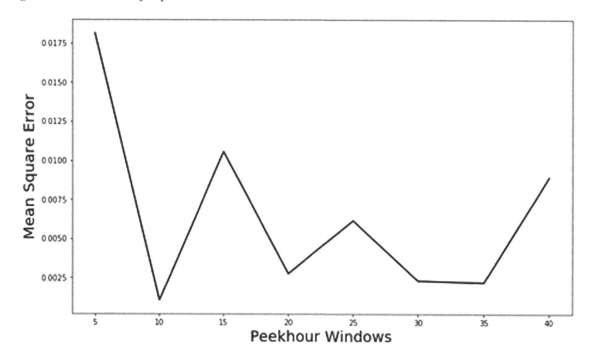

Figure 15. Forecast results for rainfall

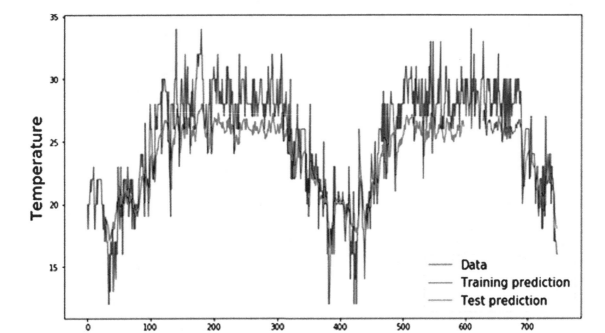

*For a more accurate representation see the electronic version.

Figure 16. Forecast results for temperature

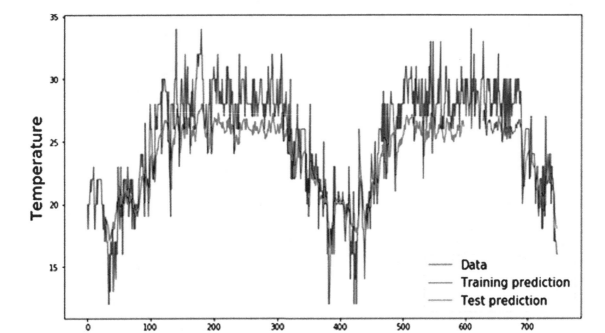

*For a more accurate representation see the electronic version.

Figure 17. Forecast results for wind

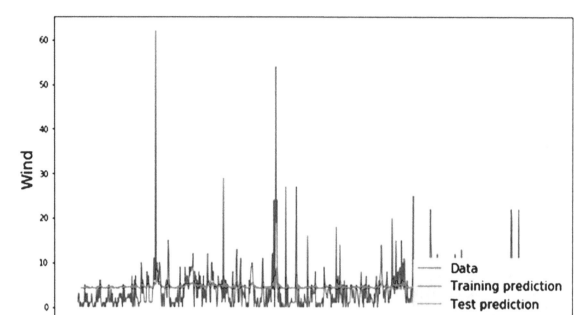

*For a more accurate representation see the electronic version.

Figure 18. Forecast results for humidity

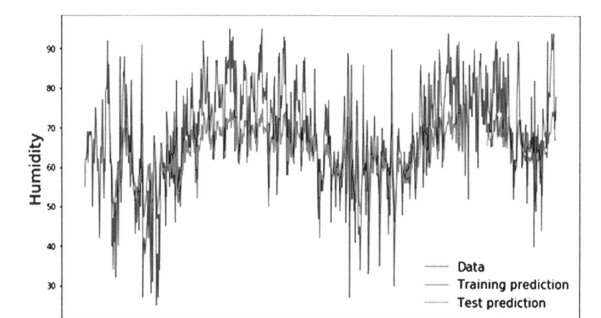

*For a more accurate representation see the electronic version.

Figure 19. Forecast results for peek hour

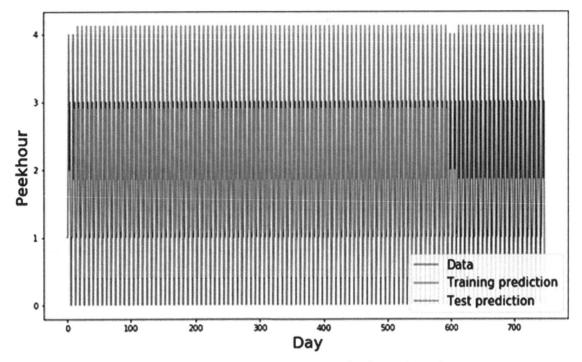

For a more accurate representation see the electronic version.

(2) different LSTM based time series forecasting models, including univariate model and multivariate model. Average MSE of univariate model is 34.6 and multivariate model MSE is 0.0169. Thus, multivariate model outperforms previous forecasting models. Still, we need a performance analysis on the multivariate model validation and accuracy level.

FUTURE RESEARCH DIRECTIONS

Traffic management system is getting tremendous attention in research and data analytics. So far in our existing research projects (Rahman & Akhter, 2015a; 2015b; 2015c), (Akhter et al., 2016) (Nawrin et. al., 2017) and (Sumit & Akhter, 2018), we have designed and implemented an intelligent traffic management system (ITMS). However, the ITMS suffers for road weight forecasting model. LSTM based neural model is developed and integrated with ITMS with adequate accuracy. Still, the model needs improvement to decide traffic concession and forecasting related information. In addition, a comparative study with different types of recurrent NNs will be done and their performance will be evaluated for both road weight classification and forecasting.

BPNN was performing well by providing classification result only but the decision for the actual weight calculation or weight mapping was missing. Calculating weight from each cluster is a chaos overlapping scenario. Thus, fuzzy inference rules need to be defined for each attribute cluster and proper road weight mapping scheme is necessary. After successful mapping, the system can be integrated with deep NN approach and trained properly. We are in the developing stage of this research.

Table 3. Grid search result for multivariate time series

Train MSE	Test MSE	Times of 5 Input Features	Times of the Output Feature
0.028920992	0.025406714	1	1
0.026516356	0.022390319	1	2
0.024315238	0.019811989	1	3
0.025987064	0.019338848	1	4
0.024452167	0.01770886	1	5
0.027919207	0.022352813	2	1
0.027617069	0.022270488	2	2
0.024305088	0.018741139	2	3
0.024172001	0.017317545	2	4
0.023365919	0.017077755	2	5
0.024284383	0.018901957	3	1
0.026065557	0.019319394	3	2
0.02451834	0.017821585	3	3
0.022848259	0.016761644	3	4
0.024695994	0.01772786	3	5
0.026662949	0.019837873	4	1
0.023789254	0.016925627	4	2
0.026161932	0.01899232	4	3
0.023919281	0.018219504	4	4
0.023917623	0.017438246	4	5
0.023218132	0.017872454	5	1
0.025626094	0.018557159	5	2
0.023848348	0.017567746	5	3
0.025666739	0.018370314	5	4
0.023310737	0.017113751	5	5

Several online web portals host real time continuous weather data streams. However, road and vehicle information are missing in there. In addition, their coverage is limited to city level congregate information and location/area/road segment based information is necessary for real time TMS decision. Internet of Things (IoT) based online sensors can be a solution for this circumstance. IoT sensors will collect information from the mobile vehicles. Moreover, sensors may need to communicate among themselves and transfer the acquired information to the TMS system. Subsequently, the TMS decision-making system can use those data for routing related decision making problem. Sensors can also be securely interconnected with an authenticated cloud server (AWS) using GSM/GPRS based HTTP protocol, and able to collect or exchange encrypted TMS data among themselves through GSM/GPRS/Bluetooth wireless communication.

Figure 20. LSTM training and testing results in MSE

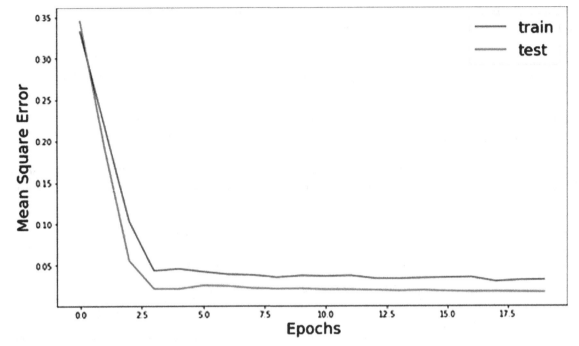

*For a more accurate representation see the electronic version.

Traffic Management System (TMS) is a research dimension, where the task priorities with decision mappings are changing dynamically. Thus, uncertain situations can force TMS to change their overall activities. (Habiba and Akhter, 2012; 2013; 2017) developed a dynamic workflow and schedule modeling for disaster management system. That model can be integrated with TMS to decide tasks flow according to their priorities in any uncertain accidental activities.

ACKNOWLEDGMENT

The authors gratefully acknowledge Mr. Md. Ashfaqul Islam and Ms. Sadia Nawrin from East West University, Bangladesh for their assistance in data collection for TMS.

REFERENCES

Akhter S, Rahman R, Islam A. (2016). Neural Network Based Route Weight Computation for Bi-directional Traffic Management System. *International Journal of Applied Evolutionary Computation, 7*(4), 45–59.

Almishari, M., Gasti, P., Nathan, N., & Tsudik, G. (2014). Optimizing Bi-Directional Low-Latency Communication in Named Data Networking. *Computer Communication Review, 44*(1).

Aloul, F., Sagahyroon, A., Nahle, A., Dehn, M. A., & Anani, R. A. (2012). GuideME: An Effective RFID-Based Traffic Monitoring System. *Proc. of IASTED-International Conference on Advances in Computer Science and Engineering (ACSE)*. 10.2316/P.2012.770-036

Angel, A., Hickman, M., Mirchandani, P., & Chandnani, D. (2003). Methods of Analyzing Traffic Imagery Collected From Aerial Platforms. *IEEE Transactions on Intelligent Transportation Systems, 4*(2), 99–107. doi:10.1109/TITS.2003.821208

ANPR. (2014, Apr 9). *Automatic Number Plate Recognition (ANPR)*. Retrieved from: http://www.gmp.police.uk/content/section.html?readform&s=353EDD067D2055288025796100399283

Dhar, A. (2008). *Traffc and Road Condition Monitoring System. M.Tech report*. Bombay: Indian Institute of Technology. Available at http://citeseerx.ist.psu.edu/viewdoc/download?doi=10.1.1.518.2687&rep=rep1&type=pdf

Dijkstra's Algorithm. (2015, May 25). Retrieved from: https://en.wikipedia.org/wiki/Dijkstra's_algorithm

Google Maps. (2015, May 10). Retrieved from: http://en.wikipedia.org/wiki/Google_Maps

Habiba, M., & Akhter, S. (2012). *MAS Workflow Model and Scheduling Algorithm for Disaster Management System. In Cloud Computing Technologies, Applications and Management*. ICCCTAM.

Habiba, M., & Akhter, S. (2013). A Cloud Based Natural Disaster Management System. *International Conference on Grid and Pervasive Computing*, 152-161. 10.1007/978-3-642-38027-3_16

Habiba, M., & Akhter, S. (2017). Exploring Cloud-Based Distributed Disaster Management With Dynamic Multi-Agents Workflow System. *Smart Technologies for Emergency Response and Disaster Management,* 167-195.

Hagan, M. T., Demuth, H. B., Beale, M. H., & Jesús, O. D. (1995). Neural Network Design (2nd ed.). Academic Press.

Hochreiter, S., & Schmidhuber, J. (1997). Long Short-Term Memory. *Neural Computation, 9*(8), 1735–1780. doi:10.1162/neco.1997.9.8.1735 PMID:9377276

HTML5 Web Sockets. (2015, May 10). *A Quantum Leap in Scalability for the Web*. Retrieved from: http://www.websocket.org/quantum.html

Moving Average Algorithm. (2016, Mar 6). Retrieved from: https://en.wikipedia.org/wiki/Moving_average

Nawrin, S., Rahman, M. R., & Akhter, S. (2017). Exploreing k-means with internal validity indexes for data clustering in traffic management system. *International Journal of Advanced Computer Science and Applications, 8*(3). doi:10.14569/IJACSA.2017.080337

Panagiotakis, S., Kapetanakis, K., & Malamos, A. G. (2013). Architecture for Real Time Communications over the Web. *International Journal of Web Engineering, 2*(1), 1–8. doi:10.5923/j.web.20130201.01

Rahman, M. A. (2012, Feb 1). ID3 Decision Tree Algorithm - Part 1. Academic Press.

Rahman, M. R., & Akhter, S. (2015a). Real Time Bi-directional Traffic Management Support System with GPS and WebSocket. *Proc. of the 15th IEEE International Conference on Computer and Information Technology (CIT-2015)*.

Rahman, M. R., & Akhter, S. (2015b). Bi-directional Traffic Management Support System With Decision Tree Based Dynamic Routing. *Proc. of 10th International Conference for Internet Technology and Secured Transactions, ICITST 2015*. 10.1109/ICITST.2015.7412080

Rahman, M. R., & Akhter, S. (2015c). BiDirectional Traffic Management with Multiple Data Feeds for Dynamic Route Computation and Prediction System. *International Journal of Intelligent Computing Research*, 7(2).

Reporter (2013, Sep-Oct). *Bluetooth and Wi-Fi Offer New Options for Travel Time Measurements*. ITS International. Retrieved from: http://www.itsinternational.com/categories/detection-monitoring-machine vision/features/bluetooth-and-wi-fi-offer-new-options-for-travel-time-measurements/

Reporter. (2016, Mar 6). Retrieved from: https://en.wikipedia.org/wiki/Moving_average

Romão, T., Rato, L., Fernandes, P., Alexandre, N., Almada, A., & Capeta, N. (2006). M-Traffic - A Traffic Information and Monitoring System for Mobile Devices. In *Proc. of International Workshop on Ubiquitous Computing (IWUC 2006)* (pp. 87-92). ICEIS Publisher.

Srivastava, N., Hinton, G., Krizhevsky, A., Sutskever, I., & Salakhutdinov, R. (2014). Dropout: A Simple Way to Prevent Neural Networks from Overfitting. *Journal of Machine Learning Research*, *15*, 1929–1958.

Sumit, S. H. (2018). *Akhter*. C-means Clustering and Deep-Neuro-Fuzzy Classification for Road Weight Measurement in Traffic Management System. Soft Computing. Springer Berlin Heidelberg; doi:10.100700500-018-3086-0

Sumit, S. H., & Akhter, S. (2018). C-means Clustering and Deep-Neuro-Fuzzy Classification for Road Weight Measurement in Traffic Management System. *Soft Computing*. doi:10.100700500-018-3086-0

Verma, N., Sobhan, M. S., & Jalil, T. (2012). *Novel Design Proposal For Real Time Traffic Monitoring & Management of Dhaka Metropolitan City with (Rcap)*. Global Engineering, Science and Technology Conference, BIAM Foundation.

Wiki-1 (2016). Retrieved from: https://en.wikipedia.org/wiki/Cross-validation_(statistics)

XPath. (2016, Mar 6). *XML Path Language*. Retrieved from: https://www.w3.org/TR/xpath/

Chapter 5
DNA Fragment Assembly Using Quantum–Inspired Genetic Algorithm

Manisha Rathee
Jawaharlal Nehru University, India

Kumar Dilip
Jawaharlal Nehru University, India

Ritu Rathee
Indira Gandhi Delhi Technical University for Women, India

ABSTRACT

DNA fragment assembly (DFA) is one of the most important and challenging problems in computational biology. DFA problem involves reconstruction of target DNA from several hundred (or thousands) of sequenced fragments by identifying the proper orientation and order of fragments. DFA problem is proved to be a NP-Hard combinatorial optimization problem. Metaheuristic techniques have the capability to handle large search spaces and therefore are well suited to deal with such problems. In this chapter, quantum-inspired genetic algorithm-based DNA fragment assembly (QGFA) approach has been proposed to perform the de novo assembly of DNA fragments using overlap-layout-consensus approach. To assess the efficacy of QGFA, it has been compared genetic algorithm, particle swarm optimization, and ant colony optimization-based metaheuristic approaches for solving DFA problem. Experimental results show that QGFA performs comparatively better (in terms of overlap score obtained and number of contigs produced) than other approaches considered herein.

DOI: 10.4018/978-1-5225-5832-3.ch005

1. INTRODUCTION

Understanding the functioning (as well as malfunctioning) of living beings require determination and interpretation of their genome sequences (Kikuchi & Chakraborty, 2006). The genome of an organism is made up of deoxyribonucleic acid (DNA) strands which encode its hereditary information and determine its body structure, functions and protein formation (Watson & Berry, 2003). DNA strands consist of two types of nitrogenous bases namely purines (adenine (A) and guanine (G)) and pyrimidines (cytosine (C) and thymine (T)). DNA has a double helical structure consisting of two strands running anti-parallel to each other and having complementary bases where a purine on one strand is paired with pyrimidine on the other and vice-versa in such a way that A is always paired with T and G is always paired with C (Watson & Berry, 2003; Watson & Crick, 1953). The process of determining the complete sequence of bases in all the strands of DNA (i.e. the genome) is termed as DNA sequencing. The genome sequences are generally very large ranging from few thousand base pairs for small viruses to 3×10^9 base pairs for humans, 1.7×10^{10} base pairs for wheat and 1.2×10^{11} base pairs for lily (Kikuchi & Chakraborty, 2006). A number of techniques are available for sequencing but none of the available techniques is capable of reading more than 1000 bases at a time, let alone reading an entire genome at once. This limitation of DNA sequencing methods is overcome by shotgun sequencing where the target DNA is replicated to generate multiple copies which are then randomly broken into a number of smaller fragments so that the fragments are short enough to be sequenced by any of the available sequencing techniques (Dorronsoro, *et al.*, 2008). After sequencing, the sequenced fragments need to be combined back to obtain the original sequence as the whole genome sequence is required for phylogenetic and genomic research activities. But, as the fragments were generated randomly, the information about ordering of the fragments on the parent strand or the strand to which a particular fragment belongs is lost thereby resulting in the DNA fragment assembly problem (Meksangsouy & Chaiyaratana, 2003). DFA problem involves reconstruction of target DNA from several hundred (or thousands) of sequenced fragments by identifying the proper orientation and order of the sequenced fragments (Meksangsouy & Chaiyaratana, 2003). The sequenced fragments are called as reads and are provided as input to the assembly procedure.

DFA is proved to a NP-Hard combinatorial optimization problem (Medvedev, *et al.*, 2007). The complexity arises due to a very large search space as there are $2^k \times k!$ possible solutions in worst case for a set containing k fragments (Kubalik, *et al.*, 2010). Therefore obtaining exact solutions using traditional optimization techniques is not possible. Metaheuristic techniques have the capability to handle large search spaces and therefore well suited to solve the hard optimization problems. In this chapter, Quantum inspired genetic algorithm (QIGA) has been adapted for performing the de novo assembly of DNA fragments using overlap-layout-consensus approach. QIGA is a relatively recent metaheuristic technique which blends the principals of quantum computing with the concepts of genetic algorithm (Han & Kim, 2002). Due to the parallel processing capabilities of QIGA, it is capable of providing better solutions (in terms of diversity, quality and convergence) with a smaller population size. Also, QIGA has an edge over other metaheuristic techniques as very less number of parameters needs to be adjusted in case of QIGA.

Quantum inspired **G**enetic algorithm-based DNA **F**ragment **A**ssembly (QGFA) has been proposed in this paper with the objective of maximizing the sum of overlaps between adjacent fragments in a layout. The main contribution of the proposed work is mentioned below:

- QIGA has been adapted for solving the DFA problem. To the best of our knowledge, none of the works existing in literature has used QIGA for solving the DFA problem.

- An improvement has been proposed in measuring operator so that only feasible solutions are generated and solution repairing is not required.

- A novel method has been proposed for computing the change in angle of rotation which is required for updating the Q-bit population in QIGA.

- Comprehensive comparison of proposed QGFA algorithm with genetic algorithm (GA), particle swarm optimization (PSO) and Ant Colony Optimization (ACO), Cuckoo Search (CS) based metaheuristic approaches for solving DFA. The experimental results show that proposed QGFA algorithm performs comparatively better in terms of overlap score and number of contigs.

The organization of the rest of the paper is as follows. DFA problem is discussed in detail and problem formulation is given in section 2. Related work is discussed in section 3. Proposed approach is presented in section 4. Experimental results are shown and discussed in section 5. Conclusion is presented in section 6.

2. DFA PROBLEM

Before proceeding into the particulars of the DFA problem, given below is the nomenclature needed for understanding the problem (Firoz, *et al.*, 2012):

1. **Fragment:** A short segment of DNA sequence of length 500-800 bps.
2. **Read:** A sequenced fragment.
3. **Prefix:** A substring consisting of first n characters of a read.
4. **Suffix:** A substring consisting of last n characters of a read.
5. **Overlap Score:** The number of matching bases between suffix of one read and prefix of another.
6. **Layout:** The order of fragments in which they must be joined to get the target sequence.
7. **Contig:** A sequence comprising contiguous overlapping fragments.
8. **Consensus:** The final sequence obtained by majority voting in each column of the layout.

As discussed previously, fragment assembly is a critical step in de novo sequencing of the genomes. DFA is concerned with determining the order and orientation of randomly generated fragments in order to construct the original DNA sequence. DFA is therefore similar to solving a large jigsaw puzzle which assembles the sequenced fragments for creating the original DNA sequence. DFA depends on the length of the sequenced fragments and the availability of the reference genome. On the basis of fragment length, DFA is categorized as Long read assembly (Chevreux, 2005; Huang, *et al.*, 2003; Huang & Madan, 1999; Sutton, *et al.*, 1995; http://www.phrap.org/phredphrap/phrap.html) and Short read assembly (Chaisson, *et al.*, 2004; Hernandez, *et al.*, 2008; Jeck, *et al.*, 2007; Simpson, *et al.*, 2009; Zerbino & Birney, 2008). On the basis of availability of reference genome, genome assembly is categorized as Comparative assembly (Pop, 2009; Phillippy, *et al.*, 2004) and De-novo assembly (Pop, 2009). Both long and short reads can be assembled by comparative as well as de-novo assembly. In this chapter, de-novo assembly is performed on long reads using Overlap-Layout-Consensus (OLC) approach which is well suited for longer reads. OLC approach views DFA problem as a Hamiltonian path problem in an undirected graph where reads are treated as vertices and edges exist between overlapping reads. The aim here is to combine the reads into contigs by finding a path that traverses each node exactly once.

OLC approach consists of three phases as shown in Figure 1 and briefly discussed below:

Overlap Phase

In this phase, all-against-all, pair-wise comparison between the reads is carried out for computing the amount of overlap. It is assumed that higher the overlap score between reads, more are the chances that fragments originated from the same region of DNA and therefore need to be adjacent in the layout (Dorronsoro, *et al.*, 2008).

Layout Phase

Based on the overlap score, this phase decides the order of fragments. This is the most complex part as it is difficult to decide the true overlap between the reads due to incomplete coverage, unknown orientation of fragments, base call errors and repeated regions (Dorronsoro, *et al.*, 2008).

Consensus Phase

This is the final phase where consensus is generated by using majority vote for determining the base to be put in each column of layout (Dorronsoro, *et al.*, 2008). The quality of consensus is decided by evaluating the distribution of the coverage. For any base location, coverage is defined as the number of fragments covering that location. Coverage measures the redundancy in the sequenced data. It computes the average number of fragments containing a given nucleotide and is defined as the total number of bases in the reads over the total length of the target DNA sequence (Setubal & Meidanis, 1997):

$$Coverage = \frac{\sum_{i=1}^{N} length\,of\,fragment_i}{target\,sequence\,length} \qquad (1)$$

Figure 1. Overlap layout consensus approach

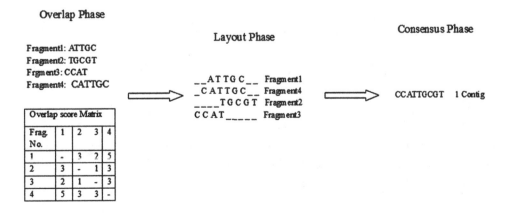

83

where N denotes the number of fragments. Higher coverage value leads to fewer gaps in the target sequence thereby resulting in a better solution. In order to reconstruct the original genome, coverage of $6\times$ to $10\times$ is required (Li, *et al.*, 1997).

2.1 Problem Formulation

Given a set of sequenced fragments $\mathcal{F}$ consisting of N fragments $\mathcal{F} = \left\{ f_1, f_2, f_3, ..., f_N \right\}$, let the length of f_i be represented by ℓ_i overlap score between f_i and f_j be denoted by $\mathcal{W}_{i,j}$. Then DFA problem is an asymmetric optimization problem where $\mathcal{W}_{i,j}$ may not be same as $\mathcal{W}_{j,i}$. The aim is to reconstruct the original sequence in such a way that total overlap among the adjacent fragments is maximized.

The DFA is formulated as an optimization problem as follows (Parsons *et al.*, 1995):

$$MAXIMIZE\left(F\right) \tag{2}$$

where $F = \sum_{i=1}^{N-1} \mathcal{W}_{i,j}$ such that $j = i + 1$ (3)

$$\mathcal{W}_{i,j} = g\left(f_i, f_j\right), \mathcal{W}_{i,j} \geq 0 \text{ and } \mathcal{W}_{i,j} \leq \min\left(\ell_i, \ell_j\right) \tag{4}$$

F is the sum of overlap scores between adjacent fragments in a layout. The overlap score between fragments is a function of fragments themselves. The value of $\mathcal{W}_{i,j}$ ranges from 0 to $\min\left(\ell_i, \ell_j\right)$. If $\mathcal{W}_{i,j} = \min\left(\ell_i, \ell_j\right)$, then one of the fragments is contained in the other fragment. The overlap score between fragments is calculated using a semi-global alignment algorithm presented in (Coull & Szymanski, 2008).

3. RELATED WORK

A large number of techniques including deterministic, stochastic and meta-heuristic have been proposed in literature to address the DFA problem. A qualitative review on DFA problem is presented by broadly categorizing the theme into non-metaheuristic and metaheuristic based approaches.

3.1 Non-Metaheuristic Approaches for DFA Problem

DFA was first introduced in (Staden, 1980; Huang, 1992) and was solved using a deterministic greedy search technique. Huang (1992) computed the overlap score using a local alignment algorithm proposed in (Smith & Waterman, 1981) and used a filtering technique presented in (Chang & Lawler, 1990) for discarding the fragments having overlap score below a given threshold. A deterministic branch-and-cut algorithm has been proposed in (Ferreira *et al.*, 2002) and a deterministic overlap graph based algorithm has been presented in (Braga & Meidanis, 2002) for solving the DFA problem. In (Churchil *et al.*, 1993; Burks *et al.* 1994), simulated annealing algorithm, a stochastic search technique has been applied for addressing the DFA problem. Angeleri *et al.* (1999) have applied neural prediction technique for addressing the DFA problem. Bocicor *et al.* (2011) have used reinforcement learning approach for dealing with the DFA problem. Fullerton *et al.* (2015) have addressed the DFA problem using modified classical graph algorithms.

3.2 Metaheuristic Approaches for DFA Problem

As discussed earlier, metaheuristic techniques are well suited for solving hard combinatorial optimization problems. A large body of literature exists where metaheuristic techniques have been used for solving the DFA problem. The first approach based on metaheuristic was presented by Parsons *et al.* (1993, 1995) where GA has been used for solving the DFA problem. Already formed contigs have been preserved or extended by using edge recombination, order crossover, transposition and inversion operators. Kikuchi & Chakraborty (2006) have improved the GA by proposing two heuristics namely chromosome reduction (CRed) for improving the efficiency of search procedure and chromosome refinement (CRef) for improving the fitness locally. ISA, a simulated annealing based meta-heuristic has been proposed in (Alba, *et al.*, 2009) where inversion procedure is applied generating the neighbor solutions. A problem aware local search (PALS) algorithm has been presented in (Alba & Luque, 2007) where a number of contigs has been considered as the primary measure while overlap score has been taken as secondary measure for evaluating the quality of solutions. Determination of overlap score and number of contigs is computationally inexpensive as in each generation only the change in values is estimated. In (Alba, *et al.*, 2008), GA is presented where greedy strategy has been used for initializing 50% of starting population and order crossover and swap mutations are used for evolving the population. In (Alba & Dorronsoro, 2008), PALS has been used in conjunction with a cellular genetic algorithm (cGA) to reap the benefits of both cGA and PALS. Prototype optimization with evolved improvement steps, POEMS, is an iterative method presented in (Kubalik *et al.* 2010) where evolutionary strategy is applied for searching the best modification for current solution (called prototype). An ant colony based approach employing asymmetric ordering representation has been proposed by Meksangsouy & Chaiyaratana (2003) for addressing the DFA problem. Firoz *et al.* (2012) have considered both noisy and noiseless instances of the problem and proposed Queen Bee evaluation based on genetic algorithm (QEGA) and Artificial Bee Colony (ABC) algorithm for the same. Rathee & Kumar (2014) has formulated DFA as a bi-objective and tri-objective optimization problem and has solved it using a multi-objective GA namely NSGA-II. Huang et al. (2015) have proposed a memetic particle swarm optimization algorithm for addressing the DNA fragment assembly problem. Huang et al. (2016) have proposed a memetic gravitational search algorithm for solving the DFA problem where tabu search has been used for population initialization, two operators have been proposed for increasing the diversity of population and simulated annealing based variable neighborhood search is applied for finding better solutions. Kchouk & Elloumi (2016) have proposed a clustering approach for performing de-novo assembly on next generation sequencing data.

4. PROPOSED APPROACH

As discussed earlier, DFA problem is proved to be NP-Hard combinatorial optimization problem and therefore exact solutions are not possible to find within a reasonable amount of computational time.

Recently, metaheuristic techniques have been shown performing better than their traditional counterparts for such problems. Due to their capability to handle large search spaces, metaheuristic techniques have been used by many researchers for solving hard optimization problems in diverse domains. In this chapter, *Q*uantum inspired *G*enetic algorithm (QIGA) has been adapted for solving the DNA *F*ragment *A*ssembly problem (QGFA) with the objective of maximizing the sum of overlap between adjacent fragments.

4.1 Overview of QIGA

Quantum inspired algorithms have recently been developed as a new class of artificial intelligence techniques. QIGA was proposed by Narayanan & Moore (1996) for the first time but first practical implementation and application of QIGA was discussed by Han & Kim (2002). QIGA combines the features of quantum computing with that of evolutionary computation in order to devise better solutions to the optimization problems. Quantum computing principles such as Q-bit, superposition and entanglement are blended with GA methodology of having an initial population, evaluating the fitness of population, performing crossover and mutation in order to evolve the population towards better regions of search space. This combined approach imparts QIGA the capability of global searching with a small population and faster convergence. QIGA and its variants have been applied in diverse domains for addressing a large class of combinatorial optimization problems (Zhang, 2011). QIGA variants can be broadly categorized as: real observation QIGA for numerical optimization (Zhang & Rong, 2007) and binary observation QIGA (bQIGA) for combinatorial optimization (Han & Kim, 2002). Since the DFA problem addressed in this chapter is a combinatorial optimization problem, bQIGA has been used in chapter.

In QIGA, chromosome is called as Q-bit chromosome and consequently the population is called as Q-bit population as Q-bits are used to represent genes in a chromosome instead of using binary, real or alphabetic representation for genes as done in the case of GA. Q-bits are smallest unit of information in quantum systems which can represent a 0 or 1 or any liner superposition of the two (Nielsen & Chuang, 2000). A pair of complex numbers $\left(\alpha, \beta\right)$ is used to denote a Q-bit as shown below

$$| \Psi >= \alpha | 0 > +\beta | 1 > \tag{5}$$

Such that

$$| \alpha |^2 + | \beta |^2 = 1 \tag{6}$$

where $| \alpha |^2$ and $| \beta |^2$ are the probabilities that, when observed, Q-bit will lead to a 0 and 1 respectively. A string of Q-bits make a Q-bit chromosome. The observation of a Q-bit chromosome results in a classical chromosome which is basically the solution representation used by conventional GA. The fitness of classical chromosomes is computed using a fitness function. Based on the fitness value of classical population, the q-bit population is moved in the direction of the best solution by applying Q-gates as variation operators. The most commonly used Q-gate operator in literature is Rotation gate operator which is defined as given below

$$U\left(\Delta\Phi_i\right) = \begin{pmatrix} \mathrm{Cos}\left(\Delta\Phi_i\right) & -\mathrm{Sin}\left(\Delta\Phi_i\right) \\ \mathrm{Sin}\left(\Delta\Phi_i\right) & \mathrm{Cos}\left(\Delta\Phi_i\right) \end{pmatrix} \qquad (7)$$

where $\Delta\Phi_i$ denotes the change in angle of rotation of ith Q-bit. Based on the sign of Φ, each Q-bit moves towards either 0 or 1. A generic quantum inspired algorithm is shown in Table 1 (Han & Kim, 2002).

4.2 QGFA

The proposed QGFA algorithm is discussed in this section. QGFA is a population based metaheuristic for solving DFA problem. Like any other evolutionary approach, QGFA also comprises of encoding the chromosomes (i.e. solution representation), evaluating the fitness of chromosomes and evolving the population towards better regions of search space.

4.2.1 Solution Representation

Solution representation is the first step in the process of optimization using metaheuristic techniques. In QIGA, Q-bits are used for representing the genes in a chromosome. The DFA problem addressed in this paper is a permutation combinatorial optimization problem where ordering and orientation of fragments in a layout needs to be determined. For a DFA problem having N fragments, each fragment is identified using an integer from 1 to N. A Q-bit solution for DFA problem is denoted by q and is encoded as shown in equation (8)

$$q = \ddots \begin{pmatrix} q(1,1) & q(1,2) & \cdots\cdots & q(1,N) \\ q(2,1) & q(2,2) & \cdots\cdots & q(2,N) \\ \vdots\cdots & \cdots\vdots & \cdots & \vdots \\ q(N,1) & q(N,2) & \cdots\cdots & q(N,N) \end{pmatrix} \qquad (8)$$

4.2.2 Population Initialization

Let the size of population be m. Then Q-bit population in j^{th} generation, $Q(j)$, is represented as:

Table 1. Generic quantum inspired algorithm

Algorithm 1: Generic Quantum Inspired Algorithm
Begin Initialize the Q-bit solutions **While** (not termination condition) Measure the Q-bit solutions. Evaluate Fitness Update Q-bit population using Q-gate operator. **End** **End**

$$Q_j = \left\{ q_1^j, q_2^j, q_3^j, \ldots, q_m^j \right\} \tag{9}$$

where

$$q_i^j = \ddots \begin{pmatrix} q_i^j(1,1) & q_i^j(1,2) & \cdots\cdots & q_i^j(1,N) \\ q_i^j(2,1) & q_i^j(2,2) & \cdots\cdots & q_i^j(2,N) \\ \vdots\cdots & \cdots\vdots & \cdots & \vdots \\ q_i^j(N,1) & q_i^j(N,2) & \cdots\cdots & q_i^j(N,N) \end{pmatrix} \text{ for } i=1,2,3,\ldots m \tag{10}$$

and

$$q_i^j(x,y) = \begin{bmatrix} \alpha_i^j(x,y) \\ \beta_i^j(x,y) \end{bmatrix} \text{ for } x, y = 1,2,3,\ldots, N \tag{11}$$

$$\left| \alpha_i^j(x,y) \right|^2 + \left| \beta_i^j(x,y) \right|^2 = 1 \tag{12}$$

At the start of algorithm, $j = 0$ and therefore the initial population denoted by $Q(0)$ is given as

$$Q(0) = \left\{ q_1^0, q_2^0, q_3^0, \ldots, q_m^0 \right\} \tag{13}$$

Such that

$$q_i^0(x,y) = \begin{bmatrix} \alpha_i^0(x,y) \\ \beta_i^0(x,y) \end{bmatrix} \text{ for } x, y = 1,2,3,\ldots, N \tag{14}$$

$$\alpha_i^0(x,y) = \beta_i^0(x,y) = \sqrt{\frac{1}{2}} \text{ for } x, y = 1,2,3,\ldots, N \text{ and } i = 1,2,3,\ldots, m \tag{15}$$

Initially, every Q-bit in a chromosome is assigned a value of $\sqrt{1/2}$ so that all the fragments have equal chances of being placed at any position in a fragment layout.

4.2.3 Quantum Measurement

Q-bit chromosomes in the Q-bit population are measured or observed in order to generate a population of classical chromosomes as fitness evaluation can be performed only on classical chromosomes. The classical chromosome in QGFA is a binary matrix of size $N \times N$ where N is the number of DNA fragments. The binary population in j^{th} generation is represented by $B(j)$ as shown in equation (16).

$$B\left(j\right) = \left(b_1^j, b_2^j, \ldots, b_m^j\right) \tag{16}$$

where

$$b_i^j = \begin{bmatrix} b_i^j\left(1,1\right) & b_i^j\left(1,2\right)\cdots & b_i^j\left(1,N\right) \\ b_i^j\left(2,1\right) & b_i^j\left(2,2\right)\cdots & b_i^j\left(2,N\right) \\ \vdots & \vdots & \vdots \\ b_i^j\left(N,1\right) & b_i^j\left(N,2\right)\cdots & b_i^j\left(N,N\right) \end{bmatrix} \text{for } i = 1, 2, \ldots, m \tag{17}$$

Such that

$$\forall x \forall y\, b_i^j\left(x,y\right) = 0 \mid 1 \tag{18}$$

$$\forall x \forall y\, if\, x = y, b_i^j\left(x,y\right) = 0 \tag{19}$$

$$\forall x \sum_{y=1}^{N} b_i^j\left(x,y\right) = 1, \ \forall y \sum_{x=1}^{N} b_i^j\left(x,y\right) = 1 \tag{20}$$

$$\sum_{x=1}^{N}\sum_{y=1}^{N} b_i^j\left(x,y\right) = N \tag{21}$$

where $b_i^j\left(x,y\right) = 1$ is interpreted as, in i^{th} solution of jth generation, fragment y is at x^{th} position in the fragment layout. Since the classical solution is in binary matrix form and DFA problem is a permutation problem, for evaluating fitness, the binary solutions need to be converted into numeric solutions. The measurement of Q-bit chromosome for constructing classical binary chromosome and conversion of binary representation to numeric representation are O(N^2) operations. The procedure for measuring operator is presented in Table 2.

Table 2. Procedure for measuring operator

Procedure 1: Measuring Operator
Input: Q-bit Chromosome q
Output: Classical Binary chromosome b
Begin for i=1:N for j=1:N if $random[0,1) < \lvert \beta(i,j) \rvert^2$ if $b(i,1:j-1) == 0 \ \&\ \& b(1:i-1,j) == 0$ then $b(i,j) \leftarrow 1$ else $b(i,j) \leftarrow 0$ **End**

The measuring procedure has been modified in this chapter so that condition given in equation (20) is fulfilled and no infeasible solutions are generated.

4.2.4 Fitness Function

Evaluating the quality of solutions is an important aspect of working of any evolutionary technique including QIGA. The fitness of a chromosome represents the probability of reproduction and survival to the next generation. Higher the fitness value, higher is the chance of producing offspring and therefore surviving to next generation. Fitness function, a heuristic specific to the problem being addressed, is used to evaluate the quality of solutions. In this chapter, the fitness function evaluates the performance of assembling the DNA fragments.

The efficiency of assembling the fragments by finding their proper order and orientation depends on the overlap score between adjacent fragments. Higher the overlap score better is the assembled sequence as it is assumed that fragments having higher overlap score are generated from the same region of DNA sequence and therefore needs to be adjacent in the fragment layout. Therefore, fitness of solutions is evaluated using equation (3).

4.2.5 Updating the Q-Bit Population

Q-gate operator is used to update the Q-bit population and make it evolve towards the best solution. In literature, rotation gate has been the most commonly used Q-gate operator. Therefore, in this chapter also Rotation gate operator is used for updating the Q-bits as shown below.

$$\begin{bmatrix} \alpha(x,y)^{j+1} \\ \beta(x,y)^{j+1} \end{bmatrix} = U(\Delta\phi_{x,y}) \begin{bmatrix} \alpha(x,y)^{j} \\ \beta(x,y)^{j} \end{bmatrix} for\, x,y = 1,2,\ldots\ldots,N \tag{22}$$

where $U\left(\Delta\phi_{x,y}\right)$ is the rotation operator as given in equation (7) and $\Delta\phi_{x,y}$ is the step size i.e. the angle by which Q-bit needs to be rotated. $\alpha\left(x,y\right)^{j+1}$ & $\beta\left(x,y\right)^{j+1}$ is the state of Q-bit after rotation and $\alpha\left(x,y\right)^{j}$ & $\beta\left(x,y\right)^{j}$ is the state before rotation.

Let b represents the current solution and best solution till current generation be represented by BS, then angle of rotation for $\left(x,y\right)^{th}$ Q-bit $\Delta\phi_{x,y}$ is computed using equation (23).

$$\Delta\phi_{x,y} = \left(BS_{x,y} - b_{x,y}\right)\left(\frac{F\left(BS\right) - F\left(b\right)}{F\left(BS\right)}\right) * 2\pi \qquad (23)$$

where $BS_{x,y}$ & $b_{x,y}$ represent the $\left(x,y\right)^{th}$ bit and $F\left(BS\right)$ & $F\left(b\right)$ represent the fitness value of BS and b respectively.

The QGFA algorithm is presented in Table 3.

5. EXPERIMENTAL RESULTS AND ANALYSIS

The experiments have been conducted on an Intel core i5 Processor with 4GB RAM in Windows8 environment. Real genome sequences frequently used for validating the models for DFA problem in existing literature have been used to test the effectiveness of proposed QGFA algorithm. The genome sequences used in this work have been taken from NCBI website. The details of the datasets are given in Table 4. Noiseless data has been used in this work. The pair wise overlap between fragments has been computed using a semi-global alignment technique presented in (Coull & Szymanski, 2008). If the overlap score between the fragments is less than thirty then it not considered as real match.

The proposed QGFA approach has been compared with other metaheuristic approaches used for addressing the DNA fragment assembly problem which include GA, PSO and ACO. The comparison is performed on the basis of overlap score (F) and number of contigs (denoted by NC). The experimental setup for all these approaches is given in Table 5. Comparison based on overlap score is shown in Table 6. And comparison in terms of number of contigs is shown in Table 7.

It can be inferred from Table 6 and Table 7 that QGFA produces DNA fragment layout having higher value of overlap score and smaller value of number of contigs. Therefore, QGFA performs comparatively better as compared to GA, PSO and ACO based DNA fragment assembly algorithms. The reason for QGFA performing better than others is that it has better exploration and exploitation capability even for smaller population sizes. Another advantage of using QGFA is that number of parameters to be adjusted is lesser in comparison to other techniques considered in this chapter. But the QGFA proposed in this chapter is computationally more expensive as compared to GA, PSO and ACO based approaches. This is due to the reason that solution representation is in matrix form which requires $O(N^2)$ computational time for quantum measurement, fitness evaluation and population updation operations while in the other techniques considered in this chapter solution representation is in vector form thus requiring only $O(N)$ computational time.

Table 3. QGFA algorithm

Algorithm 2: QGFA
Input: Set of fragments $\mathcal{F}$, Number of Fragments N, Maximum number of generations Gen_{max}, Population Size m, Overlap Score matrix $\mathcal{W}$
Output: Best layout of the fragments

Begin
Initialize generation number $j = 0$
Initialize Q-bit population $Q(j) = \left\{ q_1^j, q_2^j, q_3^j, \ldots, q_m^j \right\}$ for $j = 0$
Measure $Q(j)$ to generate $B(j) = \left\{ b_1^j, b_2^j, b_3^j, \ldots, b_m^j \right\}$ using **Procedure 1**
For each $b_i^j \in B(j), i = 1, 2, \ldots, m$
Evaluate fitness value F_i of b_i^j using **equation (3)**
End for
Determine current best solution $CBS = b_i^j$ $such\,that\,F_i = \max\limits_{j=1,2,\ldots,m} F_j$
Initialize best solution $BS = CBS$
While ($j < Gen_{max}$)
Update $Q(j)$ using **equation (22)** and **(23)**
Measure $Q(j)$ to generate $B(j) = \left\{ b_1^j, b_2^j, b_3^j, \ldots, b_m^j \right\}$ using **Procedure 1**
For each $b_i^j \in B(j), i = 1, 2, \ldots, m$
Evaluate fitness value F_i of b_i^j using **equation (3)**
End for
Determine current best solution $CBS = b_i^j$ $such\,that\,F_i = \max\limits_{j=1,2,\ldots,m} F_j$
if $F(CBS) > F(BS)$
$BS = CBS$
End if
End while
Return BS
End

Table 4. Details of dataset

Instances	Coverage	Mean Fragment Length	No. of Fragments	Original Sequence LENGTH (in bps)
X60189_4	4	395	39	3835
X60189_5	5	386	48	
X60189_6	6	343	66	
X60189_7	7	387	68	
M15421_5	5	398	127	10089
M15421_6	6	350	173	
M15421_7	7	383	177	
j02459_7	7	700	352	48502
BX842596_4	4	708	442	77292
BX842596_7	7	703	773	

Table 5. Experimental setup

Parameter	Value
Population size	100
Number of Generations	2000
Selection (GA)	Binary tournament
Crossover (GA)	Ordered two point crossover (P_c=0.75)
Mutation (GA)	Insertion (P_m=0.10)
Inertia weight (PSO)	0.65
Cognitive element (PSO)	2
Social parameter (PSO)	2
Pheromone importance α (ACO)	0.5
Heuristic importance β (ACO)	1
Evaporation coefficient ρ (ACO)	0.2

6. CONCLUSION AND FUTURE WORK

DNA fragment assembly is a critical step in whole genome sequencing using shotgun sequencing technique. Assembly process aims to reconstruct the original DNA sequence by determining the proper order and orientation of the fragments in a layout. DNA fragment assembly problem has been proved to be NP-Hard and therefore finding exact solutions is not possible. A number of techniques have been proposed in literature for addressing this problem but due to its importance and complexity, better techniques are still needed. In this chapter, Quantum inspired Genetic algorithm has been adapted to addressed the DNA Fragment Assembly problem (QGFA) as in literature quantum inspired metaheuristic techniques have been proved performing better than traditional metaheuristic techniques. The efficacy

Table 6. Comparison in terms of overlap score

Instances	Overlap Score (F)			
	QGFA	*GA*	*PSO*	*ACO*
X60189_4	12428	11527	11976	12105
X60189_5	14731	13978	14433	14489
X60189_6	18836	18008	18291	18302
X60189_7	21685	20986	21489	21505
M15421_5	38791	37417	38578	38593
M15421_6	48412	47198	47582	47896
M15421_7	55896	52355	53498	54325
j02459_7	116109	108643	112557	113914
BX842596_4	227957	211135	217915	218332
BX842596_7	442861	418568	421186	426748

Table 7. Comparison in terms number of contigs

Instances	Number of Contigs (NC)			
	QGFA	*GA*	*PSO*	*ACO*
X60189_4	1	3	2	2
X60189_5	1	2	2	2
X60189_6	1	2	1	1
X60189_7	1	1	1	1
M15421_5	3	9	7	6
M15421_6	2	6	6	3
M15421_7	1	5	4	2
j02459_7	3	13	9	7
BX842596_4	5	16	11	11
BX842596_7	2	8	5	4

of proposed QGFA approach has been evaluated by comparing it with other metaheuristic approaches used for solving the DNA fragment assembly problem. Simulation results show that QGFA based assembly is comparatively better in terms of the overlap score and the number of contigs produced. But the proposed QGFA approach is computationally more expensive as compared to other approaches. This is due to the reason that solution is represented using a matrix due to which quantum measurement, fitness evaluation and updating the population operations become computationally expensive. Devising novel methods for solution representation which maintain the inherent capabilities of Q-bit representation and are computationally less expensive can be considered as a future work.

REFERENCES

Alba, E., & Dorronsoro, B. (2008). *Cellular genetic algorithms*. Heidelberg, Germany: Springer-Verlag.

Alba, E., & Luque, G. (2007). *A new local search algorithm for the DNA fragment assembly problem*. Paper presented in Evolutionary Computation in Combinatorial Optimization, EvoCOP'07, Valencia, Spain. doi:10.1007/978-3-540-71615-0_1

Alba, E., Luque, G., & Minetti, G. (2008). Seeding strategies and recombination operators for solving the DNA fragment assembly problem. *Information Processing Letters, 108*(3), 94–100. doi:. ipl.2008.04.00510.1016/j

Angeleri, E., Apolloni, B., de Falco, D., & Grandi, L. (1999). DNA fragment assembly using neural prediction techniques. *International Journal of Neural Systems, 9*(6), 523–544. doi:10.1142/S0129065799000563 PMID:10651335

Bocicor, M. I., Czibula, G., & Czibula, I. G. (2011). A reinforcement learning approach for solving the fragment assembly problem. In *Proceedings of 13th International Symposium on Symbolic and Numeric Algorithms for Scientific Computing* (pp. 191-198). Academic Press. 10.1109/SYNASC.2011.9

Braga, M. D. V., & Meidanis, J. (2002). An algorithm that builds a set of strings given its overlap graph. *Lecture Notes in Computer Science, 2286*, 52–63. doi:10.1007/3-540-45995-2_10

Burks, C., Engle, M., Forrest, S., Parsons, R. J., Soderlund, C., & Stolorz, P. (1994). *Stochastic optimization tools for genomic sequence assembly*. London, UK: Academic Press. doi:10.1016/B978-0-08-092639-1.50038-1

Chaisson, M., Pevzner, P., & Tang, H. (2004). Fragment assembly with short reads. *Bioinformatics (Oxford, England), 20*(13), 2067–2074. doi:10.1093/bioinformatics/bth205 PMID:15059830

Chang, W., & Lawler, E. (1990). Approximate string matching in sublinear expected time. In *Proceedings of the 31st IEEE Symposium on Foundations of Computer Science* (pp. 118-124). IEEE. 10.1109/FSCS.1990.89530

Chevreux, B. (2005). *MIRA: An automated genome and EST assembler* (Ph.D thesis). German Cancer Research Center, Heidelberg, Germany.

Churchill, G., Burks, C., Eggert, M., Engle, M., & Waterman, M. (1993). *Assembling DNA sequence fragments by shuffling and simulated annealing (Tech. Rep. No. LAUR 93-2287)*. Academic Press.

Coull, S. E., & Szymanski, B. K. (2008). Sequence alignment for masquerade detection. *Computational Statistics & Data Analysis, 52*(8), 4116–4131. doi:10.1016/j.csda.2008.01.022

Dorronsoro, B., Alba, E., Luque, G., & Bouvry, P. (2008). A self-adaptive cellular memetic algorithm for the DNA fragment assembly problem. In *Proceedings of IEEE Congress on Evolutionary Computation* (pp. 2651-2658). IEEE. 10.1109/CEC.2008.4631154

Ferreira, C. E., de Souza, C. C., & Wakabayashi, Y. (2002). Rearrangement of DNA fragments: A branch-and-cut algorithm. *Discrete Applied Mathematics, 116*(1/2), 161–177. doi:10.1016/S0166-218X(00)00324-3

Firoz, J. S., Rahman, M. S., & Saha, T. K. (2012). Bee algorithms for solving DNA fragment assembly problem with noisy and noiseless data. In *Proceedings of the Conference on Genetic and Evolutionary Computation, GECCO'12*. Philadelphia: GECCO. 10.1145/2330163.2330192

Han, K., & Kim, J. (2002). Quantum inspired evolutionary algorithm for a class of combinatorial optimization. *IEEE Transactions on Evolutionary Computation*, *6*(6), 580-593.

Hernandez, D., Francois, P., Farinelli, L., Osteras, M., & Schrenzel, J. (2008). De novo bacterial genome sequencing: Millions of very short reads assembled on a desktop computer. *Genome Research*, *18*(5), 802–809. doi:10.1101/gr.072033.107 PMID:18332092

Huang, K. W., Chen, J. L., Yang, C. S., & Tsai, C. W. (2015). A memetic particle swarm optimization algorithm for solving the DNA fragment assembly problem. *Neural Computing & Applications*, *26*(3), 495–506. doi:10.100700521-014-1659-0

Huang, K. W., Chen, J. L., Yang, C. S., & Tsai, C. W. (2016). A memetic gravitation search algorithm for solving DNA fragment assembly problems. *Journal of Intelligent & Fuzzy Systems*, *30*(4), 2245–2255. doi:10.3233/IFS-151994

Huang, X. (1992). A contig assembly program based on sensitive detection of fragment overlaps. *Genomics*, *14*(1), 18–25. doi:10.1016/S0888-7543(05)80277-0 PMID:1427824

Huang, X., & Madan, A. (1999). CAP3 sequence assembly program. *Genome Research*, *9*(9), 868–877. doi:10.1101/gr.9.9.868 PMID:10508846

Huang, X., Wang, J., Aluru, S., Yang, S. P., & Hillier, L. (2003). PCAP: A whole-genome assembly program. *Genome Research*, *13*(9), 2164–2170. doi:10.1101/gr.1390403 PMID:12952883

Jeck, W. R., Reinhardt, J. A., Baltrus, D. A., Hickenbotham, M. T., Magrini, V., & Mardis, E. R. (2007). Extending assembly of short DNA sequences to handle error. *Bioinformatics (Oxford, England)*, *23*(21), 2942–2944. doi:/btm45110.1093/bioinformatics

Jones, D. F., Mirrazavi, S. K., & Tamiz, M. (2002). Multiobjective meta-heuristics: An overview of the current state-of-the-art. *European Journal of Operational Research*, *137*(1), 1–9. doi:10.1016/S0377-2217(01)00123-0

Kchouk, M., & Elloumi, M. (2016, December). A clustering approach for denovo assembly using Next Generation Sequencing data. In *Bioinformatics and Biomedicine (BIBM), 2016 IEEE International Conference on* (pp. 1909-1911). IEEE. 10.1109/BIBM.2016.7822812

Kikuchi, S., & Chakraborty, G. (2006). Heuristically tuned GA to solve genome fragment assembly problem. In *Proceedings of IEEE Congress on Evolutionary Computation CEC'06* (pp. 1491-1498). IEEE. 10.1109/CEC.2006.1688485

Kubalik, J., Buryan, P., & Wagner, L. (2010). Solving the DNA fragment assembly problem efficiently using iterative optimization with evolved hypermutations. In *Proceedings of the 12th Annual Conference on Genetic and Evolutionary Computation, GECCO'10*, (pp. 213-214). GECCO. 10.1145/1830483.1830522

Li, P., Kupfer, K. C., Davies, C. J., Burbee, D., Evans, G. A., & Garner, H. R. (1997). PRIMO: A primer design program that applies base quality statistics for automated large-scale DNA sequencing. *Genomics*, *40*(3), 476–485. doi:10.1006/geno.1996.4560 PMID:9073516

Mallén-Fullerton, G. M., Quiroz-Ibarra, J. E., Miranda, A., & Fernández-Anaya, G. (2015). Modified Classical Graph Algorithms for the DNA Fragment Assembly Problem. *Algorithms*, *8*(3), 754–773. doi:10.3390/a8030754

McCombie, W. R., & Martin-Gallardo, A. (1994). Large-scale, automated sequencing of human chromosomal regions. In *Automated DNA sequencing and analysis*. San Diego, CA: Academic Press. doi:10.1016/B978-0-08-092639-1.50028-9

Medvedev, P., Georgiou, K., & Myers, E. W. (2007). Computability and equivalence of models for sequence assembly. In *Proceedings of Workshop on Algorithms in Bioinformatics (WABI)*. WABI. 10.1007/978-3-540-74126-8_27

Meksangsouy, P., & Chaiyaratana, N. (2003). DNA fragment assembly using an ant colony system algorithm. In *Proceedings of Congress on Evolutionary Computation CEC'03* (Vol. 3, pp. 1756-1763). CEC. 10.1109/CEC.2003.1299885

Narayanan, A., & Moore, M. (1996). Quantum-inspired genetic algorithm. *Proceedings of IEEE International Conference on Evolutionary Computation*, 61–66. 10.1109/ICEC.1996.542334

Nielsen, M., & Chuang, I. (2000). *Quantum computation and quantum information*. Cambridge University Press.

Parsons, R. J., Forrest, S., & Burks, C. (1993). Genetic algorithms for DNA sequence assembly. *ISMB-93 Proceedings, 1*, 310-318.

Parsons, R. J., Forrest, S., & Burks, C. (1995). Genetic Algorithms, operators and DNA fragment Assembly. *Machine Learning*, *21*(1/2), 11–33. doi:10.1023/A:1022613513712

Phillippy, P. M., Delcher, A. L., & Salzberg, S. L. (2004). Comparative genome assembly. *Briefings in Bioinformatics*, *5*(3), 237–248. doi:10.1093/bib/5.3.237 PMID:15383210

Pop, M. (2009). Genome assembly reborn: Recent computational challenges. *Briefings in Bioinformatics*, *10*(4), 354–366. doi:10.1093/bib/bbp026 PMID:19482960

Rathee, M., & Kumar, T. V. (2014). Dna fragment assembly using multi-objective genetic algorithms. *International Journal of Applied Evolutionary Computation*, *5*(3), 84–108. doi:10.4018/ijaec.2014070105

Setubal, J., & Meidanis, J. (1997). *Introduction to computational molecular biology*. PWS Publishing Company.

Simpson, J. T., Wong, K., Jackman, S. D., Schein, J. E., Jones, S. J. M., & Birol, I. (2009). ABYSS: A parallel assembler for short read sequence data. *Genome Research*, *19*(6), 1117–1123. doi:10.1101/gr.089532.108 PMID:19251739

Sivanandan, S. N., & Deepa, S. N. (2008). *Introduction to genetic algorithms*. Springer.

Smith, T., & Waterman, M. (1981). Identification of common molecular subsequences. *Journal of Molecular Biology*, *147*(1), 195–197. doi:10.1016/0022-2836(81)90087-5 PMID:7265238

Staden, R. (1980). A new computer method for the storage and manipulation of DNA gel reading data. *Nucleic Acids Research*, *8*(16), 3673–3694. doi:10.1093/nar/8.16.3673 PMID:7433103

Sutton, G. G., White, O., Adams, M., & Kerlavage, A. (1995). TIGR assembler: A new tool for assembling large shotgun sequencing projects. *Genome Science & Technology*, *1*(1), 9–19. doi:10.1089/gst.1995.1.9

Waston, J. D., & Crick, F. H. C. (1953). Molecular structure of nucleic acids: A structure for deoxyribose nucleic acid. *Nature*, *171*(4356), 737–738. doi:10.1038/171737a0 PMID:13054692

Watson, J. D., & Berry, A. (2003). *DNA: The secret of life*. Knopf.

Zerbino, D. R., & Birney, E. (2008). Velvet: Algorithms for de novo short read assembly using de Bruijn graphs. *Genome Research*, *18*(5), 821–829. doi:10.1101/gr.074492.107 PMID:18349386

Zhang, G. (2011). Quantum-inspired evolutionary algorithms: A survey and empirical study. *Journal of Heuristics*, *17*(3), 303–351. doi:10.100710732-010-9136-0

Zhang, G. X., & Rong, H. N. (2007). Real-observation quantum-inspired evolutionary algorithm for a class of numerical optimization problems. In Lecture Notes in Computer Science: Vol. 4490. ICCS2007, Part IV (pp. 989-996). Springer.

Chapter 6
Effective Prevention and Reduction in the Rate of Accidents Using Internet of Things and Data Analytics

Sowmya B. J.
Ramaiah Institute of Technology, India

Chetan Shetty
Ramaiah Institute of Technology, India

Seema S.
Ramaiah Institute of Technology, India

Srinivasa K. G.
CBP Government Engineering College, India

ABSTRACT

Hundreds of lives in India are lost each day due to the delayed medical response. In the present scenario, the victims completely rely on the passersby for almost every kind of medical help such as informing the hospital or ambulance. This project aims to automate the process of detecting and reporting accidents using accident detection kits in vehicles. The kit has a system on chip and various sensors which sense various parameters that change drastically during the occurrence of accidents such as the vibration levels, orientation of vehicles with respect to the ground. The accident is said to occur when these values cross the permissible threshold limit. As soon as this happens, the latitude and longitude of the accident spot is tracked using the GPS module present in the kit. The nearest hospital and police station is computed by the GPS module, which uses the latitude and longitude values as the input. The accident notifications are sent to the concerned hospital and police station over the web interface accordingly. The assignment of particular ambulance and the required traffic policemen to the accident cases is done using the web

DOI: 10.4018/978-1-5225-5832-3.ch006

interface. The android application guides the ambulance driver as well as the policemen to the accident spot and also helps in the detailed registration of the accidents. The closest doctor facility and police headquarters is processed by the GPS module, which utilizes the scope and longitude esteems as the information. The accident warnings are sent to the concerned healing facility and police headquarters over the web interface as needs be. The task of specific rescue vehicle and policemen to the accident cases is finished utilizing the web interface. An intelligent analysis of the last five years' rich dataset uncovers the patterns followed by the accidents and gives valuable insights on how to deploy the existing resources such as ambulances and traffic-police efficiently. Various types of analysis are done to identify the cause-effect relationships and deal with this in a better way. Such technical solutions to the frequently occurring problems would result in saving many lives as well as making the cities safer and smarter.

1. INTRODUCTION

Hundreds of accidents occur in the country everyday causing an immense damage to lives and property. These accidents go unnoticed and unattended by the police and medical help such as ambulance all over the world. This is due to the absence of a mechanism, which can detect the accidents, notify all the nearest concerned authorities such as the police station, hospitals, insurance agents etc. Things haven't changed much in the context of accidents in the last few decades.

The product which is proposed as the solution is Accident Detection Kit, which has a Raspberry Pi as the System on Chip and some of the sensors such as Vibration or Shock sensors, Tilt sensors, Fire and Smoke sensors etc. each dedicated to the sensing of certain parameters which help in the detection of accidents further. The values sensed by them are continuously monitored and on encountering that they have crossed the threshold, the accident is said to occur. The threshold is set based on the testing which was performed on a model car which has undergone certain conditions which could be considered to be as accidents such as extreme vibrations, tilting of vehicles to an angle that sliding or falling becomes very likely, release of smoke/fire near the engine of the vehicle etc. On detecting the occurrence of accident, the location of the accident spot is tracked in terms of latitude and longitude using GPS Module.

The EC2 instance of Amazon Web Services as in is deployed to collect the data from the Raspberry Pi as discussed by (Ignacio, Stefano, Marco, & Maurizio, 2013). The cloud computes the nearest police station as well as the nearest hospital using Google Maps API and the output of GPS module and hence, allots these accident cases to their nearest concerned authorities. The accident details are sent to the hospitals and police station over on their web interfaces so that they can choose the ambulance and police staff to be sent to the accident spot respectively. Automated SMSs are sent to the associated ambulance driver and police staff, intimating them with the details of the accident. The android application eases the process of reaching to the accident spot by guiding the ambulance drivers and the policemen to the associated accident spot in real time. The police staffs also have the option to register the accidents after they examine the situation. This helps in a better monitoring of the accidents which happen in the country and also in the maintenance of a centralized data repository which would be of extreme use further.

The accidents are analyzed to know the cause-effect behavior as discussed by Miyaji (2014) and the generated reports are sent weekly as well as monthly to the respective authorities for further actions using automated e-mail system. This helps in a better understanding of how the deployment of resources such as the police staffs, ambulances etc. can be done. It helps in smarter planning of cities by identifying the suitable sites to build the hospitals, preferably in the areas which are the most prone to accidents so that the time taken by the ambulances to reach the hospital would be lesser. Similarly, the schools, colleges and old-age homes could be constructed or relocated to the areas which are very less prone to accidents to ensure safety of lives. Also, the cab services can improve their patrolling or stationing in the areas with more drunken-driving accidents expecting the people to book their cabs after they drink. Such business strategies could also be made using the inferences drawn from the analysis.

Different Objectives for the Modules

1. Ambulance Service Provider controls both ambulances and hospitals registered under him. Each area consists of an Ambulance Service Provider. Whenever an accident occurs, the corresponding Ambulance Service Provider gets a notification about occurrence of accident in that area. He then assigns ambulance and also books beds in nearby hospital.
2. The drivers of ambulances would get notifications about accidents from corresponding Ambulance Service Provider. He also gets details about the assigned hospital so that they can reach the accident spot faster and admit victim in assigned hospital.
3. This spot of accident is tracked and sent to ambulance driver so that he can reach accident spot. Also the location is shown on graphical user interface (Google maps API) so that he can change travelling directions depending on the traffic to reach accident spot faster.
4. The GPS module which is in-built to get position, altitude, speed etc.
5. The concerned car insurance and life insurance organizations can also be intimated with the notifications regarding the accidents. The blood banks can also be notified in case of any medical urgencies leading to the requirement of blood.

2. LITERATURE SURVEY

Internet of Things offers a great and advanced connection between the many devices, system as well as the services. This goes beyond the machine-to-machine (M2M) communication and includes many protocols, domains as well as applications. (Shah, Nair, Parikh, & Shah, 2015) used piezoelectric sensors which sense the vibrations statically as well as dynamically. They have used a combination of GPS and GSM module to fetch the location. Wakure, Patkar, Dagale, Priyanka, and Solanki (2014) used AVR microcontroller along with accelerometer to detect the accidents. They also used airbag and alcohol sensor to detect the accidents mostly occurred in the four wheelers. Patil, Rawat, Singh, Dixit (2016) discussed about detection of accidents using FPGA, ARM processor and Raspberry Pi. They have designed an intelligent system to control the movement of ambulances on the roads with no loss of time. Poongundran and Jeevabharathi (2015) have designed a vehicle monitoring and tracking system using Raspberry Pi, Thermistor, Shock sensor and Gas Sensor. Hussain, Sharma, Bhatnagar, & Goyal (2011) have discussed about several units such as Vehicle Unit, Ambulance Unit, Traffic Unit, Hopsital Unit and Central Server and implemented them using Arduino as the System on chip. Sonika, Sekhar and Jaishree (2014) have used the same units such as hospital unit, ambulance unit etc and simulated them using nodes in Network Simulation tool NS2. They have found the shortest path for the ambulance to cover in case of occurrence of accidents using Radio Frequency transmitters. Bai, Wu and Tsai (2012) designed a fall monitor system using accelerometers which could analyze the actions of humans such as jumping, waling, sitting etc. The similar kind of approach can also be designed for the monitoring of vehicles too. Prabha, Sunitha and Anitha (2014) discussed that ARM is used by them for the detection of accidents. They used a sensor and used it to detect the accidents. The GSM is used to send the SMS having latitude and longitude values to the number which is pre-saved in the EEPROM. A paper on IoT Based Accident Prevention & Tracking System for Night Drivers as discussed by Lakshmi & Balakrishnan, (2012). They discussed the accident detection mechanism and used KNN algorithm to find the nearest hospital. They have designed an automatic alarm device for the traffic accidents. They have also talked about the chances of false accidents for which a solution is very important to be incorporated.

Kumar and Toshniwal (2015) used clustering initially to partition the working data into multiple groups and then, they have used Probit model to identify the relationships between various characteristics related to accidents. Poisson models and negative binomial models are used by many people, researchers and analysts to mine the relationship between the traffic accidents and the causes of accidents. Rovsek et al. (2017) analyzed the crash data from 2005 to 2009 of Slovenia using classification and regression tree algorithm. Kashani et al. (2011) also used classification and regression tree algorithm to analyze crash records obtained from information and technology department of the Iran traffic police from 2006 to 2008. Depaire et al. (2008) had used latent class clustering on two road user traffic accident data from 1997 to 1999 of Belgium. He divided the data into seven clusters and then performed the analysis. Chang and Chen (2005) analyzed the national freeway data from Taiwan. They have used CART and negative binomial regression model for this analysis. Abdel & Radwan (2000) used an unrelated Negative Binomial regression model to predict the total number of property damages and the injury crashes. Karlaftis and Tarko (1998) used cluster analysis to categorize the accident data into many categories and then analyzed the results obtained from the cluster analysis using the Negative Binomial. They have also revealed the impact of the driver age on the road accidents.

Sangeetha et al. (2014) emphasize the requirements on the ambulance side i.e., reaching the accident site in time. This is accomplished by controlling the traffic lights whenever an ambulance is detected nearby traffic junctions so as to provide a clear path to the ambulance by giving green signal to the lane in which the ambulance is currently travelling. The authors have constructed 2 units namely: ambulance unit, to communicate the position of the ambulance and traffic junction unit, to control the traffic lights as and when the ambulance comes near its vicinity. In the ambulance unit, a GPRS 3G modem is installed so as to provide position of the ambulance as well as to receive the coordinates of the accident site. The position is represented in terms of latitude and longitude, which is displayed on the LCD. In the traffic junction unit, the signal received from the ambulance will cause the circuitry to change the traffic signals as and when necessary. Hence the basic ideology in this work is the automatic control of traffic lights. In this work, other important transportation vehicles which have to reach on time to the delivery site will suffer due to the disruption in the traffic lights and also it will take time to decode the actual position based on latitude and longitude to pin point the actual location and to provide the said location to the ambulance driver.

Shruti Gotadki et al. (2104) have implemented intelligent ambulance system by providing mechanisms to measure vital patient information such as heart rate and body temperature. The ambulance is also provided with the capability of changing traffic signals to provide a smoother ride of ambulance. A visual system is designed and implemented in the hospitals concerned so that the necessary preparations can be made as suitable for the victim and as quickly as possible. The design of the work is as follows. There are 3 main parts namely Ambulance unit, Hospital unit and Traffic signal unit. In the ambulance unit sensors to measure patient parameters such as heart beat/pulse rate and body temperature is embedded on to the micro controller. It also has an analog to digital converter and a Zigbee module. Zigbee module maintains high energy efficiency as a result it works well on low power batteries. The analog to digital converter converts the analog signal detected from the embedded sensors and converts it to appropriate digital signals so that necessary operations can be carried on. The microcontroller reads the parameters and displays on the LCD. It is then sent to the Zigbee module to send the information to the hospital. The traffic signal unit consists of RFID reader, microcontroller, relay driver and light signal. RFID reader detects the signals emitted by the ambulance and each ambulance will have unique RFID. Based on the received signals, the signals are passed on to the microcontroller which is then passed on t the relay to change the traffic signal as and when necessary. The hospital unit consists of Zigbee which is connected to a visual system to display the patient parameters so that the hospital staff can make the necessary preparations even before the arrival of the patient.

Numerous analysts did their examinations on accident discovery framework. Aishwarya explained an IoT based vehicle accident avoidance and framework for night drivers in this paper gives Eye Blink Monitoring System (EBM) that alarms the subject amid condition of drowsiness. Transportation has extraordinary significance in our everyday life and IoT based vehicle accident location framework utilizing GPS and WIFI has picked up consideration. At the point when accident happens, this framework sends short message to WhatsApp of a versatile number by means of Wi-Fi over web. Message will give longitude and scope esteems. From these qualities area of mishap can be resolved (Aishwarya et.al, 2105). Sadhana B clarified Smart head protector keen security for motorcyclist utilizing raspberry pi and open CV. The thought is acquired in the wake of realizing that there is expanded number of deadly street accident throughout the years. This undertaking is intended to present security frameworks for the motorcyclist to wear the cap legitimately. Keen Helmet - Intelligent Safety Helmet for Motorcyclist is a venture attempted to expand the rate of street security among motorcyclists. The thought is gotten after realizing that there is expanded number of harmful street accidents throughout the years. Through the investigation recognized, it is broke down that the caps utilized isn't in wellbeing highlights for example, not wearing a cap string and not utilize the proper size (Shabrin et al., 2016). The primary goal of the referred paper is to computerize every one of the gadgets i.e. home machines through web utilizing Raspberry Pi, and in addition we can have the security for the framework by utilizing sensors like PIR, LPG, temperature sensors. The calculation is produced in Python dialect, which is default programming dialect of Raspberry Pi. To limit the measure of carbon outflows that we contribute towards the total carbon discharges of this world, Use of Sustainable power Sources in Household application has dependably been the best strategy. By creating distinctive codes the correspondence between the remote clients, the web server, the raspberry pi card and the home parts are conceivable (Ghorpade et al., 2016). A productive car security framework is actualized for hostile to robbery and accident location, utilizing an installed framework comprising of a Global Positioning System (GPS) and a Wi-Fi Module. The framework in case of robbery will send predefined message to the proprietor of vehicle. The client (in the event that he feels his vehicle is getting stolen) can begin following the position of focused vehicle on Google Earth on a committed vehicle tracker application. Utilizing GPS locator, the target's present area is resolved and sent, alongside different parameters got by vehicle's information port, through Web through Wifi module that is associated with PC or cell phone. Since the fundamental medium of correspondence is web (framework to client and the other way around), the term IoT or 'Web of Things' is actualized here. The proprietor will have the decision of slicing the supply of fuel to the motor on the off chance that he needs to make prompt move catch the criminal. This highlight will be available on the vehicle tracker application. The other part of the venture is the accident location. The procedure is same as in robbery identification, i.e., when accident takes put; the accelerometer's readings will trigger the framework to begin sending directions of the accident site to the law requirement experts and healing centers, because of which crisis move can be made by them instantly (Karande et al., 2016). The minimal effort and adaptable home control and observing framework utilizing a Raspberry PI module and a Static Relay, with web availability for getting to and controlling gadgets and machines remotely utilizing Smartphone android application. The proposed framework does not require a committed server PC as for comparative frameworks and offers a novel correspondence convention to screen and control the home condition with something beyond the exchanging usefulness. To exhibit the practicality and viability of this framework, gadgets, for example, Static transfers and a Wi-Fi switch can be coordinated with the home control framework (Anitha et al., 2016).

3. ARCHITECTURE

The architecture can be roughly divided in to Internet of Things and Data Analytics part. The Internet of Things part aims to provide solutions after the occurrence of accidents whereas the Data Analytics part proves to be helpful in the pre-accident context. The Internet of Things part consists of the accident detection kit, web interface and android application. The Accident Detection Kit has Raspberry Pi 2 (Model B) as the System on chip. To power it up, a single 2.0 USB connector was used. The SD card was set up with NOOBS and Raspbian OS, which worked in the similar way as the Linux Operating system does. The board has 10/100 Ethernet RJ45 jack for internet connectivity which was used to communicate with the cloud in real time. The Vibration Sensor LM393 served the purpose of detecting the vibrations produced in the vehicle as a result of movements and collisions. They use piezoelectric effect to measure the changes to electrical charge and provide the output in terms of voltages. The sensitivity of the sensor was adjusted by the potentiometer available in the sensor itself. The Tri-Axis tilt sensor, MPU 6050, with programmable full-scale range and digital output was used for measuring the orientation of the vehicles with respect to the ground. Depending on the electric current which is produced from the piezoelectric walls, the direction of inclination of the vehicle and magnitude along the X, Y and Z axes was also determined. The GPS Module, s1216 – R1 is used as the GPS Module, which uses NMEA-0183 protocol for the communication. It has an antenna which communicates with the satellite and finally, the output is obtained as the latitude and the longitude values as discussed by Shah, Nair, Parikh, & Shah (2015). The fire sensor is used to detect the presence of fire, which might have caused due to the combustion of fuel in the vehicle.

The Google Maps API is used on the cloud to compute the nearest hospital and the police station. The cloud performs this using the latitude and longitude values and performs a nearby search for the desired entity. The accident notifications are sent to the concerned hospital and police station over the web interface accordingly. The assignment of particular ambulance and the required traffic policemen to the accident cases is also done using the web interface. The android application guides the ambulance driver as well as the policemen to the accident spot and also helps in the detailed registration of the accidents. The web interface and android application runs with the cloud instance and is hosted on the same. The five years' data set is stored on the cloud referred to as history data. The Data Analytics is implemented on this data using the R analytical tool after identifying the variables which are closely related and dependent. The output of analytics part is a set of various demographic plots which give a

Figure 1. Architecture design of the system

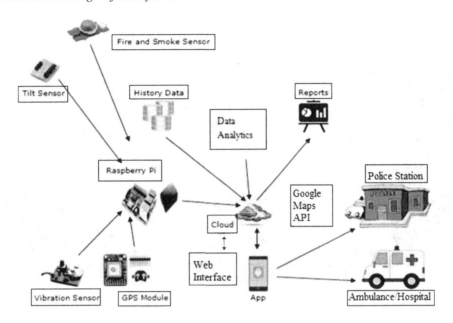

richer and better insight into this concern. These accident analysis reports are mailed to the police station at regular intervals of time so that they can take some steps to overcome or control these problems.

4. IMPLEMENTATION

The implementation can be roughly divided into two parts, namely the Internet of Things part and Data Analytics part. The Internet of Things part consists of the accident detection, tracking of the location using GPS module, finding the nearest hospital and police station, sending them notifications using the web interface, guiding the policemen and the ambulance drivers to the accident spot using the Android application. The data analytics part gives us insights into the trends which are followed by the accidents. The initial part here is the detection of accident for which the authors used a model car to the set up of the sensors as shown in the figure 2. The Raspberry Pi 2 is used as the System on chip. The sensors are used help in the detection of accidents by sensing the parameters such as vibration, tilting, presence of fire etc. EC2 instance of Amazon Web Services is used as the cloud and it does the computations as well as serves as the storage for the data. It hosts the websites and the database too.

Accident Detection Part Using the Accident Detection Kit Having SoC and Sensors

Step 1: The Raspberry Pi, model 2 B Board is configured.
Step 2: The GPS module is configured to work in association with the System on chip.
Step 3: Connect the accident detection kit to the MySQL database and AWS cloud.

Figure 2. Model car with system on Chip and the sensors

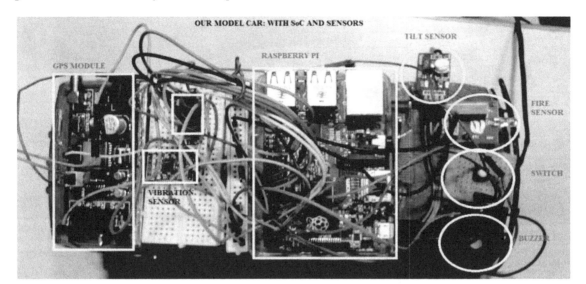

Step 4: The vibration sensor is set up on the model car, which is interfaced to the Raspberry Pi board (SoC). The vehicle is moved and the vibrations caused usually are noted. The vibrations caused when the vehicle collides are also noted.

Step 5: The tilt sensor is set up in the car, which is interfaced to the Raspberry Pi board. The tilting of the vehicle is done along all the three axes, namely X, Y and Z axes. The variations caused in the values of the angles are noted.

Step 6: The fire sensor is set up, ideally near the engine.

Step 7: The test cases for the accident cases are written, considering the conditions such as extreme vibrations, tilting and sensing of fire. This makes sure that all kinds of accidents are detected.

Step 8: The vehicle is titled and is made to collide. As soon as the parameters are noted to be unusual, the buzzer present in the kit starts buzzing. This buzzing happens for 15 seconds and it indicates that there might be an accident in the vehicle.

In cases when the person in the vehicle is fine and doesn't need any kind of help, he can press the switch present near the buzzer in lesser than 15 seconds. Such cases aren't updated in the cloud and are just cancelled as soon as the switch is pressed. This help in taking care of the false accidents and reducing the burden on the cloud too.

In case if he's not fine, the switch will not be pressed at all and this will be considered as an accident and will be hence updated to the cloud after 15 seconds have passed. The various possibilities are shown in Figure 3.

Step 9: Fetch the latitude and longitude using the GPS module as soon as the accident occurs and store them on the cloud.

Figure 3. Accidents caused due to different reasons

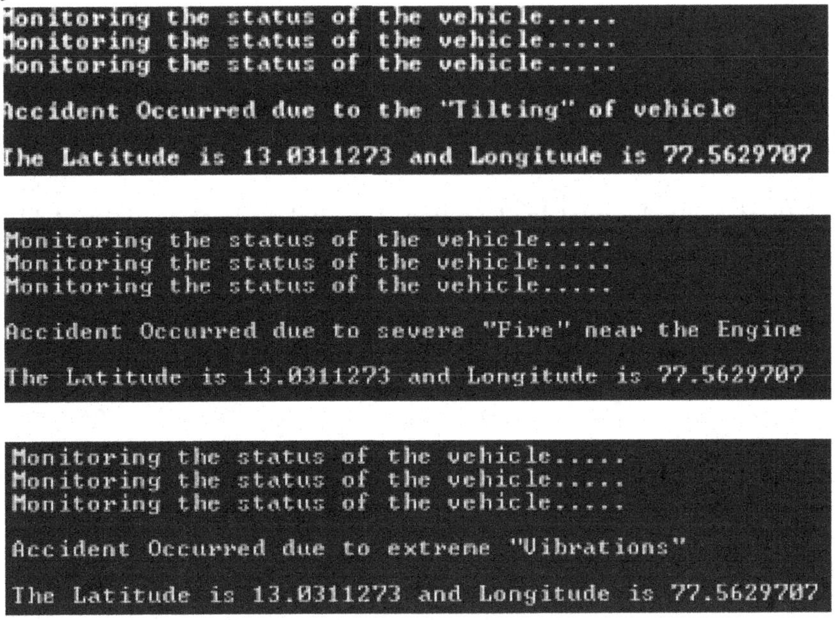

Finding Out the Hospital and the Police Station Which Are the Nearest to the Accident Spot

The nearest hospital and the nearest police station is found using the Google Maps Script which takes the latitude and longitude values as the input. The pseudo code for searching the nearest hospital using the latitude and longitude as input is as below:

Step 1: The radius for searching the hospital and police station is set to 500 meters initially.

Radius=500 meters

Step 2: Perform a nearby search of type hospital and police station, with source as the address of accident location and within the range as mentioned in the radius. The output of this is the latitude and longitude of the nearest hospital and police station.

Nearest Hospital= nearby search (type='hospital', source=Address, distance=Radius)

Nearest Police Station = nearby search (type='police', source=Address, distance=Radius)

Step 3: If the hospital is found in that range, then go to Step 4, else go to step 6.
Step 4: Get the address of the hospital and police station using Reverse Geo-coding of the location co-ordinates.

Hospital Address = Reverse Geo-code (Nearest Hospital)

Police Station Address = Reverse Geo-code (Police Station)

Step 5: Obtain the shortest path between the accident spot and the hospital as well as the time required to travel from the accident spot to the nearest hospital.

Duration from accident spot to hospital=getDuration (Hospital Address., vicinity, Address)

Distance from accident spot to hospital =getDistance(Hospital Address., vicinity, Address)

Duration from accident spot to police station =getDuration(Police Station Address., vicinity, Address)

Distance from accident spot to police station =getDistance(Police Station Address., vicinity, Address)

Go to step 7

Step 6: Increment the value of Radius by 100 meters. Go to step 3
Step 7: Update the distance and duration in database and commit the changes.

Here, the latitude and longitude for the accident location was 13.0311273 and 77.5629707 respectively. The nearest hospital based on this location is M S Ramaiah Narayana Heart Centre and the nearest police station is Yeshwanthpur police station. This is shown in the figure 4 below. Even the location is geo-coded and stored as the address with the distance and the time duration required to travel from the hospital or police station to the accident spot.

Notifying the Nearest Hospital and the Police Station Using the Web Interface

The hospitals as well as police stations are supposed to register on the website in prior. Only single registration is required for one hospital or a police station. The hospitals have to provide the details of ambulances which they have. These details include the ambulance vehicle numbers, names of drivers and the driver's contact information. Similarly, the police stations have to provide information such as the number of police staff working at that particular branch and their contact details. Once logged in, they get a list of all such accidents which have been allotted to them, meaning that these accidents have occurred in places near to them and hence, are concerned for those cases. These new cases would appear under the New Cases tab as shown in the figure 5.
    The concerned person at the hospital checks this and needs to pick an ambulance from the list of available ambulances at his hospital which appears in the form of a drop-down menu and hence, assigns particular ambulance to the accident case. As soon as this happens, the associated ambulance driver receives a notification in the form of SMS to log in to the android application as shown in the figure 8. Similarly, the concerned person at the police station has the option to pick the available police staff

Figure 4. Fetching the nearest hospital and police station using Google Maps API and storing them on to the cloud database

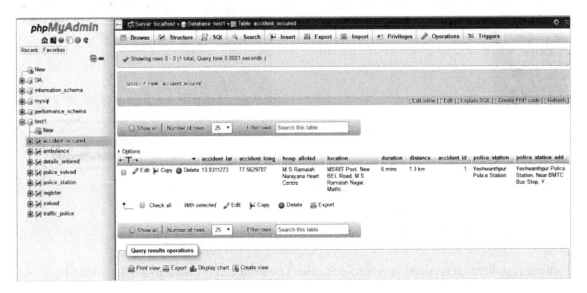

and assign him/her to the accident case. The associated staff gets an SMS requesting him to login to the android application using his/her credentials.

Once, the SMS has been sent to the allotted ambulance driver and the police staff, the status of accident changes from new to pending for the hospital's and the police station's account respectively as shown in the figure 6. New accidents which occur now would also again appear under the new cases only.

On the arrival of the ambulance to the hospital after picking the victim, the status of the accident changes from pending to solved finally. Similarly, when the police staffs reach the accident spot and register the accidents using android application, the status of the case changes from pending to solved. All the cases which were solved in the past get saved under the solved cases and hence, is a kind of repository for the hospitals and police station too.

Figure 5. Snapshot of SMS received

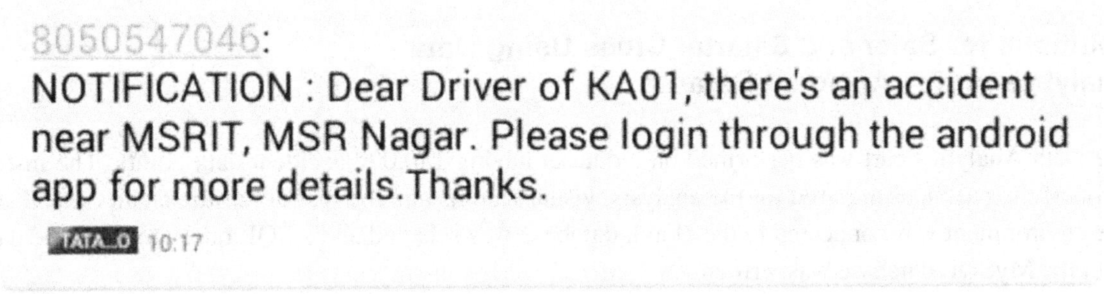

8050547046:

NOTIFICATION : Dear Driver of KA01, there's an accident near MSRIT, MSR Nagar. Please login through the android app for more details.Thanks.

TATA_O 10:17

Figure 6. The case appears under Pending Cases

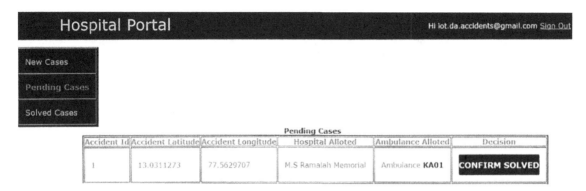

Guiding the Associated Ambulance Driver and the Police Staffs Using the Android Application

The android application is coded in Android Studio. The front end is coded in XML and the back end is Java with MySQL, which is hosted on the cloud. The connection between Java and cloud is established using JDBC. The android application allows the user to login. The user of the android application would be the ambulance drivers or the policemen who have to report to the accident spot after being allotted by the hospital and police station respectively. On entering the valid login credentials, the accident identifier to which they are allotted is found. The login credentials are very simple, such as the vehicle number for the ambulance drivers and the employee id for the policemen. This ensures that there is minimal delay introduced in picture as there's no delivery of OTPs and all which saved time. Using the accident id, the latitude and longitude values of the accident location is found from the database, which is further represented by the red marker as shown in figure 7.

The android application uses Google Maps API to find out the shortest route from the current location to the destination. The API key to get this functionality is achieved by publishing the app to the Google Developers Console. The destination for the ambulance driver and the policemen is the accident location. As shown at the bottom right in the figure 7, the options to get the real time travelling direction are also available. The direction appears on the phone as shown in the figure 8.

The policemen can also register the accident by providing further details after they reach the accident spot. That option is also available in the android application. They can describe the parameters related to accidents, which help in the analysis late, such as type of accident, severity, phase of day when accident occurred, if it is a hit and run case, the vehicle number, number of vehicles involved, number of pedestrians injured, number of motorcycles, heavy and public vehicles involved etc.

Solutions for Safer and Smarter Cities Using Data Analytics on the Accident Dataset

The Data Analytics part was performed on a dataset having 140,000 accident data points. The installation of the packages required for the analysis, visualizations and the mailing of the results was done. The environment was connected to the cloud, database was selected and a SQL query to fetch the data from the MySQL database was written.

Figure 7. The accident location appears in the android application

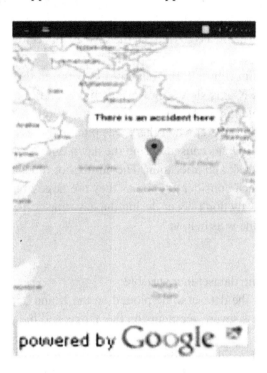

Figure 8. Travelling directions using Google Maps API

Various graphs were plotted to visualize the relationship between the various columns. These graphs were added to a PDF file and then mailed to the concerned person at the police station using mailR package and related functions. The idea is to find out the severity of accidents as discussed by (Esmaeili, Khalili, & Pakgohar, 2012).

In the first graph as shown in figure 9, the relationship between the severity of accidents and the phase of day is identified. The X-axis shows the various light conditions such as complete dark with no street lights, dusk, dawn, late night, day and dark with street lights. The accidents were extremely higher in number and were more severe, when there was pitch-darkness and street lights were absent. The number of highly severe accidents caused during the dawn time is more than the number of severe accidents occurred during the dusk and afternoon. The number of moderate accidents occurred during the dawn and dusk are very much considerable too as they are large in number. The least, moderately and highly severe accidents mostly don't occur during the day time.

The pseudo code for the same is as below:

Step 1: Import the libraries.
Step 2: Extract or read the entire dataset in a variable.
Step 3: Identify the column of the dataset to be plotted on the X and Y axes. Here it is the number of highly, moderately and less severe accidents on the Y-axis and the phase of day when they occur on the X-axis.
Step 4: Count the frequency of accidents and plot the results in the form of a bar graph.
Step 5: Add the main tag to the image, which usually appears at the top of the bar graph as well as the labels for the X and Y axes.
Step 6: Set the legend and specify the various colors to be shown for each of them.

As shown in figure 10, the maximum number of highly and moderately severe accidents occurred due to the consumption of alcohol. The number of accidents occurred die to collision with vehicles and absence of traffic lights is also quite considerable. The accidents which have happened due to the falling of vehicles in the ghats are also very severe. The number of least severe accidents occurred due to the absence of traffic lights, colliding with pedestrians and animals is almost negligible. Using this analysis, some solutions can be derived such as the cab companies can improve their services expecting the people to book their cabs after consuming alcohol. The concerned department can rework on the construction of boundaries near the ghats to reduce the number of accidents.

The pseudo code for the same is as below:

Step 1: Import the libraries.
Step 2: Extract or read the entire dataset in a variable.
Step 3: Identify the column of the dataset to be plotted on the X and Y axes. Here it is the number of highly, moderately and less severe accidents on the Y-axis and the cause of accidents on the X-axis.
Step 4: Count the frequency of accidents and plot the results in the form of a bar graph.
Step 5: Add the main tag to the image, which usually appears at the top of the bar graph as well as the labels for the X and Y axes.
Step 6: Set the legend and specify the various colors to be shown for each of them

Figure 9. Analysis of the severity of accidents and the phase of day when they occurred

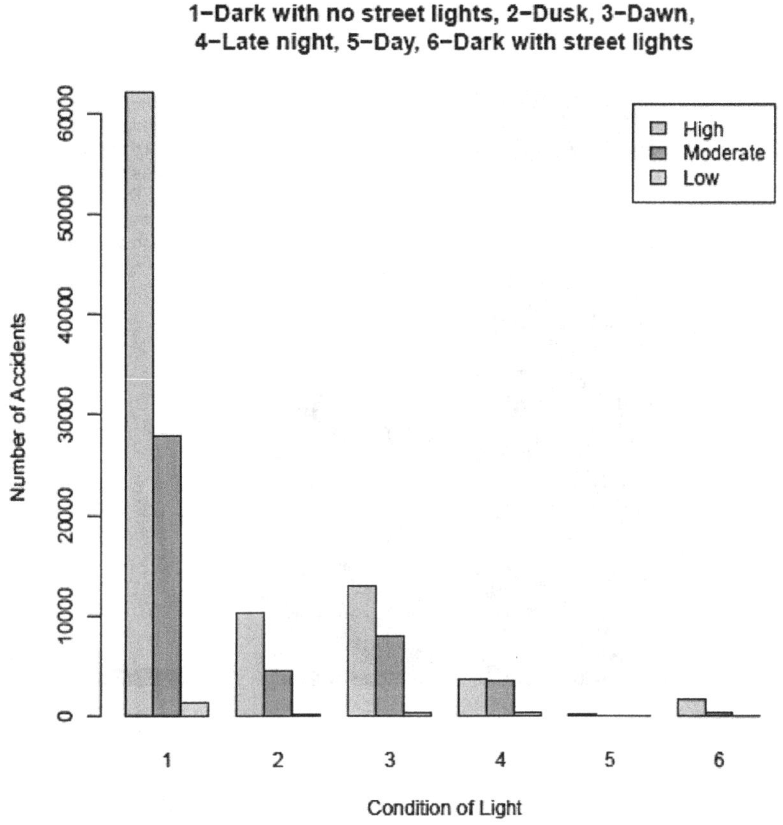
1-Dark with no street lights, 2-Dusk, 3-Dawn,
4-Late night, 5-Day, 6-Dark with street lights
High
Moderate
Low
Number of Accidents
0
10000
20000
30000
40000
50000
60000
1
2
3
4
5
6
Condition of Light

The X-axis in the figure 11 corresponds to the severity of the accidents being highly, moderately and least severe. The majority of severe accidents occur in the speed zones where allowable driving speed is 60 km/hr. The reason could be too many vehicles moving in those zones causing mayhem and commotion in the dense roads. The number of accidents happened in the zones where allowable speed is nearly 50 and 100 km/hr is also pretty much considerable. The majority of moderately severe accidents occur in the zones where the driving limit is 70 km/hr, followed by the places with a speed limit of 40 km/hr. One important inference from this is that maximum accidents don't occur in the high speed zones but they are in the average speed zones only. The number of less severe accidents is comparatively quite less in number and have mostly occurred in the areas with a speed limit of 50km/hr. Overall, the accidents are very unevenly distributed here.

The pseudo code for the same is as below:

The pseudo code for the same is as below:

Step 1: Import the libraries.
Step 2: Extract or read the entire dataset in a variable.
Step 3: Identify the column of the dataset to be plotted on the X and Y axes. Here it is the number of highly, moderately and less severe accidents on the Y-axis and the speed zone in which they occur is showed on the X-axis.

Figure 10. Analysis of the type of accident and severity

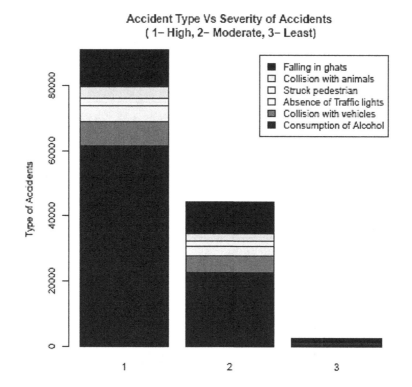

Step 4: Count the frequency of accidents and plot the results in the form of a bar graph.
Step 5: Add the main tag to the image, which usually appears at the top of the bar graph as well as the labels for the X and Y axes.
Step 6: Set the legend and specify the various colors to be shown for each of them

The X-axis in the figure 12 corresponds to the age and sex who consumes alcohol. The majority of accidents which is indicated in the y-axis is for the age group 20-29 and more of Male Gender. That is more than 90%. Above 50% of accidents are in the age group 30-39 and again it is more number of male. Above 60 less number of accidents.

The pseudo code for the same is as below:

Step 1: Import the libraries.
Step 2: Extract or read the entire dataset in a variable.
Step 3: Identify the column of the dataset to be plotted on the X and Y axes. Here it is the Age group of different categories teenagers, 20-29, 30-39, 40-49, 50-59 and above 60 and Number of accidents on the Y-axis.
Step 4: Count the frequency of accidents and plot the results in the form of a bar graph.
Step 5: Add the main tag to the image, which usually appears at the top of the bar graph as well as the labels for the X and Y axes.
Step 6: Set the legend and specify the various colors to be shown for each of them

Figure 11. Analysis of the severity of accidents based on the speed zones in which they have occurred

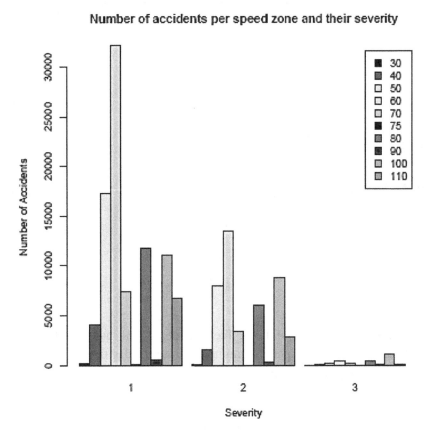

Figure 12. Analysis of the number of Accidents involving Sex and Age by consuming Alcohol

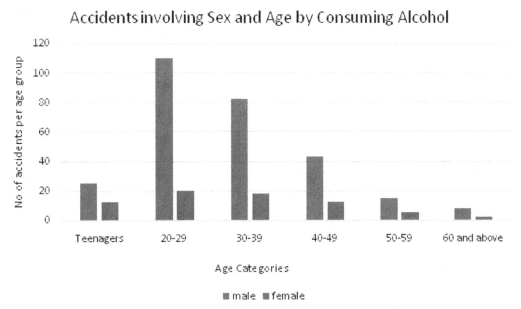

Figure 13. Analysis of Teenages death by time of day

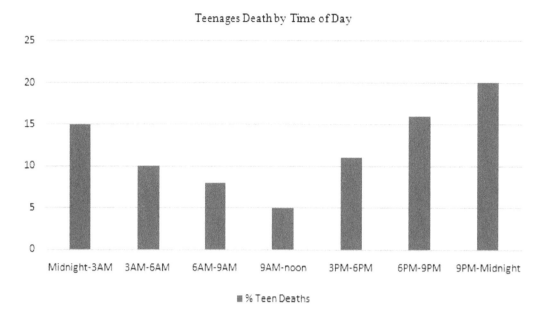

The X-axis in the figure 13 corresponds to the Teenages death. The majority of accidents of teenagers and death are in the duration of Mid night and minimal during the day time.

The pseudo code for the same is as below:

Step 1: Import the libraries.
Step 2: Extract or read the entire dataset in a variable.
Step 3: Identify the column of the dataset to be plotted on the X and Y axes.
Step 4: Count the frequency of accidents and plot the results in the form of a bar graph.
Step 5: Add the main tag to the image, which usually appears at the top of the bar graph as well as the labels for the X and Y axes.
Step 6: Set the legend and specify the various colors to be shown for each of them

The Accident caused by different vehicles and analysis is given in the figure 14. Most of the accidents are due to the 2 wheelers.

The overall analysis of the cause of accidents was also done which is shown in the figure 15. Most of the accidents, closer to 60% of the total, occurred due to the consumption of alcohol. A large number of accidents have occurred due to the absence of traffic lights while driving. The number of accidents which have occurred due to the collision with the vehicles and the animals is also considerable. The least number of accidents have occurred due to the falling of vehicles in the ghats. A large number of accidents have also occurred leading to the striking of the pedestrians on the roads.

The pseudo code for the same is as below:

Step 1: Import the libraries.
Step 2: Extract or read the entire dataset in a variable.
Step 3: Identify the column of the dataset to be represented in the form of pie chart.

Figure 14. Analysis of the Accidents caused by different vehicles

Accidents Caused By Different Vehicles

Bicycle
3%

Others
11%

2 Wheeler
24%

Truck/Lorry
20%

3 Wheeler
6%

Car
11%

Jeep
8%

Tempo/Vans
7%

Bus
10%

▪ Others ▪ Truck/Lorry ▪ Bus ▪ Tempo/Vans ▪ Jeep ▪ Car ▪ 3 Wheeler ▪ 2 Wheeler ▪ Bicycle

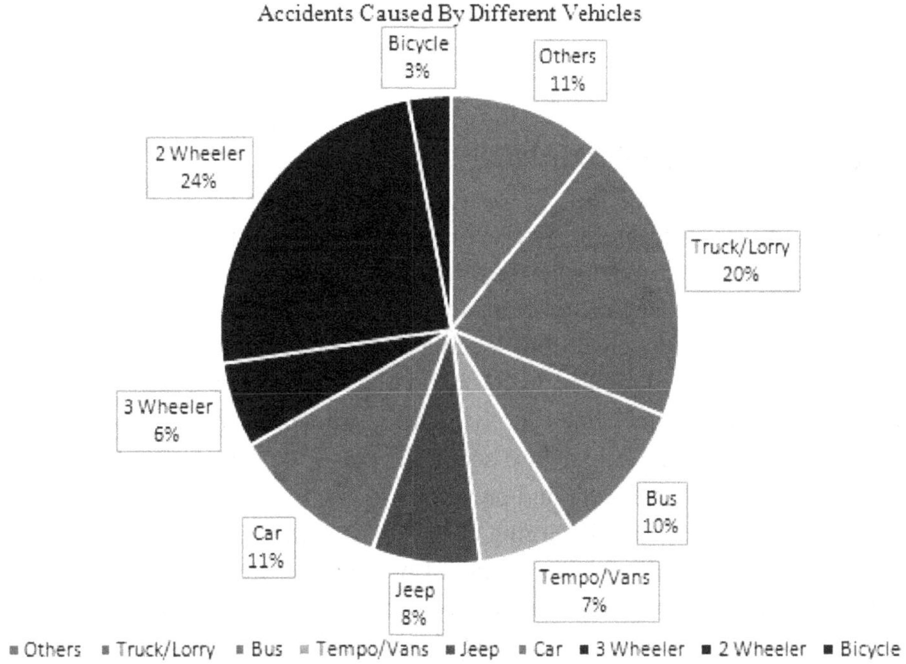

Figure 15. Analysis of the overall causes of the accidents

**1-Consumption of Alcohol 2-Collision with vehicles
3-Absence of Traffic lights 4-Struck pedestrian
5-Collision with animals 6-Falling in ghats**

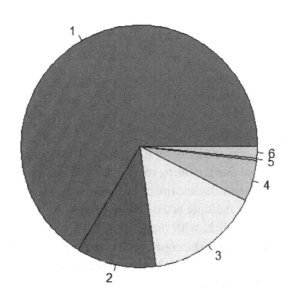

Step 4: Count the frequency of accidents and plot the results in the form of a bar graph.
Step 5: Add the main tag to the image, which usually appears at the top of the bar graph.
Step 6: Set the legend and specify the various colors to be shown for each of them.

5. COMPARISON AND PERFORMANCE

The existing products similar to this are very rare. Most of them are very static and are installed in very less vehicles due to constraints such as poor performance, non-functioning of sensors etc. The kit designed by the authors is very well-functioning and compact. The existing related work involves detection of accidents by placing sensors in the vehicle and sending SMS. The sending of SMS doesn't take care of the entire process. The authors' solution to this problem makes the entire process easy and hassle free. The information regarding accidents being sent to the nearest hospital and police station using Google Maps API is a novel idea and carries immense social impacts. The sensors used for the project work at a great degree of temperature, moisture and pressure which ensures that the kit doesn't malfunction in certain adverse conditions such as submerging of vehicle in water etc. Most of the related works use GSM Modules for communication, which is a kind of one-way communication and hinders the communication from the other side. The authors have used Ethernet Module to overcome this and using so, they are able to have a proper flow of the both sided communication. The response time of updating the cloud is also very minimal. The usual response time with 3G speed is 1 second and with 2G speed is 3 seconds. The login to the website and android application takes minimum delay. The redirection of android app to the page where the user gets the travelling directions and the related information requires 5 seconds to open with 3G internet speed and 8 seconds with 2G speed. These timing measurements are on an average and completely depend on the speed of internet. The registration of accidents using the android application is also a new idea. The sole purpose of doing this is to obtain and store more information about the accidents so that preventive steps and measures can be taken well in advance. The collection of this accident data serves as the target data for the analysis. The idea of generating reports after analysis and sending it to the concerned person at the police stations is also new and it hardly takes 30 seconds for the script to run.

CONCLUSION

Accidents are one of the most devastating tragedies with the ever-rising trends and these trends have to be necessarily uncovered in order to mine the factors which add severity to them. This product is highly important, quite innovative and very challenging to be used in the country. The product at this time is able to detect the accidents caused due the tilting of vehicles as a consequence of collision, extreme and abnormal vibrations produced in the vehicles, fire caused due to the combustion of fuel in the engine etc. The product also works fine when multiple accident conditions occur. The false alarm is also present, implemented using a buzzer and switch, with the purpose of not notifying anyone when the switch is pressed indicating that the victim is safe. The concerned people at hospital and police station are notified. The allotted ambulance driver as well as police staff is guided to the accident spot. Hence, the Internet of Things as well as Data Analytics helps to save more lives. It also attempts to reduce the number of drunken driving cases. The timely arrival of the ambulances and the policemen to the accident spots can be ensured as the communication becomes quickly. The accident records updated by the policemen serve as a solid proof for the occurrence of the accidents. This solution is an attempt to use technology to solve problems in an eco-friendly and cost-effective manner. The product is very user-friendly, durable and fault tolerant.

FUTURE WORK

The Accident Detection Kit consists of many sensors and is able to sense and record the values properly, but it would be better if the decision is taken using more sensors such as pressure sensors, accelerometers etc. This would strengthen the decision making on the system on chip. The product may need to undergo some customization based on the make and model of the vehicle in which it has to be installed. Some modification will also be required in case of two-wheelers. The app can be used to notify some of the few more concerned authorities such as the blood bank, insurance agents etc. This would make sure that the requirement of blood reaches the concerned department in lesser time. Also, the accident records serve as a proof for the claiming of insurances, which makes the process easy and hassle-free. The commuters can get the real time notifications about the severity of the zone they are traveling in. Alternate routes which are less severe can be suggested to them in such cases to ensure the safety of their lives. Even the website can also be created for the other authorities such as insurance companies and blood banks in the same way as we have for police and hospital at this time. The police stations can have an option to download the weekly and monthly reports generated after the analysis. The data analysis part aims to improve the approach of solving the method of collection and analysis of accident related information. The sensitive areas such as schools, old age homes, orphanages and hospitals can be relocated to the areas which are least prone to accidents. Similarly, the hospitals can be constructed or relocated to the areas which are very much prone to accidents. This would save the travelling time of victims in the ambulances. The real time monitoring of the victim's health condition can also be done by measuring the various parameters such as the blood pressure, heart beat etc. This data can be sent to the hospital prior to the arrival of the victim to plan better well in advance. This analysis can be used to implement protective measure to ensure road-safety of elderly citizens, wildlife and also. This analysis can also be used to identify the areas where consumption of alcohol is found to be the leading cause of accident occurrences. Such areas would be the target for the cab companies as the drunken people would prefer to book their cabs to commute from one place to another. These results can be used by the policy-makers to design the policies which ensure road safety and life safety too.

REFERENCES

Abdel-Aty, M. A., & Radwan, A. E. (2000). Modeling traffic accident occurrence and involvement. *Accident; Analysis and Prevention*, *32*(5), 633–642. doi:10.1016/S0001-4575(99)00094-9 PMID:10908135

Aishwarya, S.R., & Rai, A., Charitha, Prasanth, M.A, & Savitha, S.C. (2015). An IoT based vehicle accident prevention and tracking system for night drivers. *International Journal of Innovative Research in Computer and Communication Engineering*, *3*(4), 3493–3499.

Anitha, T., & Uppalaigh, T. (2016). Android based home automation using Raspberry pi. *International Journal of Innovative Technologies.*, *4*(1), 2351–8665.

Bai, Y., Wu, S., & Tsai, C. (2012). Design and implementation of a fall monitor system by using a 3-axis accelerometer in a smart phone. *Proceedings of the 16th International Symposium on Consumer Electronics (ISCE).*

Bermudez, I., Traverso, S., Mellia, M., & Munao, M. (2013). Exploring the cloud from passive measurements: The Amazon AWS case. Proceedings of IEEE INFOCOM, 230-234.

Chang, L. Y., & Chen, W. C. (2005). Data mining of tree-based model to analyze freeway accident frequency. *Journal of Safety Research*, *36*(4), 365–375. doi:10.1016/j.jsr.2005.06.013 PMID:16253276

Depaire, B., Wets, G., & Vanhoof, K. (2008). Traffic accident segmentation by means of latent class clustering. *Accident Analysis and Prevention, 40*(4).

Ghorpade, D. D., & Patki, A. M. (2016). IoT Based Smart Home Automation Using Renewable Energy Sources. *International Journal of Advanced Research in Electrical Electronics and Instrumental Engineering*, *5*(7), 6065–6072.

Gotadki, S., Mohan, R., Attarwala, M., & Gajare, M. P. (2014). Intelligent Ambulance. *International Journal of Engineering and Technical Research*, *2*(4).

Hussain, F., Sharma, A., Bhatnagar, S., & Goyal, S. (2011). GPS and GSM based Accident Monitoring System. *International Journal of Scientific Research and Management Studies*, *2*(12), 473–480.

Karande, I., Deshpande, G., Kumbhar, S., & Deshmukh, A. V. (2016). Intelligent Anti-Theft Tracking and Accident Detection System for Automobiles Based on Internet of Things. *International Journal of Innovative Research in Computer and Communication Engineering*, *4*(3), 4142–4149.

Karlaftis, M. G., & Tarko, A. P. (1998). Heterogeneity considerations in accident modeling. *Accident; Analysis and Prevention*, *30*(4), 425–433. doi:10.1016/S0001-4575(97)00122-X PMID:9666239

Kashani, T., Mohaymany, A. S., & Rajbari, A. A. (2011). data mining approach to identify key factors of traffic injury severity. *PROMET- Traffic & Transportation, 23*(1). Retrieved from http://www.fpz.unizg.hr/traffic/index.php/PROMTT/article/view/144/51

Kumar, S., & Toshniwal, D. (2015). A data mining framework to analyze road accident data. *Journal of Big Data*, *2*(26).

Lakshmi, C. V., & Balakrishnan, J. R. (2012). Automatic Accident Detection via Embedded GSM message interface with Sensor Technology. *International Journal of Scientific and Research Publication*, *2*(4).

Miyaji, M. (2014). Study on the reduction effect of traffic accident by using analysis of Internet survey, Internet of Things (WF-IoT). *IEEE World Forum on Internet of Things (WF-IoT)*, 325-330.

Patil, M., Rawat, A., Singh, P., & Dixit, S. (2016). Accident Detection and Ambulance Control using Intelligent Traffic Control System. *International Journal of Engineering Trends and Technology*, *34*(8).

Poongundran, A. A., & Jeevabharathi, M. (2015). Vehicular Monitoring and Tracking Using Raspberry Pi. *International Journal of Innovative Research in Science, Engineering and Technology*, *4*(2), 2319–8573.

Prabha, C., Sunitha, R., & Anitha, R. (2014). Automatic Vehicle Accidents Detection and Messaging System Using GSM and GPS Modem. *International Journal of Advanced Research in Electrical, Electronics and Instrumentation Engineering*. Retrieved from http://www.rroij.com/open-access/automatic-vehicle-accident-detection-andmessaging-system-using-gsm-and-gpsmodem.php?aid=44586

Rovsek, V., Batista, M., & Bogunovic, B. (2017). Identifying the key risk factors of traffic accident injury severity on Slovenian roads using a non-parametric classification tree. *Transport*, *32*(3), 272–281. doi:10.3846/16484142.2014.915581

Sangeetha, K., Archana, P., Ramya, M., & Ramya, P. (2014). Automatic Ambulance Rescue with Intelligent Traffic Light System. *IOSR Journal of Engineering*, *4*(2), 53–57. doi:10.9790/3021-04255357

Shabrin, S. B., Nikharge, B. J., Poojary, M. M., & Pooja, T. (2016). Smart helmet– intelligent safety for motorcyclist using raspberry pi and open CV. *International Research Journal of Engineering and Technology*, *3*(3), 2395–0056.

Shah, D., Nair, R., Parikh, V., & Shah, V. (2015). Accident Alarm System using GSM, GPS and Accelerometer. *International Journal of Innovative Research in Computer and Communication Engineering*, *3*(4).

Sonika, S., Sekhar, K. S., & Jaishree, S. (2014). Intelligent accident identification system using GPS and GSM modem. *International Journal of Advanced Research in Computer and Communication Engineering*, *3*(2).

Wakure, A. R., Patkar, A. R., Dagale, M. V., & Solanki, P. P. (2014). Vehicle Accident Detection and Reporting System Using GPS and GSM. *International Journal of Engineering Research and Development*, *10*(4), 25–28.

Chapter 7
Nature–Inspired Algorithms for Bi–Criteria Parallel Machine Scheduling

Kawal Jeet
D. A. V. College, India

ABSTRACT

Nature has always been a source of inspiration for human beings. Nature-inspired search-based algorithms have an enormous computational intelligence and capabilities and are observing diverse applications in engineering and manufacturing problems. In this chapter, six nature-inspired algorithms, namely artificial bee colony, bat, black hole, cuckoo search, flower pollination, and grey wolf optimizer algorithms, have been investigated for scheduling of multiple jobs on multiple potential parallel machines. Weighted flow time and tardiness have been used as optimization criteria. These algorithms are very efficient in identifying optimal solutions, but as the size of the problem increases, these algorithms tend to get stuck at local optima. In order to extract these algorithms from local optima, genetic algorithm has been used. Flower pollination algorithm, when appended with GA, is observed to perform better than other counterpart nature-inspired algorithms as well as existing heuristics and meta-heuristics based on MOGA and NSGA-II algorithms.

INTRODUCTION

The problem of scheduling n jobs on m parallel potential machines for optimizing bi-criteria, namely, maximum tardiness (minimize) and weighted flow time (minimize) is one of the important problems that is often encountered by engineers. The number of possible job sequences obtained by allocation of these n jobs on m machines is exponentially large and identifying best sequence out of them especially when m or n is large is NP-hard (Mazdeh, Zaerpour, Zareei, & Hajinezhad, 2010). Nature-inspired algorithms such as Artificial Bee Colony (ABC) (Akbari, Hedayatzadeh, Ziarati, & Hassanizadeh, 2012), Bat (Yang, 2011), Black hole (BH) (Hatamlou, 2013), Cuckoo Search (CS) (Yang & Deb, 2009), Flower Pollination (FPA) (Yang, Karamanoglu, & He, 2013), Grey Wolf Optimizer (GWO) (Mirjalili, Saremi, Mirjalili, & Coelho, 2016) algorithms have the ability to handle such optimization problems.

DOI: 10.4018/978-1-5225-5832-3.ch007

One of the possible applications of the problem under consideration is scheduling of large number (n) of processes on multiple processors (m) by the operating system. In such a system, numbers of processors (CPU) (as machines) are available all the time in parallel and number of processes (jobs) are to be scheduled on these processors. Each of the process (job) has its own processing time and priority. The processes are to be scheduled on available parallel processors such that there is maximum tardiness as well as weighted flow time for the processes are minimum. This could lead to increase in the throughput rate for the running processes. Further, use of parallel processors enhances production as the work does not stop when some processors fail or maintenance occurs.

The multi-objective formulations of ABC, BAT, BH, CS, FPA, and GWO algorithms obtained by the combination of weighted objectives or auxiliary archive for managing possible solutions along with their hybrids with GA have been developed and applied to the problem of scheduling jobs on machines running in parallel in order to optimize bi-criteria, namely, maximum tardiness and weighted flow time. The algorithms are applied on randomly generated sample for scheduling 40 and 60 jobs on 2, 3 and 6 machines. The proposed approaches are compared to existing meta-heuristics based on MOGA (Deb, 2014) and NSGA-II (Deb, Pratap, Agarwal, & Meyarivan, 2002) algorithms as well as existing heuristic (Nailwal, Gupta, & Sharma, 2015).

BACKGROUND

Scheduling of jobs on parallel machines is one of the prominent problems generally encountered in manufacturing and production engineering and has gained increasing attention in the past few decades. Numerous engineers and researchers are working on optimisation of different criteria for scheduling multiple jobs on multiple machines. In addition, novel meta-heuristic techniques have been actively used for scheduling of jobs on multiple potential machines. Some of the recent works eminent in the field are discussed in Table 1. Optimization criteria and heuristic being followed have also been listed in Table 1.

RESEARCH OBJECTIVES

The main objectives of the proposed work are listed below:

- To experimentally evaluate the behaviour of recent-inspired algorithms such as ABC, Bat, BH, CS, FPA and GWO algorithms on scheduling of n jobs on m potential parallel machines.
- To evaluate the impact of adding crossover and mutation operator to these nature-inspired algorithms.
- To investigate use of auxiliary archive to maintain Pareto Front and hypercubes to maintain best solutions.
- Comparison of job schedules obtained by applying these hybrid nature-inspired algorithms to that of existing search-based approaches by taking summation of maximum tardiness and weighted flow time as comparison criteria.

Table 1. Literature review

Research Work	Criteria Optimized	Heuristic Followed
(Rahimi-Vahed, Javadi, Rabbani, & Tavakkoli-Moghaddam, 2008)	Minimize the weighted mean completion time and weighted mean tardiness	Multi-Objective Scatter Search (MOSS)
(Eren, 2010)	Minimize the weighted sum of total completion time and total tardiness.	SSPRT (Shortest Sum of Setup, Processing and Removal Times), SSRT (Shortest sum of Setup and Removal Times) and EDD (Earliest Due Date) sequence.
(Berrichi, Amodeo, Yalaoui, Châtelet, & Mezghiche, 2009)	Minimize the makespan and unavailability.	Evolutionary GA
(Berrichi, Yalaoui, Amodeo, & Mezghiche, 2010)	Production and Maintenance	Multi-Objective Ant Colony Optimization (MOACO)
(Mazdeh, et al., 2010)	Minimize the total tardiness and machine deteriorating cost	Tabu search
(Rashidi, Jahandar, & Zandieh, 2010)	Minimize the makespan and maximum tardiness	Hybrid GA
(Shokrollahpour, Zandieh, & Dorri, 2011)	Minimize the weighted sum of makespan and mean completion time	Imperialist Competitive Algorithm
(Zhang, Gao, & Li, 2013)	Maximize the schedule efficiency and the schedule stability	Hybrid Genetic Algorithm and Tabu Search
(Guo, Cheng, & Wang, 2014)	Parallel machine scheduling with step deteriorating jobs and setup times	Hybrid discrete cuckoo search algorithm
(Li, Pan, & Tasgetiren, 2014)	Minimize makespan, the total workload of machines and the workload of the critical machine	Discrete Artificial Bee Colony
(Faccio, Ries, & Saggiorno, 2015)	resources utilisation; JIT production;	Simulated Annealing
(Tosun & Marichelvam, 2016)	Makespan	Bat Algorithm
(Jeet, Dhir, & Singh, 2016)	Maximum tardiness and weighted flow time	Black hole Algorithm
(Jeet, Dhir, & Sharma, 2016a)	Maximum tardiness and weighted flow time	Flower pollination algorithm
(Jeet, Dhir, & Sharma, 2016b)	Maximum tardiness and weighted flow time	Artificial Bee Colony Algorithm
(Jeet, 2017)	Maximum tardiness and weighted flow time	Grey Wolf Optimizer Algorithm

MAIN FOCUS OF THE CHAPTER

Nature-Inspired Algorithms

Human beings are always inspired by nature and this is evident from the recent technological advances in various fields of science and engineering. Over the past couple of decades, a large number of complex research problems have found their solutions in nature-inspired algorithms such as Artificial Bee Colony (ABC), BAT, Black Hole (BH), Flower Pollination (FPA), Cuckoo Search (CS), Grey Wolf Optimizer (GWO) algorithms, etc. General steps to execute any nature-inspired algorithm (Yang, 2010) are described in block diagram shown in Figure 1. These algorithms are widely used for solving a number of optimization problems in various computer science areas ranging from wireless networks to job shop scheduling.

Single-Objective vs. Multi-Objective Optimization

Optimization means to identify best possible solution to a given problem. An optimization algorithm could be classified on the basis of number of objectives to be optimized as:

- Single-objective optimization algorithm
- Multi-objective optimization algorithm

In case of single-objective optimization, the main goal of optimization is to find the best solution having optimum value of a single objective function. The optimum value could be minimum or maximum depending on the problem under consideration.

- **Local Minima:** A local minima xl $\in$ X of an objective function $F : X \rightarrow R$ is an element with F(x1) < F(x) for all x neighbouring xl. Further it could be interpreted as

$\forall x1 \in X, \exists \eta > 0$ such that F(x1) $\leq$ F(x), $\forall x1 \in X$ |x-x1|<η

- **Global Minima:** A global minima xl $\in$ X of an objective function $F : X \rightarrow R$ is an element with F(x1) < F(x) for all x $\in$ X.

Figure 1. Block diagram of nature-inspired algorithms

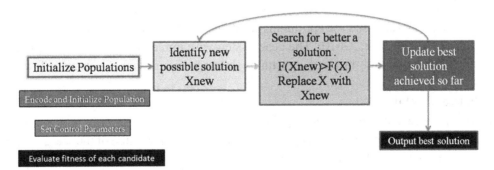

- **Local Maxima:** A local maxima $x1 \in X$ of an objective function $F : X \to R$ is an element with $F(x1) > F(x)$ for all x neighbouring $x1$. Further it could be interpreted as
  $\forall x1 \in X, \exists \eta > 0$ such that $F(x1) \geq .F(x), \forall x1 \in X \ |x\text{-}x1| < \eta$
- **Global Maxima:** A global maxima $x1 \in X$ of an objective function $F : X \to R$ is an input element with $F(x1) > F(x)$ for all $x \in X$.

In the present research, main focus is on local and global minima. In case of a multi-objective optimisation, the conflicting objectives are optimized and there is no unique optimal solution. Different objectives when optimized results in a set of compromised solutions called non-dominated or Pareto-optimal solutions of Pareto front. For a minimization approach, Pareto front is made up of job sequence with (non-dominance) relationships between solutions defined as Equation 1.

$$F(x1) > F(x2) \text{ if } \forall i \ f_i(x1) \geq f_i(x2) \land \exists i \ f_i(x1) > f_i(x2) \tag{1}$$

where $F(x)$ indicates the overall fitness of job sequence x, and $f_i(x)$ is the value of ith fitness function (optimization objective) for job sequence x. The above equation indicates that the job sequence $x2$ is considered better than $x1$ if it is proved better according to at least one of the individual fitness (objective) functions (f_i) and no worse according to the rest. In other words, $x2$ dominates $x1$. The Pareto front is the set of elements that are not dominated by any possible element of the solution space. The Pareto front thus denotes the best results achievable.

Methods for Executing Multi-Objective Optimization

There are several methods for performing and implementing multi-objective optimization. In this work, two techniques have been used for the same. Simplest of these is objectives weighted aggregation approach. In this approach, g fitness objectives are combined to make a single objective (F) as shown in Equation 2 (Konak, Coit, & Smith, 2006).

$$F = \sum_{k=1}^{g} w_k o_k \ \text{ and} \sum_{k=1}^{g} w_k = 1 \tag{2}$$

Here w_k is the weight of kth objective that is generated randomly from a uniform distribution, and o_k is the value of kth objective evaluated for candidate job sequence. Rest of the approach follows single-objective optimization. Although, weighted aggregation approach discussed above might not be able to produce certain portions of Pareto front (C. C. Coello, Lamont, & Van Veldhuizen, 2007) but still it has been found to be extensively used for optimizing multiple objectives due to its simplicity and ease of implementation (Marler & Arora, 2010). The general step-wise implementation of the approach (on the basis of block diagram of nature-inspired algorithms shown in Figure 1) is discussed below:

Step 1 [Initialize population]:
    Step 1.1: Encode and initialize the population of candidate solutions.
    Step 1.2: Set the common parameters to be used in the implementation of these algorithms. These values are obtained by manual tuning after repeated execution of these algorithms.

Step 1.3: Evaluate fitness of each candidate job sequence in the population using combined objective function F.

Repeat Steps 2-4 until the stopping criteria is met.

Step 2 [Identify new possible solution]: Identify neighbour of each current candidate job sequence.
Step 3 [Search for a better solution]:
Step 3.1: Calculate the fitness of this neighbour solution by using weighted sum approach.
Step 3.2: If neighbour candidate solutions is better than the current candidate solution then replace the current solution with this neighbour, else ignore it. This step is required to locally search for better job sequence. It moves the current candidate randomly in search for a better solution.
Step 4 [Update best solution]: Rank the candidate job sequence solutions on the basis of their combined fitness function (F). Update the best candidate job sequence obtained.
Step 5 [Output]: Output the best solution as output job sequence.

This is referred as Proposed Approach 1. The algorithms developed on the basis of this weighted aggregation based approach are named as Multi-Objective Artificial Bee Colony (MOWABC), BAT (MOWBAT), Black Hole (MOWBH), Cuckoo Search (MOWCS), Flower Pollination (MOWFPA) and Grey Wolf Optimizer (MOWGWO).

Although the algorithms defined under Proposed Approach 1 are very efficient in identifying optimal solutions but as the size of the problem increases (like other optimization algorithms), these algorithms tend to get stuck at local optima. Hence, the outputs of these algorithms are not globally optimal. In order to extract these algorithms from local optima, GA is used. The resulting hybrid approach is referred as Proposed Approach 2. The algorithms are respectively named MOWABCGA, MOWBATGA, MOWBHGA MOWCSGA, MOWFPGA, and MOWGWOGA. GA is added after Step 3 of Proposed Approach 3. In this way, before selecting the best job sequence for the current iteration, GA is applied to the current population.

GA is observed to be the main judicious choice for the same. The improvement in quality of job sequence by adding GA in these basic algorithms is inspired by Darwin's theory of survival of the fittest (Goldberg, 2006). Each individual in the population is called a chromosome. Each individual chromosome in the population competes for resources. More fit chromosomes from one population are given a chance to reproduce new and better population. This is due to the fact that GA is initially a discrete technique that is suitable for combinatorial problems (Colorni, et al., 1996).

Although the weighted aggregation approach is quite successful in solving various multi-objective optimization problem but the approach has some serious shortcomings. They return a single objective which is highly dependent on the weights. At the same time, in case of conflicting objectives, allocation of weights is difficult. In case of random selection of weights, the output is highly unpredictable.

Hence, to overcome these problems, the use of Pareto optimization approaches have been investigated (resulting in solutions in the form of Pareto front) for optimizing the job sequence of systems obtained by using nature-inspired algorithms. In order to store this Pareto front, an auxiliary archive is used. Also, hyper-cubes are used to maintain and select the best solutions during each iteration of the algorithm (C. A. C. Coello, Pulido, & Lechuga, 2004). Step-wise implementation of this approach is discussed below:

Step 1 [Initialize population]:

    Step 1.1: Encode and initialize the populations of individuals.

    Step 1.2: Set parameters to be used in the implementation of these algorithms.

    Step 1.3: Evaluate fitness of each candidate in the population using multiple objective functions under consideration.

    Step 1.4: Store the solutions that represent non-dominated vectors in the temporary repository named REP.

    Step 1.5: Generate hyper-cubes of the search space explored so far, and locate the candidate solution using these hyper-cubes as a coordinate system where coordinates of each job sequence are defined according to the values of its objective functions (Coello et al. 2004).

    Step 1.6: Select the best solution achieved so far.

    Repeat Steps 2 to 4 for a predefined number of iterations (stopping criteria).

Step 2 [Identify new possible solution]: Identify the neighbour of each current candidate solution.

Step 3 [Search for a better solution]:

    Step 3.1: Calculate the fitness of this neighbouring solution taking into consideration the non-dominance of the solutions.

    Step 3.2: If this neighbour solution is better than the current candidate solution then replace candidate solution with this better neighbour. This step is required to search locally for better candidate solutions. It moves the current candidate randomly in search of a better solution.

Step 4 [Update best solutions]: Update REP as well as the geographical representation of solutions within hyper-cubes by inserting all the currently non-dominated locations into the auxiliary archive (REP) and eliminating dominated individuals.

Step 5 [Output]: REP contains the possible Pareto front i.e., the possible non-dominated solutions as output.

This is referred as Proposed Approach 3. The algorithms developed on the basis of this auxiliary archive based approach are named as Multi-Objective Artificial Bee Colony (MOABC), BAT (MOBAT), Black Hole (MOBH), Cuckoo Search (MOCS), Flower Pollination (MOFPA) and Grey Wolf Optimizer (MOGWO).

Although, Proposed Approach 3 is very efficient in identifying optimal solutions, but as the size of the problem increases, these algorithms tend to get stuck at local optima and the outputs are hence not globally optimal. In order to recover these algorithms from local optima, GA is used for the reasons discussed above. The resulting hybrid approach is referred as Proposed Approach 4. The nature-inspired algorithms are named MOABCGA, MOBATGA, MOBHGA, MOCSGA, MOFPGA, and MOGWOGA.

Application of Nature-Inspired Algorithms for Job Scheduling

Search-Based Artificial Bee Colony, BAT, Black Hole, Cuckoo Search, Flower Pollination and Grey Wolf Optimizer algorithms along with their hybrids have been investigated for scheduling of jobs on parallel machines. In order to use any search-based technique to solve a research problem at hand, the two key pre-requisites (Harman, 2007) are:

- The choice of representation of the problem.
- The definition of the fitness functions.

The simplicity of such search-based techniques has made them attractive. With just these two simple pre-requisites, search-based optimization algorithms could be implemented to solve variety of engineering problems. It is one of the fields that have flourished a lot in the past two decades.

Problem Representation

The entire search-based techniques proposed in this work need an appropriate representation of the problem. In this proposed work, the problem is represented as population of floating point numbers. Each individual candidate is having number of positions equal to the number of jobs to be scheduled. Each position in the representation of individual is a decimal number with the integer part indicating the machine number to which the job has been allocated and decimal part indicating the order in which this job is allocated to that machine.

A possible representation of scheduling of 4 jobs on 2 machines could be:

Job 1 2 3 4

Representation 2.1 1.1 2.2 1.2

It means the representation has string of 4 floating point numbers each for each job. Job 1 has been allocated to machine 2 at first followed by job 3. Job 2 has been assigned to machine 1 followed by job 4.

The following assumptions, notations and decision variables have been drawn for the formulation of the problem.

Assumptions

The problem draws following assumption.

- A job could be processed on any machine.
- All jobs are available at time zero.
- Jobs can execute independent of each other.
- A job could not pre-empt any other job.
- All the machines are always available.

Notations

Following notations are used for the formulation of problem of job scheduling on parallel machines.

n: Number of jobs to be scheduled

m: Number of potential parallel machines

i: Job under consideration

d_i: Due date of the ith job where $i =1,2,.....,n$

j: Order of processing of ith job on a machine, where $j =1, 2,....,n$

k: Machine to which a job has been allocated, where $k = 1,2,....,m$

p_i: Processing time of ith job

w_i: Weightage of ith job. It may indicate priority or importance of the job.

a_{ik} Time at which machine k is allocated to i^{th} job

c_i: Time of completion of ith job

Ti: Tardiness of ith job

Fitness Functions

Multiple jobs are scheduled on multiple parallel machines while optimizing following fitness functions or objectives.

Maximum Tardiness (T_{max}) is the tolerance time up to which tardy job is permitted by the system, i.e., $T_{max} = \max T_i$, where $i=1$ to n

Weighted Flow Time (WFT) = Sum of weighted completion times of the jobs = $\sum_{i=1}^{n} w_i c_i$

Decision Variables

$$x_{ijk} = \begin{cases} 1, & \text{if job } i \text{ is allocated to machine } k \text{ on postion } j \\ 0, & \text{otherewise} \end{cases}$$

$$y_{ik} = \begin{cases} 1, & \text{if job } i \text{ is assigned to machine k} \\ 0, & \text{otherewise} \end{cases}$$

$$z_{irk} = \begin{cases} 1, \text{if job r immediately follows job i on machine k} \\ 0, \text{otherwise} \end{cases}$$

It could be deduced that $z_{irk}=1$ if $x_{ijk} = 1$ and $x_{r(j+1)k} = 1$

Mathematical Formulation

The mathematical formulation for the given problem is as follows:

Minimise: $T_{max}=\max T_i$

Minimise WFT=Min($\sum_{k=1}^{m} \sum_{j=1}^{n} \sum_{i=1}^{n} x_{ijk} * w_i * c_i$)

The constraints followed while scheduling jobs are described below.
T_{max} is greater than equal to difference in completion time and due date for all the jobs.

$$T_{max} \geq c_i - d_i, \forall i$$

All i jobs have been allocated to a machine k at some position j.

$$\sum_{i=1}^{n}\sum_{k=1}^{m}\sum_{j=1}^{n} x_{ijk} = n$$

Allocation time of process r is equal to completion time of process i provided r follows i on machine k.

$$a_{rk} = z_{irk} * c_i$$

Variables are either 0 or 1 (binary).

$$x_{ijk}, y_{ik}, z_{irk} \in \{0,1\}$$

Job i is assigned to only one machine and that too only once.

$$\sum_{k=1}^{m} y_{ik} = 1 \text{ where } i = 1, 2, \dots, n$$

Parameter Tuning for Job Scheduling

In order to use the nature-inspired algorithms under consideration for the process of job scheduling discussed above, parameters associated with each of the algorithms under consideration are to be tuned. Table 2 lists common parameters to be tuned for each of the algorithm whereas Table 3 lists parameters along with their tuned values specific to each of these six algorithms and their hybrids. These values are obtained by repeated execution of these algorithms and have been manually tuned. Further Table 4 lists parameters associated with hybrid of the algorithms under consideration with that of Genetic Algorithms. The algorithms thus developed on the basis of underlying approaches have been discussed as Algorithm 1-6.

EXPERIMENTAL SETUP

This section elaborates experiential setup for implementation and analysis of the proposed nature-inspired algorithms namely ABC (Jeet, Dhir, et al., 2016b), BAT, BH (Jeet, Dhir, & Singh, 2016), CS, FPA (Jeet, Dhir, et al., 2016a), and GWO (Jeet, 2017) algorithms as multi-objective formulations for job shop scheduling on parallel potential machines with some of the already known search-based techniques such as MOGA, NSGA-II algorithms and exist in the heuristic proposed by Nailwal et al. (2015). All the underlying techniques have been implemented in Matlab 8.

Nature-Inspired Algorithms for Bi-Criteria Parallel Machine Scheduling

Table 2. Common control parameters for the nature-inspired algorithms applied for job sequence

Parameter	Value	Description
Number of variables to be optimized (n)	Number of entities to be clustered	The value of ith variable in the candidate job sequence indicates the cluster to which i^{th} entity has been allocated
Population size (Pop)	$5*n$	Manually tested by repeated executions of the algorithms. Increasing population size beyond this value leads to drastic degradation in performance
Population	Candidate job sequence	Randomly generated as discussed
Generations	$10 * n$ or when value of objectives does not change for 200 consecutive iterations	Stopping criteria

Table 3. Specific control parameters for the nature-inspired algorithms applied for job sequence

Algorithm	Factor	Value	Description
ABC	Size of colony	10*Number of entities to be clustered.	Employee bees and Onlooker bees together.
	Number of food sources (Pop)	Size of colony/2	Half of the colony size.
	Trial	100	Discard job sequence which could not be further improved for 100 trials.
BAT	f_{min}	0	Minimum and maximum frequency that has been assigned to each bat representing candidate job sequence.
	f_{max}	Number of parameters to be optimized/10	
	A	Random numbers between 0 and 1	Obtained by repeated execution of the algorithm and has been manually tuned and tested.
	R		
CS	Pa	0.25	Fraction of worst nests to be abandoned.
FPA	P	0.8	Switching probability to control local pollination and global pollination.
GWO	r1	Random numbers between 0 and 1	The random numbers r1 and r2 are used to model grey wolves encircling the prey during the hunt. The parameter a is calculated as $a=2-1*(2/t)$, where t is current iteration.
	r2		
	A_i where i=1, 2 and 3	$A_i =2*a*r1-a$	
	C_i where i=1, 2 and 3	$C_i =2*r2$	

Samples Under Study

The techniques discussed in this work have been applied to randomly generated samples. The samples are based on scheduling of 40 and 60 jobs on 2, 3 and 6 machines. Upper (UB) and lower bounds (LB) for processing time of these jobs have been selected to be 80 and 20 units respectively. Due date for the jobs have been selected randomly and has to be greater than the processing time of job discussed above. Weight/priority of the job is also generated randomly between lower bound and upper bound.

Table 4. Specific control parameters for GA applied for developing hybrids for job sequence

Parameter	Value	Description
Selection algorithm	Tournament (Size 2)	Candidate sequences *Parent1* and *Parent2* are selected for crossover using this method. It could be efficiently coded, works on parallel architectures and allows the selection size to be easily adjusted
Crossover function	Arithmetic	Child=R1 * Parent1+ R2 * Parent2 where *R1*, *R2* are independent random numbers between 0 and 1 It always produces feasible offspring for a convex solution space Ideal value for job sequence (found by manual testing): 0.6
Mutation function	Uniform	Ideal value for job sequence (found by manual testing): 0.02
Population size	Pop	*Pop* of Table 2
Population	Candidate job sequence	Modified by the previous phases of nature-inspired algorithms

Algorithm 1: Artificial Bee Colony Algorithm for Job Sequence

Step 1 [Initialize population]:

    Step 1.1: Encode and initialize the population of possible candidate job sequence. Each individual is called a *bee*.

    Step 1.2: Designate first half of the job sequences from the population as *employee bees* and another half as *onlooker bees*.

    Step 1.3: Set trial counter of all the *bees* to 0. Set parameters as shown in Table 2 and Table 3.

    Step 1.4: Evaluate fitness of each employee job sequence using bi-criteria T_{max} and WFT.

Repeat steps 2 to 4 until the stopping criteria is met (as shown in Table 2).

//Employee phase

Step 2 [Identify new possible solutions]: For each iteration t, produce new job sequence for each employee bee using equation

$x_i^j\left(t+1\right) = x_i^j\left(t\right) + \varnothing_i^j\left(x_i^j\left(t\right) - x_k^j\left(t\right)\right)$ where $x_i^j\left(t+1\right)$ is the new cluster to which j^{th} entity in the ith candidate job sequence could be allocated, $\varnothing$ is a random number between $[-1,1]$, i, $k \in (1,2......Pop)$ (*Pop* is the number of candidate job sequence as shown in Table 3), k is determined randomly and should be different from i, t is the current iteration.

Step 3 [Search for a better solution]:

    Step 3.1: Evaluate fitness of this new job sequence $x_i(t+1)$.

    Step 3.2: If the fitness of new job sequence is lesser than the existing job sequence, replace existing job sequence with this new job sequence and reset trial counter to 0 (as shown in Table 3), else if the current solution cannot be improved further, increment its trial counter.

//Onlooker phase

    Step 3.3: Calculate the probability p_i of a candidate job sequence solution (*employee bee*) to be selected as follows:

$$p_i = \frac{F_i}{Pop}$$ F_i is the fitness (fitness) of the ith employee job sequence; *Pop* is the size of population.

Step 3.4: Each *onlooker bee* of the second half of the population produces new solutions from the current candidate solution (similar to Step 2).

Step 3.5: Apply greedy selection process on the newly created and existing *onlooker bees* to select onlooker bees with lesser fitness (greater fitness).

//Scout Phase

Step 4 [Update the best solution]:

Step 4.1: If a candidate job sequence can't be improved further for pre-specified number of iterations called Trial (as shown in Table 3), then replace it with a new job sequence.

Step 4.2: This newly created solution is compared to existing solutions and best solution (least fitness) achieved so far is memorized.

Step 5 [Output]: Output the candidate job sequence having least fitness.

Population Generation

The approaches under consideration are Search-based meta-heuristic approaches that aims to find an optimal solution from an initial population (Pop) of randomly generated possible solutions. For sequencing of *n* jobs on *m* potential parallel machines, initial population of candidate job sequences are generated as below.

To create integer part for encoded job sequence:

```
For each candidate job sequence p (out of Pop)
        For each job i (out of n)
                Randomly allocate to machine j (out of m machines)
        Endfor
Endfor
```

To create floating point part of each position in the job sequence to be encoded:

```
For each candidate job sequence p (out of Pop)
        For each machine j (out of m)
                Find jobs allocated to machine j
Create permutation of jobs allocated to the machine j.
        Endfor
Endfor
```

Algorithm 2: BAT Algorithm for Job Sequence

Step 1 [Initialize population]:

   Step 1.1: Encode and initialize the population of possible job sequence (x). Each individual job sequence is called a *bat*. Set parameters as shown in Table 2 and Table 3.

   Step 1.2: Each bat is assigned an initial velocity (v) (having dimension equal to the number of entities to be clustered) and frequency (f) between $f_{min}=0$ and $f_{max}=10\%$ of Number of entities to be clustered (n). Each bat i is assigned Loudness A_i and pulse rate r_i.

   Step 1.3: Evaluate fitness of each bat job sequence using fitness.

   Step 1.4: Select current best job sequence (*best*) on the basis of fitness.

Repeat steps 2 to 4 until the stopping criteria is met (as shown in Table 2).

Step 2 [Identify new possible solutions]: For each bat job sequence (x_i), update their frequency, velocity and location as shown below:

$f_i(t+1) = f_{min} + (f_{max}-f_{min})$ * *rand* where *rand* is a random number between $[0,1]$

   $v_i(t+1) = v_i(t) + (x_i(t)-best)$ * $f_i(t)$

   $x_i(t+1) = x_i(t) + v_i(t)$

where t is the current iteration

If *rand*>r_i then perform local search

$x_i(t+1)=x_i(t) + rand1$ * $A_i(t)$, where *rand1* is a random number between $(-1,1)$

Step 3 [Search for a better solution]:

   Step 3.1: Evaluate fitness (fitness) of location of each new bat job sequence $x_i(t+1)$.

   Step 3.2: If *rand*<A_i and if fitness of $x_i(t+1)$ is lesser than that of $x_i(t)$, then replace $x_i(t)$ with $x_i(t+1)$.

   Step 3.3: Update A_i and r_i as,

$A_i(t+1)=0.9$ * $A_i(t)$

$r_i(t+1)=r_i(t)$ * $(1 - \exp(-0.9$ * $t))$ where t is the current iteration

Step 4 [Update the best solution]: Update best job sequence (least fitness) achieved so far (*best*).

Step 5 [Output]: Output the candidate job sequence having the least value of fitness.

Assessment Criteria

In order to compare the techniques discussed above, total cost (sum of T_{max} and *WFT*), has been used as assessment criteria. Since, the problem of job scheduling is to be performed taking into consideration bi-criteria namely T_{max} and *WFT*, so these are multi-objective in nature and lead to Pareto front as an output. The Pareto front is the set of elements that are not dominated by any possible element of the solution space. The Pareto front thus denotes the best results achievable. In this case, *Total cost* (sum of

*T*max and WFT) of the solution has been used as criteria to assess the quality of the job sequence. The lower the value of this cost, the better is the job sequence solution.

Analysis and Evaluation of Results

Total cost (sum of maximum tardiness and weighted flow time) of resultant optimized schedules for randomly generated samples have been shown in Table 5. It provides evidence about the extent to which the approaches under consideration are successful in efficiently sequencing jobs while evaluating *Total cost* as an assessment criterion.

Total Cost as Assessment Criteria for Proposed Approach 1

If *Total cost* is used as an evaluation criterion, MOWFPA lead to the lowest value in 5 out of 6 test problems as compared to other counterparts (MOWABC, MOWBAT, MOWBH, MOWCS, and MOWGWO). Other observations regarding *Total cost* of job sequences obtained by the application of algorithms defined under Proposed Approach 1 are:

- Most of them performed better than Nilwal et al (2015)
- MOWFPA performs better than MOGA for 5 out of 6 test problems.
- MOWABC, MOWBAT, MOWBH, MOWCS and MOWGWO do not perform better than MOGA.
- MOWFPA performs better than NSGA-II for 4 out of 6 test problems.
- MOWABC, MOWBAT, MOWBH, MOWCS and MOWGWO do not perform better than NSGA-II.

Algorithm 3: Black Hole Algorithm for Job Sequence

Step 1 [Initialize population]:

    Step 1.1: Encode and initialize the population of candidate job sequence. Each individual is called a *star*.

    Step 1.2: Set parameters as shown in Table 2.

    Step 1.3: Evaluate the fitness of each candidate in the population on the basis of fitness.

    Step 1.4: Designate the solution with the least value of fitness as Black Hole (x_{BH}).

Repeat Steps 2-4 until the stopping criteria is met (as indicated in Table 2).

Step 2 [Identify new possible solutions]: For each iteration t, identify new location $(x_i(t+1))$ for each ith star job sequence $(x_i(t))$ as

$$x_i(t+1) = x_i(t)) + rand*(x_{BH} - x_i(t))$$

where *rand* is a random number between 0 and 1.

Step 3 [Search for a better solution]:

    Step 3.1: Evaluate fitness of each new location of star job sequence $x_i(t+1)$.

    Step 3.2: If new location of candidate star solution is better (lower fitness) than the current location, then replace the current star job sequence with this new solution else, ignore it. This step is required to locally search for a better sequence. It moves the current candidate randomly in search for a better solution.

Step 4 [Update the best solution]:

Step 4.1: If the new location of star job sequence $x_i(t+1)$ is better (lower fitness) than the current Black Hole (x_{BH}), then designate this new solution as new Black Hole (x_{BH}).

Step 4.2: Calculate the radius of the event of horizon (R) of the Black Hole job sequence.

$$R = \frac{F_{BH}}{\sum_{i=1}^{Pop} F_i}$$

where F_{BH} is the fitness (fitness) for Black Hole job sequence and F_i is the fitness of ith star job sequence calculated using fitness. *Pop* is the size of the population under consideration (Refer Table 2).

Step 4.3: If a star enters this event horizon, it is absorbed by the Black Hole. It means, if ($F_{BH} - F_i < R$), the star job sequence is discarded as it is regarded to be entered in event horizon of Black Hole and is thus vanished. Generate new job sequence to balance the size of the population.

Step 5 [Output]: Output the candidate job sequence having least value of fitness.

Algorithm 4: Cuckoo Search Algorithm for Job Sequence

Step 1 [Initialize population]:

Step 1.1: Encode and initialize the population of possible job sequence. Each individual is called a *nest*.

Step 1.2: Set parameters as shown in Table 2. Define abandon fraction (*pa*) (0.25 for job sequence as shown in Table 3).

Step 1.3: Select current best job sequence on the basis of fitness. Repeat steps 2 to 4 until the stopping criteria is met (as shown in Table 2).

Step 2 [Identify new possible solutions]: Select job sequence *i* by using step vector drawn from Lévy distribution.

Step 3 [Search for a better solution]:

Step 3.1: Randomly select a job sequence *j*.

Step 3.2: If the fitness of job sequence x_i is lower than x_j, replace x_j with x_i.

Step 4 [Update best solution]: Abandon fraction of job sequence (*pa*) and generate new job sequence. Identify the best job sequence (with least fitness) so far.

Step 5 [Output]: Output job sequence with least value of fitness.

Algorithm 5: Flower Pollination Algorithm for Job Sequence

Step 1 [Initialize population]:

   Step 1.1: Encode and initialize the population of possible job sequence (x). Each individual job sequence is called *flower*.

   Step 1.2: Set parameters as shown in Table 2. Define switching probability (p) (0.8 for job sequence).

   Step 1.3: Select current best job sequence (*best*) using fitness.
Repeat steps 2 to 4 until the stopping criteria is met (as shown in Table 2)

Step 2 [Identify new possible solutions]: For all the flower job sequences (x_i) repeat

Step 2.1: Generate a random number r between 0 and 1.

Step 2.2: If $r > p$

//Perform global search

 $x_i(t+1)=x_i(t) +L\ (best - x_i(t))$ where L is step vector following Lévy distribution, t is the current iteration.

         Else

     //Perform local search

           $x_i(t+1)=x_i(t) +\mathcal{E}\ (x_a(t) - x_b(t))$, where $x_a(t)$ and $x_b(t)$ are randomly selected flower

           job sequences, $\mathcal{E}$ is drawn from uniform distribution between 0 and 1.

Step 3 [Search for a better solution]: If fitness of $x_i(t+1)$ is lesser than that of $x_i(t)$, then replace $x_i(t)$ with $x_i(t+1)$.

Step 4 [Update best solution]: Identify the best job sequence (with least fitness) achieved so far.

Step 5 [Output]: Output job sequence with least value of fitness.

Algorithm 6: Grey Wolf Optimizer Algorithm for Job Sequence

Step 1 [Initialize population]:

Step 1.1: Encode and initialize the population of possible job sequence. Each individual job sequence is called a *grey wolf*.

   Step 1.2: Set parameters as shown in Table 2 and Table 3.

   Step 1.3: Select current best (x_α), second best (x_β) and third best (x_γ) job sequences on the basis of their fitness values.
Repeat steps 2 to 4 until the stopping criteria is met (as shown in Table 2).

Step 2 [Identify new possible solutions]: For each wolf job sequence xi, find new position for wolf $x_i(t+1)$ as shown below:

                $a =2-1*2(1/t)$ t is the current iteration.

         $A_i=2*a*r_1-a$ r_1 and r_2 are random numbers between 0 and 1.

         $C_i=2*r_2$ A_i and C_i are coefficient vectors where $i=1,2$ and

3.

138

$$D_\alpha = C_1 * x_\alpha - x_i(t)$$
$$D_\beta = C_2 * x_\beta - x_i(t)$$
$$D_\gamma = C_3 * x_\gamma - x_i(t)$$
$$x_{i1}(t) = x_\alpha - A_1 * D_\alpha$$
$$x_{i2}(t) = x_\beta - A_2 * D_\beta$$
$$x_{i3}(t) = x_\gamma - A_3 * D_\gamma$$
$$x_i(t+1) = (x_{i1}(t) + x_{i2}(t) + x_{i3}(t))/3$$

Step 3 [Search for a better solution]: If fitness value of new position of wolf $x_i(t+1)$ is better than its old position $x_i(t)$ then replace $x_i(t)$ with $x_i(t+1)$.

Step 4 [Update best solution]: Update x_α, x_β and x_γ.

Step 5 [Output]: Output job sequence represented by x_α.

Total Cost as Assessment Criteria for Proposed Approach 2

If *Total cost* is used as an evaluation criterion, MOWFPAGA leads to the lowest value in 2, MOWBHGA in 3 and MOWGWOGA in 1 out of 6 test problems when compared amongst them.

Other observations regarding *Total cost* of job sequences obtained by the application of algorithms defined under Proposed Approach 2 are:

- All the algorithms performed better than their respective counterparts in Proposed Approach 1 in most of the test cases.
- Most of them performed better than Nilwal et al (2015)
- MOWFPAGA performs better than MOGA for 5 out of 6 test problems.
- MOWGWOGA performs better than MOGA for 4 out of 6 test problems.
- MOWBHGA performs better than MOGA for 3 out of 6 test problems.
- MOWBAT and MOWCS perform better than MOGA in 1 out of 6 test problems.
- MOWABCGA does not perform better than MOGA.
- MOWFPAGA performs better than NSGA-II for 3 out of 6 test problems.
- MOWGWOGA performs better than NSGA-II for 2 out of 6 test problems.
- MOWBHGA performs better than NSGA-II for 4 out of 6 test problems.
- MOWABCGA, MOWBAT and MOWCS perform better than NSGA-II in 1 out of 6 test problems.

Figure 2 plots *Total cost* for job sequence obtained by applying Proposed Approach 1 and 2 for all the sample test cases (for easy comparison). By analyzing Table 5 and Figure 2, it could be easily observed that the use of GA in Proposed Approach 2 has improved its efficiency depicted by the lower value of *Total cost*.

Total Cost as Assessment Criteria for Proposed Approach 3

If *Total cost* is used as an evaluation criterion, MOFPA leads to the lowest value in all the test cases as compared to other counterparts in this approach namely MOABC, MOBAT, MOBH, MOCS and MOGWO.

Other observations regarding *Total cost* of job sequences obtained by the application of algorithms defined under Proposed Approach 3 are:

Table 5. Least 'Total cost' solution for the sample under study

Number of Machines		2		3		6	
Number of Jobs		40	60	40	60	40	60
Algorithms defined under Proposed Approach 1	MOWABC	1462.87	2229.10	1025.78	1518.10	537.38	747.45
	MOWBAT	1500.67	2305.89	1050.78	1547.82	540.65	750.74
	MOWBH	1504.11	2265.12	1003.17	1532.27	538.71	774.85
	MOWCS	1510.34	2303.61	1045.89	1551.38	539.51	777.92
	MOWFPA	1376.46	2032.210	800.81	1350.50	453.10	671.929
	MOWGWO	1495.43	2003.25	1004.54	1484.83	467.22	742.65
Algorithms defined under Proposed Approach 2	MOWABCGA	1403.812	2096.055	927.203	1405.895	456.223	694.74
	MOWBATGA	1410.67	2098.31	930.62	1410.22	460.83	692.53
	MOWBHGA	1330	2104.08	810.75	1318.43	441.54	682.35
	MOWCSGA	1413.57	2095.27	932.47	1408.93	462.69	680.16
	MOWFPGA	1350.27	2010.94	860.52	1346.06	435.22	660.38
	MOWGWOGA	1400.43	**1970.46**	870.56	1380.78	457.84	720.83
Algorithms defined under Proposed Approach 3	MOABC	1488.38	2065.25	985.328	1463.37	490.22	738.21
	MOBAT	1495.34	2064.98	987.93	1478.39	495.73	670.43
	MOBH	1412.56	2121.92	965.84	1409.07	481.44	698.98
	MOCS	1490.73	2070.82	982.36	1480.25	498.54	700.82
	MOFPA	1386.28	2042.413	831.248	1357.97	451.87	674.804
	MOGWO	1450.73	2162.71	923.66	1496.15	525.63	731.20
Algorithms defined under Proposed Approach 4	MOABCGA	1325.27	2014.53	825.863	1315.25	432.36	675.61
	MOBATGA	1330.82	2021.54	831.72	1320.42	440.93	669.51
	MOBHGA	**1305.41**	2004.03	807.81	1310.07	**430.81**	676.18
	MOCSGA	1333.58	2037.74	833.58	1325.63	436.57	665.33
	MOFPGA	1320.27	2000.03	**728.439**	**1304.07**	**430.81**	**669.18**
	MOGWOGA	1320.08	2012.39	850.35	1372.44	450.78	640.74
Existing Approaches	Nailwal et al. (2015)	1558.88	2316.87	1070.15	1577.70	526.17	781.71
	MOGA	1320.72	2047.72	880.99	1383.62	465.15	679.67
	NSGA –II	1350.16	2035	850.74	1364.14	443.19	731.03

- Most of them performed better than Nilwal et al (2015)
- MOFPA performs better than MOGA in 3 out of 6 test problems.
- MOBAT performs better than MOGA for 1 out of 6 test problems.
- MOABC, MOBH, MOCS and MOGWO do not perform better than MOGA.
- MOFPA performs better than NSGA-II for 2 out of 6 test problems.
- MOBAT performs better than NSGA-II for 1 out of 6 test problems.
- MOABC, MOBH, MOWCS and MOGWO do not perform better than NSGA-II.

Total Cost as Assessment Criteria for Proposed Approach 4

If *Total cost* is used as an evaluation criterion, MOFPAGA leads to the lowest value in 4 and MOBHGA in 2 out of 6 test cases as compared to other counterparts.

Other observations regarding *Total cost* of job sequences obtained by the application of algorithms defined under Proposed Approach 4 are:

- All the algorithms performed better than their respective counterparts in Proposed Approach 3 .
- All of them performed better than Nilwal et al (2015)
- MOFPGA, MOBHGA and MOGWOGA perform better than MOGA and NSGA-II in all test cases.
- MOABCGA, MOBATGA, MOCSGA perform better than MOGA for 5 out of 6 test problems.
- Most of these algorithms perform better than NSGA-II.

Figure 3 plots *Total cost* for job sequence obtained by applying Proposed Approach 3 and 4 for all the sample test cases (for easy comparison). By analyzing Table 5 and Figure 3, it could be easily observed that use of GA in Proposed Approach 4 has improved its efficiency depicted by the lower value of *Total cost*.

Figure 4 displays the *Total cost* for job sequence observed by application of Proposed Approach 2 and Proposed Approach 4 for all the sample test cases. It is observed that in most of the cases Proposed Approach 4 performs better than Proposed Approach 2.

Figure 2. Plots comparing the Total cost of job sequences obtained by applying Proposed Approach 1 (MOWABC, MOWBAT, MOWBH, MOWCS, MOWFPA, and MOWGWO) and Proposed Approach 2 (MOWABCGA, MOWBATGA, MOWBHGA, MOWCSGA, MOWFPGA, and MOWGWOGA) for all the test problems

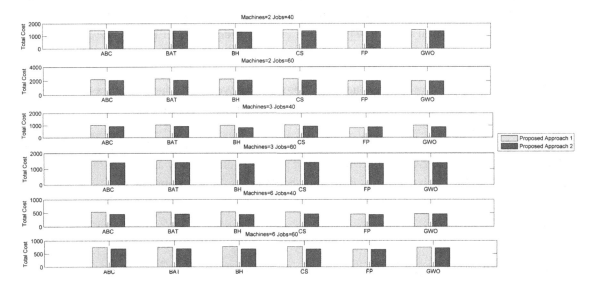

Overall, multi objective approach hybrid with the auxiliary archive as well as GA is the most proficient. As far as Proposed Approach 1 (based on weighted objectives) and Proposed Approach 3 (based on auxiliary archive) are concerned, approach based on the auxiliary archive (Proposed Approach 3) performs better than the approach based on weighted objectives (Proposed Approach 1). This is explained by the fact that the weighted objectives based approach returns a single objective which is highly dependent on the randomly selected weights of the objectives under consideration. At the same time, in case of conflicting objectives, allocation of weights is sometimes difficult. In case of random selection of weights, the output is highly unpredictable. In case of auxiliary archive based approach (Proposed Approach 3), an auxiliary archive has been used to store the Pareto front. In this way, search space is expected to be efficiently utilized leading to better optimization results.

Further, the use of GA with weighted objectives based Proposed Approach 1 leads to a better approach (Proposed Approach 2) even when compared to auxiliary archive based Proposed Approach 3. Table 5 and Figure 5 clearly presents *Total cost* of job sequences obtained by applying algorithms defined under Proposed approach 2 and 3 (for all the samples under study). It could be observed that algorithms defined under weighted objectives based approach hybrid with GA (Proposed Approach 2) perform better than auxiliary archive based approach (Proposed Approach 3).

Figure 6 plots the *Total cost* for job sequence obtained by application of Propose Approach 4 along with the existing Nailwal et al (2015), MOGA and NSGA-II algorithm based approaches for all the sample test cases. It is seen that algorithms defined under Proposed Approach 4 leads to the best job sequences. MOFPGA is observed to perform best out of all the algorithms under consideration (for all the approaches).

THREATS TO VALIDITY

Threats to validity refer to the factors that can bias our empirical study. With respect to current research work, there are two kinds of threats, namely, internal and external validity.

Internal validity refers to the biases in the results related to proposed approaches. The internal threats to validity have been taken into account in the tuning of parameters. In order to mitigate this threat, the execution of the approaches is repeated and the parameters involved in the approaches under consideration are manually tuned.

Another internal threat to validity is due to randomization involved in the search-based algorithms under consideration. In order to mitigate this threat, the algorithms are executed repeatedly (Neumann, Swan, Harman, & Clark, 2014).

External validity refers to the degree to which the results can be generalised to a wider class of subjects from which the sample has been drawn. The test problems under study are less in number and this may affect the degree to which the results could be generalised to other proprietary .

Figure 3. Plots comparing the Total cost of job sequences obtained by applying Proposed Approach 3 (MOABC, MOWBAT, MOBH, MOCS, MOFPA, and MOGWO) and Proposed Approach 4 (MOABCGA, MOBATGA, MOBHGA, MOCSGA, MOFPGA, and MOGWOGA) for all the test problems

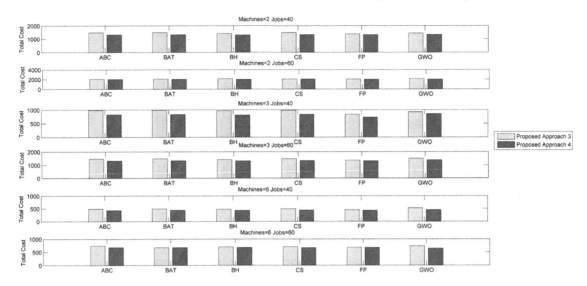

Figure 4. Plots comparing the Total cost of job sequences obtained by applying Proposed Approach 2 (MOWABCGA, MOWBATGA, MOWBHGA, MOWCSGA, MOWFPGA, and MOWGWOGA) and Proposed Approach 4 (MOABCGA, MOBATGA, MOBHGA, MOCSGA, MOFPGA, and MOGWOGA) for all the test problems

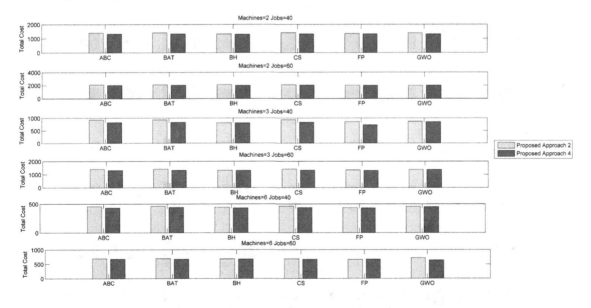

Figure 5. Plots comparing the Total cost of job sequences obtained by applying Proposed Approach 2 (MOWABCGA, MOWBATGA, MOWBHGA, MOWCSGA, MOWFPGA, and MOWGWOGA) and Proposed Approach 3 (MOABC, MOWBAT, MOBH, MOCS, MOFPA, and MOGWO) for all the test problems

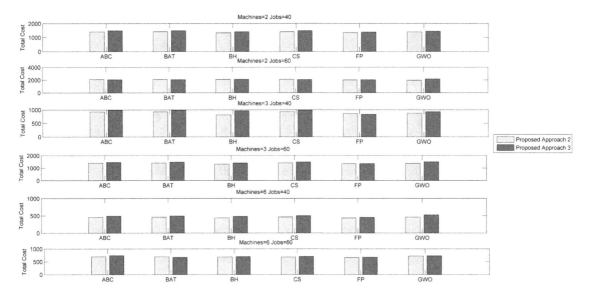

Figure 6. Plots comparing Total cost of job sequences obtained by applying Proposed Approach 4 (MOABCGA, MOBATGA, MOBHGA, MOCSGA, MOFPGA, and MOGWOGA) and existing Nailwal et al. (2015), MOGA and NSGA-II algorithm based approaches for all the test problems

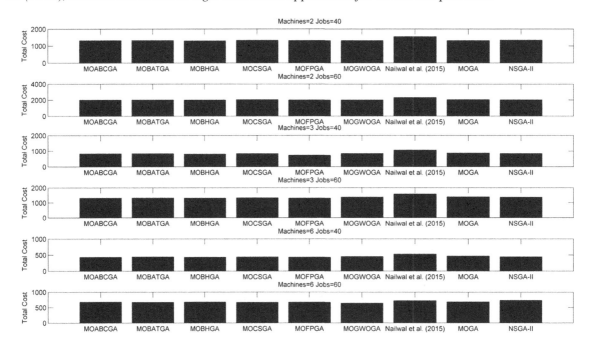

CONCLUSION

This work proposes the application of multi-objective nature-inspired algorithms such as Artificial Bee Colony, BAT, Black Hole, Cuckoo Search, Flower Pollination, and Grey Wolf Optimizer algorithms formulated as weighted aggregation based and auxiliary archive-based approaches to store best possible job sequence (in the form of non-dominated Pareto front) during each iteration. Hybrids of these algorithms with GA have also been investigated. Two objectives (Maximum Tardiness and Weighted Flow Time) have been considered for application of these approaches. These hybridised approaches have been tested on randomly generated samples of scheduling of *n* jobs on *m* parallel machines. The results are compared to that of existing search-based multi-objective approaches based on MOGA and NSGA-II algorithms as well as existing heuristic.

It is observed that multi-objective formulation of nature-inspired algorithms under consideration developed using auxiliary archive performs better than corresponding weighted aggregation-based formulations. The results further indicate that multi-objective Flower Pollination algorithm developed using auxiliary archive outperforms other counterparts (ABC, BAT, BH, CS, GWO). GA based hybrid approaches perform better than their respective non-hybrid counterparts. In addition, it is empirically evident that multi-objective auxiliary archive and GA based hybrid of Flower Pollination algorithm (MOFPGA) produces better job sequence than all other hybrids as well as existing Two-Archive, MOGA and NSGA-II algorithms-based approaches.

FUTURE WORK

In future, other evolutionary optimization approaches, such as PSO, could be investigated for optimizing nature-inspired algorithms discussed in this work for obtaining even better job sequence. Other novel better nature-inspired algorithms (such as Whale Optimization Algorithm) will be investigated for better performance.

REFERENCES

Akbari, R., Hedayatzadeh, R., Ziarati, K., & Hassanizadeh, B. (2012). A multi-objective artificial bee colony algorithm. *Swarm and Evolutionary Computation*, 2, 39–52. doi:10.1016/j.swevo.2011.08.001

Berrichi, A., Amodeo, L., Yalaoui, F., Châtelet, E., & Mezghiche, M. (2009). Bi-objective optimization algorithms for joint production and maintenance scheduling: Application to the parallel machine problem. *Journal of Intelligent Manufacturing*, 20(4), 389–400. doi:10.100710845-008-0113-5

Berrichi, A., Yalaoui, F., Amodeo, L., & Mezghiche, M. (2010). Bi-objective ant colony optimization approach to optimize production and maintenance scheduling. *Computers & Operations Research*, 37(9), 1584–1596. doi:10.1016/j.cor.2009.11.017

Coello, C. A. C., Pulido, G. T., & Lechuga, M. S. (2004). Handling multiple objectives with particle swarm optimization. *IEEE Transactions on Evolutionary Computation*, 8(3), 256–279. doi:10.1109/TEVC.2004.826067

Coello, C. C., Lamont, G. B., & Van Veldhuizen, D. A. (2007). *Evolutionary algorithms for solving multi-objective problems*. Springer Science & Business Media.

Colorni, A., Dorigo, M., Maffioli, F., Maniezzo, V., Righini, G., & Trubian, M. (1996). Heuristics from nature for hard combinatorial optimization problems. *International Transactions in Operational Research, 3*(1), 1–21. doi:10.1111/j.1475-3995.1996.tb00032.x

Deb, K. (2014). *Multi-objective optimization. In Search methodologies* (pp. 403–449). Springer.

Deb, K., Pratap, A., Agarwal, S., & Meyarivan, T. (2002). A fast and elitist multiobjective genetic algorithm: NSGA-II. *IEEE Transactions on Evolutionary Computation, 6*(2), 182–197. doi:10.1109/4235.996017

Eren, T. (2010). A bicriteria m-machine flowshop scheduling with sequence-dependent setup times. *Applied Mathematical Modelling, 34*(2), 284–293. doi:10.1016/j.apm.2009.04.005

Faccio, M., Ries, J., & Saggiorno, N. (2015). Simulated annealing approach to solve dual resource constrained job shop scheduling problems: Layout impact analysis on solution quality. *International Journal of Mathematics in Operational Research, 7*(6), 609–629. doi:10.1504/IJMOR.2015.072274

Goldberg, D. E. (2006). *Genetic algorithms*. Pearson Education India.

Guo, P., Cheng, W., & Wang, Y. (2014). Parallel machine scheduling with step-deteriorating jobs and setup times by a hybrid discrete cuckoo search algorithm. *Engineering Optimization*, 1-22.

Harman, M. (2007). *The current state and future of search based software engineering*. Paper presented at the 2007 Future of Software Engineering. 10.1109/FOSE.2007.29

Hatamlou, A. (2013). Black hole: A new heuristic optimization approach for data clustering. *Information Sciences, 222*, 175–184. doi:10.1016/j.ins.2012.08.023

Jeet, K. (2017). Fuzzy Flow Shop Scheduling Using Grey Wolf Optimization Algorithm. *Indian Journal of Social Research, 7*(2), 167–171.

Jeet, K., Dhir, R., & Sharma, S. (2016a). Bi-criteria parallel machine scheduling using nature-inspired hybrid flower pollination algorithm. *International Journal of Metaheuristics, 5*(3-4), 226–253. doi:10.1504/IJMHEUR.2016.081153

Jeet, K., Dhir, R., & Sharma, S. (2016b). Meta-Heuristic Algorithms to Solve Bi-Criteria Parallel Machines Scheduling Problem. *International Journal of Applied Evolutionary Computation, 7*(2), 76–96. doi:10.4018/IJAEC.2016040105

Jeet, K., Dhir, R., & Singh, P. (2016). Hybrid Black Hole Algorithm for Bi-Criteria Job Scheduling on Parallel Machines. *International Journal of Intelligent Systems & Applications, 8*(4), 1–17. doi:10.5815/ijisa.2016.04.01

Konak, A., Coit, D. W., & Smith, A. E. (2006). Multi-objective optimization using genetic algorithms: A tutorial. *Reliability Engineering & System Safety, 91*(9), 992–1007. doi:10.1016/j.ress.2005.11.018

Li, J.-Q., Pan, Q.-K., & Tasgetiren, M. F. (2014). A discrete artificial bee colony algorithm for the multi-objective flexible job-shop scheduling problem with maintenance activities. *Applied Mathematical Modelling, 38*(3), 1111–1132. doi:10.1016/j.apm.2013.07.038

Marler, R. T., & Arora, J. S. (2010). The weighted sum method for multi-objective optimization: New insights. *Structural and Multidisciplinary Optimization, 41*(6), 853–862. doi:10.100700158-009-0460-7

Mazdeh, M. M., Zaerpour, F., Zareei, A., & Hajinezhad, A. (2010). Parallel machines scheduling to minimize job tardiness and machine deteriorating cost with deteriorating jobs. *Applied Mathematical Modelling, 34*(6), 1498–1510. doi:10.1016/j.apm.2009.08.023

Mirjalili, S., Saremi, S., Mirjalili, S. M., & Coelho, L. S. (2016). Multi-objective grey wolf optimizer: A novel algorithm for multi-criterion optimization. *Expert Systems with Applications, 47*, 106–119. doi:10.1016/j.eswa.2015.10.039

Nailwal, K. K., Gupta, D., & Sharma, S. (2015). Fuzzy bi-criteria scheduling on parallel machines involving weighted flow time and maximum tardiness. *Cogent Mathematics, 2*(1), 1019792. doi:10.1080/23311835.2015.1019792

Neumann, G., Swan, J., Harman, M., & Clark, J. A. (2014). *The executable experimental template pattern for the systematic comparison of metaheuristics.* Paper presented at the International conference companion on Genetic and evolutionary computation companion. 10.1145/2598394.2609850

Rahimi-Vahed, A., Javadi, B., Rabbani, M., & Tavakkoli-Moghaddam, R. (2008). A multi-objective scatter search for a bi-criteria no-wait flow shop scheduling problem. *Engineering Optimization, 40*(4), 331–346. doi:10.1080/03052150701732509

Rashidi, E., Jahandar, M., & Zandieh, M. (2010). An improved hybrid multi-objective parallel genetic algorithm for hybrid flow shop scheduling with unrelated parallel machines. *International Journal of Advanced Manufacturing Technology, 49*(9-12), 1129–1139. doi:10.100700170-009-2475-z

Shokrollahpour, E., Zandieh, M., & Dorri, B. (2011). A novel imperialist competitive algorithm for bi-criteria scheduling of the assembly flowshop problem. *International Journal of Production Research, 49*(11), 3087–3103. doi:10.1080/00207540903536155

Tosun, Ö., & Marichelvam, M. (2016). Hybrid bat algorithm for flow shop scheduling problems. *International Journal of Mathematics in Operational Research, 9*(1), 125–138. doi:10.1504/IJMOR.2016.077560

Yang, X.-S. (2010). *Nature-inspired metaheuristic algorithms.* Luniver Press.

Yang, X.-S. (2011). Bat algorithm for multi-objective optimisation. *International Journal of Bio-inspired Computation, 3*(5), 267–274. doi:10.1504/IJBIC.2011.042259

Yang, X.-S., & Deb, S. (2009). *Cuckoo search via Lévy flights.* Paper presented at the World Congress on Nature & Biologically Inspired Computing, NaBIC 2009 10.1109/NABIC.2009.5393690

Yang, X.-S., Karamanoglu, M., & He, X. (2013). Multi-objective flower algorithm for optimization. *Procedia Computer Science, 18*, 861–868. doi:10.1016/j.procs.2013.05.251

Zhang, L., Gao, L., & Li, X. (2013). A hybrid genetic algorithm and tabu search for a multi-objective dynamic job shop scheduling problem. *International Journal of Production Research, 51*(12), 3516–3531. doi:10.1080/00207543.2012.751509

KEY TERMS AND DEFINITIONS

Black Hole: A region in space with so much mass concentration that no object can escape its gravitational pull.

Employee Bee: This bee is associated with a particular food source and carries information about it.

Global Pollination: Pollination occurs by utilizing cross pollination which is done with the help of insects and animals who can take Lévy flight.

Grey Wolf: Predators at the top of the food chain who mostly prefer to live in a group of sizes 5-12 on average. They follow a very strict social dominant hierarchy. Four types of grey wolves named alpha, beta, delta, and omega are employed which are simulating the leadership hierarchy.

Levy Flight: It occasionally performs Lévy steps that help the algorithm to get rid of local valleys. Lévy step is depicted as shown in Equation: $L \approx 1 / s^{(1+\beta)}$ where β refers to the Lévy exponent. Parameter s, u and v are described as $s = u / |v|^{(1+\beta)}$, $u \approx N\left(0, \sigma^2\right)$, $v \approx N\left(0,1\right)$ where σ is a function of β.

Local Pollination: Pollination occurs on the basis of self-pollination and makes use of wind and diffusion.

Onlooker Bee: This bee waits in the dance area for making a decision to choose a food source on the basis of information shared by employee bees.

Scout Bee: This bee goes on a random search to discover new sources.

Chapter 8
Hybrid Honey Bees Meta–Heuristic for Benchmark Data Classification

Habib Shah
King Khalid University, Saudi Arabia

Nasser Tairan
King Khalid University, Saudi Arabia

Rozaida Ghazali
Universiti Tun Hussein Onn Malaysia, Malaysia

Ozgur Yeniay
Hacettepe University, Turkey

Wali Khan Mashwani
Kohat University of Science and Technology, Pakistan

ABSTRACT

Some bio-inspired methods are cuckoo search, fish schooling, artificial bee colony (ABC) algorithms. Sometimes, these algorithms cannot reach to global optima due to randomization and poor exploration and exploitation process. Here, the global artificial bee colony and Levenberq-Marquardt hybrid called GABC-LM algorithm is proposed. The proposed GABC-LM will use neural network for obtaining the accurate parameters, weights, and bias values for benchmark dataset classification. The performance of GABC-LM is benchmarked against NNs training with the typical LM, PSO, ABC, and GABC methods. The experimental result shows that the proposed GABC-LM performs better than that standard BP, ABC, PSO, and GABC for the classification task.

DOI: 10.4018/978-1-5225-5832-3.ch008

INTRODUCTION

Artificial Neural Networks (ANNs) are the most novel and powerful mathematical tools suitable for solving complex linear and nonlinear, engineering and economical problems such as prediction, forecasting and classification (Chakravarty, Dash, Pandi, & Panigrahi, 2011; Ghazali, Jaafar Hussain, Mohd Nawi, & Mohamad, 2009). NNs are being used extensively for solving universal problems intelligently like continuous, discrete, telecommunications fraud detection and clustering (Charalampidis & Muldrey, 2009; Hilas & Mastorocostas, 2008; Rao, Satchidananda, & Rajib, 2012). NNs are being applied for different optimization and mathematical problems such as classification, object and image recognition, signal processing, temperature and weather forecasting and bankruptcy (Aussem, Murtagh, & Sarazin, 1994; Bakhta & Ghalem, 2014; Behnam & Isa, 2013; Ch. Sanjeev Kumar, Ajit Kumar, Satchidananda, & Sung-Bae, 2013; Chen, Duan, Cai, & Liu, 2011).

The main task of BP algorithm is to update the network weights for minimizing output error using BP processing because the accuracy of any approximation depends upon the selection of proper weights for the neural networks (NNs)(Ramakanta, Ravi, & Patra, 2010). It has high success rate in solving many complex problems, but it still has some drawbacks, especially when setting parameter values like initial values of connection weights, value for learning rate, and momentum. If the network topology is not carefully selected, the NNs algorithm can get trapped in local minima, or it might lead to slow convergence or even network failure. In order to overcome the disadvantages of standard BP, much global optimization population-based technique, GA (Geretti & Abramo, 2011), improved BP (Nawi, Ransing, & Ransing, 2006), DE (Slowik & Bialko, 2008), BP-ant colony(Chengzhi, Yifan, Lichao, & Yang, 2008), and PSO (Hongwen & Rui, 2006).

Dynamic Swarm ABC algorithm, Typical ABC, Differential Operators Embedded ABC, (Harish, Jagdish Chand, Arya, & Kusum, 2012; D. Karaboga & Akay, 2007; Tarun Kumar & Millie, 2011), he Hybrid Ant Bee Colony (HABC), Genetic Algorithm and Back Propagation Neural Network, Improved Artificial Bee Colony (IABC), G-HABC (Suruchi, 2016) and the Global Hybrid Ant Bee Colony (HABC) algorithm, are population-based algorithms that can provide the best possible solutions for different mathematical problems by using inspiration techniques from nature. A common feature of population-based algorithms is that the population consisting of feasible solutions to the difficulty is customized by applying some agents on the solutions depending upon information of their robustness. Therefore, the population is encouraged towards improved solution areas of the solution space. Population-based optimization algorithms are categories into two sections namely evolutionary algorithm (EA) (Xinyan & Jianguo, 2011), and I-based algorithm (Aydin, Wu, & Liang, 2010) . In EA, the major plan underlying this combination is to take the weight matrices of the ANNs as individuals, to change the weights by some operations such as crossover and mutation, and to use the error produced by the NNs as the fitness measure that guides selection (Yan-fei & Xiong-min, 2010). In S based algorithm, ABC has the advantage of global optimization and easy recognition. It has been successfully used in solving combinatorial optimization problems such as clustering and MLP training for XOR problems (Davidović, Šelmić, Teodorović, & Ramljak; Dervis Karaboga, Akay, & Ozturk, 2007; Habib Shah et al., 2017). ABC algorithm is an easily understandable technique for training MLP on classification problems. This algorithm uses randomly selected natural techniques with a colony to train NNs by optimal weights.

Global Artificial Bee Colony-Levenberq-Marquardt (GABC-LM) is a hybrid technique that proposed here for Boolean function classification problems by using inspiration techniques from nature swarm bees with LM. In this study, GABC-LM algorithm is used successfully to train MLP on Boolean function classification task. The performance of the algorithm is compared with standard LM, ABC, PSO and ABC algorithm.

LEARNING ALGORITHMS OF ARTIFICIAL NEURAL NETWORKS

An artificial neutral network (ANN) is an artificial model that is based on the human biological neural network systems, such as the brain. The brain has approximately 100 billion neurons, which communicate through electro-chemical signals, where the neurons are connected through synapses (Sayad, 2010). Each neuron receives thousands of connections with other neurons, constantly receiving incoming signals to reach the cell body, where the response is sent through the axon. The simple biological neuron model is given in Figure 1 as;

MLP is a universal approximate and mathematical model that contains a set of processing elements known as artificial neurons (Hornik, Stinchcombe, & White, 1989). The network which is also known as feed forward neural network was introduced in 1957 to solve a non-linear XOR, and was then successfully applied to different combinatorial problems (Hornik et al., 1989). The basic building of MLP is constructed by neurons, which have some categories as input, hidden and output layers, as shown in Figure 1. The weight values between input and hidden nodes and between hidden and output, nodes are randomly initialized. The network is highly used and tested on a different job. Figure 2 shows the basic architecture MLP (Rosenblatt, 1958).

The output value of the MLP can be obtained by the following formula:

$$Y = f_i \left(\sum_{j=1}^{n} w_{ij} x_j + b_i \right) \tag{1}$$

Figure 1. Biological neuron model

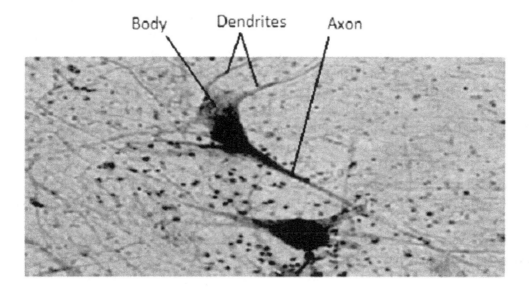

Figure 2. Multilayer perceptron model

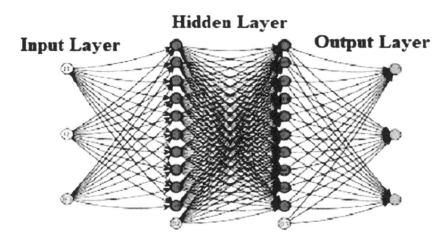

where Y is the output of the node x is the jth input to the node, w is the connection weight between the input node and output node, bi is the threshold (or bias) of the node, and fi is the node transfer function. Usually, the node transfer function is a non-linear function such as: a sigmoid function, a Gaussian functions. Network error function E will be minimized as

$$E(w(t)) = \frac{1}{n} \sum_{j=1}^{n} \sum_{k=1}^{k} (d_k - o_t)^2 \qquad (2)$$

where E (w (t)) is the error at the tth iteration; w(t) is the weight in the connections at the tth iteration; j shows training set, dk is the desired output; ot is the actual value of the k-th output node; K is the number of output nodes; and n is the no of patterns.

NN learning is a process of obtaining new knowledge or adjusting the existing knowledge through the training process. BP is currently the most widely and well known used algorithm for training MLP (Rumelhart, McClelland, & University of California, 1986). The combination of weights which minimizes the error function is considered to be a solution of the learning problem. This step by step mathematical procedure adjusts the weights according to the error function. So, the adjustment of weights which decrease the error function is considered to be the optimal solution of the problem. In the input layer only inputs propagate through weights and passing through hidden layers and get output by some local information. For the BP error, each hidden unit is responsible for some part of the error.

Although the BP algorithm is a powerful technique applied to classification, combinatorial problems and for training, MLP. However, as the problem complexity increases, the performance of BP falls off rapidly because gradient search techniques tend to get trapped at local minima. When the nearly global minima are well hidden among the local minima, BP can end up bouncing between local minima, especially for those non-linearly separable pattern classification problems or complex function approximation problem (Gori & Tesi, 1992; Kacem & Haouari, 2009). second shortcoming is that the convergence of the algorithm is very sensitive to the initial value. So, it often converges to an inferior solution and gets trapped in a long training time.

EVOLUTIONARY ALGORITHMS

Evolutionary Algorithms (EA) is a set of approaches based on the social insects, biological evolution, population based or biological behavior of members in environment (Bäck, 1996 ; Rajashree & Pradipta Kishore, 2016; Xinyan & Jianguo, 2011). Swarm Intelligence (SI) is an issue of EA where the dynamics within the group becomes the individual reason for its continued existence (R.C. Eberhart & Y. Shi, 2001; Yan-fei & Xiong-min, 2010). Common feature of population-based algorithms is that the population consisting of feasible solutions to the difficulty is customized by applying some agents on the solutions depending onuponhe information of their robustness. Therefore, the population is encouraged towards improved solution areas of the solution space. Population-based optimization algorithms are categories into two sections namely evolutionary algorithm (EA) and SI-based algorithm (Bonabeau, Dorigo, & Theraulaz, 1999; R.C. Eberhart & Y. Shi, 2001). EA, the major plan underlying this combination is to take the weight matrices of the ANN as individuals, to change the weights by some operations such as crossover and mutation, and to use the error produced by the ANN as the fitness measure that guides selection. The efficiency and agent-based technique made researchers to focus and developed new social insect's approaches for solving different problems.

There are many types of EA algorithms such as ACO (Dorigo & Di Caro, 1999), PSO (Kennedy & Eberhart, 1995), Binary Particle Swarm Optimization (BPSO), Birds Flocking, Bee Colony Optimization (BCO) (Rathipriya, Thangavel, & Bagyamani, 2011; Teodorovic, Lucic, Markovic, & Orco, 2006), Fish Schooling, Binary Cuckoo Search algorithm, Cat Swarm Optimization and Cuckoo Search Optimization (CSO) algorithm (Chakravarty, Bisoi, & Dash, 2016; Halima, Abdesslem, & Salim, 2014; Vazquez, 2011; Xin-She & Deb, 2009). The BCO further extends to Artificial Bee Colony algorithm (ABC) (D. Karaboga & Akay, 2007), Hybrid Bee Colony (HBCO) algorithm, Bee Optimization (BO) Bee Swarm Optimization (BSO) and others Hybrid Evolutionary algorithms (Akbari, Mohammadi, & Ziarati, 2009; Davidović et al.; Wali Khan, 2013). The scientists have persistent ABC algorithm because of it is characterized by a honey bee behavior pattern. The ABC which is successfully applied for several problems becomes to extend by scientific researchers to the Global Artificial Bee Colony (GABC) algorithm (Peng, Wenming, & Jian, 2011), the Modified Artificial Bee Colony (MABC) algorithm (Zhang, Guan, Tang, & Tang, 2011), an Improved Artificial Bee Colony (IABC) algorithm (H. Shah & Ghazali, 2011), PSO-ABC (Sharma, Pant, & Bhardwaj, 2011), the Global Hybrid Ant Bee Colony (GHABC) algorithm (H. SHah, R. Ghazali, N. M. Nawi, & M. M. Deris, 2012b), a Hybrid Artificial Bee Colony (HABC) algorithm (Ozturk & Karaboga, 2011), the Hybrid Ant Bee Colony (HABC) algorithm, the Discrete Artificial Bee Colony (DABC) algorithm (Yu-Yan, Jun-Hua, & Min, 2011), a Combinatorial Artificial Bee Colony(CABC) algorithm (D. Karaboga & Gorkemli, 2011), the parallel Artificial Bee Colony (PABC) algorithm (Narasimhan, 2009), the Novel Artificial Bee Colony (NABC) algorithm (Wei-Ping & Wan-Ting, 2011), an Application Artificial Bee Colony (AABC) algorithm (Nguyen Tung & Nguyen Quynh, 2010), and so other types are the recent improvement for different mathematic, statistical and engineering problems.

Swarm Intelligence

Since the last two decades, swarm intelligence (SI) has been the focus of many researches because of its unique behaviour inherent from the social insects (Akbari et al., 2009). Bonabeau has defined the SI as "any attempt to design algorithm or distributed problem-solving devices inspired by the collective behaviour of social insect colonies and other animal societies" (Bonabeau et al., 1999). He mainly focused on the behaviour of social insects alone such as termites, bees, wasps, and different ant species. However, swarm can be considered as any collection of interacting agents or individuals. Ants are individual agents of ACO (Dorigo & Di Caro, 1999). An immune system can be considered as a group of cells and molecules as well as a crowd is a swarm of people (Tao, 2008). PSO and ABC are popular population-based stochastic optimization algorithms adapted for the optimization of non-linear functions in multidimensional space (Imran, Manzoor, Ali, & Abbas, 2011; D. Karaboga & Gorkemli, 2011).

Artificial Bee Colony (ABC) Algorithm

Artificial Bee Colony algorithm (ABC) was proposed for optimisation, classification, and NNs problem solution based on the intelligent foraging behaviour of honey bee swarms (D. Karaboga & Akay, 2007; Dervis Karaboga et al., 2007). Therefore, ABC is more successful and most robust on multimodal functions included in the set with respect to DE, modified PSO, and GA (Ashena & Moghadasi, 2011; Imran et al., 2011). ABC algorithm provides solution in organised form by dividing the bee objects into different tasks such as employed bees, onlooker bees, and scout bees. These three bees/tasks determine the objects of problems by sharing information to others bees. The common duties of these artificial bees are as follows.

Employed bees: Employed bees use multidirectional search space for food source with initialization of the area. They get information and all possibilities to find food source and solution space. Sharing of information with onlooker bees is performed by employee bees. An employed bee produces a modification of the source position in her memory and discovers a new food source position. Provided that the nectar amount of the new source is higher than that of the previous source, the employed bee memorizes the new source position and forgets the old one.

Onlooker bees: Onlooker bees evaluate the nectar amount obtained by employed bees and choose a food source depending on the probability values calculated using the fitness values. For this purpose, a fitness-based selection technique can be used. Onlooker bees watch the dance of hive bees and select the best food source according to the probability proportional to the quality of that food source.

Scout bees: Scout bees select the food source randomly without experience. If the nectar amount of a food source is higher than that of the previous source in their memory, they memorize the new position and forget the previous position. Whenever employed bees get a food source and use the food source very well again, they become scout bees to find the new food source by memorising the best path. The detailed pseudo-code of ABC algorithm is shown as follows.

1:   Initialise the population of solutions x_i, where $i = 1, 2, \cdots, SN$.
2:   Evaluate the population.
3:   Cycle=1.
4:   Repeat from step 2 to step 13.
5:   Produce new solutions (food source positions) v_{ij} in the neighbourhood of x_{ij} for the employed bees using the formula

$$v_{ij} = x_{ij} + \varphi_{ij}\left(x_{ij} - x_{kj}\right) \tag{3}$$

where, k is a solution in the neighbourhood of i, φ is a random number in the range $\left[-1,1\right]$ and evaluate them.

6: Apply the Greedy Selection process between process.

7: Calculate the probability values p_i for the solutions x_i by means of their fitness values by using formula

$$p_i = \frac{fit_i}{\displaystyle\sum_{k=1}^{n} fit_k} \tag{4}$$

The calculation of fitness values of solutions is defined as

$$fit_i = \begin{cases} \dfrac{1}{1+fit_i}, & \text{for} \quad f_i \geq 0 \\ 1+\text{abs}\left(fit_i\right), & \text{for } f_i < 0 \end{cases}. \tag{5}$$

Normalise p_i values into $\left[0,1\right]$

8:    Produce the new solutions (new positions) υ_i for the onlookers from the solutions x_i, selected depending on p_i, and evaluate them

$$v_{ij} = x_{ij} + \varphi_{ij}\left(x_{ij} - x_{kj}\right) \tag{6}$$

9:    Apply the Greedy Selection process for the onlookers between x_i and v_i.

10:   Determine the abandoned solution (source), if exists, replace it with a new randomly produced solution x_i for the scout using the following equation

$$x_{ij}^{\text{rand}} = x_{ij}^{\min} + \text{rand}\left(0,1\right)\left(x_{ij}^{\max} - x_{ij}^{\min}\right) \tag{7}$$

11:   Memorise the best food source position (solution) achieved so far
12:   cycle=cycle+1
13:   **until** cycle= Maximum Cycle Number (MCN)

GLOBAL ARTIFICIAL BEE COLONY (GABC) ALGORITHM

The performance of ABC, HABC, PSO-ABC, GABCS and other population-based technique optimal solution depends at the updating technique or neighbour agent information (Peng et al., 2011; H. Shah, R. Ghazali, N. Nawi, & M. Deris, 2012a). In standard ABC algorithm the update process used in the onlooker stage is the same as that in the employed bee stage. The onlookers use their own selection criteria depend on previous information. The equations (3 and 6) are used by employed and onlooker bee. Different techniques used to update the neighbour information equation to get better performance. Population-based optimization algorithms have the necessary properties of exploration and exploitation. In population-based algorithms, the exploration refers to the ability to explore the different unidentified sections through the solution space to discover the global optimum. Furthermore, the exploitation refers to the ability to apply the knowledge of the previous good solutions to find better solution.

The ABC algorithm performance depends on three important equations (3, 6 and 7) which are performed by employed and Onlooker's bees, and the selection condition performed by Scout bees. Here GABC will collect the properties of exploration and exploitation with intelligent behavior of ABC algorithm. The GABC algorithm will update the solution step and will convert to best solution on the basis of neighborhood values. These modified steps will be in employed, Onlooker and Scout Section. Furthermore, in ABC algorithm, the employed bee and onlookers exploit their solutions based on the neighbor information of each individual with intensity of ant technique.

Usually, in bee swarm, the experienced foragers can use previous knowledge of position and nectar quantity of food source to regulate their group directions in the search space. Furthermore, in social insect's technique the best food can be finding through experience or neighbor cooperation. So GABC agents employed, scout and onlookers can be improved by their best food source. The GABC approach will merge their best finding approaches in standard ABC by the following steps. The GABC will merge their best finding approaches with original ABC by the following steps.

Step 1: It modifies the employed section as

$$v_{ij} = x_{ij} + \varphi_{ij}\left(x_{ij} - x_{kj}\right) + y \tag{8}$$

$$y = c_1 \text{rand}\left(0,1\right)\left(x_j^{\text{best}} - x_{ij}\right) + c_2 \text{rand}\left(0,1\right)\left(y_j^{\text{best}} - x_{ij}\right) \tag{9}$$

Step 2: Repeat the above formula with onlookers section.

where y shows Best_Food_Source, C_1 and C_2 are two constant values which is C_1 is 2.5 and C_2 is -3.5 for this study, x_j^{best} is the j-th element of the global best solution found so far, y_j^{best} is the j-th element of the best solution in the current iteration, φ_{ij} is a uniformly distributed real random number in the range $\left[-1,1\right]$.

Step 3: Modified the scout section as

$$x_{ij}^{rand} = x_{ij}^{min} + \text{rand}(0,1)\left(x_{ij}^{max} - x_{ij}^{min}\right) \tag{10}$$

If $\text{rand}(0,1) \leq 0.5$, then

$$x_{ij}^{mutation} = x_{ij} + \text{rand}(0,1)\left(1 - \frac{iter}{iter_{max}}\right)^b + \left(x_j^{best} - x_{ij}\right) \tag{11}$$

Ελσε

$$x_{ij}^{mutation} = x_{ij} + \text{rand}(0,1)\left(1 - \frac{iter}{iter_{max}}\right)^b + \left(y_j^{best} - x_{ij}\right) \tag{12}$$

Then comparing the fitness value of random generated solution x_{ij}^{rand} and mutation solution $x_{ij}^{mutation}$ the better one is chosen as a new food source, where b is a scaling parameter which is a positive integer within the range of [2,5].

LEVENBERQ–MARQUARDT LEARNING ALGORITHM

The Levenberq–Marquardt learning algorithm which was separately developed by Kenneth Levenberq and Donald Marquardt provides a numerical solution to the problem of minimizing a nonlinear function. It is speedy and has established convergence (Levenberg, 1944). LM algorithm was designed to approach second-order training speed without having to compute the Hessian matrix (Moré, 1978). In the ANN field, this algorithm is suitable for training small- and medium-sized problems only.

Fortunately, it inherits the speed advantage of the Gauss–Newton algorithm and the stability property of the steepest descent technique. It's more robust than the Gauss–Newton algorithm, because in many cases, it can converge well even if the error surface is much more complex than the quadratic situation (Ngia & Sjoberg, 2000). Although the LM algorithm tends to be a bit slower than Gauss–Newton algorithm (in convergent situation), it converges much faster than the steepest descent method. The basic idea of the LM algorithm is that it performs a combined training process: around the area with complex curvature, the LM algorithm switches to the steepest descent algorithm, until the local curvature is proper to make a quadratic approximation; then it approximately becomes the Gauss–Newton algorithm, which can speed up the convergence significantly (Yu & Wilamowski, 2010).

The LM is one of the most efficient algorithms, which successfully solves the problems existing in both gradient descent technique and Gauss-Newton method for training NN. However, the drawback of LM algorithm is the calculation of the Husseini Matrix inversion process needs to be calculated each time for updating weights and there will be several updates needs in iteration. The LM algorithm has good performance using small size network training, but it may be failed in large problem's solutions such as an image recognition problem due to the several inversion calculations in single iteration. This can make LM algorithm slowly. Furthermore, for large size training the Jacobi matrix has to be stored for computation process, which needs big memory size, which is leading to huge cost.

THE PROPOSED GLOBA L ARTIFICIAL BEE COLONY-LEVENBERQ-MARQUARDT

The GABC algorithm has a global ability to find global optimistic result and the LM algorithm (Habib Shah et al., 2012a) has a strong ability to find local optimistic result. Combining the step of GABC with LM, a new hybrid algorithm is proposed in this article for training NN. The key point of this hybrid GABC-LM algorithm is that the GABC is used at the initial stage of searching for the optimum using global best methods, Then, the training process is continued with the LM algorithm (Peng et al., 2011). The LM algorithm interpolates between the Newton method and gradient descent method where it approximates the error of the network with a second order expression. The flow-diagram of the ABC-LM model is shown in Figure 3. In the initial stage, ABC algorithm finishes its training, then, LM algorithm starts training with the weights of ABC algorithm and then LM trains the network for 100 epochs more.

SIMULATION RESULTS AND DISCUSSION

In this work, swarms intelligent-based combine technique based on GABC-LM algorithm is used to train feed-forward artificial neural networks. In order to calculate the performance of the GABC-LM with ABC and LM algorithms in terms of Mean Square Error (MSE), Standard Deviation (S.D) of Mean Square Error and success rate using boolean function for classification, where simulation experiments performed by Matlab 2010a software.

Figure 3. GABC-LM algorithm flow diagram

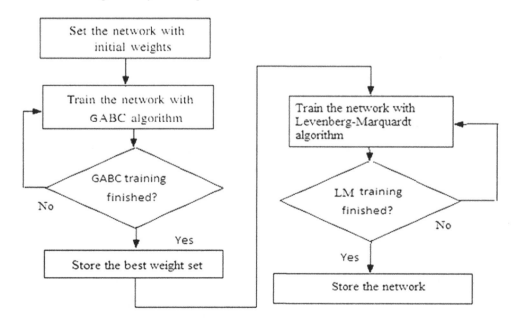

The stopping criteria minimum error is set to 0.0001 LM while ABC and GABC-LM stopped on MCN with 100 epochs. During the experimentation, 10 trials were performed for training. The sigmoid function is used as activation function for network output. During the simulation, when the number of inputs, hidden and output nodes of the NNs and running time varies, the performance of training algorithms were stable, which is important for the designation of NNs in the current state. The value of c_1 and c_2 were selected 2.5 and -3.5 respectively. From the simulation experiment, the GABC-LM performance can be affected by c_1 and c_2. So the best values selected for these two constant values.

From table 1, the 2-2-1 NNs structure for XOR6 has six parameters including weights and without bias. The colony range is [100,-100] with 7500 MCN and dimension 6. The XOR9 problem has the same NNs structure included three biases with colony size [10,-10], where MCN and D are 100 and 9 respectively. The NNs 2-3-1+4 (bias) is set with MCN 75 and D 13 for the XOR13 classification task. The NNs 3-3-1+4 (bias) is set with MCN 1000 and D 16 for 3-bit parity problem with parameter [10,-10].

The 4-bit encoder/decoder problem was defined for 4-2-4 NNs shape with dimension 22, where 1000 MCN. The simulation runs thirty times with randomly foods while the above information from table 4 is used for training NNs. The average of MSE for training NNs by the GABC-LM, ABC and LM algorithms are shown in table 1. Table 2 shows the Mean S.D of ABC, LM, GABC and GABC-LM algorithms. The success rate of ABC, GABC, GABC-LM and LM algorithms are given in table 4.

The testing Mean Square Error for XOR6, XOR9, XOR13, 3-bit Parity and 4-bit encoder/decoder are 0.000421, 1.01E-09, 2.11E-09, 4.12E-07 and 1.10E-06 respectfully using GABC-LM algorithm.

Table 1. Parameters of the problems considered in the experiments. D: a dimension of the problem, MCN: maximum cycle numbers, nns structure.

Problem	Colony Range	NN Structure	D	MCN	Epoch
XOR6	[100,-100]	2-2-1	6	7500	32000
XOR9	[10,-10]	2-2-1+ Bias(3)	9	100	500
XOR13	[-10,10]	2-3-1+ Bias(4)	13	75	250
3-Bit	[-10,10]	3-3-1+bias(4)	16	1000	1600
Enc/Dec	[10,-10]	4-2-4+Bias(6)	22	1000	2100

Table 2. Average of Mean Square Error using ABC,LM,GABC,GABC-LM algorithms

Problems\ Methods	PSO	ABC	LM	GABC	GABC-LM
XOR6	0.097255	0.007051	0.1107	0.12076	0.000641
XOR9	0.057676	0.006956	0.0491	0.000106	1.12E-09
XOR13	0.014549	0.006079	0.0078	0.000692	2.21E-09
3-Bit Parity	0.040365	0.006679	0.0209	0.00062	5.12E-07
4-bit End/Dec	0.022389	0.008191	0.0243	0.000294	1.10E-06

Table 3. Average of Mean of Standard Deviation using ABC,LM,GABC,GABC-LM algorithms

Problems\ Methods	PSO	ABC	LM	GABC	GABC-LM
XOR6	0.027367	0.00223	0.0637	0.014712	0.000940
XOR9	0.06153	0.002402	0.0646	0.003447	1.91E-10
XOR13	0.024627	0.003182	0.0223	0.00087	1.13E-09
3-Bit Parity	0.049018	0.00282	0.043	0.00156	2.12E-06
4 bit Enc/De	0.031639	0.001864	0.0424	0.00018	6.44E-07

Table 4. Success rate of ABC, LM, GABC and GABC-LM algorithm

Problems \ Methods	PSO	ABC	LM	GABC	GABC-LM
XOR6	59	100	60.12	100	**100**
XOR9	60	100	66.66	100	**100**
XOR13	63	100	96.66	100	**100**
3-Bit Parity	93	100	73.33	100	**100**
4-bit Enc/Dec	80	100	73.33	100	**100**

CONCLUSION

The GABC-LM algorithm collects the exploration and exploitation processes successfully, which proves the high performance of training MLP. It has the powerful ability of searching global optimal solution. So, the proper weights of the MLP may speed up the initialisation and improve the classification accuracy of the trained NNs. The simulation results show that the proposed GABC-LM algorithm can successfully train Boolean data for classification purpose, which further extends the quality of the given approach. The performance of GABC-LM is compared with the traditional LM, PSO, DE and ABC algorithms. GABC-LM shows significantly higher results than LM, PSO, DE and ABC algorithms during experiment. GABC-LM also shows higher accuracy in classification. The proposed frameworks have successfully classified the XOR6, XOR9, XOR13, 3-bit Parity and 4-bit encoder/decoder classification problems.

ACKNOWLEDGMENT

The authors would like to thank King Khalid University of Saudi Arabia for supporting this research under the grant number R.G.P.2/7/38.

REFERENCES

Akbari, R., Mohammadi, A., & Ziarati, K. (2009, 14-15 Dec. 2009). *A powerful bee swarm optimization algorithm.* Paper presented at the Multitopic Conference, 2009. INMIC 2009. IEEE 13th International.

Ashena, R., & Moghadasi, J. (2011). Bottom hole pressure estimation using evolved neural networks by real coded ant colony optimization and genetic algorithm. *Journal of Petroleum Science Engineering, 77*(3–4), 375–385. doi:10.1016/j.petrol.2011.04.015

Aussem, A., Murtagh, F., & Sarazin, M. (1994). Dynamical recurrent neural networks and pattern recognition methods for time series prediction: Application to seeing and temperature forecasting in the context of ESO's VLT astronomical weather station. *Vistas in Astronomy, 38*, 357-374.

Aydin, M. E., Wu, J., & Liang, Z. (2010). *Swarms of Metaheuristic Agents: A Model for Collective intelligence.* Paper presented at the P2P, Parallel, Grid, Cloud and Internet Computing (3PGCIC), 2010 International Conference on.

Bäck, T. (1996). *Evolutionary Algorithms in Theory and Practice: Evolution Strategies, Evolutionary Programming, Genetic Algorithms.* New York: Oxford University Press.

Bakhta, M., & Ghalem, B. (2014). Clustering by Swarm Intelligence in the Ad-Hoc Networks. *International Journal of Applied Evolutionary Computation, 5*(3), 1–13. doi:10.4018/ijaec.2014070101

Behnam, Z., & Isa, M. (2013). A New Radial Basis Function Artificial Neural Network based Recognition for Kurdish Manuscript. *International Journal of Applied Evolutionary Computation, 4*(4), 72–87. doi:10.4018/ijaec.2013100105

Bonabeau, E., Dorigo, M., & Theraulaz, G. (1999). *Swarm Intelligence: From Natural to Artificial Systems.* Oxford University Press.

Ch. Sanjeev Kumar, D., Ajit Kumar, B., Satchidananda, D., & Sung-Bae, C. (2013). Differential Evolution-Based Optimization of Kernel Parameters in Radial Basis Function Networks for Classification. *International Journal of Applied Evolutionary Computation, 4*(1), 56–80. doi:10.4018/jaec.2013010104

Chakravarty, S., Bisoi, R., & Dash, P. K. (2016). A Hybrid Kernel Extreme Learning Machine and Improved Cat Swarm Optimization for Microarray Medical Data Classification. *International Journal of Applied Evolutionary Computation, 7*(3), 71–100. doi:10.4018/IJAEC.2016070104

Chakravarty, S., Dash, P. K., Pandi, V. R., & Panigrahi, B. K. (2011). An Evolutionary Functional Link Neural Fuzzy Model for Financial Time Series Forecasting. *International Journal of Applied Evolutionary Computation, 2*(3), 39–58. doi:10.4018/jaec.2011070104

Charalampidis, D., & Muldrey, B. (2009). Clustering using multilayer perceptrons. *Nonlinear Analysis: Theory, Methods & Applications, 71*(12), e2807–e2813.

Chen, C., Duan, S., Cai, T., & Liu, B. (2011). Online 24-h solar power forecasting based on weather type classification using artificial neural network. *Solar Energy, 85*(11), 2856–2870. doi:10.1016/j.solener.2011.08.027

Chengzhi, C., Yifan, W., Lichao, J., & Yang, L. (2008). *Research on optimization of speed identification based on ACO-BP neural network and application.* Paper presented at the Intelligent Control and Automation, 2008. WCICA 2008. 7th World Congress on.

Davidović, T., Šelmić, M., Teodorović, D., & Ramljak, D. (n.d.). Bee colony optimization for scheduling independent tasks to identical processors. *Journal of Heuristics,* 1-21. doi:10.100710732-012-9197-3

Dorigo, M., & Di Caro, G. (1999). Ant colony optimization: a new meta-heuristic. *Evolutionary Computation, 1999. CEC 99. Proceedings of the 1999 Congress on.*

Eberhart, R. C., & Shi, Y. J. K. (2001). Swarm Intelligence. Morgan Kaufmann.

Geretti, L., & Abramo, A. (2011). The Synthesis of a Stochastic Artificial Neural Network Application Using a Genetic Algorithm Approach. In W. H. Peter (Ed.), Advances in Imaging and Electron Physics (Vol. 168, pp. 1-63). Elsevier.

Ghazali, R., Jaafar Hussain, A., Mohd Nawi, N., & Mohamad, B. (2009). Non-stationary and stationary prediction of financial time series using dynamic ridge polynomial neural network. *Neurocomputing, 72*(10–12), 2359–2367. doi:10.1016/j.neucom.2008.12.005

Gori, M., & Tesi, A. (1992). On the problem of local minima in backpropagation. *Pattern Analysis and Machine Intelligence. IEEE Transactions on, 14*(1), 76–86. doi:10.1109/34.107014

Halima, D., Abdesslem, L., & Salim, C. (2014). A Binary Cuckoo Search Algorithm for Graph Coloring Problem. *International Journal of Applied Evolutionary Computation, 5*(3), 42–56. doi:10.4018/ijaec.2014070103

Harish, S., Jagdish Chand, B., Arya, K. V., & Kusum, D. (2012). Dynamic Swarm Artificial Bee Colony Algorithm. *International Journal of Applied Evolutionary Computation, 3*(4), 19–33. doi:10.4018/jaec.2012100102

Hilas, C. S., & Mastorocostas, P. A. (2008). An application of supervised and unsupervised learning approaches to telecommunications fraud detection. *Knowledge-Based Systems, 21*(7), 721–726. doi:10.1016/j.knosys.2008.03.026

Hongwen, Y., & Rui, M. (2006). *Design A Novel Neural Network Clustering Algorithm Based on PSO and Application.* Paper presented at the Intelligent Control and Automation, 2006. WCICA 2006. The Sixth World Congress on.

Hornik, K., Stinchcombe, M., & White, H. (1989). Multilayer feedforward networks are universal approximators. *Neural Networks, 2*(5), 359–366. doi:10.1016/0893-6080(89)90020-8

Imran, M., Manzoor, Z., Ali, S., & Abbas, Q. (2011). *Modified Particle Swarm Optimization with student T mutation (STPSO).* Paper presented at the Computer Networks and Information Technology (ICCNIT), 2011 International Conference on.

Kacem, I., & Haouari, M. (2009). Approximation algorithms for single machine scheduling with one unavailability period. *4OR: A Quarterly Journal of Operations Research, 7*(1), 79-92. doi:10.100710288-008-0076-6

Karaboga, D., & Akay, B. (2007). *Artificial Bee Colony (ABC) Algorithm on Training Artificial Neural Networks.* Paper presented at the Signal Processing and Communications Applications, 2007. SIU 2007. IEEE 15th.

Karaboga, D., Akay, B., & Ozturk, C. (2007). Artificial Bee Colony (ABC) Optimization Algorithm for Training Feed-Forward Neural Networks Modeling Decisions for Artificial Intelligence. Springer Berlin.

Karaboga, D., & Gorkemli, B. (2011). *A combinatorial Artificial Bee Colony algorithm for traveling salesman problem*. Paper presented at the Innovations in Intelligent Systems and Applications (INISTA), 2011 International Symposium on.

Kennedy, J., & Eberhart, R. (1995). Particle swarm optimization. *Neural Networks, 1995. Proceedings., IEEE International Conference on*.

Levenberg, K. (1944). A method for the solution of certain problems in least squares. *Quarterly of Applied Mathematics*, 2(2), 164–168. doi:10.1090/qam/10666

Moré, J. (1978). *The Levenberg-Marquardt algorithm: Implementation and theory numerical analysis*. Springer.

Narasimhan, H. (2009). *Parallel artificial bee colony (PABC) algorithm*. Paper presented at the Nature & Biologically Inspired Computing, 2009. NaBIC 2009. World Congress on.

Nawi, N. M., Ransing, M. R., & Ransing, R. S. (2006). *An Improved Learning Algorithm Based on The Broyden-Fletcher-Goldfarb-Shanno (BFGS) Method For Back Propagation Neural Networks*. Paper presented at the Intelligent Systems Design and Applications, 2006. ISDA '06. Sixth International Conference on.

Ngia, L. S. H., & Sjoberg, J. (2000). Efficient training of neural nets for nonlinear adaptive filtering using a recursive Levenberg-Marquardt algorithm. *Signal Processing. IEEE Transactions on*, 48(7), 1915–1927. doi:10.1109/78.847778

Nguyen Tung, L., & Nguyen Quynh, A. (2010). *Application Artificial Bee Colony Algorithm (ABC) for Reconfiguring Distribution Network*. Paper presented at the Computer Modeling and Simulation, 2010. ICCMS '10. Second International Conference on.

Ozturk, C., & Karaboga, D. (2011). *Hybrid Artificial Bee Colony algorithm for neural network training*. Paper presented at the Evolutionary Computation (CEC), 2011 IEEE Congress on.

Peng, G., Wenming, C., & Jian, L. (2011). *Global artificial bee colony search algorithm for numerical function optimization*. Paper presented at the Natural Computation (ICNC), 2011 Seventh International Conference on.

Rajashree, D., & Pradipta Kishore, D. (2016). Prediction of Financial Time Series Data using Hybrid Evolutionary Legendre Neural Network: Evolutionary LENN. *International Journal of Applied Evolutionary Computation*, 7(1), 16–32. doi:10.4018/IJAEC.2016010102

Ramakanta, M., Ravi, V., & Patra, M. R. (2010). Application of Machine Learning Techniques to Predict Software Reliability. *International Journal of Applied Evolutionary Computation*, 1(3), 70–86. doi:10.4018/jaec.2010070104

Rao, B. T., Satchidananda, D., & Rajib, M. (2012). Functional Link Artificial Neural Networks for Software Cost Estimation. *International Journal of Applied Evolutionary Computation*, 3(2), 62–82. doi:10.4018/jaec.2012040104

Rathipriya, R., Thangavel, K., & Bagyamani, J. (2011). Usage Profile Generation from Web Usage Data Using Hybrid Biclustering Algorithm. *International Journal of Applied Evolutionary Computation, 2*(4), 37–49. doi:10.4018/jaec.2011100103

Rosenblatt, F. (1958). The Perceptron: A probabilistic model for information storage and organization in the brain. *Psychological Review, 65*(6), 386–408. doi:10.1037/h0042519 PMID:13602029

Rumelhart, D. E., McClelland, J. L., & University of California, S. D. P. R. G. (1986). *Parallel distributed processing: Psychological and biological models.* MIT Press.

Sayad, S. (2010). *Artificial Neural Network.* Retrieved from http://www.saedsayad.com/data_mining_map.htm

SHah., H., Ghazali, R., Nawi, N. M., & Deris, M. M. (2012b). *Global Hybrid Ant Bee Colony Algorithm for Training Artificial Neural Networks.* Paper presented at the International Conference on Computational Science and Applications, Alvador de Bahia, Brazil.

Shah, H., & Ghazali, R. (2011). *Prediction of Earthquake Magnitude by an Improved ABC-MLP.* Paper presented at the Developments in E-systems Engineering (DeSE). 10.1109/DeSE.2011.37

Shah, H., Ghazali, R., Nawi, N., & Deris, M. (2012a). Global Hybrid Ant Bee Colony Algorithm for Training Artificial Neural Networks Computational Science and Its Applications – ICCSA 2012. Springer.

Shah, H., Tairan, N., Mashwani, W. K., Al-Sewari, A. A., Jan, M. A., & Badshah, G. (2017). Hybrid Global Crossover Bees Algorithm for Solving Boolean Function Classification Task. Cham: Academic Press. doi:10.1007/978-3-319-63315-2_41

Sharma, T. K., Pant, M., & Bhardwaj, T. (2011). *PSO ingrained Artificial Bee Colony algorithm for solving continuous optimization problems.* Paper presented at the Computer Applications and Industrial Electronics (ICCAIE), 2011 IEEE International Conference on.

Slowik, A., & Bialko, M. (2008). *Training of artificial neural networks using differential evolution algorithm.* Paper presented at the Human System Interactions, 2008 Conference on.

Suruchi, C. (2016). Application of Genetic Algorithm and Back Propagation Neural Network for Effective Personalize Web Search-Based on Clustered Query Sessions. *International Journal of Applied Evolutionary Computation, 7*(1), 33–49. doi:10.4018/IJAEC.2016010103

Tao, G. (2008). *Artificial immune system based on normal model and immune learning.* Paper presented at the Systems, Man and Cybernetics, 2008. SMC 2008. IEEE International Conference on.

Tarun Kumar, S., & Millie, P. (2011). Differential Operators Embedded Artificial Bee Colony Algorithm. *International Journal of Applied Evolutionary Computation, 2*(3), 1–14. doi:10.4018/jaec.2011070101

Teodorovic, D., Lucic, P., Markovic, G., & Orco, M. D. (2006). *Bee Colony Optimization: Principles and Applications.* Paper presented at the Neural Network Applications in Electrical Engineering, 2006. NEUREL 2006. 8th Seminar on.

Vazquez, R. A. (2011). *Training spiking neural models using cuckoo search algorithm.* Paper presented at the Evolutionary Computation (CEC), 2011 IEEE Congress on.

Wali Khan, M. (2013). Comprehensive Survey of the Hybrid Evolutionary Algorithms. *International Journal of Applied Evolutionary Computation, 4*(2), 1–19. doi:10.4018/jaec.2013040101

Wei-Ping, L., & Wan-Ting, C. (2011). *A novel artificial bee colony algorithm with diversity strategy.* Paper presented at the Natural Computation (ICNC), 2011 Seventh International Conference on.

Xin-She, Y., & Deb, S. (2009). *Cuckoo Search via Lévy flights.* Paper presented at the Nature & Biologically Inspired Computing, 2009. NaBIC 2009. World Congress on.

Xinyan, G., & Jianguo, Z. (2011). *Multi-agent based hybrid evolutionary algorithm.* Paper presented at the Natural Computation (ICNC), 2011 Seventh International Conference on.

Yan-fei, Z., & Xiong-min, T. (2010). *Overview of swarm intelligence.* Paper presented at the Computer Application and System Modeling (ICCASM), 2010 International Conference on.

Yu, H., & Wilamowski, B. M. (2010). Levenberg Marquardt Training (2nd ed.). CRC Press.

Yu-Yan, H., Jun-Hua, D., & Min, Z. (2011). *Apply the discrete artificial bee colony algorithm to the blocking flow shop problem with makespan criterion.* Paper presented at the Control and Decision Conference (CCDC), 2011 Chinese.

Zhang, D., Guan, X., Tang, Y., & Tang, Y. (2011). *Modified Artificial Bee Colony Algorithms for Numerical Optimization.* Paper presented at the Intelligent Systems and Applications (ISA), 2011 3rd International Workshop on.

Chapter 9
Guided Search-Based Multi-Objective Evolutionary Algorithm for Grid Workflow Scheduling

Ritu Garg
National Institute of Technology Kurukshetra, India

ABSTRACT

The computational grid provides the global computing infrastructure for users to access the services over a network. However, grid service providers charge users for the services based on their usage and QoS level specified. Therefore, in order to optimize the grid workflow execution, a robust multi-objective scheduling algorithm is needed considering economic cost along with execution performance. Generally, in multi-objective problems, simulations rely on running large number of evaluations to obtain the accurate results. However, algorithms that consider the preferences of decision maker, convergence to optimal tradeoff solutions is faster. Thus, in this chapter, the author proposed the preference-based guided search mechanism into MOEAs. To obtain solutions near the pre-specified regions of interest, the author has considered two MOEAs, namely R-NSGA-II and R-ε-MOEA. Further, to improve the diversity of solutions, a modified form called M-R-NSGA-II is used. Finally, the experimental settings and performance metrics are presented for the evaluation of the algorithms.

INTRODUCTION

Real world optimization problems very often involve multiple objectives that have to considered simultaneously. The applications scheduling problem in computational grid environment often requires multiple objectives to be considered like makespan, economic cost, reliability etc. (Topcuoglu, Hariri, & Wu, 2002; Kumar, Dutta, & Mookerjee, 2009). As in many real world multi objective problems (MOP), it is obvious that these objectives are conflicting in nature and it is very difficult to handle number of conflicting objectives at the same time. Since enhancement in one objective may cause the deterioration

DOI: 10.4018/978-1-5225-5832-3.ch009

in another and no solution exist that is best with respect to all the objectives; rather every solution is a tradeoff among the identified objectives. There are mainly two methods to find out the tradeoff: weighted sum method and Pareto optimal method. The MOPs are generally solved by priori approaches which basically transform the multiple objectives into single objecting or weighted sum function. In weighted sum method, each objective function is linked with a weighting coefficient and then minimization of weighted sum of all the objectives is performed in order to obtain the single preferred solution. However, this is usually not applicable if the decision maker (DM) does not explicitly know how to weight the different objectives before the optimal alternatives are known. At the same time, it is difficult to estimate the weights, as small change in weights may change the solution drastically.

On the other hand, in posteriori approaches, the aim is to find the set of Pareto optimal solutions. Subsequently, the set of Pareto optimal solutions are passed to user\DM that makes a single choice according to his/her preferences, which is also called as posteriori articulation of preferences. A good Pareto optimal front (POF) must provide convergence (solutions close to optimal) as well as diversity (uniformly cover all possible ranges of optimal solutions) Usually, the Pareto optimal solutions are preferred over single solution in the real life applications. However, it becomes a critical issue if the optimization process involves computationally expensive function evaluations corresponding to large scale complex problems.

In order to reduce the total number of evaluations for faster convergence towards the efficient POF, a guided search that takes into account the user/DM preferences or reference points (RP) during optimization seems to be promising. In reference point approach, DM requires to specify reference points\ preferences in terms of aspiration and reservation levels for all objective functions. Moreover, the user may have some specific preferences for the solution or they may be having the rough idea about what he/she would prefer. Thus, in this case, instead of providing Pareto optimal front in the entire solution space, it is preferable to provide Pareto solutions close to user\DM preferences, which is also called prior articulation of preferences. Further, RP approach makes it possible to find Pareto optimal solutions corresponding to multiple preferences simultaneously. Additionally, RP based approaches are applicable to MOPs with large number of objectives because preference relation gives a finer order of vectors of objective space in comparison to Pareto dominance relation. With this motivation, several algorithms with the focus to search towards the reference areas in objective space have been proposed. Some applications using RP based evolutionary multi objective optimization particularly R-NSGA-II are logistic network design (Cheshmehgaz, Islam, & Desa, 2014) reversible logic circuit design (Wang, 2014) and workflow scheduling in cloud (Verma & Buyya, 2005) etc.

Application Workflows in Grid

Grid computing is a novel paradigm that provides the global computing infrastructure for users to access the services over a network. The term Grid is analogous to an electric power grid that provides consistent, pervasive, dependable and transparent access to electricity irrespective of its source. Grid computing is a variant of parallel and distributed computing that involves the integrated and collaborative use of wide range of heterogeneous and distributed resources for executing large-scale computing applications. The resources may include expensive computational systems, high-speed networks, storage devices, databases, scientific instruments, softwares etc. owned and managed by different organizations. However, in order to meet the computational requirements of large and diverse groups of users, the grid computing systems need to address various challenging issues that are inherent to the grid environment.

Some of these issues are heterogeneity, site autonomy, scalability, adaptability, co-allocation, quality of service (QoS) and meeting computational constraints.

Further, in order to support the efficient execution of grid applications, the application scheduling is of prime concern. Due to variations in administrative policies, heterogeneity in resources and diversity in user requirements, the application scheduling becomes more cumbersome. Most of the scheduling algorithms proposed for conventional parallel and distributed computing systems are in general applicable to homogeneous and dedicated resources. Therefore, they are not suitable to heterogeneous and dynamic grid computing systems.

To date, most grid applications lie in scientific and business domain where complex applications are modeled as workflows (Yu & Byya, 2005). As per Workflow Management Coalition (WfMC), workflows are defined as "The automation of a business process, in whole or part, during which files, information or tasks are passed from one to other participant for action, as per the predefined rules" (Hollingsworth, 1994).

The workflows are normally described as the set of tasks to be processed in a well-defined order. It is expressed as an automation of processes or tasks coordinated by control and data dependencies, in order to achieve an overall goal. The dependency refers to the existence of precedence relationship among the tasks i.e. execution of a task cannot be initiated until all its parents are done. There are many grid applications like WIEN2k- a quantum chemistry application (Blaha et al., 2001), Invmod- a hydrological application (Theiner, & Rutschmann, 2005), GriPhyN- a physics application, Montage- for astronomy (Montage, n.d.), LEAD- a meteorological analysis and weather forecasting application, which uses workflow technology to carry out large-scale experiments.

Due to the growing popularity of workflow technology in grid applications, many workflow management system projects have been designed and developed, for instance GridFlow (Cao et al., 2003), DAGMan (Tannenbaum et al., 2001), GrAds (Berman et al., 2005), Pegasus (Deelman et al., 2003), Askalon (Fahringer et al., 2005), Taverna (Oinn et al., 2004) etc. that manage and execute the workflow applications on computational resources. In order to execute the scientific workflows in grid, an efficient mapping (or scheduling) of workflow tasks on distributed grid resources is essential.

Workflow Scheduling

The scheduling of workflow applications in grid environment is a process that maps and manages the execution of interdependent tasks on the available grid resources while preserving task dependencies and meeting data transfer requirements. It allocates appropriate resources to workflow tasks so that the execution can be accomplished while satisfying the user-defined objectives. The scheduling of workflow applications lie in the category of NP-hard problems (Ullman, 1975) and therefore no known algorithm exists that are able to provide optimal solution within polynomial time complexity. Thus, researchers have used heuristics or meta-heuristics approaches in order to cope with the complexity and to obtain optimal or near optimal solutions. The heuristics are used often to improve efficiency or effectiveness of the optimization algorithms. It provides an approximate solution with small computation overhead. Alternatively, the meta-heuristics try to improve the candidate solution iteratively with respect to given quality measure. They make few or no assumptions about the problem that is to be optimized and searches the near optimal solution from large space of candidate solutions.

Workflow Scheduling as MOP

The scheduling of workflow applications in grid is one of the challenging issues. Depending upon the user demands and objective functions, several issues arise such as minimization of makespan, total economic cost etc. Many list heuristics have been devoted to this problem typically restricted to optimizing single objective, namely minimizing execution time (makespan) (Braun et al., 2001; Blythe et al., 2005) or total cost (Yu, Buyya, & Tham, 2005). Some isolated algorithms try to optimize across two criteria. A linear programming-based technique is proposed (Wieczorek et al., 2008) that considers one objective at a time. It provides a single solution to the user, but fails to produce the tradeoff front.

Recently, the research focus has shifted towards managing multiple objectives simultaneously. Mostly, the research on multi-objective grid scheduling problems, as in Talukder, Kirley, & Buyya (2009) and Izakiam et al. (2009), linearly combine the different objectives into a scalar cost function using the weight factors, which convert the problem into a single objective problem prior to optimization. It produces only a single solution. The weight selection method being abstract and empirical, in general, it is very difficult to accurately select these weights, as small perturbations in weights leads to different solutions. However, in multi-dimensional parameter space, it is not possible to find a single solution that simultaneously optimizes all the objectives; hence, the algorithm, which gives number of alternative solutions lying close to the Pareto optimal front (deb, 2011) (explained in section 4) is of great practical value. Further, in order to generate the Pareto optimal solutions through the aforementioned approaches, multiple runs of the algorithm are needed to be executed after varying the weights, which requires considerably large time. We proposed the use of multi-objective optimization approach to generate Pareto optimal solutions for grid workflow (dependent tasks) scheduling.

Although there are advantages of finding Pareto optimal front with complete range of each objective, but this makes it difficult for the decision maker (DM) to select the final solution as per his/her preference. So far, in literature little interest has been paid to choose the final solution from the set of Pareto optimal solutions. Further, the DM is perhaps only interested in few Pareto optimal solutions as per his\ her preference. For example, the financial institution Morgan Stanley, which is a user community having various branches. Each branch has a specific computational time and cost requirements that needs to be satisfied by resources in the grid. Thus, in the light of requirements submitted by user/DM, all Pareto optimal solutions may not be of interest and therefore all Pareto optimal solutions need not be generated.

Hence, in this chapter, we have generated the preferred set of solutions for the DM near his/her region(s) of interest that is specified as reference point(s). During simulation experiments, we can accommodate all reference points proposed by various users in single simulation run. Towards this goal, we have applied two evolutionary algorithms considering the two objectives makespan and economic cost that are conflicting in nature. The first one is an existing algorithm proposed by Deb et al. (2006) popularly called, reference point based non-dominated sort genetic algorithm (R-NSGA-II) and the second one is our algorithm which is a reference point based variant of ε-MOEA (Deb, Mohan, & Mishra, 2003) that we have named as R-ε-MOEA. Further, to improve the diversity of the solutions, we proposed the modified version of R-NSGA-II (called M-R-NSGA-II, henceforth) to solve the problem of workflow scheduling.

The rest of the chapter is organized as follows. Section 3 describes the related work. In Section 4, we briefly introduced the approach of multi-objective optimization. Thereafter, section 5 specifies the description of problem by illustrating the resource model and workflow application model considered. In section 6, we explained the reference point based non-dominated sort genetic algorithm (R-NSGA-II) and reference point based variant of ε-MOEA (R-ε-MOEA) algorithm. Section 7 describes the implementation of considered MOEAs for workflow scheduling. Then section 8 discusses the simulation and result analysis and finally section 9 concludes the chapter with the summary of contributions.

RELATED WORK

Many heuristics have been developed in the past for workflow scheduling in grid. Most of the classical optimization algorithms consider minimization of execution time, opportunistic load balance, minimization of cost etc. as reported in (Braun et al., 2001; Blythe et al., 2005). However, these works only attempt to minimize the single objective.

The case where multiple objectives are considered, usually they are either converted to a *constrained single objective problem* or modeled as a *weighted single objective problem*. The solution proposed by Tsiakkouri et al. (2005) addresses a similar problem of bi-criteria budget-constrained workflow scheduling. They converted the problem into single objective problem i.e. minimization of makespan only and the second criteria (budget) is considered as constraint. The algorithm works in two-phases. The first phase optimizes the schedule for a single criterion (makespan) only; the second phase produces the final solution for both criteria, keeping the budget within the defined constraint. A guided local optimization approach is applied to transform the intermediate solution to the final solution. Further, Smith, Siegel, and Maciejewski, (2008) proposed robust static scheduling algorithm for distributed computing systems based on the specified quality of service (QoS) constraints. Work in Wieczorek et al. (2008) proposed a new bi-criterion workflow-scheduling algorithm that performs optimization based on a flexible sliding constraint, and they apply a dynamic programming method to the entire workflow to enable an extensive exploration of the search space within the optimization process. Here the importance is given to primary objective while the second objective is considered as a constraint. Thus, we are able to get single solution that optimizes one objective only while meeting the other objective as a constraint.

Further, the work presented in Yu and Buyya (2006) proposes workflow scheduling for utility grids using weighted sum method. The solution is provided by introducing the genetic algorithm approach for constraint-based bi-criteria scheduling. By applying weighted sum to both objectives, the problem actually gets converted into single objective problem and we are able to get single solution.

However, in multi-objective optimization problem with conflicting objectives, user may need range of solutions rather than single solution. For example, user may prefer solution with higher value of execution time but with large savings in cost or vice versa. Thus, we need to generate the trade-off optimal solutions or non-dominated solutions, known as the Pareto optimal front. Research work by Yu, Kirley, & Buyya (2007) proposed evolutionary algorithms namely NSGA-II, SPEA and PAES for multi-criteria workflow scheduling. The presented algorithms aim at providing a set of alternative solutions (a Pareto set) rather than a single solution. Talukder, Kirley, & Buyya, (2009) proposed multi-objective differential evolution (MODE) for workflow scheduling with the aim to generate a set of trade-off solutions within the user specified constraints, which will offer more choices to user while estimating QoS requirements. The set of Pareto optimal solutions are then passed to user/DM, who then use his/her QoS requirements to make a single choice.

Moreover, user may have some specific preferences for the solution. For example, he/she may have some specific computational time and cost requirements. Thus, instead of providing Pareto optimal front in the entire solution space, it is beneficial to provide Pareto solutions close to his/her preference. With this motivation, we have proposed the multi-objective workflow-scheduling problem that satisfies the users preferences (given in terms of reference points) within the QoS constraints using the Referenced Point based NSGA-II (R-NSGA-II) and Reference point based variant of ε-MOEA (R-ε-MOEA) approaches. Using these approaches, we are able to get Pareto optimal solutions in the user specified region rather than the Pareto front in the entire region as obtained by NSGA-II (Yu, Kirley, & Buyya, 2007). Further, for multiple users with different regions of interest (preferences), we are getting number of optimal solutions in the multiple regions of user's interest simultaneously in single run of the algorithm. Finally, this allows us to obtain preferred and Pareto optimal solutions in an interactive manner with the decision maker.

MULTI-OBJECTIVE OPTIMIZATION: A BRIEF OVERVIEW

In this section, we formally define the concept of multi objective optimization, Pareto dominance and Pareto optimal front for better understanding of the work. Normally, multi-objective optimization problem (Deb, 2011) is defined as the simultaneous optimization of multiple conflicting objectives.

Mathematically a minimization problem can be expressed as follows:

$$\text{Minimize } f_i(s) \quad i = 1, 2, ...M \tag{1}$$

where f_i is the ith objective function, s is a decision vector representing a solution and M is the number of objectives considered. The multi-objective optimization problems commonly use the concepts called usual Pareto Dominance and ε-Pareto Dominance that are defined as:

Usual Pareto Dominance

Let us consider M objective functions $f(s) = (f_1(s), f_2(s), ..., f_M(s))$ and two solution vectors s_1 and s_2. Then solution s_1 is said to dominate other solution s_2 (also written as $s_1 \prec s_2$) if an only if

1. $\forall i \in \{1, 2, ..., M\} : f_i(s_1) \leq f_i(s_2)$
2. $\exists j \in \{1, 2, ..., M\} : f_j(s_1) < f_j(s_2)$

E-Pareto Dominance

On the other hand, the solution s_1 ε-dominate solution s_2 if and only if

1. $\forall i \in \{1, 2, ..., M\} : \lfloor f_i(s_1) / \varepsilon_i \rfloor \leq \lfloor f_i(s_2) / \varepsilon_i \rfloor$
2. $\exists j \in \{1, 2, ..., M\} : \lfloor f_j(s_1) / \varepsilon_j \rfloor < \lfloor f_j(s_2) / \varepsilon_j \rfloor$

Figure 1, demonstrates that the solution M dominate only the area MNOPM as per the usual Pareto domination, whereas the ε-Pareto dominance allows solution M to ε-dominate the complete area RSOQR.

The two solutions are said to be non-dominated whenever none of them dominates the other. Figure 2 depicts some dominated and non-dominated solutions assuming that both f_1 and f_2 are minimization objectives. Solution A is better than solution D in terms of both objectives. Thus, based on the conditions of Pareto dominance, solution A dominates solution D. Similarly, solution B dominates solution D and solution E with respect to both objectives. Further, solutions A and B are non-dominated because A is better than B in terms of f_1 and B is better than A in terms of f_2. The set of non-dominated solutions (Solution A, B & C) is called Pareto set or Pareto optimal front (POF) representing the trade-off between conflicting criteria. Every solution in this set is an acceptable solution.

A Pareto front represents a powerful tool for DMs as it represents the possible space of non-dominated solutions that cannot be seen until the Pareto front is known. A high quality Pareto front needs to fulfill two properties i.e. convergence and diversity in order to provide a true picture of tradeoffs to the user\DM.

- **Convergence:** Discover Pareto solutions as close as possible to the Pareto-optimal solutions.
- **Diversity:** Solutions in the Pareto set should be as uniformly distributed as possible covering all the possible ranges of optimal solutions.

Figure 1. The illustration of usual Pareto dominance and ε-Pareto dominance

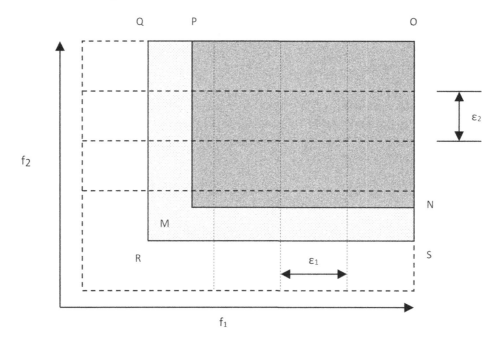

Figure 2. Solutions in Pareto optimal front

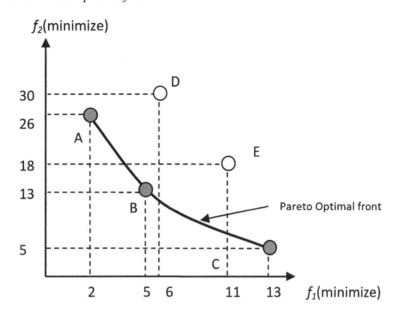

SYSTEM MODEL AND PRELIMINARIES

The task-scheduling problem in grid consists of computing environment and application model. In this section, we formally describe the mathematical model used to represents the resources in grid computing environment, precedence constrained parallel tasks applications (workflows) and problem definition.

Resource Model

We considered the grid computing system model represented as set $R = \{r_1, r_2,...., r_m\}$, consisting of m number of heterogeneous computing resources interconnected by fully connected communication links where communication is assumed to be performed without contention. The resources may have different memory sizes, processing capabilities delivered at different prices. Task executions once started on the processor is considered to be non-pre-emptive. Here the terms resource and processor are used interchangeably.

Further, communication links may have different bandwidths. To consider bandwidth linkage between any two resources, an $m \times m$ data transfer time matrix is used, where each entry $B_{s,j}$ represents the time needed to transfer a unit data between processors r_s and r_j. Further, each resource r_j have different properties:

- γ_j represents the computing speed illustrated by unitary instruction execution time.
- c_j its economic cost that represents the usage cost of resource r_j per unit time.

Workflow Model

A workflow application/job consisting of bag of tasks with precedence constraint and is represented as directed acyclic graph (DAG), $G = (T, E)$ where

- T is the set of vertices representing n different tasks $t_i \in$ T, $(1 \le i \le n)$ that can be executed on any available processor.
- E is the set of directed edges $e_{ij} = (t_i, t_j) \in$ E, $(1 \le i \le n, 1 \le j \le n, i \ne j)$ representing dependencies among the tasks t_i and t_j indicating that a task t_j cannot start its execution before t_i finishes and send all the required output data to task t_j.
- The weight $w(t_i)$ is assigned to task t_i representing the size/computing requirement of ith task expressed as number of instructions (MI) that need to be executed by the task.
- Weight $w(e_{ij})$ assigned to edge e_{ij} represents the amount of data required to be transfer from task t_i to t_j if they are not executed on the same resource.

In the DAG, *entry task* does not have any predecessor; similarly, the exit *task* does not possess any successor. We assumed that a DAG has one entry and one exit task. If the DAG has more than one entry or exit tasks, then one pseudo entry and exit task are added to the DAG along with edges of zero weights connecting them to original entry and exit tasks respectively.

Problem Definition

We considered the problem of scheduling workflow applications that deals with assigning various precedence constrained tasks in the workflow to different available grid resources. In the current work, each schedule (solution) is represented as the *task assignment string* corresponding to the *scheduling order string*. The task assignment string is the allocation of each task to the available time slot of the resource capable of executing the task, and the scheduling order string encodes the order to schedule the tasks. The ordering of tasks in the scheduling order string must satisfy the precedence constraints (or task dependencies). In order to describe the optimal schedule S: T→R that maps every task t_i onto a suitable resource r_j, we define some attributes as follows:

- Execution time or Computation cost of task

$$ET(t_i, r_j) = w(t_i).\gamma_j \qquad (2)$$

where $ET(t_i, r_j)$ represents the execution time for processing task t_i on resource r_j.

- Communication time /Communication cost

$$C_{p,i}^{s,j} = w(e_{pi}).B_{s,j} \qquad (3)$$

where $c_{p,i}^{s,j}$ represents the transfer time of sending the output data from parent task t_p to current task t_i if they are scheduled on resource r_s and r_j respectively. The communication time between two tasks is assumed to be zero if they are allocated to the same resource.

- The Earliest Start Time

$$EST(t_i, r_j) = \begin{cases} 0, & \text{if } t_i \text{ is entry task} \\ \max\{RAT(r_j), \ DRT(t_i,r_j)\}, & \text{otherwise} \end{cases} \tag{4}$$

where $EST(t_i,r_j)$ represents the earliest start time of task t_i on resource r_j. Here $RAT(r_j)$ represents the resource available time and $DRT(t_i,r_j)$ represents the data ready time for task t_i over resource r_j which is defined as

$$DRT(t_i, r_j) = \max_{t_p \in pred(t_i)} \begin{cases} EFT(t_p,r_s) & \text{if } r_s=r_j \\ \{EFT(t_p,r_s)+C_{p,i}^{s,j}\}\}, & \text{otherwise} \end{cases} \tag{5}$$

where the set $pred(t_i)$ represents the direct predecessor tasks of task t_i.

- The Earliest Finish Time

$$EFT(t_i, r_j) = EST(t_i, r_j) + ET(t_i, r_j) \tag{6}$$

where $EFT(t_i, r_j))$ represents the earliest finish time of a task t_i on some resource r_j.

- Overall Makespan of grid workflow

$$makespan = EFT(t_{exit}, r_j) \tag{7}$$

where $EFT(t_{exit}, r_j))$ represents the earliest finish time of the last completed task (i.e. exit task) on some resource r_j, considering the start time of the workflow as zero.

- For the economic cost, we used the "pay per use" paradigm (Smith, Siegel, & Maciejewski, 2008) where users have to pay a fixed price per unit time of the resource usage. Let $C_{i,j}$ is the execution cost spent to process a task t_i on resource r_j and is defined as:

$$C_{i,j} = c_j \cdot ET(t_i, r_j) \tag{8}$$

In order to handle the workflow-scheduling problem in grid, we considered the two conflicting objectives of minimization of makespan and economic cost. Therefore, grid workflow scheduling problem is formulated as:

$$\textit{Minimize } Time(S) = \{EFT(t_{exit})\} \tag{9}$$

$$\textit{Minimize } Cost(S) = \sum_{\forall i} C_{i,j} \tag{10}$$

subject to the condition that

Cost(S) < B and Time(S) < D

where B is the cost constraint (Budget) and D is the time constraint (Deadline) that are specified by the user for workflow execution.

GRID WORKFLOW SCHEDULING AUGMENTED MOEA

The multi-objective evolutionary algorithms (MOEA) are well-known meta-heuristic global search techniques and have been successfully applied to solve the non-linear continuous objective functions as well as combinatorial optimization problems like knapsack problem (Florios, Mavrotas, Diakoulaki, 2010). In this chapter, we have proposed the use of two MOEA's to solve the problem of workflow scheduling where DM or user has some preferences for the solutions. The first one is an existing algorithm called Reference Point Based Non-Dominated Sort Genetic Algorithm (R-NSGA-II) and second is our algorithm named as Reference point based variant of ε-MOEA (R-ε-MOEA) which are extension of NSGA-II and ε-MOEA with some pre specified preferences or reference points by the users. For the comparison purpose, we have also implemented NSGA-II (Deb et al., 2002).

R-NSGA-II

In order to solve workflow-scheduling problem where user has some specific QoS requirements or pre-specified preferences for solutions, R-NSGA-II (Deb et al., 2006) is very suitable. In R-NSGA-II, a user or decision maker simply provides some clues in terms of reference directions or reference points that represent the region of interest of the user. Therefore, the algorithm is able to generate the solutions in the region of user interest rather than wasting time to find complete set of Pareto optimal solutions that are not of user's interest. Moreover, the user can specify multiple reference points. The generic overview of R-NSGA-II procedure is shown in Figure 3.

In order to incorporate the idea of reference point in NSGA-II, modified crowded operator called preference operator is used to select the subset of solutions from the last front that cannot be accommodated entirely to preserve the population size in the next iteration. This preference operator uses the preference distance measurement instead of crowding distance as in NSGA-II. The preference distance represents how the solutions are closest to the reference points. Solutions that are closet to RP will receive a higher selection probability. The modification performed is shown in Figure 4 by R-NSGA-II nitching (diversity) strategy.

$$d_{x,R} = \sqrt{\sum_{i=1}^{M}\left(\frac{f_i(x)-f_i(R)}{f_i^{\max}-f_i^{\min}}\right)^2} \tag{11}$$

Figure 3. Overview of R-NSGA-II procedure

R-NSGA-II Algorithm
Step 1. Generate initial parent population P
Step 2. Evaluate each solution once
Step 2. Repeat the loop
Step 3. Generate offspring population Q from parent population by applying selection, crossover and mutation operators
Step 4. Combine parent and offspring populations PvQ
Step 5. Place each individual in its respective front by applying fast non-dominated sort on the combined population
Step 6. Calculate preference distance of each front's individual from reference point Rusing nitching strategy specified in Figure 4
Step 7. Make new parent population by selecting representative individuals which are in the better front and having the least preference distances
Step 8. Increment the loop counter. If it is less than the maximum number of iterations, then go to step 2, otherwise output the obtained solutions from current parent population

Figure 4. Overview of Nitching strategy

Nitching strategy
1. Assign rank to each solution with respect to each reference point R according to calculated Euclidean distance   // as per Eq. (11)
2. Determine preference distance of each solution by selecting minimum rank with respect to all reference points.
3. Make clusters of solutions by applying ε-clearing idea and retain one random solution from each cluster.

where $d_{x,R}$ represents the normalized Euclidean distance from solution x to the reference point R, M - number of objectives, f_i^{max} - maximum value of ith objective in the population, f_i^{min} - minimum value of ith objective in the population.

The ε-clearing idea mentioned in the Figure 4 is similar to ε-dominance strategy (Laumanns et al., 2002), which is used to control the spread\diversity of solutions close to the preferred Pareto optimal regions. This spread of solutions is maintained by the ε-values that state the tolerance or precision specified by the user corresponding to different objective function values. The choice of ε-value is application specific and can be specified different for each objective. The R-NSGA-II nitching strategy is shown by example in the Figure 5. In this example, there are four solutions and two reference points and accordingly preference distance of each solution is determined.

The R-NSGA-II algorithm has the capability of good convergence while meeting the user preferences because it uses non-dominated procedure of NSGA-II, but it does not give uniform diversity between solutions closest to a reference point. Therefore, we made change in the original R-NSGA-II nitching strategy to get good spread of preferred solutions. We called this algorithm modified R-NSGA-II (M-R-NSGA-II). In this, instead of retaining the random solution from each group, the solution that is very closest to a reference point is retained and others are discarded as shown in Figure 6.

Figure 5. R-NSGA-II Nitching strategy

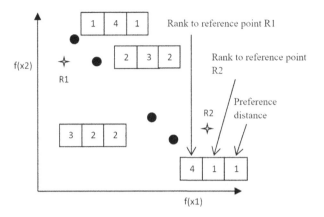

(i) Assignment of ranks and preference distance

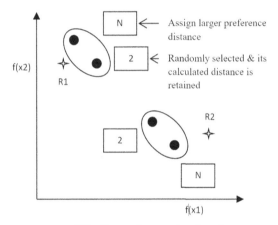

(ii) Grouping and selection

Figure 6. Modified R-NSGA-II Nitching strategy

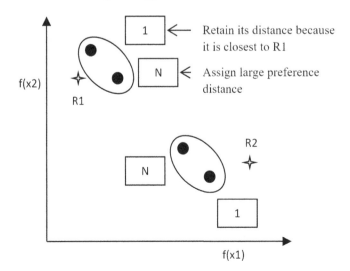

R-ε-MOEA

Further, in order to solve the problem of workflow scheduling, we have proposed the reference point based variant of ε-MOEA (R-ε-MOEA) which is an extension ε-MOEA (Deb, Mohan, Mishra, 2003; Singh & Garg, 2011) with some pre specified preferences by the users. It is based on the idea of ε-dominance, where the concept of ε-dominance does not permit non-dominated solutions having differences less than ε_I in the ith objective, thus it maintains uniform diversity among solutions as shown in Figure 1.

In R-ε-MOEA, two populations are evolved simultaneously namely a parent population P(t) and an archive population E(t). Here, t represents the iteration counter. The complete procedure of R-ε-MOEA is illustrated in Figure 7.

The algorithm begins with randomly generated initial population P(0). Afterwards, we identify the ε-non-dominated solutions from P(0) and store them as archive population E(0). Further, we select two solutions each from P(t) and E(t) to perform crossover and mutation. In order to select a solution from P(t), we randomly choose two members from P(t) and perform the dominance checking (usual dominance). The solution that dominates the other is selected. If none dominates the other, one solution is selected randomly. We name the selected solution as *p* henceforth. To select a solution from E(t), a random solution is chosen and is called *e*. After selecting *p* and *e*, *m* offspring solutions are generated using crossover and mutation operations. We denote the offspring solutions as c_i, i = *1, 2,..., m*. In Figure 7, the case of one offspring is illustrated. Further, the offspring solutions c_i have been compared with P(t) and E(t) for their possible inclusion. The entire procedure is repeated for the specified number of iterations. Finally, the solutions in the archive population are the obtained solutions.

Figure 7. Procedure of R-ε-MOEA

R-ε-MOEA Algorithm

Step 1. Initialize the parent population of size N in a list P(0);

Step 2. Identify the ε-non-dominated solutions of P(0) and store them as archive population E(0);

Step 3. Set the iteration counter t = 0;

Step 4. Repeat the loop

    a. Select a solution *p* from P(t) by applying the dominance checking on two randomly selected solutions;

    b. Select a solution *e* from E(t) randomly;

    c. Generate an offspring *c* by applying crossover and mutation operators on selected solutions *p* and *e*;

    d. Update archive E(t) with *c* on the basis of ε-domination check with members of E(t) by applying ***inclusion-check-archive(c)***;

    e. Update population P(t) with *c* on the basis of usual domination check with members of P(t) by applying ***inclusion-check-EA(c)***;

Step 5. Increment the loop counter. If it is less than the maximum number of iterations, then go to step 4, otherwise output the obtained solutions from archive population;

Inclusion Checking of Offspring in an Archive Population

As mentioned above, the produced offspring c is to be included in the archive population. In order to decide its possible inclusion, the offspring c is compared with each member of archive population based on ε-dominance. An identification array B is assigned to every solution of archive population E(t) and offspring c. This identification array B is described as follows:

$$B = B_1, B_2, ..., B_M \qquad (12)$$

$$B_i = \left\lfloor (f_i - f_i^{\min}) \backslash \varepsilon_i \right\rfloor \qquad (13)$$

where M is the total number of objectives, $f_i^{\min}$ is the minimum value of the ith objective and ε_i is the allowable tolerance in the ith objective. The identification array B divides the whole search space into grids or hyper-boxes and each hyper-box having ε_i size in the ith objective. After the calculation of identification array for both offspring and members of archive population, inclusion checking of offspring is performed and accordingly update in archive population is performed. During inclusion checking and update, reference points are considered to reject a solution that is far away from them. The whole process of possible inclusion of offspring in archive population is specified in Figure 8.

If the B_a array corresponding to any member a of archive population dominates the B_c array for offspring c ($B_a \prec B_c$) i.e. the offspring is ε-dominated by this archive member, thus it is not accepted in the archive population. On the other side, if B_c dominates B_a ($B_c \prec B_a$), a is replaced by the offspring c. If neither of the above two cases occur ($B_a ! \prec B_c \&\& B_c ! \prec B_a$), it means that the offspring and archive members are ε-non-dominated, and then further two more cases are checked. First, if the offspring has the same B vector as that of an archive member ($B_a = B_c$), then they are checked for their usual domination. If the offspring dominates the archive member ($c \prec a$) or the offspring is non-dominated with the archive member ($c ! \prec a \&\& a ! \prec c$), but it is closer to the B vector than archive member in terms of Euclidean distance (Eu_dist[c, B_c] <Eu_dist[a, B_a]), then offspring replaces that archive member in the archive population. This condition ensures that only one solution would exist in each grid or hyper-box thus maintaining diversity among solutions. Second, if the offspring does not share the same B vector with any archive member ($B_a != B_c$) then furthermore two cases are checked. i) If the current size of archive population is less than or equal to maximum size (cur_archive_size<= MAX_ARCHIVE_SIZE) then the offspring c is accepted. ii) Otherwise, delete an archive solution, which is far remote with respect to reference points after inclusion of offspring.

Inclusion Checking of Offspring in an EA Population

Likewise, in archive population, the offspring is also included in EA population to search the objectives space. Here, each offspring is compared with all EA population members. If the offspring dominates one or more members of EA population i.e. ($c \prec EA_i$) then the offspring replaces one of them randomly. For this purpose, a domination array (dom_arr) is used to store the location of all EA solutions that are dominated by offspring c. On the other side if the offspring is dominated by any member of EA (any $EA_i \prec c$), it is discarded. Finally, when both the above mentioned cases fail i.e. the offspring is non-

Figure 8. Offspring inclusion checking in archive population

inclusion-check-archive (c)

1. Assign an identification array B to every solution *a* of archive population E(t) and offspring *c*; Let B_a and B_c are identification arrays corresponding to archive and offspring respectively
2. If (B_a π B_c) then
   Offspring *c* is not accepted;
3. If (B_c π B_a) then
   Offspring *c* replaces archive solution *a*;
4. If (B_a ! π B_c&&B_c ! π B_a) then
   If (B_a = B_c) then
      If (c π a) || ((c ! π a&&a ! π c) && (Eu_dist[c, B_c] <Eu_dist[a, B_a])) then
      Offspring *c* replaces archive solution *a*;
   Else If (B_a != B_c) then
         If (cur_archive_size<= MAX_ARCHIVE_SIZE) then
         Offspring *c* is accepted;
   Else
      Include *c* in archive;
      Delete an archive solution which is far away from the reference points;
      Else
      Offspring *c* is not accepted;

dominated with all the EA members (c ! $\prec$ EA$_j$&&EA$_j$! $\prec$ c), an EA solution is deleted which is far away from the reference points after inclusion of offspring in EA population. The complete process is specified in Figure 9.

IMPLEMENTATION OF MOEA TO WORKFLOW SCHEDULING

In order to use the considered MOEA's for workflow scheduling problem, we need to define the population formulation, fitness assignment and the genetic operators. The algorithm starts with a population of randomly generated candidate solutions and move towards the better set of solutions (Pareto optimal front) over the number of generations. Its implementation for workflow task scheduling is given below.

Population Formulation and Fitness Assignment

In the considered MOEA's, the population of solutions (chromosomes) is formulated as two strings called task assignment string (S) and scheduling order string (O). Initially, the resource on which a task will execute is defined in S randomly. The O describes tasks' ordering sequence and is generated randomly while preserving the precedence constraints among workflow tasks. Let us consider an example workflow shown in Figure 10 corresponding to workflow model mentioned in section 4.

Figure 9. Offspring inclusion checking in EA population

inclusion-check-EA (c)
1. Set i = 1;
2. until (i<= size_EA) repeat
    If ($c \pi$ EA$_i$) then
        Store location of ith solution of EA in dom_arr;
        i = i + 1;
3. if (size(dom_arr) >= 1)
        Offspring replaces a random member of EA having location in dom_arr;
    Else if (any EA$_i$ π c)
        Offspring is not accepted;
4. If (c ! π EA$_j$&&EA$_j$! π c) then   //for all j solutions in EA
        Include *c* in EA;
        Delete a solution in EA which is far away from reference points;

Figure 10. An example workflow represented as DAG

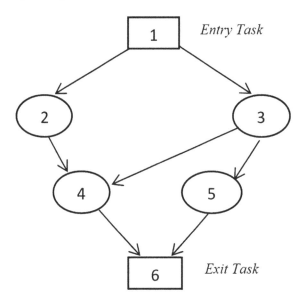

Figure 11 depicts the random S and O formulation for the sample DAG in Figure 10 by considering availability of three resources. We formed the fitness functions $F_{time}(S)$ and $F_{cost}(S)$ that are used to evaluate the individuals of the population. These fitness functions are designed according to makespan and economic cost of the schedule using Equation (9) and (10) respectively by adding the penalty, where the penalty is added to respective objective functions only on the violation of constraints (i.e. deadline and budget), otherwise not.

Figure 11. Population formulation

Task Assignment String

{[t₁→r₂], [t₂→r₃], [t₃→r₁], [t₄→r₃], [t₅→r₁], [t₆→r₂]}

Scheduling Order String

{t₁, t₃, t₂, t₄, t₅, t₆}

Selection Operator

In order to preserve superior chromosomes, selection of individuals (chromosomes) play very important role. We have used binary tournament selection due to its wide use in the literature. In binary tournament selection, one of two individuals is selected by playing tournament among them based on their fitness values. Thus individual having good fitness value get more chance to survive in the next generation.

Crossover and Mutation Operator

Crossover is used to generate new solutions by rearranging the part of existing fittest solutions. We have used one-point crossover for task assignment string. The probability of crossover is determined by experimentation and is set to 0.8. Figure 12 describes the crossover operation on two task assignment strings. The position of crossover point is chosen randomly. Then, the resources on the right side of the crossover point for both the strings are exchanged as shown in Figure 12.

Further, mutation operator is used to explore the search space that could not be exploited by crossover operator in order to exit from local optimum. For mutation, single chromosome is selected to generate new chromosome that possibly is genetically better. We have used the replacing mutation, where an individual task is moved to another resource randomly. As shown in Figure 13, a task t_5 is moved to

Figure 12. Crossover operation on two task assignment strings

Crossover Point

{[t₁→r₂], [t₂→r₃], [t₃→r₁], [t₄→r₃], [t₅→r₁], [t₆→r₂]}

{[t₁→r₁], [t₂→r₂], [t₃→r₃], [t₄→r₂], [t₅→r₃], [t₆→r₁]}

⇩ **Crossover Operation**

{[t₁→r₂], [t₂→r₃], [t₃→r₃], [t₄→r₂], [t₅→r₃], [t₆→r₁]}

{[t₁→r₁], [t₂→r₂], [t₃→r₁], [t₄→r₃], [t₅→r₁], [t₆→r₂]}

Figure 13. Mutation operation

$$\{[t_1 \rightarrow r_2], [t_2 \rightarrow r_3], [t_3 \rightarrow r_3], [t_4 \rightarrow r_2], [t_5 \rightarrow r_3], [t_6 \rightarrow r_1]\}$$

Mutation Operation

$$\{[t_1 \rightarrow r_2], [t_2 \rightarrow r_3], [t_3 \rightarrow r_3], [t_4 \rightarrow r_2], [t_5 \rightarrow r_2], [t_6 \rightarrow r_1]\}$$

resource r_2 that was on resource r_3 previously. The probability of mutation was set to 0.5. In general, mutation should be applied with significant low rate but we have applied it with high rate because it shows effective results in grid environment as shown by Yu and Buyya (2006). The crossover and mutation operators are applied on S (i.e. task matching string) only.

SIMULATION STRATEGY

Simulation Model

We have used the GridSim (Buyya & Murshed, 2002) toolkit in our experiments to simulate the scheduling of workflow applications. The GridSim is flexible enough to support simulation of grid entities like resources, users, application tasks and schedulers along with their behavior using discrete events. It is a common practice in computing research community that in simulator based experiments the randomly generated task graphs are used to mimic the real task graphs. Therefore, we have also worked on the similar lines.

In our test environment, we have simulated the complex workflow applications represented by randomly generated task graphs consisting of 20 tasks on eight virtual resources that are managed by different organizations in the grid. Links between resources are established through a router so that direct communication can take place between resources. The computational rating (Million instructions per second) of processing elements varies from Pentium II to Pentium IV and computational cost (in dollars) of each resource is generated randomly where cost is inversely proportional to computational rating.

In order to generate valid deadline and budget constraints, we have considered maximum and minimum time\cost for workflow execution. $Cost_{max}$ represents the cost paid to execute the workflow with minimum time ($Time_{min}$), while $Time_{max}$ represents the time required to execute the workflow at cheapest cost ($Cost_{min}$). To generate $Time_{min}$ and $Cost_{max}$ we have implemented HEFT (Topcugolu, Hariri, & Wu, 2002). It is a well-known time optimization algorithm in which workflow tasks are allocated to heterogeneous resources such that minimum execution time can be obtained irrespective of the utility cost of resources. However, $Time_{max}$ and $Cost_{min}$ is generated by implementing Greedy Cost that is a cost optimization algorithm in which workflow tasks are allocated on the cheapest heterogeneous resources irrespective of the task execution time. Thus, the deadline (D) and budget (B) constraints are specified as:

$$D = Time_{max} - P(Time_{max} - Time_{min}) \tag{14}$$

$$B = Cost_{max} - P(Cost_{max} - Cost_{min}) \qquad\qquad (15)$$

The value of parameter P was varied from 0.1 to 0.7 in order to generate *loose* (P=0.1), *intermediate* (P=0.4) and *stiff* (P=0.7) deadline and budget constraints. Loose constraint means that the user requires relatively large deadline and budget values while stiff constraint represents values close to optimal solutions obtained by time optimization and cost optimization algorithms individually. Since, we know that both the objectives are conflicting in nature, so getting solutions in stiff constraint is very challenging.

In order to show the effectivity and validity of the proposed algorithms, we have implemented the highly competitive technique namely NSGA-II. Yu, Kirley, and Buyya (2007), declared that the NSGA-II and SPEA with seeding are powerful approaches to obtain complete set of Pareto optimal solutions. However, we are not considering SPEA as its computational time is very large (Deb, Mohan, & Mishra, 2003).

Further, we have evaluated the considered algorithms with single reference point as well as multiple (two) reference points. The objective values for these reference points are also established using the knowledge of $Time_{max}$, $Time_{min}$, $Cost_{max}$ and $Cost_{min}$ in order to generate valid schedules (solutions). The parameter values used for considered algorithms NSGA-II, R-NSGA-II, M-R-NSGA-II and R-ε-MOEA are given below:

1. The size of the population = 10.
2. Probability of Crossover = 0.8 with One-point crossover operator.
3. Probability of Mutation = 0.5 with Replacing mutation operator.
4. Binary tournament selection operator.
5. Number of iterations = 200.
6. Number of offspring per iteration (R-ε-MOEA) = 10.
7. Furthermore, the different ε-values are used for each objective function according to the scale of objective functions.

We have made two models of our MOEA algorithms for workflow scheduling. In the first model, initial population is generated *randomly*. While in the second model, initial population is *seeded* with two solutions obtained by heuristics namely LOSS-II and modified GAIN-II and the rest of the population is generated randomly. LOSS-II and modified GAIN-II are used to generate solution with minimum makespan (total time) while meeting budget constraint and minimum total cost while meeting deadline constraint respectively.

The model in which all initial solutions are randomly generated, algorithms are denoted as NSGA-II, R-NSGA-II, M-R-NSGA-II and R-ε-MOEA while the model in which two initial solutions are seeded and rest are randomly generated, algorithms are denoted as NSGA-II~, R-NSGA-II~, M-R-NSGA-II~and R-ε–MOEA~.

Performance Metrics: GD, Spacing and Computation Time

In order to evaluate the performance of considered algorithms R-NSGA-II~, M-R-NSGA-II~ and R-ε–MOEA~, we need to estimate the extent of minimization of obtained solutions for each objective and spacing among the solutions. Thus, we have used two performance metrics namely Generational Distance

(GD) and Spacing by Deb and Jain (2002). Further, the computation time taken by each algorithm is also measured. For the performance comparison, we have obtained the Pareto optimal solutions by our experiments averaged over ten runs for the randomly generated task graphs.

GD is the popularly used convergence measure that represents the closeness of obtained solution set Q from a known set called reference front P*. In the workflow-scheduling problem, we have generated the set P* by merging the solutions of all algorithms over five runs. Further, the Spacing measure is used to find the diversity (spread) in obtained solutions. The mathematical expression for GD and Spacing metrics is defined by Equations (16) and (17) respectively.

$$GD = \frac{\left(\sum_{i=1}^{|Q|} d_i^2\right)^{1/2}}{|Q|}$$

(16)

$$Spacing = \sqrt{\frac{1}{|Q|}\sum_{i=1}^{|Q|}(d_i - \overline{d})^2}$$

(17)

In Equation (16), the parameter d_i is the Euclidean distance between the solution in Q and the nearest member of set P*. The value 0 for GD indicates that the obtained front is equal to true Pareto optimal front P*. While in Equation (17), the parameter d_i is the distance measure representing the minimum value of the sum of absolute difference in the objective function values between the solution and any other solution in set Q. Further, $\overline{d}$ is the mean of above distance measures d_i. Corresponding to Spacing metric, the value 0 indicates that all the solutions of obtained front are equidistantly spaced. Thus, an algorithm having small value for both GD and Spacing metric is better. Further, we have normalized the Euclidean distance and the distance value before using them in Equations (16) and (17) respectively because in our problem both objectives are of different scale.

Simulation Results

In order to compare the performance of algorithms, we have run the algorithms over 200 generations at each constraint level with the initial population size of 10. The Pareto optimal solutions obtained with NSGA-II and NSGA-II~ for bi-objective workflow scheduling problem are shown in Figure 14.

The results clearly specify that the initial population with seeding (NSGA-II~) gives good and fast convergence with better spread in comparison to population with all solutions generated randomly (NSGA-II). The seeding allows MOEA algorithms to find the true front because it contains two already optimized boundary solutions. Therefore, for the next set of experiments we are considering the comparison between our MOEA approaches with only seeded population.

In the next experiment, we compare considered multi-objective workflow scheduling approaches i.e. NSGA-II~, R-NSGA-II~, M-R-NSGA-II~ and R-ε–MOEA~ on different constraint levels and the results are shown in Figure 15, 16 and 17. In Figure 15 and 16, non-dominated solutions generated by R-NSGA-II~, M-R-NSGA-II~ and R-ε–MOEA~ on loose and intermediate constraints are only in region of user interest rather than generation of non-dominated solution over the entire Pareto front as produced

Figure 14. Pareto optimal solutions obtained with NSGA-II and NSGA-II~ on intermediate constraint

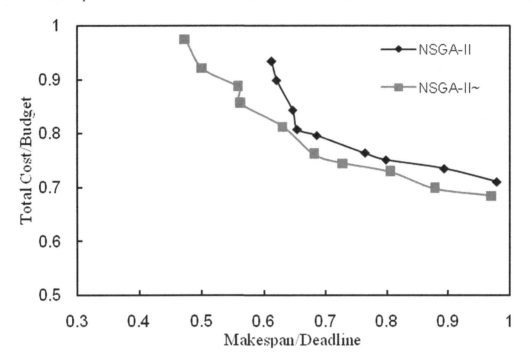

by NSGA-II~. Further, it shows that the convergence of Pareto solutions obtained with R-ε–MOEA~ is better as compared to others. Moreover, the solutions generated close to the reference point by M-R-NSGA-II~ and R-ε–MOEA~ have better diversity than R-NSGA-II~ because of its good nitching strategy and the use of ε value. Figure 17 on stiff constraint shows that the solutions obtained by algorithms are in same region with slight difference. This is due to the reason that only a few non-dominated solutions exist with very small value of budget and deadline constraint i.e. at tight constraints.

Furthermore, the comparison results obtained with the considered algorithms based on the metrics described previously in section 8.2 and computation time taken by each algorithm on different constraint levels i.e. loose, medium and tight constraint are shown in Table 1, 2 and 3 respectively.

On loose constraint (shown in Table 1), average value of the GD metric for R-ε–MOEA~ is smallest, which clearly states that R-ε–MOEA~ has better convergence towards the reference front. Further, the average value obtained with Spacing metric for M-R-NSGA-II~ is least and the value for R-ε–MOEA~ is less and close to that obtained by M-R-NSGA-II~. So in terms of diversity both M-R-NSGA-II~ and R-ε–MOEA~ are good and comparable, but better than R-NSGA-II~. The average computational time taken by R-ε–MOEA~ is much less as compared to other algorithms. Overall, it shows that R-ε–MOEA~ performs better in terms of solution spread, closeness to reference front with small computation time for workflow scheduling in grid environment.

On intermediate constraint, Table 2 shows similar results. The results clearly specify that R-ε–MOEA~ provides solutions with best convergence at small computational time and it is having comparable diversity among solutions to M-R-NSGA-II~. In Table 3, results on stiff constraint level are listed. Here the average value of GD metric for R-ε–MOEA~ got the least value. Hence, it is having better convergence. Variation in values (depicted by standard deviation) is there because on stiff constraint only few number

Figure 15. Pareto optimal solutions obtained with considered MOEA's on Loose constraint

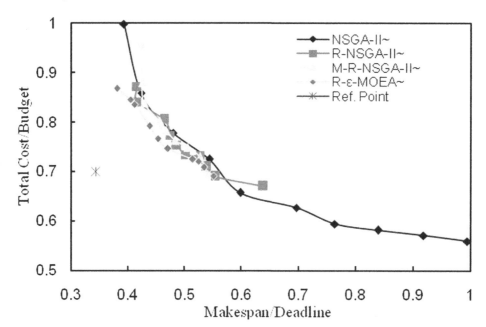

Figure 16. Pareto optimal solutions obtained with considered MOEA's on Intermediate constraint

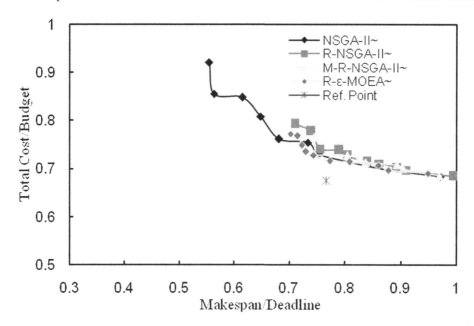

Figure 17. Pareto optimal solutions obtained with considered MOEA's on Stiff constraint

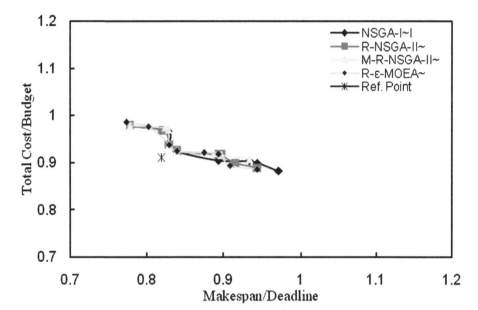

of non-dominated solutions exit. In case of spacing metric both M-R-NSGA-II~ and R-ε–MOEA~ gives less value, hence having good diversity among solutions. The computation time taken by R-ε–MOEA~ is significantly less as on other constraint levels.

Next, Figure 18 shows the solutions obtained by the algorithms when user have more than one preference region. Results clearly specify that the considered algorithms are able to generate Pareto optimal solutions in the multiple regions of interest of the user simultaneously but with the same computation overhead.

Further, we have evaluated the performance of the proposed approaches by varying the size of the task graph. We have considered the higher number of tasks as 50, 100 representing medium and large size workflow applications respectively at different constraints. Figure 19 & 20 shows the distribution of solutions obtained by each algorithm on intermediate constraint. The results clearly specify that most of the solutions corresponding to R-ε-MOEA~ are falling in the better minimization region with respect to the reference point as compared to other considered algorithms with more uniform spacing. With the increase in the number of tasks, performance of the R-ε-MOEA~ increases. It is due to the existence

Table 1. GD, Spacing and computation time results of considered MOEA's for workflow scheduling on loose constraints

Evaluation Metrics	R-NSGA-II~		M-R-NSGA-II~		R-ε-MOEA~	
	Average	Std. Dev	Average	Std. Dev	Average	Std. Dev
GD	0.0610	0.0089	0.0601	0.0092	**0.0242**	0.0096
Spacing	0.0670	0.0091	**0.0527**	0.0087	0.0564	0.0086
Computation Time (Nanosecond)	1.82×10^8	0.0446×10^6	1.80×10^8	0.0123×10^6	**1.46×10^8**	0.0097×10^6

Table 2. GD, Spacing and computation time results of considered MOEA's for workflow scheduling on intermediate constraints

Evaluation Metrics	R-NSGA-II~		M-R-NSGA-II~		R-ε-MOEA~	
	Average	Std. Dev	Average	Std. Dev	Average	Std. Dev
GD	0.0490	0.0076	0.0335	0.0082	**0.0215**	0.0079
Spacing	0.0827	0.0096	0.0672	0.0092	**0.0660**	0.0089
Computation Time (Nanosecond)	1.81×10^8	0.0563×10^6	1.80×10^8	0.0458×10^6	**1.48×10^8**	0.0348×10^6

Table 3. GD, Spacing and computation time results of considered MOEA's for workflow scheduling on stiff constraints

Evaluation Metrics	R-NSGA-II~		M-R-NSGA-II~		R-ε-MOEA~	
	Average	Std. Dev	Average	Std. Dev	Average	Std. Dev
GD	0.0238	0.0029	0.0246	0.0028	**0.0220**	0.0025
Spacing	0.0848	0.0118	**0.0649**	0.0102	0.0792	0.0284
Computation Time (Nanosecond)	1.78×10^8	0.0423×10^6	1.79×10^8	0.0494×10^6	**1.38×10^8**	0.0418×10^6

Figure 18. Pareto optimal solutions obtained with considered MOEA's with two reference points on intermediate constraint

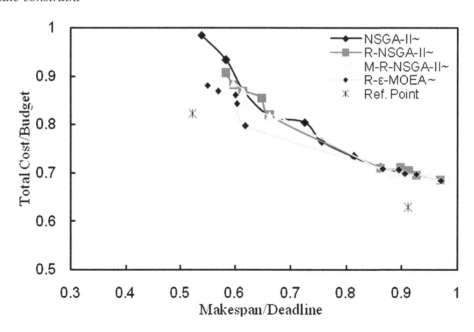

Figure 19. Pareto optimal solutions obtained with considered MOEA's for Medium size task graph (Number of tasks=50)

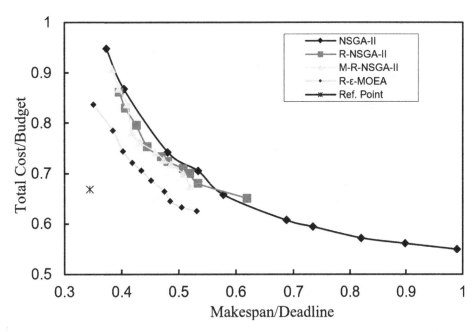

Figure 20. Pareto optimal solutions obtained with considered MOEA's for Large size task graph (Number of tasks=100)

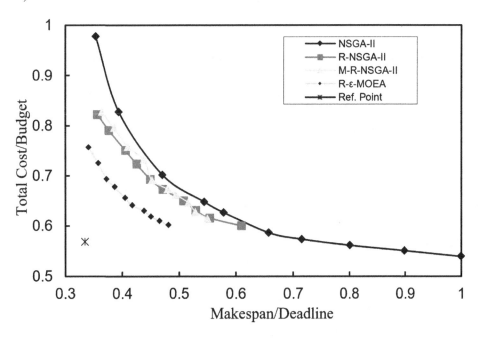

Table 4. GD, Spacing and computation time results of considered MOEA's for different size of application task graphs on intermediate constraints

No of Tasks	Evaluation Metrics	R-NSGA-II~		M-R-NSGA-II~		R-ε-MOEA~	
		Average	Std. Dev	Average	Std. Dev	Average	Std. Dev
50	GD	0.0246	0.0054	0.0238	0.0046	**0.0104**	0.0038
	Spacing	0.0632	0.0057	0.0620	0.0045	**0.0614**	0.00043
	Computation Time (Nanosecond)	3.34×10^8	0.0397×10^6	3.43×10^8	0.0404×10^6	**2.21×10^8**	0.0323×10^6
100	GD	0.0173	0.0023	0.0169	0.0025	**0.0076**	0.0020
	Spacing	0.0557	0.0098	0.0546	0.0094	**0.0539**	0.0085
	Computation Time (Nanosecond)	7.75×10^8	0.0343×10^6	7.78×10^8	0.0354×10^6	**4.56×10^8**	0.0276×10^6

of large number of non-dominated solutions at higher number of tasks and the use of ε-dominance for selecting offspring rather than simply using of the concept non-dominance from the large solution space (non-dominated solution set). Table 4 shows the comparison of results among the three algorithms corresponding to metrics considered previously. The results clearly specify that the R-ε–MOEA~ provide better convergence and uniform spacing with small computation overhead.

SUMMARY

The current work emphasizes on the planning and optimizing the workflow scheduling in grid environment. Existing bi-criteria workflow scheduling algorithms generate the wide spread alternative Pareto solutions which are then passed to DM to select the one according to his/her preference. Based on the role of DM, multi objective optimization can be categorized into priori or posteriori approach. In priori approach, preference information is given before the solution process. While in posteriori approach, well distributed Pareto solutions are first obtained and then DMs preference information is used to select the final solution. In the current chapter, we have applied the priori approach to find the trade-off scheduling solutions in the regions of the interest of the DM. By applying reference point based evolutionary algorithms, we are able to obtain the number of scheduling solutions that minimizes the execution time and economic cost in the close vicinity of each desired region of interest simultaneously with small computation overhead.

REFERENCES

Berman, F., Casanova, H., Chien, A., Cooper, K., Dail, H., Dasgupta, A., ... YarKhan, A. (2005). New grid scheduling and rescheduling methods in the GrADS project. *International Journal of Parallel Programming, 33*(2-3), 209–229. doi:10.100710766-005-3584-4

Blaha, P., Schwarz, K., Madsen, G. K. H., Kvasnicka, D., & Luitz, J. (2001). *WIEN2k: An Augmented Plane Wave plus Local Orbitals Program for Calculating Crystal Properties*. Vienna University of Technology.

Blythe, J., Jain, S., Deelman, E., Gil, Y., Vahi, K., Mandal, A., & Kennedy, K. (2005). Task scheduling strategies for workflow-based applications in grids. In *Cluster Computing and the Grid, 2005. CCGrid 2005. IEEE International Symposium on* (Vol. 2, pp. 759-767). IEEE. 10.1109/CCGRID.2005.1558639

Braun, T. D., Siegel, H. J., Beck, N., Bölöni, L. L., Maheswaran, M., Reuther, A. I., ... Freund, R. F. (2001). A comparison of eleven static heuristics for mapping a class of independent tasks onto heterogeneous distributed computing systems. *Journal of Parallel and Distributed Computing, 61*(6), 810–837. doi:10.1006/jpdc.2000.1714

Buyya, R., & Murshed, M. (2002). GridSim: A Toolkit for Modeling and Simulation of Grid Resource Management and Scheduling. *Concurrency and Computation, 14*(13-15), 1175–1220. doi:10.1002/cpe.710

Cao, J., Jarvis, S. A., Saini, S., & Nudd, G. R. (2003). Gridflow: Workflow management for grid computing. In *Cluster Computing and the Grid, 2003. Proceedings. CCGrid 2003. 3rd IEEE/ACM International Symposium on* (pp. 198-205). IEEE.

Cheshmehgaz, H. R., Islam, M. N., & Desa, M. I. (2014). A polar-based guided multi-objective evolutionary algorithm to search for optimal solutions interested by decision-makers in a logistics network design problem. *Journal of Intelligent Manufacturing, 25*(4), 699–726. doi:10.100710845-012-0714-x

Deb, K. (2011). Multi-objective optimisation using evolutionary algorithms: an introduction. In *Multi-objective evolutionary optimisation for product design and manufacturing* (pp. 3–34). Springer London. doi:10.1007/978-0-85729-652-8_1

Deb, K., Agrawal, S., Pratap, A., & Meyarivan, T. (2002). A fast and elitist multi objective genetic algorithm: NSGA-II. *IEEE Transactions on Evolutionary Computation, 6*(2), 182–197. doi:10.1109/4235.996017

Deb, K., & Jain, S. (2002). Running Performance Metrics for Evolutionary Multi-Objective Optimization. *Proceedings of the Fourth Asia-Pacific Conference on Simulated Evolution and Learning (SEAL'02)*, 13-20.

Deb, K., Mohan, M., & Mishra, S. (2003). *A Fast Multi-objective Evolutionary Algorithm for Finding Well-Spread Pareto-Optimal Solutions, KanGAL Report Number: 2003002*. Kanpur, India: Indian Institute of Technology.

Deb, K., Sundar, J., Udaya Bhaskara, R. N., & Chaudhuri, S. (2006). Reference point based multi-objective optimization using evolutionary algorithms. *International Journal of Computational Intelligence Research, 2*(3), 273–286. doi:10.5019/j.ijcir.2006.67

Deelman, E., Blythe, J., Gil, Y., Kesselman, C., Mehta, G., Vahi, K., ... Koranda, S. (2003). Mapping abstract complex workflows onto grid environments. *Journal of Grid Computing, 1*(1), 25–39. doi:10.1023/A:1024000426962

Fahringer, T., Jugravu, A., Pllana, S., Prodan, R., Seragiotto, C., & Truong, H. L. (2005). ASKALON: A tool set for cluster and Grid computing. *Concurrency and Computation, 17*(2-4), 143–169. doi:10.1002/cpe.929

Florios, K., Mavrotas, G., & Diakoulaki, D. (2010). Solving multiobjective, multiconstraint knapsack problems using mathematical programming and evolutionary algorithms. *European Journal of Operational Research, 203*(1), 14–21. doi:10.1016/j.ejor.2009.06.024

Hollingsworth, D. (1994). *Workflow Management Coalition*. The Workflow Reference Model, TC00-1003.

Izakian, H., Ladani, B. T., Zamanifar, K., & Abraham, A. (2009). A novel particle swarm optimization approach for grid job scheduling. In Information Systems, Technology and Management (pp. 100-109). Springer Berlin Heidelberg. doi:10.1007/978-3-642-00405-6_14

Kumar, S., Dutta, K., & Mookerjee, V. (2009). Maximizing business value by optimal assignment of jobs to resources in grid computing. *European Journal of Operational Research, 194*(3), 856–872. doi:10.1016/j.ejor.2007.12.024

Laumanns, M., Thiele, L., Dev, K., & Zitzler, E. (2002). Combining Convergence and Diversity in Evolutionary Multi-Objective Optimization. *Evolutionary Computation, 10*(3), 263–282. doi:10.1162/106365602760234108 PMID:12227996

Montage. (n.d.). *Montage: An Atronomical Image Mosaic Engine—NASA Space Act Award Winner 2006*. Retrieved from http://montage.ipac.caltech.edu

Oinn, T., Addis, M., Ferris, J., Marvin, D., Senger, M., Greenwood, M., ... Li, P. (2004). Taverna: A tool for the composition and enactment of bioinformatics workflows. *Bioinformatics (Oxford, England), 20*(17), 3045–3054. doi:10.1093/bioinformatics/bth361 PMID:15201187

Singh, D., & Garg, R. (2011, July). A robust multi-objective optimization to workflow scheduling for dynamic grid. In *Proceedings of the International Conference on Advances in Computing and Artificial Intelligence* (pp. 183-188). ACM. 10.1145/2007052.2007090

Smith, J., Siegel, H. J., & Maciejewski, A. A. (2008). A stochastic model for robust resource allocation in heterogeneous parallel and distributed computing systems. In *Parallel and Distributed Processing, 2008. IPDPS 2008. IEEE International Symposium on* (pp. 1-5). IEEE. 10.1109/IPDPS.2008.4536431

Talukder, A. K. M., Kirley, M., & Buyya, R. (2009). Multiobjective differential evolution for scheduling workflow applications on global Grids. *Concurrency and Computation, 21*(13), 1742–1756. doi:10.1002/cpe.1417

Tannenbaum, T., Wright, D., Miller, K., & Livny, M. (2001). Condor: a distributed job scheduler. In Beowulf cluster computing with Linux (pp. 307-350). MIT Press.

Theiner, D., & Rutschmann, P. (2005). An inverse modelling approach for the estimation of hydrological model parameters. *Journal of Hydroinformatics*.

Topcuoglu, H., Hariri, S., & Wu, M. Y. (2002). Performance-effective and low-complexity task scheduling for heterogeneous computing. *Parallel and Distributed Systems. IEEE Transactions on, 13*(3), 260–274.

Tsiakkouri, E., Sakellariou, R., Zhao, H., & Dikaiakos, M. (2005). Scheduling Workflows with Budget Constraints. Core GRID Integration Workshop, 347-357.

Ullman, J. D. (1975). NP-complete Scheduling Problems. *Journal of Computer and System Sciences, 10*(3), 384–393. doi:10.1016/S0022-0000(75)80008-0

Verma, A., & Kaushal, S. (2015). Cost-time efficient scheduling plan for executing workflows in the cloud. *Journal of Grid Computing, 13*(4), 495–506. doi:10.100710723-015-9344-9

Wang, X. (2014, October). Reference point-based evolutionary multi-objective optimization for reversible logic circuit synthesis. In *Biomedical Engineering and Informatics (BMEI), 2014 7th International Conference on* (pp. 955-959). IEEE. 10.1109/BMEI.2014.7002910

Wieczorek, M., Podlipnig, S., Prodan, R., & Fahringer, T. (2008). Bi-criteria scheduling of scientific workflows for the grid. In *Cluster Computing and the Grid, 2008. CCGRID'08. 8th IEEE International Symposium on* (pp. 9-16). IEEE. 10.1109/CCGRID.2008.21

Yu, J., & Buyya, R. (2005). A taxonomy of workflow management systems for grid computing. *Journal of Grid Computing, 3*(3-4), 171–200. doi:10.100710723-005-9010-8

Yu, J., & Buyya, R. (2006). Scheduling Scientific Workflow Applications with Deadline and Budget Constraints using Genetic Algorithms. *Scientific Programming, 14*(3-4), 217–230. doi:10.1155/2006/271608

Yu, J., Buyya, R., & Tham, C. K. (2005). Cost-based scheduling of scientific workflow applications on utility grids. In *e-Science and Grid Computing, 2005. First International Conference on*. IEEE.

Yu, J., Kirley, M., & Buyya, R. (2007). Multi-objective planning for workflow execution on grids. In *Proceedings of the 8th IEEE/ACM International conference on Grid Computing* (pp. 10-17). IEEE Computer Society. 10.1109/GRID.2007.4354110

Chapter 10
An Optimal Configuration of Sensitive Parameters of PSO Applied to Textual Clustering

Reda Mohamed Hamou
Dr. Moulay Tahar University of Saida, Algeria

Abdelmalek Amine
Dr. Tahar Moulay University of Saida, Algeria

Mohamed Amine Boudia
Dr. Tahar Moulay University of Saida, Algeria

Ahmed Chaouki Lokbani
Dr. Tahar Moulay University of Saida, Algeria

ABSTRACT

The clustering aims to minimize intra-class distance in the cluster and maximize extra-classes distances between clusters. The text clustering is a very hard task; it is solved generally by metaheuristic. The current literature offers two major metaheuristic approaches: neighborhood metaheuristics and population metaheuristics. In this chapter, the authors seek to find the optimal configuration of sensitive parameters of the PSO algorithm applied to textual clustering. The study will go through in dissociable steps, namely the representation and indexing textual documents, clustering by biomimetic approach, optimized by PSO, the study of parameter sensitivity of the optimization technique, and improvement of clustering. The authors will test several parameters and keep the best configurations that return the best results of clustering. They will use the most widely used evaluation measures like index of Davies and Bouldin (internal) and two external: the F-measure and entropy, which are based on recall and precision.

DOI: 10.4018/978-1-5225-5832-3.ch010

INTRODUCTION

Currently, due to the exponentially increasing amount of electronic textual information, the major problem for computer scientists is access to the content of textual information. This requires the use of more specific tools to access and siphon through the content of texts in a faster and more effective way.

Text Mining aims to develop new and effective algorithms for processing, searching, and extracting knowledge from textual and unstructured documents. One of the techniques widely used is called clustering.

Nature is a source of inspiration for researchers in various fields. These inspirations offer a natural framework to solve these problems in a flexible and adaptive way. The swarm intelligence is a field of interdisciplinary research that is relatively recent.

We are interested in studying the algorithms that are based on the specific movements of a swarm of agents to solve a problem. We chose the PSO algorithm ("particle swarm optimization") that uses a set of particles characterized by their position and velocity to optimize one or more fitness functions in a search space. This algorithm was initially proposed as a meta-heuristic for solving optimization problems.

In this paper, we use textual clustering by applying the PSO algorithm for multi-objective optimization (minimizing the intra-class distance and maximizing distances extra-class) and study the sensitivity parameters of the PSO for improvement on the quality of the textual clustering.

The study will go through in dissociable steps:

1. The representation and indexing of textual documents
2. Clustering by biomimetic approach
3. Optimized by PSO
4. Study the sensitivity parameter.

REPRESENTATION OF TEXTUAL DOCUMENTS

The machine learning algorithms cannot process directly the unstructured data: image, video, and of course, the texts written in natural language. Thus, we are obliged to pass by an indexing step.

The indexing step is simply a representation of the text as a vector where each entry corresponds to a different word and the number at that entry corresponds to how many times that word was present in the document (or some function of it); this is very delicate and very important at the same time: a poor or bad representation will lead certainly to bad results.

We will represent each text as a vector where each entry corresponds to a different word and the number at that entry corresponds to how many times that word was present in the document (or some function of it). In this way, we shall have a vector which represents the text and which is exploitable by machine learning algorithms at the same time. The main characteristic of the vector representation is that every language is associated with a particular dimension in the vector space. Two texts using the same textual segments are projected on identical vectors.

Several approaches for the representation of texts exist in the literature, among whom the bag-of-words representation which is the simplest and the most used, the bag-of-sentences representation, the n-gram representation which is a representation independent from the natural language and conceptual representation.

Choice of Term

In our study, we use the n-gram method. The n-grams of character consider spaces because the not grip of spaces introduces the noise. Many works have shown the efficiency of n-grams as a method of representation of texts.

This method has many strong points, we made a comparison between the n-gram and other methods of representation of texts and we get the following points:

1. N-grams capture the stems of the words automatically without going through the research phase of lexical roots.
2. N-grams are language independent.
3. The n-gram method tolerates the spelling mistakes and the noise which can be caused by using of OCR (Optical Character Recognition) for example
4. The key limitation of n-gram feature extraction is that the length of the n-gram increases and the dimensionality of feature set will increase.

Weighting

When the matrix document - term (document = text, term = token) is ready, we calculate the weighting of matrix document-term by using one of the coding known (tf-idf, or tfc). The weight of a term tk in the text i (message or email)is calculated as:

TF-IDF

$$Tf - Idf\left(t_k, i\right) = Nb * \log\left(A/B\right) \tag{1}$$

Nb: The number of occurrences of the term tk in the text i (message or email);
A: The total number of documents (message or email) in the corpus
B: The number of text (message or email) in which the term tk appears at least once.

TFC

$$tfc\left(t_k, p_i\right) = \frac{tf - idf\left(t_k, p_i\right)}{\sqrt{\sum_{i=1}^{|p|} tf - idf\left(t_k, p_i\right)^2}} \tag{2}$$

In all areas of computing in which you want to automatically analyze a set of data, it is necessary to have an operator can accurately assess the similarities or dissimilarities that exist within the data. On this basis, it becomes possible to order the elements of the set, prioritize or to extract invariants.

To describe this operator in our area which is supervised and unsupervised classification of text document we use the term "similarity". This similarity is expressed by several types of vector distances.

Similarity Metrics

To automatically analyze a set of data, it is necessary to have an operator to estimate exactly the similarities or differences between them; for that, we use the similarity metrics. We say that two documents are close if the distance between them is small. If the distance between D1 and D2 is small then the similarity is big.

To describe this operator in our field which is the textual clustering we use the term "similarity".

This similarity is expressed by several types of vector distances. Distances used our chapter are:

Let $X=[x_1, x_2, \ldots \ldots x_n]$

and

$Y=[y_1, y_2, \ldots \ldots y_n]$ two vectors of R

The Minkowski distance between vectors X and Y are defined by:

$$d_p\left(X, Y\right) = \sqrt[p]{\sum_{i=1}^{n}\left|x_i - y_i\right|^p} \quad avec\, p \in N \tag{3}$$

If $p = 1$, the Minkowski distance is called Manhattan distance and is given by:

$$d_1\left(X, Y\right) = \sum_{i=1}^{n}\left|x_i - y_i\right| \tag{4}$$

and if $p = 2$, it is called Euclidean distance and is defined by

$$d_2\left(X, Y\right) = \sqrt[2]{\sum_{i=1}^{n}\left(x_i - y_i\right)^2} \tag{5}$$

Chebyshev distance given by the formula:

$$Chebyshev\left(x, y\right) = \max_i\left(\left|x_i - y_i\right|\right) \tag{6}$$

The Cosine distance given by the formula:

$$Cosine\left(X, Y\right) = \frac{X.Y}{|X||Y|} = \sum_{i=1}^{n}x_i.y_i \Big/ \sqrt{\sum_{i=1}^{n}x_i^2}\sqrt{\sum_{i=1}^{n}y_i^2} \tag{7}$$

THE CLUSTERING OF DATA BY THE PSO

PSO is relatively recent; the first articles pertaining to PSO date from 1995. It is a method that uses a population of agents, here called particles, but, as will be seen, by compared with other heuristics from the same family, it has some interesting features, among others, notion that efficiency which is due to the collaboration rather than competition.

The Particle Swarm Optimization (PSO) was proposed by Kennedy and Eberhart (1995). This method is inspired by the social behavior of animals living in the swarm. The example most commonly used is the behavior of schools of fish or flock of birds or bees living in swarm (exploitation of food sources, building shelves, etc.). Indeed, it can be observed in these animals relatively complex dynamic movement, while than individually each individual has limited intelligence and local knowledge only of its position in the swarm. An individual of the swarms have for knowledge the position and the speed of its nearest neighbors. Each individual therefore uses not only its own memory, but also local information on its closest neighbors to decide its own movement. Simple rules, such as going to the same speed as the other, moving in the same direction or remain close to their neighbors are examples of behaviors that are sufficient to maintain the cohesion of the swarm, and allow the implementation of complex collective behaviors and adaptive. The overall swarm intelligence is the direct result of local interactions between individual particles of the swarm. The performance of the whole system is higher than the sum of the performance of its parts.

The quality of a solution of the search space in an optimization problem is determined by the value of the objective function at that point.

Informal Description (Bonabeau,1999)

The version history may be easily described from the point of view of a particle. At the start of the algorithm, a swarm is randomly distributed in space research, each particle also having a random speed. Then, at each time step:

- Each particle is able to assess the quality of its position it has achieved so far(which can sometimes actually be the current position) and quality (the value in this position of the function to be optimized).
- Each particle is able to interview a number of its congeners (his informants, including itself) and get each of them its own best performance (and the quality there of).
- At each time step, each particle chooses the best of the best performances of which it has knowledge, changes speed based on this information and own data and moves accordingly.

Once the best informant detected, each particle directed his next move by combining three trends: follow its own speed, back to his best performance, go to the best performance of his informants.

The change of velocity is a simple linear combination of three trends with confidence coefficients (Hamane, 2009):

- Trend "adventurous" or also called physical component, are to continue under the current speed.
- Trend "conservative" or also called cognitive component returning more or less to the best position already found.

- Trend "overreaction" or also called social component, directing approximately to the best informant.

Neighborhood Particle (Rioland, 2007)

It is then necessary to define the neighborhoods and their structure, there are two types:

The Geographical Neighborhoods

Neighbors of a particle are its nearest neighbors. This type of neighborhood requires the use of a distance to recalculate at each iteration (or all k iterations) neighbors of each particle. Below is an example where the neighbors of a particle are the two particles that are nearest.

Figure 1. Schematic diagram of the displacement of a particle

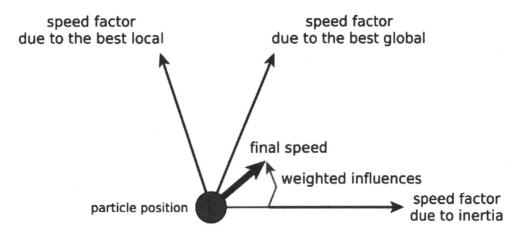

Figure 2. Example of neighborhood

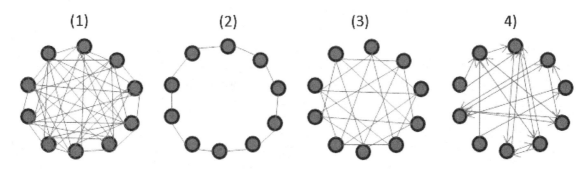

The Social Neighborhoods

Neighborhoods are established at initialization and do not change thereafter. There are different structures of social neighborhoods, we present a few.

If you use a neighborhood in rows and columns then two particles of the swarm are neighbors if they belong to the same row or the same column. If using a circular neighborhood, the neighbors of a particle are, for example, both of which are positioned to the left and two that are positioned to the right. The principle of the particle swarm optimization has been especially designed from social models. In fact, each particle is based on its own experience and that of its neighbors. To move it takes into account its history (his best position) and is attracted by the current best particle in its neighborhood. This is the model of individual behavior within a tribe.

This is the social neighborhood is most used for several reasons:

- It is easier to program,
- It is less time consuming calculation,
- Anyway, in case of convergence, a social neighborhood tends to become a geographical neighborhood (Clerc, 2003).

Formal Description

We begin by describing the method of calculating the velocity V_n, and the position X_n, of a particle Π_n in this field. These two elements are given for iteration given by Equations 7 and 8, where p_n is the best position visited by particle Π_n and l_n is the best position visited by his informants, w is the inertia factor, c_1 and c_2 are the confidence factors of the algorithm and r_1 and r_2 are real numbers chosen randomly in the interval [0,1].

$$V_n\left(t\right) = w.v_n\left(t-1\right) + c_1.r_1\left(p_n - x_n\left(t-1\right)\right) + c_2.r_2\left(l_n - x_n\left(t-1\right)\right) \tag{8}$$

$$X_n\left(t\right) = X_n\left(t-1\right) + V_n\left(t\right) \tag{9}$$

This model is called model *lBest* (local best model). When the notion of Neighborhood of a particle is extended to the entire population, the best position visited by the informants is the best overall position g and is obtained the model *gbest* (global best model) whose formula for calculating the speed given by the following equation:

$$V_n\left(t\right) = w.v_n\left(t-1\right) + c_1.r_1\left(p_n - x_n\left(t-1\right)\right) + c_2.r_2\left(g - x_n\left(t-1\right)\right) \tag{10}$$

w is usually a constant called, inertia coefficient, c_1 and c_2 are constants, called acceleration coefficients, r_1 and r_2 are two random numbers drawn uniformly in [0,1] for each iteration and for each dimension to allow a better exploration of the search space (Cooren,2008).

$w.v_n\left(t-1\right)$ corresponds to the physical component of displacement. The parameter w controls the influence of the direction of movement on the future movement. It should be noted that in some applications, the parameter w can be variable (Siarry, 2008).

$c_1.r_1(p_n - x_n\left(t-1\right))$ corresponds to the cognitive component of displacement. c_1 controls the cognitive behavior of the particle.

$c_2.r_2\left(l_n - x_n\left(t-1\right)\right)$ corresponds to the social component of displacement. c_1 control the social aptitude of the particle.

The combination of parameters w, c_1 and c_2 can adjust the balance between diversification and intensification phases of the research process (Shi, 1998) It should be noted that the term velocity is abusive here because the vectors V_i are not homogeneous speed. It would be more appropriate to speak of "direction of displacement". However, to respect the analogy with the animal world, it instead uses the term "speed" (Eberhart, 1995).

Clustering Data by PSO

In recent years, the PSO method has been shown to be both effective and quick to resolve some optimization problems. The latter has been successfully applied in many research fields such as data classification (Jain,1988). Thus, it is possible to view the clustering problem as an optimization problem that locates the optimal centroids of data rather than finding an optimal partition. This view gives us a possibility to apply the PSO clustering problem, the aim of clustering algorithm by PSO as by other methods is to find the centroids of clusters making:

- High homogeneity of each class
- Good separation of classes

The clustering algorithm consists of two step

- The first step in global search (initialization)
- A second refinement step (optimization)

Algorithm Adopted

It is assumed that each particle in the swarm represents a possible solution for clustering of documents it is represented by a matrix $x_i = \{c_1, c_2, ... c_i .... c_k\}$ is the vector or centroid of ith cluster and k is the number of cluster.

At each iteration the particles adjust their centroids vectors (position and velocity) according to their best positions and the best position of their informants according to the following equations:

$$V_{ij}\left(t\right)=w.v_{ij}\left(t-1\right)+c_1.r_1\left(p_{ij}-x_{ij}\left(t-1\right)\right)+c_2.r_2\left(g_{ij}-x_{ij}\left(t-1\right)\right) \tag{11}$$

$$X_{ij}\left(t\right)=X_{ij}\left(t-1\right)+V_{ij}\left(t\right) \qquad j\in\left\{1,2,.....,D\right\} \tag{12}$$

The average distance between the centroids and documents is used as fitness function to evaluate the solutions represented by each particle, the fitness function is given by the following formula:

$$f=\frac{\sum_{i=1}^{N_c}\left[\dfrac{\sum_{j=1}^{P_i}d\left(o_i,m_{ij}\right)}{P_i}\right]}{N_c}\left(Xiaohui,2005\right) \tag{13}$$

m_{ij} is the jth document vector belonging to the ith cluster;

o_i is the centroid vector, of the ith cluster;

$d\left(o_i,m_{ij}\right)$ is the distance between the centroid o_i and Document m_{ij} .

P_i is the number of documents belonging to the ith cluster.

N_c is the number of clusters.

Our algorithm can be summarized as following:

1. In the initial state, each particle, chosen randomly, k vectors member documents as vectors cluster centroids.
2. For each particle
    a. Assigning each document of the set to appropriate cluster (minimum With its centroid distance)
    b. Calculate the fitness chosen to be according to equation (13).
    c. Generating the new position and velocity for each particle using Equations (11) and (12).
3. Repeating step (2) until the stopping criterion satisfaction

EXPERIMENTS AND RESULTS

We experimented 500 documents of Benchmarks "Reuters 21578" represented by the 2-grams and indexed by two coding approaches namely Tf-Idf and TFC.

The quality of clustering achieved by each method must be evaluated either by internal indices (which concern the classification itself) or external compares with other classification. The internal indice used in our study concerns the Davies and Bouldin, and external indices used relate entropy and the f-measure.

Davies and Bouldin Indice

Davies and Bouldin indice is a function based on the minimization of the ratio of dispersions intra clusters and inter-clusters separation. This indice ensures that the clusters are compact. This indice has a small value for a good grouping and is defined as follows:

$$DB = \frac{1}{n}\sum_{i=1}^{n} max_{i \neq j} \left\{ \frac{S_n(Q_i) + S_n(Q_j)}{S(Q_i, Q_j)} \right\} \tag{14}$$

where

- n : Number of clusters
- S_n : The average distance of all objects in the cluster their centroid.
- $S(Q_i, Q_j)$: The distance between the centers of the clusters.

F-Measure and Entropy

To calculate the purity of the clusters and the quality of clustering, we use two well-known measure, which the entropy and the f measure based on the following functions:

$$precision(i, k) = \frac{N_{i,k}}{N_k} \tag{15}$$

$$recall(i, k) = \frac{N_{i,k}}{N_{c_i}} \tag{16}$$

where

- N is the total number of documents.
- i is the number of predefined class.
- K is the number of clusters.
- N_{ci} is the number of documents in class i.
- N_k is the number of documents in cluster k.
- N_{ik} number of documents of class i in cluster k.

Entropy and F-measure of the partition P are defined as follows:

$$F(p) = \sum \frac{N_{c_i}}{N} \max_{i=1} k \frac{\left(1 + ^2\right) \times \text{racall}(i, k) \times \text{precision}(i, k)}{^2 \times \text{racall}(i, k) + \text{precision}(i, k)} \tag{16}$$

$$E(p) = \sum_{k=1}^{K} \frac{N_k}{N} \times \left(-\sum \text{precision}(i, k) \times \log\left(\text{precision}(i, k)\right)\right) \tag{17}$$

Study of the Sensitivity Parameters for the PSO Clustering

To extract the best result of clustering by the PSO we need to experiment by changing parameters that can intervene in the quality of the results one by one (each time we change a parameter we set the other to their best values) and see their influence by measuring each change the quality of clustering result.

The parameters of PSO are numerous and each is influenced on the results of the method.

Size of the Swarm

Studies have shown that more we increase the number of particles, the method converges more in a reduced number of iterations. But the disadvantage is that more we increase the size of the swarm more computation time per iteration is enormous. Whence a number of particles through is better in most cases, some researchers have tried to find the optimal size depending on the size of the problem and led to the following formula (Sandou, 2009):

$$\text{Swarm size} = 10 + \sqrt{D}$$

D is the size of the corpus.

To ensure the quality of our method with this value we will proceed to a successive change of this parameter (including the value of $10 + \sqrt{D}$, which is in our case 32).

From Table 1 we find that:

- The best F-measure is presented with a number of swarm = 32, and the best fitness.

Table 1. Influence of the size of the swarm

Swarm size	# cluster	Fitness	Indice D.B	Entropy	F-measure	Convergence of fitness
10	45	1.97	2.64	0.25	0.40	0.009
20	19	0.54	1.71	0.30	0.76	0.005
32	*12*	*0.37*	*1.99*	*0.30*	*0.77*	*1.9 E-05*
40	47	1.21	1.32	0.29	0.76	0.002
50	49	1.18	1.74	0.26	0.62	0.0006

- The value of entropy in this case = 0.30 (with 12 clusters) and the smallest is 0.26 with (49 clusters) so the information loss of 0.30 compared to 12 clusters is good.
- The DB indice aims the minimization of the ratio of dispersions intra clusters and inter-cluster separation, given the reduced number of cluster (12) in the swarm size 32 and comparing it with the smallest index 1.32 (for 47 cluster), this indice reflects a good clustering.

Based on these results we will fix in the following swarm size to 32.

Size of the Neighborhood

In most studies researchers take the neighborhood size between 3 and 5 (usually 4) (Clerc, 2005) as the optimal value. To ensure the quality of the method which in our case is based on geographical neighborhood we will proceed to a successive change of this parameter and indicate the results:

Parameter of Velocity Change

The velocity change follows the following formula:

$$V_{ij}(t) = w.v_{ij}(t-1) + c_1.r_1(p_{ij} - x_{ij}(t-1)) + c_2.r_2(g_{ij} - x_{ij}(t-1)) \tag{18}$$

The parameters of this formula are determined by performing a variety of tests to have a kind of PSO without parameters.

- $c_1 = c_2 = 1.4960$;
- r_1 and r_2 are random value between 0 and 1;

About inertia, a large value of w is synonymous with a greater range of motion and therefore global exploration of the search space. In contrast, allow value of w is synonymous with low amplitude of movement and therefore local exploration. Fix this factor is therefore to find a compromise between exploitation and exploration of the search space. Commonly found in the literature the value of w

Table 2. Influence of neighborhood size

neighborhood size	# clusters	fitness	Indice of DB	Entropy	F-measure	Convergence of fitness
2	39	1.02	1.87	0.28	0.68	0.001
3	42	1.69	1.61	0.29	0.71	0.004
4	*12*	*0.37*	*1.99*	*0.30*	*0.77*	*1.9 E-5*
5	37	1.23	1.67	0.27	0.74	0.01
6	25	0.81	1.66	0.30	0.77	4.2 E-5
avec Gbest	50	0.54	1.56	0.27	0.71	0.006

=0.7298. Good results have been found for a value decreasing linearly from 0.9 to 0.4 so the inertia factor is given by:

$$w = w_{max} - \frac{w_{max} - w_{min}}{Maximum\,iteration\,number} \times\ current\,iteration$$

w_{max} =0.9 and w_{min} =0.4

Stopping Criterion

The stopping criterion can be either a number of iterations fixed in advance or almost nil variation of velocity (and subsequently the fitness). We will make successive tests to extract the number of iterations assuring convergence. The parameters giving the best results of clustering precedents are set. Regarding the number of cluster we suppose a maximum number of clusters and the method goes minimize (initialization of the number of cluster to a maximum value and an adjustment is made to achieve optimal cluster number).

From Table 3 we note that the stability of the method is achieved from iteration 125 viewed the very low fitness value from this.

After stability, better fitness and F-measure, is presented in the iteration150, with a good entropy, and DB indice relative to the number of cluster(12). So the number of iteration is set in the following to 150.

We also note that there's a peak in the method to75th iteration, the results of this iteration are interesting and will be studied later.

Behavior of a Particle

The behavior of a particle (in terms of fitness value) during the execution of the method until150 iterations is summarized in Table 4.

Table 3. Influence of number of iterations

Number of iterations	# clusters	fitness	DB Indice	Entropy	F-measure	Convergence of fitness
25	50	0.94	3.03	0.26	0.21	0.026
50	50	0.84	3.15	0.25	0.15	0.0096
75	*14*	*0.39*	*1.66*	*0.37*	*0.83*	*0.002*
100	44	1.15	2.40	0.30	0.52	0.0049
125	41	1.06	1.92	0.32	0.56	6.16 E -05
150	*12*	*0.37*	*1.99*	*0.35*	*0.77*	*1.91 E -05*
200	42	1.2	2.5	0.29	0.52	5.5 E -05

Table 4. Behavior of a particle during iterations

Iteration	25	50	75	100	125	135	145	150
Particle 1	0,04	0,11	0,12	0,55	0,03	0,0388	0,03886	0,03886
Particle 2	0,7	0,079	0,52	0,15	0,01	0,019	0,01905	0,01905
Particle 3	0,049	0,2	0,21	0,4	0,01	0,019	0,01907	0,01907
Particle 4	0,28	0,28	0,29	0,74	0,02	0,021	0,02087	0,02087

We note that in early of iterations, the variation of the particles is interesting. The stability of the particles begins from the iteration125.

Results of Classification

All PSO parameters studied are fixed at their optimal values.

With the TFC Coding

According to the results of the previous table we see that the best results for the coding TFC with150 iterations are those of the Chebyshev distance with a reduced computation time, high F-measure and low entropy.

Figure 3. Behavior of a particle

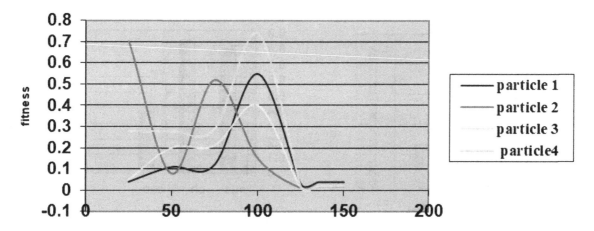

Table 5. TFC Coding

Distance	# cluster	Entropy	F-Measure
Euclidienne	12	0.30	0.77
Chebyshev	*5*	*0.06*	*0.89*
Cosinus	47	0.62	0.41

With the Tf-Idf Coding

According to the results of the previous table we see that the best results for the coding TFIDF with150 iterations are those of the Chebyshev distance with a reduced computation time a high F-measure and low entropy.

Comparison

Also in the field of biomimicry, we compared the best results of the PSO method with those of cellular automata and immune systems. The best evaluation is given to the PSO having regarded its greatest f-measure by cons in terms of computation time cellular automata have ample advantage (learning in less than one second for 1000 documents). The analysis results coincide with the literature given that the PSO is a metaheuristic with a high temporal complexity.

Table 6. Results of coding TFIDF

Distance	# cluster	Comput. Time (S)	Entropy	F-Measure
Euclidienne	8	4076	0.31	0.78
Tcheby	*3*	*1338*	*0.05*	*0.84*
Cosinus	36	4599	0.64	0.38

Figure 4. Comparison of three distances for Tf-Idf coding

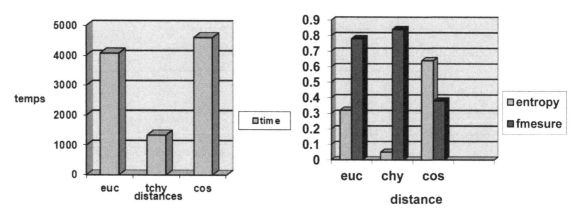

Table 7. Results of comparison with other biomimetic methods

	F-measure	# Class	Comput. Time
PSO	0,89	5	1066
Cellular Automata	0,51	43	0,786
Immune System	0,45	30	8,125

CONCLUSION AND PERSPECTIVES

Through all the tests and experiments performed we note that the size of the swarm is a very sensitive issue for PSO because every time we increase this size, the quality of clustering increases. After several trials on parameter, we fixed on optimal value of 32. The size of the neighborhood is also interesting, a neighborhood size=4 was set after several tests.

The stability of the method must be guaranteed to get good results that are why we madeseveral tests on the number of iterations to determine the sufficient number for the stability that has been fixed in our case150. Despite that there's a peak of the method with 75 iterations.

The best results in 2 types of coding used are obtained with the Chebyshev distance; this distance has proven by its simplicity enormous efficiency with the PSO method, it allowed us to have a very small execution time and very good value assessments.

In this paper we study the clustering of documents from another point of view, we consider the problem as an optimization problem which aims to minimize an objective function that guarantee the intra-clusters dispersion and separation between clusters in the classification.

The optimization method used is a biomimetic method, inspired by the displacement of the swarms of insects or poisons known PSO (particle Swarm Optimization). This method is relatively young, has proved its effectiveness in the area of clustering, due to its easy programming, its accuracy and its interesting results.

In our case we made an unsupervised classification of 500 documents, after several tests and experiments on the parameters of the method, the results were very encouraging and proved the effectiveness of the latter, the major drawback of this method is the enormous computational time as all meta-heuristics.

Our results are only the beginning of research for clustering with PSO, the results can be enriched with comparison with other types of coding and large corpus. For the problem of computing time, parallel programming is envisaged.

REFERENCES

Bhuyan, J. N. (1991). Genetic algorithm for clustering with an ordered representation. *Proceedings of the fourth International Conference on Information Retrieval*, 408-417.

Bonabeau, E., Dorigo, M., & Theraulaz, G. (1999). Swarm Intelligence: From natural to artificial systems (No.1). Oxford University Press.

Boudia, M. A., Hamou, R. M., & Amine, A. (2016). A New Approach Based on the Detection of Opinion by SentiWordNet for Automatic Text Summaries by Extraction. *International Journal of Information Retrieval Research*, 6(3), 19–36. doi:10.4018/IJIRR.2016070102

Boudia, M. A., Hamou, R. M., Amine, A., & Rahmani, A. (2015). A New Biomimetic Method Based on the Power Saves of Social Bees for Automatic Summaries of Texts by Extraction. *International Journal of Software Science and Computational Intelligence*, 7(1), 18–38. doi:10.4018/IJSSCI.2015010102

Boudia, M. A., Hamou, R. M., Amine, A., Rahmani, M. E., & Rahmani, A. (2015, May). A new multi-layered approach for automatic text summaries mono-document based on social spiders. *In IFIP International Conference on Computer Science and its Applications_x000D_* (pp. 193-204). Springer, Cham. 10.1007/978-3-319-19578-0_16

Clerc, M. (2003). TRIBES Un exemple d'optimisation par essaim particulaire sans paramètres de réglage. OEP'03 (Optimisation par Essaim Particulaire), Paris, France.

Clerc, M. (2005), L'optimisation par essaims particulaires, versions paramétriques et adaptatives. Hermès Science.

Cooren, Y., Clerc, M., & Siarry, P. (2008). Initialization and Displacement of the Particles in TRIBES, a Parameter-Free Particle Swarm Optimization Algorithm, Springer. *Studies in Computational Intelligence*, *136*, 199–219.

Deneubourg, J.-L., Goss, S., Franks, N. R., Sendova-Franks, A., Detrain, C., & Chretien, L. (1990) The dynamics of collective sorting: robot-like ant and ant-like robots. *Proceedings of the First International Conference on Simulation of Adaptive Behavior.*

Dziczkowski, G., & Wegrzyn-Wolska, K. (2008). Tool of the Intelligence Economic: Recognition Function of Reviews Critics - Extraction and Linguistic Analysis of Sentiments. *ICSOFT (ISDM/ABF) 2008*, 218-223.

Eberhart, R. C., & Kennedy, J. (1995). Particle Swarm Optimization. *Proceedings of IEEE International Conference on Neural Networks*, 4, 1942–1948. 10.1109/ICNN.1995.488968

Eberhart, R. C., & Shi, Y. (2000). Comparing inertia weights and constriction factors in particle swarm optimization. *Proceedings of the 2000 Congress on Retrieval Information.* 10.1109/CEC.2000.870279

Falkenauer, E. (1994). A new representation and operators for genetic algorithms applied to grouping problems. *Evolutionary Computation*, *2*(2), 1994. doi:10.1162/evco.1994.2.2.123

Fayyad, U. M. (1996). Data mining and knowledge discovery: Making sense out of data. *IEEE Expert*, *11*(5), 20–25. doi:10.1109/64.539013

Fogel, D. B., & Simpson, P. K. (1993) Evolving fuzzy clusters. *Proceedings of ICNN93.*

Frawley, W. J., Piatetsky-Shapiro, G., & Matheus, C. (1991). Knowledge Discovery. In *Databases, chapter Knowledge Discovery In Databases: An Overview.* Cambridge, MA: AAAI Press/MIT Press.

Goldberg, D. E. (1989). Genetic algorithm in search, Optimization and machine Learning. Addison-Wesley.

Goss, S., Aron, S., Deneubourg, J. L., & Pasteels, J. M. (1989). _Self-Organized Shortcuts *Proceedings of the Argentine Conference, Naturwissenchaften*, 76, 579-581.

Hamane, R., Itoh, T., & Tomita, K. (2009). Approximation Algorithms for the Highway Problem under the Coupon Model. *IEICE Transactions on Fundamentals of Electronics, Communications and Computer Science*, *92*(8), 1779–1786. doi:10.1587/transfun.E92.A.1779

Hamou, Abdelmalek, & Mohamed. (2012). Visualization and clustering by 3D cellular automata: Application to unstructured data. *International Journal of Data Mining and Emerging Technologies, 2*(1).

Hamou, R. M. (2012). A New Biomimetic Approach Based on Social Spiders for Clustering of Text, Software Engineering Research, Management and Applications 2012. *Studies in Computational Intelligence, Springer, 430/2012*, 17–30. doi:10.1007/978-3-642-30460-6_2

Hamou, R. M., Lehireche, A., Lokbani, A. C., & Rahmani, M. (2010). Representation of textual documents by the approach wordnet and n-grams for the unsupervised classifcation (clustering) with 2D cellular automata:a comparative study. *Journal of Computer and Information Science, 3*(3), 240-255.

Hamou, R. M., Lehireche, A., Lokbani, A. C., & Rahmani, M. (2010). Clustering Based on the n-grams by Bio Inspired Method (Immune Systems). *International Refereed Research Journal (Researchers Worls), 1*(1).

Holland, J. H. (1975). Adaptation in Natural and Artificial Systems. University of Michigan Press.

Jain A.K., & Dubes, R.C. (1988). *Algorithms for Clustering Data*. Prentice Hall Advanced Reference Series.

Jalam, R. (2003). *Apprentissage automatique et catégorisation de textes multilingues* (PhD thesis). Université Lumière Lyon 2.

Jones, D. R., & Beltramo, M. A. (1991). Solving partitioning problems with genetic algorithms. In *Proceedings of the Fourth International Conference on Genetic Algorithms*. San Diego, CA: Morgan Kaufmann.

Kirkpatrick, S., Gelatt, C. D., & Vecchi, M. P. (1983). Optimization by Simulated Annealing. *Science, 220*(4598), 671–680. doi:10.1126cience.220.4598.671 PMID:17813860

Lawrence, S., & Giles, C. L. (1998). Context and Page Analysis for Improved Web Search. *IEEE Internet Computing, 2*(4), 38–46. doi:10.1109/4236.707689

Lewis, D. (1992). *Representation and Learning in Information Retrieval* (Ph.D. thesis). Department of Computer Science, University of Massachusetts.

MacQueen, J. B. (1967). Some methods for classification and analysis of multivariate observations. *Proceedings of Fifth Berkeley Symposium, 2*.

Proctor, G., & Winter, C. (1998). Information flocking: Data visualisation in virtual worlds using emergent behaviours. *Proceedings First International Conference Virtual Worlds*, 1434.

Raghavan, V. V., & Birchard, K. (1979) A clustering strategy based on a formalism of the reproductive process in natural systems. In *Proceedings of the Second International Conference on Information Storage and Retrieval*. ACM. 10.1145/511706.511709

Reynolds, C. W., & Flocks, H. (1987). A distributed behavioural model. *Computer Graphics (SIGGRAPH '87 Conference Proceedings), 21*(4).

Rioland, A., &Eudes, A. (2007). *Raport de projet Optimisation par essaim particulaire pour un problème d'ordonnancement et d'affectation de ressources*. Institut Superieur D'informatique De Modelisation et de Leurs Applications.

Salton, G., & Buckley, C. (1988). Term-weighting approaches in automatic text retrieval. *Information Processing & Management*, *24*(5), 513–523. doi:10.1016/0306-4573(88)90021-0

Sandou, G. (2009). *Optimisation par essaim pour la synthèse de lois de commande: du PID à la synthèse H¥ Supélec*. Département Automatique.

Shannon, C. (1948). A mathematical theory of communication. Bell System Technical Journal, 27. *The Bell System Technical Journal*, 17.

Shi, Y., & Eberhart, R. C. (1998). Parameter Selection in Particle Swarm Optimization. *Proceedings of the 7th Annual Conference on Evolutionary Programming*.

Siarry, P., & Michalewicz, Z. (Eds.). (2008). Advances in Metaheuristics for Hard Optimization. Springer.

Xiaohui, C., & Potok, T. E. (2005). Document Clustering Analysis based on Hybrid PSO+K-means Algorithm. *The Journal of Computer Science*, *1*(3), 27 – 33.

Chapter 11

An Improved Hybridized Evolutionary Algorithm Based on Rules for Local Sequence Alignment

Jayapriya J.
National Institute of Technology, India

Michael Arock
National Institute of Technology, India

ABSTRACT

In bioinformatics, sequence alignment is the heart of the sequence analysis. Sequence can be aligned locally or globally depending upon the biologist's need for the analysis. As local sequence alignment is considered important, there is demand for an efficient algorithm. Due to the enormous sequences in the biological database, there is a trade-off between computational time and accuracy. In general, all biological problems are considered as computational intensive problems. To solve these kinds of problems, evolutionary-based algorithms are proficiently used. This chapter focuses local alignment in molecular sequences and proposes an improvised hybrid evolutionary algorithm using particle swarm optimization and cellular automata (IPSOCA). The efficiency of the proposed algorithm is proved using the experimental analysis for benchmark dataset BaliBase and compared with other state-of-the-art techniques. Using the Wilcoxon matched pair signed rank test, the significance of the proposed algorithm is explicated.

INTRODUCTION

The Ultimate goal of Bioinformatics is to better understand the functionality of living cells at the molecular level. They are basically three analysis in molecular level namely sequence, structural and functional analysis. Amongst them sequence analysis is considered as the important one as it paves way for other two analysis. The first step in this is to align the sequences locally or globally where both are regard as important for biologist. In analysis, sequences are represented as the combination of alphabet (Xiong,

DOI: 10.4018/978-1-5225-5832-3.ch011

2006). Figure 1 shows the overview of bioinformatics domain. This figure explains the three analysis and its applications. Apart from these applications there are many in sequence analysis. As sequence analysis is the first phase of the investigation, many researches are developed in this area.

Sequence alignment is a process in which sequences are arranged in such a way that similar residues are found in the same column. Initially, two sequences are aligned to find the similarity between them is known as pair-wise alignment (PA). As an extension of PA, Multiple Sequence Alignment (MSA) came into exists, where in this more than two sequences are aligned. These sequences can be aligned locally or globally depending upon the information needed for the analysis. The main applications of sequence alignment are to construct phylogenetic tree, to find motif (conserved patterns), gene promoter. These identified motifs give more information that is used to study the relationship between the sequences and its consequences. The different forms of sequence alignment are depicted in Figure 2. The sequences in the pair-wise alignment in the figure 2 represents protein and in the MSA, DNA sequences. Both the alignment can be done for all types of molecular sequences. MSA reveals additional biological information than pair-wise alignment. Likewise local alignment gives information as global alignment. Local alignments are more useful for dissimilar sequences that are suspected to contain regions of similarity. A locally aligned sequence is used to find the motif patterns. In MSA process, three major tasks are scoring; creating an alignment and assessing its significances. Depending upon the type of alignment scoring function are chosen. Any statistical test applied on the bases of dataset comparison.

Exhaustive and heuristic algorithms are two forms of traditional alignment approaches. Dynamic programming sequence matching algorithm is used in exhaustive method. This method was first used for pair-wise alignment. These types of methods are used only for small number of sequences dataset. Many heuristic algorithms has been encouraged to solve the above mentioned problem. This can be classified into Progressive Alignment (PA), Iterative Alignment (IA) and Block-based Alignment (BA) types. BA method (Mohsen et al., 2011) is used to find the conserved domains and motifs. It is not done through PA and IA methods.

Figure 1. Overview of bioinformatics domain

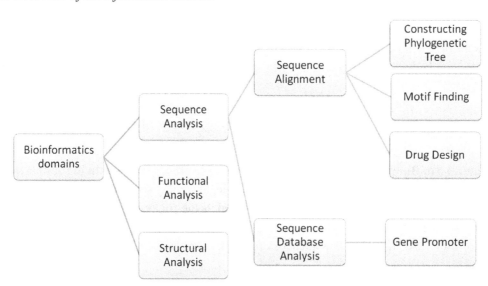

Figure 2. Different forms of sequence alignment

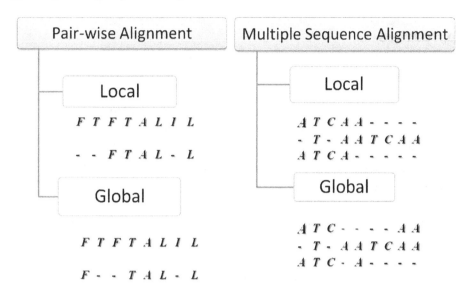

The PA algorithms initially start aligning most similar pairs of sequence and then continue with less similar ones. Even though PA is fast, it is not suitable for aligning sequences of different lengths. Some of the progressive type algorithms are T-Coffee (Notredame C et al., 2000), DBClustal (Thompson J D et al., 2000), PRALINE (Simossis V A et al., 2005), where PRALINE is more sophisticated and accurate alignment program, but extremely slow in terms of time. This problem is overcome by the iterative alignment. The main idea of this is to repeatedly modify suboptimal solutions to find the optimal solution. This chapter proposes one type of iterative approach to align the sequences locally.

The main objectives of this Chapter are:

- To proposes an efficient algorithm to align long and large number of multiple molecular sequences.
- To align the sequence set locally that is used to find motif.

This chapter is organized as follows. First, in Background section the basic approaches used in this chapter and the literature review is presented. In Section Main Focus of the Chapter, the problem and its solution as proposed algorithm is explained. Section Solution and Recommendations explicate the experimental analysis of the proposed algorithm and proved its significance. Eventually, the chapter is concluded with the conclusion and future research directions.

BACKGROUND

Related Approaches

Need for Evolutionary Algorithms

In general, biological problems are computational intensive one. Many bio-inspired algorithms are used in solving these kind of biological problems. Each algorithm has its own merits and demerits. Apart from many algorithms, one of the swarm intelligence namely, Particle Swarm Optimization (PSO) is used efficiently for biological computational intensive problems. This is because it has less parameter and avoids local optima problem.

Evolutionary Algorithms for Sequence Alignment

In general, more information is gathered from global/ local alignment depending upon the need of biologist. An important advantage of Evolutionary Algorithm (EA) based approach over progressive methods is that, different fitness function can be tested without modifying the alignment procedure. There are many works proposed using EA like (Notredame C et al., 2000; Rasmussen TK et al., 2003; Lee Z J et al., 2008; KayaM et al., 2014). Tsiligaridis in 2016 proposed a hybrid genetic algorithm that proves it is stochastic approach and very beneficial for MSA in terms of their performance.

Notredame C et al., (1996) has proposed a genetic algorithm, namely Sequence Alignment by Genetic Algorithm(SAGA) with sum of pairs as objective function using tertiary structure datasets. Notredame C et al., (2000) has proposed a progressive alignment based method using position-specific scoring scheme. Yin et al., in (2002) has proposed a new approach for Multiple Sequence Alignment using Genetic Algorithms (MSAGA). This algorithm uses the fitter spanning tree for sequence alignment. Rasmussen T K et al., (2003) has proposed improved Hidden Markov Model with PSO using SP as objective function. Edgar (2004) has proposed a new computer program called MUSCLE for multiple sequence alignment problem using two distance measures. For unaligned pair k-mer distance and for aligned pair the Kimura distance are employed. Lee et al., (2008) has developed a hybrid algorithm with GA (Genetic Algorithm) & ACO (Ant Colony Optimization) using Sum-of-Pairs (SP) score. Nazin et al., (2012) has developed a progressive alignment method using GA and the Weighted Sum of Product (WSOP) as objective function for small sequence length. Chang et al., (2012) has proposed a consistency based approach with the homology extension in order to significantly improve the multiple sequence alignment of alpha helical TMPs. Sun et al., (2012) has proposed a quantum behaved particle swarm optimization (QPSO) that is analyzed mathematically and then anticipated an improved version using the HMMs. Fan et al., (2012) has proposed an improved genetic algorithm for multiple sequence alignment that represents three ways to get better genetic algorithm.

Hamidi et al., (2013) has proposed a protein multiple sequence alignment based on secondary structure similarity. Here, initially the sequences are divided into groups according to their secondary structure similarities after that the sequences in each group are aligned with each other. Finally, the alignment results from all the groups are aligned together. Katoh et al. (2013) has anticipated a major update of the MAFFT multiple sequence alignment program. This version has several new features like adding unaligned sequences in an existing alignment, adjustment of direction in nucleotide alignment, constrained alignment and parallel processing. Orobitg et al. (2013) has proposed an improved GA algorithm using Q score as objective function. Kaya et al. (2014) has proposed multi-objective GA (MSAGMOGA) algorithm with affine gap, SP and column score as objective function for MSA problem.

Zemali et al., in 2016 has introduces a new bio-inspired approach to solve such problem. This approach named BA-MSA is based on Bat Algorithm. Bat Algorithm (BA) is a recent evolutionary algorithm inspired from Bats behavior seeking their prey. The proposed approach includes new mechanism to generate initial population. It consists in generating a guide tree for each solution with progressive approach by varying some parameters. The generated guide tree will be enhanced by Hill-Climbing algorithm. In addition, to deal with the premature convergence of BA, a new restart technique is proposed to introduce more diversification when detecting premature convergence. In 2016, Jayapriya et al. has proposed a Particle Swarm Optimization with Cellular Automata algorithm for aligning multiple molecular sequences. In this paper, a novel preprocessing technique is proposed for unequal length of sequences. This algorithm yields better global alignment when compared to other state-of-the-art techniques but for only medium length sequences. Lalwani et al., in 2017 has proposes Two-Level Particle Swarm Optimization (TL-PSO), an efficient PSO variant that addresses two levels of optimization problem. Level one works on optimizing dimension for entire swarm, whereas level two works for optimizing each particle's position. In 2017, Hussein et al., has proposed a Flower Pollination Algorithm (FPA) for the multiple sequence alignment problem. In essence, EA based methods reduced the time for computational intensive problems.

There are many algorithms that use bio-inspired concepts for this particular problem where each has its own merits and demerits. From the above study, it is concluded that there is a tradeoff between the computational time and accuracy. In additional to this, there is another deal among the number of sequences and its varying length. So the MSA is considered as challenging problem which leads to the development of new algorithms. When PSO and CA algorithm implemented separately for the MSA problem some issues were found. Here the drawback of PSO is dominance of global alignment and in CA convergence rate is slow. When these algorithms are combined together (PSOCA) the convergence of solution is fast by PSO and the local alignment is also considered because of CA (Jayapriya et al., 2016). The issues in this algorithm are, it doesn't suits for long and large number of sequences and it is global alignment. Considering these two issues, this chapter proposes an Improvised version of PSOCA algorithm. All the algorithms for MSA are evaluated according to a particular scoring function which is the objective function for finding one of the best solutions. The scoring function, Sum of Pairs (SP) and Total Column Score (TC) are considered in most of the algorithms for evaluating the alignment. The Sum-of-Paris is given as

$$SP = \sum_{i=1}^{n-1} \sum_{j=i+1}^{n} S(l_i, l_j) \tag{1}$$

where $S(l_i, l_j)$ is the score of induced pair-wise alignment.

The number of correctly aligned columns divided by number of columns is the reference alignment is known as Total Column (TC).

PROPOSED WORK TECHNIQUES

Particle Swarm Optimization Technique

The objective of this algorithm is to find an optimal solution for any computational intensive problem using the behavior of bird flock that is searching for food. Kenny and Eberhart proposed this algorithm in 1995. The main idea of the PSO algorithm is considering each bird as particle that represents a solution and group of birds as swarm that represents a population. Let us consider $X_i = (X_{i1}, X_{i2...,}X_{id})$ represents each particle in dimension d and $V_i = (V_{i1}, V_{i2...,}V_{id})$ represents the flying velocity of each particle. Initially the position of the particles is given as $P_i = (p_{i1}, p_{i2}...p_{id})$ i.e., particle best position and $P_g = (p_{g1}, p_{g2...}p_{gd})$ as global best position discovered in each iteration or generation. With the above definitions, two properties of variables are found for each particle P as follows: The velocity is given by

$$V_{id}(t + 1) = wV_{id}(t) + c_1\varphi_1(P_d(t) - X_{id}(t)) + c_2\varphi_2(g_d(t) - X_{id}(t)) \qquad (2)$$

where $w, c_1, \varphi_1, c_2, \varphi_2$ are constants, t represents a generation. The position is given by

$$X_{id}(t + 1) = X_{id}(t) + V_{id}(t + 1) \qquad (3)$$

The following is the general algorithm for PSO.

Algorithm 1: PSO

1. Initialize the swarm from the solution space
2. Repeat
   a. Evaluate the fitness of individual particles
   b. Modify gbest, pbest and velocity
   c. Move each particle to a new position.
3. Until convergence is achieved or termination criteria are satisfied

Initial solutions are generated. Next step, for each iterations the fitness function is evaluated for each particle i.e., solution. Depending upon the local best solution (pbest) identified by the fitness function, all the particles are modified. This is done repeatedly until some condition is attained. Each time global best solution (gbest) is stored and at the last iteration it is considered as the one of the best solution for particular problem. Depending upon the problem the fitness function is chosen.

Cellular Automata

CA was introduced by John von Neumann (Neumann et al., 1966). This is sequence of cells interact with neighbor and set the definite state. Cellular automata are:

- Discrete in both space and time,
- Homogeneous in space and time (same update rule at all cells at all times),
- Local in their interactions.

Basically, it is made up of four attributes, namely state space, a neighborhood, a number of states and rules. Parallelism locality and homogeneity are the fundamental properties of CA. This may be in one- or two- dimensional form. CA obeys one common transition function synchronously at discrete time steps. It has similar interconnected cells, which interact locally with their neighbors to solve problems. This is in the form of regular uniform lattice which may be infinite in size and can be expanded in the same direction (MizasC et al., 2008). The four basic components of CA can be given as: cell space, which is the connection between each cell, cell state as 4 states (DNA / RNA) or 20 states (protein). Figure 3 explains the general rules and its next state value in a pictorial representation.

Problem Statement

Arrange the molecular sequences in such a way that more residues are aligned in the same column. This is represented as equation 3,

$$AS = S_{il_{i=1}}^{n} \cup \{-\} \tag{4}$$

where AS denotes aligned sequences, n is the number of sequences, S_{il} is the set of sequence that consists of alphabets {A,T,C,G} for DNA or {A,T,U,G} for RNA or S_A– {B,J,O,U,X,Z} for protein, where S_A is a set of 26 alphabet. And the symbol {-} represents, the gap in the sequences. This symbol is used in between the sequences for the alignment process.

PSOCA Algorithm

The PSOCA algorithm uses a PSO technique along with CA rules for aligning the sequence. The equations (1) & (2) of PSO are applied for changing the positions of each particles'. In Figure 4, sample particles for this problem are shown. Figure 4 (a) shows the sample DNA sequence set in which the partitioned is highlighted in a box and Figure 4(b) represents the initial population of that partitioned sequence set. This represents a DNA sequence with gaps filled according to the following procedure. In additional to

Figure 3. Rule set of 1D Grid: courtesy of Wolfram (2002)

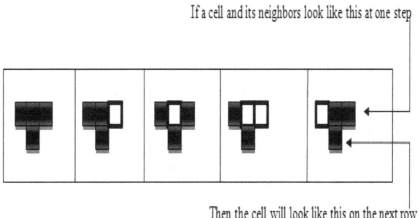

Figure 4. Particles in the population

ATCT-ACTACGCA—GAAA- -AGACGA- -C-GCGCA- - CGCGCG-TG-T-CG-GCGCAAAA- - -TCGACGG-C-CAG-C-
AG-GACTATCG-AGCGACGGGCG—CGCATATATG- -CGGG- -TAAAAAAGG- -ATCTAT - -AATA- - -TCAGCTAG
ACTG--AGCTA-CGATGC-AGCCG-CC-GG-CGCGGCGATC-GCATG-CTGT-CGTA-CG-TGAA-AACAG-TACGT-AG

(a) Sample DNA sequence set

A	T	C	T	A	-	C	T	A	C
A	G	-	G	A	C	T	A	T	C
A	C	T	G	A	G	-	-	C	T

A	T	C	T	A	-	C	T	A	C
A	G	-	G	A	C	T	A	T	C
A	C	T	G	-	-	A	G	C	T

A	T	-	C	T	A	C	T	A	C
A	G	-	G	A	C	T	A	T	C
A	C	T	G	-	-	A	G	C	T

A	T	C	T	A	C	T	-	A	C
A	G	G	A	C	T	-	A	T	C
A	C	T	G	-	-	A	G	C	T

A	-	T	C	T	A	C	T	A	C
A	G	-	G	A	C	T	A	T	C
A	C	T	G	A	G	C	-	-	T

A	T	C	T	A	-	C	T	A	C
A	G	G	A	-	C	T	A	T	C
A	C	T	G	A	-	-	G	C	T

(b) Particles for a partition segment

this, the consensus of the alignment is considered as a CA rule for aligning all the particles. A set of *n* sequences is taken and checked for the length. If the length is not the same, gaps are inserted in all the sequences using some basic calculations. Otherwise, it goes to the PSOCA algorithm process instantly.

Depending upon the maximum length of the sequences, 20 percentages of the gaps are filled in each sequence. Efficient alignment can be achieved when 20% of the length of the sequences is filled with gaps for all different sequences (Chellapilla et al., 1999). After inserting gaps, sequences of equal length are generated to which the consensus should be found. Randomly any two sequences are chosen to find the consensus. In response to this, other sequences are modified either by inserting or removing gaps. This consensus is considered as CA rule. Here, each cell is measured as an alphabet either $S_A=(A,T,C,G)$ or $S_A=(A,T,U,G)$ or $S_A=(S-\{B,J,O,U,X,Z\})$ where S is an alphabet. All the cells communicate and change states synchronously. In this proposed algorithm, one-dimensional (1D) CA is used for representing DNA/RNA/protein sequences. In general, CA can be represented as binary (0, 1) states or more than that. Here, 1D CA consists of four states per cell for DNA & RNA and 20 states per cell for protein sequences.

Algorithm 2: PSOCA

Input: Unaligned Sequences of any length
    Output: Aligned Sequences

1. Call Preprocessing
2. Generate a set of initial particles ie. randomly aligned sequences
3. Repeat
    a. Find the consensus of the particles
    b. Determine the lbest particle using the scoring function
    c. Randomly select two sequences & find consensus in that lbest particle using that as CA rule.
    d. Using this CA rule, align all the particles
    e. Memorize the gbest particles

4.   Until condition is met

Algorithm 3: PreprocessingSequences

1.   Find the lengths of all the sequences

$$L^n_{i=1} = (L_1, L_2 \ldots L_n)$$

2.   Find maximum length among them is found, $ma=\max (L)$
3.   Gap percentage for each sequence is computed for inserting gap $G_p=0.2 - ma$
4.   Find a new maximum length, $ml=G_p+ma$
5.   Calculate the number of gaps that should be inserted in each sequence depending upon m, $s^n_{gi=1} = $

$ml - L^n_{i=1}$

First, the unequal sequences, are made equal using a preprocessing technique proposed in (Jayapriya et al, 2016). If the sequence set has equal length then it directly goes to the PSOCA algorithm. The preprocessing algorithm is given in Algorithm 3. Depending upon the maximum length of the sequences, the gaps are inserted and length of the sequence is made same for all sequences in the set. In the preprocessing step, first the maximum length in the sequence set identified. As per the study, 20 percentage gaps with respect to its length can be inserted. According to this calculation, the number of gaps should be inserted in sequences are found. In general, the sequences may or may not have same length in the sequence set. Next, initial population is created. Randomly gaps are inserted to generate the initial population. Sequence consensus is found for each particle generated in the population. CA rule with respect to the consensus is given in the following equation,

$$C_iR_{s1}=C_i(S_{i1}U\{-\}) \tag{5}$$

where C_iR_{s1} is the CA rule for each particle, C_i is the consensus of each particle.

Consensus of any sequence set shows the maximum frequencies of a base in each column. This is shown in the Figure 5. In this four sequence are taken and the consensus is given as C in the last row.

Amongst, these consensuses, the best one is taken as CA rule. Depending upon this rule all the particles i.e. sequence sets are modified. The main advantage using CA rule is it depends on the neighboring cells and it changes. This is very important for local alignment. These steps are repeated until specified iterations that leads to an optimal solution i.e. aligned sequence set.

SOLUTIONS AND RECOMMENDATIONS

Issues in PSOCA

The algorithm 3 works well for the medium length sequences and used to align globally. Molecular sequences that are aligned locally are also used for the sequences analysis by biologist. As there is tremendous increase in the molecular sequences, there is a demand for an efficient algorithm to align long

Figure 5. Sequence Consensus of a particle in the population

S_1	A	T	C	G	T	A	C
S_2	A	-	-	G	T	C	C
S_3	A	T	C	G	T	-	-
S_4	A	T	C	T	T	A	C
C	*A*	*T*	*C*	*G*	*T*	*A*	*C*

and large number of sequences. To the overcome these issues this algorithm is improvised by including some steps so that it will align long and large number of sequences locally. This chapter proposes an improvised evolutionary algorithm namely IPSOCA.

Proposed Algorithm

Initially, the sequence alignment problem is solved using PSO algorithm. The problem with this approach it is avoids local optima. To enhance this algorithm, cellular automata based rules are incorporated with this PSO algorithm. But this algorithm do not aligned the long and large number of sequences locally. To solve the above issues, this chapter proposes an improvised PSOCA algorithm. This approach partitions the sequences into small segments to align the sequences locally considering the neighbors.

The following algorithm shows the steps that are involved in IPSOCA.

Algorithm 4: IPSOCA

Input: $S= \{S_{11}, S_{212......} S_{n1n}\}; p_{gap}>=0; p_{alp}>=0$, where p_{gap} denotes penalty for gap and p_{alp} denotes penalty of a letter of the alphabet

Output: $AS = S_{il i=1}^{n} \cup \{-\}$

1. Call PreprocessingSequences
2. Generate a set of initial particles ie. randomly aligned sequences
3. Each particle ie. sequence set is partition into number of small sequences
4. Repeat. For each partition in a particle
   a. Find the consensus of the particles
   b. Determine the lbest particle using the scoring function
   c. Randomly select two sequences & find consensus in that lbest particle using that as CA rule.
   d. Using this CA rule, align all the particles
   e. Memorize the gbest particles
5. Until condition is met

First, unequal lengths in the sequence set are preprocessed to make them equal. Here, the sequences are divided into small segments. This is given in the following equation 6,

$$S_{part} = \left[S_{si} + S_{si+1} + S_{si+2} \ldots\ldots + S_{sk} \right] \tag{6}$$

where S_{part} is the partition sequence set, S_s is the sequence set in which i is the 1st sequence set and k is the number of partition in the sequence set. This is because to align the sequence set locally. For each partition sequence set, consensus is found and used as CA rule. The initial population of the sequence set is generated randomly for each partition. The following equation7 represents the initial population,

$$S_{IPi}{}^{k} = \begin{bmatrix} \left[S_{si,j}, S_{si,j+1}, S_{si,j+2} \ldots\ldots S_{si,j+pop} \right] \\ \left[S_{si+1,j}, S_{si+1,j+1}, S_{si+1,j+2} \ldots\ldots S_{si+1,j+pop} \right] \\ \vdots \\ \vdots \\ \left[S_{sk,j}, S_{sk,j+1}, S_{sk,j+2} \ldots\ldots S_{sk,j+pop} \right] \end{bmatrix} \tag{7}$$

And finally the whole sequences are combined as a final alignment. Each aligned sequence set is evaluated using a standard scoring function particular for sequence alignment. The equation (1) is used using penalty for the gaps.

Experimental Results

Result Analysis for PSOCA

PSOCA algorithm used BaliBase (Benchmark Alignment database) to evaluate and reveal its efficiency. Datasset has different length with various identity based on the type of the sequences.

Here, in this experiment five references are taken each having various sequence lengths. In this dataset, six sequence set are taken from reference1, three sequence set of reference 2, two sequence set of reference 3, three sequence set of reference 4 and six sequence set of reference 5 depending upon their length of the sequence. The results of these data set using PSOCA algorithm are shown and explained in following subsections.

The parameters used are

- **S:** Number of sequences which varying depending upon the dataset given in the Table 2.
- **Populations:** 10 to 100 varying according to the number of sequences.
- **Generations:** 10 to 200 varying according to the dataset.

The population is initialized depending upon the number of sequences in each dataset. As the number of sequence increases the population size also increases. This supports to increase the search space. In the similar manner, generation is initialized for various dataset. Initially, we start our experiment with the sequences that has fewer in number and less in length. Gradually, we increased the number of sequences and then its length. The average of TC and scoring function for about 200 iterations are taken.

The dataset with medium sequence length of various references in BaliBASE dataset are used. As the analysis was continued with fewer sequences with medium sequence length, the proposed algorithm yields better result than other state-of- the art algorithms. This is because the CA rules depend on the neighboring cells in the alignment. This is shown in Figure 6. This result shows that for the dataset ac5, 1ad3, kinase, 1bgl of reference1 the TC score obtained by the PSOCA algorithm is better than others. These sequences have an average length as 1725.

Table 1 shows the average scores of SP and TC for the dataset. The result depicts that PSOCA algorithm has the higher SP and TC scores when compared with other algorithms given in the Table 1. The overall average scores are high for each reference set when PSOCA is used.

Figure 7 shows the comparative study of the scoring function SP and TC for all the different methods using benchmark dataset. This analysis shows that the PSOCA algorithm yields better alignment for dataset 1bgl_ref1 which has medium length of sequence. Figure 8 depicts the convergence rate for different sequence length with 200 generation. From this it is clear that when the sequence length is less than 300 it takes more generations for convergence, when the sequence length range is 1000-2000 it convergences soon than 300 length. And when the sequence length range is 2000-3000 it convergence faster than other two range. This result concludes that the PSOCA algorithm works well for the medium length sequences.

The statistical significance of the performance is checked using Wilcoxon matched pair signed rank test using MATLAB function (signrank). This test is nonparametric one that is often regarded as being similar to a matched pairs`. This is used to determine the magnitude of difference between matched groups. Here, the SP and TC score's are employed for this test. Here, the p-value shows the difference in p-value between the scores of all the algorithms. This test result shows that the proposed algorithm is significant for the MSA problem.

Figure 6. Comparison of TC score for medium sequence length

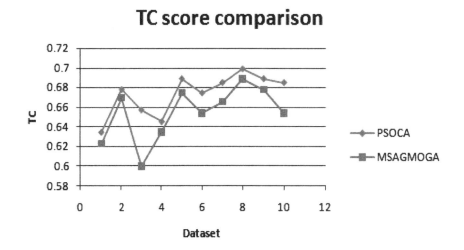

Table 1. Average score comparison

Algorithms	Ref1		Ref2		Ref3		Ref4		Ref5	
	SP	TC	SP	TC	SP	TC	SP	TC	SP	TC
PSOCA	0.718	0.655	0.690	0.684	0.690	0.660	0.670	0.659	0.689	0.678
PSO	0.675	0.634	0.655	0.675	0.654	0.645	0.655	0.640	0.677	0.660
GA	0.680	0.654	0.642	0.634	0.639	0.630	0.645	0.635	0.656	0.650
MSAGA	0.689	0.649	0.654	0.653	0.649	0.620	0.660	0.645	0.623	0.617
MSAGMOGA	0.690	0.657	0.640	0.656	0.639	0.625	0.630	0.620	0.645	0.634
MUSCLE	0.680	0.645	0.670	0.659	0.660	0.650	0.620	0.615	0.638	0.629

Figure 7. Comparison TC and SP of different method

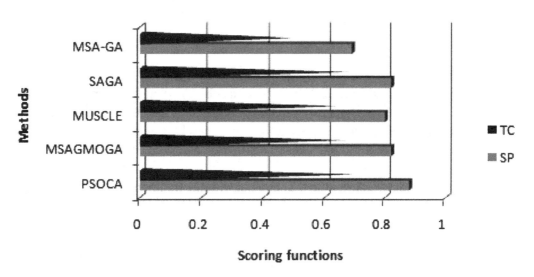

Result Analysis for the Proposed Algorithm IPSOCA

The proposed algorithm IPSOCA proves its efficiency by experimental analysis using the following benchmark dataset give in Table 2,3 & 4. Dataset are available in online. Analysis is done in three different comparison. First, the proposed algorithm is compared with the PSO variants and then with recent approaches FPA and TLSIA. These algorithms use two different types of dataset, one is long and small number of sequences and another one is small and large number of sequences.

Dataset Description

The dataset used of length ranges from 10,000 – 25500 bp for analysis. The sequences are named with accession number for references. Table 2 & 3 contains about ten sequences. In table 4, ten sequence set

Figure 8. Convergence rate for PSOCA

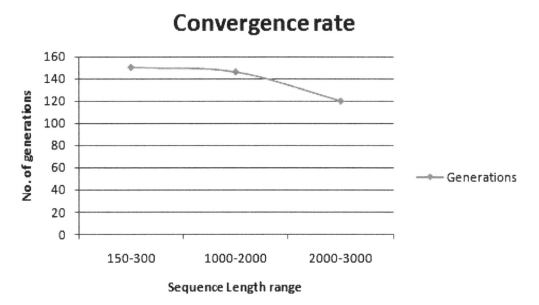

from benchmark dataset with various number of sequences in each. These sequences are taken from different references in BaliBase(Benchmark Alignment database) where the name mentions it. It has length in the range of 300-600 bp. Here, two different sequences set are taken for the analysis like Dataset 1 & 2 has long and less number of sequences; Dataset 3 has large number of sequences and small length. This is because; it is needed to prove that the proposed algorithm IPSOCA works well for both the types of sequence set.

Firstly, the proposed IPSOCA algorithm is compared with the traditional PSO, PSOCA. This comparison is used to study the result obtained by the variants of PSO algorithm. The following Figure 9 depicts the two scoring function comparison with the variants of PSO algorithm. From the figure, it is understood that the peaks of the scoring function i.e. similarity is high for the proposed algorithm IPSOCA. From the base algorithm PSO, each variant has been enhanced according the alignment problem. The parameters used for the experimental analysis are 200 generations and 100 populations. This is because the PSO algorithm convergence fast and depending upon the dataset the number of generations and populations are varied.

For comparison, two recent approaches have been taken namely FPA and TLSIA. These approaches are implemented and the results are compared with the proposed algorithm. These approaches not only recent ones but they are also based on evolutionary algorithm. The scoring function TC and SP of Dataset 1 & 2 are found for FPA, TLSIA and the proposed algorithm IPSOCA. This is shown in the following Figure 10.

The Figure 10 concludes that the proposed algorithm yields better alignment than the recent algorithms. Even though, TLSIA is a variant of PSO algorithm the proposed algorithm IPSOCA works well because of the CA rule on the segmented sequences.

Here, the scoring function are monitored before and after partition the sequences for the proposed algorithm. This is depicted in Figure 11. The peaks in the figure proves that the proposed algorithm, which is segmented the sequences aligns the sequence efficiently.

Table 2. Dataset 1

Accession No.	Length of the sequence
NZ JMGY01000049	10239 bp
NZ JMGY01000048	10486 bp
NZ AVDZ02000069	10483 bp
NZ JNST01000086	10320 bp
NZ JPZF01000014	10095 bp
NZ ASPB01000040	10051 bp
NZ AXSS02000051	10388 bp
NZ AKHN02000122	10294 bp
NZ AKJC01000359	10105 bp
NZ ACNQ01000005	10449 bp

Table 3. Dataset 2

Accession No.	Length of the sequence
NZ AKIW01000021	25107 bp
NZ JHHT01000128	25045 bp
NZ JFYU01000056	25240 bp
NZ JRYY01000008	25290 bp
NZ AYLV01000059	25140 bp
NZ KE332468	25260 bp
NZ AMWR01000108	25386 bp
NZ JFZD01000066	25082 bp
NZ AXSV02000066	25195 bp
NZ AHOR02000030	25312 bp

Table 4. Dataset 3

Dataset	No. of Sequence	Length	Average % identity
1ajSA_ref2	20	368	35
1pamA_ref2	19	473	35
1ped_ref2	19	358	39
2myr_ref2	19	540	32
Kinase_ref3	23	278	28
4enk_ref2	18	387	48
2myr_ref2	19	411	32
1vl_ref2	24	437	30

Figure 9. Scoring function comparison for PSO variants

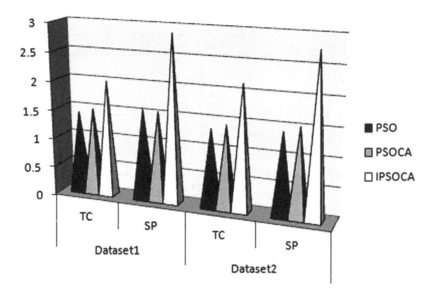

Figure 10. Scoring function comparison with recent approaches

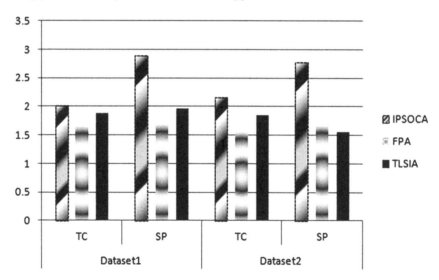

The TC score comparison for the dataset 3 is shown in Figure 12. The proposed algorithm IPSOCA shows the higher similarity than the state-of-the-art techniques. From this result it is shown that the improvised algorithm also suits for large and small length sequences set.

Statistical Significance Comparison With Proposed and Other Algorithms

Finally to prove the overall performance of the proposed algorithm, the statistical test has performed for all algorithms. The statistical test used here is Wilcoxon Signed Rank Test. When the basic statistical test do not suits the problem, then WSR test is undergone. This is a non-parametric statistical hypothesis

Figure 11. TC comparison of before and after segmenting sequences

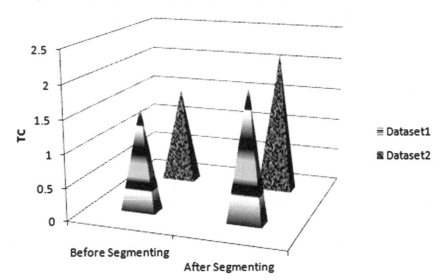

Figure 12. TC score comparison for dataset 3

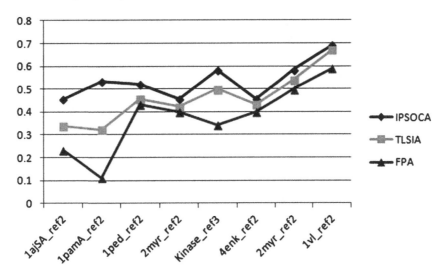

test to compare two related samples that is matched. Here data are assumed to be paired and obtain from the population. Randomly the pair is chosen for test. For this first the hypotheses are formed. Basically, two hypotheses are framed namely null hypothesis and alternative hypothesis. The former tells that there is no similarity between the test data that is given as H_o and the latter shows that is some significance between the test cases. In general, the researchers try to prove that null hypothesis is false. Here, the significance is measured using p-value that is a function which observes the sample results. If p-value is low, the null hypothesis is rejected but when high the alternative hypothesis is rejected. Here the following Table 5, shows that the significant calculation between the proposed and the other algorithm for dataset 1. Likewise, the WSRT is compared for all the dataset.

The result obtained in the table shows the similarity of the proposed algorithm is significant. First, twenty sample TC score of IPSOCA and FPA are taken for the calculation. Signed between the pairs are identified and given in the column, SIGN. In the ABS column, the absolute difference of the pairs is presented. As a next step, rank is found and given the column R and finally signed rank is given in SIGN R. Figure 13 show the p-value and h obtained for the tested data using MATLAB. These values shows that the proposed algorithm is significant than the other algorithm and null hypothesis is rejected.

Time Complexity

The time complexity of the proposed algorithm IPSOCA is calculated for each step. The preprocessing step takes $O (n*m)$ where n is the number of sequences and m is the maximum length of the sequences. Initial population phase takes $O (G*P)$, where G is the number of generations (iterations) and P is the number of population used for experimental analysis.

As the sequences are partition into segments, additionally it takes some time for computation. Hence, its time complexity is given as O $(G*P*S)$. Finding consensus and CA rule implementation takes O $(n*m)$. Among these various phases time complexity, the largest is $O (G*P*S)$. So this is considered as time complexity of the proposed algorithm IPSOCA. Even though the time complexity is more than PSOCA, the proposed IPSOCA algorithm aligns long and large number of algorithms efficiently.

Table 5. Wilcoxon Sign Rank Test Calculation

IPSOCA	FPA	SIGN	ABS	R	SIGN R
1.78	1.89	-1	0.11	19	-19
2.13	1.82	1	0.31	18	18
2.54	1.3	1	1.24	4	4
2.14	1.7	1	0.44	15	15
2.94	1.9	1	1.04	8	8
2.45	1.7	1	0.75	11	11
2.57	1.837	1	0.733	11	11
2.14	1.478	1	0.662	11	11
2.748	1.873	1	0.875	9	9
2.593	1.43	1	1.163	4	4
2.9	1.47	1	1.43	1	1
2.38	1.4	1	0.98	6	6
2.58	1.78	1	0.8	6	6
2.59	1.47	1	1.12	3	3
2.19	1.84	1	0.35	5	5
2.5784	1.478	1	1.1004	3	3
2.78	1.374	1	1.406	2	2
2.47	1.384	1	1.086	2	2
1.79	1.83	-1	0.04	2	-2
2.79	1.374	1	1.416	1	1

Figure 13. WSRT result

```
>> [p,h]=signrank(x,y)

p =

   1.4013e-04
|

h =

     1
```

CONCLUSION AND FUTURE RESEARCH DIRECTIONS

Multiple molecular sequences alignment is one of the important task in sequence analysis. Local alignment of long and large number of sequences gives information about the sequences relationship and used to find the motif. As there is trade -off between computational time and accuracy, many evolutionary algorithms are used for solving these problems.

This chapter emphasis the local sequence alignment problem and provides an efficient algorithm. An improvised evolutionary algorithm using CA rule based on PSO is proposed for aligning multiple molecular sequence locally. This improvised algorithm divides the sequences into partition and aligned. The main advantage in dividing the sequences is, it is aligned locally and long sequences can be easily aligned using the CA rule. To prove the efficient of the proposed algorithm, it compared with the state-of-the-art algorithms. And also, the significance of the algorithm is proved statistically by employing Wilcoxon signed rank test. The result shows that the proposed improvised algorithm aligns long and large number of sequences efficiently. The time complexity of the proposed algorithm IPSOCA is O (G*P*S). In this chapter, the experimental analysis is done for the variants of PSO algorithm also and proved that the proposed algorithm is better than other ones.

Future Research Directions

The results show that the proposed algorithm is efficient for long and large number of sequences. This proposed algorithm yields better local alignment for more sequences but its takes more computational time. As the number of sequences increases with length of the sequences, the proposed algorithm can be implemented in parallel to reduce the computational time. When the proposed algorithm is implemented in parallel, the time complexity is reduced to O (G). Any recent parallel approach can be used efficiently. They are recent parallel techniques namely Graphics Processing Unit, Hadoop, Field Programmable Gate Array etc.

In another way, the proposed algorithm can be implemented in any parallel approach for the Next generation sequences. These sequences are short DNA sequences from the genome sequences. These kinds of sequences are very large and long where serial methods take exponential time complexity. These sequences are very much useful for the DNA analysis.

ACKNOWLEDGMENT

The authors would like to thank Ministry of Human Resource Development, Government of India for providing financial support for this research.

REFERENCES

Chang, J. M., Di Tommaso, P., Taly, J. F., & Notredame, C. (2012). Accurate multiple sequence alignment of transmembrane proteins with PSI-Coffee. *BMC Bioinformatics*, *13*(Suppl 4), S1. doi:10.1186/1471-2105-13-S4-S1 PMID:22536955

Chellapilla, K., & Fogel, G. B. (1999). Multiple sequence alignment using evolutionary programming. In *Evolutionary Computation, 1999. CEC 99. Proceedings of the 1999 Congress on* (Vol. 1). IEEE.

Das, S., Abraham, A., & Konar, A. (2008). Swarm intelligence algorithms in bioinformatics. In *Computational Intelligence in Bioinformatics* (pp. 113–147). Springer Berlin Heidelberg. doi:10.1007/978-3-540-76803-6_4

Edgar, R. C. (2004). MUSCLE: Multiple sequence alignment with high accuracy and high throughput. *Nucleic Acids Research*, *32*(5), 1792–1797. doi:10.1093/nar/gkh340 PMID:15034147

Fan, H., Wu, R., Liao, B., & Lu, X. (2012). An Improved Genetic Algorithm for Multiple Sequence Alignment. *Journal of Computational and Theoretical Nanoscience*, *9*(10), 1558–1564. doi:10.1166/jctn.2012.2244

Gondro, C., & Kinghorn, B. P. (2007). A simple genetic algorithm for multiple sequence alignment. *Genetics and Molecular Research*, *6*(4), 964–982. PMID:18058716

Hamidi, S., Naghibzadeh, M., & Sadri, J. (2013, August). Protein multiple sequence alignment based on secondary structure similarity. In *Advances in Computing, Communications and Informatics (ICACCI), 2013 International Conference on* (pp. 1224-1229). IEEE. 10.1109/ICACCI.2013.6637352

Hussein, A. M., & Abdullah, R. (2017, May). Protein multiple sequence alignment by basic flower pollination algorithm. In *Information Technology (ICIT), 2017 8th International Conference on* (pp. 833-838). IEEE.

Issa, M., & Hassanien, A. E. (2017). Multiple Sequence Alignment Optimization Using Meta-Heuristic Techniques. In *Handbook of Research on Machine Learning Innovations and Trends* (pp. 409–423). IGI Global. doi:10.4018/978-1-5225-2229-4.ch018

Jayakumar, J., & Arock, M. (2016). Cellular Automata-Based PSO Algorithm for Aligning Multiple Molecular Sequences. *International Journal of Applied Evolutionary Computation*, *7*(1), 1–15. doi:10.4018/IJAEC.2016010101

Katoh, K., & Standley, D. M. (2013). MAFFT multiple sequence alignment software version 7: Improvements in performance and usability. *Molecular Biology and Evolution*, *30*(4), 772–780. doi:10.1093/molbev/mst010 PMID:23329690

Kaya, M., Sarhan, A., & Alhajj, R. (2014). Multiple sequence alignment with affine gap by using multi-objective genetic algorithm. *Computer Methods and Programs in Biomedicine, 114*(1), 38–49. doi:10.1016/j.cmpb.2014.01.013 PMID:24534604

Kenndy, J., & Eberhart, R. C. (1995). Particle swarm optimization. In *Proceedings of IEEE International Conference on Neural Networks* (Vol. 4, pp. 1942-1948). IEEE. 10.1109/ICNN.1995.488968

Lalwani, S., Kumar, R., & Gupta, N. (2017). Efficient Two-Level Swarm Intelligence Approach for Multiple Sequence Alignment. *Computer Information, 35*(4), 963–985.

Lei, X. J., Sun, J. J., & Ma, Q. Z. (2009). Multiple sequence alignment based on chaotic PSO. In *Computational Intelligence and Intelligent Systems* (pp. 351–360). Springer Berlin Heidelberg. doi:10.1007/978-3-642-04962-0_40

Mizas, C., Sirakoulis, G. C., Mardiris, V., Karafyllidis, I., Glykos, N., & Sandaltzopoulos, R. (2008). Reconstruction of DNA sequences using genetic algorithms and cellular automata: Towards mutation prediction? *Bio Systems, 92*(1), 61–68. doi:10.1016/j.biosystems.2007.12.002 PMID:18243517

Mohsen, M. S., & Abdullah, R. (2011). HS-MSA: New algorithm based on Meta-heuristic harmony search for solving multiple sequence alignment. *Int. J. Comput. Sci. Inform. Security, 9*, 70–85.

Naznin, F., Sarker, R., & Essam, D. (2012). Progressive alignment method using genetic algorithm for multiple sequence alignment. *Evolutionary Computation. IEEE Transactions on, 16*(5), 615–631.

Neumann, J. V., & Burks, A. W. (1966). *Theory of self-reproducing automata.* Academic Press.

Notredame, C., & Higgins, D. G. (1996). SAGA: Sequence alignment by genetic algorithm. *Nucleic Acids Research, 24*(8), 1515–1524. doi:10.1093/nar/24.8.1515 PMID:8628686

Notredame, C., Higgins, D. G., & Heringa, J. (2000). T-Coffee: A novel method for fast and accurate multiple sequence alignment. *Journal of Molecular Biology, 302*(1), 205–217. doi:10.1006/jmbi.2000.4042 PMID:10964570

Orobitg, M., Cores, F., Guirado, F., Roig, C., & Notredame, C. (2013). Improving multiple sequence alignment biological accuracy through genetic algorithms. *The Journal of Supercomputing, 65*(3), 1076–1088. doi:10.100711227-012-0856-9

Rasmussen, T. K., & Krink, T. (2003). Improved Hidden Markov Model training for multiple sequence alignment by a particle swarm optimization—evolutionary algorithm hybrid. *Bio Systems, 72*(1), 5–17. doi:10.1016/S0303-2647(03)00131-X PMID:14642655

Shi, Y., Liu, H., Gao, L., & Zhang, G. (2011). Cellular particle swarm optimization. *Information Sciences, 181*(20), 4460–4493. doi:10.1016/j.ins.2010.05.025

Simossis, V. A., & Heringa, J. (2005). PRALINE: A multiple sequence alignment toolbox that integrates homology-extended and secondary structure information. *Nucleic Acids Research, 33*(suppl 2), W289–W294. doi:10.1093/nar/gki390 PMID:15980472

Sirakoulis, G. C., Karafyllidis, I., Mizas, C., Mardiris, V., Thanailakis, A., & Tsalides, P. (2003). A cellular automaton model for the study of DNA sequence evolution. *Computers in Biology and Medicine*, *33*(5), 439–453. doi:10.1016/S0010-4825(03)00017-9 PMID:12860467

Sun, J., Wu, X., Fang, W., Ding, Y., Long, H., & Xu, W. (2012). Multiple sequence alignment using the Hidden Markov Model trained by an improved quantum-behaved particle swarm optimization. *Information Sciences*, *182*(1), 93–114. doi:10.1016/j.ins.2010.11.014

Thompson, J. D., Plewniak, F., Thierry, J. C., & Poch, O. (2000). DbClustal: Rapid and reliable global multiple alignments of protein sequences detected by database searches. *Nucleic Acids Research*, *28*(15), 2919–2926. doi:10.1093/nar/28.15.2919 PMID:10908355

Tsiligaridis, J. (2016). Hybrid Genetics Algorithms for Multiple Sequence Alignment. In *Handbook of Research on Modern Optimization Algorithms and Applications in Engineering and Economics* (pp. 346–366). IGI Global. doi:10.4018/978-1-4666-9644-0.ch013

Wolfram, S. (2002). *A new kind of science* (Vol. 5). Champaign: Wolfram media.

Xiong, J. (2006). *Essential bioinformatics*. Cambridge University Press. doi:10.1017/CBO9780511806087

Xu, F., & Chen, Y. (2009). A method for multiple sequence alignment based on particle swarm optimization. In Emerging Intelligent Computing Technology and Applications. With Aspects of Artificial Intelligence (pp. 965-973). Springer Berlin Heidelberg.

Yin, P. Y., & Shyu, S. J. (n.d.). *MSAGA: Multiple Sequence Alignment Using Genetic Algorithms*. Academic Press. doi:10.1007/978-3-642-04020-7_104

Zambrano-Vega, C., Nebro, A. J., Durillo, J. J., García-Nieto, J., & Aldana-Montes, J. F. (2017). Multiple Sequence Alignment with Multiobjective Metaheuristics. A Comparative Study. *International Journal of Intelligent Systems*, *32*(8), 843–861. doi:10.1002/int.21892

Zemali, E. A., & Boukra, A. (2016). Using a Bio-Inspired Algorithm to Resolve the Multiple Sequence Alignment Problem. *International Journal of Applied Metaheuristic Computing*, *7*(3), 36–55. doi:10.4018/IJAMC.2016070103

KEY TERMS AND DEFINITIONS

Cellular Automata: Cellular automata is set of units in a mathematical model that governs with simple rules for replication and destruction, which is used to model complex systems in living things or parallel processors.

Evolutionary Algorithm: All bio-inspired process is considered as Evolutionary algorithm to solve computational intensive problems.

Global Alignment: Global alignment considers the whole sequences to find the similarity between the sequences.

Local Alignment: Local alignment arranges the sequences to find the similarity of the small portions of the sequences.

Molecular Sequence: Molecular sequences are DNA, RNA, and protein where it is represented using letters of the alphabet.

Multiple Sequence Alignment: Aligning 'n' number of sequences to find the similarity between the sequences set is known as multiple sequence alignment, where n > 2.

Pair-Wise Alignment: Aligning two sequences to identify the similarity between them is known as pair-wise alignment.

Scoring Function: Scoring function is a defined function used to evaluate the solution of any particular problem.

Sequence Alignment: A sequence alignment is a way of arranging the sequences like DNA, RNA, or protein in such a way that maximum column have same residue to identify regions of similarity.

Chapter 12
Bi-Objective Supply Chain Optimization With Supplier Selection

Kanika Gandhi
University of Skövde, Sweden

P. C. Jha
University of Delhi, India

ABSTRACT

Supplier selection is one of the most important decisions within SCM since suppliers have emerged as value adding partners in industrial relationship. In the current study, supplier selection on the basis of information pertaining to quality and delivery time is explained. The cost aspects are taken care while coordinating procurement and distribution in the echelons. The deteriorating nature of the product creates imprecision in demand and fuzziness in different stages of the coordination. A fuzzy bi-objective mixed integer non-linear model is developed, where the first objective minimizes the combined cost of holding, processing, and transportation in all the echelons and the second objective maximizes combination of lot acceptance percentage and on-time delivery percentage. The solution process converts the model into crisp form and solves using a fuzzy goal programming technique.

INTRODUCTION

Supply chain management is termed as synchronization of the requirements of key business processes from ultimate customer through ultimate supplier with the flow of product, service and information in order to create a balance among high customer service, low transportation & inventory management and low unit cost. Keeping good synchronization as priority, supplier selection can be regarded as one of the most important activities. A careful assessment with respect to strengths and weakness of suppliers is required before ranking them. In the supply chain coordination most, appropriate suppliers should be selected as per their performance and hence, can have a potential capability to increase customers' satisfaction. A big part of company's financial resources are consumed in selecting the best supplier,

DOI: 10.4018/978-1-5225-5832-3.ch012

therefore, selecting suppliers with good price may become a challenge for supply chain coordination. To reduce the transportation cost, it has to be depended upon capacity of vehicle with third party logistics (3PL) providers. Since numerous criteria can be appraised during the decision-making process in supply chain (SC) coordination, this problem shows more complexities in presence of multiple products, transportation policies and suppliers' performance. Thus, the problem is a bi-objective problem with several conflicting aspects such as cost, quality, and delivery.

Hence, to improve the overall performance firms have to collate all the actions of the supply chain in a coordinated method. In real business world, the information of parameters & variables and the objective function are often uncertain since most of the input information is not precisely known. With the imprecise demand, fuzzy set theory can be used to handle uncertainty and vagueness. The fuzzy set theory is used during solution process of integrated model for procurement, inventory management, transportation policy and selection of supplier to procure goods. The goods are transported on the basis of vehicle capacity. Here 3PL provides flexible approach based on cost of full vehicle (truck) and transportation cost per weight. On the other side, selection of supplier also plays a vital role in improving the efficiency and reduced cost. To summarize the coordination of inventory, procurement and transportation mechanism to minimize the costs incurred, our work includes: (1) constructing a fuzzy bi-objective two stage optimization model that involves the computation of cost incurred during holding, procurement, transportation and inspection; (2) process to choose best supplier on the basis of maximum delivery time percentage and acceptance percentage; (3) fuzzy set theory to manage many imprecise parameters in the model; (4) proposing transportation policy based on overhead quantity and truck capacity; (5) finding strategies to minimize inventory as well as ensuring no shortage.

BACKGROUND

The supplier selection in its nature is a multi-criteria decision-making (MCDM) problem as many inconsistent criteria may influence valuation and selection of suppliers.. Dickson (1966) identified and ranked 23 criteria for selecting the supplier. The top six criteria were respectively quality, delivery, performance history, warranty policy, production facilities and capacity, and price. However in practice, the importance of those criteria may change from one industry to another. The methodologies on supplier selection stated by Ho, Xu, and Prasanta (2010) were divided into two main groups such as individual approaches and integrated approaches. An improved integrated approach for supplier selection problem is discussed by Bhattacharya, Geraghty, and Young (2010). The approach consisted of AHP, quality function deployment (QFD) and cost factor measure (CFM). Further, a multi-objective model for supplier selection in multi-service outsourcing is developed by Feng, Fan, and Li (2011). An approach based on ANP under fuzzy environment within multi-person decision-making schema is developed (Büyüközkan and Çiftçi, 2011). An integrated method including DEMATEL, ANP and TOPSIS in fuzzy environment for green supplier evaluation is proposed by Büyüközkan and Çiftçi (2012). Two optimization mathematical models for supplier clustering and selection are constructed by Che (2012). For solving the first model, integrated k-means and simulated annealing algorithm with the Taguchi method were proposed and for solving the second model, simulated annealing algorithm was used with the weights obtained from AHP method. For constructing the structure of criteria, AHP is used by (Chen and Chao 2012) and then for the decision matrices, they used consistent fuzzy preference relations (CFPR). They made an application in an electronic company regarding 15 criteria. Kuo and Lin (2012) presented a supplier selection method, which also considers green indicators due to environmental protection issues, by using an analysis network process (ANP) as well as data envelopment analysis (DEA). ANP which is able to consider the interdependency between criteria releases the constraint of DEA that the users cannot set up criteria weight preferences.

Further, some more literature on supplier selection and fuzzy optimization has been discussed. A fuzzy multi-objective linear model for a supplier selection problem is developed, to overcome the vangueness of information involved in the selection process (Amid Ghodsypour, and O'Brien 2006). Some approaches are also classified according to the fuzzy parameter in a multi objective programming model (Arikan and Gungor 2007). When the model has fuzzy aspiration levels attained to the objective functions and/or right hand side constants then fuzzy programming models can be generated by using fuzzy operators (Suer, Arikan, and Babayigit 2009). A two stage model consisting of satisfying technique and fuzzy preference programming is proposed by Chamodrakas, Batis, and Martakos (2010). A combined methodology for supplier selection and performance evaluation shown by Mithat, Cuneyt, and Cemal (2011). Dotoli and Falagario (2012) addressed the strategic purchasing function in supply chains, i.e. optimal supplier selection. They presented a hierarchical extension of the data envelopment analysis (DEA) for application in a multiple sourcing strategy context. An integer programming model to study a procurement setting in which suppliers offer total quantity discounts and transportation costs are based on truckload shipping rates proposed by Mansini et al. (2012). Parthiban, Zubar and Katakar (2013) showed that sourcing decisions are one of the strategic decisions because they enable companies to reduce costs and improve profit figures. They consider main task in sourcing is vendor selection keeping recent challenges such as shortened product life cycle, just-in-time environment and cost of finished goods. A model to attempt simultaneously minimizes total purchasing and ordering costs, a number of defective units, and late delivered units ordered from suppliers is proposed by Shirkouhi et al. (2013). The piecewise linear membership functions are applied to represent the decision maker's fuzzy goals for the supplier selection and order allocation problem. A multiple sourcing supplier selection problem is considered as a multi criteria decision making problem is proposed with informational vagueness by Arikan (2013). In the study fuzziness stems from the aspiration levels of the monetary cost, quality requirements, delivery targets and the demand level.

MAIN FOCUS OF THE CHAPTER

As it is evident in the literature, most studies have rarely paid attention to supplier selection problem models that simultaneously consider uncertainty in information (incompleteness) and several conflicting criteria under conditions of multiple products and transportation policies and multiple sourcing. The main focuses of this paper are outlined: (1) to propose an extended fuzzy bi-objective optimization model including new aspects of suppliers that show performance as quality and delivery for selling their products, new aspects of buyers that want to consider several conflicting criteria such as minimizing total procurement and transportation costs, the net number of inventory items, and net order quantity from suppliers subject to real constraints regarding buyer's demand, suppliers' capacity, inspection, (2) Due to the inherent conflict of the two objectives consisting of the total purchasing, transportation, holding and inspection costs, and the performance of the supplier on the bases of on-time delivery and lot acceptance percentage, we employ fuzzy goal programming approach to solve an extended mathematical model of a supplier selection and cost minimization.

Problem Definition

To manage the coordination among different entities for minimizing their cost and at the same time measuring the suppliers' performances in the environment of uncertainty, the current paper shows a fuzzy bi-objective mixed integer non-liner model. The first objective of the proposed model minimizes the cost of integration of procurement and distribution in two stages. This comprises of multi source (suppliers), one warehouse (processing point) & multi destination (buyers), incorporating transportation policies. The second objective focuses on performance and selection of suppliers on the bases of on-time delivery percentage and acceptance percentage of the ordered quantity.

The first stage of first objective explains procurement cost as per optimum procured quantity from the active suppliers, fuzzy holding cost at warehouse of the transported quantity from different suppliers. At the warehouse, receiving of goods and their processing takes time for which the holding cost is imposed on the transported quantity. The second stage shows the cost of inspection, fuzzy cost of holding and cost of transportation of goods from warehouse to different destinations which is completed through two modes of transportation as full truck load (TL) mode and truck load (TL) & less than truck load (LTL) mode. In truck load transportation mode, the cost is fixed of one truck up to a given capacity. In this mode company may use less than the capacity available but cost per truck will not be deducted. However, sometimes the weighted quantity may not be large enough to corroborate the cost associated with a TL mode. In such situation, a LTL mode may be used. LTL is defined as a shipment of weighted quantity which does not fill a truck. In such case transportation cost is taken on the bases of per unit weight. The second objective is to find best suppliers with the combination of fuzzy on-time delivery percentage and fuzzy acceptance percentage of the ordered quantity.

The model integrates inventory, procurement and transportation mechanism to minimize all costs discussed above and also chooses the best supplier. The total cost of the model becomes fuzzy due to fuzzy holding cost and consumption. On the other hand, performance level is also fuzzy as percentage of on-time delivery and acceptances are fuzzy. Hence, the model discussed above is fuzzy bi-objective mixed integer non-linear model. In the solution process, the fuzzy model is converted into crisp and further fuzzy goal programming approach is employed where each objective could be assigned a different weight.

PROPOSED MODEL FORMULATION

Assumptions

1. The planning horizon is finite.
2. The consumption at destinations is uncertain, and no shortages are allowed.
3. Initial inventory level is positive at the beginning of planning horizon.
4. Inventory deteriorates with constant rate and inspection cost is also assumed to be constant.
5. No transportation is considered from supplier to warehouse as that is being taken care by supplier.

Sets

1. Product set with cardinality P and indexed by i

2. Periods set with cardinality T and indexed by t
3. Supplier set with cardinality J and indexed by j
4. Destinations with cardinality M and indexed by m

Parameters

$\tilde{C}$: Fuzzy total cost

C_0 & C_0^* : Aspiration & Tolerance level of fuzzy total cost

$\widetilde{PR}$: Fuzzy performance of supplier

PR_0 & PR_0^* : Aspiration & Tolerance level of fuzzy performance of supplier

$\widetilde{HS}_{it}$ & $\overline{HS}_{it}$: Fuzzy & Defuzzified holding cost per unit of product i for t^{th} period at warehouse

ϕ_{it} : Unit purchase cost for i^{th} product in t^{th} period

s : Cost per weight of transportation in LTL policy

β_t : Fixed freight cost for each truck load in period t

$\widetilde{HD}_{imt}$ & $\overline{HD}_{imt}$: Fuzzy & defuzzified holding cost per unit of product i for t^{th} period at destination m

λ_{imt} : Inspection cost per unit of product i in period t at destination m

$\widetilde{CR}_{imt}$ & $\overline{CR}_{imt}$: Fuzzy & defuzzified consumption at destination m for product i in period t

ISN_{i1} : Inventory level at warehouse in beginning of planning horizon for product i

IDN_{im1} : Inventory level at destination m in beginning of planning horizon for product i

η : Deterioration percentage of ith product at destination m

w_i : Per unit weight of product i

ω : Weight transported in each full truck

$\widetilde{DT}_{ijt}$ & $\overline{DT}_{ijt}$: Fuzzy & defuzzified percentage of on-time delivery time for product i in period t for supplier j

$\widetilde{AC}_{ijt}$ & $\overline{AC}_{ijt}$: Fuzzy & defuzzified percentage of acceptance for product i in period t for supplier j

CP_{ij} : Capacity at supplier j for product i

Decision Variables

IS_{it} : Inventory levels at warehouse at the end of period t for product i

ID_{imt} : Inventory levels at destination m at the end of period t for product i

X_{it} : Optimum ordered quantity of product i ordered in period t

L_{mt} : Total weighted quantity transported in stage I & II respectively in period t to destination m

J_{mt} : Total number of truck loads in period t

y_{mt} : Weighted quantity in excess of truckload capacity

u_{mt} : Usage of modes, either TL & LTL mode (value is 1) or only TL mode (value is 0)

V_{ijt}: If ordered quantity is transported by supplier j for product i in period t then the variable takes value 1 otherwise zero

D_{imt}: Demand for product i in period t from destination m

Fuzzy Optimization Model Formulation

Crisp mathematical programming approaches provide no such mechanism to quantify the uncertainties of fuzzy dependent environment with respect to uncertain independent variables. Fuzzy optimization is a flexible approach that permits more adequate solutions of real problems in the presence of vague information by defining the mechanisms to quantify uncertainties directly. Therefore, we formulate fuzzy optimization model for vague aspiration levels on cost, consumption, on-time delivery percentage and acceptance percentage the decision maker may decide the aspiration and tolerance levels on the basis of past experience and knowledge.

Formulation of Objectives

Initially a bi-objective fuzzy model is formulated which discusses about fuzzy total cost and performance of the suppliers. The first objective of the model minimizes the total cost, consisting of procurement cost of goods from supplier, holding cost at warehouse for ordered quantity, transportation cost from warehouse to destinations, cost of holding at destinations and finally inspection cost of the reached quantity at destination.

$$\text{Minimize } \widetilde{C} = \sum_{t=1}^{T}\sum_{j=1}^{J}\sum_{i=1}^{P}\phi_{ijt}X_{ijt}V_{ijt} + \sum_{t=1}^{T}\sum_{i=1}^{P}\widetilde{HS}_{it}\,X_{it} +$$

$$\sum_{t=1}^{T}\sum_{m=1}^{M}\left[\left(sy_{mt} + j_{mt}\beta_{mt}\right)u_{mt} + \left(j_{mt}+1\right)\beta_{mt}\left(1-u_{mt}\right)\right]$$

$$+\sum_{t=1}^{T}\sum_{m=1}^{M}\sum_{i=1}^{P}\widetilde{HD}_{imt}\,ID_{imt} + \sum_{i=1}^{P}\sum_{t=1}^{T}\sum_{m=1}^{M}\lambda_{imt}X_{it}$$

The second objective discusses the performance of suppliers and maximizes the performance percentage of supplier as per on-delivery time percentage and acceptance percentage of ordered quantity.

$$\text{Maximize } \widetilde{PR} = \sum_{t=1}^{T}\sum_{j=1}^{J}\sum_{i=1}^{P}\left(\widetilde{DT}_{ijt} + \widetilde{AC}_{ijt}\right)V_{ijt}$$

Formulation of Objectives

All the suppliers must have enough capacity to fulfill the orders. The following equation ensures that the active supplier shall have enough capacity to complete the orders from processing point.

$$X_{ijt} \leq CP_{ij}V_{ijt} \quad \forall i,j,t$$

Goods reach at warehouse (processing point) is procured from all the active suppliers.

$$X_{it} = \sum_{j=1}^{J} X_{ijt} \quad \forall i,t$$

Next equation ensures that only one supplier can be active for a particular product in a period. However, same supplier can be active again in next period.

$$\sum_{j=1}^{J} V_{ijt} = 1 \quad \forall i,t$$

Next three equations calculate ending inventory at processing point, who acquires quantity from suppliers and ships further to all demand points and ensures no shortages.

$$IS_{it} = IS_{it-1} + X_{it} - \sum_{m=1}^{M} D_{imt} \quad \forall i, t > 1$$

$$IS_{it} = ISN_{it} + X_{it} - \sum_{m=1}^{M} D_{imt} \quad \forall i, t = 1$$

$$\sum_{t=1}^{T} IS_{it} + \sum_{t=1}^{T} X_{it} \geq \sum_{t=1}^{T}\sum_{m=1}^{M} D_{imt} \quad \forall i$$

Following equation is an integrator and calculates the weighted quantity which is to be transported from processing point to demand points.

$$L_{mt} = \sum_{i=1}^{P} \omega_i X_{it} \quad \forall t,m$$

The next equation finds out transportation policy as per the weighted quantity. Here, the costs of TL policy and TL&LTL policy are compared as per the weight.

$$L_{mt} \leq \left(y_{mt} + j_{mt}w \right) u_{mt} + \left(j_{mt} + 1 \right) w \left(1 - u_{mt} \right) \quad \forall\, m, t$$

The calculation of overhead quantity in TL&LTL policy is calculated by comparing total weighted quantity with total number of full truck loads as per weight is discussed in following equation.

$$L_{mt} = y_{mt} + j_{mt}w \quad \forall m,\, t$$

Next three equations ensure no shortages at any destination and keeping some inventory in hand.

$$ID_{imt} = ID_{imt-1} + D_{imt} - \overset{\sim}{CR}_{imt} - \eta ID_{imt} \quad \forall\, i, m, t > 1$$

$$ID_{imt} = IDN_{imt} + D_{imt} - \overset{\sim}{CR}_{imt} - \eta ID_{imt} \quad \forall\, i, m, t = 1$$

$$\left(1 - \eta \right) \sum_{t=1}^{T} ID_{imt} + \sum_{t=1}^{T} D_{imt} \geq \sum_{t=1}^{T} \overset{\sim}{CR}_{imt} \quad \forall\, i, m$$

Lastly, describing the nature of decision variables and enforcing the binary and non-negative restrictions to them.

$$X_{ijt}, X_{it}, L_{mt}, D_{imt} \geq 0;\ V_{ijt}, u_{mt} \in \left[0,1 \right];\ IS_{it}, ID_{imt}, y_{mt}, j_{mt}\ \text{are integer}$$

SOLUTION ALGORITHM

Fuzzy Solution Algorithm

In following algorithm by Zimmermann (1976) specifies the sequential steps to solve the fuzzy mathematical programming problems.

Step 1: Compute the crisp equivalent of the fuzzy parameters using a defuzzification function. Here, ranking technique is employed to defuzzify the parameters as $F_2(A) = \left(a_l + 2a_m + a_u \right) / 4$, where a_l, a_m, a_u are the Triangular Fuzzy Numbers (TFN).

Let $C\overline{R}_{imt}$ be the defuzzified value of $C\tilde{R}_{imt}$ and $\left(CR^1_{imt}, CR^2_{imt}, CR^3_{imt}\right)$ for each i, m & t be triangular fuzzy numbers then, $\overline{CR}_{imt} = \left(CR^1_{imt} + 2CR^2_{imt} + CR^3_{imt}\right)/4$. Similarly, $H\overline{S}_{it}$ and $H\overline{D}_{imt}$ are defuzzified aspired holding cost at warehouse and destination.

Step 2: Since industry is highly volatile and customer demand changes in every short span, a precise estimation of cost and performance aspirations is a major area of discussion. Hence the better way to come out of such situation is to incorporate tolerance and aspiration level with the main objectives. So the model discussed in section 4.4.3 can be re-written as follows:

Find X

$$X \in S$$

$$(1-\eta)\sum_{t=0}^{T} ID_{imt} + \sum_{t=0}^{T} D_{imt} \underset{\sim}{\geq} \sum_{t=0}^{T} \overline{CR}_{imt} \quad \forall\, i, m$$

$$C(X) \underset{\sim}{\leq} C_0$$

$$PR \underset{\sim}{\geq} PR_0$$

$$X_{ijt}, X_{it}, L_{mt}, D_{imt} \geq 0;\ V_{ijt}, u_{mt} \in [0,1];\ IS_{it}, ID_{imt}, y_{mt}, j_{mt}\ \text{are integer}$$

Step 3: Define appropriate membership functions for each fuzzy inequalities as well as constraint corresponding to the objective functions.

$$\mu_C(X) = \begin{cases} 1 & ; C(X) \leq C_0 \\ \dfrac{C_0^* - C(X)}{C_0^* - C_0} & ; C_0 \leq C(X) < C_0^* , \\ 0 & ; C(X) > C_0^* \end{cases}$$

$$\mu_{PR}(X) = \begin{cases} 1 & ; PR \geq PR_0 \\ \dfrac{PR - PR_0^*}{PR_0 - PR_0^*} & ; PR_0^* \leq PR < PR_0 , \\ 0 & ; PR < PR_0^* \end{cases}$$

$$
\mu_{ID_{imt}}(X) = \begin{cases} 1 & ; ID_{imt}(X) \geq \overline{CR_0} \\[2ex] \dfrac{ID_{imt}(X) - \overline{CR_0}^*}{\overline{CR_0} - \overline{CR_0}^*} & ; \overline{CR_0}^* \leq ID_{imt}(X) < \overline{CR_0} \\[2ex] 0 & ; ID_{imt}(X) > \overline{CR_0}^* \end{cases}
$$

where $\overline{CR_0} = \sum\limits_{t=1}^{T} \sum\limits_{m=1}^{M} \overline{CR}_{imt}$ is the aspiration and $\overline{CR_0}^*$ is the tolerance level to inventory constraints.

Step 4: Employ extension principle to identify the fuzzy decision, which results in a crisp mathematical programming problem given by

Maximize α

Subject to $\mu_c(X) \geq w_1 \alpha,$

$\mu_{PR}(X) \geq w_2 \alpha,$

$\mu_{ID_{imt}}(X) \geq \alpha,$

$X \in S$

where α represents the degree up to which the aspiration of the decision-maker is met. The above problem can be solved by the standard crisp mathematical programming algorithms.

Step 5: Following Bellman and Zadeh (1970), while solving the problem following steps 1-4, the objective of the problem is also treated as a constraint. Each constraint is considered to be an objective for the decision-maker and the problem can be looked as a fuzzy bi-objective mathematical programming problem. Further, each objective can have a different level of importance and can be assigned weight to measure the relative importance. The resulting problem can be solved by the weighted min max approach. On substituting the values for $\mu_{PR}(x)$ and $\mu_c(x)$ the problem becomes

Maximize α

subject to

$$
\begin{aligned} PR(x) &\geq PR_0 - (1 - w_1\alpha)(PR_0 - PR_0^*) \\ C(x) &\leq C_0 + (1 - w_2\alpha)(C_0^* - C_0) \end{aligned} \quad \text{(P1)}
$$

$\mu_{ID_{imt}}(X) \geq \alpha$

$$X \in S$$

$$w_1 \geq 0, w_2 \geq 0, \ w_1 + w_2 = 1, \ \alpha \in \left[0,1\right]$$

Step 6: If a feasible solution is not obtained for the problem in Step 5, then we can use the fuzzy goal programming approach to obtain a compromised solution given by Mohamed (1997). The method is discussed in detail in the next section.

Fuzzy Goal Programming Approach

On solving the problem, we found that the problem (P1) is not feasible; hence the management goal cannot be achieved for a feasible value of $\alpha \epsilon[0,1]$. Then, we use the fuzzy goal programming technique to obtain a compromised solution. The approach is based on the goal programming technique for solving the crisp goal programming problem given by Mohamed (1997). The maximum value of any membership function can be 1; maximization of $\alpha \epsilon[0,1]$ is equivalent to making it as close to 1 as best as possible. This can be achieved by minimizing the negative deviational variables of goal programming (i.e., η) from 1. The fuzzy goal programming formulation for the given problem (P1) introducing the negative and positive deviational variables ηj & ρj is given as

Minimize u

subject to $\mu_{PR}(X) + \eta_1 - \rho_1 = 1$

$$\mu_C(X) + \eta_2 - \rho_2 = 1$$

$$u \geq w_j * \eta_j \qquad j = 1,2$$

$$\eta_j * \rho_j = 0 \qquad j = 1,2$$

$$w_1 + w_2 = 1$$

$$\alpha = 1 - u$$

$$\eta_j, \rho_j \geq 0 \, ; X \in S \, ; \ u \in [0,1] ; w_1, w_2 \geq 0$$

CASE STUDY

The retail chain industry is developing exponentially because of its ability to deliver a extensive variety of high quality Fast-moving consumer goods (FMCG) or consumer packaged goods (CPG) to consumers as per the requirement. This step could be accomplished by building stability into the products through processing, packaging, and by adding additives that enable food items to remain fresh and wholesome throughout the distribution process. Examples include non-durable goods such as soft drinks, toiletries, and grocery items. Though the absolute profit made on FMCG products is relatively small, they are generally sold in large quantities, and so the cumulative profit on such products can be substantial. Food spoilage is caused by two main factors, namely; Natural decay in foods, and Contamination by micro-organisms. In the current study, we are considering the problem of a Variance retail chain co. (name changed), who purchases various products from different suppliers and process them in different sizes and designs at their processing point (warehouse) to increase their shelf life so that deterioration could be reduced at retail stores and then transported to its different retail stores. In the case, we are discussing a tiny problem of three suppliers (source pt.) and three retail outlets (destinations) with a processing point (warehouse). Four products as Powder milk (P1), Sugar cubes (P2), noodles (P3) and Pasta (P4) are considered for managing procurement & distribution for 3 months. In the case the two major objectives of the company are to manage optimal order quantity from suppliers of deteriorating type products, as the consumption at retail outlets is uncertain, reducing fuzziness in environment so that company will be able to precise consumption and cost for future and to choose the best supplier, who could deliver the required quantity on-time with the acceptable lot. Company needs to reduce cost of procurement, inventory carrying cost at warehouse during stage I, and in stage II, cost of transportation from warehouse to retail outlets, inspection cost of reached quantity at outlets, and ending inventory carrying cost at outlets. At the same time Co. needs to select best supplier who can supply ordered quantity on time with acceptable quality lot.

To solve company's problem, a fuzzy optimization model is developed, which is converted into crisp form and fuzzy goal programming approach is employed to reach at feasible and optimal solution. The data provided by the company is as follows:

The purchase cost of each product is as, for P1 cost is Rs.100, Rs.110, Rs.125 per 1kg, P2 is Rs.130, Rs.135, Rs.145 per 2kg, P3 is costing Rs.115, Rs.123, Rs.132 per 1kg, and P4 is costing Rs.134, Rs.138, Rs.126 per 0.5kg. Initial inventory at warehouse in starting of the planning horizon are 90, 120, 90, and 99 packets of all the four products. Similarly initial inventory at destination 1 is 100, 98, 65, and 90 packets, at destination 2, the initial inventory is 90, 67, 50 and 40 packets and at destination 3, the initial inventory is 60, 80, 70 and 57 packets. The inspection cost per unit is Rs.0.5 for P1, Rs.1 for P2, Rs.0.75 for P3 and Rs.6 for P4. While transporting weighted quantity from warehouse to destination, TL & LTL policies may be used. In such case, cost per full truck for destination 1 is Rs.1150, Rs.1250, and Rs.1400, for destination 2 is Rs.1400, Rs.1000, and Rs.1150 and destination 3 is Rs.1070, Rs.1100, and Rs.1300. Capacity per truck is 670kg. In the case of LTL policy, per extra unit from full truck capacity is costing Rs.5. Ending inventory deterioration fraction is 7% at destination.

Table 1. Holding cost at warehouse (in INR) per packet

Product Type	Period 1		Period 2		Period 3	
	De-Fuzzy	Fuzzy	De-Fuzzy	Fuzzy	De-Fuzzy	Fuzzy
P1	3.5	3,4,3	3.8	3.5,4.2,3.3	3.3	3,3.5,3.2
P2	3.3	3,3.8,2.6	4	3.8,4.2,3.8	3.5	3,3.8,3.4
P3	4.4	4,4.8,4	3.7	3.5,4,3.3	3	2.8,3.5,2.2
P4	4.2	4,4.5,3.8	3.2	3,3.5,2.8	3.1	2.9,3.5,2.5

Table 2. Fuzzy holding cost at retail outlets (in INR) per packet

Product Type	Destination 1			Destination 2			Destination 3		
	Period 1	Period 2	Period 3	Period 1	Period 2	Period 3	Period 1	Period 2	Period 3
P1	3,3.5,4	3.3,3.8,2.7	2.9,3.2,3.1	3,3.2,3	3.3,3.8,2.7	3,3.2,3.8	3,3.5,2.8	3.3,3,3.1	2.5,3.2,3.1
P2	3,2.6,3.4	2.6,3,3.4	2.3,2.9,3.1	3,3.9,4.4	3,4.2,4.2	3.5,3.5,3.9	3,2.6,3	2.6,3,3	2.3,2.9,2.3
P3	3.8,4,3.8	3.1,3.4,2.9	2.3,2.8,3.3	3,3.6,3	2,2.6,2	2.3,2.8,2.1	3,3.8,3.4	3.4,2.3,3.6	2.3,2.8,2.1
P4	3.9,4,3.7	2.7,3,2.5	2.7,3,2.9	3.5,3.9,3.9	2.7,2.5,3.1	2,2.4,3.6	3.9,3.5,3.5	2.7,2.5,2.7	2,2.4,2.4

Table 3. De-fuzzified holding cost at retail outlets (in INR) per packet

Product Type	Destination 1			Destination 2			Destination 3		
	Period 1	Period 2	Period 3	Period 1	Period 2	Period 3	Period 1	Period 2	Period 3
P1	3.5	3.4	3.1	3.1	3.4	3.3	3.2	3.1	3.0
P2	2.9	3	2.8	3.8	3.9	3.6	2.8	2.9	2.6
P3	3.9	3.2	2.8	3.3	2.3	2.5	3.5	2.9	2.5
P4	3.9	2.8	2.9	3.8	2.7	2.6	3.6	2.6	2.3

Table 4. Fuzzy consumption at retail outlets (in INR) per packet

Product Type	Destination 1			Destination 2			Destination 3		
	Period 1	Period 2	Period 3	Period 1	Period 2	Period 3	Period 1	Period 2	Period 3
P1	155,169,143	134,144,138	175,184,173	170,190,170	140,150,140	189,185,181	160,155,166	145,140,167	200,190,200
P2	140,155,150	179,184,173	176,183,178	156,145,174	180,179,206	178,165,180	170,160,170	210,189,196	135,149,135
P3	155,165,155	177,183,177	160,168,160	160,150,168	175,170,181	175,170,197	170,179,180	178,175,168	205,198,195
P4	166,172,170	160,172,156	160,164,152	176,172,136	150,155,176	187,180,193	186,180,190	150,145,156	203,200,177

Table 5. De-fuzzified consumption at retail outlets (in INR) per packet

Product Type	Destination 1			Destination 2			Destination 3		
	Period 1	Period 2	Period 3	Period 1	Period 2	Period 3	Period 1	Period 2	Period 3
P1	150	140	179	180	145	185	159	148	195
P2	150	180	180	155	186	172	165	196	142
P3	160	180	164	154	174	178	177	174	199
P4	170	165	160	164	159	184	184	149	195

Table 6. Fuzzified on-time delivery and acceptance percentage

Product Type	On-Time Delivery			Acceptance Percentage		
	S1	S2	S3	S1	S2	S3
P1	0.91,0.95,0.87	0.95,0.93,0.91	0.93,0.95,0.93	0.90,0.95,0.84	0.91,0.95,0.87	0.93,0.97,0.89
P2	0.95,0.93,0.99	0.89,0.96,0.83	0.90,0.95,0.84	0.89,0.93,0.97	0.89,0.96,0.87	0.88,0.92,0.96
P3	0.92,0.96,0.80	0.86,0.96,0.94	0.91,0.95,0.91	0.89,0.91,0.89	0.86,0.95,0.92	0.91,0.97,0.91
P4	0.88,0.93,0.90	0.90,0.95,0.96	0.89,0.96,0.95	0.88,0.93,0.98	0.90,0.95,0.84	0.89,0.93,0.97

Table 7. De-fuzzified on-time delivery & acceptance percentage in all the periods

Product Type	On-Time Delivery Percentage			Acceptance Percentage			Supplier's Capacity (in Packets)		
	S1	S2	S3	S1	S2	S3	S1	S2	S3
P1	0.92	0.93	0.94	0.91	0.92	0.94	250	300	130
P2	0.95	0.91	0.91	0.93	0.92	0.92	120	220	170
P3	0.91	0.93	0.93	0.90	0.92	0.94	350	130	340
P4	0.91	0.94	0.94	0.93	0.91	0.93	230	120	240

Results and Managerial Implications

The model helps company to provide minimum total cost incurred coordinating all the entities. Rs.786103.4 is the total cost consists holding cost at warehouse as Rs.4981.1, procurement cost of Rs.714041, holding cost at destination of Rs.5189.597, cost of transportation is Rs.49840 and finally inspection cost is Rs.12051.75. It is observed from the results that highest proportion is of cost of procurement, which clearly validates the requirement of supplier selection. Further, keeping a valid track of transportation polices is equally important as next highest portion in the cost is occupied by the transportation cost only. To prevent the over valuation of cost, the aspiration and tolerance level have been considered as Rs.701385 and Rs.820000. As validated with the help of cost, the suppliers' performance is second objective of the model which is combination of on-time delivery and acceptance percentage of the suppliers. The higher the performance is better the performance of the company. Keeping the aspiration level of suppliers' performance as 11 and tolerance as 10, the performance level of suppliers is 10.5. The model tries to activate the high performers to procure ordered quantity so that uncertainty in the environment can be managed. Nearby 55% of the aspiration level of cost and performance has been attained which makes the environment more certain and crisp for future decisions.

The ordered quantity head in table 8 the positive quantity indicates the active supplier to supply goods as he has the highest performance percentage among the three suppliers on the bases of on-time delivery, acceptance percentage and capacity. It can help reduced procurement cost in company and a smooth process in further stages.

The demanded quantity from destinations depends upon the consumption there, which is fuzzy in nature and is managed using triangular fuzzy numbers. The demand from destinations for source is shown in table 8 under demand at destination head. The demanded quantity will provide an idea of order quantity from suppliers. This will maintain a low inventory level and will optimally utilize the space resources.

Table 9 shows ending inventory at warehouse and at different destinations, which ensures no shortages in the case of unexpected demand. It is clearly observed that inventory towards end of the planning horizon is either zero or very low, which explains the consumption of available quantity in inventory.

While transporting weighted quantity to destination, the policy type, number of trucks and overhead weights are to be checked as each of them incurs cost to the company. In the table 10 it is observed that in period 2 and 3, only TL policy is used as 2010kg can be transported by 3 trucks. In this case, LTL policy will become expensive. But in period 1 TL&LTL policy is employed, as it has positive overhead quantity. In the case of TL&LTL policy, if overhead weighted quantity is transported through full truckload, the cost of transportation will become much higher than using LTL policy.

In table 10 the transportation mode is TL & LTL* explains that 2010Kg is transported with full trucks and reaming 62 kg is transported with LTL policy.

Table 8. Optimum ordered quantity from supplier (S1-S3) and Demand at destination (D1-D3)

| Product Type | Optimum Ordered Quantity | | | | | | | | | Demand at Destination | | | | | | | | |
| | Period 1 | | | Period 2 | | | Period 3 | | | Period 1 | | | Period 2 | | | Period 3 | | |
	S1	S2	S3	S1	S2	S3	S1	S2	S3	D1	D2	D3	D1	D2	D3	D1	D2	D3
P1	0	0	421	0	0	419	0	0	344	229	90	157	0	248	94	165	92	200
P2	387	0	0	401	0	0	412	0	0	123	215	168	131	68	124	164	172	137
P3	0	0	607	0	0	519	0	0	617	267	107	107	29	174	174	522	206	240
P4	0	0	540	0	0	540	0	0	450	154	171	169	96	115	119	428	185	191

Table 9. Inventory at warehouse & destination (in packets)

| Product Type | Warehouse Inventory | | | Destination Inventory | | |
| | | | | D1, D2, D3 | D1, D2, D3 | D1, D2, D3 |
	Period 1	Period 2	Period 3	Period 1	Period 2	Period 3
P1	35	112	0	159, 0,54	18,96,0	3,3,4
P2	2	80	19	66,118,77	16,0,5	0,0,0
P3	216	358	7	161,0,0	9,0,0	343,26,39
P4	144	355	1	69,44,40	0,0,9	251,0,4

Table 10. Transported quantity, no. of trucks, transportation mode, overhead quantity

	Destination 1			Destination 2			Destination 3		
	Period 1	**Period 2**	**Period 3**	**Period 1**	**Period 2**	**Period 3**	**Period 1**	**Period 2**	**Period 3**
Transported Quantity	2072	2010	2010	2072	2010	2010	2072	2010	2010
No. of Trucks	3	3	3	3	3	3	3	3	3
Transportation Mode	TL & LTL*	TL	TL	TL & LTL	TL	TL	TL & LTL	TL	TL
Overhead Quantity	62	0	0	62	0	0	62	0	0

CONCLUSION

Cost management and supplier selection are two important decisions any supply chain partner has to make. However, due to the inherent interdependency between these two decisions, they cannot be optimized separately. Hence to optimize the two, all the partners need to consider the main objectives with regard to supplier selection such as quality & on-time delivery service level maximization and cost minimization. As mentioned in defining the objectives of this study, the aim of this research was to find optimum quantity from the best suppliers under uncertain conditions. In this regard, a fuzzy bi-objective mixed integer nonlinear model was defined with objective functions as cost and combination of timely delivery & acceptance of lot, keeping the constraints as capacities of supplier, warehouse and truck. The parameters as holding cost, consumption, delivery time and acceptance percentage are fuzzy in nature. Hence to handle the issues of imprecision and fuzziness, the model is converted into crisp form with the help of membership functions of fuzzy modeling. The parameters are also converted into crisp form with the help of triangular fuzzy numbers. To obtain the solutions, fuzzy goal programming approach is employed. The proposed model can be used to simultaneously determine optimum procured quantity from the best chosen supplier, how many trucks should be chosen for transporting procured weights from each warehouse to destination, the cost size as per procurement, holding, transportation and inspection. The computational results show that proposed model is sensitive to the problem parameters.

Furthermore, future research might include choice between selection of supplier for procurement and manufacturing i.e. buy or build of the demanded products. This decision may be dependent on the parameters like cost, quality and manufacturing capacity. The point is that build or buy would allow additional economies in purchasing costs

REFERENCES

Arikan, F. (2013). A fuzzy solution approach for multi objective supplier selection. *Expert Systems with Applications*, *40*(3), 947–952. doi:10.1016/j.eswa.2012.05.051

Arikan, F. Z., & Gungor, Z. (2007). A two-phased solution approach for multi-objective programming problems with fuzzy coefficients. *Information Sciences*, *177*(23), 5191–5202. doi:10.1016/j.ins.2007.06.023

Bellman, R. E., & Zadeh, L. A. (1970). Decision-making in a fuzzy environment. *Management Science*, *17*(4), 141–164. doi:10.1287/mnsc.17.4.B141

Bhattacharya, A., Geraghty, J., & Young, P. (2010). Supplier selection paradigm: An integrated hierarchical QFD methodology under multiple-criteria environment. *Applied Soft Computing*, *10*(4), 1013–1027. doi:10.1016/j.asoc.2010.05.025

Büyüközkan, G., & Çiftçi, G. (2011). A novel fuzzy multi-criteria decision framework for sustainable supplier selection with incomplete information. *Computers in Industry*, *62*(2), 164–174. doi:10.1016/j.compind.2010.10.009

Büyüközkan, G., & Çiftçi, G. (2012). A novel hybrid MCDM approach based on fuzzy DEMATEL, fuzzy ANP & fuzzy TOPSIS to evaluate green suppliers. *Expert Systems with Applications*, *39*(3), 3000–3011. doi:10.1016/j.eswa.2011.08.162

Chamodrakas, I., Batis, D., & Martakos, D. (2010). Supplier selection in electronic marketplaces using satisficing and fuzzy AHP. *Expert Systems with Applications*, *37*(1), 490–498. doi:10.1016/j.eswa.2009.05.043

Che, Z. H. (2012). Clustering and selecting suppliers based on simulated annealing algorithms. *Computers & Mathematics with Applications (Oxford, England)*, *63*(1), 228–238. doi:10.1016/j.camwa.2011.11.014

Chen, Y., & Chao, R. (2012). Supplier selection using consistent fuzzy preference relations. *Expert Systems with Applications*, *39*(3), 3233–3240. doi:10.1016/j.eswa.2011.09.010

Dickson, G. W. (1966). An analysis of vendor selection: Systems and decisions. *Journal of Purchasing*, *2*(1), 5–17. doi:10.1111/j.1745-493X.1966.tb00818.x

Dotoli, M., & Falagario, M. (2012). A Hierarchical Model for Optimal Supplier Selection in Multiple Sourcing Contexts. *International Journal of Production Research*, *50*(11), 2953–2967. doi:10.1080/00 207543.2011.578167

Feng, B., Fan, Z., & Li, Y. (2011). A decision method for supplier selection in multi-service outsourcing. *International Journal of Production Economics*, *132*(2), 240–250. doi:10.1016/j.ijpe.2011.04.014

Ho, W., Xu, X. D., & Prasanta, K. (2010). Multi-criteria decision making approaches for supplier evaluation and selection: A literature review. *European Journal of Operational Research*, *202*(1), 16–24. doi:10.1016/j.ejor.2009.05.009

Kuo, R. J., & Lin, Y. J. (2012). Supplier selection using analytic network process and data envelopment analysis. *International Journal of Production Research*, *50*(11), 2852–2863. doi:10.1080/00207543.2 011.559487

Lee, H. L. (2000). Creating value through supply chain integration. *Supply Chain Management Review*, *4*(4), 30–36.

Mansini, R., Tocchella, B., & Savelsbergh, M. (2012). The supplier selection problem with quantity discounts and truck load shipping. *Omega*, *40*(4), 445–455. doi:10.1016/j.omega.2011.09.001

Mithat, Z., Cuneyt, C., & Cemal, C. (2011). A combined methodology for supplier selection and performance evaluation. *Expert Systems with Applications*, *8*, 2741–2751.

Mohamed, R. H. (1997). The relationship between goal programming and fuzzy programming. *Fuzzy Sets and Systems*, *89*(2), 215–222. doi:10.1016/S0165-0114(96)00100-5

Parthiban, P., Zubar, H. A., & Katakar, P. (2013). Vendor selection problem: A multi-criteria approach based on strategic decisions. *International Journal of Production Research*, *51*(5), 1535–1548. doi:10.1080/00207543.2012.709644

Shirkouhi, S. N., Shakouri, H., Javadi, B., & Keramati, A. (2013). Supplier selection and order allocation problem using a two-phase fuzzy multi-objective linear programming. *Applied Mathematical Modelling*, *37*(22), 9308–9323. doi:10.1016/j.apm.2013.04.045

Suer, G. A., Arikan, F., & Babayigit, C. (2009). Effects of different fuzzy operators on bi objective cell loading problem in labor intensive manufacturing cells. *Computers & Industrial Engineering*, *56*(2), 476–488. doi:10.1016/j.cie.2008.02.001

Zimmermann, H. J. (1976). Description and optimization of fuzzy systems. *International Journal of General Systems*, *2*(4), 209–215. doi:10.1080/03081077608547470

Chapter 13
Overview and Optimized Design for Energy Recovery Patents Applied to Hydraulic Systems

Marwa Elhajj
University of Versailles, France

Rafic Younes
Lebanese University, Lebanon

Sebastien Charles
Universite de Versailles Saint Quentin en Yvelines, France

ABSTRACT

Due to their large application quantities with extremely low efficiency, pollutant emissions, high fuel consumption, and oil price, researches on the environment protection and the energy saving of construction machinery, especially hydraulic excavators, become very necessary and urgent. In this chapter, the authors proposed a complete study for the excavators' hydraulic energy recovery systems. This study is divided into two parts. In the first one, an overview for the energy saving principles is discussed and classed based on the type of the energy recovered. In the second part and once the energy recovery system is selected, the authors proposed a new approach to design the energy recovery system under a typical working cycle. This approach, the global optimization method for parameter identification (GOMPI), uses an optimization technique coupled with the simulated model on simulation software. Finally, results concluded that applying GOMPI model was an efficient solution as it proves its accuracy and efficiency to design any energy recovery patent applied to hydraulic systems.

DOI: 10.4018/978-1-5225-5832-3.ch013

INTRODUCTION

The excavator is a machinery dedicated to long-time and high-power work. Its load power varies periodically in a large range that's why the working condition of the engine changes periodically too. The output power's variation of an excavator in digging working condition is shown in Figure 1. Due to these fluctuations, engine cannot always remain in a high efficiency state and results to energy losses and high fuel consumption.

Furthermore, the energy loss in the hydraulic system mainly refers to the losses of pressure and flow of the oil. In a typical working cycle, when lowering, the fluid draining from the actuator chamber of the excavator's arm to the tank has a pressure greater than the pressure of the fluid already within the tank. This fluid still contains some energy that is wasted upon entering the low-pressure tank.

When slewing stoppage, the fluid draining from the hydraulic motor of the excavator's turret to the tank still contains some energy, since the pressure of the fluid is much greater than the pressure within the tank.

Normally, the wasted energy is lost as heat energy on the surface of excavator's components. This heat increases the components' temperature and accordingly reduces their lives (Weidong et al., 2011). Moreover, energy is too valuable to waste and reducing fuel consumption directly leads to reduced emissions of global warming gases as well as costing the customer less in fuel.

In this study, we treat the energy saving systems applied on hydraulic systems and their optimized design.

In section 2 we present an overview on the energy recovery systems. Following that, and in order to design an excavator's energy recovery system, a new approach (GOMPI) is proposed then applied in section 3. The conclusions are given in the last section.

OVERVIEW ON ENERGY RECOVERY SYSTEMS APPLIED ON HYDRAULIC SYSTEMS

A lot of researches have been reported during the last two decades in the field of energy saving in heavy goods vehicles. USA, Europe, and Japan have spent a huge amount of capital on related projects and many valuable results are now available and can be used to provide solutions for construction machinery. Some studies tend to save the wasted energy in storage devices, some tend to optimize the whole system; some automate the machine and some change completely the hydraulic circuit.

Due to a wide variety of energy recovery principles and type of storages, it was thought to divide these solutions into five categories: 1) potential energy saving; 2) kinetic energy saving; 3) hybrid systems; 4) system's control and automation; and 5) non-conventional machinery. Then each category, in turn, was divided into subcategories respecting to the type of the storage device. To recover the potential energy, we propose three subcategories: a) storing the energy in storage devices (hydraulic, electrical and hydro-electric storage devices); b) sharing power between actuators; and c) storing the energy in a hybrid system that combines the two subcategories a and b. To recover the kinetic energy, we present one subcategory based on storing the energy in storage devices (hydraulic, electrical, and hydro-electric storage devices). The third category contains each solution that combines potential and kinetic energy recovery. The category four is divided into two subcategories: control of the system and automation of the machinery. Category five only contains the non-conventional systems.

Figure 1. Output power of the system's engine in digging working condition (Lin et al., 2010)

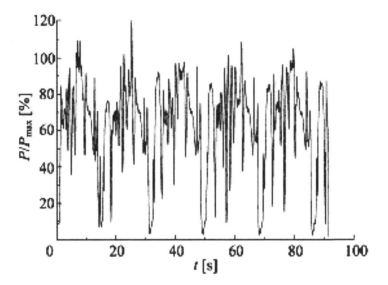

The classification of the energy recovery system, principles, categories and subcategories are shown in Figure 2.

In the following section, we explain the repartition and the principle of each category and subcategory.

Category 1: Potential Energy Saving

When the actuator of the construction machinery goes down, and due to large mass associated with the heavy arm of hydraulic excavators (the boom), the fluid draining from this actuator's chamber to the tank has a pressure greater than the fluid's pressure already in the tank. This fluid still contains some energy that is lost as heat energy in the system (Wang et al. 2012). This wasted energy, called the potential energy, reduces the efficiency of the hydraulic system. To save this energy, three subcategories are presented: 1) storing the energy in storage devices, 2) sharing power between actuators and 3) storing energy in hybrid system that combines the two subcategories 1 and 2

Subcategory 1: Storing the Energy in Storage Devices

The principle of this subcategory is to store the energy, when lowering, in storage devices by using hydraulic, or electrical or hydro-electrical components. This stored energy is to be reutilized when the actuator is lifted up. The principle of this subcategory is shown in Figure 3.

Electrical Storage Devices

This section contains all the patents that store the potential energy in electrical storage components such the capacitors and batteries. Nyman et al. (2004) described a way to enable the energy recuperation in electrically powered warehouse truck. They combined the use of a hydraulic pump as a motor with a counter balance technique. When lowering the load the hydraulic pump drives the electric motor, which acts as a generator and charges the electric batteries. Simulation results show that this technique can

Figure 2. Classification of the energy recovery systems of hydraulic systems

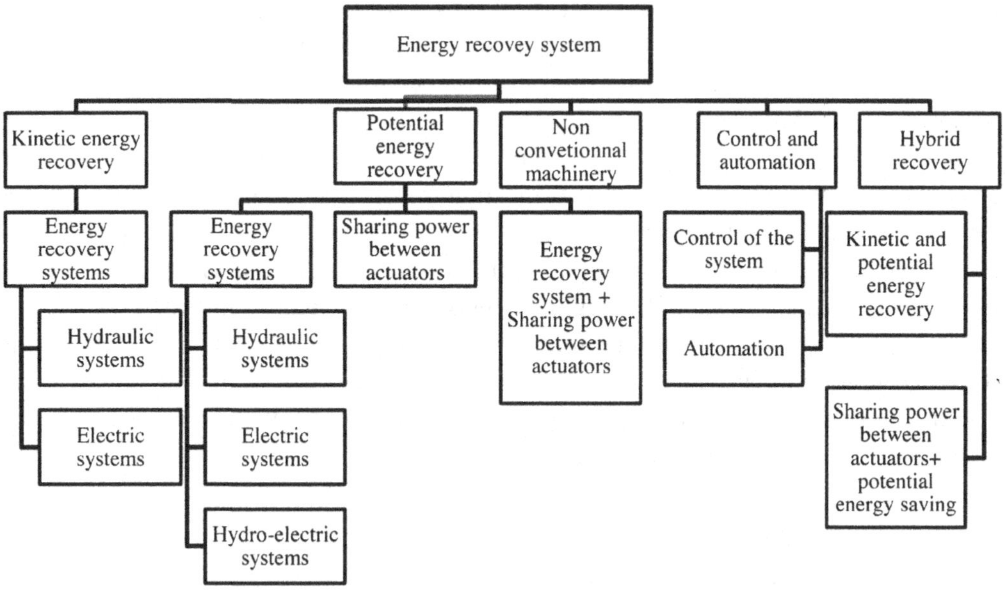

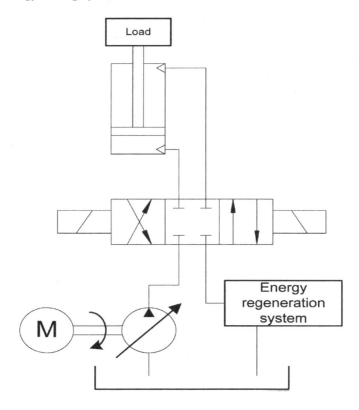

Figure 3. Potential energy saving system

save 40–60% of the lifting energy. Andersen et al. (2005) studied a similar system and compare different systems and control strategies. Weidong et al. (2011) proposed that by opening the reversal valve, pressure oil passes a throttle, then it will separate into two parts. The one returns receipt through another throttle, and the other one drives motor which links with generator and produces electrical energy. A new system proposed by Tao Wang and al. ng et al. 2012) is based on the combination of the throttle and the regeneration device together to decouple the functions of velocity control and energy regeneration. Its basic idea is to govern the cylinder velocity by adjusting the opening of the throttle and regenerate the potential energy by controlling the electromagnetic torque of the generator. Qing Xiao and al. (Xiao et al., 2008) presented a system that is consisted of a combustion engine and an electric motor in a parallel hybrid style. The mechanical power of the engine outputs to the hydraulic pump directly, which reduces energy conversion loss comparing with the serial hybrid system. The electric motor, which can work as a motor or generator, outputs energy together with the engine or converts the engine's redundant mechanical energy to electrical energy and stores in the capacitor. All these innovations improve fuel economy and reduce the emission of warning gases.

Hydraulic Storage Devices

This part includes all the patents and researches that store the potential energy in hydraulic storage component such the accumulators. The hydraulic accumulator stores a volume of hydraulic oil under high pressures so that it is immediately available as a source of energy. In 1989, Komatsu Company produced a solution recovering the potential energy of the hydraulic cylinders, by the back pressure, with an accumulator. Liang, Sun, and Virvalo studied the energy recovery system connected to the hydraulic accumulator that can save and restore the hydraulic energy in cranes hydraulic system. By applying this invention, the energy savings is up to 20.5% (Xingui et al., 2001). A similar system was studied by Nyman and Rydberg (2001). In 2000, the company Komatsu developed a new solution (Nishimura, 1989) based on an hydraulic storage device to save the energy. Glenn R. Wendel (2000) described a circuit applied on shovel 41 tons that comprises the original circuit; energy storage circuit comprises a high-pressure accumulator and a pump variable displacement auxiliary. The system performance is about 75% energy recovery, energy savings about 28% on a classic cycle. Bradford J. Holt et al. (2003) proposed that the energy stored under pressure in the accumulator may be used for energy regeneration. No expensive additional hardware, such as pumps, hydraulic transformers, complicated valves, or extremely large accumulators is required. This invention needed only the addition of a few control valves. Bruun presented in 2004 an application called "Eco Mate" based on a hydraulic accumulator energy regeneration system installed onto a 50 ton Caterpillar hydraulic excavator (Rydberg, 2004). It allowed a reduction in fuel consumption by about 37% and seems to be an interesting solution because of the views of the few changes of components and architecture of the system. Mark John Cherney and al. (Cherney et al. 2006) proposed a system based on the use of an accumulator to store the energy than using it when need it in the inlet of the pump. This solution could lead to a decrease in the size and energy requirements of the engine without a consequential loss in performance for the hydraulic circuit. This makes possible to reduce the hydraulic pump size and benefit from increased fuel efficiency without a consequential reduction in performance for the hydraulic circuit. Jiao Zhang et al. (2007) presented a system based on the use of two accumulators: accumulator HP (High Pressure) and accumulator LP (Low Pressure). Kenneth Korane (2008) described a typical excavator energy-recovery circuit harnesses flow from the lift cylinders. Return flow drives a hydraulic motor that, in turn, drives a secondary hydraulic pump that charges an accumulator. Flow from the accumulator supplements the main pump during lift cycles. Such energy-recovery systems make it possible to reduce pump size by 25%, with resulting fuel cost savings as high as 30 to 35%. Sun and Virvalo (Sun et al. 2001) studied an energy saving system of the hydraulic boom. The main parts of the system consist of one hydraulic accumulator and a hydraulic pump/motors. If the pressure in the accumulator is not enough for lifting the load, additional pressure is taken from the supply unit, meanwhile the accumulator still supplies part of the pressure, thus the power consumption of the supply unit is much smaller than that without the accumulator-pump-motor system. The efficiency of the boom hydraulic system can rise up to 34%. A similar system called the hydraulic accumulator balancing (HAB) system was presented in (Sun et al. 2005).

Hydro-Electrical Storage Devices

Since the time for the recovery power of the potential energy in hydraulic excavator is only 2–3 s as presented in Figure 4, it is important to find the adequate storage devices.

Hydraulic accumulators systems have an order of magnitude advantage in terms of the power density over electric batteries. They have the ability of accepting exceptionally high rates of charging and discharging. A combination of high efficiency and high charging/discharging rates enables effective regeneration and re-use of energy in heavy engineering vehicles. In general, the major advantages of the proposed hydraulic drive over other solutions are the higher efficiency, higher power performance and relatively minor modifications to the drive train. Accumulator has the seamless interface and it can be easily integrated into a hydraulic circuit by hydraulic pumps/motors. But the major disadvantage of a hydraulic accumulator is that the energy storage density is severely limited relative to other competing technologies (Lin et al., 2010) (Figure 5). Hydraulic storage devices are not attractive for storage of large amounts of energy and usually need large installation space. However, hydraulic accumulators have an order of magnitude advantage in terms of the power density over electric storage devices. Hence, hydraulic accumulators are ideal for those confronted with frequent, short start–stop cycles in enough spaces.

Due to their high internal resistance, both fuel cells as well as batteries have a low power density and are only marginally suitable for recovering energy (Xingui et al., 2001; Nishimura, 1989). As for batteries, they store energy by chemical reactions which will generally take much longer time to recharge and regenerate the energy in such a short time. As well, batteries cannot be charged with large power which is always required in the off-highway vehicles, especially the hydraulic excavators. For these reasons, it is possible to use capacitor to save the energy. The capacitor is charged and discharged by migration of ions and electrons, it can be charged rapidly, it is free of heat generation and deterioration, enabling long life, maintenance-free care but too expensive.

Therefore, some authors proposed a new energy storage device that combines the advantages of the electric and hydraulic components. When the boom goes down, the potential energy can be converted into both electric and hydraulic energy.

Tianliang Lin (Lin et al., 2012; Lin et al., 2010) proposed a new innovation on electro-hydraulic energy regeneration systems. When lowering, the potential energy can be converted into electric and hydraulic energy. As the hydraulic accumulator can quickly store the energy, the change rate and amplitude of the charging current are much smaller. Hence, we can use a battery instead of a capacitor even if the recovery time is short. Simulation results show that it is possible to increase the efficiency of the generator and downsize the generator with the hydraulic accumulator in the Accumulator-Motor Generator Energy Regeneration system (AMGERS). An estimated 41% of the total potential energy could be

Figure 4. Regenerative power of the boom of the 7-ton hydraulic excavator in digging working condition (Lin et al., 2010)

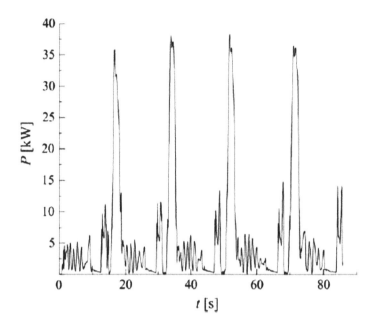

Figure 5. Response of the accumulator, flywheel and battery in function of energy storage amount

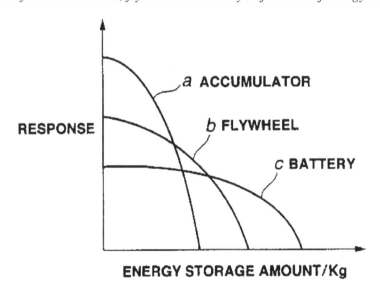

regenerated at the lowering of the boom in AMGERS. It is also shown that the AMGERS features better speed control of the boom and response characteristics than the MGERS. Michael H and Grace et al. (1976) presented an invention related to a system for converting the potential energy into useful energy such as battery charging current and particularly to an electric control for such a system which permits adjustment of the rate of descent of the elevated load. Hydraulic motor drives an electrical alternator and charge the battery to thereby convert the potential energy of the descending carriage into electrical energy to charge the battery. The accumulator is added to store the energy from the pump when it doesn't feed the actuators. It can then, at the opening of the dispenser, an addition power at start up.

Subcategory 2: Sharing Power Between Actuators

This section contains the patents and papers that are based on sharing the back pressure of the cylinder to perform other hydraulic functions without additional storage devices. Calin Raszga studied a hydraulic system that has gravitational load energy recuperation by opening a recuperation piloted valve with a pilot pressure supplied by a hydraulic pump so as to drive a recuperation hydraulic motor with a source of fluid pressurized by gravity from the load (Bergquist et al., 2007). Normally, the prime mover drives the pump that supplies the load and the other pumps that supply the other loads. During the retraction, the recuperation hydraulic motor drives the mechanical drive train of this prime mover. In this case, the engine allows the reduction of the driving force applied by the engine, thereby reducing fuel consumption. Randy N Peterson and Baker et al. (2010) proposed on their study that the machine transmits a message to the engine to change its speed as required. Also this method supports regeneration by using the back pressure of actuator to the inlet of the pump. Using regeneration requires less flow from the pumps, therefore less power used by the pumps. The engine can operate more efficiently while saving fuel too.

Subcategory 3: Storing Energy in Hybrid Systems That Combine the Two Subcategories 1 and 2

This subcategory contains the system that combines the two subcategories 1 and 2 presented above. Published by Caterpillar, David P. Smith (2004) described a circuit to recover directly the back pressure of cylinder for supplying a second one. As well, the potential energy in this circuit is stored in an accumulator. This innovation seems to be interesting and applicable to the hoisting function in principle of energy exchange between the cylinders, but it requires major changes in the system architecture, including the addition of numerous valves with the complexity of corresponding control. Rabie Khalil (2010) studied in his patent a hydraulic transformer that uses a pair of variable displacement gear pumps. The two gear pumps are disposed on a common shaft and receive fluid in parallel from a common high pressure source. Both first and second pumping mechanisms may be reversible and selectively operated as both a pump and a motor. The accumulator is used to store pressurized fluid for future use as a source of fluid power. In most cases, the pump and engine are out of service, which improve the fuel economy and emissions.

The second category of the energy saving is the regeneration of the kinetic energy.

Category 2: Kinetic Energy Saving

Hydraulic excavators have the characteristics of frequent starts/stops which generated significant amounts of breaking energy. During the swing braking, the hydraulic motor cannot be stopped immediately due to the application of the still rotating inertia. The fluid draining from the hydraulic motor to the tank still contains some energy, since the pressure of the fluid is much greater than the pressure in the tank. This energy, called the kinetic energy, is lost in the form of heat and it reduced the efficiency of the hydraulic system (Yoshino, 2008). This part is dedicated to study the kinetic energy saving and its single category to store it. This stored energy is reutilized during swing when accelerating.

The principal of the kinetic energy saving is presented in Figure 6.

Storing the Energy in Recovery Storage Devices

Electrical Storage Devices

The company Hiroshi Kondo filed a patent in 2007 on the use of an electric motor for rotating a shovel. In this patent, an electrical generator is mounted with a clutch of the transmission of rotation to recover the kinetic energy. The excavator can thus be driven by the hydraulic motor or by the electric motor whose energy is stored in a battery. Toshiba machines E-1 propose an hybrid swing system]. In this system, an electric system for regenerating inertia energy is added to the hydraulic system. Hydraulic braking force is not generated during deceleration and all inertia energy can be converted into electrical energy. By utilizing the energy accumulated by the regenerative action and synchronizing the hydraulic motor with the electric motor during acceleration, the capacity of the hydraulic motor can be reduced to about half, compared with the conventional systems as well as the capacity of the hydraulic pump can be decreased. It is aiming at reducing the total fuel consumption during excavator operation by 30% or more. Hitachi presented a system outline of the hybrid wheel loader (Lin et al. 2010). Engine drives the hydraulic pump and electric generator in parallel and the pump drives the hydraulic system of the working front that consist of the boom, the arm and so on, and the generator drives electric motor and then the wheel movement. Since the ratio of travelling in total working process of the wheel loader is quite large, it has preferred effect on the power saving. In practice, the system regenerates the braking energy into electric power and saves it in battery as the wheel loader is decelerating and use the power to assist

Figure 6. Kinetic energy regeneration system

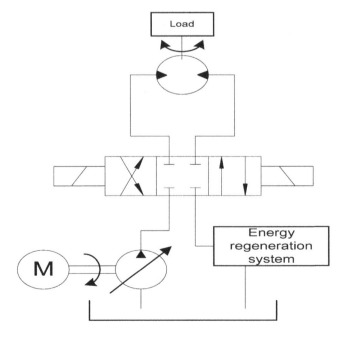

the engine as it is in acceleration. Compared with the conventional wheel loader, the fuel consumption can be cut down by 30–40%. New Holland Construction (Lin et al., 2010) previewed its hybrid 7-ton parallel hydraulic excavator at the 2006 Internet show. It used a 288 V lithium battery to store energy produced by the engine and generator. This excavator is able to produce as much power as a conventional 7-ton excavator without sacrificing any digging performance. It achieves regenerative charging through an electric swing motor, which produce additional electrical power through the regenerative braking. According to New Holland, both fuel consumption and CO_2 emission are reduced by 40% versus a 7-ton conventional excavator. Komatsu hybrid system also presented a new hybrid hydraulic excavator (Hiroaki, 2008). The kinetic energy is recovered as electric energy and stored in a capacitor. This energy is reused through the inverter during turning and is also used as assist energy during engine acceleration in excavation work. As a result, the engine revolution speed can be kept low also during idling to reduce fuel consumption.

Hydraulic Storage Devices

Many studies attempt to store the kinetic energy in hydraulic accumulators. Caterpillar created an excavator that stores the kinetic energy in hydraulic accumulators during the deceleration of the turret. This energy is reused during the acceleration phase. This innovation uses 25% less fuel compared to a regular excavator. Sun Hui et al. (2010) proposed that the stored energy is used to provide the total command power during loader launching or provide auxiliary traction power during shovelling operation mode, which avoid the engine working in the regions of low efficiency and significant emissions. The braking energy recovery rate under typical operation cycle is 60.03%, which is similar to the experimental results. Ford's Hydraulic Launch Assist (HLA) system is mounted downstream of the conventional power train on a four-wheel drive motor vehicle. HLA can quickly provide high torque even at low speed. A decrease in emissions is also significant and up to 80% of the initial kinetic energy is returned to the vehicle as hydraulic fluid flows from the accumulator. HLA presents many benefits: fuel economy, high efficiency braking, reduced maintenance costs and emissions. Regenerative Drive System (RDS) is a system similar to HLA with the same benefits. It consists of a hydraulic pump/motor connected to the axial transmission, two batteries, sensors and intelligent control software. When braking, the driver does not have to use the brake pedal; it can simply release the accelerator pedal. Thus provided the RDS braking and stores the energy normally lost. In response to the request of the driver via the accelerator pedal, the RDS control system manages the release of energy. During these processes, the requirement of the engine power is reduced, which reduces fuel consumption and potentially engine size and, therefore, emissions of pollutants. Amitesh Kumar (2012) has developed a system similar to HLA and RDS called HRBS based on implementing a strategy for storage and retrieval of subtle energy.

Category 3: Hybrid Systems

This category contains all the innovations that combine potential and kinetic energy recovery solutions. Komiyama et al. (2007) described a system formed by new regeneration hydraulic motors and two generators which are connected to the regeneration hydraulic motors and generated electric power. The engine drives a generator that supplies the batteries. The cylinders of boom, arm and bucket are each fed by an assembly comprising an electric motor and a hydraulic pump. When lowering, the hydraulic pump becomes a motor and thus rotates the electric motor. This electric motor becomes in turn a generator that recharges the battery or the capacitor. During decelerating phases, this electric motor also serves as a generator that recharges the electric storage devices (battery or capacitor). This innovation reduces the total fuel consumption but increases the cost by using many components. Brunn (2003) proposed also an innovation for saving the kinetic and potential energy in hydraulic storage devices. When lowering the boom and when decelerating of the hydraulic motor, the potential and the kinetic energy are stored in an accumulator. Endo Hiroshi et al. (2000) presented a recovery hybrid system. This system combines the potential energy recovery system in hydraulic devices and sharing actuator's back pressure to supply another one. Others proposed solution based on storing the kinetic and potential energy in electrical storage devices. Koji Kawashima et al. (2010) considered that at the time of decelerating the upper turning body, a motor functions as a dynamo which generates regeneration power to supply it t to the capacitor system. In addition when lowering the boom, the hydraulic fluid returned from the boom cylinder is used to drive the dynamo so that regeneration power is generated and supplied to the capacitor system. In 2003, Hitachi launched the world's first hybrid wheel loader and a 20-ton hybrid excavator in May 2008. The ZAXIS 200 (Lin et al., 2010) hybrid hydraulic excavator is powered by a parallel hybrid system, and the potential and kinetic energy is converted into electric energy to be stored in the capacitor. The fuel saving is up to 25%. Others innovation proposed storing kinetic and potential energy in batteries (Naruse et al., 2004). In Naruse et al. (2004), the hybrid recovery system reduces energy consumption by about 40%.

Category 4: Automation and Optimal Control Strategies

Optimizing the energy consumption of a system does not always require a structural changes and / or technology. Sometimes, it is possible to reduce the losses by driving optimally the components to perform their required work. This paper will focus on presenting two types of solutions that can lead to a significant reduction in fuel consumption: 1) Optimal control strategies and 2) Automation strategies.

Subcategory 1: Optimal Control Strategies

This subcategory includes the proposals that are based on new control systems. Andruch and Lumkes proposed the use of a pump for each actuator. This innovation reduces power consumption significantly, 46% on a standard cycle. It does not lead to overconsumption of energy if several features are used simultaneously. However, the price of the pumps is a significant drawback, especially for small shovels dedicated to renting. Jing and Yang et al. (2012) proposed the diesel engine cylinder deactivation technology. Based on working conditions, some of cylinders are cut off from fuel supply to deactivate the cylinders as load variation. This technology can reduce fuel consumption by about 11% under economic mode, and about 13% under heavy load condition. In the field of the adaptation of the power delivered by the vehicle depending on the workload, and since 1980, many excavators used the principle of the call charge, the Load Sensing (LS). These systems continuously measure the needs in terms of flow and hydraulic pressure to control the speed of the main motor (Hirata et al., 1990; Yi et al., 2013). Caterpillar created many excavators using this principle, most recently in 2013 . These two excavators used the load-sensing system with proprietary electronic actuation to provide excellent efficiency and controllability with little hydraulic loss. PC1250-7 from Komatsu used the Electronic Open-Centre Load-Sensing systems (EOLSS) to reduce the losses (Hirata et al., 1990). By producing just the amount of flow the load is demanding at the moment and under just sufficient pressure, it is possible to reduce the power losses from the system to a minimum. The other advantage is that LS maintains a constant pressure drop cross the orifice that controls the load with the highest pressure level, independent of changes in that pressure. However, and since a load sensing system is a feedback control system, there is a risk of instability. Yuan Yi et al. (2013) presented new solution in the field of control system: the proportion multi-channel valves. In general, excavators require multiple set of hydraulic systems and multiple mechanisms to jointly complete the required action. This innovation forms a combination valves to control the plurality of hydraulic systems and loads. The application of multi-channel valves gained optimal distribution of oil supply and good composite operability. Sem Zarotti et al. (2010) presented the modeling of two systems: 1) An open circuit with three fixed displacement pumps; 2) A circuit with only a single variable displacement pump incorporating a control LS.. By using the LS, energy loss of hydraulic oil is prevented and the relief noise is diminished. Yamashita (Yamashita, 2001) presents invention to provide a flow rate control device capable of making the relief cut-off control only where required for various works of different conditions performed by a hydraulic excavator including excavating, crushing and land readjusting works. Many working hydraulics systems are controlled exclusively by valves. Valve control allows a simple realization of open loop motion control and load holding tasks, in which the hydraulic actuators are usually supplied by a central pressure source. Displacement-controlled hydrostatic transmissions DC are an exception to this rule. The displacement-controlled circuit decouples the actuators by controlling each cylinder with a separate pump. Further, the pump flow rate is essentially independent of pressure. By applying this innovation, the efficiency is improved, throttling losses are eliminated thus reducing the overall machine fuel consumption. But the cost is increased because of the system require a dedicated pump/motor for each actuator. A comparison of the performance of a classical LS and the same system whose movement is controlled by linear actuators, DC system, on a digging cycle type is done (Budny et al., 2003). The results show that the performance of the system passes from 12.5% for LS to 30.9% for DC system. Tien-Hoang Huu and al. presents an innovation formed from four independent metering valves. It combines with control variable displacement pump to control the speed of hydraulic cylinder and saving energy. The energy can be saved up to 25% of energy consumption comparing to the conventional system. The performance of cylinder velocity is better than conventional system too.

Some authors present the Topography with Integrated Energy Recovery (Andruch et al., 2010) (TIER) in combination with an appropriate electronic control system. This technique is capable to sum flows from multiple changing sources, isolate faulty fluid conduit sections, and adaptively change operating mode (load sensing, displacement control, and modes unique to the TIER system). TIER can be used to recover energy and improve the cycle efficiency by about 33% compared to using industry standard spool valves in pressure-compensated load sensing systems. A significant advantage of this invention is the ability to use and operate the hydraulic systems to achieve better energy efficiency, reliability and performance.

Subcategory 2: Automation Strategies

Normally hydraulic excavator has three links (boom, arm and bucket) used for excavating, dumping, finishing, and lifting work. The management of these three elements independently is usually long because it requires great skill and an intellectual approach depending on the task. Operators who control hydraulic excavators must be trained for many years to do such work quickly and skilfully. Even though no one in this special field thinks that automation can out-perform an experienced operator over a short period, it is accepted that automation will continue to perform during a longer period at exactly the same level as at where it started, whereas operators have shown to be regular humans, suffer after more or less time of fatigue, have more difficulty in maintaining concentration and show a reduced performance over a longer period of time. Moreover, the operators have to run work in various dangerous and dirty environments (chemical and nuclear wastes). For all these reasons, authors attempt to automate the machines.

The automation of hydraulic excavators has been carried out by several researchers (Singh, 1997). Wohlford et al. (1989) describes a backhoe that has been tele-operated for dealing with buried hazardous wastes. Similarly, Burks describes a modified tracked excavator that has been developed to deal with buried waste (Thompson et al., 1995). Kojima have described a tele-operated backhoe used to dig deep foundations (Kraft, 1994). Nakano et al. have demonstrated a prototype controller for a backhoe excavator that allows an operation to control the bucket in Cartesian coordinates, and, to perform slope control. Researchers at the University of British Columbia have proposed a system that provides force-feed-back in rate mode using a 6 DOF magnetically levitated hand controller (Lawrence et al., 1997). Bullock (1992) demonstrates a simple scheme to deal with the stiffness of soil. Researchers at the University of Lancaster, England have developed an automated excavator (LUCIE) that uses a rule based method to dig trenches (Bradley et al. 1993). A tele-operated mini-excavator developed by Salcudean et al. (1997) at the University of British Columbia uses a position-based impedance control to assist a human operator in guiding the bucket during the digging process. Singh reports on a system in which pure position control is used during the digging process (Singh, 1995). Koivo suggests a geometric method to plan trajectories for the tip of an excavator bucket when the ground plane can be assumed to be level Takahashi has demonstrated a scaled model wheel loader that uses a camera to determine the place to start digging in the rock pile (Hirochi, 1995). Chang and Lee (Chang et al., 2002) automated straight-line motions on a 13-ton robotic excavator. Budny et al. (2003) studied the optimal control of an excavator bucket positioning for a minimum time process (Figure 7). Stentz et al. (1999) studied the excavator with two scanning laser range finders to recognize and localize the truck, measure the soil face, and detect obstacles (Figure 8). The excavator's software decides where to dig in the soil, where to dump in the truck, and how to quickly move between these points while detecting and stopping for obstacles.

The control of excavator's manipulator is an important task in autonomous research of hydraulic excavator. To control an excavator's manipulator, firstly, the full kinematic and dynamic model of the excavator's manipulator which three degrees of freedom should be studied (Lee et al., 2001). The trajectory of the bucket is designed and the desired angle joint of each links are determined by using inverse kinematic. The control of robotic excavator is difficult from the standpoint of the following problems: parameter variations in mechanical structures (inertial force and gravitational force), various nonlinearities in hydraulic actuators, and disturbance due to the contact with the ground. To solve these problems, several research works have been performed. Seward et al. used a high-level controller that was based on rules obtained by observation of skilled operators, and a Proportional-Integral-Derivative (PID) low-level motion controller (Bredley et al., 1998). Quang Hoan et al. used the PID controller to control the desired trajectory of the bucket. Lee used the proportional control together with a fuzzy control technique. Sepehri and et al. (1994) analyzed the phenomenon of coupling in the hydraulic actuator and proposed a Feed forward scheme that compensates coupling and load variation by using a simple valve model and measured pressure. Yokota et al. (1996) used disturbance observer and a Proportional-Integral controller and applied it to a mini excavator. Chang and Lee (2002) used Time-Delay Control (TDC) and compensators based on the dynamics of the robotic excavator and applied it to straight-line motions of a 13-ton robotic excavator. Chang and Park (1998) proposed the Time-Delay Control with Switching Action (TDCSA) to control a heavy-duty robotic excavator. The switching action is based on sliding mode control (SMC) and it compensates for the error of the time delay estimation (TDE) and makes the TDC more robust. Sung-Uk Lee et al. (2001) applied this method to automate the straight-line motion of an excavator (21 tons). A comparison between TDC and TDCSA shows that the control performance of TDCSA is better than that of TDC.

Category 5: Non-Conventional Excavators

In this category, we present the innovations based on a significant change of the conventional system. Michael H. Grace and al. (Grace et al. 1976) and Hideki Kinugawa and al. (Kinugawa et al. 1999) proposed a solution where the engine driving the hydraulic pump of the excavator is replaced by an electric motor driven by a battery. When lowering the load, the hydraulic motor connected to an electrical generator recharges the battery. The hydraulic excavator driven by a battery is less noise and reduces the exhaust gases as compared with hydraulic excavators of an internal combustion engine. It is a suitable solution for operation in a city area where buildings are thickly settled. In 1999, Kobe- shi and al. (Kagoshima et al. 2001) proposed to replace the thermal motor of the main pump by an electric motor, the hydraulic motor of the turret by an electric motor and the hydraulic cylinder of the arrow by an electric motor providing the tune rotation. Thus, the kinetic energy during deceleration of the turret and the potential energy of the boom during the descent could be recovered by saving this energy in electrical storage devices. This energy is used to recharge the battery as the electric motors may easily become generators. However, this solution may be less expensive overall because it avoids the addition of many components (hydraulic motor, electric generator).

Recovering energy seems to be an efficient solution to reduce the wasted energy, fuel consumption and pollution. In the following section, we propose a new method to design the energy system and identify all the unknown parameters of the circuit.

Figure 7. Vertical projection of the excavator (Budny et al., 2003)

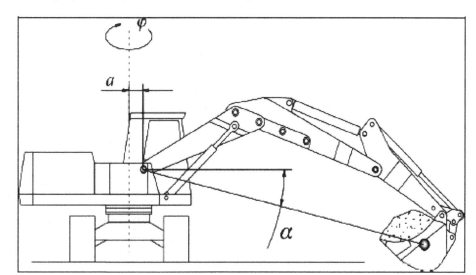

Figure 8. Excavator with two scanning laser range finders (Stentz et al., 1999)

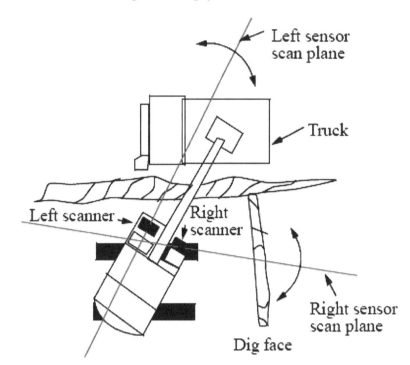

OPTIMIZED DESIGNS FOR ENERGY RECOVERY PATENTS APPLIED ON HYDRAULIC SYSTEMS

Different principles are accessible to recover the energy on hydraulic excavators. However many factors affect energy saving effects, mainly include driving circles, energy control strategy, vehicle construction as well as propelling system's main components' parameters design condition (Yueyuan et al., 2006; Filipi et al., 2004). Inappropriate installed recovery system may be caused by unseemly parameter matching, a low installed power would make excavator not catch expected operation, and a high one would increase factory price of excavator. For that reason, it becomes a necessity to design the selected energy recovery system (XIAO et al., 2008; Peng et al., 2001; Katrasnik et al., 2007; Li-Zhongli et al., 2010). The energy recovery system lies on several unknown parameters. Usually, these parameters are in connection with the specific excavator models and the chosen overall energy recovery system. However, the identification of these unknown parameters by direct measurement is characterized by complicated calculation and lack of universality (Zhi et al., 2011). As well, direct calculation methods are seriously influenced by optimal sequence (Wang et al., 2011). Recently, Liu Zhi and al. proposed a new method based on generalization of the energy transfer in different hybrid system. This method is used to design a 7t hydraulic excavator. However, it does not reflect the real operation of the excavator, since Liu proposed many preconditions in order to simplify the application of the method.

In hydraulic excavators, several important parameters are constrained by the technical requirements, others should be chosen carefully. Moreover, the hybrid excavator's working cycles were non-linear and impossible to describe by some specific formulas, the only things we could know were the parameters we set and the result we measured. By considering these adverse conditions, after comparing the popular optimized algorithms, Genetic Algorithm (GA) seems to be a successful method to design hybrid systems, since this method did not need a precise certain equation for a whole complex system. Xiaoliang Lai et al. (2013) used the GA to design a parallel hydraulic hybrid excavator. Xin Wang et al. (2011) proposed the GA to calibrate the driving system of hydraulic hybrid vehicle.

In general, GA is used to solve a constrained optimization problem for which an OBJ is to be minimized or maximized subject to constraints.

In our case, we believe that designing the energy recovery system must meet two goals:

1. The operation of the system without the energy recovery circuit and the operation of the new system with recovery circuit must be the same, since the goal is to design the new system without changing the operation of the standard one.
2. The benefit from the energy gained by integrating the energy recovery system must be the maximum. Referring to these two goals, the OBJ can be expressed as follows (1):

$$OBJ = k1 \sum_{i=0}^{n} \left(di, rs - di, s \right)^2 - k2 \sum_{i=0}^{n} Ei \qquad (1)$$

where n is the total count of simulation steps, $d_{i,rs}$ is the displacement of the actuator of the circuit equipped with the energy regeneration system at the ith simulation step, $d_{i,s}$ is the displacement of the actuator of the standard circuit at the ith simulation step, E_i is the energy gained by integrating the energy recovery system at the ith simulation step, k_1 and k_2 are two constant used as weighting coefficient. Since these two goals presented above have the same importance, we consider that k1 and k2 are equal to 1

The OBJ is subject to two constraints:

1. **Inequality Constraint:** The unknown parameters are bounded as follows (2):

$$O_{i\,min} \leq O_i \leq O_{i\,max} \qquad (2)$$

where O_i is the ith unknown parameter, $O_{i\,min}$ and $O_{i\,max}$ are the lower and upper bounds respectively of O_i.

2. **Equality Constraint:** The variation of outputs depends on the values of the unknown parameters and the time such as (3):

$$(d_{1,rs}, ..., d_{i,rs}, ..., d_{1,s}, ..., d_{i,s}, ..., E_1, ... E_i) = f(O_1, ..., O_i, t) \qquad (3)$$

where $d_{i,rs}$ is the displacement of the actuator of the circuit equipped with the energy regeneration system at the ith simulation step, $d_{i,s}$ is the displacement of the actuator of the standard circuit at the ith simulation step, E_i is the energy gained by integrating the energy recovery system at the ith simulation step, Oi is the ith unknown parameter and t is the time.

To solve this constrained optimization problem, we proposed a complete method, GOMPC, in order to design and identify all the unknown parameters of the energy recovery system.

The Proposed Solution

The proposed method, the GOMPC, uses an optimization technique coupled with the simulated model on simulation software. In this paper two optimization techniques: the Genetic Algorithm (GA) and the two-levels of Genetic Algorithm are applied then compared on an energy recovery system. In this process, these two optimization methods generate a set of calibrated parameters, passes them onto the simulation model, which returns the physical outputs (Hamby, 1995) (Elhajj et al., 2014). The optimization tools then uses the GA's and the two-levels of GA's OBJ to minimize the difference between the operation of the circuit without energy recovery system and the circuit with energy recovery system and maximize the power gained by integrating the energy recovery system. GOMPC consists on establishing a representative operating scenario to generate experiences on the circuit without energy recovery system. We consider that all the parameters of this circuit are known. On the other hand, we use this same scenario to feed energy recovery system to generate simulation outputs. However, in this phase, not all the parameters of the recovery system are known. In order to design the energy recovery system, the GA and the two-levels of GA are lunched. The principle of this method is presented in Figure 9.

GOMPC Applied on a Hydraulic Excavator

GOMPC consists of several hierarchical steps. In this paper, the case study is the system of the excavator's lifting function, and the patent applied is the patent proposed by Calin Raszga and Bergquist (2007). It consists on using the back pressure of the actuator, when lowering, to drive an hydraulic motor. This hydraulic motor drives in turn the pump of the hydraulic excavator.

The first step of the GOMPC is the modeling of the circuit with and without the energy recovery system.

Figure 9. The principle of the GOMPC to design the energy

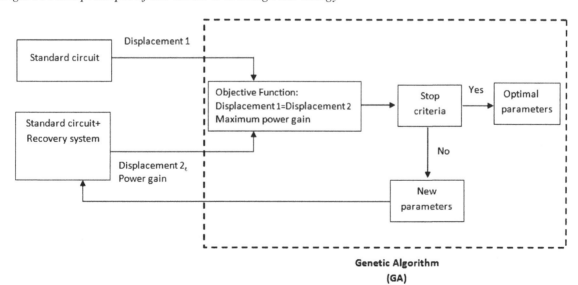

Step 1: Modeling the standard and hybrid system on a prototype circuit.

In our study, we model the two systems (the circuit without and with the energy recovery system) on Simulink by using SimHydraulic library . Simulink provides a general interface linked with Matlab. This coupling ensures the data exchange between the GA or the two-levels of GA compiled on Matlab and the modeled system on the simulation software. This interface facilitates the exchange of data and increases the flexibility of the complex model optimization in order to reach the optimal solution.

The modeling of the lifting function of the hydraulic circuit without the energy recovery system is illustrated in Figure 10. The operating cycle chosen for this study is based on typical working cycle. The first phase is the start. It allows positioning the excavator and / or its arm depending on the profile to achieve. Then, the lifting of the arm is performed. The third phase of the movement consists on the lifting's stop. The next phase allows the lowering down of the arm before the complete stop of movement.

According to this typical working cycle, the signal that feeds the 4/3 directional control valve of the standard system should be like presented in Figure 11.

The model of the circuit with energy recovery system is illustrated in Figure 12. The principle of this saving energy method is to use directly the back pressure of the cylinder to perform other hydraulic functions without additional storage devices. When lowering, the back pressure passes through the 2/2 directional control valve in order to drive a recuperation hydraulic motor. According to the principle of the recuperation, the signal that feeds the 2/2 distributor should be like presented in Figure 13. Distributor 2/2 is opened to store the potential energy only when the arm is lowering down. Otherwise, this distributor is closed.

Step 2: Identification of the unknown parameters to calibrate.

Once the hybrid system is modeled on Simulink, we define the parameters to calibrate and the range of their lower and upper values. Herein, we identify three unknown parameters. These parameters, d, s and m represent respectively the displacement of the hydraulic motor, the maximum area of fluid that can passes into distributor 2/2 and the maximum surface of the opened section. They were calibrated by assigning to each parameter the variability range as shown in Table 1. Most of ranges have been selected according to estimation in terms of physical meaning of the parameters and to the basis of the authors' experience.

Once the two circuits are modeled on Simulink and the unknown parameters of the energy recovery system are defined, we can apply the GA and the two-levels of GA.

Step 3: Definition of GA and two-levels of GA and their characteristics.

GA is one of the powerful tools for optimization problem; it has a great robustness and ability to find the global optimum solution. It searches more globally (Wang 1997) and could be coupled with simulation software (Liu et al. 2009). With the increase of problems' dimensions, the calculate efficiency of standard GA can't be satisfied. Thus, people are trying to research more efficient GA in order to reduce the computation time. Given that the time using the GA solving the optimization problem is simple but too long; many researchers have tried to combine many methods of GAs. This new optimization method is called the Hierarchical Genetic Algorithm (HGA) (Cantú-Paz 1998).

Figure 10. Hydraulic gravitational load standard system

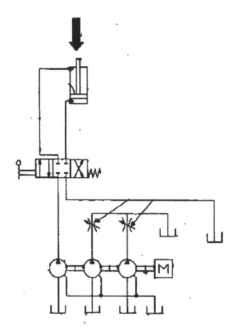

Figure 11. Signal that feeds the distributor 4/3 of the standard system

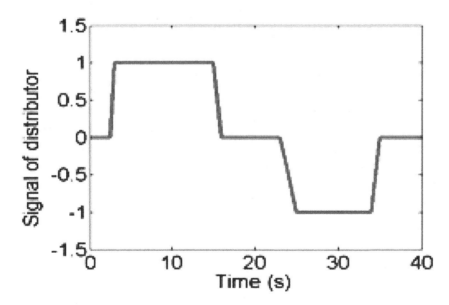

When many methods of GAs are combined they form a hierarchy. Hierarchical implementations can reduce the execution time more than any of their components alone. HGA accelerates the search of the standard GA, maintains the diversity of population prevents premature, and solves such a complicated problem efficiently and effectively. To benefit from the simplicity of GA and the advantages of HGA, we proposed in our study, the two-levels of GA.

Figure 12. Hydraulic gravitational load energy recovery system

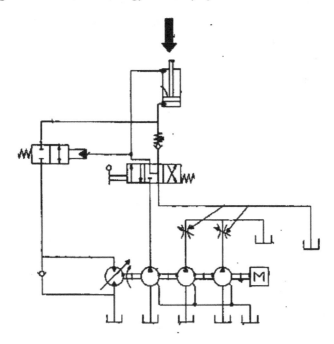

Figure 13. Signal that feeds the distributor 2/2 of the hybrid system

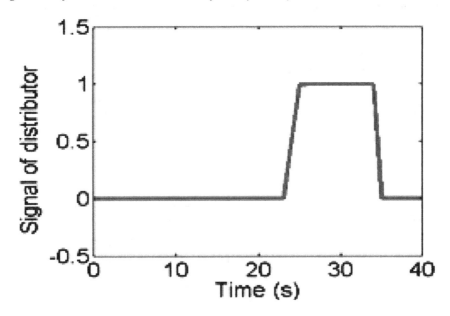

Table 1. Ranges for the parameters to calibrate

	d (cm3/rev)	s (m2)	m (mm)
Lower bound	2	2ᵉ-6	8
Upper bound	10	10ᵉ-5	50

This method is composed from two levels (Figure 14): in the first one GA is applied in parallel on many populations. After a large number of generations, the best individual of each population will be treated as an individual of a new population; in the second level, we apply the GA to this new population in order to get the optimal values.

In this step, the characteristics of the standard GA and the two-levels of GA (probability of the cross over, selection and mutation, OBJ, stop criteria, etc…) are defined.

Characteristics of the standard GA are presented below:

- Number of population: 1
- Size of the population: 40
- Rate of selection: 0.1
- Rate of mutation: 0.7
- Rate of crossover: 0.2
- Formula of the (OBJ) (5):

$$OBJ= OBJ=k1\sum_{i=0}^{n}\left(di,rs - di,s\right)^2 - k2\sum_{i=0}^{n}Ei \tag{5}$$

where n is the total count of simulation steps, $d_{i,rs}$ is the displacement of the actuator of the circuit equipped with the energy regeneration system at the ith simulation step, $d_{i,r}$ is the displacement of the actuator of

Figure 14. The topology of the two-levels of GA

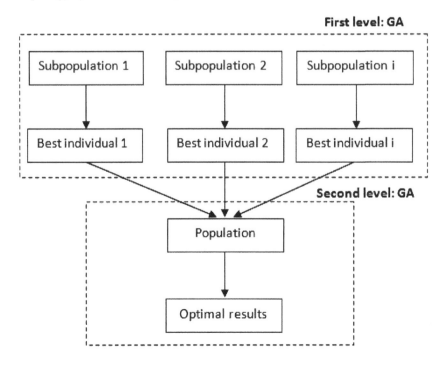

the standard circuit at the ith simulation step, E_i is the energy gained by using the energy recovery system at the ith simulation step, k_1 and k_2 are two constant used as weighting coefficient.

- **Stop Criteria:** GA stops when the value of the OBJ is smaller than 0.001 or when the generation's number of the GA exceeds 150.

Characteristics of the first level of the two-levels of GA are presented below:

- **Number of Population:** 5
- **Size of Population:** 40
- **Rate of Selection:** 0.1
- **Rate of Mutation:** 0.7
- **Rate of Crossover:** 0.2
- **Formula of the OBJ:** Same as formula (5)
- **Stop Criteria:** GA stops when the value of the OBJ is smaller than 0.001 or when the generation's number exceeds 15.

Characteristics of the second level of the two-levels of GA are presented below:

- **Number of Population:** 1
- **Size of Population:** 40
- **Rate of Selection:** 0.1
- **Rate of Mutation:** 0.7
- **Rate of Crossover:** 0.2
- **Formula of the OBJ:** Same as formula (5)
- **Stop Criteria:** GA stops when the value of the OBJ is smaller than 0.001 or when the generation's number exceeds 15.
  Step 4: Launching the GA and two-levels of GA.

The final step of GOMPC is launching these two optimization methods then collecting the results.

Results

We applied our GOMPC method and for each proposed optimization method about 10 times. Briefly, by applying the first method, one population runs executing the standard GA. In this process, GA generates a set of parameters, and then passes them onto the simulation model on Simulink, which in turn passes back the physical outputs. After 150 generations, GA begins to converge to the optimized solution. The best five runnings are presented in Table 2. As for the second method, the two-levels of GA, its first level is composed from five populations. Each one runs in parallel executing the standard GA. The principle of exchange between the simulation software and the optimization method is the same as those in the first method. After a few generations and for each population, GA begins to converge and the best five individual will form a new population. This population will pass to the second level. In the second level, GA is applied to this new population. After 150 generations, the optimized solution is reached. The best five trials and their (OBJ)'s values of the second level were selected then represented in Table 2.

Comparing the five best runnings of each method, the OBJs of the Run1 are the smallest ones. Hence, we consider that the optimal solutions for the GA and the two-levels of GA are those of the Run 1. Comparing the Run 1's OBJ by applying GA and two-levels of GA, it is evident to note that, even with less number of generations, the second method seems to be more efficient than GA and requires less computation time to converge. Figure 15 represents the arm's displacement curves of the circuit with and without the energy recovery system of Run 1 applying the two-levels of GA. From this figure, we can see that the displacement of these two circuits almost matches adequately. Therefore, the first goal of the OBJ is achieved. As for the others physical outputs, and theoretically, when lowering (time from 25s to 32s), pressure of the fluid is higher because it still contains some energy. In this phase, distributor 2/2 should be opened so as to recover this energy by driving an hydraulic motor. As we see in Figure 16 and Figure 17, the flow and the pressure at the inlet of the hydraulic motor increase from 0 l/mn to 18 l/mn and from 0 bar to 25 bar respectively. In this phase, the recuperation hydraulic motor drives the mechanical drive train of the prime mover that drives in turn the pump that supplies the load. The power

Figure 15. Evolution curves of the actuator's displacement with and without energy recovery system of Run 1 by applying two-levels of GA

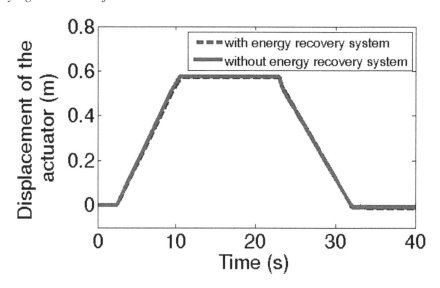

Table 2. Results of the best five runs applying GOMPC by using the GA and the two-levels of GA

Run	d (rev/cm3)		s (m²)		m (mm)		OBJ	
	GA	Two-levels of GA	GA	Two-levels of GA	GA	Two-levels of GA	GA	Two-levels of GA
Run 1	5.109	5.0194	8.9936 e-6	9.2175e-6	22.3	11.23	12396771.2	12124003.7
Run 2	5.154	5.2283	8.872 e-6	8.4293ᶜ-6	17.8	16.3	12416293.5	12192212.3
Run 3	5.501	5.0095	9.299 e-6	8.9592e-6	11.4	10	12498289.7	12285982.7
Run 4	4.998	5.0364	9.1037 e-6	8.643e-6	18.1	25.3	12598376.2	12364424.2
Run 5	5.037	5.4064	8.94231 e-6	8.4064e-6	22.4	24.3	12700311.4	12400776.9

Figure 16. Evolution curve of the flow at the hydraulic motor inlet in the of the energy recovery system of Run 1 by applying two-levels of GA

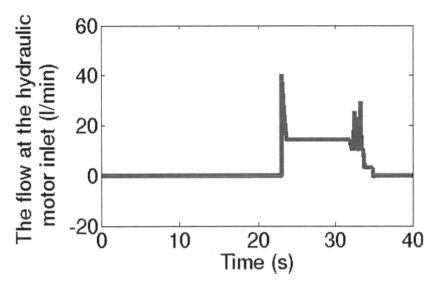

gained by integrating this energy recovery system is presented in Figure 18. The power increases from 0 kW to 2 kW, when lowering the arm.

From results presented above, we can confirm that GOMPC is an integrated solution for designing the energy recovery system. This method is always able to find the unknown parameters of the new added components. It respects two goals: having the same displacement of the arm with and without the energy recovery system and having the maximum power gained.

Figure 17. Evolution curve of the pressure at the hydraulic motor inlet of the of the energy recovery system of Run 1 by applying two-levels of GA

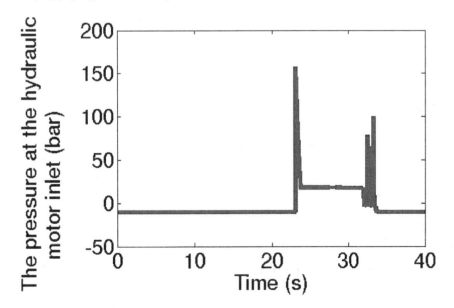

Figure 18. Evolution curve of the power gain by using the energy recovery system of Run 1 by applying two-levels of GA

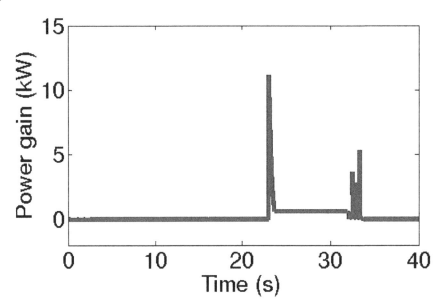

CONCLUSION

In this paper, we present an overview on the energy recovery systems applied on hydraulic circuits, their principals, their classifications and their categories. After that, we propose a framework for an integrated optimized method to design and to identify the components' unknown parameters of the energy recovery system. This method, the GOMPC, combines between the simulated model and an optimization method. In this paper two optimization methods (GA and two-levels of GA) are presented then compared. We apply GOMPC on an energy recovery patent based on sharing the back pressure of the actuators. The results revealed that applying the two-levels of GA in combination with a simulation software is an efficient method that leads to the most accurate results and to have the optimal design.

Since GOMPC was a successful solution to our case study, we believe that it could be a useful technique for designing any energy recovery system in hydraulic excavator.

REFERENCES

966L Wheel Loader, Caterpillar, AEHQ6211-01 (07-2011)

Amitesh Kumar, E. R. (2012). Hydraulic Regenerative Braking System. *International Journal of Scientific & Engineering Research, 3*(4).

Andersen, T. O., Hansen, M. R., & Pedersen, H. C. (2005). Regeneration of potential energy in hydraulic forklift trucks. *Fluid Power Transmission and Control ICFP, 2005*, 302–306.

Andruch, J., III, & Lumkes, J. H., Jr. (2010). *U.S. Patent Application 13/498,769*. US Patent Office.

Andruch & Lumkes Jr. (n.d.). Balance of Power: hydraulic-powered add to vehicle efficiency, reduce emissions. *Technology Today*.

Baker, T. L., Egelja, A. M., Peterson, R. N., VerKuilen, M. T., & Yoshino, T. (2010). *U.S. Patent No. 7,832,208*. Washington, DC: U.S. Patent and Trademark Office.

Bergquist, U., Girard, J. R., & Raszga, C. L. (2007). *U.S. Patent No. 7,249,457*. Washington, DC: U.S. Patent and Trademark Office.

Bradley, D. A., & Seward, D. W. (1998). The development, control and operation of an autonomous robotic excavator. *Journal of Intelligent & Robotic Systems*, *21*(1), 73–97. doi:10.1023/A:1007932011161

Bradley, D. A., Seward, D. W., Mann, J. E., & Goodwin, M. R. (1993). Artificial intelligence in the control and operation of construction plant the autonomous robot excavator. *Automation in Construction*, *2*(3), 217–228. doi:10.1016/0926-5805(93)90042-V

Bruun, L. (2003). *U.S. Patent No. 6,584,769*. Washington, DC: U.S. Patent and Trademark Office.

Budny, E., Chłosta, M., & Gutkowski, W. (2003). Load-independent control of a hydraulic excavator. *Automation in Construction*, *12*(3), 245–254. doi:10.1016/S0926-5805(02)00088-2

Budny, E., Chlosta, M., & Gutkowski, W. (2003). Optimal control of an excavator bucket positioning. *NIST Special Publication*, 481-488.

Bullock, D. M., & Oppenheim, I. J. (1992). Object-oriented programming in robotics research for excavation. *Journal of Computing in Civil Engineering*, *6*(3), 370–385. doi:10.1061/(ASCE)0887-3801(1992)6:3(370)

Cantú-Paz, E. (1998). A survey of parallel genetic algorithms. *Calculateurs paralleles, reseaux et systems repartis*, *10*(2), 141-171.

Chang, P. H., & Lee, S. J. (2002). A straight-line motion tracking control of hydraulic excavator system. *Mechatronics*, *12*(1), 119–138. doi:10.1016/S0957-4158(01)00014-9

Chang, P. H., & Park, S. H. (1998, June). The development of anti-windup scheme and stick-slip compensator for time delay control. In *American Control Conference, 1998. Proceedings of the 1998* (Vol. 6, pp. 3629-3633). IEEE. 10.1109/ACC.1998.703290

Cherney, M. J., & Radke, D. D. (2006). *U.S. Patent No. 7,124,576*. Washington, DC: U.S. Patent and Trademark Office.

Elhajj, M., Younes, R., Charles, S., & Padiolleau, E. (2014). Calibration of the Parameters of a Model of an Engineering System Using the Global Optimization Method. *International Journal of Applied Evolutionary Computation*, *5*(3), 28. doi:10.4018/ijaec.2014070102

Endo, H., Maruta, K., & Yoshida, N. (2000). *U.S. Patent No. 6,151,894*. Washington, DC: U.S. Patent and Trademark Office.

Filipi, Z., Louca, L., Daran, B., Lin, C.-C., Yildir, U., Wu, B., ... Chapp, R. (2004). Combined Optimisation of Design and Power Management of the Hydraulic Hybrid Propulsion System for the 6 × 6 Medium Truck. *International Journal of Heavy Vehicle Systems*, *11*(3/4), 372–402. doi:10.1504/IJHVS.2004.005458

Grace, M. H., & Karazija, A. (1976). *U.S. Patent No. 3,947,744*. Washington, DC: U.S. Patent and Trademark Office.

Hamby, D. M. (1995). A comparison of sensitivity analysis techniques. *Health Physics, 68*(2), 195–204. doi:10.1097/00004032-199502000-00005 PMID:7814253

Hirata, T., Izumi, E., Tanaka, Y., Watanabe, H., & Yoshida, K. (1990). *U.S. Patent No. 4,967,557*. Washington, DC: U.S. Patent and Trademark Office.

Hirochi. (1995). A Stereo Vision System using Multi Slit Lights for Underground Vehicle. *Proc. of the 2nd Asian Conference on Computer Vision, 2*, 326-330.

Holt, B. J., Krone, J., & Nippert, A. (2003). *U.S. Patent No. 6,655,136*. Washington, DC: U.S. Patent and Trademark Office.

Hui, S., & Junqing, J. (2010). Research on the system configuration and energy control strategy for parallel hydraulic hybrid loader. *Automation in Construction, 19*(2), 213-220.

Huu, Ahamad, Jong, Kyoung, & Jin. (2012). *Tracking control of hydraulic actuator with energy saving using independent metering valves*. 16th International conference on mechatronics technology, Tianjin, China.

Inoue, H. (2008). Introduction of PC200-8 hybrid hydraulic excavators. Komatsu Technical Report. Vol.54 NO.161. "Hydraulic excavator equipped with generator operated by revolution", Kondo Hiroshi.

Kagoshima, M., & Kinugawa, H. (2001). *U.S. Patent No. 6,199,307*. Washington, DC: U.S. Patent and Trademark Office.

Kagoshima, M., Komiyama, M., Nanjo, T., & Tsutsui, I. A. (2007). Development of new hybrid excavator. *Kobelco Technology Review*, (27), 39–42.

Kar-Erik Rydberg. (2004). Hydraulic Accumulators as Key Components. In *Energy Efficient Mobile Systems*. Linköping University.

Katrasnik, T., Trenc, F., & Opresnik, S. R. (2007). Analysis of energy conversion efficiency in parallel and series hybrid powertrains. *Vehicular Technology. IEEE Transactions on, 56*(6), 3649–3659.

Kawashima, K., & Sugiyama, Y. (2010). *U.S. Patent Application 13/376,932*. US Patent Office.

Khalil, R. E. (2010). *U.S. Patent No. 7,775,040*. Washington, DC: U.S. Patent and Trademark Office.

Kinugawa, H., & Komiyama, M. (1999). *U.S. Patent No. 5,913,811*. Washington, DC: U.S. Patent and Trademark Office.

Koivo, A. J. (1992). Controlling an Intelligent Excavator for Autonomous Digging in Difficult Ground. *Proc. the 9th International Symposium on Automation and Construction*.

Korane, K. (2008). *Energy recovery systems on hydraulic excavators*. Hydraulics and Pneumatics, Parker Hanninfin.

Kraft TeleRobotics. (1994). *Haz-Trak: Force Feedback Excavator and Material Handling System*. Kraft TeleRobotics, Inc.

Lai, X., & Guan, C. (2013). A Parameter Matching Method of the Parallel Hydraulic Hybrid Excavator Optimized with Genetic Algorithm. *Mathematical Problems in Engineering*, 2013.

Lawrence, P. D., Salcudean, S. E., Sepehri, N., Chan, D., Bachmann, S., Parker, & Frenette, R. (1997). Coordinated and force-feedback control of hydraulic excavators. In Experimental Robotics IV (pp. 181-194). Springer Berlin Heidelberg.

Lee, C. C. (1993). *A Study on the Design of Fuzzy Logic Controller for Bucket Tip Leveling of Hydraulic excavator* (PhD thesis). Seoul National University. (in Korean)

Lee, S. U., & Chang, P. H. (2001). Control of a heavy-duty robotic excavator using time delay control with switching action with integral sliding surface. In *Robotics and Automation, 2001. Proceedings 2001 ICRA. IEEE International Conference on* (Vol. 4, pp. 3955-3960). IEEE.

Li-Zhongli, Wang-Ximing, & Gao-Jianping. (2010). Study in Work Condition Matching of Dynamical System of Hybrid Power Vehicle. [in Chinese]. *Journal of Henan University of Science & Technology*, *31*(5), 24–28.

Liang, X., & Virvalo, T. (2001). Energy reutilization and balance analysis. *Proceedings of the Fifth International Conference on Fluid Power Transmission and Control (ICFP)*.

Lin, T., & Wang, Q. (2012). Hydraulic accumulator-motor-generator energy regeneration system for a hybrid hydraulic excavator. *Chinese Journal of Mechanical Engineering*, *25*(6), 1121–1129. doi:10.3901/CJME.2012.06.1121

Lin, T., Wang, Q., Hu, B., & Gong, W. (2010). Research on the energy regeneration systems for hybrid hydraulic excavators. *Automation in Construction*, *19*(8), 1016–1026. doi:10.1016/j.autcon.2010.08.002

Lin, T., Wang, Q., Hu, B., & Gong, W. (2010). Development of hybrid powered hydraulic construction machinery. *Automation in Construction*, *19*(1), 11–19. doi:10.1016/j.autcon.2009.09.005

Liu. (2009). A improved parallel genetic algorithm based on fixed point theory for the optimal design of multi-body model vehicle suspensions. In *Computer Science and Information Technology, 2009. ICCSIT 2009. 2nd IEEE International Conference on* (pp. 430-433). IEEE.

Nakano, E., Tsuda, N., Inuoe, K., Kayaba, K., & Kimura, H. (1992). Development of an advanced way of improvement of the maneuverability of a backhoe machine. *Proc. 9th International Symposium on Automation and Robotics in Construction*. 10.22260/ISARC1992/0029

Naruse, M., Ohtsukasa, N., Tanaka, J., & Haga, S. (2004). *U.S. Patent No. 6,725,581*. Washington, DC: U.S. Patent and Trademark Office.

Nishimura, S. (1989). *Position energy recovering activating device for hydraulic excavator*. Komatsu.

Nyman, J., Bärnström, J., & Rydberg, K. E. (2004). Use of accumulators to reduce the need of electric power in hydraulic lifting systems. *Scandinavian International Conference on Fluid Power, SICFP03*.

Nyman, J., & Rydberg, K. E. (2001). Energy saving lifting hydraulic systems. *7th Scandinavian International Conference on Fluid Power*, 163-177.

Peng-Tianhao. (2001). Research on Pump-engine Match in Hydraulic Excavator. *China Journal of Highway and Transport*, *14*(4), 118–120.

Potential Energy recovery reproducing device for hydraulic operated excavator. (1989). Komatsu.

Qing, X. I. A. O., & Qing-feng, W. A. N. G. (2008). Parameter matching Method for Hybrid Power System of Hydraulic Excavator [in Chinese]. *China Jounal of Hightway and Transport*, *21*(1), 121–126.

Salcudean, S. E., Tafazoli, S., Lawrence, P. D., & Chau, I. (1997, July). Impedance control of a teleoperated mini excavator. In *Advanced Robotics, 1997. ICAR'97. Proceedings., 8th International Conference on* (pp. 19-25). IEEE. 10.1109/ICAR.1997.620156

Sepehri, N., Lawrence, P. D., Sassani, F., & Frenette, R. (1994). Rosolved-mode teleoperated control of heavy-duty hydraulic machines. ASME Journal of Dynamic System. *Measurement and Control*, *116*(2), 232–240. doi:10.1115/1.2899215

Singh, S. (1995, May). Learning to predict resistive forces during robotic excavation. In *Robotics and Automation, 1995. Proceedings., 1995 IEEE International Conference on* (Vol. 2, pp. 2102-2107). IEEE. 10.1109/ROBOT.1995.526025

Singh, S. (1997). State of the art in automation of earthmoving. *Journal of Aerospace Engineering*, *10*(4), 179–188. doi:10.1061/(ASCE)0893-1321(1997)10:4(179)

Smith, D. P. (2004). *U.S. Patent No. 6,748,738*. Washington, DC: U.S. Patent and Trademark Office.

Stentz, A., Bares, J., Singh, S., & Rowe, P. (1999). A robotic excavator for autonomous truck loading. *Autonomous Robots*, *7*(2), 175–186. doi:10.1023/A:1008914201877

Sun, W., & Virvalo, T. (2001). Accumulator-pump-motor as energy saving in hydraulic boom. *8th Scandinavian International Conference on Fluid power*, 163-177.

Sun, W., & Virvalo, T. (2005). Simulation study on a hydraulic –accumulator-balancing-energy saving system in hydraulic boom. *50th National Conference on fluid power*, 371-381.

Thompson, D. H., Killough, S. M., Burks, B. L., & Draper, J. V. (1995). *Design of the human computer interface on the telerobotic small emplacement excavator*. Academic Press.

Wang, Q. J. (1997). Using genetic algorithms to optimise model parameters. *Environmental Modelling & Software*, *12*(1), 27–34. doi:10.1016/S1364-8152(96)00030-8

Wang, T., & Wang, Q. (2012). Design and analysis of compound potential energy regeneration system for hybrid hydraulic excavator. *Proceedings of the Institution of Mechanical Engineers. Part I, Journal of Systems and Control Engineering*, *226*(10), 1323–1334. doi:10.1177/0959651812456642

Wang, X., Yu, A., & Chen, W. (2011). Optimal matching on driving system of hydraulic hybrid vehicle. *Procedia Engineering*, *15*, 5294–5298. doi:10.1016/j.proeng.2011.08.981

Weidong, L., Kaikai, S., Wei, L., & Jun, X. (2011, August). Research on Potential Energy Recovery of 16T Wheeled Hybrid Excavator. In *Digital Manufacturing and Automation (ICDMA), 2011 Second International Conference on* (pp. 996-998). IEEE.

Wendel, G. R. (2000). *Regenerative hydraulic systems for increased efficiency*. San Antonio, TX: Southwest Research Institute.

Wohlford, W. P., Bode, B. D., & Griswold, F. D. (1989). *New capability for remote controlled excavation* (No. 891859). SAE Technical Paper.

Xiao, Q., Wang, Q., & Zhang, Y. (2008). Control strategies of power system in hybrid hydraulic excavator. *Automation in Construction*, *17*(4), 361–367. doi:10.1016/j.autcon.2007.05.014

Yamashita, K. (2001). *U.S. Patent No. 6,202,411*. Washington, DC: U.S. Patent and Trademark Office.

Yang, J., Quan, L., & Yang, Y. (2012). Excavator energy-saving efficiency based on diesel engine cylinder deactivation technology. *Chinese Journal of Mechanical Engineering*, *25*(5), 897–904. doi:10.3901/CJME.2012.05.897

Yi, Y., & Yu, T. (2013, January). The Load Sensing Principle of Proportion Multi-channel Valve and its Application in Excavator. In *Proceedings of the 2013 Third International Conference on Intelligent System Design and Engineering Applications* (pp. 1469-1472). IEEE Computer Society. 10.1109/ISDEA.2012.351

Yokota, S., Sasao, M., & Ichiryu, K. (1996). Trajectory Control of the boom and arm system of hydraulic excavators. Transactions of the Japan Society of Mechanical Engineers [Japanese]. *Part C*, *62*(593), 161–167.

Yoshino, K. (2008). *U.S. Patent No. 7,401,464*. Washington, DC: U.S. Patent and Trademark Office.

Yueyuan, W., Cheng, L., & Yi, L. (2006). Factors Influencing Hybrid Electric Vehicle System Efficiency. *Journal of Jilin University*, *36*, 20–24.

Zarotti, S., & Eugenio, L. R. P. (2010). Hydraulic Excavator Working Cycle: From Field Test to Simulation Model. *7th International Fluid Power Conference*, Aachen.

Zhang, J., Ma, P., Schwab, M., Patel, K. N., & Shang, T. (2007). *Design and analysis for recovering potential energy*. Caterpillar.

Zhi, L., Shaoju, L., Zhonghua, H., & Qiong, H. (2011, August). Hydraulic Excavator Hybrid Power System Parameters Design. In *Digital Manufacturing and Automation (ICDMA), 2011 Second International Conference on* (pp. 602-605). IEEE.

Chapter 14
Wireless Robotics Networks for Search and Rescue in Underground Mines:
Taxonomy and Open Issues

Alok Ranjan
National Institute of Technology Rourkela, India

H. B. Sahu
National Institute of Technology Rourkela, India

Prasant Misra
TCS Research & Innovation, India

ABSTRACT

To ensure the safety of miners, reliable and continuous monitoring of underground mine environment plays a significant role. Moreover, such a reliable communication network is essential to provide speedy rescue and recovery operations in case of an emergency situation in a mine. However, due to the hostile nature and unique characteristics of underground mine workings, emergency response communication and disaster management are very challenging tasks. This chapter presents an overview of evolving technology wireless robotics networks (WRN) which may be a promising alternative to support search and rescue (SAR) operation in underground mine emergencies. The chapter first outlines the introduction followed by a detailed discussion on the current state of the art on WRNs and their development in the context of underground mines. Finally, this chapter provides some insights on open research areas targeting the current wireless research design community and those interested in pursuing such challenging problems in this field.

DOI: 10.4018/978-1-5225-5832-3.ch014

1. INTRODUCTION

Underground mining occupation is considered as *high-stressed* work environment, compared to a normal work environment, which consists of several unique features such as narrower work space, high humidity, poor visibility, dusty and hazardous gas concentration, etc. (Bandyopadhyay, Chaulya, & Mishra, 2010; Misra et al., 2010). The miners working underground are highly exposed to health hazards and risks of either fatal injuries or minor causalities. Therefore, to provide a safe work environment to the mine personnel is of paramount importance for the mine management. However, reliable operation of mine communication and monitoring systems are *restricted* in performance due to the unique features of underground mines. The different challenges to achieve wireless communication with particular reference to Wireless Robotics Networks (WRN) is discussed later in the chapter.

Disasters either natural or man-made have always been a matter of concern and are hard to predict. It can affect a large number of people, causing loss of lives and serious injuries, infrastructure damages, and also hampers our environment and surroundings. In the context of underground mines, *unforeseen disasters* have been a challenge to the mine management. Moreover, providing a timely rescue support to the affected persons in the working districts is another significant concern to the management (Ranjan, Sahu, & Misra 2016). Though several mine accidents have been reported and remained in news headlines, there are many small injuries and events which remained unnoticed across the world. For example, in the year of 2006-2007, there were around11,800 minor injuries and 69 fatal injuries in US mines (Kamruzzaman, Fernando, Jaseemuddin, & Farjow, 2017). Every year miners die due to serious injuries. A comparative illustration of mine accidents in coal and metal mines of India can be seen in the Figures 1 and 2. It is reported that a miner in routine operation is five times more exposed to occupational hazards than a person working in the normal industry (Kamruzzaman et al., 2017). In case of any emergency situation in underground mine workings, the first ever question in front of mine management and rescue team is, *where exactly are the miners trapped?* In addition, there are few more questions which have to be answered in the aftermath of mine disaster to support timely rescue operation and are as follows (Alok Ranjan, Sahu, & Misra, 2016):

- How many miners have been trapped?
- What are the different mine environmental parameters such as temperature, noxious gas concentration, and humidity percentage?
- Is there any communication infrastructure working?
- And knowledge of escape route plans.

Hence, locating the miners' positions, mine asset and explosives tracking and environmental monitoring are crucial tasks for the mine management for both routine operations and during any emergency scenario. Following are some of the major causes that have led to the frequent occurrence of accidents in underground mines and need to be monitored in a timely manner (Forooshani et al., 2013; Ranjan, Sahu, & Misra, 2015).

Mine Fire

Every day for carrying out mining activity, several mine equipment is used such as drilling machine, surface miner, belt conveyors, mine trucks, shuttle car, load haul and dump (LHD), etc. Proper maintenance of mine machinery is necessary as a small ignition or excessive of friction from the drum, wheels/axles, dysfunctional bearings, etc. may lead to a mine fire. Except this, there is also a chance of spontaneous heating of coal seams which may cause the fire. Excessive heat from the surroundings due to exothermal process is another concern for the mine management which need to be monitored (Sahu, Panigrahi, & Mishra, 2004). Therefore, an early monitoring and warning of spontaneous combustion of coal are significant to further minimize the risk of material losses as well loss of lives.

Gas Explosions

In an underground mine working hazardous gases are present. For coal mines, methane and carbon monoxide remain a matter of concern, whereas for metal mines such as copper and zinc, hydrogen sulphide and carbon monoxide have been potentially dangerous. Methane is highly flammable in nature and generally trapped in the coal structure and associated strata. With extraction, the mobilization of methane takes place, and it moves upwards due to its lower density and so is found in the roof/roof cavities in the mines. There are different mechanisms of measuring the presence of concentrations of noxious gases, of which the most common methods are using safety lamps which is *manual* and using electric automatic gas detector. Sensor based gas detection is also carried out in a few mines. A number of mines have also adopted environmental telemonitoring systems (Alok Ranjan, Sahu, & Misra, 2015a). Considering the explosive nature of such gases, any error either mechanical or man-made such as wrong measurements may lead to a fire, firedamp, and coal dust explosions inside mine workings. By analyzing the statistics of mine disasters, one can easily find out that *methane* and *coal dust explosions* have been a major cause of mine accidents which resulted in several losses of lives and injuries to the mine personnel (DGMS, 2016).

Drilling and Blasting

In a daily routine, blasting and drilling are performed and are part of mine production. Blasting is performed to fragment the ore chunks for further mineral exploration. To this objective, *explosives* are used and placed inside the ore body with the help of drilling operation. Though drilling and blasting are a daily routine operation, they have caused serious injuries to the mine personnel due to *fly rock* propagation, and *premature explosion* motivated from careless planning, a faulty fuse or sometimes use of degenerated explosives. Moreover, misfires of explosive have also resulted in injuries to the miners. In addition to drilling and blasting operation, it is reported that blasting affects the strata caused by seismic activity. It is worthy to understand that the *undesired seismic activity* in strata may lead to unpleasant behavior of crack propagation in the rock, hence results in unforeseen disaster over time. Ground support and analysis of strata behavior is very significant as this may lead to the collapse of mine walls and also may cause for roof fall resulting in loss of lives and infrastructure damage. There are several disasters reported caused by roof falls and side wall collapses (DGMS, 2016). Therefore, a timely and reliable monitoring system is required to monitor and analyze the mine-induced seismic behavior which may further cause instability in strata behavior.

The remainder of the chapter unfolds as follows. Section 2, includes the introduction of underground mines followed by features of underground mine environments in the following subsections. Characteristics of the underground mine communication channel are also discussed as a subsection of section 2. In Section 3, a brief background of WRNs for SAR operation is presented followed by different perspective of WRN to be used in underground mines for SAR operation. A detailed discussion on the state-of-the-art work based on WRNs in underground mines is presented in Section 4. An outline of some major implications for WRN operation in underground mines is discussed in Section 5. The future research directions are presented in Section 6, and Section 7 concludes our work.

2. UNDERGROUND MINES: AN INSIGHT

When an ore body occurs at greater depth, it becomes uneconomic to exploit by opencast methods. In such cases, the ore body is extracted by adopting underground mining. Underground mines are an interconnected network of cross cuts, uneven structures, tunnels, sub-stations, shafts, escape routes and rail tracks. Different types of support systems are present either in the form of wood, metal, hydraulic props and bolted reinforcement (Bandyopadhyay, Chaulya, & Mishra, 2010). Figure 3 depicts the schematic diagram of the underground mine.

2.1 Features of Underground Mine Environment

In an underground mine, miners are continuously exposed to the risks of life and health hazards due to a dynamic and unpredictable set of conditions posed by the tunnels. Situational awareness of the environmental conditions and two-way voice communications would be one approach to ensure the safety of miners. The environment inside an underground mine tunnel also has poor visibility due to the pres-

Figure 1. Fatal injuries in different mines (DGMS 2016)

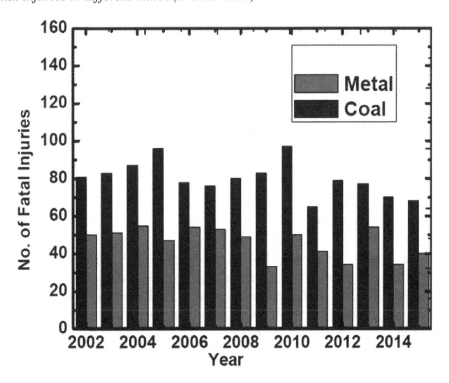

Figure 2. Serious injuries in different mines (DGMS 2016)

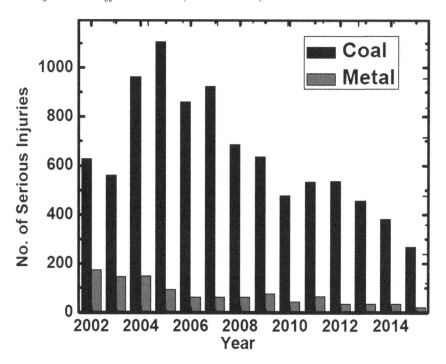

ence of airborne dust, smoke, poor lighting and the obstructions to a clear line of sight in mine galleries. Other physical factors present in the underground mines like humidity, the disorientation of minerals, temperature and gas concentration *strictly* opposed the use of standard communication systems for a normal environment. Following are some major characteristics of underground mines that may affect the performance of communication systems (Bandyopadhyay et al., 2010; Misra, Kanhere, Ostry, & Jha, 2010; Ranjany, Misraz, Dwivediz, & Sahuy, 2016; Yarkan, Guzelgoz, Arslan, & Murphy, 2009):

2.1.1 Uneven Structure

The underground mines do not have smooth surface throughout the mine. The hanging wall and footwall wall conditions vary from mine to mine and have a discontinuity in the thickness. This leads to the poor signal strength at the receiver end because of scattering and reflection phenomena inside underground mines.

2.1.2 Poor Line of Sight (LOS)

A direct LOS provides a better signal strength at the receiver because the signal transmitted by the transmitter is partially affected by parameters like attenuation, transmission delay, loss of packets. Attenuation and propagation delay affect the overall communication where there is no line of sight path (NLOS) between the transmitter and receiver. Moving vehicles, equipment, mine personnel, blockages are also sometimes caused NLOS hence, restricts the reliable operation of communication devices.

Figure 3. General layout of underground mine environment

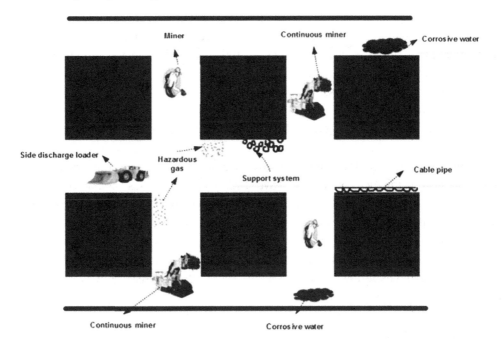

2.1.3 Noise

Noise due to the operation of mining equipment inside the underground mine degrades the signal quality; transmitted by a transmitter. This may affect the performance of a communication system seriously. Noise in the signal added either externally or internally reduces the coverage range of the communication system. However, in the case of the rescue operation, this is somewhat reduced due to power failures, electronic devices and other mechanical rescue equipment carried by the rescue team may add noise to the transmitted signal.

2.1.4 Gaseous Environment

Different gases are present inside the mine workings. The main concerns in coal mines are methane which is highly flammable and have been responsible for a number of accidents due to fire and explosion across the globe. Other toxic gases are also there which may also cause degradation of signal quality.

2.1.5 Warm Conditions and Humidity

Usually, as we go deeper, the temperature rises due to the geothermic gradient. Moreover, there is the release of heat to the mine air due to auto-compression, machinery, strata movement, etc. A mining environment also has relative humidity predominantly due to seepage. This high humidity can affect the signal propagation for communication between the transmitter and receiver. The communication devices should be intrinsically safe for normal operations and activities as per the mining regulations.

2.1.6 Tunnel as a Waveguide

It has been observed that an underground mine tunnel behaves as waveguide at certain frequencies thus the transmitted signal has enhanced coverage range. A High coverage range of communication can achieve due to waveguide effect inside the mine tunnel. This causes less propagation effect for a communication system operating on these frequencies.

2.2 Characteristics of Underground Mine Communication Channel

Underground wireless channels for communication is quite different than the terrestrial WSN channels. Communications using electromagnetic wave (EM) propagation has been actively researched and implemented as compared to other digital communication possibilities (Wait & Fuller, 1971; Weldon & Rathore, 1999). Understanding the underground mine characteristics as well as challenges faced by wired and wireless communication is necessary for developing a reliable system. Some major properties of underground channels that affect the performance of wireless communication systems in underground mines can be summarized as follows (Bandyopadhyay et al., 2010; Misra et al., 2010; Alok Ranjan et al., 2016).

2.2.2 Extreme Path Loss

The attenuation rate is high for the communication system which operates at higher frequencies compared to the lower frequencies device. Path loss is directly dependent on the distance between the transmitter and the receiver.

2.2.3 Reflection/ Refraction

It is found that due to the consideration of low loss dielectric the tunnel acts as a waveguide for the signal. When the transmitted signals strike on the walls, the signals are partially reflected and back into the planar guide and also partially refracted into the surroundings. This causes the loss of the received power at the receiver.

2.2.4 Multipath Fading

During the mining operation, a lot of mine equipment spread over the working area. Due to this multipath and scattering comes into effect. This multipath signal propagation affects the signal and causes for the fading in the transmitted signals. Also, due to the scattering effect, the signal fades faster in the near region of the transmitter at high frequencies.

2.2.5 Propagation Velocity

In a normal environment, the radio wave propagates with a better velocity compared to the environments having the obstructions and complex infrastructures. This affects the signal propagation inside mine tunnels. The dielectric properties of the medium change with the environment considered for the radio communication. This dielectric behavior of the mine tunnels alters the signal characteristics.

2.2.6 Waveguide Effect

In an ideal condition for the tunnel scenario, the waveguide effect guides the signal for better propagation of electromagnetic signals. But in the case of mine tunnels, due to absorption of signals and coupling of modes the tunnel leads to the signal attenuation. Hence, the received power at the receiver gets decreased.

2.2.7 Noise

In a normal mining operation inside the underground mines, different equipment is used for production purposes. This equipment produces a considerable amount of noise in the mine environment. This noise degrades the overall signal quality of the communication devices. Drill machines, mine trucks, electric motors and continuous miner are some major source of the noise inside the tunnel. It is noticed that the mining equipment lies in the same frequency range in which most of the communication devices work. This caused for additional loss in the received power.

3. WIRELESS ROBOTICS NETWORKS: BACKGROUND

Robotics has been a very interesting research area with the main objective of making human lives simple and is used to assist people in the events such as daily work, during an emergency situation, medical treatment, and search and rescue operations, etc. (Ko & Lau, 2009; Murphy, 2004; Penders et al., 2011; Schneider, 2009). Due to the availability of low-cost hardware solutions with optimized protocol stacks; robotics based research has gained tremendous interests and widens the scope of *interdisciplinary* research directions. Therefore, researchers have been motivated towards solving problems on different aspects of networked robotics for different social driven tasks and goals (Gazi & Passino, 2011; Hainsworth, 2001; Sahin & Winfield, 2008; Xue, Ma, & Wei, 2014). However, most of the proposed solutions are *limited* to theoretical aspects and are limited in real time deployment constraints and resource sharing. Considering the different emerging applications of robotics networks such as during fire situation, military application, oil and mine exploration, and disasters; it would be interesting to the research community to understand the robotics network *behavior* in the desired application environment. As part of this interesting research discussion of robotics networks in a different environment, a careful realization of communication among robots in case of collaborative tasks, deployment planning, message passing and the reliable network link is crucial. To this, more systematic measurements and modeling of communication network will be required in the near future targeting different applications.

Though robotics based networks have been an area of interest of researchers over a couple of decades, research on the *wireless networks of robots with controlled mobility* is underdeveloped. On the other hand, the field of wireless networks especially the Wireless Sensor Networks and Mobile Ad-Hoc Networks have been explored widely and deployed in several application areas such as in agriculture fields, industry environment, battlefield, health care, volcano monitoring, underground mines, and smart sensing, etc. (Sammarco, Paddock, Fries, & Karra, 2007; Wang, Zhang, & Wang, 2006; Werner-Allen et al., 2006; Yang, Zhang, & Liu, 2010; Yarkan et al., 2009). Nevertheless, recently researchers have attempted to connect the dots between wireless network technology and robotics networks in different applications. This new research area is known as *"Wireless Robotics Networks (WRN)" or "Automated Robotics Networks (ARN)."* WRN is a network of autonomous robots connected through wireless links to perform different assigned tasks while maintaining certain network performance to offer a better quality of service (QoS). Unlike the teleoperated robotics networks, WRN exchange data with other robots or sensor devices over radio frequency (RF) links. This is further useful to extend the service area by the robots and to perform coordination tasks efficiently.

Going back to the experimental deployment of robotics networks in different application scenario; the first ever network of robots in the practical scenario was used in the year of 2001 during the SAR operation at the well-known *World Trade Centre, USA*. The SAR mission consisted of four robots to help in speedy recovery from the disaster (Murphy, 2014). A group of Unmanned Aerial Vehicles (UAV) was used in Portugal during a forest fire in 2003 (Murphy, 2014). It is crucial for WRN to be deployed in such challenging environment that a reliable communication link should always be maintained as the link might get affected due to different propagation factors like dynamic link behavior due to mobility, multipath effects and terrain profiles, etc.

3.1 Wireless Robotics Networks for Underground Mines: A Search and Rescue Perspective

Apart from the different novel application of WRNs, the underground mining is another potential area. It is motivated by the fact of occurrence of underground mine disasters across the world. The mine accidents leading to disasters may be caused due to several reasons among which most frequents are roof fall, gas explosion, and mine fire, etc. In such circumstances, a timely SAR operation would not only help in a reduced number of loss of lives but would also act as the first responder to the situation. However, due to the hostile nature of mine environment (see section 2) a speedy operation of rescue efforts is a challenge to the mine management. This is because of the lack of real-time information of mine working parameters such as hazardous gas concentration, temperature, geo-structure deformations after the disaster, and knowledge of escape routes to the rescue team, etc. Therefore, *prior* and *post* knowledge of environmental features of mine workings will significantly help the rescue team to achieve a timely rescue operation. To this timely rescue concern, a mobile sensing platform could be deployed in the disaster-affected area of mine workings to get real-time information of environmental parameters. Nonetheless, to achieve such desired tasks communication and data exchange among different robots and to the surface/base station or vice versa is a significant challenge.

In past few years, researchers have proposed mobile robot platforms equipped with multiple sensors to collect the environmental parameters in underground coal mines. These robots are used to disseminate the different collected data to the rescue team through a communication network. If the accident site is safe to enter for the rescuers, then further rescue plan is executed. However, if the mine accident area is found to be *risky,* then proper precautions will be followed by the rescuers. Hence, this will make rescue operation much safer rather entering the mine accident area without any information.

Though research efforts have been made to design a mobile robotics network for SAR operation in underground mines, different concerns related to overall system design is underdeveloped and very few findings have been reported. Such as due to the hostile nature of mine workings, the WRN system should be explosion proof, water proof in case of operation in flooding scenario, and should be rugged enough. In addition to these system design challenges; *reliable communication, localization of robots* and *data transmission* is another concern for WRNs to be deployed in underground mines for SAR purposes. It is worthy to mention here that there are different government agencies which are responsible for approving any system to be used and install in the underground mine workings. Hence, the developed WRN system should be certified by the appropriate agency of the country.

SAR operation in underground mines is different than the operation performed at ground levels, and SAR in urban environments. Therefore, a careful realization of the WRN deployment in a mining environment is crucial. *SAR operation can be further classified in four different aspects of WRNs and is shown in Figure 4. Unmanned Surface Vehicle (USV)* can be useful in a scenario where the mine workings are flooded and further makes it difficult to access by the rescuers. In such scenario, USV is capable of floating at the water surface. Hence, this will help to locate the particular mine area of rescuers' interests. Moreover, depending on the payload capacity it could be further utilized to transport some assets to the victims as well to the rescue team. On the other hand, *Unmanned Ground Vehicle (UGV)* is useful in the scenario of roof falls, gas explosion and in drifts. In addition, it can also assist the rescue team where it is hard to access some parts of the mine workings such as *grizzly area* and *unsafe zone* due to weak roof support conditions. Considering such events, UGV can be utilized to collect the data either by capturing the images of that particular location or providing real-time video to the BS or temporary command centre. Unlike the USV, *Unmanned Underwater Vehicle (UWV)* has the ability to perform the SAR operation deep in the water and provides data dissemination to the rescue team. This type of WRN technique exchange data with other robots while connected over RF link or through an optical cable. Moreover, such technique can perform the desired tasks either in manual mode, semi-automatic mode or fully automatic mode. However, such WRN platform is challenged by different communication parameters such reliability, time-bound services and communication coverages. The other WRN technique suitable for underground mines SAR is *Unmanned Aerial Vehicle (UAV)*. Such technique is having several advantages and have been used in different civil applications such as to provide broadband services during natural disasters, extension of communication coverage, as a relay node, and capacity enhancement of network in temporary sports events, etc. (Gupta, Jain, & Vaszkun, 2016; Hayat, Yanmaz, & Muzaffar, 2016). Nonetheless, it is important to discuss here that being a resource constrained and high-stressed work environment, *navigation* of UAVs in mine workings will be a concern. Therefore, a detailed study on the type of UAV suitable for mine environment considering the *size of UAV, communication technique, flight time,* and *obstacle avoidance* is necessary.

Though different researchers have performed detailed analysis of SAR operation in mine environment and can be seen in the following sections. To the best of the knowledge of authors research on UAV based SAR operation in underground mines is not reported or discussed in any literature. Hence, this chapter attempts to present a comprehensive discussion of using a UAV in mines. To this potential application of UAVs in underground mine space, it could be utilized as a *message ferrying agent* and may serve the purpose of maintaining wireless network communication in case of wireless nodes get damaged/malfunction due to the roof falls, rib falls, and physically damaged due to mine equipment mobility, etc. UAVs have the advantage of rapid deployment, capable of collecting data from the sensor/gateway nodes, image capturing and video transmission, etc. However, modeling the communication scenario for UAV and performance analysis of such on-demand temporary communication platform considering different characteristics of underground mine workings (see section 2) will be a *challenge* to the researchers. Also, the developed aerial platform should be intrinsically safe to be used in underground mine space which further makes the practical deployment of UAVs in mines as a challenge.

Figure 4. Different techniques for WRN based SAR operation in underground mines

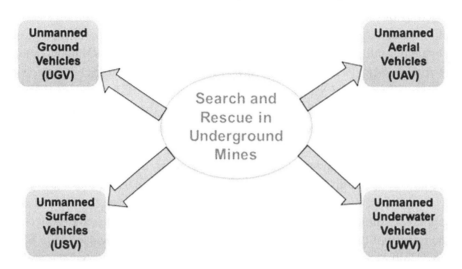

4. STATE OF THE ART

Accidents in mines are a common phenomenon since the early days of mine occupation, be open pit or underground mines. Due to the increased demand for raw materials, mines are becoming larger and *deeper* in both coal and metal mines. To boost production from underground mines, large-scale mechanization is taking place, particularly for extraction and transportation. Hence, the risks involved in such occupation is comparatively *high* than the normal work environment of an industry. WRN has a great potential to assist the underground mining activity in both normal routine operation and during an emergency scenario. In this section, the current state-of-the-art on WRNs for SAR in underground mines is discussed in detail. We find that while there exists a significant amount of contributions on SAR using robotics networks, there are limited studies which specifically covers the autonomous operation of robotics networks. Hence such studies do not exactly come under the classification of WRN. However, the scope of the autonomous operation in present robotics platforms is there and have also been reported by the researchers.

Experimental deployments of mobile robots for SAR operation in underground mines is dated back to 2001. The United States has been involved using different mobile robots for mine recovery operation and rescue. Initial deployments of mobile robots in mines ranged in a variety of robotics platforms available during the deployment time and included Allen- Vanguard, Inuktun versatrax, Remotec Wolverine, and Inuktun ASRVGTV Extreme. However, due to the different unique features of underground mine rescue operation, it is suggested that in the near future certain modifications in system design and communication technology is required for reliable operation of SAR (Murphy, Kravitz, Stover, & Shoureshi, 2009).

Commonwealth Scientific and Industrial Research Organization (CSIRO), Australia developed a robot named "Numbat" (Figure 5) in 1990 and further discussed the mechanism of teleoperation user interface intended for autonomous activity by the robot (Hainsworth, 2001). The developed robot is designed for the purpose of SAR operation in mine environment and can be remotely controlled from a control station over the fiber-optic network. The design of the robot is reported as water proof and explosion proof. However, the real-time deployment of Numbat is not performed and is limited to the laboratory setup.

Figure 5. Numbat mobile robot developed by CSIRO

Kasprzyczak, Trenczek, & Cader (2012) developed a mobile robot "GMRI" for monitoring the hazardous gas concentration in underground mine environments such as methane and fumes. Further traction tests are performed with a view of real-time deployment in underground mines. The initial results found to be satisfactory. However, proper lighting mechanism to address the obstacles in dark environment and recognition of materials is reported as a future work along with long-range communication distance between the mobile robot and operator.

In another effort by LESZEK Kasprzyczak, Szwejkowski PAWEŁ, and Cader (2016), a mobile inspection platform "MPI" is developed to monitor the underground mine environment and functionally tested in the "Central Mines Rescue Station (CSRG)," Chorzowska, Bytom. Later the developed system is also experimentally evaluated in the rescue operation performed by the CSRG's rescuers in Królowa Luiza Underground Mine (Figure 6). MPI in the experiment covered a distance of 250 meters and was capable of climbing on-ramp with 30^0 inclinations to the ground. The developed mobile robot passes through the complex mine infrastructure such as rocks, rail tracks, and other obstacles efficiently.

For the data transmission, the developed robot MPI has two mechanisms: *optical fiber* based communication and *Wireless Fidelity (Wi-Fi)*. The Wi-Fi communication technique is used when the robot is moving forward to the mine accident location where rescue operation has to be performed. Whereas the optical cable based communication is used when the robot enters the excavation area or narrower mine workings. The reason to use optical fiber based communication in such workings may be motivated by the fact of reliable communication coverage as the mine workings pose several challenges for the wireless communication network. In addition, communication devices operating at higher signal frequency goes through higher signal attenuation compared to the lower frequency (Alok Ranjan, Misra, Dwivedi, & Sahu, 2017). Hence, for a better signal reception at the command center optical fiber based communication is used in the excavation area. Nevertheless, the developed robot MPI has both the functionalities, i.e., autonomous and semi-autonomous which is suitable for underground mine SAR operation.

Figure 6. MPI robot

Jingchao Zhao, Gao, Zhao, and Liu (2017) proposed and developed two mobile robots platform named "MSROBOTS" with an operating control unit (OCU) for remotely sensing the underground coal mine parameters and rescue operation. The platform consisted of two gas sensors for monitoring hazardous gases such as methane, two cameras to capture images of the mine workings, a two-way audio system for voice data transmission and a 1 km long fiber optic cable for communication and control. The developed robots are explosion proof and also suitable for flooding scenario due to water proof design. Moreover, a novel mechanical manipulator is also proposed and integrated into the platform having 3 degrees of freedom and uses two motors for operation.

The authors carried out a detailed analysis of the various design aspects of the robots to be used in SAR operation in coal mines. MSROBOTS has a battery life of 8 hours and can communicate over 2 km distance in a series. It is reported that the platform can collect ten different types of environmental information such as different gas concentration, humidity, temperature, air pressure, and wind speed, etc. The collected data is then transmitted through OCU by a fiber-optic network. The mechanical manipulator is used to remove any obstacles in between the path such as cables and steel roll bars. Further, authors carried an experiment to demonstrate the ability of the manipulator and sensing platform in a coal mine in China and successfully performed wire cut and data collection. However, it is suggested that the manipulator should have a steel case to protect the motor from any explosion as the device has to be intrinsically safe to be used in the underground mine environment.

For communication in between the two robots, a networked communication structure is followed. The robots can be operated in three different modes: viz. *telecontrol, semi-automatic and automatic*. The MSROBOTS (see Figure 7) communicates with the OCU using a router mounted and housed inside the platform and then the second mobile robot placed in the deep excavated area and the hazardous zone is communicated over a fiber-optic cable connected to the OCU unit. Further, a detailed analysis and discussion on electric system design, navigation control assembly, mechanical manipulator, explosion proof design approach and water proof design can also be seen in the work. The developed mobile robot

Figure 7. Developed mobile robot (a) rear view of the robot, (b) side view

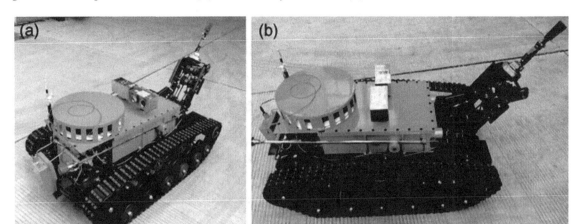

platform is intrinsically safe in operation and is approved by the *Mining Products Safety Approval and Certification Centre in China*. However, the MSROBOTS platforms are heavy, hence is less flexible in movement in the mine working. In addition, OCU unit needs to be more user-friendly and simpler in access to the rescuers for speedy rescue operations.

To monitor the underground coal mine environment due to the catastrophic events, recently a team from different organizations jointly working on a project called "TELERESCUER" (Novak et al., 2017). The project is maintained by a consortium of members from Silesian University of Technology (Poland), the VSB – Technical University of Ostrava (Czech Republic), the Universidad Carlos III de Madrid (Spain), COPEX (Poland), SIMMERSION GMBH (Austria) and SKYTECH RESEARCH (Poland). The objective of this project is to save the lives of rescuers as well as provide a speedy rescue operation to those affected by the mine disaster and have been trapped. As discussed in above section, the mine workings considered to be high-stressed work environment due to the unique characteristics of mine environment. After a disaster, it is dangerous to send the rescuers without proper planning and prior knowledge of different mine environment parameters such as wind speed, air pressure, and noxious gas concentrations, etc.

A detailed analysis of the control system of TELERESCUER (see Figure 8) is discussed with an emphasis on controlled mobility and communication modes. For better autonomy and teamwork of the consortium, it is suggested that a dedicated operating system (OS) such as Robotics Operating System (ROS) is necessary. Therefore, the initially developed control system was redesigned again for implementation in ROS. This provided the flexibility of independent research and development activity carried out by an individual team member. Several tests were performed to analyze the detailed behavior of each component of the mobile robot for better coordination in ROS.

The proposed mobile robot has both communication modes, i.e., semi-automatic and automatic. Fiber-optic cable and Wi-Fi are used for communication purpose. Nevertheless, the Wi-Fi is intended to use as a backup communication plan in case the link is lost in between the operator and mobile robot. Whereas the fiber-optic cable is used as a primary link between the operator and mobile robot. The initial understandings from a detailed analysis of each component behavior in ROS suggested that the initial control system need to be changed for reliable operation of a mobile robot according to the ROS

Figure 8. A 3D view of TELERESCUER

protocol. In addition, special software is used for 3D mapping and visualization which is described in detail in reference.

Molyneaux, Carnegie, & Chitty's work (2016) considered different aspects of WRN failures in underground mines from past learnings and literature survey and addressed three crucial problems. These problem considerations include tethered communication, locomotion systems and considerations of an underground mine working features. Further, a novel locomotion chassis and wireless mesh communication module is proposed and discussed.

The proposed and designed mobile robot "HADES" has a unique chassis of dimensions 400 × 600 × 700 mm (height × width × length) to pass through complex terrains of mine roadways and debris (see Figure 9). It senses the environmental parameters and transmits to the command center. The system consists of 4 spoked wheel system and is capable of overcoming the challenge of passing through discontinuous debris and rail tracks (*a typical scenario of underground mine roadways and workings*). The wheel radius is taken as 400 mm with the view to overcome the maximum height of mine rail track (114 mm, British Standard 60A) and a maximum height of staircase (220 mm NZ Build Code).

The authors chose *purged, and pressurized* enclosure chassis design over flameproof or explosion proof design consideration as such considerations will *increase* the weight of the mobile robots. However, it is reported that the enclosed design is made in accordance with the Australia and New Zealand standard for Equipment protection by pressurized enclosure 'p guidelines. Hence, is secure to be used in underground mine environment reported in the study.

For wireless communication module in HADES, an *XBee-Pro* module operating at 2.4 GHz of signal frequency is used supporting wireless mesh architecture. As a case study Pike River Mine tunnel features are chosen to estimate the number of nodes required for reliable coverage. A Total of 40 nodes are estimated to achieve wireless data transmissions by the mobile robot. A node enclosure dimension for the study is 40 × 50 × 50 mm with a battery capacity of 5 hours in a continuous access mode and 24 hours for standby operation. However, the wireless communication module is limited to simulation studies with a maximum communication range of 60 meters. A microphone and speaker module are also incorporated in the mobile robot for two-way communication purpose. Further, dedicated software is developed for optimized performance of the mobile robot using ROS. However, the practical deployment of the proposed, designed robot in underground mine workings is reported as the future work. Nevertheless, the initial deployment of HADES and performance analysis of the robot was performed in the commercial clean-fill dumping area. The initial findings of the study suggest that the mobile robot overcome the debris with a maximum height of 300 mm, but struggled a bit on loose gravel at slopes with an angle of 45 degrees to the surface.

In another effort of WRN based SAR operation in underground mines the researchers (Xue et al., 2014) carried out an analysis of wireless communication mechanism based on Wi-Fi communication technique for data transmission among robots. However, practical concerns of mine workings features were not considered in the proposed architecture and were limited to simulation setup.

Jie Zhao, Liu, Liu, and Zhu, (2008) proposed a concept of mobile robot platform capable of autonomous operation for SAR in underground mines. The theoretical formulation of SAR is discussed considering underground mine features. They proposed a robot named marsupial which carries a baby robot within it. Hence, it is claimed that it overcomes the drawback of the single robot-based rescue operation in underground mines. Further different design considerations for the marsupial robot and associated challenges are outlined. However, the work neither detailed any test results nor provides any analytical insight of mobile robot working mechanism and different design considerations such as locomotion, chassis and communication technology used.

Recently a project on the autonomous mobile radio (AMR) to maintain a reliable wireless communication link with the lead teleoperated robot was carried out at the Colorado School of Mines, USA (Hulbert, 2012). The project *"Mine Safety and Rescue through Sensing Networks and Robotics Technology" (MineSENTRY)* was aimed to extend the communication coverage in SAR operation in underground mines while providing significant information of mine environment such as gas concentrations, and heat, etc. AMR platforms are developed to create an ad-hoc communication network which can adapt the dynamic conditions to maintain a reliable communication link between the operator and main teleoperated robot.

To maintain a clear line of sight (LoS) between the operator and lead teleoperated robot, the operator remained at underground mine entrance (Figure 10) which helped to keep the lead robot to be in communication range of wireless communication link. Then several AMRs are used to create a mesh

Figure 9. Proposed mobile robot- HADES

Figure 10. A concept of MinesENTRY Project

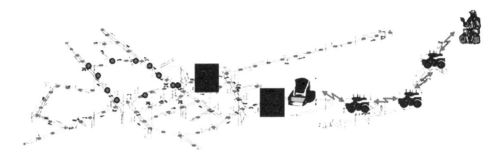

network for data dissemination at the command centre. Hence, the AMRs acted as wireless nodes in the network extending the communication range to support a deeper SAR operation in mines.

Different tests were carried out at Edgar Mine in Idaho Springs, Colorado which is an experimental mine of the university. The initial tests carried out in the test mines confirmed satisfactory results. However, to design an effective controller for the AMRs was reported as the challenge for reliable performance in the mine environment. Different design issues with particular reference to mine safety guidelines and pose estimations of AMR were reported as a future scope of the project.

5. CHALLENGES FOR WIRELESS ROBOTICS NETWORKS IN UNDERGROUND MINES

In a post-disaster condition, inspection of mine environmental parameters usually requires a team of human experts. This direct diagnostic mechanism may *seriously* affect the rescuers due to the presence of fumes, dust, and noxious gas concentration such as carbon monoxide and methane. Also, the excess amount of methane in mine air may further cause for the gas explosion. Therefore, rescuers are highly exposed to *risks* during a rescue operation in an underground mine. To this safety concern of rescuers, it is significant to remotely sense the different environmental parameters such as air pressure, dust concentration, ground conditions, and noxious gas concentrations, etc. Once the path to be followed by the rescuers is found to be safe, then rescuers may move forward to the location of a mine accident.

Several researchers in past one decade have significantly contributed towards the safety of rescuers and miners and proposed different mobile robotics platforms. These mobile robotics platforms have the ability to remotely sense the mine environment and transmit the sensed data over a fiber-optic link or wireless link. Since the underground mine workings pose different challenges for wireless communication network (Forooshani, Bashir, Michelson, & Noghanian, 2013; Ranjan et al., 2016); it is important to understand different associated challenges for the reliable and robust performance of these WRN platforms for SAR operation in underground mines. In this section, we have discussed different implications for WRN to be deployed in underground mine workings. In addition, since most of the current state-of-the-art on WRN for SAR operation in underground mines can be operated in two modes, i.e., remotely controlled (semi-automatic) and automatic, we have considered both the operation modes while discussing different challenges for WRN in mines and have been outlined as follows.

5.1 Controlled Mobility

An underground mining gallery consists of several features like rail tracks, power cables, water pipes, mining equipment, ventilation systems, etc. Underground mine workings are narrower in space and ranges in between few meters of width and height (Chehri & Mouftah 2012, Ranjan, Misra & Sahu 2017) . Due to this space limitation, the mobility of the mobile robots is a challenge. It is reported that due to the excessive height of robot, Wolverine V2 could not complete a mission in mine gallery (Molyneaux et al., 2016). After a disaster different sized grit and gravel may present which adds another complexity in the existing uneven terrain profiles for mobile robots. In addition, mine workings may have flowing or standing water, mud, mine equipment and also have different sized support systems, especially in excavation areas. In such scenario, controlled mobility of the robots is a challenge to the researchers for autonomous operations. It is very significant that the design of autonomous robots should be in such a fashion that it can avoid the obstacles in between the path and change its pathway accordingly without affecting the scheduled tasks.

5.2 Smart Vision

Typically, mine tunnel roadways are poorly lighted, hence has poor visibility. Whereas in excavation area or near the face (areas where mineral extraction is going on) the visibility is comparatively less than mine roadways or in some cases the mine workings are not having any light sources (*gaseous coal mines, degree 3 coal mines*) (Ranjan & Sahu, 2014). Considering such *practical deployment concerns* for autonomous robots, it is desired that the camera mounted with the robot should be capable to take images in poorly lighted conditions as well as in no light mining areas. One approach to this problem may be adding an additional light source to the robotics platform that can be used whenever required to take the image file or capturing video.

5.3 Reliable Communication

A mine tunnel structure greatly affects the performance of wireless communication systems due to the tilt of sidewalls, crosscuts, curvatures and changes in mine dimensions (Ranjan, Misra, & Sahu, 2017). Longitudinal attenuation increases due to wall roughness and uneven tunnel cross sections. Curvatures in tunnels introduce some additional loss which is highly dependent on the frequency of operation and some other geometrical parameters like tunnel width, wave polarization, and radius of curvature (Bandyopadhyay, Mishra, Kumar, Selvendran, & Chaulya, 2007). Moisture content available due to seepage from strata is also one factor which affects the path of the signal that has also been observed in literature (Peplinski, Ulaby, & Dobson, 1995). In literatures (Ndoh, Delisle, & Le, 2003; Ranjan, Sahu, & Misra, 2015b), the authors studied the effects of the geographical roughness of the sidewalls and how this discontinuity is affecting the wireless signal propagation characteristics in underground mine galleries has been studied. Results obtained concluded that multipath, reflection, and diffractions are critical issues to be addressed in future. According to (Schiffbauer & Brune, 2006), the electrical properties of the mine vary from mine to mine which caused for variations in attenuation of operating frequencies. This indicates that *every mine has its own set of features* which affects the performance of communication systems. However, the same device gives satisfactory performance in another mine. Due to the obstructions in mines, the signal power decreases significantly. It was observed that the RMS delay spread in an empty mine gallery was less than 25 ns and 103 ns when the tunnel was occupied by miners, equipment, and vehicles. This RMS delay and losses in power decrease the data rate in underground mines (Hämäläinen, Talvitie, Hovinen, & Leppänen, 1998).

The Fiber-optic based remote control provides satisfactory performance but restricted by the communication coverage due to cable length. Also, the cable is vulnerable to *breakage* due to tunnel geometry and *tangling* which may further cause in unreliable performance. Most of the available mobile robots for mining scenario are unable to maintain a robust communication link to the base station or command centre (Murphy, 2014). Hence, these platforms are limited in performance in accomplishing certain scheduled tasks. The presence of objects within the environment and mobility of the communication nodes make a comparative difference in a propagation environment of wireless communication and wired communication. Therefore, the link quality may vary significantly when the autonomous robot is mobile compared to the stationary robot involved in environmental sensing. Citing the above discussions on reliable wireless communication networks in underground mine galleries, it is desired that the autonomous robots should be flexible and maintain certain communication requirements through adaptive mechanisms and cooperative control.

It is to be understood that an improved communications range would allow the mobile robots to travel farther into the mine workings, and access those unattended areas also which are hard to access by the rescuers while exchanging invaluable sensed data to the command centre.

5.4 Design Considerations

The first ever rescue robots in underground mines were deployed in the year of 2001 at Jim Walter mine of No. 5, and since then different rescue robots have been deployed in nine major underground mine disasters. However, the success rate of these rescue robots are affected due to the safety concerns, hence denied by the three underground mine managements during SAR operations (Murphy et al., 2009). The reason for denying mobile robots to be used in SAR operation was lack of explosion proof design considerations and rough terrain which was reported as impassable terrain for those mobile robots (Murphy, 2014).

Design of autonomous robots should be such that it is not vulnerable in a harsh and hostile environment of underground mines. As discussed earlier, an underground mine has very harsh environment for daily activities which includes productivity and monitoring of mine workings. This is because of presence of high relative humidity, warm conditions, and hazardous gas concentrations. A device should be designed in such a manner so that it is *intrinsically safe* and can be used in such hostile environment. Mine Safety and Health Administration (MSHA) and National Institute for Occupational Safety and Health (NIOSH) have given a set of regulations and safety parameters for designing different electronics systems to be used in mine workings (Ranjan & Sahu, 2014). Therefore, WRN platforms to be used in mine workings should be intrinsically safe and certified by the competent authorities. Table 1 briefs different design considerations for WRN platforms for underground mine environments.

6. FUTURE RESEARCH DIRECTIONS

Research on WRN based SAR operation particularly in underground mines is underdeveloped and is being actively researched. On the other hand, WSN and MANET have been actively researched in different applications and is now a quite mature technology compared to WRN (Yick, Mukherjee, & Ghosal,

Table 1. Major design considerations for WRN platforms in underground mines

Consideration	Design Goals
Size	System should be optimum in size and light weighted so that robots can be easily portable and moved freely without any difficulty
Design	Rugged and should be enough to resist shocks
Safety	The system should be intrinsically safe from operational heat and short circuit
Protection and immunity	Dust proof, immune to moisture, corrosion proof and also has wide range of temperatures
Reliability and fault tolerance	Should always be maintained
Obstacle avoidance	The mobile robots should be capable of detecting any obstacles and changing their path accordingly

2008). We learned from the current-state-of-the-art that the present mobile robots have both *fiber-optic* and *wireless communication* modules to carry out collaborative tasks during SAR operation either in semi-automatic mode or fully automatic. However, very few works have been reported in which the autonomous operation of mobile robots exploiting wireless communication technology is discussed. The fiber-optic cable is used as a *primary link* in between the mobile robots and operator, whereas in most cases the Wi-Fi has been considered as a *backup link* and have been used while getting inside the underground mine gallery. Though fiber-optic based communication in mine environment is satisfactory, it is still vulnerable to *safety risks* of rescuers. For example, the rescuers have to remotely operate the mobile robots over the fiber-optic link, hence is limited in coverage due to the cable length. Considering the *post disaster* situation in underground mines, it is hard to predict the ground conditions and strata behavior and it may so happen that the rescuers might have to face *unfavorable* conditions such as *rib falls* due to structural deformations.

Motivated from such safety risks to the rescuers; an approach to extend the communication and monitoring coverage area through *autonomous robots* communicating over *RF links* might serve the purpose. The autonomous robots may act as a router/gateway sensor node which will collect the necessary information of the mine environment and transmit the sensed data to the nearest gateway in the communication range of that mobile robot. This mechanism will not only increase the communication and monitoring coverage area, but will also improve the safety of the rescuers which is a primary concern. However, to achieve such research objectives more systematic measurements and real time deployments in different underground mines is needed in the near future.

The work required for such kind of complex autonomous mobile robot development require engagements of experts from different domains such as robotics engineers, mechatronics, electrical and automatic control, software developers and finally mining experts, which widens the scope of collaborative *interdisciplinary research*. Therefore, to achieve the objective of reliable performance of autonomous robots in underground mines and their deployment, there is a need of strong R&D collaborations among universities, industries and government agencies all together.

7. CONCLUSION

Mobile robots play a significant role in the aftermath of mine disaster or in emergency operations. It helps to find the survivors trapped in a disaster affected area and acts as the first responder to the event. Moreover, it remotely senses the environmental parameters and informs the rescuers. Several autonomous mobile robots have been designed and are under development. However, the reliable performance of the deployed robots in mine environments is affected due to the unique features of underground mine environment. The main challenges faced by the researchers is consideration of different design factors with particular reference to underground mine workings. For example, the developed autonomous robot should be intrinsically safe in operation and immune to heat, humidity and dust while providing a reliable sensing information over RF links to the rescuers.

In this work, an overview of WRNs for SAR operation in the context of underground mines is presented. A detailed taxonomy of SAR in underground mines based on WRNs concept is also discussed followed by the different associated challenges for autonomous robots in mines. The different classifications of problems for WRN are highlighted with particular reference to underground mine workings.

REFERENCES

Bandyopadhyay, L. K., Chaulya, S. K., & Mishra, P. K. (2010). *Wireless Communication in Underground Mines*. RFID-Based Sensor Networking. doi:10.1007/978-0-387-98165-9

Bandyopadhyay, L. K., Mishra, P. K., Kumar, S., Selvendran, D., & Chaulya, S. K. (2007). Studies on radio frequency propagation characteristics for underground coalmine communications. *Indian Journal of Radio & Space Physics*, *36*(5), 418.

Chehri, A., & Mouftah, H. (2012). An empirical link-quality analysis for wireless sensor networks. In *Computing, Networking and Communications (ICNC), 2012 International Conference on* (pp. 164–169). Academic Press. 10.1109/ICCNC.2012.6167403

DGMS Standard Note. (2016). Retrieved from http://dgms.gov.in/writereaddata/UploadFile/STD-NOTE-1-1-2016636047840119597695.pdf

Forooshani, A. E., Bashir, S., Michelson, D. G., & Noghanian, S. (2013). A survey of wireless communications and propagation modeling in underground mines. *IEEE Communications Surveys and Tutorials*, *15*(4), 1524–1545. doi:10.1109/SURV.2013.031413.00130

Gazi, V., & Passino, K. M. (2011). *Swarm stability and optimization*. Swarm Stability and Optimization; doi:10.1007/978-3-642-18041-5

Gupta, L., Jain, R., & Vaszkun, G. (2016). Survey of Important Issues in UAV Communication Networks. *IEEE Communications Surveys and Tutorials*, *18*(2), 1123–1152. doi:10.1109/COMST.2015.2495297

Hainsworth, D. W. (2001). Teleoperation user interfaces for mining robotics. *Autonomous Robots*, *11*(1), 19–28. doi:10.1023/A:1011299910904

Hämäläinen, M., Talvitie, J., Hovinen, V., & Leppänen, P. (1998). Wideband radio channel measurement in a mine. In *Spread Spectrum Techniques and Applications, 1998. Proceedings., 1998 IEEE 5th International Symposium on* (Vol. 2, pp. 522–526). IEEE. 10.1109/ISSSTA.1998.723839

Hayat, S., Yanmaz, E., & Muzaffar, R. (2016). Survey on Unmanned Aerial Vehicle Networks for Civil Applications: A Communications Viewpoint. *IEEE Communications Surveys and Tutorials*, *18*(4), 2624–2661. doi:10.1109/COMST.2016.2560343

Hulbert, J. N. (2012). *Local navigation of mobile robots in mining environments*. Colorado School of Mines. Arthur Lakes Library.

Kamruzzaman, S. M., Fernando, X., Jaseemuddin, M., & Farjow, W. (2017). Reliable Communication Network for Emergency Response and Disaster Management in Underground Mines. *Smart Technologies for Emergency Response and Disaster Management*, 41–85. 10.4018/978-1-5225-2575-2.ch002

Kasprzyczak, L., Szwejkowski, P., & Cader, M. (2016). Robotics in mining exemplified by Mobile Inspection Platform. *Mining--Informatics, Automation and Electrical Engineering, 54*.

Kasprzyczak, L., Trenczek, S., & Cader, M. (2012). Robot for monitoring hazardous environments as a mechatronic product. *Journal of Automation Mobile Robotics and Intelligent Systems, 6*, 57–64.

Ko, A. W. Y., & Lau, H. Y. K. (2009). Intelligent robot-assisted humanitarian search and rescue system. *International Journal of Advanced Robotic Systems*, *6*(2), 121–128. doi:10.5772/6792

Misra, P., Kanhere, S., Ostry, D., & Jha, S. (2010). Safety assurance and rescue communication systems in high-stress environments: A mining case study. *Communications Magazine, IEEE*, *48*(4), 66–73. doi:10.1109/MCOM.2010.5439078

Molyneaux, L., Carnegie, D. A., & Chitty, C. (2016). HADES: An underground mine disaster scouting robot. In *SSRR 2015 - 2015 IEEE International Symposium on Safety, Security, and Rescue Robotics*. IEEE. 10.1109/SSRR.2015.7443019

Murphy, R. R. (2004). Human-robot interaction in rescue robotics. *IEEE Transactions on Systems, Man and Cybernetics. Part C, Applications and Reviews*, *34*(2), 138–153. doi:10.1109/TSMCC.2004.826267

Murphy, R. R. (2014). *Disaster Robotics. Statewide Agricultural Land Use Baseline 2015* (Vol. 1). Academic Press. 10.1017/CBO9781107415324.004

Murphy, R. R., Kravitz, J., Stover, S. L., & Shoureshi, R. (2009). Mobile robots in mine rescue and recovery. *IEEE Robotics & Automation Magazine*, *16*(2), 91–103. doi:10.1109/MRA.2009.932521

Ndoh, M., Delisle, G. Y., & Le, R. (2003). A novel approach to propagation prediction in confined and diffracting rough surfaces. *International Journal of Numerical Modelling: Electronic Networks. Devices and Fields*, *16*(6), 535–555. doi:10.1002/jnm.521

Novak, P., Babjak, J., Kot, T., Bobovsky, Z., Olivka, P., & Moczulski, W. (2017). *Telerescuer-reconnaissance mobile robot for underground coal mines*. Academic Press.

Penders, J., Alboul, L., Witkowski, U., Naghsh, A., Saez-Pons, J., Herbrechtsmeier, S., & El-Habbal, M. (2011). A Robot Swarm Assisting a Human Fire-Fighter. *Advanced Robotics, 25*(1–2), 93–117. doi:10.1163/016918610X538507

Peplinski, N. R., Ulaby, F. T., & Dobson, M. C. (1995). Dielectric properties of soils in the 0.3-1.3-GHz range. *Geoscience and Remote Sensing. IEEE Transactions on, 33*(3), 803–807.

Ranjan, A., Misra, P., Dwivedi, B., & Sahu, H. B. (2017). Studies on Propagation Characteristics of Radio Waves for Wireless Networks in Underground Coal Mines. *Wireless Personal Communications*, 1–14. doi:10.100711277-017-4636-y

Ranjan, A., Misra, P., & Sahu, H. B. (2017). Experimental measurements and channel modeling for wireless communication networks in underground mine environments. In *Antennas and Propagation (EUCAP), 2017 11th European Conference on* (pp. 1345–1349). Academic Press. 10.23919/EuCAP.2017.7928854

Ranjan, A., Misra, P., & Sahu, H. B. (2017). On the importance of link characterization for wireless sensor networks in underground mines. In *2017 9th International Conference on Communication Systems and Networks (COMSNETS)* (pp. 1–2). Academic Press. 10.1109/COMSNETS.2017.7945456

Ranjan, A., & Sahu, H. B. (2014). *Advancements in communication and safety systems in underground mines: present status and future prospects*. Academic Press.

Ranjan, A., & Sahu, H. B. (2014). Communications Challenges in Underground Mines. *Search & Research, 5*(2), 23–29.

Ranjan, A., Sahu, H. B., & Misra, P. (2015a). Performance Evaluation of Underground Mine Communication and Monitoring Devices: Case Studies. In J. K. Mandal, S. C. Satapathy, M. Kumar Sanyal, P. P. Sarkar, & A. Mukhopadhyay (Eds.), *Information Systems Design and Intelligent Applications* (Vol. 339, pp. 685–694). Springer India; doi:10.1007/978-81-322-2250-7_69

Ranjan, A., Sahu, H. B., & Misra, P. (2015b). Wave propagation model for wireless communication in underground mines. In *Bombay Section Symposium (IBSS)*, (pp. 1–5). IEEE. 10.1109/IBSS.2015.7456655

Ranjan, A., Sahu, H. B., & Misra, P. (2016). Wireless Sensor Networks: An Emerging Solution for Underground Mines. *International Journal of Applied Evolutionary Computation, 7*(4), 1–27. doi:10.4018/IJAEC.2016100101

Ranjany, A., Misraz, P., Dwivediz, B., & Sahuy, H. B. (2016). Channel modeling of wireless communication in underground coal mines. In *2016 8th International Conference on Communication Systems and Networks (COMSNETS)* (pp. 1–2). Academic Press. 10.1109/COMSNETS.2016.7440023

Sahin, E., & Winfield, A. (2008). Special issue on swarm robotics. *Swarm Intelligence, 2*(2), 69–72. doi:10.100711721-008-0020-6

Sahu, H. B., Panigrahi, D. C., & Mishra, N. M. (2004). Assessment of spontaneous heating susceptibility of coal seams by differential scanning calorimetry. *Journal of Mines, Metals and Fuels, 52*(7–8), 117–121.

Sammarco, J. J., Paddock, R., Fries, E. F., & Karra, V. K. (2007). A Technology Review of Smart Sensors With Wireless Networks for Applications in Hazardous Work Environments. Department of Health and Human Services, Centers for Disease Control and Prevention. National Institute for Occupational Safety and Health, Pittsburgh Research Laboratory.

Schiffbauer, W. H., & Brune, J. F. (2006). *Coal mine communications.* American Longwall Mag.

Schneider, D. (2009). Robin Murphy roboticist to the rescue. *IEEE Spectrum, 46*(2), 36–37. doi:10.1109/MSPEC.2009.4772558

Wait, J., & Fuller, J. (1971). On radio propagation through earth. *Antennas and Propagation. IEEE Transactions on, 19*(6), 796–798. doi:10.1109/TAP.1971.1140048

Wang, N., Zhang, N., & Wang, M. (2006). Wireless sensors in agriculture and food industry. Recent development and future perspective. *Computers and Electronics in Agriculture, 50*(1), 1–14. doi:10.1016/j.compag.2005.09.003

Weldon, T. P., & Rathore, A. Y. (1999). *Wave propagation model and simulations for landmine detection.* Department of Electrical & Computer Engineering University of North Carolina-Charlotte.

Werner-Allen, G., Lorincz, K., Ruiz, M., Marcillo, O., Johnson, J., Lees, J., & Welsh, M. (2006). Deploying a wireless sensor network on an active volcano. *IEEE Internet Computing, 10*(2), 18–25. doi:10.1109/MIC.2006.26

Xue, X., Ma, H., & Wei, J. (2014). Setting-up Wireless Communication System for Mine Rescue Robots. In Mechanical Components and Control Engineering III (Vol. 668–669, pp. 366–369). Academic Press. doi:10.4028/www.scientific.net/AMM.668-669.366

Yang, W., Zhang, Y., & Liu, Y. (2010). Constructing of wireless emergency communication system for underground coal mine based on WMN technology. *Journal of Coal Science and Engineering (China), 16*(4), 441–448. doi:10.100712404-010-0420-0

Yarkan, S., Guzelgoz, S., Arslan, H., & Murphy, R. R. (2009). Underground mine communications: A survey. *IEEE Communications Surveys and Tutorials, 11*(3), 125–142. doi:10.1109/SURV.2009.090309

Yick, J., Mukherjee, B., & Ghosal, D. (2008). Wireless sensor network survey. *Computer Networks, 52*(12), 2292–2330. doi:10.1016/j.comnet.2008.04.002

Zhao, J., Gao, J., Zhao, F., & Liu, Y. (2017). A Search-and-Rescue Robot System for Remotely Sensing the Underground Coal Mine Environment. *Sensors (Basel), 17*(10), 2426. doi:10.339017102426 PMID:29065560

Zhao, J., Liu, G., Liu, Y., & Zhu, Y. (2008). Research on the application of a marsupial robot for coal mine rescue. In Lecture Notes in Computer Science (including subseries Lecture Notes in Artificial Intelligence and Lecture Notes in Bioinformatics) (Vol. 5315, pp. 1127–1136). Springer. doi:10.1007/978-3-540-88518-4_120

Chapter 15
Solving Job Scheduling Problem in Computational Grid Systems Using a Hybrid Algorithm

Tarun Kumar Ghosh
Haldia Institute of Technology, India

Sanjoy Das
Kalyani University, India

ABSTRACT

Grid computing is a high performance distributed computing system that consists of different types of resources such as computing, storage, and communication. The main function of the job scheduling problem is to schedule the resource-intensive user jobs to available grid resources efficiently to achieve high system throughput and to satisfy user requirements. The job scheduling problem has become more challenging with the ever-increasing size of grid systems. The optimal job scheduling is an NP-complete problem which can easily be solved by using meta-heuristic techniques. This chapter presents a hybrid algorithm for job scheduling using genetic algorithm (GA) and cuckoo search algorithm (CSA) for efficiently allocating jobs to resources in a grid system so that makespan, flowtime, and job failure rate are minimized. This proposed algorithm combines the advantages of both GA and CSA. The results have been compared with standard GA, CSA, and ant colony optimization (ACO) to show the importance of the proposed algorithm.

1. INTRODUCTION

A computational Grid aims to aggregate the power of heterogeneous, geographically distributed, multiple-domain-spanning computational resources to provide high performance or high-throughput computing. It also provides dependable, consistent, pervasive, and inexpensive access to computational resources existing on the network. Job scheduling is one of the major challenges in computational Grids to efficiently exploit the capabilities of dynamic, autonomous, heterogeneous and distributed resources for execution of different types of jobs. Also, the size of a Grid has been ever increasing. Therefore, the job scheduling in such complex systems is a challenging problem.

DOI: 10.4018/978-1-5225-5832-3.ch015

The Grid scheduler, often known as Grid resource broker, acts in three phases: resource discovery phase, resource allocation phase and job execution phase. The resource discovery phase involves identifying the available resources from the resource pool, whereas the resource allocation phase involves selection of suitable resources and allocating the selected resources to the jobs. The third phase is executing the jobs at resource locations. The Grid scheduler searches the fittest resource for a job so that certain criteria (like minimization of makespan or execution time, best utilization of the resources, and maximization of user satisfaction) are met.

In this chapter, a hybrid algorithm is proposed which combines the advantages of Genetic Algorithm (GA) and Cuckoo Search Algorithm (CSA) to minimize three key performance issues, viz. makespan, flowtime and job failure rate, of a computational Grid system. Genetic Algorithm (GA) is one of the widely used evolutionary heuristic algorithms for the constrained optimization problems, but the disadvantage of the algorithm is that it can easily be trapped in local minima. In order to avoid such local minima problem, the Cuckoo Search Algorithm (CSA) can be used to perform the local search more efficiently.

This chapter is organized as follows. Section 2 briefly outlines the relevant past works done on job scheduling in computational Grid environment. In Section 3, the framework of Grid job scheduling problem has been defined. Sections 4 - 6 highlight GA, CSA and ACO methods. Section 7 describes our proposed hybrid technique for scheduling jobs in computational Grid systems. Section 8 exhibits the results obtained in this study. Finally, Section 9 concludes the chapter.

2. RELATED WORKS

Due to various complex characteristics of resources and jobs, the job scheduling in Grid is a NP-complete problem. Meta-heuristic methods have proven to be efficient in solving such problems. Various meta-heuristic algorithms have been designed to schedule the jobs in computational Grid (Thilagavathi et al., 2012). These sorts of approaches make realistic assumptions based on a priori knowledge of the concerning environment and of the system load characteristics. The most commonly used meta-heuristic algorithms are Genetic Algorithms (GA), Particle Swarm Optimization (PSO), Simulated Annealing (SA), Ant Colony Optimization (ACO) and Cuckoo Search Algorithm (CSA). In general, meta-heuristic approaches manage to obtain much better performance, but take a longer execution time (Bianco et al., 2015).

The Genetic algorithm (GA) is a meta-heuristic algorithm that imitates the principle of genetic process in living organisms. GA mimics the evolutionary process by applying selection, crossover, and mutation to generate solution from the search space. The GA is a very popular algorithm to solve various types of combinatorial optimization problems. GAs for the Grid scheduling problems have been studied by Abraham et al. (2000); Kolodziej et al. (2012); Braun et al. (2001); Zomaya and The (2001); Di Martino and Mililotti (2004); Moghaddam et al. (2012); Page and Naughton (2005); Gao et al. (2005); Xhafa et al. (2008); Aggarwal et al. (2005). Prakash and Vidyarthi (2015) have proposed a new technique to maximize the availability of resources for job scheduling in computational Grid using GA. Enhanced Genetic-based scheduling for Grid computing is proposed in (Kolodziej and Xhafa, 2011).

The PSO algorithm is a population-based optimization technique that tries to find the optimal solution using a population of particles. Each position of a particle in the search space corresponds to a potential solution of the problem. Particles cooperate to find the best position (best solution) in the search space (solution space). The PSO algorithm is proved to be a good mechanism to apply for the Grid scheduling (Zhang et al., 2008; Karimi, 2014). Ghosh and Das (2016) have proposed a modified binary PSO algorithm for scheduling independent jobs in Grid. Liu et al. (2009) proposed an approach for scheduling using a fuzzy PSO algorithm.

The Simulated Annealing (SA) is a variant of local search to find a good solution to an optimization problem by trying random variations of the current solution. Traditional local search (e.g. steepest descent for minimization) always moves in a direction of improvement. The SA allows non-improving moves to avoid getting stuck at a local optimum with a probability that decreases as the computation proceeds. The slower the cooling schedule, or rate of decrease, the more likely the algorithm is to find an optimal or near-optimal solution. Goswami et al. (2011) have proposed a local search based approach using SA as a periodical optimizer to other dynamic, space shared and schedule based scheduling policies. Such meta-heuristic has also been studied for Grid scheduling by Abraham et al. (2000), and Yarkhan and Dongarra (2002). Wang et al. (2010) have proposed a Genetic-Simulated Annealing (GSA) algorithm which combines GA with SA algorithm for Grid job scheduling.

The Ant Colony Optimization (ACO) algorithm is an intelligent algorithm inspired by ants' feeding action in natural world. The algorithm imitates the pheromone's effect during ants' feeding action to achieve the optimization solution of NP-complete problem. That is, ants choose the path due to the concentration of pheromone and pseudo-random probability rules. Through pheromone evaporation and emancipation process, the ant colony achieves the exchange of information between individuals. An ACO implementation of the problem has been given by Zhu et al. (2010), Molaiy et al. (2014) and Ritchie (2003). Lorpunmanee et al. (2007) have also implemented an ACO algorithm for dynamic job scheduling in Grid environment. Tiwari and Vidyarthi (2014) have examined the effect of inter process communication in auto controlled ACO based scheduling on computational Grid.

The Cuckoo Search Algorithm (CSA), a relatively new meta-heuristic optimization method, is based on the obligate brood parasitic behavior of the cuckoo and its method in egg laying and breeding. The job scheduling in computational Grids using CSA has been investigated by Prakash et al. (2012), Rabiee and Sajedi (2013), and Ghosh et al. (2017) for optimization of various parameters.

A large number of researches have been carried out using hybrid methods which combine two or more meta-heuristic algorithms in order to achieve a result that is not achievable using a single algorithm. Buyya et al. (2000) addressed the hybridization of GA, SA and Tabu Search (TS) heuristics. For the scheduling in Grid computing, hybridization of the GA and TS has been proposed by Xhafa et al. (2009). In fact, our original work (Ghosh and Das, 2016) of this chapter has proposed a hybrid algorithm using GA and CSA to solve job scheduling problem in computational Grid systems, where two important parameters makespan and flowtime were minimized.

3. PROBLEM DEFINITION

In a general setting, a Grid scheduler will be permanently running as follows: receive new incoming jobs, check for available resources, select the appropriate resources according to availability, performance criteria and produce a planning of jobs to selected resources. Here, we have assumed that jobs submitted to the Grid are independent and are not preemptive (they cannot change the resource they has been assigned to once their execution is started, unless the resource is dropped from the Grid.) The jobs are of different computational sizes. The computational requirement (job length) of each job is presented in Millions of Instructions (MI). The computing capacity of each resource is measured in Millions of Instructions Per Second (MIPS).

In order to make realistic simulations of job scheduling in Grid systems, we have considered the use of a simulation model of Ali et al. (2000). To formulate the problem using such simulation model, an estimation of the computational load of each job, the computing capacity of each resource, and an estimation of the prior load of each one of the resources are required. Such simulation model is known as *Expected Time to Compute (ETC)* model which is an *n x m* matrix in which *n* is the number of jobs and *m* is the number of resources. Each row of the ETC matrix specifies the estimated execution time for a given job on each resource. Similarly, each column of the ETC matrix indicates the estimated execution time of a given resource for each job. *ETC[i, j]* is the expected execution time of job *i* on the resource *j*. The size of the ETC matrix is *no_of_jobs* x *no_of_resources*. For the simulation studies, characteristics of the ETC matrices were varied in an attempt to represent a range of possible heterogeneous environments.

Our performance evaluation criteria used to evaluate the performance of the proposed hybrid algorithm are makespan, flowtime and job failure rate. These performance criteria are defined below.

Makespan: One of the most common measures in evaluating the performance of a scheduling algorithm is the makespan. The makespan is the total application execution time. The total application execution time is measured from the time the first job is sent to the Grid, until the last job comes out of the Grid. The makespan includes the total computation time taken at the resource, total time to send the jobs to resource and receiving results from resources, and time taken to schedule the jobs. Makespan is an indicator of the general productivity of the Grid system, small values of makespan mean that the scheduler is providing good and efficient planning of jobs to resources. The makespan is given by

$$makespan_{Min} = \min_{S_i \in Sched} \left\{ \max_{j \in Jobs} F_j \right\}$$

where F_j denotes the time when job *j* finalizes, *Sched* is the set of all possible schedules and *Jobs* represents the set of all jobs to be scheduled.

Flowtime: It is another common measure for evaluating the performance of a scheduling algorithm. The flowtime is the sum of finalization times of all the jobs. It is defined as

$$flowtime_{Min} = \min_{S_i \in Sched} \left\{ \sum_{j \in Jobs} F_j \right\}$$

Note that makespan is not affected by any particular execution sequence of the jobs in a concrete resource; while in order to minimize flowtime of a resource, jobs should be executed in an increasing order of their expected time to compute.

Fault Rate: The fault handler module in the scheduler calculates the failure rate *FR* of each resource with the information such as number of jobs submitted and successfully completed. It is calculated using the formula

$$FR(R_j) = \frac{J_f}{J_{sub}}$$

where J_f is the number of jobs failed to be executed previously in resource R_j and J_{sub} is the number of jobs submitted to resource R_j for execution. The failure rate ranges from 0 to 1. Here, one of the objectives is to minimize the job failure rate.

4. GENETIC ALGORITHM

Developed in 1975 by John Holland, the Genetic Algorithm (GA) is a stochastic search optimization technique that mimics the evolutionary processes in biological systems. The GA combines exploitation of best solutions from past searches with the exploration of new areas of the solution space. The GA for scheduling problems can be organized as follows: First, an initial population is generated either randomly or using other heuristic algorithm. A population consists of a set of chromosomes where each represents a possible solution. A solution is a mapping sequence between jobs and resources. The chromosomes are evaluated and a fitness value is associated with each. The fitness value indicates degree of goodness of individual chromosome compared to others in the population. Next, the population evolves, that is, a new generation is obtained by using the genetic operators, namely selection, crossover and mutation (Haupt et al., 2004). Finally, the chromosomes from this modified population are evaluated again. This completes one iteration of the GA. The GA stops when a predefined number of iterations are reached or all chromosomes converge to the same mapping. The major steps of GA can be written as:

Step 1: Generate the initial population $P(t = 0)$ of n individuals (chromosomes).
Step 2: Evaluate the fitness of each individual of the population. Evaluate $(P(t))$.
Step 3: Select a subset of m pairs from $P(t)$. Let $P_1(t) = \text{Select}(P(t))$.
Step 4: With probability p_c, cross each of the m chosen pairs. Let $P_2(t) = \text{Cross}(P_1(t))$ be the set of off-springs.
Step 5: With probability p_m, mutate each offspring in $P_2(t)$. Let $P_3(t) = \text{Mutate}(P_2(t))$.
Step 6: Evaluate the fitness of each offspring. Evaluate $(P_3(t))$.
Step 7: Create a new generation from individuals in $P(t)$ and $P_3(t)$. Let $P(t + 1) = \text{Replace}(P(t); P_3(t))$; $t = t + 1$.
Step 8: If terminating conditions are not met, go to *Step 3*. Termination criteria of the search can be a maximum number of iterations or convergence to a sub-optimum.

5. CUCKOO SEARCH ALGORITHM

Yang and Deb in 2009 developed the Cuckoo Search Algorithm (CSA) based on the Lévy flight behavior and brood parasitic behavior (Yang et al., 2009). The CSA has been proven to deliver excellent performance in constrained optimizations. Cuckoo birds have an aggressive reproduction in which females hijack and lay their fertilized eggs in other birds' nests. If the host bird discovers that the egg does not belong to it, it either throws away or abandons its nest and builds a new one elsewhere.

Each egg in a nest represents a solution, and a cuckoo egg represents a new solution. The aim is to employ the new and potentially better solutions (cuckoos) to replace not-so-good solutions in the nests. In the simplest form, each nest has one egg. The algorithm can be extended to more complicated cases in which each nest has multiple eggs representing a set of solutions (Yang et al., 2009; Yang et al., 2010). The CSA is based on three idealized rules:

- Each cuckoo lays one egg at a time, and dumps it in a randomly chosen nest;
- The best nests with high quality of eggs (solutions) will transmit to the next generations;
- The number of available host nests is fixed, and a host can discover an unknown egg with probability $p_a \in [0, 1]$. In this case, the host bird can either throw the egg away or abandon the nest to build a completely new nest in a new location (Yang et al., 2009).

For simplicity, the last assumption can be approximated by a fraction p_a of the n nests being replaced by new nests, having new random solutions. For a maximization problem, the quality or fitness of a solution can simply be proportional to the objective function.

When generating new solutions $x_i(t + 1)$ for the *ith* cuckoo, the following Lévy flight is performed

$$x_i(t+1) = x_i(t) + \alpha \oplus L\acute{e}vy(\lambda) \tag{1}$$

where $\alpha > 0$ is the step size, which should be related to the scale of the problem of interest. The product $\oplus$ means entry-wise multiplications (Yang et al., 2010). In this paper, we consider a Lévy flight in which the step-lengths are distributed according to the following probability distribution

$$L\acute{e}vy(u) = t^{-\lambda}, 1 < \lambda \leq 3 \tag{2}$$

which has an infinite variance. Here, the consecutive jumps/steps of a cuckoo essentially form a random walk process which obeys a power-law step-length distribution with a heavy tail.

Based on the above mentioned rules, the basic steps of the CSA can be summarized as:

Step 1: Determine fitness function $f(x)$, $x = (x_1, \ldots, x_d)^T$
Step 2: Generate initial population of n host nests x_i $(i = 1, \ldots, n)$
Step 3: Get a cuckoo (say, i) randomly and generate a new solution by Lévy flights.
Step 4: Evaluate its quality / fitness. Let it be F_i
Step 5: Choose a nest among n (say, j) randomly.
Step 6: If $(F_i > F_j)$ replace j by the new solution;
Step 7: A fraction (p_a) of worse nests is abandoned and new ones are built at new locations using Lévy flights.
Step 8: Keep the best solutions (or nests with quality solutions).
Step 9: Rank the solutions and find the current best
Step 10: If terminating conditions are not met, go to *Step 3*. Termination criteria of the search can be a maximum number of iterations or convergence to a sub-optimum.

6. ANT COLONY OPTIMIZATION

Proposed by Dorigo, et al in 1991 (Dorigo et al., 1991) the Ant Colony Optimization (ACO) algorithm has been used as a discrete optimization technique. The ACO is inspired by the real ants' foraging behavior. Real ants are capable of finding the shortest path from their nest to a food source without using any visual signal. Instead, they communicate information about the food source through depositing a chemical substance called pheromone on the paths. The following ants are attracted by the pheromone. Since the shorter paths have higher traffic densities, these paths are having higher concentration of pheromones. Hence, the probability of ants following these shorter paths would be higher than that of those following the longer ones. As time passes, the oldest pheromone-paths evaporate and at some time, only the shortest path will remain with a good amount of pheromones.

The quantity of pheromone is stored into a matrix which specifies the probability for each decision to lead to a good solution. All the decisions are initialized with a uniform probability. Then a certain number of routines (ants) are started to construct different solutions (paths) iteratively. At each decision point, a probability is generated for each of the admissible choices as follows:

$$P_{x,y} = \frac{[\tau_{x,y}]^\alpha [\eta_{x,y}]^\beta}{\sum_{l \in \Omega_x} [\tau_{x,l}]^\alpha [\eta_{x,l}]^\beta} \tag{3}$$

where x is the present point in the decision process, and y is the possible destination, η is a problem-related local heuristic (i.e., calculated every time a probability is generated), while τ is the global heuristic determined by the pheromone. Both contributions, weighted through α and β, control the decision of the ant. Ω_x contains all the choices at the present point x. At the end of each iteration, the results are evaluated and the pheromones are updated using the following:

$$\tau_{x,y} = (1-\rho).\tau_{x,y} + \sum_{l=1}^{m} \Delta\tau^{(l)}_{x,y} \tag{4}$$

where $0 < \rho < 1$ is the evaporation rate and the deltas are computed as $\Delta\tau^{(l)}_{x,y} = R/S$, if the path from x to y was in the solution, 0 if not, with R as pheromone delivery rate and S as the cost of the result. The number of ants at point x is m. After each iteration, some pheromones evaporate on all the paths. This allows forgetting paths explored and never revisited, avoiding early convergence to local minima.

In Grid job scheduling, the ACO algorithm can be summarized as:

Step 1: Initially associate each path connecting job-source(x) to resource-destination(y) with a pheromone path $\tau_{x,y}$.
Step 2: Put m ants on an initial point (job-source).
Step 3: Each ant constructs its own path. The probability of going from the present point x to the destination point y is calculated using Equation no. (3).
Step 4: Evaluation of the quality of the result.

Step 5: Update of the pheromones using Equation no. (4), firstly evaporating the pheromone-paths on all the paths and then incrementing it by a factor proportional to the quality of the result found.

Step 6: If terminating conditions are not met, go to *Step 2*. Termination criteria of the search can be a maximum number of iterations or convergence to a sub-optimum.

7. PROPOSED HYBRID ALGORITHM

The GA can provide better results as compared to many other heuristic algorithms for constrained optimization problems, but the disadvantage of the algorithm is that it can easily be trapped in local minima. In order to avoid this local minima problem, the CSA can be used to perform the local search more efficiently, because it uses only a single parameter apart from the population size. Therefore, our proposed algorithm combines the advantages of both GA and CSA.

In the present study, we have employed pipelining type hybrid method because of its advantages. In the hybrid algorithm, we apply GA to all individuals in the population from which we select the *n* best vectors based on the fitness values to generate the initial population for local search via CSA. There after this population is refined by CSA and the best population obtained through this local search are sent back to GA. This search continues till it reach maximum number of generations or it satisfies pre-defined criterion. The steps of hybrid algorithm are summarized as follows:

Step 1: *Initialization*: Initialize the parameters. Find out the no. of jobs that need to be scheduled and the no. currently available resources.

Step 2: *Creation*: Generate the initial population of *n* individuals (chromosomes).

Step 3: *Fitness*: Evaluate the fitness of each individual of the population.

Step 4: *Local Search*: Perform local search using CSA and memorize the improved solutions obtained so far.

Step 5: *Genetic Operations*: Apply genetic operations: selection, crossover, mutation for each solution (individual) obtained.

Step 6: *Fitness*: Evaluate the fitness of each offspring (possible solution).

Step 7: *Termination Condition*: If terminating conditions are not met, go to *Step 3*. Termination criteria of the search can be a maximum number of iterations or obtaining near optimum solution.

8. EXPERIMENTS AND RESULTS

For evaluation of performance of the proposed hybrid algorithm, the approach is compared with GA, CSA and ACO algorithms outlined earlier for the job scheduling problem in computational Grid systems. The goal of scheduler in these methods is to minimize the makespan, flowtime and job failure rate. The algorithms are developed using MATLAB Release 2013A and run on a PC with 2.6 GHz processor and 4 GB of RAM. In order to optimize the performance of the proposed method and other methods, fine tuning has been performed and best values for their parameters are selected which have been given in Table 1. Also we have used the benchmark that proposed in Ali et al. (2000) for simulating the heterogeneous computing environment.

Table 1. Parameter settings for the algorithms

Algorithm	Parameter Name	Parameter Value
GA	Number of individuals	25
	Number of iterations	1000
	Crossover probability (p_c)	0.8
	Mutation probability (p_m)	0.07
	Scale for mutations	0.1
CSA	Number of nests	20
	Number of iterations	1000
	Mutation probability value (p_a)	0.25
	Step size (α)	1.5
ACO	Number of iterations	1000
	Evaporation rate (ρ)	0.015
	Weight for local heuristic (α)	1
	Weight for global heuristic (β)	1
Hybrid	Number of iterations	1000
	Other parameters are same as GA and CSA	

The simulation model in Ali et al. (2000) is based on expected time to compute (ETC) matrix for 512 jobs and 16 resources. The instances of the benchmark are classified into 12 different types of ETC matrices according to the three following metrics: job heterogeneity, resource heterogeneity, and consistency. In ETC matrix, the amount of variance among the execution times of jobs for a given resource is defined as job heterogeneity. Resource heterogeneity represents the variation that is possible among the execution times for a given job across all the resources. Also an ETC matrix is said to be consistent whenever a resource R_i executes any job J_j faster than resource R_k; in this case, resource R_i executes all jobs faster than resource R_k. In contrast, inconsistent matrices characterize the situation where resource R_i may be faster than resource R_k for some jobs and slower for others. Partially-consistent matrices are inconsistent matrices that include a consistent sub-matrix of a predefined size (Ali et al., 2000). Instances consist of 512 jobs and 16 resources and are labeled as *u-x-yy-zz* as follows:

- *u* means uniform distribution used in generating the matrices.
- *x* shows the type of inconsistency; *c* means consistent; *i* means inconsistent and *p* means partially-consistent.
- *yy* indicates the heterogeneity of the jobs; *hi* means high and *lo* means low.
- *zz* represents the heterogeneity of the resources; *hi* means high and *lo* means low.

The makespan, flowtime and job failure rate using GA, CSA, ACO and our proposed algorithms are compared in Tables 2, 3 and 4 respectively. The results are obtained as an average of 50 simulations. In Table 2, the first column indicates the instance name, the second, third, fourth and fifth columns indicate the average makespan (in second) achieved by GA, CSA, ACO and our proposed hybrid method respectively. The results show that our hybrid algorithm has minimized makespan best among four

Table 2. Comparison of statistical results for average makespan (in second) obtained by GA, CSA, ACO and the proposed hybrid methods

Instance	GA	CSA	ACO	Hybrid Algorithm
u-c-hi-hi	21506993	12551328	13561023	**10162378**
u-c-hi-lo	235597	203262	224293	**191597**
u-c-lo-hi	696238	423628	464123	**372102**
u-c-lo-lo	8129	7087	7573	**6276**
u-i-hi-hi	21042093	21461852	23120826	**6648885**
u-i-hi-lo	244892	224163	287102	**148879**
u-i-lo-hi	692501	712591	848693	**227879**
u-i-lo-lo	8249	7905	9585	**4512**
u-p-hi-hi	21250898	18234472	22064596	**8325138**
u-p-hi-lo	242296	218783	267796	**163103**
u-p-lo-hi	712313	701179	772783	**293345**
u-p-lo-lo	8241	8027	8639	**5221**

Table 3. Comparison of statistical results for average flowtime (in second) obtained by GA, CSA, ACO and the proposed hybrid methods

Instance	GA	CSA	ACO	Hybrid Algorithm
u-c-hi-hi	311862093	215387342	199343215	**179386672**
u-c-hi-lo	3558439	3115598	3319643	**2817588**
u-c-lo-hi	10301965	6516653	6822124	**5506458**
u-c-lo-lo	123897	100856	114627	**92551**
u-i-hi-hi	313532344	254789678	342186522	**197739373**
u-i-hi-lo	3697318	3413533	4334351	**3103582**
u-i-lo-hi	10534875	8746577	12476144	**3396673**
u-i-lo-lo	123421	102457	140212	**87467**
u-p-hi-hi	314513842	283823464	324346914	**223221475**
u-p-hi-lo	3659248	3539285	3937228	**2929089**
u-p-lo-hi	10541032	8644573	11438789	**4341537**
u-p-lo-lo	121102	99458	127226	**78657**

algorithms. In Table 3, the first column indicates the instance name, the second, third, fourth and fifth columns indicate the average flowtime (in second) achieved by all four algorithms. The results again indicate that our hybrid algorithm has given the best results among all algorithms. Table 4 shows the performances of all four algorithms based on hit count which is the measure of fault tolerance. The results show that the hybrid algorithm has more number of jobs successfully completed without failure. In other words, this algorithm shows least job failure rate among all four algorithms. Figures 1, 2 and 3 show the comparison of statistical results using different algorithms for average makespan (in second), average flowtime (in second) and average hit count for the 12 considered cases respectively.

Table 4. Comparison of statistical results for average hit count obtained by GA, CSA, ACO and the proposed hybrid methods

Instance	GA	CSA	ACO	Hybrid Algorithm
u-c-hi-hi	345	340	333	**389**
u-c-hi-lo	332	327	322	**378**
u-c-lo-hi	288	280	278	**345**
u-c-lo-lo	282	292	290	**356**
u-i-hi-hi	351	338	334	**392**
u-i-hi-lo	339	323	318	**369**
u-i-lo-hi	291	281	291	**338**
u-i-lo-lo	280	281	283	**364**
u-p-hi-hi	363	332	352	**395**
u-p-hi-lo	341	320	318	**373**
u-p-lo-hi	285	279	280	**324**
u-p-lo-lo	281	278	273	**354**

Figure 1. Mean makespan comparison among GA, CSA, ACO and our proposed hybrid algorithm

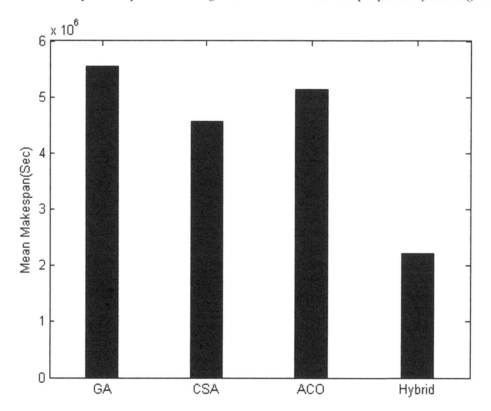

Figure 2. Mean flowtime comparison among GA, CSA, ACO and our proposed hybrid algorithm

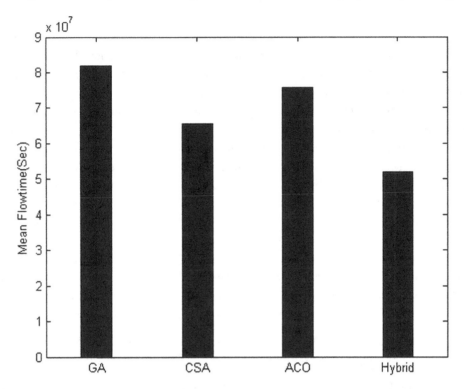

Figure 3. Average hit count comparison among GA, CSA, ACO and our proposed hybrid algorithm

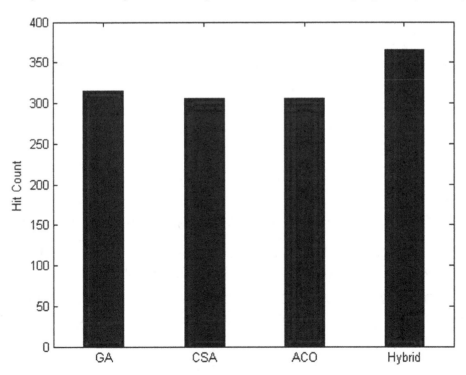

9. CONCLUSION

Job scheduling in computational Grid is an NP-complete problem. Therefore, using meta-heuristic techniques is an appropriate approach in order to cope with its difficulty in practice. This chapter investigates the job scheduling algorithms in Grid environments as optimization problems. A new hybrid algorithm combining GA and CSA has been proposed to schedule the jobs in computational Grids. The goal of the proposed scheduler in this chapter is minimizing makespan, flowtime and job failure rate. The performance of the proposed method was compared with GA, CSA and ACO through carrying out exhaustive simulation tests on different settings. Experimental results show that our proposed algorithm surpasses other existing techniques in all cases. There are other important performance evaluation criteria such as processing cost, resource utilization rate and communication delay which may be studied further.

REFERENCES

Aggarwal, M., & Kent, R. (2005). Genetic Algorithm Based Scheduler for Computational Grids. *Proceedings of the 19th International Symposium on High Performance Computing Systems and Applications (HPCS '05)*. 10.1109/HPCS.2005.27

Ali, S., Siegel, H. J., Maheswaran, H. D., & Ali, S. (2000). Representing Task and Machine Heterogeneities for Heterogeneous Computing Systems. *Tamkang Journal of Science and Engineering, 3*(3), 195–207.

Bianco, L., Caramia, M., Giordani, S., & Mari, R. (2015). Grid scheduling by bilevel programming: A heuristic approach. *European Journal of Industrial Engineering, 9*(1), 101–125. doi:10.1504/EJIE.2015.067450

Braun, T. D., Siegel, H. J., Beck, N., Boloni, L. L., Maheswaran, M., Reuther, A. I., ... Yao, B. (2001). A comparison of eleven static heuristics for mapping a class of independent tasks onto heterogeneous distributed computing systems. *Journal of Parallel and Distributed Computing, 61*(6), 810–837. doi:10.1006/jpdc.2000.1714

Buyya, R., Abraham, A., & Nath, B. (2000). Nature's heuristics for scheduling jobs on computational grids. *Proceedings of 8th IEEE International Conference on Advanced Computing and Communications (ADCOM2000)*, 45–52.

Di Martino, V., & Mililotti, M. (2004). Sub optimal scheduling in a grid using genetic algorithms. *Parallel Computing, 30*(5-6), 553–565. doi:10.1016/j.parco.2003.12.004

Dorigo, C. A., & Maniez, M. (1991). *Distributed optimization by ant colonies*. Elsevier Publishing.

Gao, Y., Rong, H., & Huang, J. Z. (2005). Adaptive Grid job scheduling with genetic algorithms. *Future Generation Computer Systems, 21*(1), 151–161. doi:10.1016/j.future.2004.09.033

Ghosh, T. K., & Das, S. (2016). A Modified Binary PSO Algorithm for Scheduling Independent Jobs in Grid Computing System. *International Journal of Next-Generation Computing, 7*(2), 144–154.

Ghosh, T. K., & Das, S. (2016). A Hybrid Algorithm Using Genetic Algorithm and Cuckoo Search Algorithm to Solve Job Scheduling Problem in Computational Grid Systems. *International Journal of Applied Evolutionary Computation, 7*(2), 1–11. doi:10.4018/IJAEC.2016040101

Ghosh, T. K., Das, S., Barman, S., & Goswami, R. (2017). Job Scheduling in Computational Grid Based on an Improved Cuckoo Search Method. *International Journal of Computer Applications in Technology. Inderscience, 55*(2), 138–146.

Goswami, R., Ghosh, T. K., & Barman, S. (2011). Local search based approach in Grid scheduling using simulated annealing. *Proceedings of IEEE International Conference on Computer and Communication Technology (ICCCT)*. 10.1109/ICCCT.2011.6075112

Haupt, R. L., & Haupt, S. E. (2004). *Practical Genetic Algorithms*. New York: John Wiley & Sons.

Karimi, M. (2014). Hybrid Discrete Particle Swarm Optimization for Task Scheduling in Grid Computing. *International Journal of Grid and Distributed Computing, 7*(4), 93–104. doi:10.14257/ijgdc.2014.7.4.09

Kolodziej, J., & Khan, S. U. (2012). Multi-level hierarchical genetic-based scheduling of independent jobs in dynamic heterogeneous grid environment. *Information Sciences, 214*, 1–19. doi:10.1016/j.ins.2012.05.016

Kolodziej, J., & Xhafa, F. (2011). Enhancing the Genetic-Based Scheduling in Computational Grids by a Structured Hierarchical Population. *Journal of Future Generation Computer Systems., 27*(8), 1035–1046. doi:10.1016/j.future.2011.04.011

Liu, H., Abraham, A., & Hassanien, A. (2009). Scheduling jobs on computational grids using a fuzzy particle swarm optimization algorithm. *Future Generation Computer Systems*.

Lorpunmanee, S., Sap, M. N., Abdullah, A. H., & Chompooinwai, C. (2007). An Ant Colony Optimization for Dynamic Job Scheduling in Grid Environment. *International Journal of Computer, Electrical, Automation. Control and Information Engineering, 1*(5), 1343–1350.

Moghaddam, S. K., Khodadadi, F., Maleki, R. E., & Movaghar, A. (2012). A Hybrid Genetic Algorithm and Variable Neighborhood Search for Task Scheduling Problem in Grid Environment. *Procedia Engineering, 29*, 3808–3814. doi:10.1016/j.proeng.2012.01.575

Molaiy, S., & Effatparvar, M. (2014). Scheduling in Grid Systems using Ant Colony Algorithm. *I.J. Computer Network and Information Security., 6*(2), 16–22. doi:10.5815/ijcnis.2014.02.03

Page, J., & Naughton, J. (2005). Framework for task scheduling in heterogeneous distributed computing using genetic algorithms. *AI Review, 24*, 415–429.

Prakash, M., Saranya, R., Rukmani Jothi, K., & Vigneshwaran, A. (2012). An Optimal Job Scheduling in Grid Using Cuckoo Algorithm. *International Journal of Computer Science and Telecommunications, 3*(2), 65–69.

Prakash, S., & Vidyarthi, D. P. (2015). Maximizing Availability for Task Scheduling in Computational Grid using GA. *Concurrency and Computation, 27*(1), 197–210. doi:10.1002/cpe.3216

Rabiee, M., & Sajedi, H. (2013). Job Scheduling in Grid Computing with Cuckoo Optimization Algorithm. *International Journal of Computer Applications, 62*(16), 975-987.

Ritchie, G. (2003). *Static multi-processor scheduling with ant colony optimization and local search* (Master Thesis). School of Informatics, Univ. of Edinburgh.

Thilagavathi, J., & Thanamani, A. S. (2012). A Survey on Dynamic Job Scheduling in Grid Environment Based on Heuristic Algorithm. *International Journal of Computer Trends and Technology, 3*(4).

Tiwari, P. K., & Vidyarthi, D. P. (2014). Observing the Effect of Inter Process Communication in Auto Controlled Ant Colony Optimization based Scheduling on Computational Grid. *Concurrency and Computation, 26*(1), 241–270. doi:10.1002/cpe.2977

Wang, J., Duan, Q., Jiang, Y., & Zhu, X. (2010). A New Algorithm for Grid Independent Task Schedule: Genetic Simulated Annealing. *World Automation Congress (WAC)*, 165–171.

Xhafa, F., Duran, B., Abraham, A., & Dahal, K. P. (2008). Tuning struggle strategy in genetic algorithms for scheduling in computational grids. *Neural Network World, 18*(3), 209–225.

Xhafa, F., Gonzalez, J. A., Dahal, K. P., & Abraham, A. (2009). A GA(TS) Hybrid Algorithm for Scheduling in Computational Grids. *Proceedings of the 4th International Conference on Hybrid Artificial Intelligence Systems*, 285–292. 10.1007/978-3-642-02319-4_34

Yang, X. S., & Deb, S. (2009). Cuckoo Search via Levy Flights. *Proceedings of World Congress on Nature & Biologically Inspired Computing*, 210-225. 10.1109/NABIC.2009.5393690

Yang, X. S., & Deb, S. (2010). Engineering Optimization by Cuckoo Search. *Int. J. Mathematical Modeling and Numerical Optimization., 1*(4), 330–343. doi:10.1504/IJMMNO.2010.035430

YarKhan, A., & Dongarra, J. (2002). Experiments with scheduling using simulated annealing in a Grid environment. *GRID-2002*, 232-242.

Zhang, L., Chen, Y., Sun, R., Jing, S., & Yang, B. (2008). A task scheduling algorithm based on PSO for grid computing. *International Journal of Computational Intelligence Research*, 4.

Zhu, P., Zhao, M., & He, T. (2010). A Novel Ant Colony Algorithm for Grid Task Scheduling. *Journal of Computer Information Systems, 6*(3), 745–752.

Zomaya, A. Y., & Yee-Hwei Teh. (2001). Observations on using genetic algorithms for dynamic load-balancing. *IEEE Transactions on Parallel and Distributed Systems, 12*(9), 899–911. doi:10.1109/71.954620

Chapter 16
An Enhanced Clustering Method for Image Segmentation

Bikram Keshari Mishra
Veer Surendra Sai University of Technology, India

Amiya Kumar Rath
Veer Surendra Sai University of Technology, India

ABSTRACT

The findings of image segmentation reflect its expansive applications and existence in the field of digital image processing, so it has been addressed by many researchers in numerous disciplines. It has a crucial impact on the overall performance of the intended scheme. The goal of image segmentation is to assign every image pixels into their respective sections that share a common visual characteristic. In this chapter, the authors have evaluated the performances of three different clustering algorithms used in image segmentation: the classical k-means, its modified k-means++, and proposed enhanced clustering method. Brief explanations of the fundamental working principles implicated in these methods are presented. Thereafter, the performance which affects the outcome of segmentation are evaluated considering two vital quality measures, namely structural content (SC) and root mean square error (RMSE). Experimental result shows that the proposed method gives impressive result for the computed values of SC and RMSE as compared to k-means and k-means++. In addition to this, the output of segmentation using the enhanced technique reduces the overall execution time as compared to the other two approaches irrespective of any image size.

1. INTRODUCTION

Digital image processing refers to the processing of digital images by means of a digital computer. A digital image consists of a limited number of elements, and each element has a particular value and a location. These elements are referred to as pixels.

Image processing is a simple method of conversion of an image to its digital form for the purpose of enhancing its visual appearance or extracting some useful information from it. The whole concept of image processing includes obtaining an *input image* by digital photography or video frame, *examining*

DOI: 10.4018/978-1-5225-5832-3.ch016

and maneuvering the image in order to spot some patterns that are normally not visible to human eye, or sharpening the image for better viewing, or retrieving those portions of the image that are of interest, and finally *outputting* the resulting image based on some image analysis.

An image may be defined as a matrix in which the picture elements or the pixels are arranged in columns and rows. Mathematically, an image is a two dimensional function, $f(x, y)$, where x and y are spatial coordinates. The amplitude of f at any pair of plane coordinates (x, y), which is the gray level or intensity of the image at that point. We will employ two vital ways to represent digital images. Assume an image $f(x, y)$ has M rows and N columns. For convenience, we shall use integer values for x and y. Hence, the values of coordinates at origin are $(x, y) = (0, 0)$. The next values along the first row of the image are $(x, y) = (0, 1)$. Figure 1 show the coordinate convention used.

Thus, the total $M*N$ digital image can be represented in the following form:

$$f(x,y) = \begin{bmatrix} f(0,0) & f(0,1) & \cdots & f(0, N-1) \\ f(1,0) & f(1,1) & \cdots & f(1, N-1) \\ \vdots & \vdots & & \vdots \\ f(M-1,0) & f(M-1,1) & \cdots & f(M-1, N-1) \end{bmatrix} \quad (1)$$

The distribution of an image into meaningful compositions, formally referred as *image segmentation*, is often a crucial step in image analysis, object illustration, visualization, and several other image processing tasks. The aim of the segmentation in image processing consists of dividing an input image into several regions with similar characteristics like color, texture, intensity, etc. The pixels that share a certain amount of common visual characteristics are clustered into same regions as compared to the other pixels.

Figure 1. Representation of digital images using coordinates

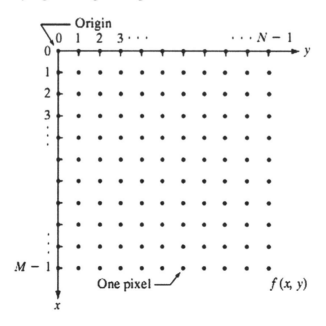

Today, image processing forms a core research area within engineering and computer science disciplines. A broad variety of computational vision problems could make good use of segmented images. For instance, after closely analyzing the segmented cancerous tissue (N. D. Khalilabad *et al.* (2017), it becomes more prominent to the naked eye from the non-cancerous ones. Similarly, radiologists work out the best path for applying radiation to a tumor while avoiding other critical structures of the body. To improve the diagnosis of heart diseases image analysis techniques are employed to radiographic images (J. Rajeswari *et al.* (2017). This image segmentation method reduces the time required for radiation treatment planning dramatically. Color image segmentation is also useful in many other applications like classification of vehicles in dedicated lanes of an intelligent transportation system (S. S. Sarikan, 2017 *et al.*). From the segmentation results, it is easily possible to identify the required region of interest.

There are primarily two approaches to carry out image segmentation; the first one is to find the pixels whose intensity rapidly changes. Those pixels are then connected to give the boundaries, which we generally term as *edge detection*. The second one is to locate the regions within the image whose intensity (color) is mostly stable, which we refer to as *region-based segmentation*. For this work, the primary focus is on the second approach and the main goal is to implement clustering approaches to image segmentation.

The basic clustering methods for image segmentation are compared and a new clustering algorithm for segmentation is introduced which is far more efficient than the classical K-Means algorithm (J. Mac Queen, 1967) and it's modified K-Means++ algorithm (David Arthur and Sergei Vassilvitskii, 2007). These algorithms have been implemented on various standard images. The major downside of K-Means and K-Means++ are discussed, and in order to curtail such difficulties and improve the segmentation quality and efficiency, a simple model known as Enhanced Clustering Algorithm has been projected. The relative performances of cluster based segmentation are analyzed by using few standard measures on the given algorithms and the amount of computational time taken by each of them is recorded.

The organization of this work is as follows: In Section II, the basic idea of relative performance of cluster based segmentation approaches is briefly discussed. Section III presents the efficient and productive works done by several researchers in this relevant area. The K-Means and K-Mean++ clustering method is briefly presented in Section IV and proposed efficient clustering method for image segmentation is mentioned in Section V. Simulation and experimental results are shown in Section VI. Finally, Section VII concludes the paper.

2. PERFORMANCE MEASURES

The performance criterion plays a vital role in the field of image segmentation. Determining the fineness of segmentation results, minimizing the noise factor present in the segmented image and performing the segmentation in a least amount of time are some of the factors that affect the outcome of segmentation. The algorithms designed for this purpose should take care of these issues. Performance measure deals with the assessment of segmentation consequences.

In general, the performance measures of image quality can be classified into two categories, viz, subjective and objective quality measurements. Subjective quality measurement are based on observer's response such as Mean Opinion Score (MOS), is really authoritative but excessively inconvenient, time consuming and expensive. For that reason, objective measurements are developed which are based on computable distortion measures such as MSE, PSNR, SC, LMSE etc that are least time consuming than MOS. In this section, the following quality measures are briefly discussed that affect the relative performance of segmentation using clustering approach.

2.1. Structural Correlation / Content (SC)

In the computer vision literature concerning image quality criterion, the most commonly used measures are variations among the original and segmented images of which the root mean square error (RMSE) or structural content (SC) being widely used. The reason for these metrics extensive popularity is the fact that these are quite simple and straight forward to implement.

Correlation, a well-known notion in image processing, calculates approximately the similarity of the organization of two signals. This measure efficiently evaluates the total weight of an original signal to that of an obtained one. It is therefore a global metric. The value of SC (Jaskirat *et al.*, 2012) to a great extent influences the quality of a segmented image. SC measure is given by:

$$SC = \sum_{i=1}^{m} \sum_{j=1}^{n} in(i,j)^2 \bigg/ \sum_{i=1}^{m} \sum_{j=1}^{n} seg(i,j)^2 \tag{2}$$

where, *in(i, j)* is the input image and *seg(i, j)* is the target segmented image and *m* & *n* are image matrix rows and columns respectively.

A smaller value of SC means that the image is of better quality.

2.2. Root Mean Square Error (RMSE)

The RMSE (Jaskirat *et al.*, 2012) is a well known parameter to evaluate the quality of segmented image. Generally speaking, RMSE gives the difference between the values predicted by a model and the values actually present in that model. In term of image processing, it corresponds to the amount of deviation present in the output segmented image as compared to that in the original input image. RMSE measure is given by:

$$RMSE = \sqrt{\frac{1}{m*n} \left[\frac{\sum_{i=1}^{m} \sum_{j=1}^{n} \left[in(i,j)\right]^2}{\sum_{i=1}^{m} \sum_{j=1}^{n} \left[in(i,j) - seg(i,j)\right]^2} \right]} \tag{3}$$

A smaller value calculated for RMSE means that the image is of good quality.

2.3. Peak Signal–to–Noise Ratio (PSNR)

This is an extensively used objective image quality measure. The key feature of this measure is its simplicity of computation. Another vital property of PSNR is that a minor spatial change of an image may lead to a large numerical distortion but no visual deformation. A small value of Peak Signal-to-Noise Ratio (PSNR) means that image is of poor quality. PSNR is defined as follow:

$$PSNR = 20\log_{10}\left(\frac{N}{RMSE}\right)dB \tag{4}$$

2.4. Mean Absolute Error (MAE)

MAE is calculated using eqn. (5) and large value of MAE means that the image is of poor quality.

$$MAE = \frac{1}{MN}\sum_{i=1}^{M}\sum_{i=1}^{N}\left(\mid f(i,j)\text{-}f^{'}(i,j)\mid\right) \tag{5}$$

3. RELATED WORKS

A huge volume of literatures can be found in the past few decades regarding the various ways in which clustering algorithms have been used on image segmentation. In this section, some of the related work are discussed that are most relevant to the approach presented in this paper.

A straightforward method is proposed by Jaskirat, Sunil & Renu, (2012) to solve the problem of generality-based image segmentation in which the performance analysis of different cluster-based image segmentation methods can be carried out. They have discussed a few parameters based on which the quality of clustering can be accessed. An improved version of K-Means algorithm called Enhanced Moving K-Means (EMKM) given by F. U. Siddiqui *et al.* (2011) is capable of generating good quality segmentation with less cluster variance. This algorithm is also less sensitive to the initial center selection. K-means clustering as proposed by P. Jeyanthi *et al.,* (2010) can be used for the feature set which is obtained using the histogram refinement method, and is based on the concept of coherency and incoherency.

The shortcomings of the standard K-Means clustering algorithm can be found in the literature proposed by Shi Na *et al.,* (2010) in which a simple and efficient way for assigning data points to clusters is proposed. This improved algorithm reduces the execution time of K-Means algorithm to a great extent. To avoid the classical K-Means algorithm for reaching to local optima, A. Hatamlou *et al.* (2012) proposed a hybrid method by combining Gravitational search algorithm (GSA) with K-Means termed as *GSA-KM*. This technique assists K-Means algorithm to escape from local optima and increases the convergence speed of GSA.

M. C. Chiang *et al.* (2011) suggested an efficient algorithm called *pattern reduction (PR)* for reducing the computational time of K-Means and its associated clustering algorithms. This algorithm reduces the execution time by compressing and removing those patterns which do not change their membership on each iteration. T. Niknam *et al.* (2011) presented an efficient hybrid evolutionary optimization algorithm based on combining Modify Imperialist Competitive Algorithm (MICA) and K-means (K), which is called *K-MICA* for optimum clustering N objects into K clusters. The convergence of the proposed hybrid algorithm to the global optimum solution is better than that of other evolutionary algorithms.

Segmentation of a document image into text and non-text regions as suggested by S. Bukhari *et al.,* (2010) is an important preprocessing step for a variety of document image analysis tasks like improving Optical Character Recognition (OCR), document compression etc. Most of the document image segmentation approaches use pixel-based or zone-based classification. As pixel-based classification is time consuming and block-based methods largely depend upon accuracy of block segmentation steps, the authors have introduced a new approach for document image segmentation by using connected component-based classification without using block-segmentation. The main objective of a model projected by K. Ravichandran & B. Ananthi (2009) is to segment human skin areas in a given color image. In this model, skin detection using cluster based technique is built to detect the vital skin areas.

In another noteworthy contribution concerning clustering, David Arthur and Sergei Vassilvitskii (2007) proposed K-Means++ which substantially outperformed the standard K-Means in terms of both speed and accuracy. In addition to this, their experimental results illustrate that K-Means++ normally performs much better if new cluster centers are selected during each iteration.

The implementation of a new adaptive technique for color-texture segmentation, a generalization of the standard K-Means algorithm is presented in detail by D.Ilea and P. Whelan in 2006. The main contribution of this work is the generalization of the K-Means algorithm that includes the primary features, which describes the color smoothness and texture complexity in the process of pixel assignment. P. M. Galaviz *et al.* (2005) proposed a new variation of the clustering method, which is based on density called OPTICS (which was initially suggested by M. Ankerst *et al.,* 1999). In this method different clusters are created based on density of the points. In addition to this, the algorithm develops a classification with regard to their parameters. A novel color image segmentation technique using density-based clustering is presented by Q. Ye et al., (2003) in which the selection of Munsell color space have resulted in encouraging segmentation results.

K.G. Srinivasa *et al.* (2016) developed a model to remove noise from image documents involving ancient texts, scripts, stone tablets etc. so that they can be digitized using Optical Character Recognition (OCR). Image processing methods like thresholding, filtering, edge detection, morphological procedures, etc. were applied to pre-process images to produce superior precision of neural network models.

Automatic selection of the best possible threshold is still a challenge in image segmentation. The fuzzy 2-partition entropy method is one of the best approaches of image threshold selection. O. Assas (2015) has proposed an enhancement to this technique using type-2 fuzzy sets to represent the imprecision in the selection of membership function related with the image. Experiments confirm that type-2 fuzzy 2-partition entropy method performs well in achieving quality image segmentation results.

4. IMAGE SEGMENTATION USING DIFFERENT CLUSTERING METHODS

Clustering is an *unsupervised learning* approach in which similar type of items are gathered and placed in one group separating them from dissimilar items which are placed in their respective groups. A variety of clustering algorithms analyzed in this paper are as follows:-

4.1. K-Means Clustering Algorithm

The K-Means Clustering algorithm is one of the simplest unsupervised learning algorithms that solve the well known clustering problem. In 1967, J. Mac Queen first proposed the K-Means algorithm for data clustering.

During every pass of the algorithm, each data is assigned to the nearest partition based upon some similarity parameter (such as Euclidean distance measure). After the completion of every successive pass, a data may switch partitions, thereby altering the values of the original partitions. Partitions which are equally spaced are preferred in this paper in order to improve the running time of the algorithm.

The initial cluster is selected first. Every pixel in the input image has its own RGB value. Each pixel is compared with the already chosen initial clusters and its nearest cluster is recorded. Then within a particular cluster the RGB mean value of all pixels is determined. This resultant mean is used as the new centroid for the given cluster. Then the algorithm returns to again assigning each pixel to its nearest cluster and the above process is repeated until pixels no longer change their corresponding groups.

Generally, during the implementation phase of this algorithm in MATLAB, an image is first converted into its matrix format, where each pixel of the image has its own RGB values. For K-means algorithm, the number of clusters is initialized first. For example, if the number of clusters K = 4, it means the image is going to be segmented into four clusters c_1, c_2, c_3 and c_4 each having its own RGB values. We select a pixel and find the distance matrix from the already initialized clusters, which is d_1, d_2, d_3, d_4 (say). Then from that, we calculate the minimum distance of that pixel from c_1, c_2, c_3 and c_4. Let's assume d_2 is the minimum distance. Hence, the pixel will be grouped in c_2 cluster. Within c_2 the mean values of all pixels is again calculated which now becomes the centroid of that cluster. The above procedure is repeated until a convergence criterion is met.

In K-Means, the Euclidean distance measure is used for calculating the distance between each pixel and the cluster centers. The Euclidean distance is given by:

$$D_{ij} = \left(\sum_{l=1}^{d} \left| x_{il} - x_{jl} \right|^2 \right)^{1/2} \tag{6}$$

The major downside of this algorithm is that, the result strongly depends on the initial selection of centroids. It is very difficult to compare the quality of the clusters produced (e.g. different initial partitions of *K* produce different results), and also very far data from the centroid may pull the centroid away from the real one.

4.2. K-Means++ Clustering Algorithm

K-Means++ was developed by David Arthur & Sergei Vassilvitskii in the year 2007. It is a simple alteration of K-Means. This algorithm provides a new way to select the initial cluster centers in which the first center is chosen randomly and thereafter the subsequent centers are selected basing on some specific probability criteria.

The initial center c_1 is randomly chosen from the given input image I_p to be segmented. The subsequent step is to choose c_i which is the next cluster center. c_i is selected such that $c_i = p' \in I_p$ with a probability defined by:

$$\left(\frac{D(p')^2}{\sum_{p \in I_p} D(p)^2} \right) \tag{7}$$

where, p is any pixel in the input image I_p and $D(p)$ is the shortest distance from p to the already chosen nearest center. The above step of selection of the next cluster center with a defined probability is repeated until K numbers of cluster centers are chosen. Once K number of initial centers is obtained, K-Means algorithm is applied to get the ultimate K clusters.

K-Means++ performs better only if it selects several new centers during each iteration, and then greedily chose the one that decreased the mentioned probability criteria. This is one of its major drawbacks.

5. PROPOSED METHOD FOR IMAGE SEGMENTATION

When clustering algorithm is applied for image segmentation, the input image initially needs to be converted to a numerical three dimensional matrix which contains the RGB value of each pixel. Clustering these massive data matrices using K-Means and its allied algorithms takes significant amount of computational time. In addition to this, the selection of initial cluster center is an important aspect for the said methods. In order to improve the execution time of clustering and select the initial cluster center more efficiently, an enhance clustering method for color image segmentation has been proposed.

In this method of clustering, the algorithm has been slightly customized and has used more effectively which works much proficiently than the already discussed two classical clustering techniques. The flow diagram (Figure 2) as well as the algorithm of the proposed methodology is outlined as follows:

5.1. The Enhanced Clustering Algorithm

The algorithm operates in two phases:

Phase I: *Selection of K Cluster Centers*

```
(1)  Take initial cluster center c_i randomly as any pixel from the input image
matrix I_p.
(2)  repeat
        {
                choose the next cluster center c_i = p' with a   maximum prob-
ability given by:
```

$$\left(\frac{D(p')^2}{\sum_{p \in I_p} D(p)^2} \right)$$

```
                            where, D(p) denotes the shortest distance from
any pixel p to the already chosen nearest  cluster center (David Arthur et
al., 2007)
            }
        until  K number of cluster centers are chosen.
```

Phase II: *The Clustering of Image*

```
(3) Compute the Euclidean distance between each pixel present in the input
image matrix I_p and all K cluster centers.
```

Figure 2. Flow diagram of the Proposed Enhanced Clustering Methodology for color Image Segmentation

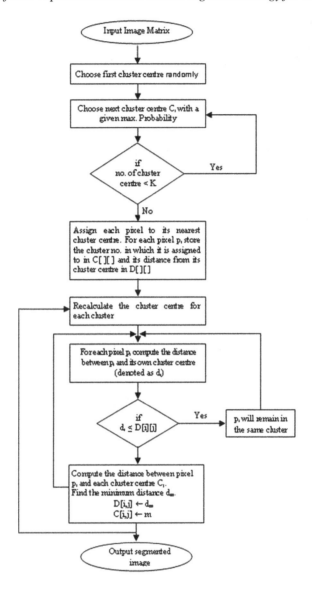

(4)   Assign each pixel to its nearest cluster center c_i.

(5)   (a)   Create two matrices C[ ][ ] and D[ ][ ].

(b) **for** each pixel p[i][j] $\in I_p$

{

Set C[i][j] $\leftarrow$ *n*   (where *n* is the cluster number in which the   pixel p[i][j] was

assigned in step (4)).

Set D[i][j] $\leftarrow$ the distance of pixel p[i][j] to its nearest cluster.

} (End of for loop)

```
(6)   Recalculate the cluster center for each cluster.
(7)   repeat
      {
            for each pixel p[i][j] e I_p
                {
                      compute the distance between p[i][j] and its cluster
center to which it belongs.
                           if  (this computed distance is less than or equal to
the previously stored distance      in matrix D[i][j])
                  then
                                 the pixel p[i][j] remains in its initial cluster.
                  else
                      {
                          for each cluster center   j
                            {
                                 find the distance d_j between center j and
pixel p[i][j]
                            }
```

$$d_m \leftarrow \min_{1 \leq j \leq K}\{d_j\}$$
$$D[i][j] \leftarrow d_m$$
$$C[i][j] \leftarrow m$$

```
                      }
                  } (End of for loop)
            Recalculate the cluster center.
      }
      until convergence is reached.
```

6. EXPERIMENTAL RESULTS

The performances of the developed algorithms were examined on a large number of benchmark RGB images with varying pixel sizes. To assess the efficiency of the projected method, the results were compared obtained from classical K-Means clustering technique of image segmentation against the segmentation results returned by K-Means++ and the proposed enhance clustering method. The outputs were compared pixel-wise. For each image, their respective SC and RMSE (Jaskirat *et al.,* 2012) values were calculated for the discussed algorithms. The results of the assessment are illustrated in Table 1 and Table 2 respectively.

All these algorithms were implemented in MATLAB 7.8.0 on Intel Core 2 Duo system. The processing time of all the above specified algorithms for segmentation of variety of images were recorded in seconds as can be seen from Table 3. In order to obtain a generalized result, experimentations were carried out on lot of images which differ mainly in their color, texture and number of pixels.

Figure 3. (a) input image (b), (c) and (d) its corresponding segmented three clustered images using Enhance Clustering Method

Table 1. *Analysis of Structural Content (SC) performance measure on K-Means, K-Means++ and proposed Enhanced clustering algorithm on different images (with K=3)*

Images	Size (in Pixel)	k-Means	k-Means++	Proposed Method
Joker	200×200	1.0605	1.0605	**1.0446**
Monalisa	200×200	1.2952	1.2862	**1.0385**
Sweet Corn	240×210	1.0093	1.0091	**1.0082**
Girl	256×256	1.0088	1.0049	1.0158
Baboon	365×286	1.1412	1.1412	**1.0195**
Boat	512×512	1.0207	1.0207	**1.0144**
House	512×512	1.0068	1.0062	**1.0047**

Table 2. Analysis of Root Mean Square Error (RMSE) performance measure on K-Means, K-Means++ and proposed Enhanced clustering algorithm on different images (with K=3)

Images	Size (in Pixel)	k-Means	k-Means++	Proposed Method
Joker	200 × 200	0.9365	0.9365	**0.7081**
Monalisa	200 × 200	0.8112	0.8573	0.9985
Sweet Corn	240 × 210	0.9598	1.2430	**0.9478**
Girl	256 × 256	0.7162	0.6938	**0.6560**
Baboon	365 × 286	1.3703	1.2463	**0.9153**
Boat	512 × 512	0.3318	0.3318	**0.2964**
House	512 × 512	0.4063	0.4063	**0.3739**

Table 3. Running time (in seconds) of K-Means, K-Means++ and proposed Enhanced clustering algorithm on different images (with K=3)

Images	Size (in Pixel)	k-Means	k-Means++	Proposed Method
Joker	200 × 200	18.5000	20.4688	**6.9688**
Monalisa	200 × 200	13.2813	15.1365	**10.3281**
Sweet Corn	240 × 210	21.1250	18.4844	**5.5156**
Girl	256 × 256	18.3125	22.3750	**7.8125**
Baboon	365 × 286	8.2344	10.6250	**7.8906**
Boat	512 × 512	158.750	172.2500	**104.9844**
House	512 × 512	171.671	83.5156	**65.7969**

Figure 4. Bar chart showing the analysis of Root Mean Square Error (RMSE) performance measure on K-Means, K-Means++ and proposed Enhanced clustering algorithm on different images (with K=3)

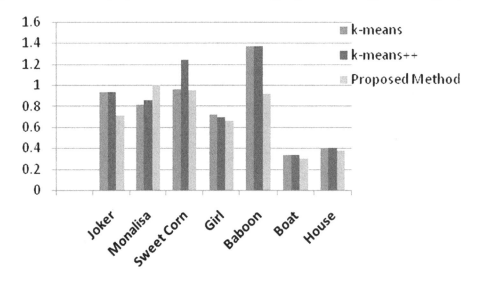

Figure 5. Line chart showing the performance comparison of computational time (in seconds) of K-Means, K-Means++ and proposed Enhanced clustering algorithm on different images (with K=3)

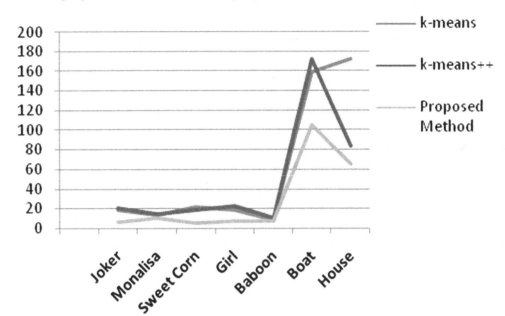

Figure 6 shows a range of input images being segmented into three numbers of clusters using proposed Enhance Clustering method. Below in Figure 3 (a) the authors have shown an input image and its corresponding segmented three clustered images in (b), (c) and (d) using their proposed technique. Here, (b) displays only those pixels which belong to cluster 1 and the rest pixels of cluster 2 and 3 are hide from view. Similarly Figure (c) contains only those pixels belonging to cluster 2 and the rest pixels of cluster 1 and 3 are put out of sight. The same case is for Figure (d). The above discussion is also intended for Figure 6 respectively.

7. CONCLUSION

In this paper, the authors have given a concise description regarding two varieties of image segmentation algorithms i.e. K-means and its modified K-means++. Thereafter, a new algorithm for segmenting image into different clusters has been initiated. The idea is to give a brief clarification of the basic structure of these methods, the loopholes obtained in the earlier methodologies, and the amount of extensions that can be done to lessen these ambiguities in order to obtain a better clustering effect on diverse input images within a short time interval.

From the experimental results it can be clearly seen that, all the three clustering algorithms can be used to produce good quality results in image segmentation. The K-Means algorithm is fairly simple to employ and results achieved is remarkable. But, this algorithm is very much sensitive to the initial cluster selection because, the pixels present very far away from the centroid can pull it to an undesirable region ultimately resulting in bad segmentation. Unlike the K-Means algorithm, the K-Means++ method is independent of any starting conditions and the preferred performance criterion of SC and RMSE is by far more impressive than the classical K-Means technique.

The proposed Enhanced Clustering methodology for image segmentation which operates in two phases – selecting K numbers of cluster centers and clustering the image into the selected K clusters, is a method which provides exceptional outcome in terms of segmentation results. The ideally selected performance criterion of SC and RMSE calculated for this algorithm is highly remarkable than that of K-Means and K-Means++ techniques as can be seen from Table 1 and 2 respectively. Most of the chosen input images possess a smaller value of SC and RMSE implying a better quality of clustering by the proposed method. A Bar chart showing the analysis of Root Mean Square Error (RMSE) performance measure on K-Means, K-Means++ and proposed Enhanced clustering algorithm on different images by choosing the initial number of clusters K as 3 can be seen from Figure 4.

Also, the segmentation using the proposed scheme results in least amount of computational time (calculated in seconds) as compared to the other two discussed approaches. This can be seen from Figure 5. This is due to the fact that, we need not have to repeatedly calculate the distance from a pixel to all other K – 1 centroids thereby reducing the execution time to a greater extent.

ACKNOWLEDGMENT

The authors are extremely thankful to Sagarika Swain who provided expertise that greatly assisted the work. The authors also express gratitude to the editors and the anonymous referees for their productive suggestions on the work.

REFERENCES

Ankerst, M., Breunig, M. M., Kriegel, H. P., & Sander, J. (1999). OPTICS: Ordering Points To Identify the Clustering Structure. *Proceedings ACM SIGMOD'99 Conference on Management of Data (SIGMOD'99)*, 49–60. 10.1145/304182.304187

Arthur, D., & Vassilvitskii, S. (2007). K-Means++: The advantages of careful seeding. *Proceedings of the eighteenth annual ACM-SIAM symposium on Discrete algorithms*, 1027–1035.

Assas, O. (2015). Improvement of 2-Partition Entropy Approach Using Type-2 Fuzzy Sets for Image Thresholding. *International Journal of Applied Evolutionary Computation*, 6(3), 33–48. doi:10.4018/IJAEC.2015070103

Bukhari, S., Al Azawi, M., Shafait, F., & Breuel, T. (2010). Document image segmentation using discriminative learning over connected components. In *Proceedings of the 8th IAPR International Workshop on Document Analysis Systems* (pp. 183–190). ACM. 10.1145/1815330.1815354

Chiang, M. C., Tsai, C. W., & Yang, C. S. (2011). A time efficient pattern reduction algorithm for K-Means clustering. Information Sciences, (181), 716–731.

Coleman, G. B., & Andrews, H. C. (1979). Image segmentation by clustering. *Proceedings of the IEEE*, 67(5), 773–785. doi:10.1109/PROC.1979.11327

Galaviz, P. M., Lopez, A. R., & Garcia, M. J. S. (2005). I.H.P. Torres. Algorithm of Clustering for Color Image segmentation. In *International Conference on Electronics, Communications and Computers (CONIELECOMP 2005)* (pp. 306–310). IEEE. 10.1109/CONIEL.2005.16

Hatamlou, A., Abdullah, S., & Nezamabadi-pour, H. (2012). A combined approach for clustering based on K-Means and gravitational search algorithms. Swarm and Evolutionary Computation, (6), 47-52.

Ilea, D., & Whelan, P. (2006). Color image segmentation using a spatial k-means clustering algorithm. *Proceedings of the Irish Machine Vision & Image Processing Conference*, 146–53.

Jeyanthi, P., & Kumar, V. (2010). Image Classification by K-means Clustering. *Advances in Computational Sciences and Technology, 3*(1), 1–8.

Kaur, J., Agrawal, S., & Vig, R. (2012). A Methodology for the Performance Analysis of Cluster Based Image Segmentation. *International Journal of Engineering Research and Applications, 2*(2), 664–667.

Khalilabad, N. D., & Hassanpour, H. (2017). Employing image processing techniques for cancer detection using microarray images. *Computers in Biology and Medicine, 81*, 139–147. doi:10.1016/j.compbiomed.2016.12.012 PMID:28061369

Mac Queen, J. (1967). Some methods for classification and analysis of multivariate observations. In *Fifth Berkeley Symposium on Mathematics, Statistics and Probability* (pp. 281–297). University of California Press.

Na, S., Xumin, L., & Yong, G. (2010). Research on K-Means clustering algorithm–An Improved K-Means Clustering Algorithm. *IEEE Third International Symposium on Intelligent Information Technology Security Informatics*, 63–67. 10.1109/IITSI.2010.74

Niknam, T., Fard, E. T., Pourjafarian, N., & Rousta, A. (2011). An efficient hybrid algorithm based on modified imperialistic competitive algorithm and K-Means for data clustering. Engineering Application of Artificial Intelligence, (24), 306–317.

Rajeswari, J., & Jagannath, M. (2017). Advances in biomedical signal and image processing – A systematic review. *Informatics in Medicine Unlocked, 8*, 13–19. doi:10.1016/j.imu.2017.04.002

Ravichandran, K., & Ananthi, B. (2009). Color Skin Segmentation Using K-Means Cluster. *International Journal of Computational and Applied Mathematics, 4*(2), 153–157.

Sarikan, S. S., Ozbayoglu, A. M., & Zilci, O. (2017). Automated Vehicle Classification with Image Processing and Computational Intelligence. *Procedia Computer Science, 114*, 515–522. doi:10.1016/j.procs.2017.09.022

Siddiqui, F. U., & Isa, N. A. M. (2011). Enhanced Moving K-Means (EMKM) Algorithm for Image Segmentation. *IEEE Transactions on Consumer Electronics, 57*(2), 833–841. doi:10.1109/TCE.2011.5955230

Srinivasa, K. G., Sowmya, B. J., Pradeep Kumar, D., & Shetty, C. (2016). Efficient Image Denoising for Effective Digitization using Image Processing Techniques and Neural Networks. *International Journal of Applied Evolutionary Computation, 7*(4), 77–93. doi:10.4018/IJAEC.2016100105

Ye, Q., Gao, W., & Zeng, W. (2003). Color Image Segmentation Using Density-Based Clustering. In *International Conference of Acoustics, Speech, and Signal Processing (ICASSP)* (pp. 345–348). IEEE.

ADDITIONAL READING

Das, A. J., Talukdar, A. K., & Sarma, K. K. (2013). An Adaptive Rayleigh-Laplacian Based MAP Estimation Technique for Despeckling SAR Images using Stationary Wavelet Transform. *International Journal of Applied Evolutionary Computation, 4*(4), 88–102. doi:10.4018/ijaec.2013100106

Gonalez, R. C., & Woods, R. E. (2001). Digital Image Processing, 2nd edition, Prentice Hall. Robert A Schowengerdt, Remote Sensing- Models and Methods for Image Processing, IIIrd edition, Elsevier Inc.

Han, J., & Kamber, M. (2001). *Data Mining Concepts and Techniques*. Morgan Kaufmann Publishers.

Majumder, S. (2017). Multiresolution SVD Based Image Watermarking Scheme Using Noise Visibility Function. *International Journal of Applied Evolutionary Computation, 8*(1), 38–48. doi:10.4018/ijaec.2017010103

Peng, L., & Gan, X. (2012). The Statistical Pattern Recognition of the Weather Conditions Based on the Gray-Scale of Image. *International Journal of Applied Evolutionary Computation, 3*(3), 78–87. doi:10.4018/jaec.2012070105

Selvakumar, J., Lakshmi, A., & Arivoli, T. (2012). Brain Tumor Segmentation and Its Area Calculation in Brain MR Images using K-Mean Clustering and Fuzzy C-Mean Algorithm, *IEEE-International Conference on Advances in Engineering, Science and Management*, pp, 186–190.

KEY TERMS AND DEFINITIONS

Cluster Analysis: Statistical procedure by which data or objects are sub-divided into groups (clusters) such that the elements in a cluster are incredibly similar (but may not be identical) to each other and very dissimilar from the elements present in other clusters.

Cluster Sampling: It is a method by which cluster groups of sample components (and not individual elements) are chosen from a population for the purpose of analyzing them.

Digital Image: It is a numerical depiction of a two-dimensional image in binary form. Generally, digital image refers to raster or bit-mapped images.

Edge Detection: An edge is a boundary or contour in an image at which a momentous alteration may be found in its physical aspect, like surface reflectance, clarification or distance of the detectable surfaces from the observer. Edge detection is generally determined by detecting discontinuities in intensity of the image.

Image Sampling: For making it appropriate for digital processing, an image function $f(x,y)$ have to be digitized both spatially and in amplitude. Normally, a digitizer is used to sample and quantize an analogue image.

Performance Metrics: Performance evaluation is based on the use of performance indicators. Such indicators express the qualities of an image segmentation method. A typical performance indicator includes – precision, robustness, flexibility, consistency and feasibility of an algorithm to time and space.

Region-Based Segmentation: It is a simple region growing-based image segmentation approach. It is also referred as *pixel-based image segmentation* as it engrosses the selection of primary pixels. In this method, the neighboring pixels of initially selected pixel-center are examined to determine whether they can be added to the region. The process is continued iteratively till convergence is reached.

APPENDIX

Structural Content (SC): $SC = \sum\limits_{i=1}^{m} \sum\limits_{j=1}^{n} in(i,j)^2 \Big/ \sum\limits_{i=1}^{m} \sum\limits_{j=1}^{n} seg(i,j)^2$

Root Mean Square Error (RMSE): $RMSE = \sqrt{\dfrac{1}{m*n}\left[\dfrac{\sum\limits_{i=1}^{m}\sum\limits_{j=1}^{n}\left[in(i,j)\right]^2}{\sum\limits_{i=1}^{m}\sum\limits_{j=1}^{n}\left[in(i,j)-seg(i,j)\right]^2}\right]}$

Peak Signal–to–Noise Ratio (PSNR): $PSNR = 20\log_{10}\left(\dfrac{N}{RMSE}\right)dB$

Mean Absolute Error (MAE): $MAE = \dfrac{1}{MN}\sum\limits_{i=1}^{M}\sum\limits_{i=1}^{N}\left(\left| f(i,j) - f^{'}(i,j) \right|\right)$

Euclidean distance measure: $D_{ij} = \left(\sum\limits_{l=1}^{d}\left| x_{il} - x_{jl} \right|^2\right)^{1/2}$

Figure 6. Column (a): input images, column (b), (c), and (d): its corresponding segmented three clustered images using proposed Enhance Clustering Method

Compilation of References

966L Wheel Loader, Caterpillar, AEHQ6211-01 (07-2011)

Abdel-Aty, M. A., & Radwan, A. E. (2000). Modeling traffic accident occurrence and involvement. *Accident; Analysis and Prevention, 32*(5), 633–642. doi:10.1016/S0001-4575(99)00094-9 PMID:10908135

Aggarwal, M., & Kent, R. (2005). Genetic Algorithm Based Scheduler for Computational Grids. *Proceedings of the 19th International Symposium on High Performance Computing Systems and Applications (HPCS '05).* 10.1109/HPCS.2005.27

Ahmed, M. J., Sarfraz, M., Zidouri, A., & Alkhatib, W. G. (2003). License Plate Recognition System. *Proceedings of The 10th IEEE International Conference On Electronics, Circuits And Systems (ICECS2003).*

Aishwarya, S.R., & Rai, A., Charitha, Prasanth, M.A, & Savitha, S.C. (2015). An IoT based vehicle accident prevention and tracking system for night drivers. *International Journal of Innovative Research in Computer and Communication Engineering, 3*(4), 3493–3499.

Akbari, R., Mohammadi, A., & Ziarati, K. (2009, 14-15 Dec. 2009). *A powerful bee swarm optimization algorithm.* Paper presented at the Multitopic Conference, 2009. INMIC 2009. IEEE 13th International.

Akbari, R., Hedayatzadeh, R., Ziarati, K., & Hassanizadeh, B. (2012). A multi-objective artificial bee colony algorithm. *Swarm and Evolutionary Computation, 2*, 39–52. doi:10.1016/j.swevo.2011.08.001

Akhter S, Rahman R, Islam A. (2016). Neural Network Based Route Weight Computation for Bi-directional Traffic Management System. *International Journal of Applied Evolutionary Computation, 7*(4), 45–59.

Alba, E., & Luque, G. (2007). *A new local search algorithm for the DNA fragment assembly problem.* Paper presented in Evolutionary Computation in Combinatorial Optimization, EvoCOP'07, Valencia, Spain. doi:10.1007/978-3-540-71615-0_1

Alba, E., Luque, G., & Minetti, G. (2008). Seeding strategies and recombination operators for solving the DNA fragment assembly problem. *Information Processing Letters, 108*(3), 94–100. doi:.ipl.2008.04.00510.1016/j

Alba, E., & Dorronsoro, B. (2008). *Cellular genetic algorithms.* Heidelberg, Germany: Springer-Verlag.

Ali, S., Siegel, H. J., Maheswaran, H. D., & Ali, S. (2000). Representing Task and Machine Heterogeneities for Heterogeneous Computing Systems. *Tamkang Journal of Science and Engineering, 3*(3), 195–207.

Almishari, M., Gasti, P., Nathan, N., & Tsudik, G. (2014). Optimizing Bi-Directional Low-Latency Communication in Named Data Networking. *Computer Communication Review, 44*(1).

Aloul, F., Sagahyroon, A., Nahle, A., Dehn, M. A., & Anani, R. A. (2012). GuideME: An Effective RFID-Based Traffic Monitoring System. *Proc. of IASTED-International Conference on Advances in Computer Science and Engineering (ACSE).* 10.2316/P.2012.770-036

Amitesh Kumar, E. R. (2012). Hydraulic Regenerative Braking System. *International Journal of Scientific & Engineering Research, 3*(4).

Andersen, T. O., Hansen, M. R., & Pedersen, H. C. (2005). Regeneration of potential energy in hydraulic forklift trucks. *Fluid Power Transmission and Control ICFP, 2005*, 302–306.

Andruch & Lumkes Jr. (n.d.). Balance of Power: hydraulic-powered add to vehicle efficiency, reduce emissions. *Technology Today*.

Andruch, J., III, & Lumkes, J. H., Jr. (2010). *U.S. Patent Application 13/498,769*. US Patent Office.

Angel, A., Hickman, M., Mirchandani, P., & Chandnani, D. (2003). Methods of Analyzing Traffic Imagery Collected From Aerial Platforms. *IEEE Transactions on Intelligent Transportation Systems, 4*(2), 99–107. doi:10.1109/TITS.2003.821208

Angeleri, E., Apolloni, B., de Falco, D., & Grandi, L. (1999). DNA fragment assembly using neural prediction techniques. *International Journal of Neural Systems, 9*(6), 523–544. doi:10.1142/S0129065799000563 PMID:10651335

Anitha, T., & Uppalaigh, T. (2016). Android based home automation using Raspberry pi. *International Journal of Innovative Technologies., 4*(1), 2351–8665.

Ankerst, M., Breunig, M. M., Kriegel, H. P., & Sander, J. (1999). OPTICS: Ordering Points To Identify the Clustering Structure. *Proceedings ACM SIGMOD '99 Conference on Management of Data (SIGMOD '99)*, 49–60. 10.1145/304182.304187

ANPR. (2014, Apr 9). *Automatic Number Plate Recognition (ANPR)*. Retrieved from: http://www.gmp.police.uk/content/section.html?readform&s=353EDD067D20552880025796100399283

Ansari, A. Q., Philip, J., Siddiqui, S. A., & Alvi, J. A. (2010). Fuzzification of intuitionistic fuzzy sets. *International Journal of Computational Cognition, 8*(3).

Arikan, F. (2013). A fuzzy solution approach for multi objective supplier selection. *Expert Systems with Applications, 40*(3), 947–952. doi:10.1016/j.eswa.2012.05.051

Arikan, F. Z., & Gungor, Z. (2007). A two-phased solution approach for multi-objective programming problems with fuzzy coefficients. *Information Sciences, 177*(23), 5191–5202. doi:10.1016/j.ins.2007.06.023

Arthur, D., & Vassilvitskii, S. (2007). K-Means++: The advantages of careful seeding. *Proceedings of the eighteenth annual ACM-SIAM symposium on Discrete algorithms*, 1027–1035.

Ashena, R., & Moghadasi, J. (2011). Bottom hole pressure estimation using evolved neural networks by real coded ant colony optimization and genetic algorithm. *Journal of Petroleum Science Engineering, 77*(3–4), 375–385. doi:10.1016/j.petrol.2011.04.015

Askari, S., Montazerin, N., & Zarandi, M. F. (2015). A clustering based forecasting algorithm for multivariable fuzzy time series using linear combinations of independent variables. *Applied Soft Computing, 35*, 151–160. doi:10.1016/j.asoc.2015.06.028

Assas, O. (2015). Improvement of 2-Partition Entropy Approach Using Type-2 Fuzzy Sets for Image Thresholding. *International Journal of Applied Evolutionary Computation, 6*(3), 33–48. doi:10.4018/IJAEC.2015070103

Atanassov, K. T. (1986). Intuitionistic fuzzy sets. *Fuzzy Sets and Systems, 20*(1), 87–96. doi:10.1016/S0165-0114(86)80034-3

Aussem, A., Murtagh, F., & Sarazin, M. (1994). Dynamical recurrent neural networks and pattern recognition methods for time series prediction: Application to seeing and temperature forecasting in the context of ESO's VLT astronomical weather station. *Vistas in Astronomy, 38*, 357-374.

Aydin, M. E., Wu, J., & Liang, Z. (2010). *Swarms of Metaheuristic Agents: A Model for Collective intelligence.* Paper presented at the P2P, Parallel, Grid, Cloud and Internet Computing (3PGCIC), 2010 International Conference on.

Azar, A. T., & Hassanien, A. E. (2015). Dimensionality reduction of medical big data using neural-fuzzy classifier. *Soft Computing*, *19*(4), 1115–1127. doi:10.100700500-014-1327-4

Bäck, T. (1996). *Evolutionary Algorithms in Theory and Practice: Evolution Strategies, Evolutionary Programming, Genetic Algorithms.* New York: Oxford University Press.

Bai, Y., Wu, S., & Tsai, C. (2012). Design and implementation of a fall monitor system by using a 3-axis accelerometer in a smart phone. *Proceedings of the 16th International Symposium on Consumer Electronics (ISCE).*

Baker, T. L., Egelja, A. M., Peterson, R. N., VerKuilen, M. T., & Yoshino, T. (2010). *U.S. Patent No. 7,832,208.* Washington, DC: U.S. Patent and Trademark Office.

Bakhta, M., & Ghalem, B. (2014). Clustering by Swarm Intelligence in the Ad-Hoc Networks. *International Journal of Applied Evolutionary Computation*, *5*(3), 1–13. doi:10.4018/ijaec.2014070101

Bakhtan, M. A. H., Abdullah, M., & Rahman, A. A. (2016). A review on License Plate Recognition system algorithms. In *International Conference on Information and Communication Technology (ICICTM)* (pp. 84 – 89). IEEE Xplore.

Bandyopadhyay, L. K., Chaulya, S. K., & Mishra, P. K. (2010). *Wireless Communication in Underground Mines.* RFID-Based Sensor Networking. doi:10.1007/978-0-387-98165-9

Bandyopadhyay, L. K., Mishra, P. K., Kumar, S., Selvendran, D., & Chaulya, S. K. (2007). Studies on radio frequency propagation characteristics for underground coalmine communications. *Indian Journal of Radio & Space Physics*, *36*(5), 418.

Battiti, R. (1994). Using mutual information for selecting features in supervised neural net learning. *IEEE Transactions on Neural Networks*, *5*(4), 537–550. doi:10.1109/72.298224 PMID:18267827

Behnam, Z., & Isa, M. (2013). A New Radial Basis Function Artificial Neural Network based Recognition for Kurdish Manuscript. *International Journal of Applied Evolutionary Computation*, *4*(4), 72–87. doi:10.4018/ijaec.2013100105

Bellman, R. E., & Zadeh, L. A. (1970). Decision-making in a fuzzy environment. *Management Science*, *17*(4), 141–164. doi:10.1287/mnsc.17.4.B141

Benitez, J. M., Castro, J. L., Mantas, C. J., & Rojas, E. (2001). A Neuro-Fuzzy Approach for Feature Selection. *IFSA World Congress and 20th NAFIPS International Conference, Joint 9th.* DOI: 10.1109/NAFIPS.2001.944742

Bergquist, U., Girard, J. R., & Raszga, C. L. (2007). *U.S. Patent No. 7,249,457.* Washington, DC: U.S. Patent and Trademark Office.

Berman, F., Casanova, H., Chien, A., Cooper, K., Dail, H., Dasgupta, A., ... YarKhan, A. (2005). New grid scheduling and rescheduling methods in the GrADS project. *International Journal of Parallel Programming*, *33*(2-3), 209–229. doi:10.100710766-005-3584-4

Bermudez, I., Traverso, S., Mellia, M., & Munao, M. (2013). Exploring the cloud from passive measurements: The Amazon AWS case. Proceedings of IEEE INFOCOM, 230-234.

Berrichi, A., Amodeo, L., Yalaoui, F., Châtelet, E., & Mezghiche, M. (2009). Bi-objective optimization algorithms for joint production and maintenance scheduling: Application to the parallel machine problem. *Journal of Intelligent Manufacturing*, *20*(4), 389–400. doi:10.100710845-008-0113-5

Berrichi, A., Yalaoui, F., Amodeo, L., & Mezghiche, M. (2010). Bi-objective ant colony optimization approach to optimize production and maintenance scheduling. *Computers & Operations Research*, *37*(9), 1584–1596. doi:10.1016/j.cor.2009.11.017

Bezdek, J. C., & Castelaz, P. F. (1977). Prototype Classification and Feature Selection with Fuzzy Sets. *IEEE Transactions on Systems, Man, and Cybernetics*, *7*(2), 87–92. doi:10.1109/TSMC.1977.4309659

Bhattacharya, A., Geraghty, J., & Young, P. (2010). Supplier selection paradigm: An integrated hierarchical QFD methodology under multiple-criteria environment. *Applied Soft Computing*, *10*(4), 1013–1027. doi:10.1016/j.asoc.2010.05.025

Bhuyan, J. N. (1991). Genetic algorithm for clustering with an ordered representation. *Proceedings of the fourth International Conference on Information Retrieval*, 408-417.

Bianco, L., Caramia, M., Giordani, S., & Mari, R. (2015). Grid scheduling by bilevel programming: A heuristic approach. *European Journal of Industrial Engineering*, *9*(1), 101–125. doi:10.1504/EJIE.2015.067450

Bisht, K., & Kumar, S. (2016). Fuzzy time series forecasting method based on hesitant fuzzy sets. *Expert Systems with Applications*, *64*, 557–568. doi:10.1016/j.eswa.2016.07.044

Biswas, S. K., Bordoloi, M., Singh, H. R., & Purkayasthaya, B. (2016). A NeuroFuzzy RuleBased Classifier Using Important Features and Top Linguistic Features. *International Journal of Intelligent Information Technologies*, *12*(3), 38–50. doi:10.4018/IJIIT.2016070103

Blaha, P., Schwarz, K., Madsen, G. K. H., Kvasnicka, D., & Luitz, J. (2001). *WIEN2k: An Augmented Plane Wave plus Local Orbitals Program for Calculating Crystal Properties*. Vienna University of Technology.

Blythe, J., Jain, S., Deelman, E., Gil, Y., Vahi, K., Mandal, A., & Kennedy, K. (2005). Task scheduling strategies for workflow-based applications in grids. In *Cluster Computing and the Grid, 2005. CCGrid 2005. IEEE International Symposium on* (Vol. 2, pp. 759-767). IEEE. 10.1109/CCGRID.2005.1558639

Bocicor, M. I., Czibula, G., & Czibula, I. G. (2011). A reinforcement learning approach for solving the fragment assembly problem. In *Proceedings of 13th International Symposium on Symbolic and Numeric Algorithms for Scientific Computing* (pp. 191-198). Academic Press. 10.1109/SYNASC.2011.9

Bonabeau, E., Dorigo, M., & Theraulaz, G. (1999). Swarm Intelligence: From natural to artificial systems (No.1). Oxford University Press.

Bonabeau, E., Dorigo, M., & Theraulaz, G. (1999). *Swarm Intelligence: From Natural to Artificial Systems*. Oxford University Press.

Boudia, M. A., Hamou, R. M., & Amine, A. (2016). A New Approach Based on the Detection of Opinion by SentiWordNet for Automatic Text Summaries by Extraction. *International Journal of Information Retrieval Research*, *6*(3), 19–36. doi:10.4018/IJIRR.2016070102

Boudia, M. A., Hamou, R. M., Amine, A., & Rahmani, A. (2015). A New Biomimetic Method Based on the Power Saves of Social Bees for Automatic Summaries of Texts by Extraction. *International Journal of Software Science and Computational Intelligence*, *7*(1), 18–38. doi:10.4018/IJSSCI.2015010102

Boudia, M. A., Hamou, R. M., Amine, A., Rahmani, M. E., & Rahmani, A. (2015, May). A new multi-layered approach for automatic text summaries mono-document based on social spiders. *In IFIP International Conference on Computer Science and its Applications_x000D_* (pp. 193-204). Springer, Cham. 10.1007/978-3-319-19578-0_16

Bradley, D. A., & Seward, D. W. (1998). The development, control and operation of an autonomous robotic excavator. *Journal of Intelligent & Robotic Systems*, *21*(1), 73–97. doi:10.1023/A:1007932011161

Bradley, D. A., Seward, D. W., Mann, J. E., & Goodwin, M. R. (1993). Artificial intelligence in the control and operation of construction plant the autonomous robot excavator. *Automation in Construction*, *2*(3), 217–228. doi:10.1016/0926-5805(93)90042-V

Braga, M. D. V., & Meidanis, J. (2002). An algorithm that builds a set of strings given its overlap graph. *Lecture Notes in Computer Science*, *2286*, 52–63. doi:10.1007/3-540-45995-2_10

Braun, T. D., Siegel, H. J., Beck, N., Bölöni, L. L., Maheswaran, M., Reuther, A. I., ... Freund, R. F. (2001). A comparison of eleven static heuristics for mapping a class of independent tasks onto heterogeneous distributed computing systems. *Journal of Parallel and Distributed Computing*, *61*(6), 810–837. doi:10.1006/jpdc.2000.1714

Bruun, L. (2003). *U.S. Patent No. 6,584,769*. Washington, DC: U.S. Patent and Trademark Office.

Budny, E., Chlosta, M., & Gutkowski, W. (2003). Optimal control of an excavator bucket positioning. *NIST Special Publication*, 481-488.

Budny, E., Chłosta, M., & Gutkowski, W. (2003). Load-independent control of a hydraulic excavator. *Automation in Construction*, *12*(3), 245–254. doi:10.1016/S0926-5805(02)00088-2

Bukhari, S., Al Azawi, M., Shafait, F., & Breuel, T. (2010). Document image segmentation using discriminative learning over connected components. In *Proceedings of the 8th IAPR International Workshop on Document Analysis Systems* (pp. 183–190). ACM. 10.1145/1815330.1815354

Bullock, D. M., & Oppenheim, I. J. (1992). Object-oriented programming in robotics research for excavation. *Journal of Computing in Civil Engineering*, *6*(3), 370–385. doi:10.1061/(ASCE)0887-3801(1992)6:3(370)

Burks, C., Engle, M., Forrest, S., Parsons, R. J., Soderlund, C., & Stolorz, P. (1994). *Stochastic optimization tools for genomic sequence assembly*. London, UK: Academic Press. doi:10.1016/B978-0-08-092639-1.50038-1

Büyüközkan, G., & Çiftçi, G. (2011). A novel fuzzy multi-criteria decision framework for sustainable supplier selection with incomplete information. *Computers in Industry*, *62*(2), 164–174. doi:10.1016/j.compind.2010.10.009

Büyüközkan, G., & Çiftçi, G. (2012). A novel hybrid MCDM approach based on fuzzy DEMATEL, fuzzy ANP & fuzzy TOPSIS to evaluate green suppliers. *Expert Systems with Applications*, *39*(3), 3000–3011. doi:10.1016/j.eswa.2011.08.162

Buyya, R., Abraham, A., & Nath, B. (2000). Nature's heuristics for scheduling jobs on computational grids. *Proceedings of 8th IEEE International Conference on Advanced Computing and Communications (ADCOM2000)*, 45–52.

Buyya, R., & Murshed, M. (2002). GridSim: A Toolkit for Modeling and Simulation of Grid Resource Management and Scheduling. *Concurrency and Computation*, *14*(13-15), 1175–1220. doi:10.1002/cpe.710

Cantú-Paz, E. (1998). A survey of parallel genetic algorithms. *Calculateurs paralleles, reseaux et systems repartis*, *10*(2), 141-171.

Cao, J., Jarvis, S. A., Saini, S., & Nudd, G. R. (2003). Gridflow: Workflow management for grid computing. In *Cluster Computing and the Grid, 2003. Proceedings. CCGrid 2003. 3rd IEEE/ACM International Symposium on* (pp. 198-205). IEEE.

Castellano, G., Castiello, C., Fanelli, A. M., & Mencar, C. (2003). Discovering Prediction Rules by a NeuroFuzzy Modeling Framework. Knowledge-Based Intelligent Information and Engineering Systems, 2773, 1242–1248.

CCTV Information. (n.d.). *An introduction to ANPR*. Retrieved 2018-02-03 from https://www.cctv-information.co.uk/i/An_Introduction_to_ANPR

Cetisli, B. (2010). Development of an adaptive neuro-fuzzy classifier using linguistic hedges: Part 1. *Expert Systems with Applications*, *37*(8), 6093–6101. doi:10.1016/j.eswa.2010.02.108

Ch. Sanjeev Kumar, D., Ajit Kumar, B., Satchidananda, D., & Sung-Bae, C. (2013). Differential Evolution-Based Optimization of Kernel Parameters in Radial Basis Function Networks for Classification. *International Journal of Applied Evolutionary Computation*, *4*(1), 56–80. doi:10.4018/jaec.2013010104

Chaisson, M., Pevzner, P., & Tang, H. (2004). Fragment assembly with short reads. *Bioinformatics (Oxford, England)*, *20*(13), 2067–2074. doi:10.1093/bioinformatics/bth205 PMID:15059830

Chakraborty, D., & Pal, N. R. (2001). Integrated feature analysis and fuzzy rule-based System identification in a neuro-fuzzy paradigm. Systems, Man, and Cybernetics, Part B. *Cybernetics*, *31*(3), 391–400. PMID:18244802

Chakraborty, D., & Pal, N. R. (2004). A neuro-fuzzy scheme for simultaneous feature selection and fuzzy rule-based classification. *Neural Networks*, *15*(1), 110–123. doi:10.1109/TNN.2003.820557 PMID:15387252

Chakravarty, S., Bisoi, R., & Dash, P. K. (2016). A Hybrid Kernel Extreme Learning Machine and Improved Cat Swarm Optimization for Microarray Medical Data Classification. *International Journal of Applied Evolutionary Computation*, *7*(3), 71–100. doi:10.4018/IJAEC.2016070104

Chakravarty, S., Dash, P. K., Pandi, V. R., & Panigrahi, B. K. (2011). An Evolutionary Functional Link Neural Fuzzy Model for Financial Time Series Forecasting. *International Journal of Applied Evolutionary Computation*, *2*(3), 39–58. doi:10.4018/jaec.2011070104

Chamodrakas, I., Batis, D., & Martakos, D. (2010). Supplier selection in electronic marketplaces using satisficing and fuzzy AHP. *Expert Systems with Applications*, *37*(1), 490–498. doi:10.1016/j.eswa.2009.05.043

Chandrashekar, G., & Sahin, F. (2014). A survey on feature selection methods. *Computers & Electrical Engineering*, *40*(1), 16–28. doi:10.1016/j.compeleceng.2013.11.024

Chang, J. M., Di Tommaso, P., Taly, J. F., & Notredame, C. (2012). Accurate multiple sequence alignment of transmembrane proteins with PSI-Coffee. *BMC Bioinformatics*, *13*(Suppl 4), S1. doi:10.1186/1471-2105-13-S4-S1 PMID:22536955

Chang, L. Y., & Chen, W. C. (2005). Data mining of tree-based model to analyze freeway accident frequency. *Journal of Safety Research*, *36*(4), 365–375. doi:10.1016/j.jsr.2005.06.013 PMID:16253276

Chang, P. H., & Lee, S. J. (2002). A straight-line motion tracking control of hydraulic excavator system. *Mechatronics*, *12*(1), 119–138. doi:10.1016/S0957-4158(01)00014-9

Chang, P. H., & Park, S. H. (1998, June). The development of anti-windup scheme and stick-slip compensator for time delay control. In *American Control Conference, 1998. Proceedings of the 1998* (Vol. 6, pp. 3629-3633). IEEE. 10.1109/ACC.1998.703290

Chang, W., & Lawler, E. (1990). Approximate string matching in sublinear expected time. In *Proceedings of the 31st IEEE Symposium on Foundations of Computer Science* (pp. 118-124). IEEE. 10.1109/FSCS.1990.89530

Charalampidis, D., & Muldrey, B. (2009). Clustering using multilayer perceptrons. *Nonlinear Analysis: Theory, Methods & Applications*, *71*(12), e2807–e2813.

Chehri, A., & Mouftah, H. (2012). An empirical link-quality analysis for wireless sensor networks. In *Computing, Networking and Communications (ICNC), 2012 International Conference on* (pp. 164–169). Academic Press. 10.1109/ICCNC.2012.6167403

Chellapilla, K., & Fogel, G. B. (1999). Multiple sequence alignment using evolutionary programming. In *Evolutionary Computation, 1999. CEC 99. Proceedings of the 1999 Congress on (Vol. 1)*. IEEE.

Chen, C., Duan, S., Cai, T., & Liu, B. (2011). Online 24-h solar power forecasting based on weather type classification using artificial neural network. *Solar Energy, 85*(11), 2856–2870. doi:10.1016/j.solener.2011.08.027

Chengzhi, C., Yifan, W., Lichao, J., & Yang, L. (2008). *Research on optimization of speed identification based on ACO-BP neural network and application*. Paper presented at the Intelligent Control and Automation, 2008. WCICA 2008. 7th World Congress on.

Chen, M. Y., & Chen, B. T. (2015). A hybrid fuzzy time series model based on granular computing for stock price forecasting. *Information Sciences, 294*, 227–241. doi:10.1016/j.ins.2014.09.038

Chen, S. M. (1996). Forecasting enrollments based on fuzzy time series. *Fuzzy Sets and Systems, 81*(3), 311–319. doi:10.1016/0165-0114(95)00220-0

Chen, S. M., Chu, H. P., & Sheu, T. W. (2012). TAIEX forecasting using fuzzy time series and automatically generated weights of multiple factors. *IEEE Transactions on Systems, Man, and Cybernetics. Part A, Systems and Humans, 42*(6), 1485–1495. doi:10.1109/TSMCA.2012.2190399

Chen, S. M., & Phuong, B. D. H. (2017). Fuzzy time series forecasting based on optimal partitions of intervals and optimal weighting vectors. *Knowledge-Based Systems, 118*, 204–216. doi:10.1016/j.knosys.2016.11.019

Chen, Y. C., Pal, N. R., & Chung, I. F. (2012). An Integrated Mechanism for Feature Selection and Fuzzy Rule Extraction for Classification. *IEEE Transactions on Fuzzy Systems, 20*(4), 683–698. doi:10.1109/TFUZZ.2011.2181852

Chen, Y., & Chao, R. (2012). Supplier selection using consistent fuzzy preference relations. *Expert Systems with Applications, 39*(3), 3233–3240. doi:10.1016/j.eswa.2011.09.010

Cherney, M. J., & Radke, D. D. (2006). *U.S. Patent No. 7,124,576*. Washington, DC: U.S. Patent and Trademark Office.

Cheshmehgaz, H. R., Islam, M. N., & Desa, M. I. (2014). A polar-based guided multi-objective evolutionary algorithm to search for optimal solutions interested by decision-makers in a logistics network design problem. *Journal of Intelligent Manufacturing, 25*(4), 699–726. doi:10.100710845-012-0714-x

Chevreux, B. (2005). *MIRA: An automated genome and EST assembler* (Ph.D thesis). German Cancer Research Center, Heidelberg, Germany.

Che, Z. H. (2012). Clustering and selecting suppliers based on simulated annealing algorithms. *Computers & Mathematics with Applications (Oxford, England), 63*(1), 228–238. doi:10.1016/j.camwa.2011.11.014

Chiang, M. C., Tsai, C. W., & Yang, C. S. (2011). A time efficient pattern reduction algorithm for K-Means clustering. Information Sciences, (181), 716–731.

Churchill, G., Burks, C., Eggert, M., Engle, M., & Waterman, M. (1993). *Assembling DNA sequence fragments by shuffling and simulated annealing (Tech. Rep. No. LAUR 93-2287)*. Academic Press.

Clerc, M. (2003). TRIBES Un exemple d'optimisation par essaim particulaire sans paramètres de réglage. OEP'03 (Optimisation par Essaim Particulaire), Paris, France.

Clerc, M. (2005), L'optimisation par essaims particulaires, versions paramétriques et adaptatives. Hermès Science.

Coello, C. A. C., Pulido, G. T., & Lechuga, M. S. (2004). Handling multiple objectives with particle swarm optimization. *IEEE Transactions on Evolutionary Computation, 8*(3), 256–279. doi:10.1109/TEVC.2004.826067

Coello, C. C., Lamont, G. B., & Van Veldhuizen, D. A. (2007). *Evolutionary algorithms for solving multi-objective problems*. Springer Science & Business Media.

Coleman, G. B., & Andrews, H. C. (1979). Image segmentation by clustering. *Proceedings of the IEEE, 67*(5), 773–785. doi:10.1109/PROC.1979.11327

Colorni, A., Dorigo, M., Maffioli, F., Maniezzo, V., Righini, G., & Trubian, M. (1996). Heuristics from nature for hard combinatorial optimization problems. *International Transactions in Operational Research, 3*(1), 1–21. doi:10.1111/j.1475-3995.1996.tb00032.x

Comelli, P., Ferragina, P., Granieri, M. N., & Stabile, F. (1995). Optical recognition of motor vehicle license plates. *IEEE Transactions on Vehicular Technology, 44*(4), 790–799. doi:10.1109/25.467963

Cooren, Y., Clerc, M., & Siarry, P. (2008). Initialization and Displacement of the Particles in TRIBES, a Parameter-Free Particle Swarm Optimization Algorithm, Springer. *Studies in Computational Intelligence, 136*, 199–219.

Coull, S. E., & Szymanski, B. K. (2008). Sequence alignment for masquerade detection. *Computational Statistics & Data Analysis, 52*(8), 4116–4131. doi:10.1016/j.csda.2008.01.022

Cowell, J., & Hussain, F. (2002). A Fast Recognition System for Isolated Arabic Characters. In *Proceedings Sixth International Conference on Information and Visualisation*. IEEE Computer Society. 10.1109/IV.2002.1028844

Dash, M., & Liu, H. (1997). Feature Selection for Classification. *Intelligent Data Analysis, 1*(1-4), 131–156. doi:10.1016/S1088-467X(97)00008-5

Das, S., Abraham, A., & Konar, A. (2008). Swarm intelligence algorithms in bioinformatics. In *Computational Intelligence in Bioinformatics* (pp. 113–147). Springer Berlin Heidelberg. doi:10.1007/978-3-540-76803-6_4

Davidović, T., Šelmić, M., Teodorović, D., & Ramljak, D. (n.d.). Bee colony optimization for scheduling independent tasks to identical processors. *Journal of Heuristics*, 1-21. doi:10.100710732-012-9197-3

Deb, K. (2011). Multi-objective optimisation using evolutionary algorithms: an introduction. In *Multi-objective evolutionary optimisation for product design and manufacturing* (pp. 3–34). Springer London. doi:10.1007/978-0-85729-652-8_1

Deb, K. (2014). *Multi-objective optimization. In Search methodologies* (pp. 403–449). Springer.

Deb, K., & Jain, S. (2002). Running Performance Metrics for Evolutionary Multi-Objective Optimization. *Proceedings of the Fourth Asia-Pacific Conference on Simulated Evolution and Learning (SEAL'02)*, 13-20.

Deb, K., Mohan, M., & Mishra, S. (2003). *A Fast Multi-objective Evolutionary Algorithm for Finding Well-Spread Pareto-Optimal Solutions, KanGAL Report Number: 2003002*. Kanpur, India: Indian Institute of Technology.

Deb, K., Pratap, A., Agarwal, S., & Meyarivan, T. (2002). A fast and elitist multiobjective genetic algorithm: NSGA-II. *IEEE Transactions on Evolutionary Computation, 6*(2), 182–197. doi:10.1109/4235.996017

Deb, K., Sundar, J., Udaya Bhaskara, R. N., & Chaudhuri, S. (2006). Reference point based multi-objective optimization using evolutionary algorithms. *International Journal of Computational Intelligence Research, 2*(3), 273–286. doi:10.5019/j.ijcir.2006.67

Deelman, E., Blythe, J., Gil, Y., Kesselman, C., Mehta, G., Vahi, K., ... Koranda, S. (2003). Mapping abstract complex workflows onto grid environments. *Journal of Grid Computing, 1*(1), 25–39. doi:10.1023/A:1024000426962

Deneubourg, J.-L., Goss, S., Franks, N. R., Sendova-Franks, A., Detrain, C., & Chretien, L. (1990) The dynamics of collective sorting: robot-like ant and ant-like robots. *Proceedings of the First International Conference on Simulation of Adaptive Behavior*.

Deng, W., Wang, G., Zhang, X., Xu, J., & Li, G. (2016). A multi-granularity combined prediction model based on fuzzy trend forecasting and particle swarm techniques. *Neurocomputing*, *173*, 1671–1682. doi:10.1016/j.neucom.2015.09.040

Depaire, B., Wets, G., & Vanhoof, K. (2008). Traffic accident segmentation by means of latent class clustering. *Accident Analysis and Prevention, 40*(4).

De, R. K., Basak, J., & Pal, S. K. (1999). Neuro-fuzzy feature evaluation with theoretical analysis. *Neural Networks*, *12*(10), 1429–1455. doi:10.1016/S0893-6080(99)00079-9 PMID:12662626

De, R. K., Pal, N. R., & Pal, S. K. (1997). Feature analysis: Neural network and fuzzy set theoretic approaches. *Pattern Recognition*, *30*(10), 1579–1590. doi:10.1016/S0031-3203(96)00190-2

DGMS Standard Note. (2016). Retrieved from http://dgms.gov.in/writereaddata/UploadFile/STD-NOTE-1-1-2016636047840119597695.pdf

Dhar, A. (2008). *Traffc and Road Condition Monitoring System. M.Tech report*. Bombay: Indian Institute of Technology. Available at http://citeseerx.ist.psu.edu/viewdoc/download?doi=10.1.1.518.2687&rep=rep1&type=pdf

Di Martino, V., & Mililotti, M. (2004). Sub optimal scheduling in a grid using genetic algorithms. *Parallel Computing*, *30*(5-6), 553–565. doi:10.1016/j.parco.2003.12.004

Diaz, D., Theodoulidis, B., & Dupouy, C. (2016). Modelling and forecasting interest rates during stages of the economic cycle: A knowledge-discovery approach. *Expert Systems with Applications*, *44*, 245–264. doi:10.1016/j.eswa.2015.09.010

Dickson, G. W. (1966). An analysis of vendor selection: Systems and decisions. *Journal of Purchasing*, *2*(1), 5–17. doi:10.1111/j.1745-493X.1966.tb00818.x

Dijkstra's Algorithm. (2015, May 25). Retrieved from: https://en.wikipedia.org/wiki/Dijkstra's_algorithm

Dorigo, M., & Di Caro, G. (1999). Ant colony optimization: a new meta-heuristic. *Evolutionary Computation, 1999. CEC 99. Proceedings of the 1999 Congress on.*

Dorigo, C. A., & Maniez, M. (1991). *Distributed optimization by ant colonies*. Elsevier Publishing.

Dorronsoro, B., Alba, E., Luque, G., & Bouvry, P. (2008). A self-adaptive cellular memetic algorithm for the DNA fragment assembly problem. In *Proceedings of IEEE Congress on Evolutionary Computation* (pp. 2651-2658). IEEE. 10.1109/CEC.2008.4631154

Dotoli, M., & Falagario, M. (2012). A Hierarchical Model for Optimal Supplier Selection in Multiple Sourcing Contexts. *International Journal of Production Research*, *50*(11), 2953–2967. doi:10.1080/00207543.2011.578167

Du, K. L., & Swamy, M. N. S. (2014). Introduction to Fuzzy Sets and Fuzzy Logic. Springer.

Dubois, D., & Prade, H. (1980). Fuzzy sets and systems: theory and applications. New York: Academic Press.

Dziczkowski, G., & Wegrzyn-Wolska, K. (2008). Tool of the Intelligence Economic: Recognition Function of Reviews Critics - Extraction and Linguistic Analysis of Sentiments. *ICSOFT (ISDM/ABF) 2008*, 218-223.

Eberhart, R. C., & Shi, Y. J. K. (2001). Swarm Intelligence. Morgan Kaufmann.

Eberhart, R. C., & Kennedy, J. (1995). Particle Swarm Optimization. *Proceedings of IEEE International Conference on Neural Networks*, *4*, 1942–1948. 10.1109/ICNN.1995.488968

Eberhart, R. C., & Shi, Y. (2000). Comparing inertia weights and constriction factors in particle swarm optimization. *Proceedings of the 2000 Congress on Retrieval Information*. 10.1109/CEC.2000.870279

Edgar, R. C. (2004). MUSCLE: Multiple sequence alignment with high accuracy and high throughput. *Nucleic Acids Research*, *32*(5), 1792–1797. doi:10.1093/nar/gkh340 PMID:15034147

Efendi, R., Ismail, Z., & Deris, M. M. (2015). A new linguistic out-sample approach of fuzzy time series for daily forecasting of Malaysian electricity load demand. *Applied Soft Computing*, *28*, 422–430. doi:10.1016/j.asoc.2014.11.043

Eiamkanitchat, N., Theera-Umpon, N., & Auephanwiriyakul, S. (2010). A Novel Neuro-fuzzy Method for Linguistic Feature Selection and Rule-Based Classification. In *Computer and Automation Engineering (ICCAE)* (pp. 247-252). IEEE.

Elhajj, M., Younes, R., Charles, S., & Padiolleau, E. (2014). Calibration of the Parameters of a Model of an Engineering System Using the Global Optimization Method. *International Journal of Applied Evolutionary Computation*, *5*(3), 28. doi:10.4018/ijaec.2014070102

Endo, H., Maruta, K., & Yoshida, N. (2000). *U.S. Patent No. 6,151,894*. Washington, DC: U.S. Patent and Trademark Office.

Eren, T. (2010). A bicriteria m-machine flowshop scheduling with sequence-dependent setup times. *Applied Mathematical Modelling*, *34*(2), 284–293. doi:10.1016/j.apm.2009.04.005

Faccio, M., Ries, J., & Saggiorno, N. (2015). Simulated annealing approach to solve dual resource constrained job shop scheduling problems: Layout impact analysis on solution quality. *International Journal of Mathematics in Operational Research*, *7*(6), 609–629. doi:10.1504/IJMOR.2015.072274

Fahringer, T., Jugravu, A., Pllana, S., Prodan, R., Seragiotto, C., & Truong, H. L. (2005). ASKALON: A tool set for cluster and Grid computing. *Concurrency and Computation*, *17*(2-4), 143–169. doi:10.1002/cpe.929

Falkenauer, E. (1994). A new representation and operators for genetic algorithms applied to grouping problems. *Evolutionary Computation*, *2*(2), 1994. doi:10.1162/evco.1994.2.2.123

Fan, H., Wu, R., Liao, B., & Lu, X. (2012). An Improved Genetic Algorithm for Multiple Sequence Alignment. *Journal of Computational and Theoretical Nanoscience*, *9*(10), 1558–1564. doi:10.1166/jctn.2012.2244

Fan, X., Lei, Y., Wang, Y., & Lu, Y. (2016). Long-term intuitionistic fuzzy time series forecasting model based on vector quantisation and curve similarity measure. *IET Signal Processing*, *10*(7), 805–814. doi:10.1049/iet-spr.2015.0496

Farhadinia, B. (2014). Correlation for dual hesitant fuzzy sets and dual interval-valued hesitant fuzzy sets. *International Journal of Intelligent Systems*, *29*(2), 184–205. doi:10.1002/int.21633

Fayyad, U. M. (1996). Data mining and knowledge discovery: Making sense out of data. *IEEE Expert*, *11*(5), 20–25. doi:10.1109/64.539013

Feng, B., Fan, Z., & Li, Y. (2011). A decision method for supplier selection in multi-service outsourcing. *International Journal of Production Economics*, *132*(2), 240–250. doi:10.1016/j.ijpe.2011.04.014

Ferreira, C. E., de Souza, C. C., & Wakabayashi, Y. (2002). Rearrangement of DNA fragments: A branch-and-cut algorithm. *Discrete Applied Mathematics*, *116*(1/2), 161–177. doi:10.1016/S0166-218X(00)00324-3

Filipi, Z., Louca, L., Daran, B., Lin, C.-C., Yildir, U., Wu, B., ... Chapp, R. (2004). Combined Optimisation of Design and Power Management of the Hydraulic Hybrid Propulsion System for the 6 × 6 Medium Truck. *International Journal of Heavy Vehicle Systems*, *11*(3/4), 372–402. doi:10.1504/IJHVS.2004.005458

Firoz, J. S., Rahman, M. S., & Saha, T. K. (2012). Bee algorithms for solving DNA fragment assembly problem with noisy and noiseless data. In *Proceedings of the Conference on Genetic and Evolutionary Computation, GECCO'12*. Philadelphia: GECCO. 10.1145/2330163.2330192

Florios, K., Mavrotas, G., & Diakoulaki, D. (2010). Solving multiobjective, multiconstraint knapsack problems using mathematical programming and evolutionary algorithms. *European Journal of Operational Research, 203*(1), 14–21. doi:10.1016/j.ejor.2009.06.024

Fogel, D. B., & Simpson, P. K. (1993) Evolving fuzzy clusters. *Proceedings of ICNN93.*

Forooshani, A. E., Bashir, S., Michelson, D. G., & Noghanian, S. (2013). A survey of wireless communications and propagation modeling in underground mines. *IEEE Communications Surveys and Tutorials, 15*(4), 1524–1545. doi:10.1109/SURV.2013.031413.00130

Frawley, W. J., Piatetsky-Shapiro, G., & Matheus, C. (1991). Knowledge Discovery. In *Databases, chapter Knowledge Discovery In Databases: An Overview.* Cambridge, MA: AAAI Press/MIT Press.

Galaviz, P. M., Lopez, A. R., & Garcia, M. J. S. (2005). I.H.P. Torres. Algorithm of Clustering for Color Image segmentation. In *International Conference on Electronics, Communications and Computers (CONIELECOMP 2005)* (pp. 306–310). IEEE. 10.1109/CONIEL.2005.16

Gao, Y., Rong, H., & Huang, J. Z. (2005). Adaptive Grid job scheduling with genetic algorithms. *Future Generation Computer Systems, 21*(1), 151–161. doi:10.1016/j.future.2004.09.033

Gazi, V., & Passino, K. M. (2011). *Swarm stability and optimization.* Swarm Stability and Optimization; doi:10.1007/978-3-642-18041-5

Geretti, L., & Abramo, A. (2011). The Synthesis of a Stochastic Artificial Neural Network Application Using a Genetic Algorithm Approach. In W. H. Peter (Ed.), Advances in Imaging and Electron Physics (Vol. 168, pp. 1-63). Elsevier.

Ghazali, R., Jaafar Hussain, A., Mohd Nawi, N., & Mohamad, B. (2009). Non-stationary and stationary prediction of financial time series using dynamic ridge polynomial neural network. *Neurocomputing, 72*(10–12), 2359–2367. doi:10.1016/j.neucom.2008.12.005

Ghorpade, D. D., & Patki, A. M. (2016). IoT Based Smart Home Automation Using Renewable Energy Sources. *International Journal of Advanced Research in Electrical Electronics and Instrumental Engineering, 5*(7), 6065–6072.

Ghosh, A., Shankar, B. U., & Meher, S. K. (2009). A novel approach to neuro-fuzzy classification. *Neural Networks, 22*(1), 100–109. doi:10.1016/j.neunet.2008.09.011 PMID:19004614

Ghosh, S., Biswas, S., Sarkar, D., & Sarkar, P. P. (2014). A Novel Neuro-Fuzzy Classification Technique for data mining. *Egyptian Informatics Journal, 15*(3), 129–147. doi:10.1016/j.eij.2014.08.001

Ghosh, T. K., & Das, S. (2016). A Hybrid Algorithm Using Genetic Algorithm and Cuckoo Search Algorithm to Solve Job Scheduling Problem in Computational Grid Systems. *International Journal of Applied Evolutionary Computation, 7*(2), 1–11. doi:10.4018/IJAEC.2016040101

Ghosh, T. K., & Das, S. (2016). A Modified Binary PSO Algorithm for Scheduling Independent Jobs in Grid Computing System. *International Journal of Next-Generation Computing, 7*(2), 144–154.

Ghosh, T. K., Das, S., Barman, S., & Goswami, R. (2017). Job Scheduling in Computational Grid Based on an Improved Cuckoo Search Method. *International Journal of Computer Applications in Technology. Inderscience, 55*(2), 138–146.

Goldberg, D. E. (1989). Genetic algorithm in search, Optimization and machine Learning. Addison-Wesley.

Goldberg, D. E. (2006). *Genetic algorithms.* Pearson Education India.

Gondro, C., & Kinghorn, B. P. (2007). A simple genetic algorithm for multiple sequence alignment. *Genetics and Molecular Research, 6*(4), 964–982. PMID:18058716

Google Maps. (2015, May 10). Retrieved from: http://en.wikipedia.org/wiki/Google_Maps

Gori, M., & Tesi, A. (1992). On the problem of local minima in backpropagation. *Pattern Analysis and Machine Intelligence. IEEE Transactions on, 14*(1), 76–86. doi:10.1109/34.107014

Goss, S., Aron, S., Deneubourg, J. L., & Pasteels, J. M. (1989). _Self-Organized Shortcuts *Proceedings of the Argentine Conference, Naturwissenchaften, 76*, 579-581.

Goswami, R., Ghosh, T. K., & Barman, S. (2011). Local search based approach in Grid scheduling using simulated annealing. *Proceedings of IEEE International Conference on Computer and Communication Technology (ICCCT)*. 10.1109/ICCCT.2011.6075112

Gotadki, S., Mohan, R., Attarwala, M., & Gajare, M. P. (2014). Intelligent Ambulance. *International Journal of Engineering and Technical Research, 2*(4).

Grace, M. H., & Karazija, A. (1976). *U.S. Patent No. 3,947,744*. Washington, DC: U.S. Patent and Trademark Office.

Grande, J., Suárez, M. R., & Villar, J. R. (2007). A Feature Selection Method Using a Fuzzy Mutual Information Measure. *Innovations in Hybrid Intelligent Systems, 44*, 56–63. doi:10.1007/978-3-540-74972-1_9

Guo, P., Cheng, W., & Wang, Y. (2014). Parallel machine scheduling with step-deteriorating jobs and setup times by a hybrid discrete cuckoo search algorithm. *Engineering Optimization*, 1-22.

Gupta, L., Jain, R., & Vaszkun, G. (2016). Survey of Important Issues in UAV Communication Networks. *IEEE Communications Surveys and Tutorials, 18*(2), 1123–1152. doi:10.1109/COMST.2015.2495297

Guyon, I., & Elisseeff, A. (2003). An Introduction to Variable and Feature Selection. *Journal of Machine Learning Research, 3*, 1157–1182.

Habiba, M., & Akhter, S. (2017). Exploring Cloud-Based Distributed Disaster Management With Dynamic Multi-Agents Workflow System. *Smart Technologies for Emergency Response and Disaster Management*, 167-195.

Habiba, M., & Akhter, S. (2012). *MAS Workflow Model and Scheduling Algorithm for Disaster Management System. In Cloud Computing Technologies, Applications and Management*. ICCCTAM.

Habiba, M., & Akhter, S. (2013). A Cloud Based Natural Disaster Management System. *International Conference on Grid and Pervasive Computing*, 152-161. 10.1007/978-3-642-38027-3_16

Hagan, M. T., Demuth, H. B., Beale, M. H., & Jesús, O. D. (1995). Neural Network Design (2nd ed.). Academic Press.

Hainsworth, D. W. (2001). Teleoperation user interfaces for mining robotics. *Autonomous Robots, 11*(1), 19–28. doi:10.1023/A:1011299910904

Halima, D., Abdesslem, L., & Salim, C. (2014). A Binary Cuckoo Search Algorithm for Graph Coloring Problem. *International Journal of Applied Evolutionary Computation, 5*(3), 42–56. doi:10.4018/ijaec.2014070103

Hämäläinen, M., Talvitie, J., Hovinen, V., & Leppänen, P. (1998). Wideband radio channel measurement in a mine. In *Spread Spectrum Techniques and Applications, 1998. Proceedings., 1998 IEEE 5th International Symposium on* (Vol. 2, pp. 522–526). IEEE. 10.1109/ISSSTA.1998.723839

Hamami, L., & Berkani, D. (2002). Recognition System for Printed Multi-Font and Multi-Size Arabic Characters. *Arabian Journal for Science and Engineering, 27*(No. 1B), 57–72.

Hamane, R., Itoh, T., & Tomita, K. (2009). Approximation Algorithms for the Highway Problem under the Coupon Model. *IEICE Transactions on Fundamentals of Electronics, Communications and Computer Science, 92*(8), 1779–1786. doi:10.1587/transfun.E92.A.1779

Hamby, D. M. (1995). A comparison of sensitivity analysis techniques. *Health Physics, 68*(2), 195–204. doi:10.1097/00004032-199502000-00005 PMID:7814253

Hamidi, S., Naghibzadeh, M., & Sadri, J. (2013, August). Protein multiple sequence alignment based on secondary structure similarity. In *Advances in Computing, Communications and Informatics (ICACCI), 2013 International Conference on* (pp. 1224-1229). IEEE. 10.1109/ICACCI.2013.6637352

Hamou, Abdelmalek, & Mohamed. (2012). Visualization and clustering by 3D cellular automata: Application to unstructured data. *International Journal of Data Mining and Emerging Technologies, 2*(1).

Hamou, R. M., Lehireche, A., Lokbani, A. C., & Rahmani, M. (2010). Clustering Based on the n-grams by Bio Inspired Method (Immune Systems). *International Refereed Research Journal (ResearchersWorls), 1*(1).

Hamou, R. M., Lehireche, A., Lokbani, A. C., & Rahmani, M. (2010). Representation of textual documents by the approach wordnet and n-grams for the unsupervised classifcation (clustering) with 2D cellular automata:a comparative study. *Journal of Computer and Information Science, 3*(3), 240-255.

Hamou, R. M. (2012). A New Biomimetic Approach Based on Social Spiders for Clustering of Text, Software Engineering Research, Management and Applications 2012. *Studies in Computational Intelligence, Springer, 430/2012*, 17–30. doi:10.1007/978-3-642-30460-6_2

Han, K., & Kim, J. (2002). Quantum inspired evolutionary algorithm for a class of combinatorial optimization. *IEEE Transactions on Evolutionary Computation, 6*(6), 580-593.

Hansen, H., Kristensen, A. W., Kohler, M. P., Mikkelsen, A. W., Pedersen, J. M., & Trangeled, M. (2002). *Automatic Recognition of License Plates*. Institute for Electronic System, Aalborg University.

Harish, S., Jagdish Chand, B., Arya, K. V., & Kusum, D. (2012). Dynamic Swarm Artificial Bee Colony Algorithm. *International Journal of Applied Evolutionary Computation, 3*(4), 19–33. doi:10.4018/jaec.2012100102

Harman, M. (2007). *The current state and future of search based software engineering.* Paper presented at the 2007 Future of Software Engineering. 10.1109/FOSE.2007.29

Hatamlou, A., Abdullah, S., & Nezamabadi-pour, H. (2012). A combined approach for clustering based on K-Means and gravitational search algorithms. Swarm and Evolutionary Computation, (6), 47-52.

Hatamlou, A. (2013). Black hole: A new heuristic optimization approach for data clustering. *Information Sciences, 222*, 175–184. doi:10.1016/j.ins.2012.08.023

Haupt, R. L., & Haupt, S. E. (2004). *Practical Genetic Algorithms*. New York: John Wiley & Sons.

Hayashi, Y., Buckley, J. J., & Czogala, E. (1992). Fuzzy Neural Network with Fuzzy Signals and Weights. *International Joint Conference on Neural Networks, IJCNN, 2*, 696 - 701. 10.1109/IJCNN.1992.226906

Hayat, S., Yanmaz, E., & Muzaffar, R. (2016). Survey on Unmanned Aerial Vehicle Networks for Civil Applications: A Communications Viewpoint. *IEEE Communications Surveys and Tutorials, 18*(4), 2624–2661. doi:10.1109/COMST.2016.2560343

Haykin, S. (1999). *Neural Networks: A Comprehensive Foundation*. Prentice Hall Inc.

Hernandez, D., Francois, P., Farinelli, L., Osteras, M., & Schrenzel, J. (2008). De novo bacterial genome sequencing: Millions of very short reads assembled on a desktop computer. *Genome Research*, *18*(5), 802–809. doi:10.1101/gr.072033.107 PMID:18332092

Hilas, C. S., & Mastorocostas, P. A. (2008). An application of supervised and unsupervised learning approaches to telecommunications fraud detection. *Knowledge-Based Systems*, *21*(7), 721–726. doi:10.1016/j.knosys.2008.03.026

Hirata, T., Izumi, E., Tanaka, Y., Watanabe, H., & Yoshida, K. (1990). *U.S. Patent No. 4,967,557*. Washington, DC: U.S. Patent and Trademark Office.

Hirochi. (1995). A Stereo Vision System using Multi Slit Lights for Underground Vehicle. *Proc. of the 2nd Asian Conference on Computer Vision, 2*, 326-330.

Hochreiter, S., & Schmidhuber, J. (1997). Long Short-Term Memory. *Neural Computation*, *9*(8), 1735–1780. doi:10.1162/neco.1997.9.8.1735 PMID:9377276

Holland, J. H. (1975). Adaptation in Natural and Artificial Systems. University of Michigan Press.

Hollingsworth, D. (1994). *Workflow Management Coalition*. The Workflow Reference Model, TC00-1003.

Holt, B. J., Krone, J., & Nippert, A. (2003). *U.S. Patent No. 6,655,136*. Washington, DC: U.S. Patent and Trademark Office.

Hongwen, Y., & Rui, M. (2006). *Design A Novel Neural Network Clustering Algorithm Based on PSO and Application*. Paper presented at the Intelligent Control and Automation, 2006. WCICA 2006. The Sixth World Congress on.

Hontani, H., & Koga, T. (2001). Character Extraction Method Without Prior Knowledge on Size and Information. *Proceedings of the IEEE International Vehicle Electronics Conference (IVEC'01)*, 67-72. 10.1109/IVEC.2001.961728

Hornik, K., Stinchcombe, M., & White, H. (1989). Multilayer feedforward networks are universal approximators. *Neural Networks*, *2*(5), 359–366. doi:10.1016/0893-6080(89)90020-8

Ho, W., Xu, X. D., & Prasanta, K. (2010). Multi-criteria decision making approaches for supplier evaluation and selection: A literature review. *European Journal of Operational Research*, *202*(1), 16–24. doi:10.1016/j.ejor.2009.05.009

HTML5 Web Sockets. (2015, May 10). *A Quantum Leap in Scalability for the Web*. Retrieved from: http://www.websocket.org/quantum.html

Huang, C. L., & Tsai, C. Y. (2009). A hybrid SOFM-SVR with a filter-based feature selection for stock market forecasting. *Expert Systems with Applications*, *36*(2), 1529–1539. doi:10.1016/j.eswa.2007.11.062

Huang, K. W., Chen, J. L., Yang, C. S., & Tsai, C. W. (2015). A memetic particle swarm optimization algorithm for solving the DNA fragment assembly problem. *Neural Computing & Applications*, *26*(3), 495–506. doi:10.100700521-014-1659-0

Huang, K. W., Chen, J. L., Yang, C. S., & Tsai, C. W. (2016). A memetic gravitation search algorithm for solving DNA fragment assembly problems. *Journal of Intelligent & Fuzzy Systems*, *30*(4), 2245–2255. doi:10.3233/IFS-151994

Huang, X. (1992). A contig assembly program based on sensitive detection of fragment overlaps. *Genomics*, *14*(1), 18–25. doi:10.1016/S0888-7543(05)80277-0 PMID:1427824

Huang, X., & Madan, A. (1999). CAP3 sequence assembly program. *Genome Research*, *9*(9), 868–877. doi:10.1101/gr.9.9.868 PMID:10508846

Huang, X., Wang, J., Aluru, S., Yang, S. P., & Hillier, L. (2003). PCAP: A whole-genome assembly program. *Genome Research*, *13*(9), 2164–2170. doi:10.1101/gr.1390403 PMID:12952883

Hui, S., & Junqing, J. (2010). Research on the system configuration and energy control strategy for parallel hydraulic hybrid loader. *Automation in Construction, 19*(2), 213-220.

Hulbert, J. N. (2012). *Local navigation of mobile robots in mining environments*. Colorado School of Mines. Arthur Lakes Library.

Hung, K. C., & Lin, K. P. (2013). Long-term business cycle forecasting through a potential intuitionistic fuzzy least-squares support vector regression approach. *Information Sciences, 224*, 37–48. doi:10.1016/j.ins.2012.10.033

Hussain, F., Sharma, A., Bhatnagar, S., & Goyal, S. (2011). GPS and GSM based Accident Monitoring System. *International Journal of Scientific Research and Management Studies, 2*(12), 473–480.

Hussein, A. M., & Abdullah, R. (2017, May). Protein multiple sequence alignment by basic flower pollination algorithm. In *Information Technology (ICIT), 2017 8th International Conference on* (pp. 833-838). IEEE.

Huu, Ahamad, Jong, Kyoung, & Jin. (2012). *Tracking control of hydraulic actuator with energy saving using independent metering valves*. 16th International conference on mechatronics technology, Tianjin, China.

Ilea, D., & Whelan, P. (2006). Color image segmentation using a spatial k-means clustering algorithm. *Proceedings of the Irish Machine Vision & Image Processing Conference*, 146–53.

Imran, M., Manzoor, Z., Ali, S., & Abbas, Q. (2011). *Modified Particle Swarm Optimization with student T mutation (STPSO)*. Paper presented at the Computer Networks and Information Technology (ICCNIT), 2011 International Conference on.

Inoue, H. (2008). Introduction of PC200-8 hybrid hydraulic excavators. Komatsu Technical Report. Vol.54 NO.161. "Hydraulic excavator equipped with generator operated by revolution", Kondo Hiroshi.

Ishibuchi, H., Fujioka, R., & Tanaka, H. (1993, May). Neural Networks That Learn from Fuzzy If-Then Rules. *IEEE Transactions on Fuzzy Systems, 1*(2), 85–97. doi:10.1109/91.227388

Issa, M., & Hassanien, A. E. (2017). Multiple Sequence Alignment Optimization Using Meta-Heuristic Techniques. In *Handbook of Research on Machine Learning Innovations and Trends* (pp. 409–423). IGI Global. doi:10.4018/978-1-5225-2229-4.ch018

Izakian, H., Ladani, B. T., Zamanifar, K., & Abraham, A. (2009). A novel particle swarm optimization approach for grid job scheduling. In Information Systems, Technology and Management (pp. 100-109). Springer Berlin Heidelberg. doi:10.1007/978-3-642-00405-6_14

Jain A.K., & Dubes, R.C. (1988). *Algorithms for Clustering Data*. Prentice Hall Advanced Reference Series.

Jalam, R. (2003). *Apprentissage automatique et catégorisation de textes multilingues* (PhD thesis). Université Lumière Lyon 2.

Jang, J. S. R. (1993). Adaptive network based fuzzy inference systems. *IEEE Transactions on Systems, Man, and Cybernetics, 23*(3), 665–685. doi:10.1109/21.256541

Jayakumar, J., & Arock, M. (2016). Cellular Automata-Based PSO Algorithm for Aligning Multiple Molecular Sequences. *International Journal of Applied Evolutionary Computation, 7*(1), 1–15. doi:10.4018/IJAEC.2016010101

Jeck, W. R., Reinhardt, J. A., Baltrus, D. A., Hickenbotham, M. T., Magrini, V., & Mardis, E. R. (2007). Extending assembly of short DNA sequences to handle error. *Bioinformatics (Oxford, England), 23*(21), 2942–2944. doi:/btm45110.1093/bioinformatics

Jeet, K. (2017). Fuzzy Flow Shop Scheduling Using Grey Wolf Optimization Algorithm. *Indian Journal of Social Research, 7*(2), 167–171.

Jeet, K., Dhir, R., & Sharma, S. (2016a). Bi-criteria parallel machine scheduling using nature-inspired hybrid flower pollination algorithm. *International Journal of Metaheuristics, 5*(3-4), 226–253. doi:10.1504/IJMHEUR.2016.081153

Jeet, K., Dhir, R., & Sharma, S. (2016b). Meta-Heuristic Algorithms to Solve Bi-Criteria Parallel Machines Scheduling Problem. *International Journal of Applied Evolutionary Computation, 7*(2), 76–96. doi:10.4018/IJAEC.2016040105

Jeet, K., Dhir, R., & Singh, P. (2016). Hybrid Black Hole Algorithm for Bi-Criteria Job Scheduling on Parallel Machines. *International Journal of Intelligent Systems & Applications, 8*(4), 1–17. doi:10.5815/ijisa.2016.04.01

Jeyanthi, P., & Kumar, V. (2010). Image Classification by K-means Clustering. *Advances in Computational Sciences and Technology, 3*(1), 1–8.

Jones, D. R., & Beltramo, M. A. (1991). Solving partitioning problems with genetic algorithms. In *Proceedings of the Fourth International Conference on Genetic Algorithms*. San Diego, CA: Morgan Kaufmann.

Jones, D. F., Mirrazavi, S. K., & Tamiz, M. (2002). Multiobjective meta-heuristics: An overview of the current state-of-the-art. *European Journal of Operational Research, 137*(1), 1–9. doi:10.1016/S0377-2217(01)00123-0

Joshi, B., & Kumar, S. (2012). A computational method of forecasting based on intuitionistic fuzzy sets and fuzzy time series. In *Proceedings of the International Conference on Soft Computing for Problem Solving (SocProS 2011) December 20-22, 2011* (pp. 993-1000). Springer Berlin/Heidelberg. 10.1007/978-81-322-0491-6_91

Joshi, B. P., & Kumar, S. (2012). Fuzzy time series model based on intuitionistic fuzzy sets for empirical research in stock market. *International Journal of Applied Evolutionary Computation, 3*(4), 71–84. doi:10.4018/jaec.2012100105

Kabir, M. (2010). A new wrapper feature selection approach using neural network. *Neurocomputing, 73*(16-18), 3273–3283. doi:10.1016/j.neucom.2010.04.003

Kacem, I., & Haouari, M. (2009). Approximation algorithms for single machine scheduling with one unavailability period. *4OR: A Quarterly Journal of Operations Research, 7*(1), 79-92. doi:10.100710288-008-0076-6

Kagoshima, M., & Kinugawa, H. (2001). *U.S. Patent No. 6,199,307*. Washington, DC: U.S. Patent and Trademark Office.

Kagoshima, M., Komiyama, M., Nanjo, T., & Tsutsui, I. A. (2007). Development of new hybrid excavator. *Kobelco Technology Review*, (27), 39–42.

Kamruzzaman, S. M., Fernando, X., Jaseemuddin, M., & Farjow, W. (2017). Reliable Communication Network for Emergency Response and Disaster Management in Underground Mines. *Smart Technologies for Emergency Response and Disaster Management*, 41–85. 10.4018/978-1-5225-2575-2.ch002

Karaboga, D., & Akay, B. (2007). *Artificial Bee Colony (ABC) Algorithm on Training Artificial Neural Networks*. Paper presented at the Signal Processing and Communications Applications, 2007. SIU 2007. IEEE 15th.

Karaboga, D., & Gorkemli, B. (2011). *A combinatorial Artificial Bee Colony algorithm for traveling salesman problem*. Paper presented at the Innovations in Intelligent Systems and Applications (INISTA), 2011 International Symposium on.

Karaboga, D., Akay, B., & Ozturk, C. (2007). Artificial Bee Colony (ABC) Optimization Algorithm for Training Feed-Forward Neural Networks Modeling Decisions for Artificial Intelligence. Springer Berlin.

Karande, I., Deshpande, G., Kumbhar, S., & Deshmukh, A. V. (2016). Intelligent Anti-Theft Tracking and Accident Detection System for Automobiles Based on Internet of Things. *International Journal of Innovative Research in Computer and Communication Engineering, 4*(3), 4142–4149.

Kar-Erik Rydberg. (2004). Hydraulic Accumulators as Key Components. In *Energy Efficient Mobile Systems*. Linköping University.

Karimi, M. (2014). Hybrid Discrete Particle Swarm Optimization for Task Scheduling in Grid Computing. *International Journal of Grid and Distributed Computing*, 7(4), 93–104. doi:10.14257/ijgdc.2014.7.4.09

Karlaftis, M. G., & Tarko, A. P. (1998). Heterogeneity considerations in accident modeling. *Accident; Analysis and Prevention*, 30(4), 425–433. doi:10.1016/S0001-4575(97)00122-X PMID:9666239

Kar, S., Das, S., & Ghosh, P. K. (2014). Applications of neuro fuzzy systems: A brief review and future outline. *Applied Soft Computing*, 15, 243–259. doi:10.1016/j.asoc.2013.10.014

Kasabov, N. K. (1996). Learning fuzzy rules and approximate reasoning in fuzzy neural networks and hybrid systems. *Fuzzy Sets and Systems*, 82(2), 135–149. doi:10.1016/0165-0114(95)00300-2

Kashani, T., Mohaymany, A. S., & Rajbari, A. A. (2011). data mining approach to identify key factors of traffic injury severity. *PROMET- Traffic & Transportation*, 23(1). Retrieved from http://www.fpz.unizg.hr/traffic/index.php/PROMTT/article/view/144/51

Kasprzyczak, L., Szwejkowski, P., & Cader, M. (2016). Robotics in mining exemplified by Mobile Inspection Platform. *Mining--Informatics, Automation and Electrical Engineering, 54*.

Kasprzyczak, L., Trenczek, S., & Cader, M. (2012). Robot for monitoring hazardous environments as a mechatronic product. *Journal of Automation Mobile Robotics and Intelligent Systems*, 6, 57–64.

Katoh, K., & Standley, D. M. (2013). MAFFT multiple sequence alignment software version 7: Improvements in performance and usability. *Molecular Biology and Evolution*, 30(4), 772–780. doi:10.1093/molbev/mst010 PMID:23329690

Katrasnik, T., Trenc, F., & Opresnik, S. R. (2007). Analysis of energy conversion efficiency in parallel and series hybrid powertrains. *Vehicular Technology. IEEE Transactions on*, 56(6), 3649–3659.

Kaur, J., Agrawal, S., & Vig, R. (2012). A Methodology for the Performance Analysis of Cluster Based Image Segmentation. *International Journal of Engineering Research and Applications*, 2(2), 664–667.

Kawashima, K., & Sugiyama, Y. (2010). *U.S. Patent Application 13/376,932*. US Patent Office.

Kaya, M., Sarhan, A., & Alhajj, R. (2014). Multiple sequence alignment with affine gap by using multi-objective genetic algorithm. *Computer Methods and Programs in Biomedicine*, 114(1), 38–49. doi:10.1016/j.cmpb.2014.01.013 PMID:24534604

Kchouk, M., & Elloumi, M. (2016, December). A clustering approach for denovo assembly using Next Generation Sequencing data. In *Bioinformatics and Biomedicine (BIBM), 2016 IEEE International Conference on* (pp. 1909-1911). IEEE. 10.1109/BIBM.2016.7822812

Kennedy, J., & Eberhart, R. (1995). Particle swarm optimization. *Neural Networks, 1995. Proceedings., IEEE International Conference on*.

Khalil, R. E. (2010). *U.S. Patent No. 7,775,040*. Washington, DC: U.S. Patent and Trademark Office.

Khalilabad, N. D., & Hassanpour, H. (2017). Employing image processing techniques for cancer detection using microarray images. *Computers in Biology and Medicine*, 81, 139–147. doi:10.1016/j.compbiomed.2016.12.012 PMID:28061369

Khayat, O., Ebadzadeh, M. M., Shahdoosti, H. R., Rajaei, R., & Khajehnasiri, I. (2009). A novel hybrid algorithm for creating self-organizing fuzzy neural networks. *Neurocomputing*, 73(1-3), 517–524. doi:10.1016/j.neucom.2009.06.013

Kikuchi, S., & Chakraborty, G. (2006). Heuristically tuned GA to solve genome fragment assembly problem. In *Proceedings of IEEE Congress on Evolutionary Computation CEC'06* (pp. 1491-1498). IEEE. 10.1109/CEC.2006.1688485

Kim, G. M. (1997). The Automatic Recognition of the Plate of Vehicle Using the Correlation Coefficient and Hough Transform. *Journal of Control Automation and System Engineering*, *3*(5), 511–519.

Kim, K. K., Kim, K. I., Kim, J. B., & Kim, H. J. (2000). Learning Based Approach for License Plate Recognition. *Proceedings of IEEE Processing Society Workshop on Neural Networks for Signal Processing*, *2*, 614-623. 10.1109/NNSP.2000.890140

Kinugawa, H., & Komiyama, M. (1999). *U.S. Patent No. 5,913,811*. Washington, DC: U.S. Patent and Trademark Office.

Kirkpatrick, S., Gelatt, C. D., & Vecchi, M. P. (1983). Optimization by Simulated Annealing. *Science*, *220*(4598), 671–680. doi:10.1126cience.220.4598.671 PMID:17813860

Ko, A. W. Y., & Lau, H. Y. K. (2009). Intelligent robot-assisted humanitarian search and rescue system. *International Journal of Advanced Robotic Systems*, *6*(2), 121–128. doi:10.5772/6792

Kohavi, R., & John, G. H. (1997, December). Wrappers for feature subset selection. *Artificial Intelligence*, *97*(1-2), 273–324. doi:10.1016/S0004-3702(97)00043-X

Koivo, A. J. (1992). Controlling an Intelligent Excavator for Autonomous Digging in Difficult Ground. *Proc. the 9th International Symposium on Automation and Construction*.

Kolodziej, J., & Khan, S. U. (2012). Multi-level hierarchical genetic-based scheduling of independent jobs in dynamic heterogeneous grid environment. *Information Sciences*, *214*, 1–19. doi:10.1016/j.ins.2012.05.016

Kolodziej, J., & Xhafa, F. (2011). Enhancing the Genetic-Based Scheduling in Computational Grids by a Structured Hierarchical Population. *Journal of Future Generation Computer Systems.*, *27*(8), 1035–1046. doi:10.1016/j.future.2011.04.011

Konak, A., Coit, D. W., & Smith, A. E. (2006). Multi-objective optimization using genetic algorithms: A tutorial. *Reliability Engineering & System Safety*, *91*(9), 992–1007. doi:10.1016/j.ress.2005.11.018

Korane, K. (2008). *Energy recovery systems on hydraulic excavators*. Hydraulics and Pneumatics, Parker Hanninfin.

Kraft TeleRobotics. (1994). *Haz-Trak: Force Feedback Excavator and Material Handling System*. Kraft TeleRobotics, Inc.

Kubalik, J., Buryan, P., & Wagner, L. (2010). Solving the DNA fragment assembly problem efficiently using iterative optimization with evolved hypermutations. In *Proceedings of the 12th Annual Conference on Genetic and Evolutionary Computation, GECCO'10*, (pp. 213-214). GECCO. 10.1145/1830483.1830522

Kulkarni, U. V., & Shinde, S. V. (2013). Hybrid fuzzy classifier based on feature-wise membership given by artificial neural network. *Fourth International Conference on Computing, Communications and Networking Technologies (ICCCNT)*. 10.1109/ICCCNT.2013.6726549

Kumar, S., Dutta, K., & Mookerjee, V. (2009). Maximizing business value by optimal assignment of jobs to resources in grid computing. *European Journal of Operational Research*, *194*(3), 856–872. doi:10.1016/j.ejor.2007.12.024

Kumar, S., & Gangwar, S. S. (2016). Intuitionistic Fuzzy Time Series: An Approach for Handling Nondeterminism in Time Series Forecasting. *IEEE Transactions on Fuzzy Systems*, *24*(6), 1270–1281. doi:10.1109/TFUZZ.2015.2507582

Kumar, S., & Toshniwal, D. (2015). A data mining framework to analyze road accident data. *Journal of Big Data*, *2*(26).

Kuo, R. J., & Lin, Y. J. (2012). Supplier selection using analytic network process and data envelopment analysis. *International Journal of Production Research*, *50*(11), 2852–2863. doi:10.1080/00207543.2011.559487

Lai, X., & Guan, C. (2013). A Parameter Matching Method of the Parallel Hydraulic Hybrid Excavator Optimized with Genetic Algorithm. *Mathematical Problems in Engineering*, 2013.

Lakshmi, C. V., & Balakrishnan, J. R. (2012). Automatic Accident Detection via Embedded GSM message interface with Sensor Technology. *International Journal of Scientific and Research Publication*, 2(4).

Lalwani, S., Kumar, R., & Gupta, N. (2017). Efficient Two-Level Swarm Intelligence Approach for Multiple Sequence Alignment. *Computer Information*, 35(4), 963–985.

Laumanns, M., Thiele, L., Dev, K., & Zitzler, E. (2002). Combining Convergence and Diversity in Evolutionary Multi-Objective Optimization. *Evolutionary Computation*, 10(3), 263–282. doi:10.1162/106365602760234108 PMID:12227996

Lawrence, P. D., Salcudean, S. E., Sepehri, N., Chan, D., Bachmann, S., Parker, & Frenette, R. (1997). Coordinated and force-feedback control of hydraulic excavators. In Experimental Robotics IV (pp. 181-194). Springer Berlin Heidelberg.

Lawrence, S., & Giles, C. L. (1998). Context and Page Analysis for Improved Web Search. *IEEE Internet Computing*, 2(4), 38–46. doi:10.1109/4236.707689

Lee, C. C. (1993). *A Study on the Design of Fuzzy Logic Controller for Bucket Tip Leveling of Hydraulic excavator* (PhD thesis). Seoul National University. (in Korean)

Lee, S. U., & Chang, P. H. (2001). Control of a heavy-duty robotic excavator using time delay control with switching action with integral sliding surface. In *Robotics and Automation, 2001. Proceedings 2001 ICRA. IEEE International Conference on* (Vol. 4, pp. 3955-3960). IEEE.

Lee, E. R., Kim, P. K., & Kim, H. J. (1994). Automatic Recognition of a Car License Plate using Color Image Processing. *IEEE International Conference on Image Processing*, 2, 301-305. 10.1109/ICIP.1994.413580

Lee, H. L. (2000). Creating value through supply chain integration. *Supply Chain Management Review*, 4(4), 30–36.

Lee, H. M., Chen, C. M., Chen, J. M., & Jou, Y. L. (2001). An Efficient Fuzzy Classifier with Feature Selection Based on Fuzzy Entropy. *IEEE Transactions on Systems, Man, and Cybernetics. Part B, Cybernetics*, 31(3), 426–432. doi:10.1109/3477.931536 PMID:18244807

Lee, L. W., Wang, L. H., & Chen, S. M. (2007). Temperature prediction and TAIFEX forecasting based on fuzzy logical relationships and genetic algorithms. *Expert Systems with Applications*, 33(3), 539–550. doi:10.1016/j.eswa.2006.05.015

Lei, X. J., Sun, J. J., & Ma, Q. Z. (2009). Multiple sequence alignment based on chaotic PSO. In *Computational Intelligence and Intelligent Systems* (pp. 351–360). Springer Berlin Heidelberg. doi:10.1007/978-3-642-04962-0_40

Leng, J., Valli, C., & Armstrong, L. (2010). A Wrapper-based Feature Selection for Analysis of Large Data Sets. *3rd International Conference on Computer and Electrical Engineering (ICCEE)*, V1-166-V1-170.

Levenberg, K. (1944). A method for the solution of certain problems in least squares. *Quarterly of Applied Mathematics*, 2(2), 164–168. doi:10.1090/qam/10666

Lewis, D. (1992). *Representation and Learning in Information Retrieval* (Ph.D. thesis). Department of Computer Science, University of Massachusetts.

Liang, X., & Virvalo, T. (2001). Energy reutilization and balance analysis. *Proceedings of the Fifth International Conference on Fluid Power Transmission and Control (ICFP)*.

Li, J.-Q., Pan, Q.-K., & Tasgetiren, M. F. (2014). A discrete artificial bee colony algorithm for the multi-objective flexible job-shop scheduling problem with maintenance activities. *Applied Mathematical Modelling*, 38(3), 1111–1132. doi:10.1016/j.apm.2013.07.038

Lin, T., & Wang, Q. (2012). Hydraulic accumulator-motor-generator energy regeneration system for a hybrid hydraulic excavator. *Chinese Journal of Mechanical Engineering, 25*(6), 1121–1129. doi:10.3901/CJME.2012.06.1121

Lin, T., Wang, Q., Hu, B., & Gong, W. (2010). Development of hybrid powered hydraulic construction machinery. *Automation in Construction, 19*(1), 11–19. doi:10.1016/j.autcon.2009.09.005

Lin, T., Wang, Q., Hu, B., & Gong, W. (2010). Research on the energy regeneration systems for hybrid hydraulic excavators. *Automation in Construction, 19*(8), 1016–1026. doi:10.1016/j.autcon.2010.08.002

Li, P., Kupfer, K. C., Davies, C. J., Burbee, D., Evans, G. A., & Garner, H. R. (1997). PRIMO: A primer design program that applies base quality statistics for automated large-scale DNA sequencing. *Genomics, 40*(3), 476–485. doi:10.1006/geno.1996.4560 PMID:9073516

Li, R. P., Mukaidono, M., & Turkse, I. B. (2002). A fuzzy neural network for pattern classification and feature selection. *Fuzzy Sets and Systems, 130*(1), 101–108. doi:10.1016/S0165-0114(02)00050-7

Liu. (2009). A improved parallel genetic algorithm based on fixed point theory for the optimal design of multi-body model vehicle suspensions. In *Computer Science and Information Technology, 2009. ICCSIT 2009. 2nd IEEE International Conference on* (pp. 430-433). IEEE.

Liu, B. (2004). *Uncertainty theory: an introduction to its axiomatic foundations.* Berlin: Springer Verlag. doi:10.1007/978-3-540-39987-2_5

Liu, H., Abraham, A., & Hassanien, A. (2009). Scheduling jobs on computational grids using a fuzzy particle swarm optimization algorithm. *Future Generation Computer Systems.*

Li-Zhongli, Wang-Ximing, & Gao-Jianping. (2010). Study in Work Condition Matching of Dynamical System of Hybrid Power Vehicle. [in Chinese]. *Journal of Henan University of Science & Technology, 31*(5), 24–28.

Lorpunmanee, S., Sap, M. N., Abdullah, A. H., & Chompooinwai, C. (2007). An Ant Colony Optimization for Dynamic Job Scheduling in Grid Environment. *International Journal of Computer, Electrical, Automation. Control and Information Engineering, 1*(5), 1343–1350.

Mac Queen, J. (1967). Some methods for classification and analysis of multivariate observations. In *Fifth Berkeley Symposium on Mathematics, Statistics and Probability* (pp. 281–297). University of California Press.

MacQueen, J. B. (1967). Some methods for classification and analysis of multivariate observations. *Proceedings of Fifth Berkeley Symposium, 2.*

Mallén-Fullerton, G. M., Quiroz-Ibarra, J. E., Miranda, A., & Fernández-Anaya, G. (2015). Modified Classical Graph Algorithms for the DNA Fragment Assembly Problem. *Algorithms, 8*(3), 754–773. doi:10.3390/a8030754

Mansini, R., Tocchella, B., & Savelsbergh, M. (2012). The supplier selection problem with quantity discounts and truck load shipping. *Omega, 40*(4), 445–455. doi:10.1016/j.omega.2011.09.001

Marcelloni, F. (2003). Feature selection based on a modified fuzzy C-means algorithm with supervision. *Information Sciences, 151*, 201–226. doi:10.1016/S0020-0255(02)00402-4

Marler, R. T., & Arora, J. S. (2010). The weighted sum method for multi-objective optimization: New insights. *Structural and Multidisciplinary Optimization, 41*(6), 853–862. doi:10.100700158-009-0460-7

Mazdeh, M. M., Zaerpour, F., Zareei, A., & Hajinezhad, A. (2010). Parallel machines scheduling to minimize job tardiness and machine deteriorating cost with deteriorating jobs. *Applied Mathematical Modelling, 34*(6), 1498–1510. doi:10.1016/j.apm.2009.08.023

McCombie, W. R., & Martin-Gallardo, A. (1994). Large-scale, automated sequencing of human chromosomal regions. In *Automated DNA sequencing and analysis*. San Diego, CA: Academic Press. doi:10.1016/B978-0-08-092639-1.50028-9

Medvedev, P., Georgiou, K., & Myers, E. W. (2007). Computability and equivalence of models for sequence assembly. In *Proceedings of Workshop on Algorithms in Bioinformatics (WABI)*. WABI. 10.1007/978-3-540-74126-8_27

Meksangsouy, P., & Chaiyaratana, N. (2003). DNA fragment assembly using an ant colony system algorithm. In *Proceedings of Congress on Evolutionary Computation CEC'03* (Vol. 3, pp. 1756-1763). CEC. 10.1109/CEC.2003.1299885

Merh, N. (2012). Stock Market Forecasting: Comparison between Artificial Neural Networks and Arch Models. *Journal of Information Technology Applications & Management, 19*(1), 1–12.

Mirjalili, S., Saremi, S., Mirjalili, S. M., & Coelho, L. S. (2016). Multi-objective grey wolf optimizer: A novel algorithm for multi-criterion optimization. *Expert Systems with Applications, 47*, 106–119. doi:10.1016/j.eswa.2015.10.039

Misra, P., Kanhere, S., Ostry, D., & Jha, S. (2010). Safety assurance and rescue communication systems in high-stress environments: A mining case study. *Communications Magazine, IEEE, 48*(4), 66–73. doi:10.1109/MCOM.2010.5439078

Mithat, Z., Cuneyt, C., & Cemal, C. (2011). A combined methodology for supplier selection and performance evaluation. *Expert Systems with Applications, 8*, 2741–2751.

Miyaji, M. (2014). Study on the reduction effect of traffic accident by using analysis of Internet survey, Internet of Things (WF-IoT). *IEEE World Forum on Internet of Things (WF-IoT)*, 325-330.

Mizas, C., Sirakoulis, G. C., Mardiris, V., Karafyllidis, I., Glykos, N., & Sandaltzopoulos, R. (2008). Reconstruction of DNA sequences using genetic algorithms and cellular automata: Towards mutation prediction? *Bio Systems, 92*(1), 61–68. doi:10.1016/j.biosystems.2007.12.002 PMID:18243517

Mladenić, D. (2006). Feature Selection for Dimensionality Reduction. *SLSFS* 2005. *LNCS, 3940*, 84–102.

Moghaddam, S. K., Khodadadi, F., Maleki, R. E., & Movaghar, A. (2012). A Hybrid Genetic Algorithm and Variable Neighborhood Search for Task Scheduling Problem in Grid Environment. *Procedia Engineering, 29*, 3808–3814. doi:10.1016/j.proeng.2012.01.575

Mohamed, R. H. (1997). The relationship between goal programming and fuzzy programming. *Fuzzy Sets and Systems, 89*(2), 215–222. doi:10.1016/S0165-0114(96)00100-5

Mohsen, M. S., & Abdullah, R. (2011). HS-MSA: New algorithm based on Meta-heuristic harmony search for solving multiple sequence alignment. *Int. J. Comput. Sci. Inform. Security, 9*, 70–85.

Molaiy, S., & Effatparvar, M. (2014). Scheduling in Grid Systems using Ant Colony Algorithm. *I.J. Computer Network and Information Security., 6*(2), 16–22. doi:10.5815/ijcnis.2014.02.03

Molyneaux, L., Carnegie, D. A., & Chitty, C. (2016). HADES: An underground mine disaster scouting robot. In *SSRR 2015 - 2015 IEEE International Symposium on Safety, Security, and Rescue Robotics*. IEEE. 10.1109/SSRR.2015.7443019

Montage. (n.d.). *Montage: An Atronomical Image Mosaic Engine—NASA Space Act Award Winner 2006*. Retrieved from http://montage.ipac.caltech.edu

Moré, J. (1978). *The Levenberg-Marquardt algorithm: Implementation and theory numerical analysis*. Springer.

Moving Average Algorithm. (2016, Mar 6). Retrieved from: https://en.wikipedia.org/wiki/Moving_average

Murphy, R. R. (2014). *Disaster Robotics. Statewide Agricultural Land Use Baseline 2015* (Vol. 1). Academic Press. 10.1017/CBO9781107415324.004

Murphy, R. R. (2004). Human-robot interaction in rescue robotics. *IEEE Transactions on Systems, Man and Cybernetics. Part C, Applications and Reviews*, *34*(2), 138–153. doi:10.1109/TSMCC.2004.826267

Murphy, R. R., Kravitz, J., Stover, S. L., & Shoureshi, R. (2009). Mobile robots in mine rescue and recovery. *IEEE Robotics & Automation Magazine*, *16*(2), 91–103. doi:10.1109/MRA.2009.932521

Nailwal, K. K., Gupta, D., & Sharma, S. (2015). Fuzzy bi-criteria scheduling on parallel machines involving weighted flow time and maximum tardiness. *Cogent Mathematics*, *2*(1), 1019792. doi:10.1080/23311835.2015.1019792

Naito, T., Tsukada, T., Yamada, K., Kozuka, K., & Yamamoto, S. (n.d.). *Robust recognition methods for inclined license plates under various illumination conditions outdoors*. IEEE/IEEJ/JSAI

Naito, T., Tsukada, T., Yamada, K., Kozuka, K., & Yamamoto, S. (2000). Robust License-Plate Recognition Method for Passing Vehicles under Outside Environment. *IEEE Transactions on Vehicular Technology*, *49*(6), 2309–2319. doi:10.1109/25.901900

Nakano, E., Tsuda, N., Inuoe, K., Kayaba, K., & Kimura, H. (1992). Development of an advanced way of improvement of the maneuverability of a backhoe machine. *Proc. 9th International Symposium on Automation and Robotics in Construction*. 10.22260/ISARC1992/0029

Napook, P., & Eiamkanitchat, N. (2015). The adaptive dynamic clustering neuro-fuzzy system for classification. *Information Science and Applications*, *339*, 721–728. doi:10.1007/978-3-662-46578-3_85

Narasimhan, H. (2009). *Parallel artificial bee colony (PABC) algorithm*. Paper presented at the Nature & Biologically Inspired Computing, 2009. NaBIC 2009. World Congress on.

Narayanan, A., & Moore, M. (1996). Quantum-inspired genetic algorithm. *Proceedings of IEEE International Conference on Evolutionary Computation*, 61–66. 10.1109/ICEC.1996.542334

Naruse, M., Ohtsukasa, N., Tanaka, J., & Haga, S. (2004). *U.S. Patent No. 6,725,581*. Washington, DC: U.S. Patent and Trademark Office.

Na, S., Xumin, L., & Yong, G. (2010). Research on K-Means clustering algorithm–An Improved K-Means Clustering Algorithm. *IEEE Third International Symposium on Intelligent Information Technology Security Informatics*, 63–67. 10.1109/IITSI.2010.74

Nauck, D., & Kruse, R. (1997). A neuro-fuzzy method to learn classification rules from data. *Fuzzy Sets and Systems*, *89*(3), 277–288. doi:10.1016/S0165-0114(97)00009-2

Nawi, N. M., Ransing, M. R., & Ransing, R. S. (2006). *An Improved Learning Algorithm Based on The Broyden-Fletcher-Goldfarb-Shanno (BFGS) Method For Back Propagation Neural Networks*. Paper presented at the Intelligent Systems Design and Applications, 2006. ISDA '06. Sixth International Conference on.

Nawrin, S., Rahman, M. R., & Akhter, S. (2017). Exploreing k-means with internal validity indexes for data clustering in traffic management system. *International Journal of Advanced Computer Science and Applications*, *8*(3). doi:10.14569/IJACSA.2017.080337

Naznin, F., Sarker, R., & Essam, D. (2012). Progressive alignment method using genetic algorithm for multiple sequence alignment. *Evolutionary Computation. IEEE Transactions on*, *16*(5), 615–631.

Ndoh, M., Delisle, G. Y., & Le, R. (2003). A novel approach to propagation prediction in confined and diffracting rough surfaces. *International Journal of Numerical Modelling: Electronic Networks. Devices and Fields*, *16*(6), 535–555. doi:10.1002/jnm.521

Neumann, G., Swan, J., Harman, M., & Clark, J. A. (2014). *The executable experimental template pattern for the systematic comparison of metaheuristics.* Paper presented at the International conference companion on Genetic and evolutionary computation companion. 10.1145/2598394.2609850

Neumann, J. V., & Burks, A. W. (1966). *Theory of self-reproducing automata.* Academic Press.

Ngia, L. S. H., & Sjoberg, J. (2000). Efficient training of neural nets for nonlinear adaptive filtering using a recursive Levenberg-Marquardt algorithm. *Signal Processing. IEEE Transactions on, 48*(7), 1915–1927. doi:10.1109/78.847778

Nguyen Tung, L., & Nguyen Quynh, A. (2010). *Application Artificial Bee Colony Algorithm (ABC) for Reconfiguring Distribution Network.* Paper presented at the Computer Modeling and Simulation, 2010. ICCMS '10. Second International Conference on.

Nielsen, M., & Chuang, I. (2000). *Quantum computation and quantum information.* Cambridge University Press.

Nieuwoudt, C., & van Heerden, R. (1996). Automatic Number Plate Segmentation and Recognition. *Seventh Annual South African Workshop on Pattern Recognition IAPR*, 88-93.

Niknam, T., Fard, E. T., Pourjafarian, N., & Rousta, A. (2011). An efficient hybrid algorithm based on modified imperialistic competitive algorithm and K-Means for data clustering. Engineering Application of Artificial Intelligence, (24), 306–317.

Nishimura, S. (1989). *Position energy recovering activating device for hydraulic excavator.* Komatsu.

Notredame, C., & Higgins, D. G. (1996). SAGA: Sequence alignment by genetic algorithm. *Nucleic Acids Research, 24*(8), 1515–1524. doi:10.1093/nar/24.8.1515 PMID:8628686

Notredame, C., Higgins, D. G., & Heringa, J. (2000). T-Coffee: A novel method for fast and accurate multiple sequence alignment. *Journal of Molecular Biology, 302*(1), 205–217. doi:10.1006/jmbi.2000.4042 PMID:10964570

Novak, P., Babjak, J., Kot, T., Bobovsky, Z., Olivka, P., & Moczulski, W. (2017). *Telerescuer-reconnaissance mobile robot for underground coal mines.* Academic Press.

Nyman, J., & Rydberg, K. E. (2001). Energy saving lifting hydraulic systems. *7th Scandinavian International Conference on Fluid Power,* 163-177.

Nyman, J., Bärnström, J., & Rydberg, K. E. (2004). Use of accumulators to reduce the need of electric power in hydraulic lifting systems. *Scandinavian International Conference on Fluid Power, SICFP03.*

Oinn, T., Addis, M., Ferris, J., Marvin, D., Senger, M., Greenwood, M., … Li, P. (2004). Taverna: A tool for the composition and enactment of bioinformatics workflows. *Bioinformatics (Oxford, England), 20*(17), 3045–3054. doi:10.1093/bioinformatics/bth361 PMID:15201187

Orobitg, M., Cores, F., Guirado, F., Roig, C., & Notredame, C. (2013). Improving multiple sequence alignment biological accuracy through genetic algorithms. *The Journal of Supercomputing, 65*(3), 1076–1088. doi:10.100711227-012-0856-9

Ozturk, C., & Karaboga, D. (2011). *Hybrid Artificial Bee Colony algorithm for neural network training.* Paper presented at the Evolutionary Computation (CEC), 2011 IEEE Congress on.

Page, J., & Naughton, J. (2005). Framework for task scheduling in heterogeneous distributed computing using genetic algorithms. *AI Review, 24*, 415–429.

Panagiotakis, S., Kapetanakis, K., & Malamos, A. G. (2013). Architecture for Real Time Communications over the Web. *International Journal of Web Engineering, 2*(1), 1–8. doi:10.5923/j.web.20130201.01

Parsons, R. J., Forrest, S., & Burks, C. (1993). Genetic algorithms for DNA sequence assembly. *ISMB-93 Proceedings, 1*, 310-318.

Parsons, R. J., Forrest, S., & Burks, C. (1995). Genetic Algorithms, operators and DNA fragment Assembly. *Machine Learning, 21*(1/2), 11–33. doi:10.1023/A:1022613513712

Parthiban, P., Zubar, H. A., & Katakar, P. (2013). Vendor selection problem: A multi-criteria approach based on strategic decisions. *International Journal of Production Research, 51*(5), 1535–1548. doi:10.1080/00207543.2012.709644

Patil, M., Rawat, A., Singh, P., & Dixit, S. (2016). Accident Detection and Ambulance Control using Intelligent Traffic Control System. *International Journal of Engineering Trends and Technology, 34*(8).

Penders, J., Alboul, L., Witkowski, U., Naghsh, A., Saez-Pons, J., Herbrechtsmeier, S., & El-Habbal, M. (2011). A Robot Swarm Assisting a Human Fire-Fighter. *Advanced Robotics, 25*(1–2), 93–117. doi:10.1163/016918610X538507

Peng, G., Wenming, C., & Jian, L. (2011). *Global artificial bee colony search algorithm for numerical function optimization.* Paper presented at the Natural Computation (ICNC), 2011 Seventh International Conference on.

Peng, H., Long, F., & Ding, C. (2005). Feature Selection Based on Mutual Information: Criteria of Max-Dependency, Max-Relevance, and Min-Redundancy. *IEEE Transactions on Pattern Analysis and Machine Intelligence, 27*(8). PMID:16119262

Peng-Tianhao. (2001). Research on Pump-engine Match in Hydraulic Excavator. *China Journal of Highway and Transport, 14*(4), 118–120.

Peng, Y., Wu, Z., & Jiang, J. (2010). A novel feature selection approach for biomedical data classification. *Journal of Biomedical Informatics, 43*(1), 15–23. doi:10.1016/j.jbi.2009.07.008 PMID:19647098

Peplinski, N. R., Ulaby, F. T., & Dobson, M. C. (1995). Dielectric properties of soils in the 0.3-1.3-GHz range. *Geoscience and Remote Sensing. IEEE Transactions on, 33*(3), 803–807.

Phillippy, P. M., Delcher, A. L., & Salzberg, S. L. (2004). Comparative genome assembly. *Briefings in Bioinformatics, 5*(3), 237–248. doi:10.1093/bib/5.3.237 PMID:15383210

Poongundran, A. A., & Jeevabharathi, M. (2015). Vehicular Monitoring and Tracking Using Raspberry Pi. *International Journal of Innovative Research in Science, Engineering and Technology, 4*(2), 2319–8573.

Pop, M. (2009). Genome assembly reborn: Recent computational challenges. *Briefings in Bioinformatics, 10*(4), 354–366. doi:10.1093/bib/bbp026 PMID:19482960

Potential Energy recovery reproducing device for hydraulic operated excavator. (1989). Komatsu.

Prabha, C., Sunitha, R., & Anitha, R. (2014). Automatic Vehicle Accidents Detection and Messaging System Using GSM and GPS Modem. *International Journal of Advanced Research in Electrical, Electronics and Instrumentation Engineering.* Retrieved from http://www.rroij.com/open-access/automatic-vehicle-accident-detection-andmessaging-system-using-gsm-and-gpsmodem.php?aid=44586

Prakash, M., Saranya, R., Rukmani Jothi, K., & Vigneshwaran, A. (2012). An Optimal Job Scheduling in Grid Using Cuckoo Algorithm. *International Journal of Computer Science and Telecommunications, 3*(2), 65–69.

Prakash, S., & Vidyarthi, D. P. (2015). Maximizing Availability for Task Scheduling in Computational Grid using GA. *Concurrency and Computation, 27*(1), 197–210. doi:10.1002/cpe.3216

Proctor, G., & Winter, C. (1998). Information flocking: Data visualisation in virtual worlds using emergent behaviours. *Proceedings First International Conference Virtual Worlds*, 1434.

Qian, G., Wang, H., & Feng, X. (2013). Generalized hesitant fuzzy sets and their application in decision support system. *Knowledge-Based Systems*, *37*, 357–365. doi:10.1016/j.knosys.2012.08.019

Qing, X. I. A. O., & Qing-feng, W. A. N. G. (2008). Parameter matching Method for Hybrid Power System of Hydraulic Excavator [in Chinese]. *China Jounal of Hightway and Transport*, *21*(1), 121–126.

Rabiee, M., & Sajedi, H. (2013). Job Scheduling in Grid Computing with Cuckoo Optimization Algorithm. *International Journal of Computer Applications, 62*(16), 975-987.

Raghavan, V. V., & Birchard, K. (1979) A clustering strategy based on a formalism of the reproductive process in natural systems. In *Proceedings of the Second International Conference on Information Storage and Retrieval*. ACM. 10.1145/511706.511709

Rahimi-Vahed, A., Javadi, B., Rabbani, M., & Tavakkoli-Moghaddam, R. (2008). A multi-objective scatter search for a bi-criteria no-wait flow shop scheduling problem. *Engineering Optimization*, *40*(4), 331–346. doi:10.1080/03052150701732509

Rahman, M. A. (2012, Feb 1). ID3 Decision Tree Algorithm - Part 1. Academic Press.

Rahman, M. R., & Akhter, S. (2015a). Real Time Bi-directional Traffic Management Support System with GPS and WebSocket. *Proc. of the 15th IEEE International Conference on Computer and Information Technology (CIT-2015)*.

Rahman, M. R., & Akhter, S. (2015b). Bi-directional Traffic Management Support System With Decision Tree Based Dynamic Routing. *Proc. of 10th International Conference for Internet Technology and Secured Transactions, ICITST 2015*. 10.1109/ICITST.2015.7412080

Rahman, M. R., & Akhter, S. (2015c). BiDirectional Traffic Management with Multiple Data Feeds for Dynamic Route Computation and Prediction System. *International Journal of Intelligent Computing Research*, *7*(2).

Rajashree, D., & Pradipta Kishore, D. (2016). Prediction of Financial Time Series Data using Hybrid Evolutionary Legendre Neural Network: Evolutionary LENN. *International Journal of Applied Evolutionary Computation*, *7*(1), 16–32. doi:10.4018/IJAEC.2016010102

Rajeswari, J., & Jagannath, M. (2017). Advances in biomedical signal and image processing – A systematic review. *Informatics in Medicine Unlocked*, *8*, 13–19. doi:10.1016/j.imu.2017.04.002

Ramakanta, M., Ravi, V., & Patra, M. R. (2010). Application of Machine Learning Techniques to Predict Software Reliability. *International Journal of Applied Evolutionary Computation*, *1*(3), 70–86. doi:10.4018/jaec.2010070104

Ranjan, A., & Sahu, H. B. (2014). *Advancements in communication and safety systems in underground mines: present status and future prospects*. Academic Press.

Ranjan, A., Misra, P., & Sahu, H. B. (2017). Experimental measurements and channel modeling for wireless communication networks in underground mine environments. In *Antennas and Propagation (EUCAP), 2017 11th European Conference on* (pp. 1345–1349). Academic Press. 10.23919/EuCAP.2017.7928854

Ranjan, A., Misra, P., & Sahu, H. B. (2017). On the importance of link characterization for wireless sensor networks in underground mines. In *2017 9th International Conference on Communication Systems and Networks (COMSNETS)* (pp. 1–2). Academic Press. 10.1109/COMSNETS.2017.7945456

Ranjan, A., Misra, P., Dwivedi, B., & Sahu, H. B. (2017). Studies on Propagation Characteristics of Radio Waves for Wireless Networks in Underground Coal Mines. *Wireless Personal Communications*, 1–14. doi:10.100711277-017-4636-y

Ranjan, A., & Sahu, H. B. (2014). Communications Challenges in Underground Mines. *Search & Research*, *5*(2), 23–29.

Ranjan, A., Sahu, H. B., & Misra, P. (2015a). Performance Evaluation of Underground Mine Communication and Monitoring Devices: Case Studies. In J. K. Mandal, S. C. Satapathy, M. Kumar Sanyal, P. P. Sarkar, & A. Mukhopadhyay (Eds.), *Information Systems Design and Intelligent Applications* (Vol. 339, pp. 685–694). Springer India; doi:10.1007/978-81-322-2250-7_69

Ranjan, A., Sahu, H. B., & Misra, P. (2015b). Wave propagation model for wireless communication in underground mines. In *Bombay Section Symposium (IBSS)*, (pp. 1–5). IEEE. 10.1109/IBSS.2015.7456655

Ranjan, A., Sahu, H. B., & Misra, P. (2016). Wireless Sensor Networks: An Emerging Solution for Underground Mines. *International Journal of Applied Evolutionary Computation*, *7*(4), 1–27. doi:10.4018/IJAEC.2016100101

Ranjany, A., Misraz, P., Dwivediz, B., & Sahuy, H. B. (2016). Channel modeling of wireless communication in underground coal mines. In *2016 8th International Conference on Communication Systems and Networks (COMSNETS)* (pp. 1–2). Academic Press. 10.1109/COMSNETS.2016.7440023

Rao, B. T., Satchidananda, D., & Rajib, M. (2012). Functional Link Artificial Neural Networks for Software Cost Estimation. *International Journal of Applied Evolutionary Computation*, *3*(2), 62–82. doi:10.4018/jaec.2012040104

Rashidi, E., Jahandar, M., & Zandieh, M. (2010). An improved hybrid multi-objective parallel genetic algorithm for hybrid flow shop scheduling with unrelated parallel machines. *International Journal of Advanced Manufacturing Technology*, *49*(9-12), 1129–1139. doi:10.100700170-009-2475-z

Rasmussen, T. K., & Krink, T. (2003). Improved Hidden Markov Model training for multiple sequence alignment by a particle swarm optimization—evolutionary algorithm hybrid. *Bio Systems*, *72*(1), 5–17. doi:10.1016/S0303-2647(03)00131-X PMID:14642655

Rathee, M., & Kumar, T. V. (2014). Dna fragment assembly using multi-objective genetic algorithms. *International Journal of Applied Evolutionary Computation*, *5*(3), 84–108. doi:10.4018/ijaec.2014070105

Rathipriya, R., Thangavel, K., & Bagyamani, J. (2011). Usage Profile Generation from Web Usage Data Using Hybrid Biclustering Algorithm. *International Journal of Applied Evolutionary Computation*, *2*(4), 37–49. doi:10.4018/jaec.2011100103

Ravichandran, K., & Ananthi, B. (2009). Color Skin Segmentation Using K-Means Cluster. *International Journal of Computational and Applied Mathematics*, *4*(2), 153–157.

Reporter (2013, Sep-Oct). *Bluetooth and Wi-Fi Offer New Options for Travel Time Measurements*. ITS International. Retrieved from: http://www.itsinternational.com/categories/detection-monitoring-machine vision/features/bluetooth-and-wi-fi-offer-new-options-for-travel-time-measurements/

Reporter. (2016, Mar 6). Retrieved from: https://en.wikipedia.org/wiki/Moving_average

Reynolds, C. W., & Flocks, H. (1987). A distributed behavioural model. *Computer Graphics (SIGGRAPH '87 Conference Proceedings), 21*(4).

Rioland, A., &Eudes, A. (2007). *Raport de projet Optimisation par essaim particulaire pour un problème d'ordonnancement et d'affectation de ressources*. Institut Superieur D'informatique De Modelisation et de Leurs Applications.

Ritchie, G. (2003). *Static multi-processor scheduling with ant colony optimization and local search* (Master Thesis). School of Informatics, Univ. of Edinburgh.

Romão, T., Rato, L., Fernandes, P., Alexandre, N., Almada, A., & Capeta, N. (2006). M-Traffic - A Traffic Information and Monitoring System for Mobile Devices. In *Proc. of International Workshop on Ubiquitous Computing (IWUC 2006)* (pp. 87-92). ICEIS Publisher.

Rosenblatt, F. (1958). The Perceptron: A probabilistic model for information storage and organization in the brain. *Psychological Review*, *65*(6), 386–408. doi:10.1037/h0042519 PMID:13602029

Rovsek, V., Batista, M., & Bogunovic, B. (2017). Identifying the key risk factors of traffic accident injury severity on Slovenian roads using a non-parametric classification tree. *Transport*, *32*(3), 272–281. doi:10.3846/16484142.2014.915581

Roy, S. S., Mittal, D., Basu, A., & Abraham, A. (2015). Stock market forecasting using lasso linear regression model. In *Afro-European Conference for Industrial Advancement* (pp. 371–381). Cham: Springer. doi:10.1007/978-3-319-13572-4_31

Rubio, A., Bermúdez, J. D., & Vercher, E. (2017). Improving stock index forecasts by using a new weighted fuzzy-trend time series method. *Expert Systems with Applications*, *76*, 12–20. doi:10.1016/j.eswa.2017.01.049

Rumelhart, D. E., McClelland, J. L., & University of California, S. D. P. R. G. (1986). *Parallel distributed processing: Psychological and biological models*. MIT Press.

Sahin, E., & Winfield, A. (2008). Special issue on swarm robotics. *Swarm Intelligence*, *2*(2), 69–72. doi:10.100711721-008-0020-6

Sahu, H. B., Panigrahi, D. C., & Mishra, N. M. (2004). Assessment of spontaneous heating susceptibility of coal seams by differential scanning calorimetry. *Journal of Mines, Metals and Fuels*, *52*(7–8), 117–121.

Salcudean, S. E., Tafazoli, S., Lawrence, P. D., & Chau, I. (1997, July). Impedance control of a teleoperated mini excavator. In *Advanced Robotics, 1997. ICAR'97. Proceedings., 8th International Conference on* (pp. 19-25). IEEE. 10.1109/ICAR.1997.620156

Salton, G., & Buckley, C. (1988). Term-weighting approaches in automatic text retrieval. *Information Processing & Management*, *24*(5), 513–523. doi:10.1016/0306-4573(88)90021-0

Sammarco, J. J., Paddock, R., Fries, E. F., & Karra, V. K. (2007). A Technology Review of Smart Sensors With Wireless Networks for Applications in Hazardous Work Environments. Department of Health and Human Services, Centers for Disease Control and Prevention. National Institute for Occupational Safety and Health, Pittsburgh Research Laboratory.

Sandou, G. (2009). *Optimisation par essaim pour la synthèse de lois de commande: du PID à la synthèse H¥ Supélec*. Département Automatique.

Sangeetha, K., Archana, P., Ramya, M., & Ramya, P. (2014). Automatic Ambulance Rescue with Intelligent Traffic Light System. *IOSR Journal of Engineering*, *4*(2), 53–57. doi:10.9790/3021-04255357

Sarfraz, M., Ahmed, M., & Ghazi, S. A. (2003). Saudi Arabian License Plate Recognition System. In *Proceedings of IEEE International Conference on Geoemetric Modeling and Graphics-GMAG'2003-UK*. IEEE Computer Society Press.

Sarfraz, M., & Ahmed, M. J. (2005). *License Plate Recognition System: Saudi Arabian Case*. In M. Sarfraz (Ed.), *Computer-Aided Intelligent Recognition Techniques and Applications* (pp. 19–32). John Wiley and Sons. doi:10.1002/0470094168.ch2

Sarikan, S. S., Ozbayoglu, A. M., & Zilci, O. (2017). Automated Vehicle Classification with Image Processing and Computational Intelligence. *Procedia Computer Science*, *114*, 515–522. doi:10.1016/j.procs.2017.09.022

Sayad, S. (2010). *Artificial Neural Network*. Retrieved from http://www.saedsayad.com/data_mining_map.htm

Schalkoff, R. (1992). *J.: Pattern Recognition: Statistical*. Structural and Neural Approaches, John Willey & Sons Inc.

Schiffbauer, W. H., & Brune, J. F. (2006). *Coal mine communications*. American Longwall Mag.

Schneider, D. (2009). Robin Murphy roboticist to the rescue. *IEEE Spectrum*, *46*(2), 36–37. doi:10.1109/MSPEC.2009.4772558

Sen, S., & Pal, T. (2007). A Neuro-Fuzzy Scheme for Integrated Input Fuzzy Set Selection and Optimal Fuzzy Rule Generation for Classification. *PReMI. LNCS*, *4815*, 287–294.

Sepehri, N., Lawrence, P. D., Sassani, F., & Frenette, R. (1994). Rosolved-mode teleoperated control of heavy-duty hydraulic machines. ASME Journal of Dynamic System. *Measurement and Control*, *116*(2), 232–240. doi:10.1115/1.2899215

Setiono, R., & Liu, H. (1997, May). Neural-Network Feature Selector. *IEEE Transactions on Neural Networks*, *8*(3), 654–662. doi:10.1109/72.572104 PMID:18255668

Setubal, J., & Meidanis, J. (1997). *Introduction to computational molecular biology*. PWS Publishing Company.

Shabrin, S. B., Nikharge, B. J., Poojary, M. M., & Pooja, T. (2016). Smart helmet– intelligent safety for motorcyclist using raspberry pi and open CV. *International Research Journal of Engineering and Technology*, *3*(3), 2395–0056.

Shah, H., & Ghazali, R. (2011). *Prediction of Earthquake Magnitude by an Improved ABC-MLP*. Paper presented at the Developments in E-systems Engineering (DeSE). 10.1109/DeSE.2011.37

Shah, H., Ghazali, R., Nawi, N., & Deris, M. (2012a). Global Hybrid Ant Bee Colony Algorithm for Training Artificial Neural Networks Computational Science and Its Applications – ICCSA 2012. Springer.

Shah, H., Tairan, N., Mashwani, W. K., Al-Sewari, A. A., Jan, M. A., & Badshah, G. (2017). Hybrid Global Crossover Bees Algorithm for Solving Boolean Function Classification Task. Cham: Academic Press. doi:10.1007/978-3-319-63315-2_41

SHah., H., Ghazali, R., Nawi, N. M., & Deris, M. M. (2012b). *Global Hybrid Ant Bee Colony Algorithm for Training Artificial Neural Networks*. Paper presented at the International Conference on Computational Science and Applications, Alvador de Bahia, Brazil.

Shah, D., Nair, R., Parikh, V., & Shah, V. (2015). Accident Alarm System using GSM, GPS and Accelerometer. *International Journal of Innovative Research in Computer and Communication Engineering*, *3*(4).

Shannon, C. (1948). A mathematical theory of communication. Bell System Technical Journal, 27. *The Bell System Technical Journal*, 17.

Sharma, T. K., Pant, M., & Bhardwaj, T. (2011). *PSO ingrained Artificial Bee Colony algorithm for solving continuous optimization problems*. Paper presented at the Computer Applications and Industrial Electronics (ICCAIE), 2011 IEEE International Conference on.

Shirkouhi, S. N., Shakouri, H., Javadi, B., & Keramati, A. (2013). Supplier selection and order allocation problem using a two-phase fuzzy multi-objective linear programming. *Applied Mathematical Modelling*, *37*(22), 9308–9323. doi:10.1016/j.apm.2013.04.045

Shi, Y., & Eberhart, R. C. (1998). Parameter Selection in Particle Swarm Optimization. *Proceedings of the 7th Annual Conference on Evolutionary Programming*.

Shi, Y., Liu, H., Gao, L., & Zhang, G. (2011). Cellular particle swarm optimization. *Information Sciences*, *181*(20), 4460–4493. doi:10.1016/j.ins.2010.05.025

Shokrollahpour, E., Zandieh, M., & Dorri, B. (2011). A novel imperialist competitive algorithm for bi-criteria scheduling of the assembly flowshop problem. *International Journal of Production Research*, *49*(11), 3087–3103. doi:10.1080/00207540903536155

Siarry, P., & Michalewicz, Z. (Eds.). (2008). Advances in Metaheuristics for Hard Optimization. Springer.

Siddiqui, F. U., & Isa, N. A. M. (2011). Enhanced Moving K-Means (EMKM) Algorithm for Image Segmentation. *IEEE Transactions on Consumer Electronics*, *57*(2), 833–841. doi:10.1109/TCE.2011.5955230

Silva, A., Caminhas, W., Lemos, A., & Gomide, F. (2012). Evolving Neural Fuzzy Network with Adaptive Feature Selection. *11th International Conference on Machine Learning and Applications*. 10.1109/ICMLA.2012.184

Simossis, V. A., & Heringa, J. (2005). PRALINE: A multiple sequence alignment toolbox that integrates homology-extended and secondary structure information. *Nucleic Acids Research*, *33*(suppl 2), W289–W294. doi:10.1093/nar/gki390 PMID:15980472

Simpson, J. T., Wong, K., Jackman, S. D., Schein, J. E., Jones, S. J. M., & Birol, I. (2009). ABYSS: A parallel assembler for short read sequence data. *Genome Research*, *19*(6), 1117–1123. doi:10.1101/gr.089532.108 PMID:19251739

Singh, S. (1995, May). Learning to predict resistive forces during robotic excavation. In *Robotics and Automation, 1995. Proceedings., 1995 IEEE International Conference on* (Vol. 2, pp. 2102-2107). IEEE. 10.1109/ROBOT.1995.526025

Singh, D., & Garg, R. (2011, July). A robust multi-objective optimization to workflow scheduling for dynamic grid. In *Proceedings of the International Conference on Advances in Computing and Artificial Intelligence* (pp. 183-188). ACM. 10.1145/2007052.2007090

Singh, H. R., Biswas, S. K., & Purkayastha, B. (2017, January). A neuro-fuzzy classification technique using dynamic clustering and GSS rule generation. *Journal of Computational and Applied Mathematics*, *309*, 683–694. doi:10.1016/j.cam.2016.04.023

Singh, S. (1997). State of the art in automation of earthmoving. *Journal of Aerospace Engineering*, *10*(4), 179–188. doi:10.1061/(ASCE)0893-1321(1997)10:4(179)

Sirakoulis, G. C., Karafyllidis, I., Mizas, C., Mardiris, V., Thanailakis, A., & Tsalides, P. (2003). A cellular automaton model for the study of DNA sequence evolution. *Computers in Biology and Medicine*, *33*(5), 439–453. doi:10.1016/S0010-4825(03)00017-9 PMID:12860467

Sivanandan, S. N., & Deepa, S. N. (2008). *Introduction to genetic algorithms*. Springer.

Slowik, A., & Bialko, M. (2008). *Training of artificial neural networks using differential evolution algorithm*. Paper presented at the Human System Interactions, 2008 Conference on.

Smith, D. P. (2004). *U.S. Patent No. 6,748,738*. Washington, DC: U.S. Patent and Trademark Office.

Smith, J., Siegel, H. J., & Maciejewski, A. A. (2008). A stochastic model for robust resource allocation in heterogeneous parallel and distributed computing systems. In *Parallel and Distributed Processing, 2008. IPDPS 2008. IEEE International Symposium on* (pp. 1-5). IEEE. 10.1109/IPDPS.2008.4536431

Smith, T., & Waterman, M. (1981). Identification of common molecular subsequences. *Journal of Molecular Biology*, *147*(1), 195–197. doi:10.1016/0022-2836(81)90087-5 PMID:7265238

Song, Q., & Chissom, B. S. (1993). Forecasting enrollments with fuzzy time series—part I. *Fuzzy Sets and Systems*, *54*(1), 1–9. doi:10.1016/0165-0114(93)90355-L

Song, Q., & Chissom, B. S. (1993). Fuzzy time series and its models. *Fuzzy Sets and Systems*, *54*(3), 269–277. doi:10.1016/0165-0114(93)90372-O

Song, Q., & Chissom, B. S. (1994). Forecasting enrollments with fuzzy time series—part II. *Fuzzy Sets and Systems*, *62*(1), 1–8. doi:10.1016/0165-0114(94)90067-1

Sonika, S., Sekhar, K. S., & Jaishree, S. (2014). Intelligent accident identification system using GPS and GSM modem. *International Journal of Advanced Research in Computer and Communication Engineering*, *3*(2).

Srinivasa, K. G., Sowmya, B. J., Pradeep Kumar, D., & Shetty, C. (2016). Efficient Image Denoising for Effective Digitization using Image Processing Techniques and Neural Networks. *International Journal of Applied Evolutionary Computation, 7*(4), 77–93. doi:10.4018/IJAEC.2016100105

Srivastava, N., Hinton, G., Krizhevsky, A., Sutskever, I., & Salakhutdinov, R. (2014). Dropout: A Simple Way to Prevent Neural Networks from Overfitting. *Journal of Machine Learning Research, 15*, 1929–1958.

Staden, R. (1980). A new computer method for the storage and manipulation of DNA gel reading data. *Nucleic Acids Research, 8*(16), 3673–3694. doi:10.1093/nar/8.16.3673 PMID:7433103

Stentz, A., Bares, J., Singh, S., & Rowe, P. (1999). A robotic excavator for autonomous truck loading. *Autonomous Robots, 7*(2), 175–186. doi:10.1023/A:1008914201877

Suer, G. A., Arikan, F., & Babayigit, C. (2009). Effects of different fuzzy operators on bi objective cell loading problem in labor intensive manufacturing cells. *Computers & Industrial Engineering, 56*(2), 476–488. doi:10.1016/j.cie.2008.02.001

Sumit, S. H. (2018). *Akhter*. C-means Clustering and Deep-Neuro-Fuzzy Classification for Road Weight Measurement in Traffic Management System. Soft Computing. Springer Berlin Heidelberg; doi:10.100700500-018-3086-0

Sun, W., & Virvalo, T. (2005). Simulation study on a hydraulic –accumulator-balancing-energy saving system in hydraulic boom. *50th National Conference on fluid power*, 371-381.

Sun, J., Wu, X., Fang, W., Ding, Y., Long, H., & Xu, W. (2012). Multiple sequence alignment using the Hidden Markov Model trained by an improved quantum-behaved particle swarm optimization. *Information Sciences, 182*(1), 93–114. doi:10.1016/j.ins.2010.11.014

Sun, W., & Virvalo, T. (2001). Accumulator-pump-motor as energy saving in hydraulic boom. *8th Scandinavian International Conference on Fluid power*, 163-177.

Suruchi, C. (2016). Application of Genetic Algorithm and Back Propagation Neural Network for Effective Personalize Web Search-Based on Clustered Query Sessions. *International Journal of Applied Evolutionary Computation, 7*(1), 33–49. doi:10.4018/IJAEC.2016010103

Sutton, G. G., White, O., Adams, M., & Kerlavage, A. (1995). TIGR assembler: A new tool for assembling large shotgun sequencing projects. *Genome Science & Technology, 1*(1), 9–19. doi:10.1089/gst.1995.1.9

Talukder, A. K. M., Kirley, M., & Buyya, R. (2009). Multiobjective differential evolution for scheduling workflow applications on global Grids. *Concurrency and Computation, 21*(13), 1742–1756. doi:10.1002/cpe.1417

Tannenbaum, T., Wright, D., Miller, K., & Livny, M. (2001). Condor: a distributed job scheduler. In Beowulf cluster computing with Linux (pp. 307-350). MIT Press.

Tao, G. (2008). *Artificial immune system based on normal model and immune learning*. Paper presented at the Systems, Man and Cybernetics, 2008. SMC 2008. IEEE International Conference on.

Tarun Kumar, S., & Millie, P. (2011). Differential Operators Embedded Artificial Bee Colony Algorithm. *International Journal of Applied Evolutionary Computation, 2*(3), 1–14. doi:10.4018/jaec.2011070101

Teodorovic, D., Lucic, P., Markovic, G., & Orco, M. D. (2006). *Bee Colony Optimization: Principles and Applications*. Paper presented at the Neural Network Applications in Electrical Engineering, 2006. NEUREL 2006. 8th Seminar on.

The MathWorks, Inc. (n.d.). *Matlab*. Retrieved 2018-02-03 from http://www.mathworks.com

Theiner, D., & Rutschmann, P. (2005). An inverse modelling approach for the estimation of hydrological model parameters. *Journal of Hydroinformatics*.

Thilagavathi, J., & Thanamani, A. S. (2012). A Survey on Dynamic Job Scheduling in Grid Environment Based on Heuristic Algorithm. *International Journal of Computer Trends and Technology, 3*(4).

Thompson, D. H., Killough, S. M., Burks, B. L., & Draper, J. V. (1995). *Design of the human computer interface on the telerobotic small emplacement excavator.* Academic Press.

Thompson, J. D., Plewniak, F., Thierry, J. C., & Poch, O. (2000). DbClustal: Rapid and reliable global multiple alignments of protein sequences detected by database searches. *Nucleic Acids Research, 28*(15), 2919–2926. doi:10.1093/nar/28.15.2919 PMID:10908355

Tiwari, P. K., & Vidyarthi, D. P. (2014). Observing the Effect of Inter Process Communication in Auto Controlled Ant Colony Optimization based Scheduling on Computational Grid. *Concurrency and Computation, 26*(1), 241–270. doi:10.1002/cpe.2977

Topcuoglu, H., Hariri, S., & Wu, M. Y. (2002). Performance-effective and low-complexity task scheduling for heterogeneous computing. *Parallel and Distributed Systems. IEEE Transactions on, 13*(3), 260–274.

Torra, V., & Narukawa, Y. (2009, August). On hesitant fuzzy sets and decision. In *Fuzzy Systems, 2009. FUZZ-IEEE 2009. IEEE International Conference on* (pp. 1378-1382). IEEE. 10.1109/FUZZY.2009.5276884

Torra, V. (2010). Hesitant fuzzy sets. *International Journal of Intelligent Systems, 25*(6), 529–539.

Tosun, Ö., & Marichelvam, M. (2016). Hybrid bat algorithm for flow shop scheduling problems. *International Journal of Mathematics in Operational Research, 9*(1), 125–138. doi:10.1504/IJMOR.2016.077560

Tsiakkouri, E., Sakellariou, R., Zhao, H., & Dikaiakos, M. (2005). Scheduling Workflows with Budget Constraints. Core GRID Integration Workshop, 347-357.

Tsiligaridis, J. (2016). Hybrid Genetics Algorithms for Multiple Sequence Alignment. In *Handbook of Research on Modern Optimization Algorithms and Applications in Engineering and Economics* (pp. 346–366). IGI Global. doi:10.4018/978-1-4666-9644-0.ch013

Ullman, J. D. (1975). NP-complete Scheduling Problems. *Journal of Computer and System Sciences, 10*(3), 384–393. doi:10.1016/S0022-0000(75)80008-0

Vazquez, R. A. (2011). *Training spiking neural models using cuckoo search algorithm.* Paper presented at the Evolutionary Computation (CEC), 2011 IEEE Congress on.

Vergara, J. R., & Este'vez, P. A. (2014). A review of feature selection methods based on mutual information. *Neural Computing & Applications, 24*(1), 175–186. doi:10.100700521-013-1368-0

Verikas, A., & Bacauskiene, M. (2002). Feature selection with neural networks. *Pattern Recognition Letters, 23*(11), 1323–1335. doi:10.1016/S0167-8655(02)00081-8

Verma, N., Sobhan, M. S., & Jalil, T. (2012). *Novel Design Proposal For Real Time Traffic Monitoring & Management of Dhaka Metropolitan City with (Rcap).* Global Engineering, Science and Technology Conference, BIAM Foundation.

Verma, A., & Kaushal, S. (2015). Cost-time efficient scheduling plan for executing workflows in the cloud. *Journal of Grid Computing, 13*(4), 495–506. doi:10.100710723-015-9344-9

Vranesic, Z. G. (1977). Multiple-Valued Logic: An Introduction and Overview. *IEEE Transactions on Computers, 26*(12), 1181–1182. doi:10.1109/TC.1977.1674778

Wait, J., & Fuller, J. (1971). On radio propagation through earth. *Antennas and Propagation. IEEE Transactions on, 19*(6), 796–798. doi:10.1109/TAP.1971.1140048

Wakure, A. R., Patkar, A. R., Dagale, M. V., & Solanki, P. P. (2014). Vehicle Accident Detection and Reporting System Using GPS and GSM. *International Journal of Engineering Research and Development, 10*(4), 25–28.

Wali Khan, M. (2013). Comprehensive Survey of the Hybrid Evolutionary Algorithms. *International Journal of Applied Evolutionary Computation, 4*(2), 1–19. doi:10.4018/jaec.2013040101

Wang, X. (2014, October). Reference point-based evolutionary multi-objective optimization for reversible logic circuit synthesis. In *Biomedical Engineering and Informatics (BMEI), 2014 7th International Conference on* (pp. 955-959). IEEE. 10.1109/BMEI.2014.7002910

Wang, J., Duan, Q., Jiang, Y., & Zhu, X. (2010). A New Algorithm for Grid Independent Task Schedule: Genetic Simulated Annealing. *World Automation Congress (WAC)*, 165–171.

Wang, L., Liu, X., Pedrycz, W., & Shao, Y. (2014). Determination of temporal information granules to improve forecasting in fuzzy time series. *Expert Systems with Applications, 41*(6), 3134–3142. doi:10.1016/j.eswa.2013.10.046

Wang, N., Zhang, N., & Wang, M. (2006). Wireless sensors in agriculture and food industry. Recent development and future perspective. *Computers and Electronics in Agriculture, 50*(1), 1–14. doi:10.1016/j.compag.2005.09.003

Wang, Q. J. (1997). Using genetic algorithms to optimise model parameters. *Environmental Modelling & Software, 12*(1), 27–34. doi:10.1016/S1364-8152(96)00030-8

Wang, T., & Wang, Q. (2012). Design and analysis of compound potential energy regeneration system for hybrid hydraulic excavator. *Proceedings of the Institution of Mechanical Engineers. Part I, Journal of Systems and Control Engineering, 226*(10), 1323–1334. doi:10.1177/0959651812456642

Wang, X., Yu, A., & Chen, W. (2011). Optimal matching on driving system of hydraulic hybrid vehicle. *Procedia Engineering, 15*, 5294–5298. doi:10.1016/j.proeng.2011.08.981

Wang, Y. N., Lei, Y., Fan, X., & Wang, Y. (2016). Intuitionistic fuzzy time series forecasting model based on intuitionistic fuzzy reasoning. *Mathematical Problems in Engineering*.

Wang, Y. N., Lei, Y., Lei, Y., & Fan, X. (2016). Multi-factor high-order intuitionistic fuzzy time series forecasting model. *Journal of Systems Engineering and Electronics, 27*(5), 1054–1062. doi:10.21629/JSEE.2016.05.13

Waston, J. D., & Crick, F. H. C. (1953). Molecular structure of nucleic acids: A structure for deoxyribose nucleic acid. *Nature, 171*(4356), 737–738. doi:10.1038/171737a0 PMID:13054692

Watson, J. D., & Berry, A. (2003). *DNA: The secret of life*. Knopf.

Weidong, L., Kaikai, S., Wei, L., & Jun, X. (2011, August). Research on Potential Energy Recovery of 16T Wheeled Hybrid Excavator. In *Digital Manufacturing and Automation (ICDMA), 2011 Second International Conference on* (pp. 996-998). IEEE.

Wei-Ping, L., & Wan-Ting, C. (2011). *A novel artificial bee colony algorithm with diversity strategy*. Paper presented at the Natural Computation (ICNC), 2011 Seventh International Conference on.

Weldon, T. P., & Rathore, A. Y. (1999). *Wave propagation model and simulations for landmine detection*. Department of Electrical & Computer Engineering University of North Carolina-Charlotte.

Wendel, G. R. (2000). *Regenerative hydraulic systems for increased efficiency*. San Antonio, TX: Southwest Research Institute.

Werner-Allen, G., Lorincz, K., Ruiz, M., Marcillo, O., Johnson, J., Lees, J., & Welsh, M. (2006). Deploying a wireless sensor network on an active volcano. *IEEE Internet Computing, 10*(2), 18–25. doi:10.1109/MIC.2006.26

Wieczorek, M., Podlipnig, S., Prodan, R., & Fahringer, T. (2008). Bi-criteria scheduling of scientific workflows for the grid. In *Cluster Computing and the Grid, 2008. CCGRID'08. 8th IEEE International Symposium on* (pp. 9-16). IEEE. 10.1109/CCGRID.2008.21

Wiki-1 (2016). Retrieved from: https://en.wikipedia.org/wiki/Cross-validation_(statistics)

Wikipedia. (n.d.). *Automatic number-plate recognition*. Retrieved 2018-02-03 from https://en.wikipedia.org/wiki/Automatic_number-plate_recognition#cite_note-29

Wohlford, W. P., Bode, B. D., & Griswold, F. D. (1989). *New capability for remote controlled excavation* (No. 891859). SAE Technical Paper.

Wolfram, S. (2002). *A new kind of science* (Vol. 5). Champaign: Wolfram media.

Wongchomphu, P., & Eiamkanitchat, N. (2014). Enhance Neuro-Fuzzy System for Classification Using Dynamic Clustering. *4th Joint International Conference on Information and Communication Technology, Electronic and Electrical Engineering (JICTEE)*, 1-6. 10.1109/JICTEE.2014.6804071

Xhafa, F., Duran, B., Abraham, A., & Dahal, K. P. (2008). Tuning struggle strategy in genetic algorithms for scheduling in computational grids. *Neural Network World, 18*(3), 209–225.

Xhafa, F., Gonzalez, J. A., Dahal, K. P., & Abraham, A. (2009). A GA(TS) Hybrid Algorithm for Scheduling in Computational Grids. *Proceedings of the 4th International Conference on Hybrid Artificial Intelligence Systems*, 285–292. 10.1007/978-3-642-02319-4_34

Xia, M., & Xu, Z. (2011). Hesitant fuzzy information aggregation in decision making. *International Journal of Approximate Reasoning, 52*(3), 395–407. doi:10.1016/j.ijar.2010.09.002

Xiaohui, C., & Potok, T. E. (2005). Document Clustering Analysis based on Hybrid PSO+K-means Algorithm. *The Journal of Computer Science, 1*(3), 27 – 33.

Xiao, Q., Wang, Q., & Zhang, Y. (2008). Control strategies of power system in hybrid hydraulic excavator. *Automation in Construction, 17*(4), 361–367. doi:10.1016/j.autcon.2007.05.014

Xin-She, Y., & Deb, S. (2009). *Cuckoo Search via Lévy flights*. Paper presented at the Nature & Biologically Inspired Computing, 2009. NaBIC 2009. World Congress on.

Xinyan, G., & Jianguo, Z. (2011). *Multi-agent based hybrid evolutionary algorithm*. Paper presented at the Natural Computation (ICNC), 2011 Seventh International Conference on.

Xiong, J. (2006). *Essential bioinformatics*. Cambridge University Press. doi:10.1017/CBO9780511806087

XPath. (2016, Mar 6). *XML Path Language*. Retrieved from: https://www.w3.org/TR/xpath/

Xu, F., & Chen, Y. (2009). A method for multiple sequence alignment based on particle swarm optimization. In Emerging Intelligent Computing Technology and Applications. With Aspects of Artificial Intelligence (pp. 965-973). Springer Berlin Heidelberg.

Xue, X., Ma, H., & Wei, J. (2014). Setting-up Wireless Communication System for Mine Rescue Robots. In Mechanical Components and Control Engineering III (Vol. 668–669, pp. 366–369). Academic Press. doi:10.4028/www.scientific.net/AMM.668-669.366

Yamashita, K. (2001). *U.S. Patent No. 6,202,411*. Washington, DC: U.S. Patent and Trademark Office.

Yan, D. (2001). A High Performance License Plate Recognition System Based on the Web Technique. *Proceedings IEEE Intelligent Transport Systems*, 325-329.

Yan-fei, Z., & Xiong-min, T. (2010). *Overview of swarm intelligence.* Paper presented at the Computer Application and System Modeling (ICCASM), 2010 International Conference on.

Yang, X.-S., & Deb, S. (2009). *Cuckoo search via Lévy flights.* Paper presented at the World Congress on Nature & Biologically Inspired Computing, NaBIC 2009 10.1109/NABIC.2009.5393690

Yang, J., Quan, L., & Yang, Y. (2012). Excavator energy-saving efficiency based on diesel engine cylinder deactivation technology. *Chinese Journal of Mechanical Engineering*, 25(5), 897–904. doi:10.3901/CJME.2012.05.897

Yang, W., Zhang, Y., & Liu, Y. (2010). Constructing of wireless emergency communication system for underground coal mine based on WMN technology. *Journal of Coal Science and Engineering (China)*, 16(4), 441–448. doi:10.100712404-010-0420-0

Yang, X. S., & Deb, S. (2010). Engineering Optimization by Cuckoo Search. *Int. J. Mathematical Modeling and Numerical Optimization.*, 1(4), 330–343. doi:10.1504/IJMMNO.2010.035430

Yang, X.-S. (2010). *Nature-inspired metaheuristic algorithms.* Luniver Press.

Yang, X.-S. (2011). Bat algorithm for multi-objective optimisation. *International Journal of Bio-inspired Computation*, 3(5), 267–274. doi:10.1504/IJBIC.2011.042259

Yang, X.-S., Karamanoglu, M., & He, X. (2013). Multi-objective flower algorithm for optimization. *Procedia Computer Science*, 18, 861–868. doi:10.1016/j.procs.2013.05.251

Yarkan, S., Guzelgoz, S., Arslan, H., & Murphy, R. R. (2009). Underground mine communications: A survey. *IEEE Communications Surveys and Tutorials*, 11(3), 125–142. doi:10.1109/SURV.2009.090309

YarKhan, A., & Dongarra, J. (2002). Experiments with scheduling using simulated annealing in a Grid environment. *GRID-2002*, 232-242.

Ye, Q., Gao, W., & Zeng, W. (2003). Color Image Segmentation Using Density-Based Clustering. In *International Conference of Acoustics, Speech, and Signal Processing (ICASSP)* (pp. 345–348). IEEE.

Yick, J., Mukherjee, B., & Ghosal, D. (2008). Wireless sensor network survey. *Computer Networks*, 52(12), 2292–2330. doi:10.1016/j.comnet.2008.04.002

Yin, P. Y., & Shyu, S. J. (n.d.). *MSAGA: Multiple Sequence Alignment Using Genetic Algorithms.* Academic Press. doi:10.1007/978-3-642-04020-7_104

Yi, Y., & Yu, T. (2013, January). The Load Sensing Principle of Proportion Multi-channel Valve and its Application in Excavator. In *Proceedings of the 2013 Third International Conference on Intelligent System Design and Engineering Applications* (pp. 1469-1472). IEEE Computer Society. 10.1109/ISDEA.2012.351

Yokota, S., Sasao, M., & Ichiryu, K. (1996). Trajectory Control of the boom and arm system of hydraulic excavators. Transactions of the Japan Society of Mechanical Engineers [Japanese]. *Part C*, 62(593), 161–167.

Yoshino, K. (2008). *U.S. Patent No. 7,401,464.* Washington, DC: U.S. Patent and Trademark Office.

Yousuf, S. A., & Sarfraz, M. (2006). Identification of Number Plates under Extreme Outdoor Factors, International Journal of Pattern Reconition and Machine Intelligence. *International Scientific*, 01(3), 69–78.

Yu, H., & Wilamowski, B. M. (2010). Levenberg Marquardt Training (2nd ed.). CRC Press.

Yu, J., Buyya, R., & Tham, C. K. (2005). Cost-based scheduling of scientific workflow applications on utility grids. In *e-Science and Grid Computing, 2005. First International Conference on*. IEEE.

Yueyuan, W., Cheng, L., & Yi, L. (2006). Factors Influencing Hybrid Electric Vehicle System Efficiency. *Journal of Jilin University, 36*, 20–24.

Yu, J., & Buyya, R. (2005). A taxonomy of workflow management systems for grid computing. *Journal of Grid Computing, 3*(3-4), 171–200. doi:10.100710723-005-9010-8

Yu, J., & Buyya, R. (2006). Scheduling Scientific Workflow Applications with Deadline and Budget Constraints using Genetic Algorithms. *Scientific Programming, 14*(3-4), 217–230. doi:10.1155/2006/271608

Yu, J., Kirley, M., & Buyya, R. (2007). Multi-objective planning for workflow execution on grids. In *Proceedings of the 8th IEEE/ACM International conference on Grid Computing* (pp. 10-17). IEEE Computer Society. 10.1109/GRID.2007.4354110

Yusuf, A. S., & Sarfraz, M. (2005). Color Edge Enhancement based Fuzzy Segmentation of License Plates. In *Proceedings of IEEE International Conference on Information Visualisation (IV'2005)-UK*. IEEE Computer Society Press.

Yu-Yan, H., Jun-Hua, D., & Min, Z. (2011). *Apply the discrete artificial bee colony algorithm to the blocking flow shop problem with makespan criterion*. Paper presented at the Control and Decision Conference (CCDC), 2011 Chinese.

Zadeh, L. A. (1965). Information and control. *Fuzzy Sets, 8*(3), 338-353.

Zadeh, L. A. (1965). Fuzzy sets. *Information and Control, 8*(3), 338–353. doi:10.1016/S0019-9958(65)90241-X

Zambrano-Vega, C., Nebro, A. J., Durillo, J. J., García-Nieto, J., & Aldana-Montes, J. F. (2017). Multiple Sequence Alignment with Multiobjective Metaheuristics. A Comparative Study. *International Journal of Intelligent Systems, 32*(8), 843–861. doi:10.1002/int.21892

Zarotti, S., & Eugenio, L. R. P. (2010). Hydraulic Excavator Working Cycle: From Field Test to Simulation Model. *7th International Fluid Power Conference*, Aachen.

Zemali, E. A., & Boukra, A. (2016). Using a Bio-Inspired Algorithm to Resolve the Multiple Sequence Alignment Problem. *International Journal of Applied Metaheuristic Computing, 7*(3), 36–55. doi:10.4018/IJAMC.2016070103

Zerbino, D. R., & Birney, E. (2008). Velvet: Algorithms for de novo short read assembly using de Bruijn graphs. *Genome Research, 18*(5), 821–829. doi:10.1101/gr.074492.107 PMID:18349386

Zhang, D., Guan, X., Tang, Y., & Tang, Y. (2011). *Modified Artificial Bee Colony Algorithms for Numerical Optimization*. Paper presented at the Intelligent Systems and Applications (ISA), 2011 3rd International Workshop on.

Zhang, G. X., & Rong, H. N. (2007). Real-observation quantum-inspired evolutionary algorithm for a class of numerical optimization problems. In Lecture Notes in Computer Science: Vol. 4490. ICCS2007, Part IV (pp. 989-996). Springer.

Zhang, L., Chen, Y., Sun, R., Jing, S., & Yang, B. (2008). A task scheduling algorithm based on PSO for grid computing. *International Journal of Computational Intelligence Research, 4*.

Zhang, G. (2011). Quantum-inspired evolutionary algorithms: A survey and empirical study. *Journal of Heuristics, 17*(3), 303–351. doi:10.100710732-010-9136-0

Zhang, J., Ma, P., Schwab, M., Patel, K. N., & Shang, T. (2007). *Design and analysis for recovering potential energy*. Caterpillar.

Zhang, L., Gao, L., & Li, X. (2013). A hybrid genetic algorithm and tabu search for a multi-objective dynamic job shop scheduling problem. *International Journal of Production Research*, *51*(12), 3516–3531. doi:10.1080/00207543.2012. 751509

Zhao, J., Liu, G., Liu, Y., & Zhu, Y. (2008). Research on the application of a marsupial robot for coal mine rescue. In Lecture Notes in Computer Science (including subseries Lecture Notes in Artificial Intelligence and Lecture Notes in Bioinformatics) (Vol. 5315, pp. 1127–1136). Springer. doi:10.1007/978-3-540-88518-4_120

Zhao, J., Gao, J., Zhao, F., & Liu, Y. (2017). A Search-and-Rescue Robot System for Remotely Sensing the Underground Coal Mine Environment. *Sensors (Basel)*, *17*(10), 2426. doi:10.339017102426 PMID:29065560

Zhi, L., Shaoju, L., Zhonghua, H., & Qiong, H. (2011, August). Hydraulic Excavator Hybrid Power System Parameters Design. In *Digital Manufacturing and Automation (ICDMA), 2011 Second International Conference on* (pp. 602-605). IEEE.

Zhu, B., & Xu, Z. (2014). Some results for dual hesitant fuzzy sets. *Journal of Intelligent & Fuzzy Systems*, *26*(4), 1657–1668.

Zhu, B., Xu, Z., & Xia, M. (2012). Dual hesitant fuzzy sets. *Journal of Applied Mathematics*.

Zhu, P., Zhao, M., & He, T. (2010). A Novel Ant Colony Algorithm for Grid Task Scheduling. *Journal of Computer Information Systems*, *6*(3), 745–752.

Zimmermann, H. J. (1976). Description and optimization of fuzzy systems. *International Journal of General Systems*, *2*(4), 209–215. doi:10.1080/03081077608547470

Zomaya, A. Y., & Yee-Hwei Teh. (2001). Observations on using genetic algorithms for dynamic load-balancing. *IEEE Transactions on Parallel and Distributed Systems*, *12*(9), 899–911. doi:10.1109/71.954620

About the Contributors

Muhammad Sarfraz is a Professor in Kuwait University, Kuwait. He received his Ph.D. from Brunel University, UK, in 1990. His research interests include Computer Graphics, Pattern Recognition, Computer Vision, Image Processing, and Soft Computing. He is currently working on various projects related to academia and industry. Prof. Sarfraz has been keynote/invited speaker at various platforms around the globe. He has advised/supervised more than 60 students for their MSc and PhD theses. He has published more than 310 publications in the form of various Books, Book Chapters, journal and conference papers. Prof. Sarfraz is member of various professional societies including IEEE, ACM, IVS, SAVE and ISOSS. He is a Chair, member of the International Advisory Committees and Organizing Committees of various international conferences, Symposiums and Workshops. He is also Editor/Guest Editor of various International Conference Proceedings, Books, and Journals. He is the reviewer, for many international Journals, Conferences, meetings, and workshops around the world. He has achieved various awards in education, research, and administrative services.

* * *

Shamim Akhter completed Ph.D. in 2009 from information processing department, Tokyo Institute of Technology, Japan. He received Ph.D, B.S. and M.S. degrees in computer science from American International University-Bangladesh (AIUB), and Asian Institute of Technology (AIT), Thailand respectively. He completed Ph.D. in 2009 from information processing department, Tokyo Institute of Technology, Japan. Currently, he is affiliated with department of computer science and engineering, East West University Bangladesh as associate professor. He served the department of computer science, American International University Bangladesh, as lecturer from 2001 - 2005, and as assistant professor 2005-2014. He also worked as assistant professor in Thompson Rivers University, Kamloops, Canada for more than six (6) months. In addition, he worked as a research associate at RS and GIS FoS, Asian Institute of Technology, Thailand, a JSPS postdoctoral research fellow at National Institute of Informatics (NII), Japan and a GCOE research assistant at Tokyo Institute of Technology, Japan. He also served as the head of computer science graduate program at American International University Bangladesh for two years. He is the author of a book, and more than 50 articles. His research interests include applied intelligent system and information processing; parallel and high-performance computing; and RS-GIS. He was a recipient of the "The Excellent Student of The Year, FY2008", Global COE Program, Photonics Integration-Core Electronics (PICE), Japan. He mentored two (2) PhD, supervised around ten (10) MSc and more than 30 undergraduate dissertations. His students/co-authors awarded student travel grant for best student paper at ICONIP, 2006, Hong Kong, the best student presentation in National Convention of IPSJ, 2010 Siga, Japan, vice chancellor award for the best thesis in 2006, and 3rd position in Falling Walls Lab in Bangladesh, 2016. He became a Member (M) of IEEE in 2006, and a Senior Member (SM) in 2014. He is also a senior member of WASET.

Abdelmalek Amine received an engineering degree in Computer Science from the Computer Science department of Djillali Liabes University of Sidi-Belabbes-Algeria, received the Magister diploma in Computational Science and PhD from Djillali Liabes University in collaboration with Joseph Fourier University of Grenoble. His research interests include big data, data mining, text mining, ontology, classification, clustering, neural networks, and biomimetic optimization methods. He participates in the program committees of several international conferences and on the editorial boards of international journals. Prof Amine is the head of GeCoDe-knowledge management and complex data-laboratory at UTM University of Saida, Algeria; he also collaborates with the "knowledge base and database" team of TIMC laboratory at Joseph Fourier University of Grenoble.

Michael Arock is an Associate Professor presently working in the Department of Computer Applications, National Institute of Technology, Tiruchirappalli. He graduated as a BSc(Mathematics) from GTN Arts College, Dindigul, Madurai Kamaraj University and as an MCA from St. Joseph's College, Bharathidasan University and earned his PhD from NITT under Bharathidasan University. His Doctoral thesis is on Design and Analysis of Parallel Algorithms on CREW PRAM and LARPBS models. His specialization is Parallel Algorithmics. His Areas of Interest include Data Structures and Algorithms, High Performance Computing and Bioinformatics. Currently, he guides four Ph.D. Scholars in the field of DNA computing, natural Language Processing and Bioinformatics. He has published 12 articles in International Journals, 2 articles in national Journals and 10 in the proceedings of International Conferences and 6 in the proceedings of national conferences /seminars. He has reviewed two books for Pearson Education and an article for an international journal. He shows interest in student counseling, in motivating for better placements and in helping them design value-based life-style. His hobbies are writing both classical and modern poems in Tamil, writing articles in Tamil and English and reading books, especially on Philosophy.

Sowmya B. J. is working as an Assistant Professor and Research Scholar in Ramaiah Institute of Technology. She holds Master of Technology in Software Engineering from Visvesvaraya Technological University. Her Research Area of Interest is Data Mining, Security, Software Engineering and IOT. She is well versed in teaching Software Engineering, Practical approach for Software Engineering, Computer Security, Computer Organization and Design and Analytics.

Kamlesh Bisht was born in 1990 in Uttarakhand, India. He received the M.Sc. degree from Kumaun University, Nainital, India in 2013. He is currently pursuing the Ph.D. degree in Mathematics at Govind Ballabh Pant University of Agriculture and Technology Pantnagar, Uttarakhand, India. He has published 4 research papers on fuzzy time series forecasting in international journals and conferences.

Saroj Biswas obtained his Bachelor of Technology degree in Computer Science and Engineering from Jalpaiguri Govt. Engineering College. He obtained his Master of Technology degree in Computer Science & Engineering from National Institute of Technical Teachers' Training and Research, Kolkata in 2008 and Ph.D. degree in Computer Science and Engineering from National Institute of Technology

Silchar in 2015. He has been working as an Assistant Professor in Computer Science & Engineering Department, NIT Silchar since 3rd May, 2010. His research interest includes Machine learning, Artificial Intelligence, Pattern Recognition and Data Mining. Four M. Tech students have completed their dissertation under him and two students are presently carrying out their M. Tech dissertation. Five Ph.D. scholars are presently doing their Ph. D. work under him. He presently runs one Deity sponsored R&D Project. He has published total 18 international journals in various reputed publication house worldwide including Elsevier, SPRINGER, World Scienticfic, IGI Global, Inderscience, etc.

Mohamed Amine Boudia received a licence degree in computer Science and Master diploma in computer modeling of knowledge and reasoning from the Computer Science department of Tahar Moulay University of Saida Algeria and PhD from the same University.. Now Dr Mohamed Amine Boudia is a teacher in Dr. Tahar Moulay University. His research interests Data Mining, Knowledge Discovery, Metaheuristic, Bio-inspired techniques, Retrieval Information, Cloud Computing and images processing.

Sanjoy Das received both his BE and ME in Mechanical Engineering and PhD in Engineering from Jadavpur University, Kolkata, India. He has more than 20 years of teaching experience and is currently an Associate Professor in the Department of Engineering and Technological Studies, University of Kalyani, India. His research interests include Optimization techniques and Tribology.

Kumar Dilip has completed his PhD and MTech from Jawaharlal Nehru University after completing his MCA from IGNOU, New Delhi. His research interests are Web mining, Data mining and Nature Inspired Computing.

Marwa Elhajj is a doctor in mechanical engineering. she holds a Phd degree from University of Versailles Saint Quentin. She holds a Master degree in Mechanical and an engineering degree in Mechanical from Lebanese University. She worked in the Laboratory of System Engineering of Versailles University (LISV). Her research focuses on modelling, simulation and optimization of mutliphysics systems.

Kanika Gandhi is a PostDoc in maintenance and Data Mining at the University of Skövde. She holds a M.Phil and PhD in Operational Research from the University of Delhi, India. Her research and expertise comprise the assessment of the relevance of context driven methodologies in the field of maintenance and supply chain systems. She has authored several conference and journal papers and participated in different research projects.

Ritu Garg is an Assistant Professor National Institute of Technology, Kurukshetra.

Rozaida Ghazali is an Associate Professor and Deputy Dean (Research and Development) at Faculty of Computer Science and Information Technology, Universiti Tun Hussein Onn Malaysia (UTHM). She graduated with a Ph.D. degree from the School of Computing and Mathematical Sciences at Liverpool John Moores University, United Kingdom in 2007, on the topic of Higher Order Neural Networks for Financial Time series Prediction. Earlier, in 2003 she completed her M.Sc. degree in Computer Science from Universiti Technology Malaysia (UTM). She received her B.Sc. (Hons) degree in Computer Science (Information System) from the Universiti Sains Malaysia (USM) in 1997. In 2001, Rozaida joined the academic staff in UTHM. Prior to this, she was a system analyst in Land and Mines Office, Kuala

Lumpur. Her research area includes neural networks, data mining, financial time series prediction, data analysis, swarm intelligence, artificial bee colony algorithm, physical time series forecasting, and fuzzy logic. He published papers in international conferences and journals.

Tarun Kumar Ghosh received his B.Tech. in Computer Science & Engineering from University of Calcutta, India, M.E. in Computer Science & Technology from B E College (DU) [now IIEST], Shibpur, Howrah, India and currently pursuing PhD in Computing from University of Kalyani. He is currently an Associate Professor in the Department of Computer Science & Engineering, Haldia Institute of Technology, West Bengal, India. His research interests include Grid Computing, Optimization, Computer Architecture and Interconnection Networks. He is author of research studies published at national and international journals, conference proceedings as well as books published by Tata McGraw-Hill.

Krishna Kumar Gupta was born in 1988 in Uttar Pradesh, India. He received the M.Sc. degree from Dr. Bhimrao Ambedkar University, Agra, India in 2009. He received the M.Phil. degree from Dr. Bhimrao Ambedkar University, Agra, India in 2010. He is currently pursuing the Ph.D. degree in Mathematics at Govind Ballabh Pant University of Agriculture and Technology Pantnagar, Uttarakhand, India. His research area is fuzzy time series forecasting.

Reda Mohamed Hamou received an engineering degree in computer Science from the Computer Science department of Djillali Liabes University of Sidi-Belabbes-Algeria and PhD (Artificial intelligence) from the same University. He has several publications in the field of BioInspired and Metaheuristic. His research interests include Data Mining, Text Mining, Classification, Clustering, computational intelligence, neural networks, evolutionary computation and Biomimetic optimization method. He is a head of research team in GecoDe laboratory. Dr. Hamou is an associate professor in technology faculty in UTMS University of Saida-Algeria.

Md. Ashfaqul Islam completed his BSc from Computer Science and Engineering Department, EWU. He is now serving as a graduate GTA in CSE, EWU. His research interests are the Neural Network and apply AI on electrical and electronic circuit's advancements.

Jayapriya J. recently completed her Ph.D. in National Institute of Technology, Tiruchirappalli. She finished her Master degree M.Sc (CS) and M.Phil (CS) in 2002 and 2004 respectively. Her area of interest are Bioinformatics, Evolutionary algorithms, Parallel computing.

Kawal Jeet is an Assistant Professor in Post-Graduate Department of Computer Science, D.A.V. College, Jalandhar, India. She received her Master' s of Technology in Computer Science from Dr B R Ambedkar National Institute of Technology, Jalandhar, India in 2012. She completed her Ph.D from this institute in 2017. Her current research interest focuses on nature-inspired computation, software modularization, Bayesian networks, and software quality. She has published her research work in more than 25 international journals and conference proceedings. She is a member of the IRED, UACEE and ACM India.

P. C. Jha is a Dean, Head of the Department and Professor in Department of Operational Research, University of Delhi, India. His area of specialization are Optimization, Software Reliability, Marketing and Supply Chain Management. He has obtained his Ph.D, and from M.Phil Department of Operational Research University of Delhi, India. He has several research papers in International and National Journal.

Srinivasa K. G. is currently working as an associate professor at CBP Government Engineering College, Jaffarpur, New Delhi. Earlier, he was a faculty in the Department of Computer Science and Engineering, M S Ramaiah Institute of Technology, Bangalore. He is the recipient of AICTE - Career Award for Young Teachers, Indian Society of Technical Education – ISGITS National Award for Best Research Work Done by Young Teachers, Institution of Engineers(India) – IEI Young Engineer Award in Computer Engineering, Rajarambapu Patil National Award for Promising Engineering Teacher Award from ISTE - 2012. He has published more than hundred research papers in International Conferences and Journals. He has visited many Universities abroad as a visiting researcher – He has visited University of Oklahoma, USA, Iowa State University, USA, Hong Kong University, Korean University, National University of Singapore are few prominent visits. He has authored two books namely File Structures using C++ by TMH and Soft Computer for Data Mining Applications LNAI Series – Springer. He has been awarded BOYSCAST Fellowship by DST, for visiting University of Melbourne.

Wali Khan Mashwani has received his M.Sc. degree in Mathematics from the University of Peshawar in 1996 and his Ph.D degree in Mathematics from the Department of Mathematical Sciences, University of Essex, Colchester, UK in 2012. He is currently working as an Associate Professor in the department of Mathematics at the Kohat University of Science & Technology (KUST), Khyber Pukhtunkawa, Pakistan. His main research areas are evolutionary computation, optimization, neural networks and their applications. Dr. Wali Khan Mashwani is currently editor of the Science International, International Journal of Communication Networks and Information Security (IJCNIS) and the guest editor of the Special Issue on Swarm Intelligence for Optimization Problems of the International Journal of Swarm Intelligence Research.

Sanjay Kumar received the B.Sc. degree from Kumaon University, Nainital, India in 1992. He received Master and Ph.D degrees in Mathematics from G.B. Pant University of Ag. & Technology in 1995 and 1998 respectively. Currently he is an Assistant Professor in department of Mathematics, Statistics & Computer Science in College of Basic Sciences & Humanities of G. B. Pant University of Agriculture & Technology Pantnagar, India. He has published 30 research papers in international journals and conferences. His current research interests are in the field of Artificial Intelligence with application of soft and non-conventional computing techniques in time series forecasting and multi-criteria decision making problems.

Bikram Keshari Mishra is currently working as a Senior Asst. Professor in the Department of Computer Science & Engineering in Silicon Institute of Technology, Bhubaneswar, Odisha, for the last ten years. His research interest includes data clustering using various data mining tools and image processing. Has contributed a few research oriented papers to some national and international journals and conference.

Prasant Misra is a Scientist in TCS Research and Innovation at TATA Consultancy Services Ltd., Bangalore. He performs research in computational sensing and systems with a focus on cyber-physical systems. He also has a background in middleware for wireless sensor networks and low-power networked embedded systems. Prasant has many years of experience in scientific and industrial research. He has worked in different roles and capabilities for: Keane Inc. (now a unit of NTT Data Corporation), Bangalore; CSIRO Sydney/Brisbane; Robert Bosch Centre for Cyber Physical Systems in the Indian Institute of Science, Bangalore. His external engagements include visiting fellow / researcher / visitor at: ETH Zurich, iMinds-IBCN Universiteit Gent, NICTA Sydney, and TIFR Mumbai. He has worked on a diverse range of problems pertaining to: location sensing/tracking technologies (for applications in wireless sensor networks, robotics, demining, hospital acquired infections), testbeds (for evaluating localization solutions), modelling / deployment / characterization studies (for underground mines), and middleware technology stacks (for IoT platforms); the outcomes of which have either resulted in open-source solutions or publications in premier sensornet/mobile computing/wireless forums. Prasant scientific excellence and leadership has been recognized and felicitated by a number of honours and awards, of which it is noteworthy to mention the: MIT TR35 - India "Top 10 Innovators under 35 in India" (published by: Massachusetts Institute of Technology and Mint-HT) in 2017, TATA Consultancy Services "Exemplary Contribution Award" in 2017, European Research Consortium on Informatics and Mathematics "Alain Bensoussan" and European Commission "Marie Skłodowska-Curie" Fellowship in 2012; and the Australian Government's AusAID "Australian Leadership Awards" (now a stream of Australia Awards) in 2008. Prasant has served on the organizing and technical committee of a number of international conferences/events. He represents TCS and India in many national and international standardization forums on "Smart Cities". He is an active speaker and thought provoker on the subject of: "IoT architecture and nuances of the last-mile". He is a senior member of IEEE and ACM, member of the executive committee of IEEE Bangalore Section, and an Associate Technical Editor of IEEE Communication Magazine. Prasant completed his postdoctoral fellowship from the Swedish Institute of Computer Science, Stockholm in 2013. He received his Ph.D. from the University of New South Wales, Sydney in 2012 and B.E. (First class with Honors) from Sambalpur University in 2006, both in the field of computer science and engineering. He is an alumnus of St. Patrick's H.S. School, Asansol.

Sadia Nawrin completed her BSc from Computer Science and Engineering Department, EWU. She is now serving as a graduate GTA in CSE, EWU. Her research interests are the Data mining and clustering algorithms and their implementation in real life applications.

Md. Rahatur Rahman is a Software Engineer specializing in delivering business solutions to support business needs. He has been in the IT industry for over 10 years and in a broad range of roles. He is highly accomplished in business analysis, software requirements analysis, software system design, development and delivery. He has had a wide range of roles including Project Manager, Team Leader, Software Engineer and IT Consultant. Also he have been working in both private and public sectors of various industries including finance, defense, health care and ecommerce and demonstrated an ability to combine his management skills with his understanding of technology, software development processes and projects to deliver business benefits. A capable leader, he possesses the ability to formulate meaningful project plans reflecting organizational goals and corporate strategy and see these through to conclusion on time and within budget.

Alok Ranjan received his Bachelor of Engineering (Hons.) in Computer Science and Engineering in 2012 from RGPV, Bhopal (India). Currently, he is a Ph.D. candidate in the Department of Mining Engineering, NIT Rourkela. He is self-motivated and loves to perform research on the wireless communication inside underground mines and confined spaces using wireless sensor devices, tracking of miners and trapped miners communication, mathematical modeling and their validations with real time data. His research methodology consists of algorithmic development, simulation and experimental evaluation over real test-bed. He is very interested in involving himself in trans-disciplinary projects where he could render and contribute his knowledge to the real world problems. His research interests are wireless sensor networks, wireless robotics networks, UAVs based emergency communication and IoT. He is a student member of IEEE and ACM.

Amiya Kumar Rath is presently working with Veer Surendra Sai University of Technology, Burla, India as Professor of Computer Science & Engg. and is actively engaged in conducting Academic, Research and development programs in the field of Computer Science and IT Engg. Contributed more than 60 research level papers to many national and International journals and conferences. Having research interests include Embedded System, Ad-hoc Network, Sensor Network, Power Minimization, Biclustering, Evolutionary Computation and Data Mining.

Manisha Rathee is currently pursuing PhD in the area of Wireless Sensor Networks after completing her M.Tech. in Computer Science and Technology from JNU, New Delhi. She has received her B. Tech. in Computer Science and Engineering from GGSIPU new Delhi. Her research interests include Nature Inspired Computing and Wireless Sensor Networks.

Ritu Rathee has completed her M.Tech. in Information Security and Management from IGDTUW, New Delhi after completing her B.Tech. in Computer Science and Engineering from GGSIPU, New Delhi. Her research interests include Information Security, Machine Learning and Nature Inspired Computing.

Heisnam Rohen Singh is a Research Scholar in NIT Silchar.

H. B. Sahu is currently working as an Associate Professor in the Department of Mining Engineering, National Institute of Technology (NIT) Rourkela, India. He received his Ph.D. from Indian School of Mines (ISM) Dhanbad, India in 2004. He has more than 20 years of experiences in teaching and research activities. His current research focuses on Environmental Impact Assessment and Management in Mining, Spontaneous Heating of Coal, Safety Risk Assessment, Solid Fuel and Clean Coal Technology. He has published more than 80 research papers in international and national journals. His name has been included in Marquis Who's Who in Science and Engineering 2011 and also in 100 Top Engineers of the World by the International Biographical Society of Cambridge, England. He has been awarded with Smt Bala Tondon Award 2015–16 by The Mining, Geological Metallurgical Institute of India (MGMI) for his outstanding contribution for upgrading the quality of life in Mining Environment. He is a Fellowof Institution of Engineers (India) and life member of professional bodies like ISTE, MEAI and MGMI.

Habib Shah is Assistant Professor of the College of Computer Science at King Khalid University, Kingdom of Saudi Arabia. Previously, he was an Assistant Professor at University of Malakand Pakistan and Islamic University, Madinah, Saudi Arabia. Prior to coming to Malaysia, he was a part time lecturer at the University Tun Hussein Onn Malaysia (UTHM). From 2010 to 2014 he worked as Graduate Research Assistant in UTHM, Malaysia. He received a BSc degree from University of Malakand in 2005, and Master in Computer Science from the Federal Urdu University of Arts Science and Technology, Karachi, Pakistan. He received his Ph.D in Information Technology from UTHM, Malaysia, in 2014. His research interests include Soft Computing, Data Mining, Artificial Neural Networks, Learning Algorithms, Swarm Intelligence, Classification, Time Series Prediction, Clustering, as well as Numerical Function Optimizations. He has more than twenty five publications in international journals, book chapters and outstanding IEEE, Elsevier and Springer conferences. Currently, he is working on three research projects awarded from the Deanship of Scientific Research, King Khalid University, KSA.

Seema Shedole works as a Professor at Ramaiah Institute of Technology Bangalore, Karnataka for 24 years. Working in the research area of data analytics and IoT applications. Have done research in the field of application of data mining in bioinformatics for cancer data.

Sakhawat Hosain Sumit completed his BSc from Computer Science and Engineering Department, East West University. He is now working as deep learning associate in a renowned AI based company. His research interests are machine learning, deep learning, data mining, intelligent agent, etc.

Özgür Yeniay is Professor and Chair of the Statistics Department at the University of Hacettepe Turkey, where he has been a faculty member since 1992. He completed his Ph.D. at Hacettepe University. His research interests lie in the area of Operations Research, Optimization and Statistics.

Index

A

Accident Detection Kit 100, 104-105, 119
Artificial Bee Colony algorithm 133, 153-154
auxiliary archive 123, 127-128, 142, 145

B

Bat Algorithm 135, 219
Bees Meta-Heuristic 149
Black Hole 122, 125, 127-128, 136, 145, 148
Black Hole Algorithm 136

C

cellular automata 210, 215, 219-220, 224, 236
character recognition 21, 29, 32-33, 329-330
classification 1-11, 13-16, 29, 59-60, 70, 75, 102, 149-152, 154, 158-160, 198, 203-204, 209, 211, 258-259, 296, 327, 329-330
cluster analysis 102, 340
Cluster Sampling 340
clustering 5, 9, 14-15, 59, 61, 68-70, 85, 102, 150, 196-197, 199-200, 203-206, 208, 211, 239, 325, 327-338, 343
color image segmentation 327, 330, 332-333
communication 59-60, 63, 76, 101, 104, 118-119, 173-174, 184, 286-288, 290-305, 310, 312, 322
computational Grid 166, 310-312, 317, 322
consensus 83, 222-225, 232
CSA and ACO 311, 317, 322
Cuckoo Search 122, 125, 127-128, 137, 145, 149, 153, 310-312, 314
Cuckoo Search Algorithm 137, 153, 310-312, 314

D

data mining 2-3, 6
digital image 325-326, 340

DNA

DNA sequence 82-83, 90, 93, 221
dual hesitant fuzzy set 37, 39

E

edge detection 21, 24, 327, 330, 340
Employee Bee 148
Enhanced Clustering Method 325
evolutionary algorithm 150, 153, 166, 215, 218-219, 224, 228, 233, 236
excavators 256, 258, 261, 263, 266-271

F

Fault Rate 313
feature selection 1-10, 13-16
Flower Pollination algorithm 122, 138, 145, 219
flowtime 310-313, 317-319, 321-322
F-measure 196, 204-205, 208-210
fragment assembly 80-82, 85-86, 91, 93-94
fuzzy logic 1, 3-8, 15

G

GA 3, 13, 38, 85-86, 91, 122-123, 127-128, 139, 141-142, 145, 150, 154, 218-219, 271-274, 276-280, 310-312, 314, 317-318, 320-322
genetic algorithm 2-3, 38, 80-81, 85-86, 93, 122, 150, 169-170, 176, 218, 271-273, 310-311, 314
global alignment 216, 219, 236
GLOBAL ARTIFICIAL BEE COLONY 149, 153, 156
Global Pollination 148
Google Maps API 100, 104, 109-111, 118
Grey Wolf 122, 125, 127-128, 138, 145, 148
Grey Wolf Optimizer Algorithm 138
grid computing 167-168, 173, 310-312

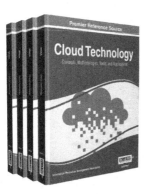

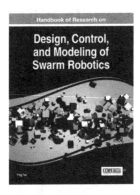

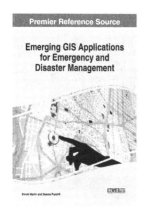
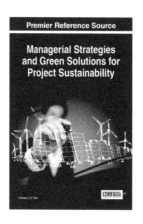

Printed in the United States
By Bookmasters